Literatures of A

Literatures of
Asia

From Antiquity to the Present

Edited and with introductions by

Tony Barnstone
Whittier College

Upper Saddle River, New Jersey 07458

Library of Congress Cataloging-in-Publication Data

Literatures of Asia: from antiquity to the present / edited and with introductions by Tony Barnstone.
    p. cm.
  Includes bibliographical references and index.
  ISBN 0-13-061368-1
    1. Oriental literature—Translations into English.   2. Vedic literature—Translations into English.   3. Indic literature—Translations into English.   4. Chinese literature—Translations into English.   5. Japanese literature—Translations into English.   I. Barnstone, Tony.

PJ409.L58   2003
808.88′0095—dc21

2002025145

Editor-in-Chief: Leah Jewell
Senior Acquisition Editor: Carrie Brandon
Editorial Assistant: Jennifer Miqueis
Managing Editor: Ann Marie McCarthy
Production Liaison: Fran Russello
Project Manager: Linda B. Pawelchak

Prepress and Manufacturing Buyer:
  Sherry Lewis
Interior Design: Delgado Design, Inc.
Cover Design: Robert Farrar-Wagner
Cover Image Credit: Willis Barnstone
Marketing Manager: Rachel Falk

This text is derived from *Literatures of Africa, Asia, and Latin America* by Willis Barnstone and Tony Barnstone.

Acknowledgements begin on page 762, which constitutes a continuation of this copyright page.

This book was set in 10/12 New Baskerville by Lithokraft II and was printed and bound by the Courier Companies. The cover was printed by Phoenix Color Corp.

© 2003 by Pearson Education, Inc.
Upper Saddle River, New Jersey 07458

Printed in the United States of America
10 9 8 7 6 5 4 3 2 1

ISBN 0-13-061368-1

Pearson Education LTD, *London*
Pearson Education Australia Pty. Limited, *Sydney*
Pearson Education Singapore, Pte. Ltd
Pearson Education North Asia Ltd, *Hong Kong*
Pearson Education Canada Ltd, *Toronto*
Pearson Educación de Mexico, S.A. de C.V.
Pearson Education—Japan, *Tokyo*
Pearson Education Malaysia, Pte. Ltd
Pearson Education, *Upper Saddle River, New Jersey*

This book is dedicated to
Arthur Sze
Sam Hamill
J. P. Seaton

CONTENTS

Section 3 ▪ Japan   458

CONTENTS BY GENRE

Poetry

SECTION 1 ■ INDIA, PAKISTAN, AND BANGLADESH

SECTION 3 ■ JAPAN

Ancient Period (to 794)

Heian Period (794–1186)

Kamakura/Nambokucho Periods (1186–1392)

Tokugawa/Edo Periods (1603–1868)

Modern Period (1868–Present)

Fiction

SECTION 1 ■ INDIA, PAKISTAN, AND BANGLADESH

SECTION 2 ■ CHINA

SECTION 3 ■ JAPAN

Prose Nonfiction

SECTION 1 ■ INDIA, PAKISTAN, AND BANGLADESH

SECTION 2 ■ CHINA

Drama

PREFACE

Literatures of Asia has been designed to present teachers and students with a textbook representative of the finest works of Asian literature, one that is amenable to many different teaching approaches. This book includes a wealth of materials so as to give teachers choices that they can tailor to their own preferences, needs, and expertise. This capaciousness will allow students to read around in authors, periods, and traditions that particularly excite them, supplementing assigned reading and providing an essential source book for their individual research. Teaching such a broad spectrum of texts may be challenging, and with this in mind I have supported the literary texts with a full apparatus: a general introduction, section introductions, and extensive headnotes. These supporting materials provide broad and specific contexts, placing literary texts within important cultural, linguistic, and historical movements. In addition, the headnotes include up-to-date bibliographies to guide students for further research.

Translations have been selected primarily for their literary quality because I firmly believe that it is a disservice to students, professors, and authors to present a great work of literature in an English translation that does not read as literature. The depth and quality of these texts demand excellent translations, so that students and professors may encounter them in a form that preserves their artistic integrity and delight. The translators featured here are among the finest in their fields, and many are themselves prominent writers. They include Burton Watson, Barbara Stoler Miller, A. K. Ramanujan, Arthur Waley, Ezra Pound, Kenneth Rexroth, Helen Craig McCullough, Donald Keene, and Robert Bly, among others. My one rule has been to include no translation that is merely adequate. In a sense, then, this text is a showcase for the art of literary translation, and my hope has been to compile an anthology that students will want to take home with them and to read around in long after the course is completed.

In addition to literary texts, *Literatures of Asia* includes selections from religious and philosophical texts that have literary merit, such as the Rig Veda; the Upanishads; Mahayana and Theravada Buddhist texts; the Bhagavad-Gita; classical Indian devotional (bhakti) verse; the *Analects* of Confucius; the Dao-De-Jing; and Zen poems, essays, and stories. These beautiful texts also provide a cosmological and cultural context for literary movements. Extensive headnotes and introductions trace religious movements and influence, giving students a broad overview of Asian religions, which, in the East as in the West, have often inspired and been an essential part of world literatures.

The book also includes important examples of the secular essay, including Mahatma Gandhi writing on passive resistance; a selection of classical Chinese and Japanese literary criticism; *ars poeticas* and meditative essays; along with a memoir by Liang Heng. These essays are themselves of immense literary importance and at the same time provide political, esthetic, philosophical, historical, and biographical supplements to the literary selections. In addition to providing context for the literary selections, the essays provide students with a valuable resource for writing and researching their own essays.

In dealing with many literatures written in many languages, a special problem is presented by the question of orthography. In the literatures of India, China, and Japan, there are alternate and warring systems of transliteration. Generally speaking, I have chosen to use those transliteration systems that are best designed for the general, nonspecialist reader, for whom a more scholarly orthography would prove less informative. However, I did not wish to tamper with the integrity of translators' choices, and so in some cases the headnote is rendered in simplified orthography (reflecting English spellings), whereas the text is maintained in scholarly orthography (reflecting the specialized phonetics of the source language). In such cases, where necessary, I attempt to avoid confusion through footnotes (the nonspecialist may not realize, for example, that the god Shiva is the same as Śiva). China presented a singular dilemma because the long-dominant Wade-Giles system, used until recently by the majority of literary translators, has now been superseded by the Pinyin system. Those Western readers who have a basic familiarity with Chinese literature may, therefore, have a hard time recognizing that the Daoist philosopher Zhuangzi (Pinyin) is the same person as Chuang Tzu (Wade-Giles), that Bo Juyi is Po Chü-i, and that Laozi is Lao Tzu. For China, therefore, I include Wade-Giles names in parentheses after Pinyin names in the headnotes and table of contents (except for those rare names, such as "Wang Wei," for which there is no difference between the systems). For Japanese terms and names, I have followed standard simplified transliteration practice, primarily eliminating long vowels (Bashō becomes Basho). When referring to Japanese nō plays, however, I use the now-archaic transliteration "noh" instead of "no" to avoid possible confusion with the English word.

Similarly, some readers may be confused by the fact that authors they may be familiar with from Japan appear here with their names inverted. The novels of Nobel Prize–winning author Mishima Yukio, for example, are commonly presented in English translation under the name Yukio Mishima, but in this text I have respected Japanese name order (last name first, first name last). Some ancient Japanese names include the preposition "no," which means "of," rather like early English usage (as in John of Gaunt). Chinese names, like Japanese names, appear with the family name first and personal name last. Transposed into English name order, for example, Mao Zedong would be rendered Zedong Mao. As with Japanese names, I have respected Chinese name order in this text.

I would like to thank the many scholars who have contributed to the project: J. P. Seaton and Chou Ping for advice on the China section; Sam Hamill for his observations on China and Japan; Richard Serrano for suggestions about China; and Brenda Schildgen and Sara Saleri for their suggestions for the Indian subcontinent. I would like to thank Mika Fukuda, who helped me regularize and simplify the orthography for the Indian subcontinent, and especially to thank Ericka Embry, David Livingston, and Ayame Fukuda for their essential help in research, typing, and organization, and in the thousand small tasks that a project like this entails. Ayame Fukuda provided essential research help and also co-wrote the introduction to Japan. Finally, I would like to thank our editor Carrie Brandon, whose good cheer and interest have made preparing this edition of *Literatures of Asia* a pleasure.

I would also like to acknowledge the following reviewers: Ali Jimale Ahmed, Queens College; Peter Edmunds, Lansing (MI) Community College; Lydia Liv, University of California, Berkeley; Michael Palencia-Roth, University of Illinois; Herman Rapaport, University of Iowa; and Lois Parkinson Zamora, University of Houston.

—TONY BARNSTONE

Literatures of Asia

General Introduction

■

Literatures of Asia brings together literary, religious, and philosophical traditions from the great civilizations of the world's largest continent. Each of these regions has given us important writings, some of them dating back as far as the third millennium. To compensate for the absence of non-Western writers, earlier anthologies represented the non-Western world with a few Chinese, Persian, and Indian texts. A century of assiduous translation, however, has made the larger world accessible to the West, reconnecting us to an enormous past and present world literature. Particularly in our multicultural society, with peoples of every background, it is vital to reveal the great traditions of Asia, and to do so in fresh, excellent literary translation or, as in the case of many colonial and postcolonial writers from India, in their original English texts. *Literatures of Asia* presents a continental view of literature and civilization. The picture that emerges is of an antiquity in a ferment of creativity and of a migration of languages and literary forms.

The great written documents of antiquity root us as readers in a past of cultural particularity, cultural marriage, and universal themes and have offered new models for modern and postmodern writers. Early in the century, when English versions of Chinese poetry were revealed through the magnificent translations of Arthur Waley and Ezra Pound, American poetics were transformed. Since then, the interpenetration of the world's literary traditions has profoundly changed the ways writers write. We live in a time when it's no less common for an American poet to write a Japanese haiku than a sonnet, and when Chinese-American novelists such as Maxine Hong Kingston and Frank Chin use Chinese classical fiction as their source and model. In the current ferment of translation, a well-read lover of literature is as likely to be a fan of the Bhagavad-Gita as of *Paradise Lost*, as likely to be reading Japanese Nobel laureate in fiction Oe Kenzaburo as Ernest Hemingway. As in the Spanish saying "the world is a handkerchief" (*el mundo es un pañuelo*), all major literatures are now intimately accessible.

A few words about my criteria for inclusion and my rationale for ordering the texts here. There are thousands of authors whose work is worthy of inclusion, and I have had to make difficult choices. Although this anthology has an immense geographic and temporal range, I have represented writers and traditions in depth rather than number. I have limited my selection to three major civilizations: India, Japan, and China, yet I wished to present a comprehensive view of each literature. So, in addition to primary literary genres and forms, I have included key religious and philosophical texts, particularly those that have intrinsic literary value, such as the Indian Bhagavad-Gita, the Chinese Zhuangzi text, and selections from Buddhist scriptures. In most cases, I have ordered the texts within each section chronologically and arranged individual sections according to a model of influence. As Hinduism was a source tradition for Buddhism, which in turn migrated from India to China and Japan, so the sections move from India, to China, and then to Japan.

The schema is a developmental one, representing a sequence of great civilizations from ancient to modern Asia and showing lines of connection between them. However, this large schema needs to be qualified. Islam, for example, came to Asia from the West and penetrated south into parts of sub-Saharan Africa. The Moguls conquered most of India in 1526, bringing in Islam and Persian and Arabic language and literary forms. Today Islam is the religion of much of Asia. Furthermore, influences are inevitably multidirectional, and each of these cultures has ancient indigenous traditions that predate the major religious and literary migrations. Both China and Japan have mythic, philosophical, literary, and religious traditions that long predate the entry of Indian Buddhism. Still, it is essential to understand the global movements of culture and how outside influences have interacted with indigenous traditions. Consider, for example, Wang Wei (701–761), the great Tang dynasty Chinese poet, who was deeply engaged with the indigenous Chinese tradition of Daoism, yet was, at the same time, a committed Buddhist who took his pen name from the reknowned Indian Buddhist Vimalakirti and whose poetry echoes Indian mystical writings.

Like the Irish bog men preserved for centuries in peat or the marvelously conserved mummies of Egypt, humanity is preserved by writing. And there is wonder in what reaches us from antiquity. Like a bead of amber containing a prehistoric insect caught in mid-crawl, each word deciphered from Chinese or Sanskrit, is precious. Ancient coins unearthed still retain monetary value, but we esteem them even more for their worth as microcosms of vanished worlds. This is the value to be found in ancient writing as well. There is an inexpressible pathos in reading the intimate words of the medieval Japanese writer Kenko, who wonders if he is alone in the history of the world in experiencing the strange feeling of having already lived this present moment, what we now call déjà vu. In fact, there is a déjà vu to reading the complaint of a Chinese woman missing her absent husband (who may be fighting the Barbarians at the northern frontier), and there is a universality to the grief of the ancient Japanese empress Jito, who writes of her sorrow after the death of her husband, Emperor Temmu.

In *Literatures of Asia,* I have gathered together the writings of the most ancient civilizations, against which the innovations of North America and Europe seem relatively recent. These texts stretch from antiquity to the present and, despite cultural differences, throughout reveal the universality of life-and-death experience. In every century and in every place, writers have recorded visions of the origins and end of the world, of the supernatural permeating ordinary life and afterlife, as in the *Rig Veda,* Japanese ghost tales, and the Bhagavad-Gita. Writers, religions, and philosophies have always tried to answer basic questions of origin, presence, and destiny and at the same time have given us intimate records of the self and the phenomenal world. The world's authors have observed the known and speculated on the unknown. *Literatures of Asia* is a record of their questioning and achievement. It encompasses a vast precinct of human knowledge, continental in scope, given to us by the writers of antiquity and by their heirs, our contemporaries, who continue to extend, and innovate, from Tokyo to Calcutta.

1

India, Pakistan, and Bangladesh

■

INTRODUCTION

The area now comprising India, Pakistan, and Bangladesh, united in the colonial period as British India, forms the major part of the region known as the Indian subcontinent. It is an area of extraordinary cultural diversity, with more than fifteen hundred languages and dialects and more than a billion people. It is customary to speak simply of Indian literature in dealing with the literatures of the subcontinent before its post-Independence partition into predominantly Hindu India and largely Muslim Pakistan (since 1947) and Bangladesh (East Pakistan from 1947–1971, Bangladesh since 1971). It has been ruled over by four great empires and four great religions—the Buddhist Mauryans, the Hindu Guptas, the Muslim Mughals, and the Christian British empire.

Civilization began in India with a culture known as the Harrapans, which flourished in the Indus basin of present-day Pakistan in the cities of Harrapa and Mohenjodaro from around 2500 to 1500 B.C. This early civilization produced cities with underground sewers, granaries, palaces, and baths, constructed out of uniformly sized bricks and planned into regular grids. Its people traded widely with the early civilizations of the Middle East

and had a system of writing that remained undeciphered until 1969. The Harrapans were most likely the ancestors of the dark-skinned Dravidians of southern India. Their civilization was overrun by lighter-skinned barbarian invaders known as the Aryans starting around 1500 B.C. The Aryans had migrated from the Russian steppes and were armed with iron weapons and fearsome chariots. The two great cities of the Harrapans were left in ruins. The Aryans dominated India from around 1500 to 500 B.C., and the complex urban civilization and writing system of the Harrapans were abandoned for a more primitive, warlike, village culture.

After centuries of eclipse, however, civilization began to emerge again between 1000 and 500 B.C. as the Aryans, merged with the Dravidian inhabitants of India, began to settle in urban centers along the great Ganges River, such as Patna and Benares. Here, the division of Indian society into four castes developed. At the top were the warriors, and below them the priests, merchants and landowners, and farmers and manual laborers. Later, the Brahmans (the priestly caste) supplanted the warriors as the predominant caste. The kings (called *rajas*) of these small states were sanctified by the priestly class.

The marriage of the Aryans and the Dravidians proved fertile both religiously and culturally. Hinduism emerged out of the synthesis of Aryan and Dravidian religions and has been central in the development of Indian literature. Out of Hinduism came two great religious offshoots, Jainism and Buddhism. The religion of the Jains was founded by Mahavira (c. 540–476 B.C.) and is particularly notable for its doctrine of nonviolence (*ahimsa*) and respect for all living beings. Buddhism was founded in India around 525 B.C. by Siddhartha Gautama (563–483 B.C.), who was given the epithet the Buddha, Sanskrit for "the enlightened one." The Buddha's teachings were an oral tradition for four hundred years, after which they were written down in a number of the Sanskrit vernacular languages. The Pali *Tipitaka* (triple basket) is the only complete version of the Indian Buddhist canon. Buddhism largely died out in India after the seventh century A.D., yielding to a revival of Hinduism and the entry of Islam. It survives largely in Tibet, China, Japan, and countries of Southeast Asia.

India was first unified under the Aryans with the conquest of much of the subcontinent by Chandragupta Maurya (321–297 B.C.), the ruler of Magadha, a small Ganges basin state centered in the city of Patna, where both the Buddha and Mahavira had preached some centuries before. Chandragupta was the founder of the Mauryan dynasty (322–185 B.C.), but it was the third Mauryan king, Asoka, who is credited with creating a golden age in ancient India. Asoka (c. 268–231 B.C.) was a convert to Buddhism who advocated nonviolent rule, vegetarianism, religious tolerance, and responsible government that performed service for the public. He sent out missionaries who spread Buddhism to Southeast Asia and Sri Lanka, but he advocated tolerance of other religions within his vast empire. With the fall of the Mauryan dynasty in 185 B.C., India again fragmented into many small states, and it wasn't until the establishment of the Gupta dynasty in A.D. 320 that India would again be united.

The most ancient Indian literature is found in the Vedas, which are written in an early form of Sanskrit called Vedic, and which record the religious beliefs of the Aryans. Of the four main Vedas, which comprise the oldest Hindu sacred texts, the Rig Veda is the scripture with the most literary value. The oral tradition of hymns that make up the Rig Veda was probably written down and compiled in the second millennium B.C. Vedic literature is vast and fascinating and includes the Brahmanas (prose commentaries on the Vedas) and later, the Upanishads, whose major texts were composed between 800 and 400 B.C. These beautiful and mystical pieces, composed of prose and verse or verse alone, are the core texts for the philosophical schools of Vedanta, which hold that all reality is united into the single macrocosmic principle of Brahman.

During the centuries between the fall of the Mauryans and the rise of the Guptas, important influxes of Greeks, Parthians, Scythians, Afghans, and Kushans settled and influenced the North, while in the Dravidian south the Tamil culture flourished, producing some of India's most extraordinary poetry. Early Tamil literature includes two epics, eight major anthologies, and ten long poems. Tamil lyric poetry is divided into two main genres, *akam* or love poems of the interior landscape and *puram* or war poems of the exterior landscape.

Like the Mauryan empire, the Gupta empire originated in the state of Magadha and spread over much of India, though it didn't conquer as much of south India as its predecessor. The third Gupta king, Chandragupta II (A.D. 375–415), was a great patron of the arts and presided over a flourishing era of literary and artistic production. His reign is considered to be India's second golden age. Although the Guptas were Hindu, like the Buddhist Mauryans they tolerated religious diversity among their conquered peoples. In around A.D. 500, the Gupta empire's northwest area fell to invaders from the north, the White Huns, and the empire from this point onward began to shrink in upon its center at the Ganges until it disappeared altogether.

The classical Indian writers of the Gupta period began to use the ancient language of Sanskrit as the formal literary language, instead of the vernacular dialects of Sanskrit—the Prakrit languages. Nonetheless, important literatures have survived from ancient times in the southern language of Tamil and in Prakrit languages—notably in Pali, the main language of Indian Buddhism. The *Gatha Saptashati*, for example, is an important compilation of seven hundred Prakrit erotic poems written between A.D. 100 and 300. Though nearly all Sanskrit literature is versified, the greatest examples of Sanskrit poetry lie in the gigantic epics, the *Mahabharata* and the *Ramayana,* which originated in Vedic times, but were adapted and edited by Brahmans in the Gupta period. It is thought that these later editors added a gloss of Hindu sanctity to what had originated as martial epics celebrating the values of the barbarian Aryans. The *Mahabharata* is the world's longest poem, over seven times the length of the

Iliad and the *Odyssey* put together. It includes one of the masterworks of world literature, the Bhagavad-Gita. This key text of Hinduism is a battle-field dialogue in which the god Krishna instructs the hero prince Arjuna on ethical and religious principles. Nonepic Sanskrit poetry includes an extensive tradition of longer poems and a diversity of minor forms. Kalidasa (fourth to fifth century A.D.) was India's "Great Poet," a resident at the brilliant court of Chandragupta II. Kalidasa's long poems figure highest in the canon. He was also the most famous Sanskrit dramatist, and his play *Shakuntala,* which is studded with beautiful short lyrical poems, is the apogee of Indian theater. Other great Sanskrit poets, those of the post-Gupta period, include Bhartrihari (seventh century A.D.?), the love poets Amaru (seventh century A.D.) and Bilhana (eleventh century A.D.), and Jayadeva (twelfth century A.D.), whose erotomystical *Gitagovinda* has been called the Indian Song of Songs. Many of these poets are included in the famous eleventh-century anthology *The Treasury of Well-Tuned Verse.* Sanskrit fairy tales and fables are collected in a number of sequences, usually with an overarching framing narrative. The most distinguished of these is the *Panchatantra,* which was collected during the Gupta era. These story cycles spread far beyond India, providing the basis for similar collections world-wide, such as *The Thousand and One Nights.*

Between the eleventh and fifteenth centuries, Sanskrit and Prakrit ceased to be the major literary languages, as a host of regional mother tongues developed major literary traditions. The key poetic movement of this time is called *bhakti,* which means "devotion." The urgent and intense-ly personal poems of the bhakti poets often addressed a particular god and are a form of devotional poetry that blends the erotic and mystical tradi-tions of Indian literature (much as English metaphysical poets used the speech of English renaissance love poetry to address God). Great bhakti poets include Mahadevi (twelfth century A.D.), Kabir (1398–1448), and Mirabai (1498–1573).

Islam arrived in the eighth century, and Islamic empires have been es-tablished in India since the twelfth century, when the Delhi Sultanate was founded. This empire lasted until 1398. The Islamic Mughal empire, founded by Babur (1483–1530), a descendant of Tamerlane, ruled in India from 1526 to 1857. Under Babur's grandson Akbar the Great (1556–1605), the Mughal empire spread across India. Like Gupta II, Akbar was religiously tol-erant and a great patron of the arts, though his powerful descendant Aurangzeb (1658–1707), who was responsible for expanding the Mughal empire through most of the subcontinent, was not as tolerant and cos-mopolitan a ruler. Under his aegis, the empire saw its majority Hindu popu-lation suffer discrimination, destruction of temples, and other forms of persecution. With Islam came Arabic and especially Persian languages and literary forms. Lalla (1320–1392), who wrote in Kashmiri; Kabir (1398–1448), who wrote in Hindi; and Ghalib (1797–1869), who wrote in Urdu and Persian, were all deeply influenced by Islam, Sufism, and Near Eastern prosody (as well as the native tradition of bhakti).

India in the modern period has been deeply influenced by the experience of British colonialism. The British had established trading stations as early as 1613, and with the conquest of Bengal in 1757, at a time when the Mughal empire was disintegrating, the British empire in India was decisively launched. The British consolidated control of India through the end of the eighteenth century. During this period, English language and Western literary models spread throughout India, particularly after Western education became widely available in the late eighteenth century. In the modern period, Indian writers have often adopted English as their literary language. Writers such as Rabindranath Tagore (1861–1941, winner of the Nobel Prize in literature in 1913) and Premchand (1880–1936) as well as activists and spiritual leaders such as Mahatma Gandhi (1869–1948), were deeply involved in the fight for independence from Great Britain, which was achieved in 1947. India was divided into India and Pakistan in August 1947, and later that year more than half a million people died in the ensuing civil war between Hindus and Muslims. A year later, Gandhi was assassinated by a Hindu fanatic. India and Pakistan have fought several wars in the twentieth century, culminating in East Pakistan's rebellion against West Pakistan, which was supported by India. West Pakistan successfully seceded and founded the state of Bangladesh. Since the subcontinent achieved independence from Colonial Britain, contemporary novelists and short story writers from India and Pakistan have become enormously successful worldwide, and the poets, though less known outside of this region, have modernized this vast and ancient tradition of verse.

The Vedic Period

(c. 1500–200 B.C.)

■ The Rig Veda (c. 1200–900 B.C.)
Sanskrit (poems)

The Vedas are the oldest books of the Indo-Aryans, the culture fused from the ancient civilization of the Indus River valley and the Indo-European-speaking Aryan (or "noble") people who invaded during the second millennium B.C. They are the source of much Indian literature and religion. The word *veda* derives from *vid*, which means "to know"; the Vedas are compilations of sacred knowledge that were supposed to have been revealed directly to the four sages by Brahma, the supreme god. There are four Vedas, the Rig Veda, the Yajur Veda, the Sama Veda, and the Atharva Veda, revealed to Agni, Vayu, Aditya, and Angiras, the four sages. Of the four, the Rig Veda (*rik* means "a verse") is the oldest, and the one with the most literary value; its ten books contain 11,000 hymns. The vedas are among the oldest literature of the world; only Egyptian and Meso-potamian literatures are probably more ancient. It is impossible to date them with certainty, but we know that they must have been completed ear-lier than the sixth or seventh century B.C., and the earliest date given for the transcription of this oral tradition of hymns is 6000 B.C. (though a more likely date would be the second or third millennium B.C.). Vyasa, tradition-ally considered the author of the Mahabharata, is thought to have been the first compiler of the vedas. Vedic literature, including the Upanishads and the vedic hymns and rituals, is the source of Hindu culture. The hymns pre-sented here worship a startling number of gods, and they paint a fascinat-ing picture of the lovers, gamblers, villages, and ceremonies of early Indian life. The literary value of these collections is secondary to their religious sig-nificance. They were (and are) used for ritual purposes—the hymns of the Rig Veda were recited, sometimes as arranged into the Sama Veda and Yajur Veda; the Atharva Veda is a compilation primarily of incantations and magic spells, mantras to be used by priests overseeing sacrifices, and hymns of atonement.

FURTHER READING: Bloomfield, M. A., tr. *Atharva Veda,* 1899. Bose, Abinash Chan-dra, tr. *Hymns from the Vedas,* 1966. Griffith, R. T. H., Max Muller, and R. Trivedi, trs. *Rig Veda,* 1889–1891, 1892, 1945. Le Mee, Jean, tr. *Hymns from the Rig Veda,* 1975. Macdonell, Arthur A., tr. *Hymns from the Rigveda: Selected and Metrically Translated,* 1922. O'Flaherty, Wendy. *The Rig Veda,* 1981. Samasrami, S., tr., *Sama Veda,* 1874–1878. Smith, H. Daniel, ed. *Selections from Vedic Hymns,* 1968.

The Creation

> Before being, before even nonbeing, there was no air, no firmament.
>   So what breathed? And where? And by whose order? And was
>   there water endlessly deep?
> This was before death or immortality. There was no division between
>   night and day, yet instinctively there was breathing, windless
>   breathing and nothing else.
> It was so dark that darkness was hidden in the dark. There was
>   nothing to show water was everywhere. And the void was a cloak
>   about the Being who sprang from heat.
> Desire pierced the Being, the mind's first seed, and wise poet saints
>   detected in their hearts the knot of being within nonbeing,
> and this rope they stretched over . . . what? Was there up? down?
>   There were seed spillers and fertile powers, impulse above and
>   energy below,
> but who can really know and say it here? Where did this creation
>   come from? The gods came later, so who can know the source?

5

No one knows creation's source. It was born of itself. Or it was not. He who looks down from the ultimate heaven knows. Or maybe not.

TRANSLATED BY TONY BARNSTONE AND WILLIS BARNSTONE

Night[1]

The goddess night has come and her eyes shine in all directions. She
    is robed in glory.
Light of the deathless goddess spills through all the valleys and peaks,
    killing darkness.
When she comes she pushes out her sister twilight, and darkness is
    chased away.
Goddess, as you approach we fly to our homes, birds to their nests.
Now the village people sleep and the clawed beasts and winged birds,   5
    even the ever-hunting hawk, are still.
Save us from the wolf and his bitch, ward off the thief, and help us
    reach night's far shore in safety.
Darkness presses on me like black paint. Let dawn banish it like a
    debt.
Daughter of the sky, you've won the battle. Please hear this hymn I
    herd toward you like cattle.

TRANSLATED BY TONY BARNSTONE AND WILLIS BARNSTONE

To Vishvakarman, Maker of the Universe

The wise father of the sun, the sky's eye, churned two arching worlds
    from primeval butter and moored their ends in the east, and the
    earth and sky spread out.
The All-Maker is strong as the universe, his mind is vast, he forms and
    orders, he is the ultimate being; offerings of prayer and rich
    liquids bring joy in heaven, there past the seven sages, where
    there is only one Being.
Father who made us, who aligned all things and knows all worlds and
    beings, you who named the gods, all creatures seek wisdom from
    you.
Like the singers who sang all things into existence when the region of
    darkness was not yet divided from light, countless ancient wise
    men have made sacrifices to you.

---

1. The goddess of night is bright with the light of heavenly objects, and she pushes out the darkness. She is the sister of twilight and dawn.

What first germ of life was planted in the waters, before earth and sky,   5
    before even the Asuras[1] and the gods, in waters where the
    company of gods were to appear?
He was the seed the waters received, all gods in one, and he sat on the
    Unborn's navel, he on whom all creatures rest.
But you will never find the one who made all creatures. Someone has
    come between you: hymn singers gorged on life who fumble
    through a cloak of fog and stammer nonsense.

TRANSLATED BY TONY BARNSTONE

The Gambler

Shivering hazelnut eardrops were born from the great tree during a
    hurricane. Now they roll on the diceboard and I'm drunk with
    gambling fever.
My wife never whined or blew up, she loved me and my friends, but I
    tossed her away with one bad throw of the dice.
Now she and her mother despise me, and no one gives a damn. A
    gambler is worth less than a boney old nag you try to dump on
    the market.
Since the thirsty dice sucked me dry, other men fondle my wife and
    my father, mother and brothers say "We don't know that man.
    Chain him up and get him out of our sight."
I swear to my friends I won't play and they take off. But the brown   5
    dice beckon as they hit the board and soon I rush off to the
    game, hot as a woman meeting her lover.
I enter the hall quivering with desire and dreaming of winning, but
    the dice smash my hopes and give my rival all the throws.
The dice seduce you. They hook and stab your flesh until you're their
    slave, mesmerized, tormented. Like children they tempt you
    with gifts, then take them back. You drown in the honey of their
    sweet magic.
In three troops of fifty the dice-game is bound by rules inflexible
    as the chariot path of the sungod Savitri. Not even the
    tantrums of rich nobles can change this. Even the king bows
    to them.
They tumble down, then bounce back up. Handless, they cow the man
    with hands. Sorcerous coals spilled on the gaming board, they're
    cold but they burn the heart to ash.

---

1. Asuras are ancient divinities, demonic enemies of the gods.

My abandoned wife groans. My mother mourns my wandering. I need   10
    money, I'm in debt and scared. At night I steal up on another
    man's house.
It kills me to see my wife in his arms, in those fine rooms, but still at
    dawn I yoke up those brown horses and when night comes
    around I'm a derelict flopping down by the fire.

General of that great dice-army, king of those troops, listen, I
    wouldn't lie! I don't have a cent. See these ten fingers spread
    wide?
Great Savitri tells me: Gambler, give up the dice and till your field.
    Love what you have already. Your cows, your wife, it's enough.
Dice, give me a break. Don't make me a slave to sorcery. Let your
    hatred and anger sleep. Tangle someone else in your net.

TRANSLATED BY TONY BARNSTONE AND WILLIS BARNSTONE

The Poet Traveler Lost in the Forest

Mother spirit of the forest, why do you vanish? Why do you flee from
    our village? Are you afraid?

When cattle low and crickets respond, you are a hunter laughing
    among bells, startling the beasts with noisy beaters.

In the twilight forest you appear as cows grazing, the shape of a
    remote house, are heard in the secret creaking of carts.

Whoever stays in the evening forest hears wild sounds. Someone
    shouts at the herds, an ax chops into a tree, someone is
    screaming.

If I come near, you do not pounce on me like an animal. No, you eat   5
    delicious fruit and lie down where you please.

Mother of wild beasts, unplowed land rich in foods, fragrances and
    balm, spirit of the forest, I sing to you.

TRANSLATED BY TONY BARNSTONE AND WILLIS BARNSTONE

The Poet to Parjanya, Bullgod of the Rain

Powerful god, I sing your praise and ask for help. You bellow and your
    luscious drops impregnate the plants.

You slaughter demons and smash trees to kindling. With your deadly
    thunderbolt you terrorize all creatures,

even the sinless flee before you, bullgod bursting with seed, and
Parjanya you execute the wicked.

Like a charioteer lashing his horses, you send your messengers of rain
tearing wildly ahead.

From the horizons a lion thunders when you fill the heavens with   5
ponderous clouds of rain.

Winds plunge over the earth, lightning splits the night, all vegetation
lunges skyward in thirst, as if after udders of milk.

When you refresh and fructify the earth with your sperm water, the
cosmos is fulfilled with food.

Before you the earth itself bows and hooved beasts quiver. Your law
spurs every species of plant into bloom. Great one, you are our
salvation.

Winds, search for rain in heaven. Let the stallion's seed swell, burst,
and flow freely over us.

You are our luminous watergod, our father, sprinkle your blessings on   10
your children,
bellow and spin through the sky over the world. Fill your chariot with
waters, tilt your waterbags over
mountains and ravines till they are one lake. Pour the enormous
buckets down. Drench heaven and earth with sweet butter,
make ponds for cows to drink, slaughter the wicked, and let the earth
be happy. You have sent the rain, now let it stop —
the deserts are pleasant woods, the plants thrive and all creatures find
the inspired poetry of food.

TRANSLATED BY TONY BARNSTONE AND WILLIS BARNSTONE

■ The Upanishads
(c. Ninth Century B.C. to First Century A.D.)
Sanskrit (poems/religious texts)

TRANSLATED BY JUAN MASCARÓ

The word *Upanishad* derives from *sad* ("to sit"), *upa* ("near"), and *ni*
("down") with a general meaning of "to sit down near the master" who
teaches the doctrine. The Upanishads range widely in age from around
800 B.C. to as late as the fifteenth century A.D., though the major ones were
composed between 800 and 400 B.C. There are as many as 150 Upanishads,
of which 108 are considered authentic. These mystical texts of Hinduism

are generally composed in Sanskrit prose interspersed with verse, though five of them are wholly in verse. The older Upanishads are among the most important, and certainly the earliest, Hindu texts treating philosophic and religious subjects and are considered the source of much Hindu faith and speculation. They are also among the most beautiful.

The Upanishads, though attached to the Vedas, present a differing perspective on the world. The rituals that are so central to Vedic religion are not important in the Upanishads. Central to the worldview of the Upanishads is the idea of Brahman, conceived of as the absolute and ultimate reality behind the world. Brahman is huge, essential, eternal, yet the Upanishads state that it is identical to the inner self, or Atman: "Concealed in the heart of all beings is the Atman, the Spirit, the Self; smaller than the smallest atom, greater than the vast spaces." By perceiving this essential unity in the world, one can be freed from the cycle of birth and rebirth, but "Who sees the many and not the ONE, wanders on from death to death." The philosophic schools of Vedanta are based upon the Upanishads.

From a literary standpoint, the Upanishads represent some of the most beautiful mystical poetry in the world, as in the Katha Upanishad's description of the Atman as a flame without smoke, the size of a thumb, or its description of Brahman as a tree of eternity with its roots in heaven and its branches reaching down to the earth. In the selections from the major Upanishads given here, we see treatments of these subjects, as well as parables and teaching stories. In the famous Katha Upanishad, we even see a youth named Nachiketas, who, like his Sumerian counterpart Gilgamesh, goes in search of what happens after death.

FURTHER READING: Mascaró, Juan. *The Upanishads*, 1965. Nikhilananda, Swami. *The Upanishads*, 1963. Younger, Paul. *Introduction to Indian Religious Thought*, 1972.

from Isa Upanishad

There are demon-haunted worlds, regions of utter darkness. Whoever in life denies the Spirit falls into that darkness of death.

The Spirit, without moving, is swifter than the mind; the senses cannot reach him: He is ever beyond them. Standing still, he overtakes those who run. To the ocean of his being, the spirit of life leads the streams of action.

He moves, and he moves not. He is far, and he is near. He is within all, and he is outside all.

Who sees all beings in his own Self, and his own Self in all beings, loses all fear.

When a sage sees this great Unity and his Self has become all beings, what delusion and what sorrow can ever be near him?

The Spirit filled all with his radiance. He is incorporeal and invulnerable, pure and untouched by evil. He is the supreme seer and thinker, immanent and transcendent. He placed all things in the path of Eternity.

from Kena Upanishad

Part 1

Who sends the mind to wander afar? Who first drives life to start on its journey? Who impels us to utter these words? Who is the Spirit behind the eye and the ear?

It is the ear of the ear, the eye of the eye, and the Word of words, the mind of mind, and the life of life. Those who follow wisdom pass beyond and, on leaving this world, become immortal.

There the eye goes not, nor words, nor mind. We know not, we cannot understand, how he can be explained: He is above the known and he is above the unknown. Thus have we heard from the ancient sages who explained this truth to us.

What cannot be spoken with words, but that whereby words are spoken: Know that alone to be Brahman, the Spirit; and not what people here adore.

What cannot be thought with the mind, but that whereby the mind can think: Know that alone to be Brahman, the Spirit; and not what people here adore.

What cannot be seen with the eye, but that whereby the eye can see: Know that alone to be Brahman, the Spirit; and not what people here adore.

What cannot be heard with the ear, but that whereby the ear can hear: Know that alone to be Brahman, the Spirit; and not what people here adore.

What cannot be indrawn with breath, but that whereby breath is indrawn: Know that alone to be Brahman, the Spirit; and not what people here adore.

from Katha Upanishad[1]

Part 2

Nachiketas. Tell me what you see beyond right and wrong, beyond what is done or not done, beyond past and future.

Death. I will tell you the Word that all the *Vedas* glorify, all self-sacrifice expresses, all sacred studies and holy life seek. That Word is OM.

That Word is the everlasting Brahman: that Word is the highest End. When that sacred Word is known, all longings are fulfilled.

It is the supreme means of salvation: it is the help supreme. When that great Word is known, one is great in the heaven of Brahman.

---

1. A dialogue in which Death acts as spiritual instructor to a youth named Nachiketas.

Atman, the Spirit of vision, is never born and never dies. Before him there was nothing, and he is ONE for evermore. Never-born and eternal, beyond times gone or to come, he does not die when the body dies.

If the slayer thinks that he kills, and if the slain thinks that he dies, neither knows the ways of truth. The Eternal in man cannot kill: the Eternal in man cannot die.

Concealed in the heart of all beings is the Atman, the Spirit, the Self; smaller than the smallest atom, greater than the vast spaces. The man who surrenders his human will leaves sorrows behind, and beholds the glory of the Atman by the grace of the Creator.

Resting, he wanders afar; sleeping, he goes everywhere. Who else but my Self can know that God of joy and of sorrows?

When the wise realize the omnipresent Spirit, who rests invisible in the visible and permanent in the impermanent, then they go beyond sorrow.

Part 4

What is here is also there, and what is there is also here.

Who sees the many and not the ONE, wanders on from death to death.

Even by the mind this truth is to be learned: there are not many but only ONE. Who sees variety and not the unity wanders on from death to death.

The soul dwells within us, a flame the size of a thumb. When it is known as the Lord of the past and the future, then ceases all fear:

This in truth is That.

Like a flame without smoke, the size of a thumb, is the soul; the Lord of the past and the future, the same both today and tomorrow:

This in truth is That.

As water raining on a mountain-ridge runs down the rocks on all sides, so the man who only sees variety of things runs after them on all sides.

But as pure water raining on pure water becomes one and the same, so becomes, O Nachiketas, the soul of the sage who knows.

Part 5

I will now speak to you of the mystery of the eternal Brahman; and of what happens to the soul after death.

The soul may go to the womb of a mother and thus obtain a new body. It even may go into trees or plants, according to its previous wisdom and work.

There is a Spirit who is awake in our sleep and creates the wonder of dreams. He is Brahman, the Spirit of Light, who in truth is called the Immortal. All the worlds rest on that Spirit and beyond him no one can go:

This in truth is That.

As fire, though one, takes new forms in all things that burn, the Spirit, though one, takes new forms in all things that live. He is within all, and is also outside.

As the wind, though one, takes new forms in whatever it enters, the Spirit, though one, takes new forms in all things that live. He is within all, and is also outside.

As the sun that beholds the world is untouched by earthly impurities, so the Spirit that is in all things is untouched by external sufferings.

There is one Ruler, the Spirit that is in all things, who transforms his own form into many. Only the wise who see him in their souls attain the joy eternal.

He is the Eternal among things that pass away, pure Consciousness of conscious beings, the ONE who fulfils the prayers of many. Only the wise who see him in their souls attain the peace eternal.

'This is That'—thus they realize the ineffable joy supreme. How can 'This' be known? Does he give light or does he reflect light?

There the sun shines not, nor the moon, nor the stars; lightnings shine not there and much less earthly fire. From his light all these give light, and his radiance illumines all creation.

Part 6

The Tree of Eternity has its roots in heaven above and its branches reach down to earth. It is Brahman, pure Spirit, who in truth is called the Immortal. All the worlds rest on that Spirit and beyond him no one can go:

This in truth is That.

The whole universe comes from him and his life burns through the whole universe. In his power is the majesty of thunder. Those who know him have found immortality.

from **Kaushitaki Upanishad**

When the fire burns, Brahman shines; and when the fire dies, Brahman goes. Its light goes to the sun, and its breath of life to the wind.

When the sun shines, Brahman shines; and when the sun sets, Brahman goes. Its light goes to the moon, and its breath of life to the wind.

When the moon shines, Brahman shines; and when the moon sets, Brahman goes. Its light goes to a flash of lightning, and its breath of life to the wind.

When a flash of lightning shines, Brahman shines; and when it goes, Brahman goes. Its light goes to the regions of heaven, and its breath of life to the wind.

✳ ✳ ✳

It is not speech which we should want to know: we should know the speaker.

It is not things seen which we should want to know: we should know the seer.

It is not sounds which we should want to know: we should know the hearer.

It is not mind which we should want to know: WE SHOULD KNOW THE THINKER.

from *Taittiriya Upanishad*

> Oh, the wonder of joy!
> I am the food of life, and I am he who eats the food of life: I am the two in ONE.
> I am the first-born of the world of truth, born before the gods, born in the centre of immortality.
>
> He who gives me is my salvation.
> I am that food which eats the eater of food.
> I have gone beyond the universe, and the light of the sun is my light.

5

from *Chandogya Upanishad*

There is a Light that shines beyond all things on earth, beyond us all, beyond the heavens, beyond the highest, the very highest heavens. This is the Light that shines in our heart.

*   *   *

OM. There lived once a boy, Svetaketu Aruneya by name. One day his father spoke to him in this way: 'Svetaketu, go and become a student of sacred wisdom. There is no one in our family who has not studied the holy *Vedas* and who might only be given the name of Brahman by courtesy.'

The boy left at the age of twelve and, having learnt the *Vedas*, he returned home at the age of twenty-four, very proud of his learning and having a great opinion of himself.

His father, observing this, said to him: 'Svetaketu, my boy, you seem to have a great opinion of yourself, you think you are learned, and you are proud. Have you asked for that knowledge whereby what is not heard is heard, what is not thought is thought, and what is not known is known?'

'What is that knowledge, father?' asked Svetaketu.

'Just as by knowing a lump of clay, my son, all that is clay can be known, since any differences are only words and the reality is clay;

Just as by knowing a piece of gold all that is gold can be known, since any differences are only words and the reality is only gold;

And just as by knowing a piece of iron all that is iron is known, since any differences are only words and the reality is only iron.'

Svetaketu said: 'Certainly my honoured masters knew not this themselves. If they had known, why would they not have told me? Explain this to me, father.'

'So be it, my child.'

'Bring me a fruit from this banyan tree.'

'Here it is, father.'

'Break it.'

'It is broken, Sir.'

'What do you see in it?'

'Very small seeds, Sir.'

'Break one of them, my son.'

'It is broken, Sir.'

'What do you see in it?'

'Nothing at all, Sir.'

Then his father spoke to him: 'My son, from the very essence in the seed which you cannot see comes in truth this vast banyan tree.

Believe me, my son, an invisible and subtle essence is the Spirit of the whole universe. That is Reality. That is Atman, THOU ART THAT.'

'Explain more to me, father,' said Svetaketu.

'So be it, my son.

Place this salt in water and come to me tomorrow morning.'

Svetaketu did as he was commanded, and in the morning his father said to him: 'Bring me the salt you put into the water last night.'

Svetaketu looked into the water, but could not find it, for it had dissolved.

His father then said: 'Taste the water from this side. How is it?'

'It is salt.'

'Taste it from the middle. How is it?'

'It is salt.'

'Taste it from that side. How is it?'

'It is salt.'

'Look for the salt again and come again to me.'

The son did so, saying: 'I cannot see the salt. I only see water.'

His father then said: 'In the same way, O my son, you cannot see the Spirit. But in truth he is here.

An invisible and subtle essence is the Spirit of the whole universe. That is Reality. That is Truth. THOU ART THAT.'

Buddhist Texts

(c. Fifth Century B.C. to A.D. 255)

■ Theravada Buddhist Texts (Fifth Century B.C. to First Century B.C.) *Pali* (religious texts)

Prince Siddhartha Gautama, known as the Buddha (Sanskrit for "the enlightened one"), probably lived from 563 B.C. to 483 B.C. His life is wreathed in legend, but it seems likely, as in the case of Christ, that a historical man existed behind the religious embroidery and controversy. He was the son of a king in what is today southern Nepal. Because of a prediction at his birth that he would become either a great king or a great religious teacher, his father raised the young prince in great luxury, wishing to assure himself a successor, and Siddhartha was shielded from the misery of the world, which might lead him toward a religious life. He married, had a son, but on excursions outside the palace, he encountered a series of men—an old man, a sick man, a corpse, and a monk—embodying the world from which he had been excluded. He abandoned his heritage and his wife and son and wandered in search of religious wisdom. After mastering yogic meditation, he tried the path of fasting and austerity, but he found neither path fully satisfactory. At last he sat down under a pipal tree and vowed not to move until he had attained enlightenment. Like Saint Anthony tempted by devils in the desert, Siddhartha overcame the wiles and attacks of the evil god Mara and attained enlightenment. Until his death at eighty, he traveled and gathered disciples of all castes and religions, spreading the word of his new religion.

The Buddha taught that religious practitioners should avoid the extremes of indulgence and self-mortification and follow instead a "middle way." He taught that life in this world is sorrow—sorrow of sickness, death, desire, and impermanence—but that there is a way out of sorrow to a different form of existence, or nonexistence (the Buddha is notoriously vague about this point), called *nirvana.* In the transitory world, beings exist and die and are reborn perpetually on the great wheel of birth and rebirth. The engine behind the world, and the means to get out of it, is *dharma.* Dharma is moral law; though the Buddha didn't deny the existence of the gods of Vedic religions, he believed that even the gods are subject to dharma and that there is no ultimate god who is creator and judge. Dharma means truth, spiritual law, way of life; those who follow the path of dharma will be rewarded in future lives, whereas those who abandon it will descend to the deepest hells. The thoughts and actions that cause us to be rewarded or punished are known as our *karma*. From a Buddhist perspective, when Milton's Satan cries, "Myself am Hell," he does so because he has departed from the path of dharma and is punished by having to live with his karma. As Emerson writes, "of their own volition, souls proceed into heaven, into hell." Those in heaven can fall and even those in hell can rise, since heavens and hells are not absolute; they belong to the world of mutability. The Buddhist practice is a method of escape from this perpetuation of misery, a way to stop the carousel ride.

Having thus analyzed the macrocosmic world, Buddhist logic then turns a microscope on the self. The self, like the world, is caught in a chain of cause and effect; if the root cause of suffering is detected, then suffering will disappear. In the *Lotus Sutra*, the Buddha writes, "As to the cause of all suffering, / it has its root in greed and desire. / If greed and desire are wiped out, / it will have no place to dwell." Since desires hold us in the world, we must analyze our selves through the intense self-scrutiny of meditation until we can eliminate this glue holding the self together. By looking in, we can discover what separates us from each other, and in tearing it away, free ourselves from the prison of the ego. These are three of the Four Noble Truths that he preached in his very first sermon: life is sorrow; desire causes sorrow; destroy desire and you may escape. The fourth truth states that this escape may be achieved through an eightfold path to liberation: right belief, right resolve, right speech, right behavior, right occupation, right effort, right contemplation, and right meditation. Through this path we may achieve nirvana. In Mahayana Buddhism, such enlightenment tends to be closer to the Upanishadic awakening to the sameness of Atman and Brahman, of self and world. In Theravada schools, however, nirvana's total cessation of desire opens a door from the self and out of the world, like a drop entering an ocean or like a fire that burns itself away. Is nirvana nothingness, complete cessation of being? Or does one cease to *become* but continue to *be* in a perfect, absolute, unchanging sphere of existence? The scripture is unclear. Nirvana is ineffable, and the Buddha spoke of it indirectly in parables because limited words can't capture its illimitable nature. A famous parable states that asking too much about the beyond is like a man with an arrow sticking in him who dies because he insists on knowing everything about the arrow, and the one who shot it, and a million other inconsequent details before allowing a doctor to pull it out and treat the wound.

The texts gathered in this section come from the Pali canon of early Buddhist texts that is religious scripture for the world's Theravada Buddhists (Mahayana texts were written later, at first mainly in Sanskrit, and subsequently in Chinese and Japanese). Pali is a vernacular dialect of classical Sanskrit, and it is the language in which oral sermons and literature of the Buddhists were set down not long after the death of the Buddha in 483 B.C. The canon is called the Tipitaka, which means triple basket; the three baskets refer to the basket of discipline, the basket of teaching, and the basket of metaphysics. This huge repository of Buddhist literature contains the doctrine of the earliest form of Buddhism, and thus in spite of sectarian differences, it contains the essential kernel of all Buddhism. Theravada Buddhism still is dominant in Burma, Sri Lanka, and Southeast Asia, whereas Mahayana is found in China, Korea, and Japan. The Pali texts presented here are of several types: there are passages from the *Visuddhi–Magga,* the finest Pali text written by Buddhaghosha, a systematic treatment of the entire Buddhist doctrine; a description of the "middle doctrine" from the *Sainyutta-Nikaya;* and passages from the *Milindapanha* (the *Questions of Milinda*), a dialogue between King Menander (Milinda) and Thera Nagasena about the essential problems of Buddhism. Also included here is the "Fire Sermon" of the *Maha-Vagga,* a famous text about the fires of passion and the source of much later literature—from Wang Wei's "Suffering from Heat" to T. S. Eliot's third section of *The Waste Land,* also titled "The Fire Sermon." Finally, there is a selection of verses from the *Dhammapada.* The *Dhammapada* is the most popular canonical text of Buddhism, consisting of 423 aphorisms attributed to the Buddha arranged by subject into twenty-six chapters. *Dhamma* is Pali for the Sanskrit dharma (defined earlier), while *pada* means "foot" or "step"; together they mean the path of truth. The *Dhammapada* is known worldwide as a condensed and evocative summation of Buddhist spiritual doctrine and is the Buddhist text most often anthologized because of its literary qualities.

FURTHER READING: Babbitt, Irving, tr. *The Dhammapada: Translated from the Pali, with an Essay on Buddha and the Occident,* 1st ed. 1936. Banerji, S. C. *An Introduction to Pali Literature,* 1964. Conze, Edward. *Buddhist Scriptures,* 1986. Geiger, Wilhelm. *Pali Literature and Language,* rev. ed. 1968. Kalupahana, David J. *A Path of Righteousness: Dhammapada: An Introductory Essay, together with the Pali Text, English Translation, and Commentary,* 1986. Lal, P., tr. *The Dhammapada,* 1967. Mascaró, Juan, tr. *The Dhammapada: The Path of Perfection,* 1973. Max Müller, F., tr. *The Dhammapada: A Collection of Verses; Being One of the Canonical Books of the Buddhists,* 1965, 1977. Radhakrishnan, S. *The Dhammapada, with Introductory Essays, Pali Text, English Translation and Notes,* 1958. Warren, Henry Clarke. *Buddhism in Translations,* 1896, 1976.

from *the Visuddhi-Magga*

TRANSLATED BY HENRY CLARKE WARREN

On Getting Angry

"My friend, who hast retired from the world and art angry with this man, tell me what it is you are angry with? Are you angry with the hair of the head, or with the hair of the body, or with the nails, etc.? Or are you angry with the earthy element in the hair of the head and the rest? Or are you angry with the watery element, or with the fiery element, or with the windy element in them? What is meant by the venerable N.N. is only the five groups, the six organs of sense, the six objects of sense, and the six sense-consciousnesses. With which of these are you angry? Is it with the form-group? Or is it with the sensation-group, perception-group, predisposition-group, or consciousness-group? Or are you angry with an organ of sense, or an object of sense, or a sense-consciousness?"

For a person who has made the above analysis, there is no hold for anger, any more than there is for a grain of mustard-seed on the point of an awl, or for a painting in the sky.

Beauty Is But Skin-Deep

. . . The story is that a certain woman had married into a family of rank, but had quarreled with her husband, and, decked and ornamented, until she looked like a goddess, had issued forth from Anuradhapura, early in the morning, and was returning home to her family. On her way she met the elder, as he was on his way from Mt. Cetiya to go on his begging-rounds in Anuradhapura. And no sooner had she seen him, than the perversity of her nature caused her to laugh loudly. The elder looked up inquiringly, and observing her teeth, realized the impurity of the body,[1] and attained to saintship. Therefore was it said:

> "The elder gazed upon her teeth,
> And thought upon impurity;
> And ere that he had left that spot,
> The stage of saintship he attained."

Then came her husband, following in her footsteps, and seeing the elder, he said: "Reverend sir, have you seen a woman pass this way?"

And the elder said:

> "Was it a woman, or a man,
> That passed this way? I cannot tell.
> But this I know, a set of bones
> Is traveling on upon this road."

* * *

For as the body when dead is repulsive, so is it also when alive; but on account of the concealment afforded by an adventitious adornment, its repulsiveness escapes notice. The body is in reality a collection of over three hundred bones, and is framed into a whole by means of one hundred and eighty joints. It is held together by nine hundred tendons, and overlaid by

---

1. By means of the tenth impurity, the teeth being reckoned as bone.

nine hundred muscles, and has an outside envelope of moist cuticle covered by an epidermis full of pores, through which there is an incessant oozing and trickling, as if from a kettle of fat. It is a prey to vermin, the seat of disease, and subject to all manner of miseries. Through its nine apertures it is always discharging matter, like a ripe boil. Matter is secreted from the two eyes, wax from the ears, snot from the nostrils, and from the mouth issue food, bile, phlegm, and blood, and from the two lower orifices of the body faeces and urine, while from the ninety-nine thousand pores of the skin an unclean sweat exudes attracting black flies and other insects.

Were even a king in triumphal progress to neglect the use of tooth-sticks, mouth-rinses, anointings of the head, baths and inner and outside garments, and other means for beautifying the person, he would become as uncouth and unkempt as the moment he was born, and would in no wise differ in bodily offensiveness from the low-caste caṇḍāla whose occupation it is to remove dead flowers. Thus in respect of its uncleanness, malodor, and disgusting offensiveness, the person of a king does not differ from that of a caṇḍāla. However, when, with the help of tooth-sticks, mouth-rinses, and various ablutions, men have cleansed their teeth, and the rest of their persons, and with manifold garments have covered their nakedness, and have anointed themselves with many-colored and fragrant unguents, and adorned themselves with flowers and ornaments, they find themselves able to believe in an "I" and a "mine." Accordingly, it is on account of the concealment afforded by this adventitious adornment that people fail to recognize the essential repulsiveness of their bodies, and that men find pleasure in women, and women in men. In reality, however, there is not the smallest just reason for being pleased.

A proof of this is the fact that when any part of the body becomes detached, as, for instance, the hair of the head, hair of the body, nails, teeth, phlegm, snot, faeces, or urine, people are unwilling so much as to touch it, and are distressed at, ashamed of, and loathe it. But in respect of what remains, though that is likewise repulsive, yet men are so wrapped in blindness and infatuated by a passionate fondness for their own selves, that they believe it to be something desirable, lovely, lasting, pleasant, and an Ego.

from *the Sainyutta-Nikaya*

TRANSLATED BY HENRY CLARKE WARREN

The Middle Doctrine

The world, for the most part, O Kaccāna, holds either to a belief in being or to a belief in non-being. But for one who in the light of the highest knowledge, O Kaccāna, considers how the world arises, belief in the non-being of the world passes away. And for one who in the light of the highest knowledge, O Kaccāna, considers how the world ceases, belief in the being of the world passes away. The world, O Kaccāna, is for the most part bound up in a seeking, attachment, and proclivity [for the groups], but a priest does not sympathize with this seeking and attachment, nor with the mental affirmation, proclivity, and prejudice which affirms an Ego. He does not doubt or question that it is only evil that springs into existence, and only evil that ceases from existence, and his conviction of this fact is dependent on no one besides himself. This, O Kaccāna, is what constitutes Right Belief.

That things have being, O Kaccāna, constitutes one extreme of doctrine; that things have no being is the other extreme. These extremes, O Kaccāna, have been avoided by The Tathāgata,[2] and it is a middle doctrine he teaches:—

On ignorance depends karma;
On karma depends consciousness;
On consciousness depend name and form;
On name and form depend the six organs of sense;
On the six organs of sense depends contact;
On contact depends sensation;
On sensation depends desire;
On desire depends attachment;
On attachment depends existence;
On existence depends birth;
On birth depend old age and death, sorrow, lamentation, misery,
  grief, and despair. Thus does this entire aggregation of misery
  arise.

But on the complete fading out and cessation of ignorance ceases karma;

On the cessation of karma ceases consciousness;
On the cessation of consciousness cease name and form;
On the cessation of name and form cease the six organs of sense;
On the cessation of the six organs of sense ceases contact;
On the cessation of contact ceases sensation;
On the cessation of sensation ceases desire;
On the cessation of desire ceases attachment;
On the cessation of attachment ceases existence;
On the cessation of existence ceases birth;
On the cessation of birth cease old age and death, sorrow,
  lamentation, misery, grief, and despair. Thus does this entire
  aggregation of misery cease.

---

2. A title for the Buddha.

from **the Mìlindapañha**

TRANSLATED BY HENRY CLARKE WARREN

The Round of Existence

"Bhante Nāgasena," said the king, "when you say 'round of existence,' what is that?"

"Your majesty, to be born here and die here, to die here and be born elsewhere, to be born there and die there, to die there and be born elsewhere, — this, your majesty, is the round of existence."

"Give an illustration."

"It is as if, your majesty, a man were to eat a ripe mango, and plant the seed; and from that a large mango-tree were to spring and bear fruit; and then the man were to eat a ripe mango from that tree also and plant the seed; and from that seed also a large mango-tree were to spring and bear fruit; thus of these trees there is no end discernible. In exactly the same way, your majesty, to be born here and die here, to die here and be born elsewhere, to be born there and die there, to die there and be born elsewhere, this, your majesty, is the round of existence."

"You are an able man, bhante Nāgasena."

Cause of Rebirth

"Bhante Nāgasena," said the king, "are there any who die without being born into another existence?"

"Some are born into another existence," said the elder, "and some are not born into another existence."

"Who is born into another existence, and who is not born into another existence?"

"Your majesty, he that still has the corruptions is born into another existence; he that no longer has the corruptions is not born into another existence."

"But will you, bhante, be born into another existence?"

"Your majesty, if there shall be in me any attachment, I shall be born into another existence; if there shall be in me no attachment, I shall not be born into another existence."

"You are an able man, bhante Nāgasena."

Rebirth Is Not Transmigration

"Bhante Nāgasena," said the king, "what is it that is born into the next existence?"

"Your majesty," said the elder, "it is name and form that is born into the next existence."

"Is it this same name and form that is born into the next existence?"

"Your majesty, it is not this same name and form that is born into the next existence; but with this name and form, your majesty, one does a deed—it may be good, or it may be wicked—and by reason of this deed another name and form is born into the next existence."

"Bhante, if it is not this same name and form that is born into the next existence, is one not freed from one's evil deeds?"

"If one were not born into another existence," said the elder, "one would be freed from one's evil deeds; but, your majesty, inasmuch as one is born into another existence, therefore is one not freed from one's evil deeds."

"Give an illustration."

"Your majesty, it is as if a man were to take away another man's mangoes, and the owner of the mangoes were to seize him, and show him to the king, and say, 'Sire, this man hath taken away my mangoes'; and the other were to say, 'Sire, I did not take away this man's mangoes. The mangoes which this man planted were different mangoes from those which I took away. I am not liable to punishment.' Pray, your majesty, would the man be liable to punishment?"

"Assuredly, bhante, would he be liable to punishment."

"For what reason?"

"Because, in spite of what he might say, he would be liable to punishment for the reason that the last mangoes derived from the first mangoes."

"In exactly the same way, your majesty, with this name and form one does a deed—it may be good, or it may be wicked—and by reason of this deed another name and form is born into the next existence. Therefore is one not freed from one's evil deeds. . . ."

"Give another illustration."

"Your majesty, it is as if a man were to ascend to the top storey of a house with a light, and eat there; and the light in burning were to set fire to the thatch; and the thatch in burning were to set fire to the house; and the house in burning were to set fire to the village; and the people of the village were to seize him, and say, 'Why, O man, did you set fire to the village?' and he were to say, 'I did not set fire to the village. The fire of the lamp by whose light I ate was a different one from the one which set fire to the village;' and they, quarreling, were to come to you. Whose cause, your majesty, would you sustain?"

"That of the people of the village, bhante."

"And why?"

"Because, in spite of what the man might say, the latter fire sprang from the former."

"In exactly the same way, your majesty, although the name and form which is born into the next existence is different from the name and form which is to end at death, nevertheless, it is sprung from it. Therefore is one not freed from one's evil deeds."

"Give another illustration."

"Your majesty, it is as if a man were to choose a young girl in marriage, and having paid the purchase-money, were to go off; and she subsequently were to grow up and become marriageable; and then another man were to pay the purchase-money for her, and marry her; and the first man were to return, and say, 'O man, why did you marry my wife?' and the other were to say, 'I did not marry your wife. The young, tender girl whom you chose in marriage, and for whom you paid purchase-money, was a different person from this grown-up and marriageable girl whom I have chosen in marriage, and for whom I have paid purchase-money;' and they, quarreling, were to come to you. Whose cause, your majesty, would you sustain?"

"That of the first man."

"And why?"

"Because, in spite of what the second man might say, the grown-up girl sprang from the other."

"In exactly the same way, your majesty, although the name and form which is born into the next existence is different from the name and form which is to end at death, nevertheless, it is sprung from it. Therefore is one not freed from one's evil deeds."

from *the Maha-Vagga*

TRANSLATED BY HENRY CLARKE WARREN

The Fire-Sermon

Then The Blessed One, having dwelt in Uruvelā as long as he wished, proceeded on his wanderings in the direction of Gayā Head, accompanied by a great congregation of priests, a thousand in number, who had all of them aforetime been monks with matted hair. And there in Gayā, on Gayā Head, The Blessed One dwelt, together with the thousand priests.

And there The Blessed One addressed the priests:—

"All things, O priests, are on fire. And what, O priests, are all these things which are on fire?

"The eye, O priests, is on fire; forms are on fire; eye-consciousness is on fire; impressions received by the eye are on fire; and whatever sensation, pleasant, unpleasant, or indifferent, originates in dependence on impressions received by the eye, that also is on fire.

"And with what are these on fire?

"With the fire of passion, say I, with the fire of hatred, with the fire of infatuation; with birth, old age, death, sorrow, lamentation, misery, grief, and despair are they on fire.

"The ear is on fire; sounds are on fire; . . . the nose is on fire; odors are on fire; . . . the tongue is on fire; tastes are on fire; . . . the body is on fire; things tangible are on fire; . . . the mind is on fire; ideas are on fire; . . . mind-consciousness is on fire; impressions received by the mind are on fire; and whatever sensation, pleasant, unpleasant, or indifferent, originates in dependence on impressions received by the mind, that also is on fire.

"And with what are these on fire?

"With the fire of passion, say I, with the fire of hatred, with the fire of infatuation; with birth, old age, death, sorrow, lamentation, misery, grief, and despair are they on fire.

"Perceiving this, O priests, the learned and noble disciple conceives an aversion for the eye, conceives an aversion for forms, conceives an aversion for eye-consciousness, conceives an aversion for the impressions received by the eye; and whatever sensation, pleasant, unpleasant, or indifferent, originates in dependence on impressions received by the eye, for that also he conceives an aversion. Conceives an aversion for the ear, conceives an aversion for sounds, . . . conceives an aversion for the nose, conceives an aversion for odors, . . . conceives an aversion for the tongue, conceives an aversion for tastes, . . . conceives an aversion for the body, conceives an aversion for things tangible, . . . conceives an aversion for the mind, conceives an aversion for ideas, conceives an aversion for mind-consciousness, conceives an aversion for the impressions received by the mind; and whatever sensation, pleasant, unpleasant, or indifferent, originates in dependence on impressions received by the mind, for this also he conceives an aversion. And in conceiving this aversion, he becomes divested of passion, and by the absence of passion he becomes free, and when he is free he becomes aware that he is free; and he knows that rebirth is exhausted, that he has lived the holy life, that he has done what it behooved him to do, and that he is no more for this world."

Now while this exposition was being delivered, the minds of the thousand priests became free from attachment and delivered from the depravities.

Here Endeth the Fire-Sermon

The Dhammapada

TRANSLATED BY JUAN MASCARÓ

from The Fool

How long is the night to the watchman; how long is the road to the
weary; how long is the wandering of lives ending in death for the
fool who cannot find the path!

If on the great journey of life a man cannot find one who is better or at least as good as himself, let him joyfully travel alone: a fool cannot help him on his journey.

'These are my sons. This is my wealth.' In this way the fool troubles himself. He is not even the owner of himself: how much less of his sons and of his wealth!

If a fool can see his own folly, he in this at least is wise; but the fool who thinks he is wise, he indeed is the real fool.

If during the whole of his life a fool lives with a wise man, he never knows the path of wisdom as the spoon never knows the taste of the soup. 5

But if a man who watches and sees is only a moment with a wise man he soon knows the path of wisdom, as the tongue knows the taste of the soup.

from Infinite Freedom

Who can trace the invisible path of the man who soars in the sky of liberation, the infinite Void without beginning, whose passions are peace, and over whom pleasures have no power? His path is as difficult to trace as that of the birds in the air.

The man who wisely controls his senses as a good driver controls his horses, and who is free from lower passions and pride, is admired even by the gods.

He is calm like the earth that endures; he is steady like a column that is firm; he is pure like a lake that is clear; he is free from Samsara, the ever-returning life-in-death.

from Life

Those who make channels for water control the waters; makers of arrows make the arrows straight; carpenters control their timber; and the holy control their soul.

from Beyond Life

How can there be laughter, how can there be pleasure, when the whole world is burning? When you are in deep darkness, will you not ask for a lamp?

Consider this body! A painted puppet with jointed limbs,[1] sometimes suffering and covered with ulcers, full of imaginings, never permanent, for ever changing.

This body is decaying! A nest of diseases, a heap of corruption, bound to destruction, to dissolution. All life ends in death.

Look at these grey-white dried bones, like dried empty gourds thrown away at the end of the summer. Who will feel joy in looking at them?

A house of bones is this body, bones covered with flesh and with blood. Pride and hypocrisy dwell in this house and also old age and death.   5

The glorious chariots of kings wear out, and the body wears out and grows old; but the virtue of the good never grows old, and thus they can teach the good to those who are good.

If a man tries not to learn he grows old just like an ox! His body indeed grows old but his wisdom does not grow.

I have gone round in vain the cycles of many lives ever striving to find the builder of the house of life and death. How great is the sorrow of life that must die! But now I have seen thee, housebuilder: never more shalt thou build this house. The rafters of sins are broken, the ridge-pole of ignorance is destroyed. The fever of craving is past: for my mortal mind is gone to the joy of the immortal NIRVANA.

Those who in their youth did not live in self-harmony, and who did not gain the true treasures of life, are later like long-legged old herons standing sad by a lake without fish.

Those who in their youth did not live in self-harmony, and who did   10
not gain the true treasures of life, are later like broken bows, ever deploring old things past and gone.

from Hasten and Strive

Let a wise man remove impurities from himself even as a silversmith removes impurities from the silver: one after one, little by little, again and again.

Even as rust on iron destroys in the end the iron, a man's own impure transgressions lead that man to the evil path.

---

1. This is a recurrent metaphor in Indian mysticism. See also Mahadevi's poem "Monkey on a Monkeyman's Stick."

Dull repetition is the rust of sacred verses; lack of repair is the rust of houses; want of healthy exercise is the rust of beauty; unwatchfulness is the rust of the watcher.

Misconduct is sin in woman; meanness is sin in a benefactor; evil actions are indeed sins both in this world and in the next.

But the greatest of all sins is indeed the sin of ignorance. Throw this *5* sin away, O man and become pure from sin.

∗   ∗   ∗

There is no fire like lust, and no chains like those of hate. There is no net like illusion, and no rushing torrent like desire.

It is easy to see the faults of others, but difficult to see one's own faults. One shows the faults of others like chaff winnowed in the wind, but one conceals one's own faults as a cunning gambler conceals his dice.

If a man sees the sins of others and for ever thinks of their faults, his own sins increase for ever and far off is he from the end of his faults.

There is no path in the sky and a monk must find the inner path. The world likes pleasures that are obstacles on the path; but the Tatha-gatas, the 'Thus-gone', have crossed the river of time and they have overcome the world.

There is no path in the sky and a monk must find the inner path. All *10* things indeed pass away, but the Buddhas are for ever in Eternity.

from Cravings

If a man watches not for NIRVANA, his cravings grow like a creeper and he jumps from death to death like a monkey in the forest from one tree without fruit to another.

And when his cravings overcome him, his sorrows increase more and more, like the entangling creeper called *birana*.

But whoever in this world overcomes his selfish cravings, his sorrows fall away from him, like drops of water from a lotus flower.

Therefore in love I tell you, to you all who have come here: Cut off the bonds of desires, as the surface grass creeper *birana* is cut for its fragrant root called *usira*. Be not like a reed by a stream which MARA, the devil of temptation, crushes again and again.

Just as a tree, though cut down, can grow again and again if its roots *5* are undamaged and strong, in the same way if the roots of craving are not wholly up-rooted sorrows will come again and again. When the thirty-six streams of desire that run towards pleasures are strong, their powerful waves carry away that man without vision whose imaginings are lustful desires. Everywhere flow the streams. The creeper of craving grows everywhere. If you see the creeper grow, cut off its roots by the power of wisdom.

The sensuous pleasures of men flow everywhere. Bound for pleasures and seeking pleasures men suffer life and old age.

Men who are pursued by lust run around like a hunted hare. Held in fetters and in bonds they suffer and suffer again.

Men who are pursued by lust run round like a hunted hare. For a monk to conquer lust he must first conquer desires.

The man who free from desires finds joy in solitude, but when free he then returns to his life of old desires, people can say of that man: 'He was free and he ran back to his prison!'

The wise do not call a strong fetter that which is made of iron, of wood or of rope; much stronger is the fetter of passion for gold and for jewels, for sons or for wives.

10

This is indeed a strong fetter, say the wise. It seems soft but it drags a man down, and it is hard to undo. Therefore some men cut their fetters, renounce the life of the world and start to walk on the path, leaving pleasures behind. Those who are slaves of desires run into the stream of desires, even as a spider runs into the web that it made. Therefore some men cut their fetters and start to walk on the path, leaving sorrows behind.

Leave the past behind; leave the future behind; leave the present behind. Thou art then ready to go to the other shore. Never more shalt thou return to a life that ends in death.

The man who is disturbed by wrong thoughts, whose selfish passions are strong and who only seeks sensuous pleasures, increases his craving desires and makes stronger the chains he forges for himself.

But he who enjoys peaceful thoughts, who considers the sorrows of pleasure, and who ever remembers the light of his life — he will see the end of his cravings, he will break the chains of death.

He has reached the end of his journey, he trembles not, his cravings are gone, he is free from sin, he has burnt the thorns of life: this is his last mortal body.

15

He is free from lust, he is free from greed, he knows the meaning of words, and the meaning of their combinations, he is a great man, a great man who sees the Light: this is his last mortal body.

I have conquered all; I know all, and my life is pure; I have left all, and I am free from craving. I myself found the way. Whom shall I call Teacher? Whom shall I teach?

The gift of Truth conquers all gifts. The taste of Truth conquers all sweetness. The Joy of Truth conquers all pleasures. The loss of desires conquers all sorrows.

Mahayana Buddhist Texts

(before A.D. 255) *Chinese* (religious texts)

"The Parable of the Burning House" from *The Lotus Sutra* is among the most famous passages, a literary landmark, in this most important of Mahayana Buddhist sutras. *The Lotus Sutra* was probably composed in a vernacular Indian or Central Asian language and later translated into Sanskrit. When it was composed remains unknown, but it was translated into Chinese in A.D. 225. The eminent sinologist Burton Watson has rendered the text in English based on a version done in A.D. 406 by the scholar and monk Kumarajiva, which is considered the most authoritative version — more dependable than the Sanskrit versions that seem to be later and less felicitous. Mahayana ("Great Vehicle") Buddhism was given this name to distinguish it from earlier forms of Buddhism, which were named Hinayana, or "Lesser Vehicle," though the more common name is Theravada ("Teachings of the Elders") Buddhism.

According to Mahayana Buddhism, the historical Buddha was merely one of many manifestations of an eternal Buddha. Mahayana Buddhism presents a cosmos significantly expanded from that of Theravada — of countless worlds inhabited by countless Bodhisattvas and lesser beings. As in Theravada, the phenomenal world is seen as empty because it is caught in the endless chain of causality and flux, as the world's inhabitants are caught within a great cycling wheel of birth and rebirth. Flux and causality keep us in this cycle of misery, and only by eliminating craving and desire and following the eightfold path of right belief, resolve, speech, behavior, occupation, effort, contemplation, and meditation, can one achieve enlightenment. Whereas Theravada suggests that such enlightenment frees us from the ordinary world, or *samsara*, Mahayana considers the world of *samsara* to be coextant with the absolute and unchanging. Enlightenment then becomes less an escape from the world than an insight into its true nature. In the parable given, the Buddha (also referred to in the poem as the Thus Come One) explains that though he had earlier taught his followers a doctrine of three vehicles or paths for the believer, this was merely an "expedient means" to help bring his followers to enlightenment. One shouldn't strive for lesser forms of enlightenment, to be a *shravaka* (a voice hearer—one who listens to the Buddha's teachings), to be a *pratyekabuddha* (one who seeks enlightenment only for him- or herself), or to be a *bodhisattva* (one who aspires to Buddhahood, but postpones his or her own entry into Nirvana in order to help others on their way). Instead, one should aim directly for Buddhahood. Here the Buddha, like the angel Raphael in *Paradise Lost,* delineates "what surmounts the reach / Of human sense" expediently, "By lik'ning spiritual to corporal forms" (*Paradise Lost* v.571–573). In this sense, the very use of parables can be seen as an expedient religious tool, a net to catch a fish; once the fish is caught, you no longer need the net.

FURTHER READING: Hurvitz, Leon. *Scripture of the Lotus Blossom of the Fine Dharma,* 1976. Watson, Burton. *The Lotus Sutra,* 1993.

from **The Lotus Sutra**

TRANSLATED BY BURTON WATSON

The Parable of the Burning House

The Buddha, wishing to state his meaning once more, spoke in verse form, saying:

> Suppose there was a rich man
> who had a large house.
> This house was very old,
> and decayed and dilapidated as well.
> The halls, though lofty, were in dangerous condition,   5
> the bases of the pillars had rotted,
> beams and rafters were slanting and askew,
> foundations and steps were crumbling.
> Walls were cracked and gaping
> and the plaster had fallen off of them.   10
> The roof thatch was in disrepair or missing,
> the tips of the eaves had dropped off.
> The fences surrounding it were crooked or collapsed
> and heaped rubbish was piled all around.
> Some five hundred persons   15
> lived in the house.
> Kites, owls, hawks, eagles,
> crows, magpies, doves, pigeons,
> lizards, snakes, vipers, scorpions,
> centipedes and millipedes,   20
> newts and ground beetles,
> weasels, raccoon dogs, mice, rats,

hordes of evil creatures
scurried this way and that.
Places that stank of excrement   *25*
overflowed in streams of filth
where dung beetles and other creatures gathered.
Foxes, wolves and jackals
gnawed and trampled in the filth
or tore apart dead bodies,   *30*
scattering bones and flesh about.
Because of this, packs of dogs
came racing to the spot to snatch and tear,
driven by hunger and fear,
searching everywhere for food,   *35*
fighting, struggling, seizing,
baring their teeth, snarling and howling.
That house was fearful, frightening,
so altered was its aspect.
In every part of it   *40*
there were goblins and trolls,
yaksha[1] and evil spirits
who feed on human flesh
or on poisonous creatures.
The various evil birds and beasts   *45*
bore offspring, hatched and nursed them,
each hiding and protecting its young,
but the yakshas outdid one another
in their haste to seize and eat them.
And when they had eaten their fill,   *50*
their evil hearts became fiercer than ever;
the sound of their wrangling and contention
was terrifying indeed.
Kumbhanda demons
crouched on clumps of earth   *55*
or leaped one or two feet
off the ground,
idling, wandering here and there,
amusing themselves according to their whim.
Sometimes they seized a dog by two of its legs   *60*
and beat it till it had lost its voice,
or planted their feet on the dog's neck,
terrifying it for their own delight.
Again there were demons
with large tall bodies,   *65*

---

1. Demons.

naked in form, black and emaciated,
constantly living there,
who would cry out in loud ugly voices,
shouting and demanding food.
There were other demons   70
whose throats were like needles,
or still other demons
with heads like the head of an ox,
some feeding on human flesh,
others devouring dogs.   75
Their hair like tangled weeds,
cruel, baleful, ferocious,
driven by hunger and thirst,
they dashed about shrieking and howling.
The yakshas and starving spirits   80
and the various evil birds and beasts
hungrily pressed forward in all directions,
peering out at the windows.
Such were the perils of this house,
threats and terrors beyond measure.   85
This house, old and rotting,
belonged to a certain man
and that man had gone nearby
and had not been out for long
when a fire   90
suddenly broke out in the house.
In one moment from all four sides
the flames rose up in a mass.
Ridgepoles, beams, rafters, pillars
exploded with a roar, quivering, splitting,   95
broke in two and came tumbling down
as walls and partitions collapsed.
The various demons and spirits
lifted their voices in a great wail,
the hawks, eagles and other birds,   100
the kumbhanda demons,
were filled with panic and terror,
not knowing how to escape.
The evil beasts and poisonous creatures
hid in their holes and dens,   105
and the pishacha demons,
who were also living there,
because they had done so little that was good,
were oppressed by the flames
and attacked one another,   110
drinking blood and gobbling flesh.

The jackals and their like
were already dead by this time
and the larger of the evil beasts
vied in devouring them.   *115*
Foul smoke swirled and billowed up,
filling the house on every side.
The centipedes and millipedes,
the poisonous snakes and their kind,
scorched by the flames,   *120*
came scurrying out of their lairs,
whereupon the kumbhanda demons
pounced on them and ate them.
In addition, the starving spirits,
the fire raging about their heads,   *125*
hungry, thirsty, tormented by the heat,
raced this way and that in terror and confusion.
Such was the state of that house,
truly frightening and fearful;
malicious injury, the havoc of fire—   *130*
many ills, not just one, afflicted it.
At this time the owner of the house
was standing outside the gate
when he heard someone say,
"A while ago your various sons,   *135*
in order to play their games,
went inside the house.
They are very young and lack understanding
and will be wrapped up in their amusements."
When the rich man heard this,   *140*
he rushed in alarm into the burning house,
determined to rescue his sons
and keep them from being burned by the flames.
He urged his sons to heed him,
explaining the many dangers and perils,   *145*
the evil spirits and poisonous creatures,
the flames spreading all around,
the multitude of sufferings
that would follow one another without end,
the poisonous snakes, lizards and vipers,   *150*
as well as the many yakshas
and kumbhanda demons,
the jackals, foxes and dogs,
hawks, eagles, kites, owls,
ground beetles and similar creatures,   *155*
driven and tormented by hunger and thirst,
truly things to be feared.

His sons could not stay in such a perilous place,
much less when it was all on fire!
But the sons had no understanding   *160*
and though they heard their father's warnings,
they continued engrossed in their amusements,
never ceasing their games.
At that time the rich man
thought to himself: *165*
My sons behave in this manner,
adding to my grief and anguish.
In this house at present
there is not a single joy,
and yet my sons,   *170*
wrapped up in their games,
refuse to heed my instructions
and will be destroyed by the fire!
Then it occurred to him
to devise some expedient means,   *175*
and he said to his sons,
"I have many kinds
of rare and marvelous toys,
wonderful jeweled carriages,
goat-carts, deer-carts,   *180*
carts drawn by big oxen.
They are outside the gate right now—
you must come out and see them!
I have fashioned these carts
explicitly for you.   *185*
You may enjoy whichever you choose,
play with them as you like!"
When the sons heard
this description of the carts,
at once they vied with one another   *190*
in dashing out of the house,
till they reached the open ground,
away from all peril and danger.
When the rich man saw that his sons
had escaped from the burning house   *195*
and were standing in the crossroads,
he seated himself on a lion seat,
congratulating himself in these words:
"Now I am content and happy.
These sons of mine   *200*
have been very difficult to raise.
Ignorant, youthful, without understanding,
they entered that perilous house

with its many poisonous creatures
and its goblins to be feared.   *205*
The roaring flames of the great fire
rose up on all four sides,
yet those sons of mine
still clung to their games.
But now I have saved them,   *210*
caused them to escape from danger.
That is the reason, good people,
I am content and happy."
At that time the sons,
seeing their father comfortably seated,   *215*
all went to where he was
and said to him:
"Please give us
the three kinds of jeweled carriages
you promised us earlier.   *220*
You said if we came out of the house
you'd give us three kinds of carts
and we could choose whichever we wished.
Now is the time
to give them to us!"   *225*
The rich man was very wealthy
and had many storehouses.
With gold, silver, lapis lazuli,
seashells, agate,
and other such precious things   *230*
he fashioned large carriages
beautifully adorned and decorated,
with railings running around them
and bells hanging from all sides.
Ropes of gold twisted and twined,   *235*
nets of pearls
stretched over the top,
and fringes of golden flowers
hung down everywhere.
Multicolored decorations   *240*
wound around and encircled the carriages,
soft silks and gauzes
served for cushions,
with fine felts of most wonderful make
valued at thousands or millions,   *245*
gleaming white and pure,
to spread over them.
There were large white oxen,
sleek, stalwart, of great strength,

handsome in form, 250
to draw the jeweled carriages,
and numerous grooms and attendants
to accompany and guard them.
These wonderful carriages
the man presented to each of his sons alike. 255
The sons at that time
danced for joy,
mounting the jeweled carriages,
driving off in all directions,
delighting and amusing themselves 260
freely and without hindrance.
I say this to you, Shariputra—
I am like this rich man.
I, most venerable of the sages,
am the father of this world 265
and all living beings
are my children.
But they are deeply attached to worldly pleasures
and lacking in minds of wisdom.
There is no safety in the threefold world; 270
it is like a burning house,
replete with a multitude of sufferings,
truly to be feared,
constantly beset with the griefs and pains
of birth, old age, sickness and death, 275
which are like fires
raging fiercely and without cease.
The Thus Come One has already left
the burning house of the threefold world[2]
and dwells in tranquil quietude 280
in the safety of forest and plain.
But now this threefold world
is all my domain,
and the living beings in it
are all my children. 285
Now this place
is beset by many pains and trials.
I am the only person
who can rescue and protect others,
but though I teach and instruct them, 290
they do not believe or accept my teachings,
because, tainted by desires,

2. "Threefold world" refers to the three worlds of desire, form, and formlessness, which are
inhabited by enlightened beings.

they are deeply immersed in greed and attachment.
So I employ an expedient means,
describing to them the three vehicles,   *295*
causing all living beings
to understand the pains of the threefold world,
and then I set forth and expound
a way whereby they can escape from the world.
If these children of mine   *300*
will only determine in their minds to do so,
they can acquire all the three understandings
and the six transcendental powers,
can become pratyekabuddhas
or bodhisattvas who never regress.   *305*
I say to you, Shariputra,
for the sake of living beings
I employ these similes and parables
to preach the single Buddha vehicle.
If you and the others are capable   *310*
of believing and accepting my words,
then all of you are certain
to attain the Buddha way.
This vehicle is subtle, wonderful,
foremost in purity;   *315*
throughout all worlds
it stands unsurpassed.
The Buddha delights in and approves it,
and all living beings
should praise it,   *320*
offer it alms and obeisance.

Classical Sanskrit, Prakrit, and Tamil Literatures

(c. 200 B.C.–A.D.1100)

■ Valmiki (c. 200 B.C.) *Sanskrit* (epic poem)

TRANSLATED BY HARI PRASAD SHASTRI

The *Ramayana* is one of the world's great epics, comparable to the *Iliad,* the *Odyssey,* or the *Aeneid.* It is ascribed to the poet Valmiki, who is honored with the title First Poet, as the *Ramayana* is called the First Poem. The dating of the *Ramayana* is extremely uncertain; estimates range from 3380 B.C. to the second century A.D. The transmission of the text is similarly confused, and versions of the epic are known in many languages. In addition to the Sanskrit epic of Valmiki, the Hindi version by Tulsidas is notable. It seems likely that Valmiki gathered material from an oral tradition about the hero Rama and expanded upon it to create a court epic, and it is thought that the last book and part of the first book of the *Ramayana* are later additions. The popularity of this epic is evidenced by the fact that it has been translated into every major Indian language, has influenced Indian writers from Kalidasa to R. K. Narayan, and is the subject of countless movies and poems and festivals of art, music, and dance; there is even a devotional (bhakti) cult of Rama.

The story of the *Ramayana* centers on the epic hero Rama, descendent of the Ikshvaku kings who ruled the kingdom of Kosala in the sixth and fifth centuries B.C. Rama's father, Dasaratha, has four sons — Rama, Bharata, Satrughna, and Lakshmana — by three wives. Rama marries Sita, daughter of the King of Videhas, after proving himself by bending a magic bow, rather like Ulysses on his return to Ithaca, or King Arthur pulling Excalibur from the stone. Rama is denied his right of succession to the throne by the wiles of Queen Kaikeyi, who wants her son Bharata set in his place. Queen Kaikeyi holds the king to a promise he had made (after she saved his life) to grant any wish she asked of him, and she arranges to have Rama exiled for fourteen years. Rama goes into exile in the Dandaka Forest with Sita and his brother Lakshmana, though his loyal brother Bharata decides to rule only as regent in Rama's absence, placing Rama's sandals on the throne as a symbol of his brother's sovereignty. In his son's absence, King Dasaratha dies of sorrow.

In the Dandaka Forest, where Rama and his brother had often been taken to slay demons by the sage Vishvamitra, they live in exile, protecting the sages of the forest and killing the giant Viradha. When the sister of the demon Ravana, Shurpanakha, falls in love with Rama and is rejected by him and by his brother, she tries to swallow Sita, whereupon the demoness is mutilated by Lakshmana, instigating a war pitting Rama and his kin (and a band of magical monkeys and bears that joins him later in the epic) against the hordes of titanic demons. After a first battle in which Rama kills fourteen thousand demons, Shurpanakha turns to her brother, ten-headed Ravana, convincing him to kidnap Sita. After the abduction, Rama and his heroic brothers wander in search of Sita, gathering allies, such as the great monkeys Sugriva and Hanuman, and eventually discovering the location of Ravana's capital city of Lanka. In an epic seige, Rama and his supernatural army attack the city of Lanka, like the Greeks trying to win kidnapped Helen back from Troy. Rama and Ravana face off like Achilles and Hector in an extended combat of cosmic proportions, and at length Rama triumphs. After all this, Rama rejects Sita in the presence of all his followers, but Sita proves her purity by throwing herself on a funeral pyre and remaining unburned.

This is the essential story of the *Ramayana,* but Book One and Book Seven add a head and a tail to this body. In Book One we are told that Rama and his brothers are the incarnations of Vishnu, who becomes human to save the gods and other celestial beings from the ravages of Ravana, who is invulnerable to all beings except humans, whom he discounts as insignificant. The monkeys and other beings who help Rama are incarnations of the gods who come to earth to help Vishnu. Book Seven has Rama desert Sita again because the people are grumbling at her becoming Queen after residing so long with Ravana. Sita stays in the hermitage of the author, Valmiki, and gives birth to twin sons, who grow up under the tutelage of Valmiki. When the two boys recite Valmiki's *Ramayana,* Rama asks Sita to prove her purity by an oath. Sita responds, "May Mother Earth embrace me in her arms to prove I have never thought a single thought outside of Rama." Sita disappears into the earth, leaving Rama heartbroken, but soon after he gives his kingdom to the twins and ascends to Heaven, where he becomes Vishnu again and is reunited with Sita.

FURTHER READING: Goldman, Robert P., tr. *The Ramayana of Valmiki: An Epic of Ancient India,* 1984. Griffith, Ralph T. H., tr. *The Ramayana of Valmiki,* 5 vols., 1870–1874. Shastri, Hari Prasad, tr. *The Ramayana of Valmiki,* 3 vols., 1952–1959.

from *The Ramayana*

The Arrival of Shurpanakha at the Hermitage

Having bathed in the Godaveri river, Rama, Sita and Lakshmana left its banks and returned to the hermitage. On reaching their retreat, Raghava[1] with Lakshmana performed their morning devotions and entered the leaf-thatched hut. In the hut, that long-armed hero with Sita at his side dwelt happily, honoured by the great Rishis,[2] and shone like the moon accompanied by the Chitra star.

One day, while Rama was reciting the traditional texts, a female demon chanced to pass that way, by name Shurpanakha who was the sister of Ravana.[3]

Approaching Rama, she observed that he resembled a God, with his radiant countenance, his long arms, his large eyes like unto lotus petals, his majestic gait resembling an elephant's, matted locks crowning his head;

---

1. Another name for Rama.

2. Great Rishi is a term for the highest class of sage.

3. Ravana is a titan, the King of Lanka, and the great villain of the epic.

youthful, full of valour, bearing the marks of royalty, his colour that of the blue lotus and alluring as the God of Love himself.

Beholding that hero, the equal of Indra, the Rakshasi[4] was overwhelmed with desire. Rama was handsome, she hideous; his waist was slender, hers thick and heavy; he had large eyes, hers squinted; his locks were beautiful, hers were red; his whole appearance was pleasing, hers repellent. Rama's voice was sonorous, hers strident; he was fair and youthful, she old and haggard; he was amiable, she sullen; he was self-controlled, she unruly; he was captivating, she odious.

Consumed with passion, the Rakshasi said to Rama: —

"With thy matted locks and ascetic guise, bearing bow and arrows, why hast thou, accompanied by thy consort, come to these woods, which are frequented by demons? What is the purpose of thy journey?"

Hearing the words of the Rakshasi, Shurpanakha, that hero, the Scourge of his Foes, with perfect candour began to relate all.

He said: — "There was a king named Dasaratha, who was as powerful as a God. I am his eldest son, known among men as Rama; this is my younger brother, Lakshmana, my faithful companion, and this, my consort, the illustrious Sita, daughter of the King of Videha.

"Bound by the will of my sire and in order to carry out my duty, I have come to dwell in the forest.

"But now I wish to know who thy father is, who thou art, and what thy race? To judge by thy charms, thou art a Rakshasi! Tell me truly, what has brought thee hither?"

Hearing the words of Rama, the Rakshasi, tormented by the pangs of love, answered: —

"Hear O Rama and I will tell thee the truth! I am Shurpanakha, a Rakshasi, who can change her form at will. I wander about in the forest, striking terror in the hearts of all beings. My brothers are Ravana, of whom thou hast doubtless heard, and the powerful and somnolent Kumbhakarna, the virtuous Bibishana a stranger to our practices,[5] and two others famed for their martial qualities, Khara and Dushana.

"I, who am more powerful than they, having seen thee, O Rama, wish to unite myself with thee, O Lord, O First of Men!

"I am endowed with power and able to range at will by thought alone; therefore do thou become my master. What is Sita to thee?

"Deformed, without beauty, she is not worthy of thee, whereas I should prove a well-matched partner, my beauty equal to thine own; do thou look on me as thy consort. This unsightly, grim-visaged human female, of lean abdomen, will be devoured by me this day in thy presence, together with that brother of thine.

---

4. Rakshasi is a term for a female titan, or demon.

5. Bibishana, brother to Ravana and Shurpanakha, is a virtuous demon who deserts his kin and joins Rama in the epic battles that follow.

"Thou and I shall wander on the summit of the mountains and through the forests together, exploring the whole region of Dandaka, according to thy whim."

Speaking thus, the Rakshasi threw impassioned glances at Rama, who, smiling, made the following astute reply.

The Mutilation of Shurpanakha

Smiling a little, Rama, in gently mocking tones, answered Shurpanakha, who had been caught in the noose of love, saying:—

"I am already wedded and this is my beloved consort; the rivalry between co-wives would prove unbearable! My younger brother however who is of a happy disposition, of agreeable appearance, virtuous and chaste, is called Lakshmana and is full of vigour. He has not yet experienced the joys of a wife's company and desires a consort. He is youthful and attractive and would therefore be a fitting husband for thee. Take my brother as thy lord, O Lady of large eyes and lovely hips, and enjoy him without a rival, as Mount Meru, the sunlight."

Hearing these words, the Rakshasi, blinded by passion, leaving Rama, at once addressed Lakshmana, saying:—

"My beauty renders me a worthy wife for thee; therefore come and we will range the Dandaka Forest and mountains happily together."

Thus accosted by the Rakshasi Shurpanakha, Lakshmana, the son of Sumitra, skilled in discourse, smiling, gave this ingenious reply:—

"How canst thou wish to become the wife of a slave, such as I? I am wholly dependent on my noble brother, O Thou whose complexion resembles the lotus, who art pleasing to look upon and chaste. O Lady of large eyes, thou art a paragon, do thou become the consort of that matchless hero. Renouncing that ugly, evil and peevish old woman, whose limbs are deformed, he will certainly devote himself to thee! O Lady of ravishing complexion and lovely limbs, what sensible man would sacrifice that unrivalled beauty of thine for an ordinary woman?"

Thinking Lakshmana's words to be sincere and not understanding his jest, that cruel and misshapen Rakshasi, in the blindness of her passion once more addressed Rama, the Scourge of His Foes, who was seated in the leaf-thatched hut with Sita, and said:—

"Is it for this hideous, evil and peevish woman, who is old and deformed, that thou dost slight me?

"I shall devour her in thy presence to-day, and shall live happily with thee without a rival."

Speaking thus, the Rakshasi, whose eyes blazed like torches, hurled herself in fury on Sita, like a great meteor descending on the planet Rohini.[6]

Then the mighty Rama restrained her, as, like the noose of death, she advanced towards Sita, and in anger addressed Lakshmana, saying:—

---

6. Rohini is the star Aldebaran.

"It is unwise to taunt those beings who are vile and cruel, O Saumitri.[7] Take heed, see, Vaidehi[8] is in danger, O Friend! Do thou maim this hideous demon of protruding belly, who is evil and filled with fury."

The valiant Lakshmana, highly incensed against the Rakshasi, thereupon drew his sword from its scabbard and, in the presence of Rama, cut off her ears and nose.

Her ears and nose severed, Shurpanakha uttered a terrible cry and ran into the forest. Being mutilated, the Rakshasi, streaming with blood, created a terrible uproar, like a tempest in the rainy season and, dripping with blood, that hideous monster, lifting up her arms, plunged howling into the deep woods.

Thereafter the injured Shurpanakha sought out her brother Khara of great might, who, surrounded by a troop of demons, was seated in Janasthana and threw herself on the ground before him, like a meteorite falling from heaven.

Wild with terror and covered with blood, Khara's sister, almost deprived of her senses, related everything concerning Raghava's arrival in the forest with his consort and Lakshmana and the circumstances of her disfigurement. . . .

Shurpanakha Upbraids Ravana and Urges Him to Destroy Rama

When Shurpanakha saw those fourteen thousand titans of dreadful deeds slain by Rama single-handed on the field of battle, together with Khara, Dushana and Trishiras, she once more emitted dreadful shrieks and roared like thunder. Perceiving the incomparable prowess of Raghava, she became exceedingly agitated and proceeded to Lanka, Ravana's capital.

There she beheld Ravana shining in glory, surrounded by his ministers on the terrace of his palace, like Indra amidst the Maruts.[9] Seated on his golden throne, blazing like a flame, Ravana resembled a great fire kindled on an altar, kept alive by sacrificial offerings. Unconquered by Gods, Gandharvas,[10] Rishis or other creatures, that warrior, who resembled death itself with wide-open jaws, bore on his person the wounds inflicted by the thunderbolts in the war between Gods and titans and on his breast the marks of Airavata's tusks.[11]

Having twenty arms, ten heads, a broad chest, wearing gorgeous attire and bearing the marks of royalty, he was adorned with a chain of emeralds and ornaments of fine gold and with his great arms, white teeth and enormous mouth resembled a mountain.

---

7. Saumitri means Son of Sumitra, i.e., Lakshmana.

8. Vaidehi means Daughter of the King of Videha, i.e., Sita.

9. Maruts are wind gods; Indra is the King of the Gods.

10. Gandharvas are the celestial musicians.

11. Airavata is the sacred elephant that carries Indra, King of the Gods.

In the combat with the Gods, Vishnu had struck him a hundred times with his discus, and he bore the marks of other weapons from that great struggle, yet his limbs were intact and had not been severed. He who was able to churn up the seas, a feat not to be performed by any other, whose missiles were the mountain crests, he the scourge of the Gods, who transgressed every moral law, the ravisher of others' wives, the wielder of celestial weapons, the destroyer of sacrifices, who descended into the city of Bhogavati and subdued the serpent Vasuki,[12] from whom, on his defeat, he stole the gentle consort; he who scaled Mount Kailasha and overcame Kuvera[13] depriving him of his aerial chariot Pushpaka, which transported him wheresoever he desired; he who in his anger destroyed the garden of Chaitaratha,[14] the lotus pool and the Nandana Grove and all the pleasurable retreats of the Gods, and with his vast arms, resembling the peaks of mountains, arrested the course of the sun and moon, twin scourgers of their foes, rising in splendour; practising asceticism in the mighty forest for a thousand years he offered his heads in sacrifice to Swyambhu[15] and obtained the boon that neither Deva, Danava, Gandharva, Pisacha, Pataya nor Uraga should be able to slay him, but of man there was no mention;[16] proud of his strength, he stole the Soma juice,[17] sanctified by mantras, before its pressing by the Twice-born in the sacrifice; this perverse wretch, Ravana of evil deeds, slayer of the brahmins, ruthless, pitiless, delighting in causing harm to others, was verily a source of terror to all beings.

The titan woman beheld her brother full of power, resplendent in gorgeous attire, adorned with celestial garlands, seated on his throne, resembling Time at the destruction of the worlds, that Indra of Demons, the proud descendant of Poulastya[18] and she, trembling with fear, in order to address him, drew near to the Slayer of his Enemies, who was seated amidst his counsellors. Distracted with terror and passion, Shurpanakha, who was wont to roam everywhere unafraid, now mutilated by the order of that magnanimous Ramachandra,[19] displaying her ravaged features before Ravana, whose large eyes appeared to shoot forth flames, uttered these bitter words to him:

Shurpanakha's Words to Ravana

Filled with anger, Shurpanakha addressed Ravana, the Oppressor of the Worlds, in harsh accents, saying:—

---

12. Vasuki is the Serpent King.

13. Kuvera is God of Wealth.

14. Chaitaratha is King of the Gandharvas, or Celestial Musicians.

15. Swyambhu is a term for Brahma, the Creator.

16. Devas are gods, Danavas are giants, Pisachas are ghosts, Uragas are Great Serpents; Ravana is invulnerable to all these mighty supernatural beings, but doesn't consider humanity enough of a threat to protect himself against it. This proves to be his Achilles heel.

17. Soma juice is used in sacred ceremonies as a beverage or libation.

18. Poulastya was one of the Seven Immortal Sages, and Ravana's grandfather.

19. Ramachandra is another name for Rama.

"O Ravana, wholly devoted to pleasure and indulging in every whim without scruple, thou art oblivious of the great calamity that threatens thee. That monarch who is given up to lust and other dissipations and who is covetous, is disregarded by his subjects, as is the fire in the crematorium. That king who does not fulfil his duties at the proper season brings ruin on his state. The Prince who, committing excess, is ruled by his consorts and readily gives credence to other's counsel, is shunned as the mud of a river is shunned by an elephant. Those rulers who are unable to protect their lands or reclaim the territory wrested from them, live without glory, like mountains submerged in the ocean.

"At enmity with the Gods, the Gandharvas and the Danavas, who are masters of themselves, doing what ought not to be done and inconstant, how art thou able to rule as king?

"O Titan, thou art childish and thoughtless and art not conversant with that which should be known to thee; how canst thou govern? Those monarchs who have neither emissaries, wealth nor policy at their disposal, resemble a common man, O Prince of Conquerors! Since kings are informed by their spies as to what is taking place abroad, they are said to be far-sighted. Meseems thou dost not discharge thy duty and that the counsellors who surround thee are inexperienced, since thou art insensible to the destruction of thy people and their territory.

"Fourteen thousand titans of dreadful deeds with Khara and Dushana have been slain by Rama single-handed; Rama of imperishable exploits has freed the ascetics of fear, established peace in the Dandaka Forest and harassed Janasthana, but thou, who art covetous and a slave to lust, art unaware of the danger that threatens thy dominion. None will help that monarch in time of peril, who is mean, violent, dissolute, haughty and perfidious. Even his own relatives will overpower a king who is excessively vain, pretentious, boastful and irascible. That monarch who fails in his duty and, under the threat of danger is lulled into a false security, will in time of adversity be swept from his kingdom like a straw. Dry wood, turf or dust have some value, but a king who is degenerate is worthless and resembles a faded wreath or a worn-out garment. That monarch who is vigilant however, conversant with what is happening and virtuous, establishes his throne in perpetuity. The king who, even while sleeping, is yet awake to the ordering of his kingdom, who manifests his anger or approval at a fitting time, is revered by all.

"O Thou, whose emissaries have failed to inform thee of the great carnage among the titans, who art bereft of wisdom, O Ravana, thou art lacking in all these great qualities.

"Disregarding others, given up to the pleasures of the senses, not able to reap the advantage of time and place or discriminate between what is good and evil, having sacrificed thy kingdom, thou wilt soon perish."

Reflecting on the infirmities his sister had ascribed to him, Ravana, the Lord of the Titans, opulent, arrogant and powerful, became absorbed in thought.

Shurpanakha Urges Ravana to Slay Rama and Wed Sita

Hearing Shurpanakha's bitter words, Ravana surrounded by his ministers enquired angrily:—"Who is Rama? What is his strength? How does he look and what is the measure of his prowess? Why has he penetrated into the lonely and inaccessible depths of the Dandaka Forest? With what weapons did he destroy the titans in that conflict, slaying Khara and Dushana as also Trishiras? Tell me truly, O Lovely One, who has disfigured thee?"

Thus addressed by the Lord of the Titans, Shurpanakha in a transport of rage began to relate the history of Rama.

She said: "Rama, the son of King Dasaratha, resembles the God of Love; his arms are long, his eyes large; clad in robes of bark and a black antelope skin, bearing a bow encircled with gold like unto Indra's, he lets fly blazing arrows resembling venomous snakes. Emitting a great shout, he discharges his formidable shafts, and in the struggle I could not distinguish him but beheld the host being decimated under the rain of his arrows, as the harvest is destroyed by the hail sent by Indra. In a short space, single-handed, standing alone, he slew fourteen thousand titans with Khara and Dushana, thus bringing peace to the sages in the Dandaka Forest and delivering them from fear. Chivalrous of soul, Rama, the Knower of Self, would not countenance the slaying of a woman and, having been mutilated at his command, I escaped.

"His brother, endowed with great valour, is renowned for his virtue; his name is Lakshmana and he is devoted to Rama. Full of fire, indomitable, victorious, powerful, intelligent and wise, he is his right hand and his very life's breath. And Rama's virtuous, tender and wedded wife, of large eyes, whose face resembles the full moon, is ever engaged in what is pleasing to her lord. With her lovely locks, well-formed nose, beautiful shoulders and her grace and dignity, one would deem her to be a forest divinity or Lakshmi herself. With a skin of the colour of molten gold, nails that are rosy and long, that surpassingly lovely woman is Sita, the slender-waisted Princess of Videha. No woman so beautiful has ever appeared in the world, either among the Gods, Gandharvas, Yakshas or Kinneras. He whose wife Sita becomes and whom she will warmly embrace will live in the world more happily than Purandara. With her natural amiability, her marvellous beauty, which is without equal on earth, she would prove a worthy consort for thee, and thou too art fit to be her lord. It was to bring thee this lady of shapely hips, softly rounded breasts and charming features, that I put forth my endeavours, when, O Mighty-armed One, I was mutilated by the ruthless Lakshmana!

"When thou dost behold Vaidehi, whose countenance resembles the full moon, thou shalt instantly be pierced with the darts of the God of Love. If thou desirest to win her, then set off speedily on thy right foot and lay siege to her heart. If, O Ravana, my counsel meets with thine approval, then, O King of the Titans, follow it without delay.

"Knowing the weakness of these people, O Valiant Chief of the Titans, make Sita, who is without blemish, thy consort. Hearing that Rama with his arrows that never missed their mark has slain the titans established in Janasthana, and of the death of Khara and Dushana, thou hast a duty to perform."

Ravana Approaches Sita

. . . Thereupon Ravana, in the guise of a mendicant, availing himself of the opportunity, rapidly approached the hermitage with the purpose of seeking out Vaidehi. With matted locks, clad in a saffron robe and carrying a triple staff and loshta, that highly powerful one, knowing Sita to be alone, accosted her in the wood, in the form of an ascetic, at dusk when darkness shrouds the earth in the absence of the sun and moon. Gazing on Sita, the consort of Rama, Ravana resembled Rahu regarding Rohini in the absence of Shasi.[20]

Beholding that monstrous apparition, the leaves of the trees ceased to move, the wind grew still, the turbulent course of the river Godaveri subsided and began to flow quietly. The ten-headed Ravana, however, profiting by Rama's absence, drew near to Sita in the guise of a monk of venerable appearance while she was overcome with grief on account of her lord.

Approaching Vaidehi in an honourable guise, as Saturn draws near to the Chitra star, Ravana resembled a deep well overgrown with grass. He stood there gazing on the glorious consort of Rama of incomparable beauty, Sita, with her brilliant lips and teeth, her countenance as radiant as the full moon, seated on a carpet of leaves, overwhelmed with grief, weeping bitterly.

On seeing the Princess of Videha alone, clad in a yellow silken sari, whose eyes resembled lotus petals, the titan, struck by Kama's arrow,[21] joyfully accosted her, feigning the gentle accents of a brahmin. Praising her beauty, unequalled in the Three Worlds, which caused her to resemble Shri,[22] he said:—

"O Thou, possessed of the brilliance of gold and silver, who art clad in a yellow silken sari and who, like a pool of lilies, art wreathed in garlands of fresh flowers, art thou Lakshmi bereft of her lotus or Kirti or a nymph of graceful aspect? Art thou Bhuti of slender hips, or Rati disporting herself in the forest?[23]

"How even, sharp and white are thy teeth, how large thy slightly reddened eyes with their dark pupils, how well proportioned and rounded are thy thighs and how charming thy legs, resembling the tapering trunk of an

---

20. That is, the demon of eclipses regarding the star Aldebaran in the absence of the moon.

21. Kama is the God of Love, who shoots arrows like Cupid.

22. Shri is the consort of Vishnu, the Goddess of Prosperity, better known as Lakshmi; Sita was said to be an incarnation of her.

23. Kirti is a celestial nymph; Bhuti is the mother of the nymph Manu; Rati is the consort of the God of Love.

elephant! How round and plump are thy cheeks, like unto the polished fruit of the Tala trees; how enchanting is thy bosom, decorated with pearls!

"O Lady of Sweet Smiles, lovely teeth and expressive eyes, as a river sweeps away its banks with its swift current so dost thou steal away my heart, O Graceful One. Slender is thy waist, glossy thine hair, thy breasts touching each other enhance thy loveliness; neither the consorts of the Gods, the Gandharvas, the Yakshas nor the Kinneras can compare with thee.[24] 'Till this hour, I have never seen any on earth so perfect; thy youth, thy beauty and thy grace are unequalled in the Three Worlds!

"Seeing thee dwelling here in solitude distresses my heart. Come with me! It is not fitting that thou shouldst remain here; this place is frequented by ruthless demons, who are able to assume different forms at will. It is for thee to reside in sumptuous and delightful palaces in the vicinity of pleasant cities, surrounded by groves of sweet smelling shrubs and green trees, where thou canst wander clad in beautiful robes, decked in fragrant garlands, with a consort worthy of thy beauty, O Charming One. O Dark-eyed Lady of Sweet Smiles, art thou wedded to one of the Rudras, the Maruts or Vasus?[25] Thou appearest divine to me, yet these are not the haunts of the Gandharvas, Devas or Kinneras, but of the Titans. How hast thou come here?

"Dost thou not fear to live amidst monkeys, lions, tigers, deer, wolves, bears, hyenas and leopards? O Fair One, dost thou not tremble before those terrible elephants, maddened with the exudation of temporal juices, in this great forest? Who art thou? To whom dost thou belong? For what reason dost thou range the Dandaka Forest alone, which is frequented by terrible titans?"

With these flattering words did the evil-minded Ravana address Sita, and seeing him in the guise of a brahmin, she entertained him with the traditional hospitality due to an uninvited guest. Leading him to a seat, she brought water to wash his feet and offered him food, saying:—"Be pleased to accept this repast!" Seeing him in the form of a Twice-born with his loshta and saffron robe, unrecognizable in his disguise, Sita welcomed him as a true brahmin, saying:—

"Be seated, O Brahmin, and accept this water for washing thy feet, also this meal, composed of ripe fruits and roasted grain, prepared for thee, which please enjoy."

Thus did she receive him with hospitable words, but Ravana, his gaze fixed on the Princess of Mithila, determined to bear her away, thus preparing his own destruction.

---

24. Yakshas are supernatural beings attendant on Kuvera, the god of wealth; Kinneras are horse-headed beings who attend Kuvera.

25. The Rudras are the sons of Aditi, Mother of the Gods; and Kashyapa, the Great Vedic Sage, grandson of Brahma; the Maruts are Gods of the Wind; the Vasus are also sons of Kashyapa and Aditi.

Sita, anxiously expecting the return from hunting of her illustrious lord, with Prince Lakshmana, searched the vast and darkening forest with her eyes but was unable to see either Rama or his brother there.

The Conversation of Ravana and Sita

Thus addressed by Ravana in the guise of a mendicant, who had resolved to bear her away, Sita reflected:—

'This person is my guest and a brahmin; if I do not answer him he may curse me!' and thinking thus, she said:—

"May good betide thee! I am the daughter of the high-souled Janaka, the King of Mithila, my name is Sita and I am the beloved consort of Rama. For twelve years, I dwelt in the palace of Ikshwaku, where all my desires were gratified and I enjoyed every comfort.

"In the thirteenth year, the king with the approval of his ministers decided to enthrone Rama. All being ready for the installation of Raghava, Kaikeyi, one of my mothers-in-law, requested a boon of her lord. Having gratified my father-in-law by her services, she extracted two promises from him, the exile of my husband and the installation of her son Bharata, saying:—'I shall neither eat, drink nor sleep if Rama is enthroned and it will prove the end of my life.'

"The Lord of the Earth, my father-in-law, hearing her speak thus, offered her diverse gifts, but Kaikeyi refused them. At that time, my lord was twenty-five years old and I eighteen. Being loyal, virtuous, honourable and devoted to the good of all, my lord, Rama, endowed with long arms and large eyes, was renowned throughout the world. Our father King Dasaratha, blinded by passion, in order to please Kaikeyi, did not install Rama, and when he came before his sire, in order to receive the crown, Kaikeyi addressed the following bitter words to him:—"O Ramachandra, hear from me the decree issued by thy father. This great kingdom is to be given to Bharata and thou art to dwell in the forest for fourteen years. Now go hence, and save thy sire from the sin of perjury."

"Then the imperturbable Rama replied: 'So be it' and acted accordingly. My lord of firm vows, accustomed to give and not to receive commands, who ever speaketh truth without prevarication, hearing these words acquiesced and has fulfilled his vow to the uttermost. His brother, the valiant Lakshmana, a Lion among Men and the companion of Rama in combat, the Destroyer of his Foes, given to asceticism, bearing his bow, followed Rama into exile with me.

"Thus Raghava, fixed in his vow, wearing matted locks, accompanied by myself and his younger brother, penetrated into the depths of the forest of Dandaka. We have all three been banished from the kingdom by Kaikeyi and, depending on our own strength, wander about in the forest. Remain here awhile, O Foremost of the Twice-born, my lord will soon return with an abundance of roots and fruit and sufficient venison, having slain deer, kine and boar. But thou, O Brahmin, tell me who thou art and what thy name, family and lineage. Why dost thou range the Dandaka Forest alone?"

Hearing the words of Sita, the consort of Rama, the mighty titan replied in these harsh words:—

"O Sita, I am that Ravana, King of the Titans, in fear of whom the world, the Gods, titans and men tremble. O Source of Delight, since I beheld thee shining like gold, clad in silk, my consorts have ceased to find favour with me. Do thou become the chief queen of those countless women, stolen away from many quarters by me.

"Lanka, my capital, set in the midst of the sea, is built on the summit of a hill. There, O Sita, wander with me in the groves and thus forget the forest. O Lovely One, if thou dost become my wife, five thousand servants adorned with diverse ornaments shall attend on thee."

The blameless daughter of Janaka, being thus addressed by Ravana, was filled with indignation and answered that titan with contempt, saying:—

"I am dependent on my lord, Rama, who is as steadfast as a rock, calm as the ocean and equal to Mahendra[26] himself, Rama, endowed with every good quality, who resembles the Nyagrodha tree[27] in stature. I am dependent on that illustrious and noble warrior, whose arms are long, whose chest is broad, whose gait is like a lion's, nay, who resembles that king of beasts; to him, the greatest of men, I give my whole allegiance. To Rama, whose countenance resembles the full moon, the son of a king, master of his passions, of immeasurable renown and power, I shall ever remain faithful.

"O Jackal, thou desirest a she-lion but art no more able to possess me than grasp the light of the sun! Thou Wretch, who seekest to carry off the beloved spouse of Raghava! Verily thou dost imagine the trees that thou seest before thee to be made of gold,[28] that thou art seeking to draw the teeth of a famished and courageous lion, that enemy of the deer, or extract the fangs of a poisonous snake. Dost thou desire to lift up the Mandara mountain with thy bare hands or live at ease after drinking poison? Thou dost seek to rub thine eyes with a needle and lick a razor with thy tongue! Thou desirest to cross the ocean with a stone round thy neck or grasp the sun and moon. O Thou who seekest to bear away the beloved wife of Rama, thou art endeavouring to carry a blazing fire in thy robe or walk on iron spikes.

"The disparity between thee and Rama is as that between a jackal and a lion, a brook and an ocean, the nectar of the Gods and sour barley gruel; between gold and iron, sandal and mud, an elephant and a cat, an eagle and a crow, a peacock and a duck, a swan and a vulture. Even shouldst thou

---

26. Mahendra is a name for Indra.

27. The Indian fig tree.

28. The trees of hell, said to be made of gold.

steal me, if that mighty archer, Rama, whose prowess is equal to the Lord of a Thousand Eyes, still lives, thou wilt no more be able to devour me than a fly can eat the clarified butter into which it has fallen."

Addressing that cruel Ranger of the Night thus, the guileless Sita shook like a leaf in the wind.

Perceiving her distress, Ravana, terrible as death, began to boast of his race, his power, his name and his exploits, in order to increase her fear.

Sita Defies Ravana

Provoked by Sita's proud words, Ravana, scowling, answered her in fierce accents: —

"O Lady of Fair Complexion, may prosperity attend thee! I am the brother of the Lord of Wealth, my name is Ravana. I am the mighty Dasha-griva[29] from whom, as all creatures before death, the Gods, Gandharvas, Pisachas, Patagas and Nagas flee in terror.[30] I have subdued my blood-brother Kuvera, who for a certain reason I incited to combat and who, vanquished by me, fled in alarm from his sumptuous abode and sought refuge on Kailasha, the Lord of Mountains.

"By virtue of my prowess I robbed him of his marvellous chariot, Push-paka, that moves according to one's will, and in it I range the skies. Seeing my dread visage, the Gods with Indra at their head flee in terror, O Maith-ili.[31] Wheresoever I roam, the wind blows temperately and the rays of the sun resemble the moon's. Where I stay, the leaves of the trees become motionless and the rivers cease to flow.

"Beyond the sea stands my magnificent capital, Lanka, inhabited by powerful titans, equal to Indra's citadel, Amaravati.

"That beautiful stronghold, encircled by dazzling battlements with golden ramparts and gates of emerald, is a city of dreams.

"Filled with elephants, horses and chariots, echoing to the sound of bugles, it is embellished by pleasant gardens planted with diverse trees, yielding fruit of every desirable taste. O Sita, O Thou Daughter of a King, in that city thou shalt dwell with me, forgetting the lot of mortal women. There thou shalt taste celestial delights! O Lady of exquisite countenance, think of Rama no more, who is but human and whose end is near. Placing his beloved son on the throne, King Dasaratha sent his heir of negligible prowess to the forest. What wouldst thou with that Rama, deprived of his kingdom, living as an ascetic in solitude, O Large-eyed Beauty? I, the Lord of all the Titans, have come to thee in person, pierced by the shafts of the God of Love. It does not befit thee to disregard me. O Timid Lady, if thou dost pass me by, thou wilt repent, like Urvashi, who thrust away Pururavas

---

29. Dashagriva is a name for Ravana, meaning Ten-necked One.

30. Pisachas are ghosts; Patagas are winged creatures; and Nagas are the Serpent Race.

31. Maithili is a name of Sita.

with her foot.[32] Rama is but a mortal and not equal to even a finger of mine in combat. By good fortune I have come to thee; do thou therefore yield thyself to me, O Fair One."

At these words, Vaidehi, her eyes flashing with anger, though alone, answered that Lord of the Titans boldly, saying:—

"Since thou claimest to be the brother of the God, Kuvera, who is held in veneration by all the Celestials, how dost thou dare to commit this infamous deed, O Ravana? Undoubtedly all the titans will meet with destruction, having so cruel, senseless and lustful a person as thee as their sovereign. The ravisher of Indra's consort, Sachi, may survive, but he who bears away the wife of Rama will never live in peace. O Titan, it were possible for the one who deprives the Bearer of the Thunderbolt of his consort of unsurpassed beauty to live on earth, but he who insults me will never escape death, were he to drink the water of immortality!"

Sita's Abduction by Ravana

Hearing those words of Sita, the mighty Ravana, striking one hand on the other, revealed his gigantic form and, skilled in speech, addressed her, saying:—

"Methinks thou hast taken leave of thy senses, hast thou not heard of my great prowess and valour? Standing in space, I am able to lift up the earth; I can drink the waters of the ocean and destroy death himself in combat. With my shafts I can pierce the sun and cleave the terrestrial globe. Thou, who dost allow thyself to be deceived by any trick and dost follow any whim, behold how I can change my shape at will."

Speaking thus, Ravana, full of wrath, his eyes glowing like burning coals, resembled a flame, and discarding his benign aspect, he, the younger brother of Kuvera, assumed a terrible shape, resembling death itself.

With smouldering eyes, a prey to anger, resplendent in ornaments of fine gold, like a dark cloud, that Ranger of the Night appeared before her with his ten heads and twenty arms. Abandoning his ascetic disguise, the King of the Titans took on his native form; wearing a blood-red robe, he fixed that pearl among women, Maithili, with his gaze, thereafter addressing her, who resembled the sun, whose hair was dark and who was clothed in a robe and jewels, saying:—

"O Fair Lady, if thou desirest a master famed throughout the Three Worlds, then surrender thyself to me. I am a husband worthy of thee; do thou serve me forever! I shall do thee great honour nor will I ever displease thee. Renouncing thine attachment to a man, place thine affection on me. What binds thee to Rama, O Thou Foolish One who deemest thyself wise;

---

32. Urvashi is a nymph mentioned in the Rig Veda, and Pururavas was the king who married her.

he who has been banished from his domain, who has failed to fulfil his destiny and whose days are numbered, Rama, who on the injunction of a woman abandoned kingdom, friends and people to inhabit a forest frequented by wild beasts?"

Speaking thus to Maithili, who was worthy of tenderness and gentle of speech, that wicked titan, inflamed by passion, seized hold of her as Budha seizes Rohini.[33] With his left hand he grasped the hair of the lotus-eyed Sita, and with his right, her thighs. Seeing Ravana with his sharp teeth like the peak of a mountain, resembling death itself, the Celestial Beings fled away in terror. Then instantly the great chariot belonging to Ravana, made of gold, to which braying mules were harnessed, appeared and, addressing Sita in harsh tones, he lifted her up and, clasping her, ascended the car.

Then the virtuous and unfortunate Sita, being overpowered by the titan, began to cry aloud, "Rama! Rama!" but he was far away in the depths of the forest. Though she possessed no love for him, Ravana, burning with passion, rose high into the air with her, as she struggled like the consort of the Indra of Serpents. . . .

Rama and Ravana Fight with Magic Weapons

Beholding Mahodara and Mahaparshwa slain and, despite his great strength, the valiant Virupaksha also struck down, a great rage seized Ravana, who urged on his charioteer with these words:—

"By slaying Rama and Lakshmana I shall remove that double scourge, the cause of the slaughter of my faithful adherents and the siege of the city. In the fight I shall cut down Rama, that tree of which Sita is the flower and the fruit, whose branches are Sugriva, Jambavan, Kumuda, Nala, also Dvivida, Mainda, Angada, Gandhamadana, Hanuman, Sushena and all the leading monkeys."[34]

Thereupon that mighty car-warrior, who caused the ten regions to resound, drove rapidly on Raghava with his chariot, and the earth, with its rivers, mountains and woods, trembled with the uproar, and the lions, gazelles and birds that inhabited it were seized with terror.

Then Ravana employed a dark and magic weapon that was formidable and terrifying and with it he consumed the monkeys, who fled hither and thither. Amidst the dust raised by their battalions, for they were unable to endure that weapon created by Brahma himself, Raghava, seeing those countless divisions taking refuge in innumerable places, pursued by Ravana's powerful shafts, stood ready waiting. . . .

* * *

. . . Thereafter, between those two warriors, each seeking to slay the other, an incomparable and unimaginable struggle ensued like unto the

---

33. That is, the planet Mercury seizes Aldebaran.

34. Sugriva is King of the Monkeys, Jambavan is King of the Bears, and all the rest are monkey warriors.

duel between Vritra and Vasava.[35] Both were furnished with excellent bows, both were skilled warriors, both brought exceptional knowledge in the science of arms to the fight. In all their maneuverings they were followed by a stream of shafts as the waves in two oceans that are whipped up by a tempest. . . . Then Rama, skilled in the use of arms, struck Ravana afresh on the forehead, as he stood in his chariot, with arrows to which he had joined a miraculous weapon, and it appeared as if five-headed serpents in the form of darts were penetrating hissing into the earth repelled by Ravana whom they sought to devour. Thereupon, having rendered Raghava's weapon void, Ravana, in a transport of rage, armed himself in his turn with the dreadful Asura weapon which he loosed joined to sharp and terrible arrows with huge points, having the heads of lions, tigers, herons, geese, vultures, falcons, jackals and wolves or resembling serpents with five heads. Others had the heads of donkeys, boars, dogs, cocks, aquatic monsters and venomous reptiles and those sharp arrows were the creation of his magic power. Struck by the Asuric shafts, that lion among the Raghus, he who resembled the God of Fire himself, responded with the Agneya Dart that was full of power and to it he joined arrows of every kind with points that burnt like fire and which resembled suns, planets, and stars in hue or great meteors like unto flaming tongues. Those formidable missiles belonging to Ravana striking against those loosed by Rama, disintegrated in space and were annihilated in their thousands.

Thereupon all the valiant monkeys with Sugriva at their head, able to change their form at will, beholding the titan's weapon destroyed by Rama of imperishable karma, let forth joyous acclamations and made a circle round him.

Then the magnanimous son of Dasaratha, the descendant of Raghu, having destroyed that weapon discharged by Ravana's own arm, was filled with felicity, whilst the leaders of the monkeys joyfully paid homage to him.

Ravana Flees from Rama

His weapon having been destroyed, Ravana, the King of the Titans, whose fury was redoubled, in his wrath instantly produced another; and he loosed the fearful Rudra Weapon, forged by Maya,[36] on Raghava. Thereafter, from his bow, innumerable spears, maces, flaming bars hard as diamond, mallets, hammers, chains and spiked clubs, like unto fiery thunderbolts, issued forth like the tempests at the dissolution of the worlds. . . .

*   *   *

∴ . . . At that instant, the younger brother of Raghava, the valiant Lakshmana, slayer of hostile warriors, armed himself with seven arrows and, with those exceedingly swift shafts, that illustrious prince severed Ravana's

---

35. Vasava is a term for Indra, who slayed the demon Vritra.
36. Maya was the artificer of the gods, like Hephaestus.

standard in many places, which bore the image of a man's head. With a single arrow, the fortunate Lakshmana of immense vigour, cut off the head adorned with brilliant earrings of the titan who drove the chariot, and with five sharp arrows severed the bow resembling the trunk of an elephant that belonged to the King of the Titans.

Thereafter Bibishana, bounding forward, with his mace slew Ravana's beautiful horses that were as tall as hills and resembled a dark cloud in hue, whereupon Dashagriva,[37] leaping quickly from his car, the steeds of which having been slain, was filled with exceeding wrath against his brother and that powerful and spirited monarch loosed a flaming spear on Bibishana like unto a thunderbolt, but ere it reached its target, Lakshmana severed it with three arrows, whereupon a great cheer arose amongst the monkeys in that formidable struggle, and that spear, wreathed in gold, fell down shattered in three fragments like unto a great meteor falling from the sky amidst a shower of flaming sparks.

Then the titan, that mighty Ravana of wicked soul, armed himself with another superior and tested spear which Death himself would have found hard to resist and which was of immense size and shone with its own effulgence. Brandished with violence by the mighty Ravana of perverse soul it gave out a lurid gleam so that it appeared like forked lightning.

Meanwhile the valiant Lakshmana, perceiving that Bibishana stood in peril of his life, placed himself quickly in front of him and that hero, stretching his bow, with a rain of darts riddled Ravana, who stood waiting to discharge the weapon he held in his hand. Under the shower of arrows with which the courageous Saumitri[38] overwhelmed him, thus frustrating his design, the titan no longer thought of striking him in return. Seeing that he had preserved his brother's life, Ravana, who was standing before him, addressed him thus:—

"O Thou whose strength renders thee arrogant, since thou hast preserved this titan, my spear shall fall on thee; having pierced thine heart, this bloodstained weapon that mine arm, equal to an iron bar, will hurl at thee will rob thee of thy life's breath and return to my hand."

Thus did Ravana speak, and in a paroxysm of rage, levelling that pick adorned with eight extremely loud bells, created magically by Maya, that was infallible, the slayer of its foes, the splendour of which flamed up as it were, hurled it at Lakshmana with a mighty shout. Loosed with terrible violence and a sound of thunder, that spear fell with force on Lakshmana in the forefront of the battle.

Then Raghava sought to mitigate the power of that weapon and said:—

"May good fortune attend Lakshmana! May this mortal impact be rendered void!"

---

37. Ravana.
38. Lakshmana.

Released by the enraged titan on that indomitable hero, the spear which resembled a venomous snake, falling with extreme violence, penetrated his great chest and so brilliant was it that it appeared like the tongue of the King of the Serpents. Loosed with force by Ravana, that spear penetrated deep into the body of Lakshmana who, with his heart pierced, fell on the earth. . . .

Lakshmana's Miraculous Recovery

Seeing the courageous Lakshmana lying on the battlefield drenched in blood, struck down by the spear discharged by the mighty Ravana, Rama entered into a terrible duel with that cruel titan whom he overwhelmed with a hail of arrows. Then he addressed Sushena and said: —

"The valiant Lakshmana, struck down by the ruthless Ravana, is writhing like a serpent, filling me with anguish! When I behold that hero, dearer to me than life itself, how, in mine affliction, can I find the strength to fight? If my brother, who is endowed with auspicious marks, that proud warrior, returns to the five elements, of what use is life or prosperity to me? My prowess is ebbing away as it were and my bow seems to be falling from my grasp; mine arrows are blunted, mine eyes blinded with tears, my limbs are heavy as when one is overcome by sleep, my thoughts wander and I long to die! In this extreme misfortune in which I am plunged, weeping, my mind distracted on seeing my brother, who is emitting inarticulate cries, lying in the dust of the battlefield, brought low by the wicked Ravana, a prey to suffering and seriously wounded in his vital parts, even victory cannot bring me felicity, O Hero. If the moon is hidden from sight what delight can it give? Of what use is it to fight? What purpose is served by living? The combat has no longer any meaning since Lakshmana is lying dead in the forefront of the battle. As that illustrious warrior followed me when I retired to the forest so will I follow him now to the abode of death. . . .

. . . As Rama was speaking thus, overwhelmed with affliction, Sushena,[39] in order to comfort him, addressed these well-considered words to him: —

"O Tiger among Men, abandon this idea that causes thee pain, this thought that pierces thine heart as a javelin in the forefront of the battle. Nay, Lakshmana, the enhancer of prosperity, has not rejoined the five elements for his features have not changed nor is he pale, rather is his countenance serene and handsome! Observe how the palms of his hands resemble the petals of a lotus and his eyes are bright. Those who appear thus have not yielded up their lives, O Lord of all Men! Do not grieve O Hero, Conqueror of thy Foes, Lakshmana lives, and the proofs are the multiple beatings of his heart united with his sighs even though his body lies stretched on the earth."

---

39. Sushena is a monkey general.

Thus spoke the extremely sagacious Sushena to Raghava and thereafter he addressed that great monkey, Hanuman, who stood near and said: —

"O Friend, go quickly, repair to the Mountain Mahodaya! Formerly thou hast heard of it from Jambavan, O Warrior! On the southern peak grow curative herbs, the plants named Vishalyakarani, Savarnyakarani, Samjivakarani and also Samdhani of great virtue. Bring them back, O Warrior, in order to revive that hero, Lakshmana. . . ."

*　*　*

. . . The mighty Hanuman hastened on his way and when he reached that high mountain, he shook the summit three times and having broken it off, balanced it, with its multitudinous trees in full flower of varying fragrance, in his two hands. Thereafter, like a dark cloud charged with rain, that monkey sprang into the air carrying the mountain peak and returned in great haste setting it down and, having rested awhile, he said to Sushena: —

"I am not conversant with the medicinal plants, O Bull among Monkeys, here is the whole summit which I have brought to thee!"

At these words of the son of Pavana, Sushena, the foremost of the monkeys, having uprooted the herb, took hold of it and there was great amazement among the monkeys witnessing Hanuman's feat which even the Gods themselves could only have accomplished with difficulty.

Then the foremost of monkeys, Sushena, having crushed that herb, held it to Lakshmana's nostrils and on inhaling it that prince, the scourge of his foes, who was riddled with arrows, instantly rose from the ground released from the darts and his sufferings. Meanwhile the monkeys beholding him standing erect cried out 'Excellent! Excellent!' and, full of joy, paid homage to him.

Then Rama, the slayer of his foes, said to Lakshmana: —

"Come, Come!" and, embracing him, pressed him close to his heart, his eyes wet with tears. Thereafter, having embraced him, Raghava said to Saumitri: — "O Hero, what good fortune to see thee return from the dead! Nay, assuredly neither life nor Sita nor victory had any attraction for me; in sooth what reason had I for living since thou hadst returned to the five elements?"

Then Lakshmana, pained, answered the magnanimous Raghava who had spoken thus and, in a voice trembling with emotion, said: —

"Bound by thy vow, O Thou who has truth for thy prowess, it does not become thee to utter such cowardly words! Nay, those who speak with sincerity do not render a promise void and the proof they give is the fulfilment of their vow! Thou shouldst not give way to despair on mine account, O Irreproachable Hero! Mayest thou redeem thy word by Ravana's death this day. Nay, when he comes within the range of thy shafts, thine adversary must not return alive, as a great elephant may not live when he falls under the sharp tooth of a roaring lion. I desire to see that wretch perish ere the orb of the day withdraws behind the Astachala Mountain, his task accomplished." . . .

The Death of Ravana

At that moment, Matali[40] sought to recall Raghava's thoughts, saying:— "How is it that thou dost act in regard to Ravana as if thou wert unaware of thine own powers? In order to bring about his end, discharge Brahma's Weapon upon him, O Lord! Foretold by the Gods, the hour of his doom is at hand!"

Prompted by Matali, Rama took up a flaming shaft that was hissing like a viper, formerly bestowed on him by the magnanimous and powerful Sage Agastya. A gift of the Grandsire, that weapon never missed its target and it had been created of yore by Brahma for Indra and bestowed on the King of the Gods for the conquest of the Three Worlds. In its wings was the wind, in its point the fire and the sun, in its haft space, and, in size, it resembled the Mountains Meru and Mandara. With its marvellous point, haft and gilding, it was composed of the essence of all the elements and was as resplendent as the sun. Resembling the Fire of Time enveloped in smoke, it was like unto an enormous snake and was capable of riving men, elephants, horses, gateways, bars and even rocks. Dreadful to behold, covered with blood from countless victims, coated with their flesh and of the temper of lightning, it emitted a thunderous sound. The disperser of hosts, it created universal alarm, and hissing like a great serpent, it was exceedingly formidable. In war, it was the provider of nourishment to herons, vultures, cranes and hordes of jackals; it was a form of death itself, the sower of terror, the delight of the monkeys, the scourge of the titans and its wings were composed of innumerable brightly coloured plumes, like unto Garuda's.[41]

That marvellous and powerful shaft that was to destroy the titan was the object of terror to the worlds, the remover of the fear of the supporters of the Ikshvakus,[42] the depriver of the glory of the foe, and it filled Rama with delight. Having charged it with the sacred formula, the valiant Rama of indescribable prowess placed that excellent weapon on his bow according to the method prescribed by the Veda and, when he made ready, all beings were seized with terror and the earth shook. Enraged, he stretched his bow with force and, deploying his whole strength, discharged that weapon, the destroyer of the vital parts, on Ravana, and that irresistible shaft like unto lightning, irrevocable as fate, loosed by the arm of one equal to the God who bears the Thunderbolt, struck Ravana's breast. Loosed with exceeding force, that missile, the supreme destroyer, pierced the breast of the

---

40. Charioteer to the god Indra. Here, he is Rama's charioteer.

41. Garuda is King of the Birds.

42. That is, Rama's followers.

wicked-hearted titan and, covered with blood, that fatal dart having extinguished his vital breaths, buried itself in the earth. Thereafter, having slain Ravana, that shaft, stained with blood which dripped therefrom, its purpose accomplished, returned submissively to the quiver.

And Dashagriva, who had been struck down suddenly, let his bow and arrow fall from his hand as he yielded up his breath. Bereft of life, that Indra of the Nairritas[43] of redoubtable valour and great renown, fell from his chariot as Vritra when struck by Indra's thunderbolt.

Seeing him stretched on the ground, the rangers of the night who had escaped the carnage, struck with terror, their sovereign being slain, fled in all directions and, from every side, the monkeys who, in the presence of the dead Dashagriva had assumed a victorious air, hurled themselves upon them, armed with trees. Harassed by the monkey divisions, the titans, terror-stricken, took refuge in Lanka and, having lost their lord, in despair, gave way to tears.

In the ranks of the monkeys, however, there arose cries of joy and shouts of triumph proclaiming Raghava's victory and Ravana's defeat, and the skies re-echoed to the music of the drums beaten by the Gods. A rain of flowers fell from heaven on to the earth, covering Raghava's chariot with a ravishing and marvellous shower of blossom. The cry of 'Well done! Well done!' came from the firmament and the celestial voices of the magnanimous Gods were raised in Rama's praise. On the death of that source of terror to all the worlds a great joy filled the Celestial Host as also the Charanas.[44]

The blessed Raghava, by slaying that Bull among the Titans, fulfilled the ambitions of Sugriva, Angada and Bibishana; peace reigned over all; the cardinal points were stilled; the air became pure, the earth ceased to tremble, the wind blew gently and the star of the day regained its full glory.

At that instant, Sugriva, Bibishana and Angada, the foremost of his friends, and Lakshmana also, approached that happy conqueror and joyfully offered him due homage. Rama, the delight of the House of Raghu, surrounded by his adherents on the battlefield, having slain his adversary by his extraordinary power, resembled Mahendra amidst the Celestial Host.

---

43. Nairritas are offspring of Nairriti, a demon.
44. Charanas are the panegyrists of the Gods.

■ The Bhagavad-Gita (c. First Century A.D.) *Sanskrit* (epic poem)

TRANSLATED BY TONY BARNSTONE[1]

The Sanskrit sacred poem Bhagavad-Gita is an episode from Vyasa's epic poem, the Mahabharata. It has come to be the bible of Hinduism. Devout Hindus recite lines from it daily, and its statement of a uniform philosophy incorporates much of the wisdom of the Upanishads and of Vedantic philosophy. It is a dialogue between the great hero Arjuna and his divine charioteer, Krishna, that takes place on the battlefield on the plain of Kurukshetra where the decisive battle between the Pandavas and the Kauravas will be fought. Arjuna, leader of the Pandavas, decides (like Achilles in a different context) not to fight, for he cannot reconcile his duty to fight with his duty to the friends and kinsmen on the opposite side. The bulk of the poem consists of Krishna's response to Arjuna, to some extent a justification for war (since death is controlled by destiny and the immortal soul does not die), but even more it is a systematic philosophical presentation of the Hindu system, emphasizing devotion to work and to the gods, pursuit of knowledge, and the shedding of selfish desires. The sustained beauty of its poetic vision is matchless: the body is merely "shabby clothes" that we discard on death for new ones; the controlled and desireless hero "withdraws his senses from sensuous pleasures" like "a tortoise retracting its limbs"; life is a fig tree with "roots in the sky and branches below," and "its leaves are Vedic hymns"; Arjuna is told to cut down this tree "with the sharp axe of detachment." In addition to its profound importance as a spiritual text, the Bhagavad-Gita is an enduring masterpiece of world literature.

FURTHER READING: Deutsch, Eliot, tr. *The Bhagavad Gita,* 1968. Edgerton, Franklin, tr. *The Bhagavad Gita,* 1944, 1964. Hill, W. Douglas P., tr. *The Bhagavadgita,* 1953. Miller, Barbara Stoler, tr. *The Bhagavad-Gita: Krishna's Counsel in Time of War,* 1986. Swami Prabhavananda and Christopher Isherwood, trs. *The Song of God: Bhagavad-gita,* intr. Aldous Huxley, 1947.

---

1. After translations and annotations by Miller, Zaehner, Radhakrishnan, van Buitenen, Mascaró, Easwaran, and Shri Purohit Swami.

from **One: Arjuna's Sorrow**

Sanjaya

Arjuna of the monkey war-banner scanned
      the battle ranks of Dhritarashtra's sons
      and raised his bow
      just as the clash of arms was to begin.

He addressed his charioteer, Krishna:
      "Drive between the two armies,
      invincible Lord,
      and halt there

so I may see these men
      drawn up eager with bloodlust
      whom I must fight
      in this enterprise, war.

I see them arrayed
      and spoiling for battle,
      happy to serve the corrupt son
      of Dhritarashtra's goals."

On hearing Arjuna's words,   5
      Krishna drove their brilliant chariot
      between the two armies
      and halted there,

facing Bhishma and Drona
      and all the world's kings
      and said "Arjuna, see the men
      of Kuru gathered here."

And Arjuna saw in each army
      fathers and grandfathers, teachers,
      uncles and brothers, son
      and grandsons, companions

and in-laws, and seeing
      all his kinsmen
      facing each other
      in battle lines

a deep pity filled his spirit
      and he exclaimed in sorrow
      "O Krishna, when I see my people
      so murderously keen

the spirit leaves my limbs and they sink,   *10*
      my mouth is seared dry,

a trembling runs through me,
and my hairs stand up in horror,

my magic bow Gandiva slips from my hands,
my skin is aflame,
I can't stand still
and my mind whirls without center.

I see evil omens, Krishna.
No good can come
from slaughtering my own family
in battle.

Victory means nothing to me,
nor kingship nor pleasure.
What good is it to be king,
to have delight or even to live?

We sought the crowns, joys,
and delights only for the sake
of the ones who stand here,
poised to abandon life and property—

these teachers, fathers and sons,
grandfathers and uncles,
in-laws, grandsons
and other kinsmen.

15

I don't care if they kill me,
I wouldn't kill them
for kingship of all the three worlds,
let alone for a paltry kingdom on earth!

How can we find it sweet to murder
our cousins the sons of Dhritarashtra?
Evil will come to us if we kill them.
though they are assassins.

It is ignoble to kill kinsmen,
and all joy will desert us
if we slaughter
Dhritarashtra's sons.

Greed possesses them and
blinds them to the sin
of fratricide and of betraying
their friends,

but we are not blind.
We see that destroying family is wrong,

20

and shall we not have the wisdom
  to refrain from this awful act?

When the family is in shambles,
  duty and ancient rituals are broken,
  and when these are lost,
  chaos desecrates our spirits.

When base chaos rules,
  women are corrupted,
  and when the women are corrupt,
  the castes mix and society fails.

In anarchy the family and those who have destroyed it
  are sucked down into hell,
  for their ancestors' spirits suffer
  when the offerings of rice and water cease.

* * *

It's better if Dhritarashtra's sons, weapons in hand,
  find me unarmed,
  offering no resistance,
  and kill me in the battle."

So spoke Arjuna on the battlefield,   25
  and sagging into his chariot
  he let bow and arrows slip from his hands,
  his spirit shipwrecked with grief.

from Two: Philosophy and the Practice of Yoga

Sanjaya

This is the counsel that Krishna
  gave to Arjuna, who was drowning
  in despair and grief,
  his eyes awash with tears.

Krishna

Why is your spirit slack in this time of crisis?
  Cowardice doesn't suit an Aryan noble.
  It is shameful on earth
  and will bar you from heaven.

Don't let this impotence triumph,
  it doesn't become you.

Strike this vile weakness from your heart
and arise, conqueror!

Arjuna

Krishna, how can I slay
    Bhishma and Drona
    with my arrows
    when they deserve my allegiance?

Better to live as a beggar eating scraps   5
    than to eat royal meals spiced with the blood
    of my sacred teachers,
    ambitious though they be.

How shall we know if our victory
    or theirs is better?
    There are the sons of Dhritarashtra;
    how can I live if I kill them?

A trembling pity assails my soul.
    My mind spins from duty to duty.
    Tell me, what is right?
    I am your student; show me the path,

for no earthly kingdom,
    not even domination over all the Gods,
    could banish this grief
    that chars my soul.

Sanjaya

Then Arjuna, the great warrior,
    said to Krishna,
    "I will not fight,"
    and fell silent.

Krishna smiled at the warror's affliction,   10
    and there
    between the two armies
    the God spoke these words:

Krishna

You speak wisely, yet you grieve for men
    who don't need your sorrow,
    for wise men mourn neither
    the living nor the dead.

Never have we not existed —
    you and I and these kings —

and the time will never come
    when we will be snuffed out.

As our spirit passes from childhood
    through youth, through old age,
    so it travels into another body at death;
    the sages know this to be true.

The senses touch matter and thus
    we feel heat, cold, pleasure and pain,
    evanescent things that come, then go.
    Rise above them, Arjuna.

When one is unmoved by these,   *15*
    when agony and ecstasy
    are the same,
    one's spirit is fit for immortality.

What isn't can't come to be
    and what is can never cease.
    Men who see reality
    perceive the line between these two.

All the universe is spun
    from one imperishable presence.
    Nothing can destroy
    this everlasting essence.

Our bodies perish, but the spirit
    which inhabits them
    is eternal and unfathomable,
    so fight the battle, Arjuna!

He who thinks the self slays
    and he who thinks the self is slain
    are both ignorant;
    it doesn't kill and is not killed.

The self is not born and does not die.   *20*
    Being cannot cease to be; it never was not.
    Unborn, undying, unchanging, primeval,
    it isn't killed with the body.

Once a man sees the self to be uncreated, eternal,
    indestructible, and immutable,
    how could he kill
    or cause anyone to kill?

As a man discards shabby clothes
    for new ones

the embodied self casts off
tattered bodies for new ones.

Weapons don't slice it,
    fire doesn't sear it,
    waters don't drench it,
    wind cannot wither it.

The self is impenetrable, incombustible,
    it can't be wet or dried.
    Eternal, pervading all, it is
    fixed, immovable, primordial.

It is named the unmanifest,   25
    the unthinkable, the unchanging.
    If you know this truth,
    you have no cause to grieve.

* * *

Arjuna
O Krishna, what are the signs of a man
    with firm concentration and pure
    insight? What would he say?
    How would he sit? How does he act?

Krishna
When his mind is free of all desires
    and he is complete in himself,
    then a man's enlightenment
    is firm.

If sorrow leaves him untouched
    and the lust for pleasure has died,
    if passion, fear and rage all cease,
    he is called a sage of firm insight.

When he is bound to nothing,
    accepting fortune and misfortune
    without joy or despair,
    his inner sight is strong.

When he withdraws his senses   30
    from sensuous pleasures
    like a tortoise retracting its limbs,
    his inner sight is firm.

Objects of the senses wither
    when a man ceases to devour them.

He may still relish their flavor,
    but with the highest vision the savor fades.

But the mind of the man who seeks
    to control his senses
    may be carried off by their whirlwind,
    Arjuna.

He should sit down, reining in the senses,
    and concentrate on me.
    One whose senses are reined in
    has firm inner sight.

Even thinking of sensuous objects
    makes your ties to them grow;
    from this attachment springs passionate desire;
    and from this passion comes rage.

From rage sprouts confusion,   *35*
    and confusion makes memory fail;
    splintered memory fractures the soul,
    and when the soul fractures, you perish.

But a man of inner power
    who passes through sensuous objects
    with his senses reined in and free of lust and anger
    will have a quiet spirit.

Serene, all sorrows flee him,
    for when his mind
    floats calmly
    it discerns the truth.

Without discipline, the soul's growth
    is stunted; without growth,
    peace abandons him,
    and without peace, joy is lost.

If the mind lusts after
    the wandering senses,
    insight is driven off
    like a ship thrown about in a typhoon.

And so, strong-armed warrior,   *40*
    he who retracts his senses
    completely
    is firm in his vision.

The disciplined master is awake
    when other creatures think it's night;

when other beings awake
the visionary master sees their night.

As the profound deeps of the sea
are unmoved by the waters pouring in,
the calm man is unchanged by rushing desires.
He is at peace, though others desire desires.

When desires drop away
and he acts free from their pull,
without *me* or *mine*,
he will find peace.

This is the ultimate state, of infinite soul, called Brahman.
Once there, delusion is dead,
even when you fly from this body
and enter Nirvana, which is also Brahman.

from Eleven: The Cosmic Vision

Arjuna

You have favored me with revelation
of the self's ultimate mystery
and your words
have banished my delusion.

You have told me of the birth
and death of all creatures,
and your own eternal greatness,
Lord whose eyes are lotus petals,

and as you describe it,
so it must be. Yet, I long
to see your divine form,
Krishna, Greatest among Men.

O Krishna, Master of Yoga,
if you think my eyes can stand it,
reveal your endless
self to me.

Krishna

Arjuna, see my forms in hundreds
and thousands, various,
divine, in countless shapes
and colors.

5

See the solar gods, Arjuna, and the storm gods, the gods of day,
    wind, water, and fire, of dawn, sun, pole-star and moon,
    and see the Horsemen, twin gods of healing,
    marvels never before witnessed.

See all the universe,
    all that moves and all that's still
    and whatever else you wish to see,
    unified in my body.

But eyes of flesh can't
    bear this vision;
    I give you supernatural eyes
    to see my divine Yogic power.

Sanjaya

Saying this, Krishna
    the great master of Yoga discipline,
    revealed to Arjuna
    his divine and ultimate form,

marvelous and manifold,   *10*
    with countless eyes and mouths,
    celestial ornaments
    and divine weapons upraised.

The infinite Lord, whose faces are everywhere,
    brilliant, boundless, containing all wonders,
    showed himself in celestial robes,
    garlanded and sweet with divine perfumes.

If a thousand suns
    were to blaze from the sky at once
    it might begin to approach
    the brilliance of that great spirit.

Arjuna saw the whole universe
    in its infinite aspects
    combined in the body
    of the God of gods.

Amazed and with his hair standing on end,
    Arjuna bowed his head before the Lord,
    joined his hands in worship,
    and spoke:

Arjuna

I see all the gods in you, O Lord,   *15*
    and all creatures; I see
    the Creator, Brahma, on his lotus throne,
    the ancient seers and heavenly serpents.

I see your infinite form everywhere,
    arms, bellies, mouths, and eyes,
    with no end, middle, or origin,
    universal Lord, manifest in all!

From your crown, mace and discus
    a mass of light permeates all things,
    and you are hard to gaze on,
    like white-hot fire and sun.

You are undying, the final revelation,
    eternal spirit, guardian of dharma's sacred law,
    the ultimate basis of all things.
    I think you must be the primal person.

I see no origin, middle or end,
    just infinite power and countless arms;
    your eyes are sun and moon
    and your fiery mouths char the universe.

Great Spirit, you fill all directions   *20*
    and all space between heaven and earth;
    and three worlds shudder
    at your fantastic and dreadful form.

Swarms of gods enter you,
    some, in terror, praise you with folded hands,
    and throngs of great seers and perfected saints
    hail and adore you with sonorous hymns.

The storm gods, solar gods, the gods of day, wind, water, and fire,
    of dawn, sun, pole-star and moon, the celestial seers
    and heavenly musicians, the twin Horsemen, and the hosts of
    demigods, demons, and perfected saints all gaze on you in awe.

Worlds shudder at your great form,
    with its many eyes, mouths, arms, thighs,
    bellies and feet, and its many terrible tusks,
    and so do I.

Vishnu, I see you touch the sky, flaming
    with many colors, your maws gaping wide
    and bulging eyes ablaze, and my spirit quakes,
    I'm unmoored and can find no peace.

Seeing jagged fangs bristling in your maws   25
    like time's devouring flames,
    I am lost and without sanctuary.
    Have mercy, Lord of gods, shelter of the universe!

All those sons of Dhritarashtra,
    the throngs of kings,
    and Bhishma, Drona,
    Karna and all our great warriors

are rushing into your terrible fanged mouths,
    and some are dangling
    from your tusks,
    their heads crushed to powder.

As swollen rivers flood headlong
    into the ocean,
    those heroic men of earth
    stream into your flaming mouths.

As moths wing rapturously into the fire,
    then burst aflame,
    these men rush
    into your mouths to die.

You lick up worlds, Vishnu,   30
    devouring them with flaming mouths;
    your dreadful rays fill the universe
    with a great inferno.

Tell me, why so cruel a form?
    Praise to you, Best of Gods, have mercy!
    Let me know your primal self,
    for I can't understand your intentions.

Krishna

I am time grown old, destroyer of worlds,
    resolved to swallow the worlds;
    even if you do nothing
    all these battle-ranked warriors will die.

So arise and seek glory, Arjuna,
    conquer your enemies and win
    a rich kingdom! I doomed these men
    an age ago; you are merely the occasion.

Slay Drona, Bhishma, Jayadratha, Karna
    and the other great warriors
    whom I've already doomed, fight
    and don't waver—you will triumph in battle!

from *Fifteen: The Supreme Spirit*

Krishna

They say there's a fig tree with roots in the sky
     and branches below;
     its leaves are Vedic hymns
     and whoever knows it knows the Vedas' wisdom.

Its branches spread above and below,
     nourished by the world's qualities,
     its twigs bud with sensual objects
     and the aerial roots cause actions in the human world.

Its form can't be known in this world,
     no end, beginning, or root source.
     Chop down this deep-rooted fig tree
     with the sharp axe of detachment,

then search for the state
     from which one doesn't return,
     saying "I seek refuge in the original Spirit,
     the First Cause of ancient creation."

Those untainted by pride, delusion, attachment   5
     or desire, focused on the inner self,
     and released from the poles of pleasure and pain,
     can transcend illusion and attain that changeless state.

Neither sun nor moon
     nor fire illuminates that state,
     my highest abode,
     from which no one returns.

A fragment of me incarnate
     in the living world is an eternal soul
     that draws in the senses and mind
     from their roots in nature.

When the Lord takes on a body
     and then escapes it,
     he brings these with him as wind
     carries scents from their sources.

Controlling the senses, ears, eyes, touch,
     taste, smell, and the mind
     as well, he enjoys
     sensual objects.

Whether he escapes or dwells within   10
     the body and he tastes the world's

qualities, fools are blind to him,
while wise eyes see him.

Sages who fight to master themselves
see him when they look inside,
but imperfect men lack the self-control
and insight to see him.

Know that my light in the sun
illuminates the universe
and I am the light
of the moon and fire.

I pierce the earth to nourish
all creatures with my strength,
and as the moon-plant Soma
my liquid light gives life to healing herbs.

I am the fire of life
that unites in all bodies
with the breaths flowing in, flowing out,
to digest the four kinds of food.

I live in every heart and from me
come memory, wisdom, and their loss.
I am the knower and what is known through the Vedas,
and also their highest truth, the Vedanta.

15

There are two spirits in the universe —
the perishable and the imperishable.
All creatures perish,
but the imperishable doesn't change.

But there is yet another spirit,
the Supreme Self,
the undying Lord who permeates
and sustains the three worlds.

As I transcend the transient
and even the imperishable,
I am known as the Supreme Self
in the sacred Vedas and in the world.

Whoever is undeluded and knows me
as the Supreme Self, knows all,
Arjuna, and adores me
with their whole spirit.

So, Arjuna, I have revealed to you
the deepest mystery.
Those who understand it will awaken
and reach their destinies.

20

■ Poems of Love and War (from the classical anthologies) (c. 100 B.C.–A.D. 250) *Tamil* (poems)

TRANSLATED BY A. K. RAMANUJAN

These poems come from anthologies of Tamil poetry that are considered classic collections of *Akam* and *Puram* poems. *Akam* means "interior" and as a poetic label it refers to poems of interiority, dealing with private life and loves. The other major type of Tamil poetry is *Puram*. These poems are poems of the "exterior": public poems, poems about war and the world at large. *Akam* poems are lyric poems in the sense that they are *overheard* poems spoken by a persona, often to another (implicit) persona. They are brief dramatic monologues in which the poet puts on masks not of real people but of dramatic types—of mismatched lovers, true lovers, unrequited lovers, and so on. The poets draw on the local animal and vegetable life to make fantastic similes—a man in love pounds on the door of his lover like a mad elephant while the women flutter inside "like a peacock in the net." The *puram* poems celebrate courage on the battlefield with the same simplicity of address and imagery, some of them, such as "Harvest of War," participating in a genre of eulogies in praise of the courage of kings.

FURTHER READING: Ramanujan, A. K. *Poems of Love and War: From the Eight Anthologies and the Ten Long Poems of Classical Tamil*, 1985; *The Interior Landscape: Love Poems from a Classical Tamil Anthology*, 1967.

Akam Poems

What She Said

Kaccipettu Nannakaiyar

My lover capable of terrible lies
at night lay close to me
in a dream
that lied like truth.

I woke up, still deceived,   5
and caressed the bed
thinking it my lover.

It's terrible. I grow lean
in loneliness,
like a water lily   10
gnawed by a beetle.

What Her Girl-Friend Said to Him

Kannan

Sir,

    not that we did not hear the noise
    you made trying to open the bolted doors,
    a robust bull elephant
    stirring in the night
    of everyone's sleep;

we did. But as we fluttered inside
like a peacock in the net,
crest broken, tail feathers flying,   5

our good mother held us close
in her innocence
thinking to quell our fears.

What She Said

Kalporu Cirunuraiyar

People say, "You will have to bear it."
    Don't they know what passion is like,
    or is it that they are so strong?

As for me, if I do not see my lover
    grief drowns my heart,

    and like a streak of foam in high waters
    dashed on the rocks

    little by little I ebb
    and become nothing.

Puram Poems

Harvest of War

Kappiyarrukkappiyanar: on Kalankaykkanni Narmuticceral[1]

Great king,

you shield your men from ruin,
so your victories, your greatness
are bywords.

---

1. Colophons for *puram* or heroic poems mention both the poet and the patron who is the subject or addressee of the poem. *Patirruppattu* poems such as this one are all about Cera kings ("Ceral").

Loose chariot wheels   *5*
lie about the battleground
with the long white tusks
of bull-elephants.

Flocks of male eagles
eat carrion   *10*
with their mates.

Headless bodies
dance about
before they fall
to the ground.   *15*

Blood glows,
like the sky before nightfall.
in the red center
of the battlefield.

Demons dance there.   *20*

And your kingdom
is an unfailing harvest
of victorious wars.

A King's Last Words, in Jail, before He Takes His Life

Ceraman Kanaikkal Irumporai

If a child of my clan should die,
if it is born dead,
a mere gob of flesh
not yet human,

they will put it to the sword,
to give the thing   *5*
a warrior's death.

Will such kings
bring a son into this world
to be kept now
like a dog at the end of a chain,   *10*

who must beg,
because of a fire in the belly,
for a drop of water,

and lap up a beggar's drink

brought by jailers,   *15*
friends who are not friends?

A Woman and Her Dying Warrior

Vanparanar

I cannot cry out.
I'm afraid of tigers.
I cannot hold you,
your chest is too wide
for my lifting.

Death
has no codes   *5*
and has dealt you wrong,
may he
shiver as I do!

Hold my wrist
of bangles,   *10*
let's get to the shade
of that hill.
Just try and walk a little.

                                                                        15

■ The Gatha Saptashati (c. A.D. 100–300) *Prakrit* (700 erotic poems compiled by King Hala)

TRANSLATED BY DAVID RAY

The Gatha Saptashati is the most celebrated Prakrit poetry anthology, compiled by the Satavahana King Hala of Pratishthanapura in Deccan, who lived between A.D. 100 and 300. The anthology consists of seven hundred stanzas, though one version has one thousand stanzas. The verses seem to be by different poets but are not attributed. It is evidence of a large body of secular Prakrit literature, and though not every poem is erotic, eroticism is the dominant strain in the anthology. The poems seem as fresh and touching today as if the seventeen-odd centuries that have passed since they were collected were a breath of wind. In a tradition noted for its erotic verse, they represent some of the finest examples.

FURTHER READING: Ray, David, tr. *Not Far from the River: Poems from the Gatha Saptasati*, 1990.

Nineteen Quatrains

[1]

Why do these prudes fear Prakrit poetry,
our music, and the blunt facts of love?
They draw back from that nectar,
yet wince as if they taste love's ashes.

[2]

Mother was angry. Father fell to his knees,
kissing her feet. I climbed on his back.
She broke into laughter, dragged him away.
Years later, I figure it out.

[3]

A small incident, but I'll always recall it.
Mother was cooking. Father said something,
made her laugh. She touched her pale face,
smudging it black as the dark spot on the moon.

[4]

She showed me how to do
everything she wanted
but in the morning
dressed behind the bamboo screen.

[5]

You'd think it would slow him,
knowing his neighbor died
in amorous sport. Still, he exerts
himself, as the entire village can hear.

[6]

Only the lady who learns
how to make love to herself
knows how to deal with that anger
that leaves her half full, half empty.

[7]

I remember this pleasure—
he sat at my feet
without speaking
and my big toe toyed with his hair.

[8]

Now that I see these dancers
I recall how much I enjoyed
that shampoo
you gave me with your feet.

[9]

The gods have parceled him out,
his beauty caught in my eye,
his talk in my ears, heart in my
heart, his thing in my thing.

[10]

Love's absence is space through the fingers.
All trickles away. Best have the hands cupped,
sweet breast at the mouth,
not one drop spilled on the ground.

[11]

O moon-faced lady,
because of your big eyes
the night had twice as many hours.
And I used them all.

[12]

O girl at the open half-door,
whom do you seek
with hot eyes and brown nipples
that stare at the roadway?

[13]

She was always a quick thinker.
But this time she surpassed herself.
"He came all this way to see you," she said,
shoving her lover toward her husband.

[14]

He worked all day, his plow
deep in the mire.
That night his wife lay restless,
her eyes wide open, counting each raindrop.

[15]

He stood at her door,
hoping to do more than sell melons
but he had not the skill
of the one who brought coconuts.

[16]

When the lady's on top
her hair's a splendid curtain, swaying.
Her earrings dangle, her necklace shakes.
And she's busy, a bee on a lotus-stalk.

[17]

When they stopped
she was embarrassed by her nakedness
but since she couldn't reach her clothes
she pulled him upon her once more.

[18]

Even an old cow
gives fresh milk
at an expert touch,
will moo with gratitude.

[19]

Our Prakrit poems end here, compiled
by King Hala. Who could refuse to be moved
by their charm, or wish sincerely
we had held our tongues, speaking of love?

■ Tales from the Panchatantra (c. A.D. 200–400) *Sanskrit* (fables)

TRANSLATED BY WILLIS BARNSTONE

The Panchatantra is the earliest Sanskrit collection of fables and is considered the grandfather of fable collections, a source for many others. In the sixth century it was translated into Pahlavi, in 570 into Syriac, and in the eighth century into Arabic, and it has continued to spread. Versions have been found in fifty languages and in more than two hundred versions, from Java to Iceland. It may have been composed by Vishnusharman, who may have lived between A.D. 200 and 400, but the original work has been lost and certainly the stories themselves are much older than their recorder. In the framing narrative, Vishnusharman is presented as a sage who purports to teach morality and the ways of the world to two dull princes who have trouble learning. Like *The Thousand and One Nights,* the Panchatantra links stories together and tells stories within stories within stories, eighty-seven in total. Its prose is interspersed with didactic poetry.

FURTHER READING: Edgerton, Franklin. *The Panchatantra Reconstructed.* American Oriental Series, vol. 3, 1924. Pawate, Chennabasappa Ishtalingappa. *The Panchatantra and Aesop's Fables: A Study in Genre,* 1986. Rice, Stanley. *Ancient Indian Fables and Stories, Being a Selection from the Panchatantra,* 1924; 1974. Ryder, Arthur W. *The Panchatantra,* 1925; reprint, 1956. Williams, Alfred. *Tales from the Panchatantra,* 1985.

The Lion Makers

In a certain town were four Brahmans who lived as close friends. Three of them had journeyed to the farthest shores of scholarship, but they lacked common sense. The other found scholarship unpleasant. But he was practical.

One day they met to talk things over. "What good is all our learning," they said, "if we can't travel, win privileges from the kings or acquire money? So at least, let's travel."

They agreed, but when they had gone a short distance, the oldest one said, "One of us, the fourth, is dull, stupid, and has nothing but common sense. Now, no one can win the favor of kings by simple sense and without serious scholarship. So we will not share our earnings with him. Let him turn around and go home." The second Brahman said, "Listen, my intelligent friend, you have no learning. Go home, please." But the third said, "No, no. We can't behave like this. We have played together since we were children. Stay with us, noble friend. You'll have your share of the money we earn."

The three scholars assented and went on with their journey. In a forest they came upon the bones of a dead lion. One of them said, "Here is a chance to test the maturity of our scholarship. Some kind of creature is lying here. Let us bring it back to life by means of great knowledge that we have honorably earned."

Then the first one said, "I know how to put together a skeleton." The second provided skin, flesh, and blood. But just when the third wanted to breathe life into the beast, the sensible man warned against doing so. "Hold on!" he cried. "This is a lion. If you bring him back to life, he will kill all of us."

"You idiot!" said one of them. "I won't reduce our scholarship to inaction."

"In that case," the man of sense answered, "wait a minute while I climb a convenient tree."

When he got up into the tree, the others restored the lion to life, and it rose up and killed the three Brahman scholars. After the lion went off, the man of sense scrambled down from the tree and went home.

And so I say, *Scholarship is less valuable than common sense.*

But the wheel bearer, who heard the story, answered, "Not at all. You reason poorly. If stricken by fate, even creatures of very great sense perish, while those of small intelligence live happily—if fate protects them. Here is a poem:

> While a hundred wits stand on a head/And a thousand wits hang
>> limply dead,
> Your humble single wit, good friend,/Is paddling in the water to the
>> end.

The Brahman's Dream of Castles in the Air

In a certain town there was a Brahman named Stingy, who begged some barley meal, ate part of it, and filled a jar with what was left over. At night he hung the vessel from a peg, placed his cot below it, and, staring at it intensely, fell into reverie.

"Here is a full jar of barley meal," he thought. "If we have a famine, I'll make a hundred rupees on it. With that money I'll buy a pair of she-goats. Every six months they will bear two more goats. After selling all the goats, I'll buy cows. When the cows calve, I'll sell the calves. After cows, buffaloes. After buffaloes, mares. From the mares I'll get many horses. The sale of them will bring me abundant gold. With the gold I will buy a mansion with an inner court. Then someone will come to my house and offer his lovely daughter as a dowry. She will bear me a son, and I will name him Moon Lord. When he is old enough to ride on my knee, I will take a book, sit on the stable roof and ponder. Just then, Moon Lord will see me, leave his mother's lap to ride on my knee, and he will go too close to the horses. Then I shall become furious and shout to my wife, 'Take the boy away!' But she will be busy with her housework and won't pay any attention to what I command. Then I will get up and kick her grievously."

Being thoroughly absorbed in his hypnotic dream, he let fly a powerful kick and smashed the jar. The barley meal smothered him, turning him white all over.

And so I say:

> Do not indulge in silly hopes.

You are absolutely right, the gold finder said. *You see:*

> The miserly and greedy do not heed/The consequenses of a deed.
> Their disappointments follow soon./Think of the father of little Lord
>> Moon.

▪ Kalidasa (c. Fourth to Fifth Centuries A.D.) *Sanskrit* (poem)

TRANSLATED BY TONY BARNSTONE

Sanskrit poet and playwright Kalidasa is considered to be the finest of the Sanskrit poets, and his play *Shakuntala* is the masterpiece of Indian drama. Nothing is known of his life, though legends abound, and there is widespread disagreement about the dating of his work, though previous scholarship indicating that he flourished as early as the second century B.C. is now discounted. There is evidence to suggest that he was associated with the Gupta king Chandragupta II, a North Indian monarch who ruled from A.D. 380 to 415. He has been given the title Great Poet (*Mahakavi*) and holds a position in Indian poetics comparable to that of Homer or Chaucer in the West. He was the author of two epic poems, *The Dynasty of Raghu* and *The Birth of Kumara*, and two shorter epics, *The Cloud Messenger* and *The Seasons;* in addition to *Shakuntala and the Ring of Recollection,* he wrote two other dramas, *Urvashi Won by Valor* and *Malavika and Agnimitra.* Close to thirty other pieces are attributed to him, probably spuriously.

Though Kalidasa is equally at home in martial and erotic poetry and drama, it is really as the grandfather of love poets that he shines. The selection presented here from *The Seasons* is one of six sections, each of which treats one of the six Indian seasons. Though some discount it as juvenalia, it is a remarkable piece, both in its passionate mood and in the ways it blends eroticism with a depiction of nature, creating an interpenetration of vegetative myth and human sexuality akin to the Sumerian *Courtship of Inanna and Dumuzi* or Chaucer's General Prologue to *The Canterbury Tales.*

FURTHER READING: Coulson, Michael, tr. *Three Sanskrit Plays,* 1981. Edgerton, Franklin and Eleanor, trs. *The Cloud Messenger: Translated from the Sanskrit Meghaduta,* 1964. Heifetz, Hank, tr. *The Origin of the Young God: Kalidasa's Kumarasambhava,* 1985. Lal, P., tr. *Great Sanskrit Plays in Modern Translation,* 1964. Miller, Barbara Stoler, ed. *Theater of Memory: The Plays of Kalidasa,* 1984. Nandargikar, Gopal Raghunath, ed. and tr. *The Raghuvamsa of Kalidasa,* 1982. Roberts, John T., tr. *The Seasons: Kalidasa's Ritusamhara,* 1990. Williams, Monier, ed. and tr. *Sakuntala: A Sanskrit Drama, in Seven Acts,* 1976.

from **The Seasons**

Winter

Winter is coming
and the lotus shrivels as new snow coats
sweet sprouts rising erect in the cornfields,
ripe rice paddies and the myrtle's bursting flowers.

Now women are sensuous and fine as sandalwood,   *5*
their skin is snow, their aureoles unadorned,
while like jasmine moons
their heavy breasts hang with pearls.

Their arms are bare
of bracelets and arm-bands.   *10*
New silk hugs the orbs of their hips
and sheer cloth rides ripe goblets of milk.[1]

They take off jeweled gold-thread belts
from their womanly hips
and from feet beautiful as lotus flowers   *15*
they discard anklets that ring like singing swans.

Rubbing black sandal oils into their skin,
painting lotuses across their faces
and scenting their tangled hair with aloe
they make up for a feast of love.   *20*

Pale and weak with desire,
the young girls are stabbed through with joy
but sink teeth into their lower lips
to bite back laughs as they seek a lover.

Beautiful breasts want to burst   *25*
from their straight chests in distress
like dew plunging from a leaf of grass
or tears in the winter dawn.

Here where the town gives way to country
this herd of does in fields flush   *30*
with rice shoots fills the men with urges
while the beautiful herons sing

and our minds are swept away
by a lake's cold pure water
decked out with flowering blue lotus   *35*
and lust-crazed geese.

Young tendrils droop and sway
in the persistent snow winds,
O sweet love vine you are pale
as a lovesick woman who's lost her man.   *40*

Knocked out by passion and their bodies' wine
the lovers sleep with their bodies twined,

---

1. The term used for breasts here means literally milk-vessels.

their limbs smelling sweet as the aroma
of flower wine on their moist lips.

Lips red with bite marks, and breasts   *45*
scratched and raw from their lovers' nails,
are passionate evidence of the adult pleasures
the young girls tasted last night.

In a handheld mirror someone paints her lotus face
in the heat of the young morning but finds,   *50*
pulling down her lip, that her lover tore it
last night when he drunk her essence;

and here is another sex-tired body:
she didn't sleep at all and her eyes are red lotuses.
Now hair tangles around her drooping shoulders   *55*
and she floats through soft sleep on warm sun waves.

Other young girls breathe in the nice aroma
as they tear faded wreaths from their dense black hair.
Their wand-like bodies bend over swollen breasts
as they pile their locks into new creations.   *60*

As she touches up her lip this girl reads
last night's frenzy in each mark on her body;
her curved eyes half-lidded, hair a dark river,
she slips her nail-torn form into a shirt.

These girls made love for so long   *65*
their slack bodies are slick with sweat,
pubic hair standing on end like their nipples
as they oil their glorious bodies.

It's winter but the women thrill, heart-rapt,
as ripe rice bursts into the village   *70*
and the herons cry that the frost has flown;
may you be so happy when your winter comes.

■ Vijjika (Vidya) (c. A.D. 659) *Sanskrit* (poems)

The poems of Vijjika (also known as Vidya) appear in Vidyakara's famous anthology *The Treasury of Well-turned Verse*. She has been identified as a queen (Vijaya-bhattarika), the wife of Chandraditya, who was the eldest son of Pulakesin II and the brother of Vikramaditya I. She may also have written a Sanskrit drama that is considered of inferior quality.

Friends

Friends, you are lucky you can talk
about what you did as lovers:
the tricks, laughter, the words,
the ecstasy.
After my darling put his hand on the knot   5
of my dress,
I swear I remember nothing.

TRANSLATED BY WILLIS BARNSTONE

Ominous Clouds

Ominous clouds
gray & swollen with water
discharge their rain.
Wind dusted with *kadamba* blossoms
toss on the storm.   5
Peacocks call and make love in the hills.
What do I care?
But when the lightning
tosses her veils around like a rival woman
the rainstorm breaks   10
my spirit.

TRANSLATED BY ANDREW SCHELLING

To Her Daughter

As children we crave
little boys
pubescent we hunger for youths
old we take elderly men.
It is a family custom.   5
But you like a penitent
pursue a whole
life with one husband.
Never, my daughter
has chastity   10
          so stained our clan.

TRANSLATED BY ANDREW SCHELLING

■ Bhartrihari (Seventh Century?)
Sanskrit (poems)

TRANSLATED BY TONY BARNSTONE

The poems collected in the *Shatakatrayam* are attributed to someone named Bhartrihari, but it is unclear whether a single author by that name ever existed, or whether these poems are by several hands. Though the collection was probably gathered between the eleventh and twelfth centuries, there is an earlier reference by the Chinese pilgrim I-ching to a grammarian named Bhartrihari who died in A.D. 650. Are they the same man? It is impossible to know. Another tale about Bhartrihari, popular but almost certainly apocryphal, says that he was a king who, disgusted with the inconstancy of women, gave up his kingship and went to live in the forest. Certainly this misogyny is apparent in the poems attributed to him. Women are an "acrid poison," a "snare," a "poisonous creeper," a "yoke," and passion is an "epileptic fit." His disgust for the body, the "fleshy protuberances" of a woman's breasts, her face as a "vile receptacle of phlegm" echoes the *Visuddhi-Magga*'s account of beauty (see Buddhist Texts, "Beauty Is But Skin-Deep," in this collection). Yet this stern denunciation of women and the pleasures of the flesh wavers in other poems, and women are seen as "heaven" instead of the evil devices of the god of love Kamadeva. If these poems were indeed written by a single man, they are a record of a man who vacillates between love and hate for the world and for women, and who, like the Chinese poet Wang Wei, always longs to be the perfect ascetic yet falls back into the net of passion. His failure, if it was real, is what humanizes him to us. Barbara Stoler Miller writes: "Bhartrihari does not simply vacillate between worldly indulgence and asceticism; his confusion is more profound. He concurrently experiences delight in the fullness of the world, anxiety over its cruel transience, and the feeling that this tension is inescapable. His ironic sense that none of life's possibilities are what they seem to be gives pattern to his irreconcilable attractions and to [his poems]."[1] In Bhartrihari, as in Kalidasa's Ri-tusamhara (*The Seasons*), woman is associated with nature, which is also beautiful and dangerous and the source of life. His moralistic poems are of significantly less interest than his erotic ones, often seeming humorless and pedantic, but he sometimes achieves a vision of humanity caught in a world of delusion that rivals Rumi, Kabir, and Saigyo.

---

1. Barbara Stoler Miller, tr. *Bhartrihari: Poems.* New York: Columbia University Press, 1967, p. xxiv.

FURTHER READING: *Bhartrihari: Poems.* Translated by Barbara Stoler Miller. With the transliterated Sanskrit text of the Satakatrayam: Niti, Sringara, Vairagya, 1967. *The Hermit & The Lovethief: Sanskrit Poems of Bhartrihari and Bilhana.* Translated by Barbara Stoler Miller, 1978. *An Old Tree Living by the River: Poems of Bhartrihari.* Translated from Sanskrit by John Cort, 1983.

Who Can See a Sexy Woman

Who can see a sexy woman—
with wild shimmering eyes,
young and proud, ripe breasts
perched over her slim belly
and her trunk dimpling in beautiful folds 5
as if wrapped around with vines
—and not lose his mind?

Three Waves Roll across Her Waist

Three waves roll across her waist,
her breasts take flight like wild geese
and her blossoming face is a bright lotus,
but a woman is a moody river
where a monster dwells. 5
Think well before you take that fatal bath.

My Love Is Nothing like the Moon

My love is nothing like the moon,
her eyes are not two lotus blooms
and her shining flesh is not gold,
but listening to what poets say
even a sage will pray at the body's altar, 5
this sack of meat and bones.

The Cycles of Day and Night

The cycles of day and night
mark our decay
but caught up in our lives
we don't see them slip away.
Pain, death, old age 5

don't make us worry;
we drink lies till we're sloshing drunk
and the mad world reels through nothingness.

The Moth Dives into Flame

The moth dives into flame,
ignorant of its fury,
and the dumb fish
eats both worm and hook,
but we who see   5
the mayhem of passion
embrace its intricate net.
Who can understand?

■ Amaru (Seventh Century) *Sanskrit* (poems)

Sanskrit poet Amaru (also known as Amaruka) is the author of the
Amaru-sataka, a collection of one hundred verses named after him, all dealing with love. Little is known of his life, but since he is quoted from a number of times after A.D. 800, he must have flourished before then. Daniel H.
H. Ingalls suggests that the majority of the hundred poems ascribed to him
are written by various authors of the seventh and eighth centuries.

Ingenue

Friends, I did as you said: stiffened, desperately lowered my willing
    eyes when his eyes called me,
Stared at his feet, shut my hungry ears on the sweets of his speech,
    threw up my hands to hide
The shiver and flush of my skin. But what could I do if this
    treacherous blouse,
With a mind of its own, suddenly gave at the seams?

TRANSLATED BY V. N. MISTRA, L. NATHAN, AND S. H. VATSYAYAN

Finesse

When he came in, she rose. No chance to sit together.
She ducked out of his arms to order betel leaf.

As he opened his mouth to speak, she called the maid.
> A fine fury,
Slapping him every turn by too much courtesy.   5

TRANSLATED BY V. N. MISTRA, L. NATHAN, AND S. H. VATSYAYAN

Somehow She Got

Somehow she got
through the day
dwelling on night's hundred pleasures.
Her dear one's returned!
But now it's time to enter the bedchamber   5
and relatives
won't stop their dull conversation.
Mad with desire the girl finally cries
something bit me
shakes her skirt wildly   10
> and knocks over the lamp—

TRANSLATED BY ANDREW SCHELLING

Regional Bhakti (Devotional) Literatures

(c. Tenth to Sixteenth Centuries)

■ Basavanna (1106–1167 or 1168) *Kannada* (poem)

TRANSLATED BY A. K. RAMANUJAN

Basavanna was a Virashaiva saint who wrote *vachanas,* or free verse mystical poems addressed to the god Shiva and written in the Dravidian language *Kannada.* Virashaivism is a monotheistic form of Hinduism. Basavanna was probably born in Manigavalli. His parents died young, and he was raised first by a grandmother, then by foster parents from whom he may have received an education in the traditional classics. Disgusted with ritual and the caste system, at sixteen he devoted himself to the worship of Shiva and, like the Buddha, left family behind for a religious life. Basavanna moved to Kappadisangama, where three rivers flow together, and began to address Shiva in his poems as "The Lord of the Meeting Rivers." Later he moved to Kalyana, married his cousin, and became a friend and courtier of King Bijjala. Basavanna was soon the center of a Virashaiva revival that was so threatening to traditionalists in the area that Bijjala found himself pressured to find an excuse to persecute the rising religion. When an outcaste man married a Brahman woman in a Virashaiva wedding, Bijjala had them executed. In the resulting riots and rounds of persecution, Bijjala was stabbed to death, the community was scattered, and Basavanna, having failed to prevent the violence, returned to Kappadisangama, where he died not long after. His poems, like those of the other great Virashaiva saints, are considered not mere literature but central psalms of the religion.

FURTHER READING: Ramanujan, A. K. *Speaking of Siva*, 1973.

The Pot Is a God

The pot is a god. The winnowing
fan is a god. The stone in the
street is a god. The comb is a
god. The bowstring is also a
god. The bushel is a god and the   5
spouted cup is a god.

Gods, gods, there are so many
there's no place left
for a foot.

There is only   10
one god. He is our Lord
of the Meeting Rivers.

▪ Mahadevi (Mahadeviyakka) (Twelfth Century) *Kannada* (poems)

TRANSLATED BY A. K. RAMANUJAN

Mahadevi was born in the Indian village of Udutati and was initiated into the worship of the god Shiva when she was ten. In the form that Shiva took at Mahadevi's temple, he was referred to by the epithet Lord White as Jasmine, and in Mahadevi's terrifically sexy poems, this lord appears as her divine lover. However, a human lover, Kaushika, the king of the region, saw Mahadevi and fell in love with her, and it seems likely that she was forced to marry him, in spite of the fact that he was a nonbeliever. Still, in her poetry, her divine lover is her true husband, sometimes represented as an illicit lover who is her true soulmate, and she writes, "Take these husbands who die, / decay, and feed them / to your kitchen fires!" At some point Mahadevi seems to have left the king and become a wandering mendicant, throwing away the clothes that covered her true self and covering herself only with her long hair. She went to Kalyana, where Allama Prabhu and Basavanna ran a school of Virashaiva religion. There, after a trial by debate with Allama, she was accepted into their company. Mahadevi is said to have died into a union with Shiva at the Holy Mountain of Shrishaila.

FURTHER READING: Ramanujan, A. K. *Speaking of Siva,* 1973.

Riding the Blue Sapphire Mountains

Riding the blue sapphire mountains
wearing moonstone for slippers
blowing long horns
O Siva
when shall I   5
crush you on my pitcher breasts?
O lord white as jasmine
when do I join you
stripped of body's shame
and heart's modesty?   10

People

People,
male and female,
blush when a cloth covering their shame
comes loose.
      When the lord of lives   5
lives drowned without a face
in the world, how can you be modest?

When all the world is the eye of the lord,
onlooking everywhere, what can you
cover and conceal?   10

Monkey on Monkeyman's Stick

Monkey on monkeyman's stick
puppet at the end of a string

I've played as you've played
I've spoken as you've told me
I've been as you've let me be   5

O engineer of the world
lord white as jasmine

I've run
till you cried halt.

I Love the Handsome One

I love the Handsome One:
he has no death
decay nor form
no place or side
no end nor birthmarks.   5
I love him O mother. Listen.

I love the Beautiful One
with no bond nor fear
no clan no land
no landmarks   10
for his beauty.

So my lord, white as jasmine, is my husband.

Take these husbands who die,
decay, and feed them
to your kitchen fires!   15

▪ Jayadeva (Twelfth Century)
Sanskrit (dramatic poetry)

TRANSLATED BY BARBARA STOLER MILLER

Jayadeva was born at Kindubilva in Bengal to a Brahman family, according to legend, and was a court poet under King Lakshmanasena. Early on he gave up scholarship for the life of a wandering mendicant. His great work is the *Gitagovinda,* an epic poem blending songs and recited passages that tells of the erotic union of Radha and the god Krishna, of Krishna's infidelity with the cowherd women, of Radha's jealousy, and of Krishna's return to her. Jayadeva's wife Padmavati is said to have danced with Jayadeva in accompaniment to his songs in the *Gitagovinda.* The name Jayadeva means "God of Triumph," and he uses this phrase in the *Gitagovinda's* songs to refer to Krishna. The *Gitagovinda* has become famous in the West as the Indian equivalent of the biblical *Song of Songs* and in India is a sacred text whose songs are canonized within the Vaishnava religion. The extant manuscripts of the *Gitagovinda* include the names of the *ragas,* or melodic formulas, that go with the various songs and, as translator Barbara Stoler Miller notes, "nightly performance of the songs in worship of Jagannatha at Puri has been continuous for more than seven hundred years."[1] Its long popularity is well-deserved. In its apotheosis of erotic drama, it remains among the world's best long poems.

FURTHER READING: Arnold, Edwin. *The Indian Song of Songs.* 6th ed., 1891. Keyt, George. *Gita Govinda,* 1947. Miller, Barbara Stoler, ed. and tr. *Love Song of the Dark Lord: Jayadeva's Gitagovinda,* 1977. Siegel, Lee. *Sacred and Profane Dimensions of Love in Indian Traditions as Exemplified in the Gitagovinda of Jayadeva,* 1978.

The Gitagovinda

from The First Part: Joyful Krishna

If remembering Hari[1] enriches your heart,
If his arts of seduction arouse you,
Listen to Jayadeva's speech
In these sweet soft lyrical songs.

       ✳   ✳   ✳

When he quickens all things   5
To create bliss in the world,
His soft black sinuous lotus limbs
Begin the festival of love
And beautiful cowherd girls wildly
Wind him in their bodies.   10
Friend, in spring young Hari plays
Like erotic mood incarnate.

---

1. Barbara Stoler Miller ed. and tr. *Love Song of the Dark Lord: Jayadeva's Gitagovinda.* New York: Columbia University Press, 1977, pp. 6–7.

1. A name for Krishna.

Winds from sandalwood mountains
Blow now toward Himalayan peaks,
Longing to plunge in the snows   *15*
After weeks of writhing
In the hot bellies of ground snakes.
Melodious voices of cuckoos
Raise their joyful sound
When they spy the buds   *20*
On tips of smooth mango branches.

from The Second Part: Careless Krishna

While Hari roamed in the forest
Making love to all the women,
Rādhā's hold on him loosened,
And envy drove her away.
But anywhere she tried to retreat   *5*
In her thicket of wild vines,
Sounds of bees buzzing circles overhead
Depressed her—
She told her friend the secret.

✳   ✳   ✳

My heart values his vulgar ways,   *10*
Refuses to admit my rage,
Feels strangely elated,
And keeps denying his guilt.
When he steals away without me
To indulge his craving   *15*
For more young women,
My perverse heart
Only wants Krishna back.
What can I do?

from The Third Part: Bewildered Krishna

Krishna, demon Kaṁsa's foe,[2]
Feeling Rādhā bind his heart with chains
Of memories buried in other wordly lives,
Abandoned the beautiful cowherd girls.

As he searched for Rādhikā[3] in vain,   *5*
Arrows of love pierced his weary mind

───────────

2. Kaṁsa was Krishna's uncle and a dangerous enemy.
3. Rādhā.

And Mādhava[4] repented as he suffered
In a thicket on the Jumna riverbank.

＊　＊　＊

Lotus stalks garland my heart,
Not a necklace of snakes!   10
Blue lily petals circle my neck,
Not a streak of poison!
Sandalwood powder, not ash,
Is smeared on my lovelorn body!
Love-god, don't attack, mistaking me for Śiva![5]   15
Why do you rush at me in rage?

Don't lift your mango-blossom arrow!
Don't aim your bow!

＊　＊　＊

Her arched brow is his bow,
Her darting glances are arrows,   20
Her earlobe is the bowstring—
Why are the weapons guarded
In Love's living goddess of triumph?
The world is already vanquished.

from The Seventh Part: Cunning Krishna

She is richly arrayed in ornaments for the battle of love;
Tangles of flowers lie wilted in her loosened hair.
> Some young voluptuous beauty
> Revels with the enemy of Madhu.[6]

She is visibly excited by embracing Hari;   5
Her necklaces tremble on full, hard breasts.

Curling locks caress her moon face;
She is weary from ardently drinking his lips.

Quivering earrings graze her cheeks;
Her belt sounds with her hips' rolling motion.   10

She laughs bashfully when her lover looks at her;
The taste of passion echoes from her murmuring.

Her body writhes with tingling flesh and trembling.
The ghost of Love expands inside with her sighing.

---

4. Krishna.

5. Kamadeva, the god of love (equivalent to Cupid in the West) was burned up by the god
Shiva (Śiva) after piercing him with the arrow of love-madness and remorse.

6. This refrain is repeated after each stanza. "The enemy of Madhu" is an epithet for Krishna.

Drops of sweat wet the graceful body   *15*
Fallen limp on his chest in passionate battle.

May Hari's delight in Jayadeva's song
Bring an end to this dark time.

✳   ✳   ✳

Friends are hostile,
Cool wind is like fire,   *20*
Moon nectar is poison,
Krishna torments me in my heart.
But even when he is cruel
I am forced to take him back.

from The Ninth Part: Languishing Krishna

Then, when she felt wasted by love,
Broken by her passion's intensity,
Despondent, haunted by Hari's
Response to her quarreling,
Her friend spoke to her.   *5*

✳   ✳   ✳

When he is tender you are harsh,
When he is pliant you are rigid,
When he is passionate you are hateful,
When he looks expectant you turn away,
You leave when he is loving.   *10*
Your perverseness justly
Turns your sandalbalm to poison,
Cool moon rays to heat, ice to fire,
Joys of loveplay to torments of hell.

from The Tenth Part: Four Quickening Arms

Fretful Rādhā, don't suspect me!
A rival has no place
When your voluptuous breasts and hips
Always occupy my heart.

✳   ✳   ✳

Your moist lips glow   *5*
Like crimson autumn blossoms;
The skin of your cheek
Is a honey-colored flower.
Fierce Rādhā, your eyes glower
Like gleaming dark lotuses;   *10*

Your nose is a sesame flower;
Your teeth are white jasmine.
Love's flower arms conquer worlds
By worshipping your face.

■ Lalla (c. 1320–1392) *Kashmiri* (poems)

TRANSLATED BY COLEMAN BARKS

Kashmiri poet and mystic Lalla is also known as Lal Didi, Mai Lal Diddi, Lal Ded (all of which mean Grandmother Lal) and, in Sanskrit, as Lalleshwari, or Lalla the great yogi. She moves between schools and doctrines to create a personal spiritual vision that draws on the Upanishads, Sufism, Vedanta, Shaivism, and other schools, and that, while idiosyncratic, teaches the lesson of nonduality, that *I* am *you* and *you* are *that*. She is famous for dancing naked while singing her songs: "Dance, Lalla," she writes, "with nothing on / but air," for "[w]hat clothes / could be so beautiful, or / more sacred" than "this glowing day"? Little is known of her life, since there are no records from her lifetime, only legends about her recorded in the eighteenth century. It is said that she left an unhappy marriage to become a student of the Hindu sage Sed Bayu. Translator Coleman Barks relates that

> It was then also that she began to ignore conventional standards of dress and to wander in a state of ecstatic clarity. One morning as children were making fun of her nakedness, a cloth merchant scolded their disrespect. Lalla asked him for two strands of cloth equal in weight. That day as she walked about, she wore a piece of cloth over each shoulder, and as she met with respect or scorn, she tied knots in one or the other. In the evening she came back to the merchant and asked him to weigh the cloth again. The scales swung in balance, of course, no matter how the cloth was knotted. Praise and blame have no substance of their own.[1]

FURTHER READING: Barks, Coleman, tr. *Lalla: Naked Song*, 1992. Grierson, Sir George, and Lionel D. Barnett. *Lalla-Vakyani, the Wise Saying of Lal Ded, A Mystic Poetess of Ancient Kashmir*, 1920. Kaul, Jayalal. *Lal Ded*, 1973. Kotru, Nil Kanth. *Lal Ded, Her Life and Sayings*, 1989. Temple, Richard Carnac. *The Word of Lalla the Prophetess*, 1924. *Lalleshwari*. Poems rendered by Muktananda and Gurumayi, 1981.

---

1. Coleman Barks, tr. *Lalla: Naked Song*. Athens, GA: Maypop Books, 1992, p. 9.

Dance, Lalla, with Nothing On

Dance, Lalla, with nothing on
but air. Sing, Lalla,
wearing the sky.
Look at this glowing day! What clothes
could be so beautiful, or   5
more sacred?

Whatever Your Name, Shiva, Vishnu

Whatever your name, Shiva, Vishnu,
the genius who inspired Scherazade,
savior of the Jains, the pure Buddha,
lotus-born God, I am sick. The world
is my disease, and You are the cure,   5
You, you, you, you, you, you, you.

The Soul, Like the Moon

The soul, like the moon,
is new, and always new again.

And I have seen the ocean
continuously creating.

Since I scoured my mind   5
and my body, I too, Lalla,
am new, each moment new.

My teacher told me one thing,
Live in the soul.

When that was so,   10
I began to go naked,
and dance.

■ Chandidas (Late-Fourteenth to Mid-Fifteenth Centuries) *Bengali* (poems)

The great Bengali poet Chandidas's life remains shrouded in mystery,
yet he was so famous that many other poets adopted his name. Of the thousands of poems attributed to Chandidas, around two hundred are thought

to be authentic. His love poems have been extremely important in the development of Bengali literature and to such seminal figures as Rabindranath Tagore. Versions of his poems can even be heard sung as folk songs by Bengali peasants. The historical trace that he left has been obscured by imitators and exists, in any case, in such "soft" historical forms as legend and song; however, it does seem that he had a career as a village priest, that he was connected to the Sahaja movement, and that he had a relationship with a village woman called Rami (or Ramini). He may have lived in the West Bengali village Nannur, or in the village of Chhatna, and it seems that he defied tradition by openly living with his lover, Rami, though he was a high-caste priest and she a lowly washerwoman. Similarly, he wrote not in the literary language, Sanskrit, but in the vulgate, Bengali, which made his poetry comprehensible to the lowest classes.

The great lovers Radha and Krishna are considered the female and male reincarnations of Vishnu; Vaishnava philosophy focuses on Vishnu, and the words derive from the same root. One of the paths to worshiping Vishnu is that of *bhakti,* in which the devotee marshals his or her emotions to find union with the god. This path has proven to be a particularly fertile source of great love poetry. Chandidas's poetry clearly fits into the bhakti tradition and is associated as well with the Sahaja movement, a Hindu method of yoga in which eroticism and lovemaking are embraced, and each man is considered Krishna, each woman Radha.

FURTHER READING: Bhattacharya, Deben. *Love Songs of Chandidas: The Rebel Poet-Priest of Bengal,* 1967.

I Pick Wild Flowers

I pick wild flowers
and make a love necklace
but their coldness and smell
fade
as my neck catches fire.   5

Gardener, why did you poison
the necklace?
You blackened my heart.
Now my whole body
chars.   10

I hear nothing.
My eyes are dead
and the flowers burn.

My heart is coal.
My ribs collapse,   *15*
descending.
My body is gone.

TRANSLATED BY TONY BARNSTONE AND WILLIS BARNSTONE

Why Tell Me What to Do?

Why tell me what to do?
Dreaming or awake I see only his black skin.
I don't even fix my tangled hair,
just pour it in my lap, and wish it were Krishna.
I call to him, sweet black Krishna,   *5*
and cry.

I leave this black hair loosely knotted
so when my dark love comes to mind
I can let it down and brood.
What can I do?   *10*
His black skin is always with me.

TRANSLATED BY TONY BARNSTONE

■ Kabir (1398–1448) *Hindi* (poems)

When Rabindranath Tagore published his translation from the medieval Hindi of the great poet Kabir, he made available to the West the fascinating poems that continue to inspire a Kabir sect, and his translations of this world-class poet remain among the very best. Kabir was born in Varanasi to a family of weavers and raised Muslim, though he seems to have studied with a Hindu guru before turning into an influential teacher himself. He did not, however, take the religious path of withdrawing from the world; he was married, had children, and earned his living as a weaver. Kabir was popularly believed to have been discipled to the famous guru Ramananda. Linda Hess recounts the legend about "how he tricked the orthodox Hindu into accepting him, a Muslim, as a student. Supposedly he stretched himself across the stairs leading to the river where Ramananda came for his bath in the predawn darkness. Tripping over Kabir's body and fearing sudden danger to his life, Ramananda cried out—as Kabir knew he would—his own mantra: 'Ram! Ram!' Kabir then claimed that the mantra had been transmitted and he must be accepted as a disciple."[1] Yet Kabir is

---

1. Kabir. *The Bijak of Kabir.* Translated by Linda Hess and Shukdev Singh; essays and notes by Linda Hess. San Francisco: North Point Press, 1983, p. 3.

neither wholly Hindu nor wholly Muslim; his peculiar brand of mysticism, while retaining the devotionalism of Vaishnava, was also influenced by Sufi mysticism. He continues to be a figure embraced by the Sikhs, the Muslims, and the Hindus.

Kabir is thought to have been illiterate, and his songs were collected by disciples. The songs associated with him continue to be sung in a lasting oral tradition. Iconoclastic, idiosyncratic, he is a riddling poet, and an aggressive one in his attempt to shock his listeners out of orthodox, calcinated beliefs, and to speak that "secret word" that will awaken the reader to the God inside.

FURTHER READING: Kabir. *The Bijak of Kabir.* Translated by Linda Hess and Shukdev Singh; essays and notes by Linda Hess, 1983; *Kabir.* Introduction and translation from the Hindi and notes by Ch. Vaudeville, 1974; *The Kabir Book: Forty-four of the Ecstatic Poems of Kabir.* Versions by Robert Bly, 1977; *One Hundred Poems of Kabir.* Translated by Rabindranath Tagore assisted by Evelyn Underhill, 1961; *Songs of Kabir from the Adi Granth.* Translation and introduction by Nirmal Dass, 1991.

Who Needs Words When You're Drunk on Love?

Who needs words when you're drunk on love?
I've got a diamond wrapped in my cloak. I won't open it again.
When the pan was near empty the scales tipped; now full why weigh it
    at all?
The swan soared to a high lake in the mountains. Why should it
    scrabble in puddles and ditches?
He lives inside. Why bother opening your eyes?   5
Kabir says, friend, my eyes are ravished by the One inside.

TRANSLATED BY TONY BARNSTONE

Shadows Fall Everywhere

Shadows fall everywhere, piling up deep, and body and mind
    disappear in dark love.
Open the window to the west and you topple into the sky of love.
Eat honey that seeps from lotus petals of your heart
and a magnificent ocean's swells will enter your body.
Can you hear the bells and conch shells?   5
Kabir says, friend, my body is his vessel.

TRANSLATED BY TONY BARNSTONE AND WILLIS BARNSTONE

How Can I Ever Speak That Secret Word?

How can I ever speak that secret word?
How can I say He is this and not that?
If I say He is inside I shame the world
but to say He's outside is a lie.
He makes the worlds inside and outside one.   5
His feet rest both on thought and dream
and he is neither manifest nor hidden, mystery nor revelation.
No words can say just what He is.

TRANSLATED BY TONY BARNSTONE

I've Played with Other Girls but My Heart Shakes

I've played with other girls but my heart shakes
as I mount the high stairs to my Master's palace.
He's to be my Lover and I can't be shy.
My heart must leap toward him. I will lower my veil and touch him
    with all my body,
my eyes like ceremonial lamps of love.   5
Kabir says, friend, to understand, love. If you don't worship the Lover
    why dress up and line your eyes with kohl?

TRANSLATED BY TONY BARNSTONE AND WILLIS BARNSTONE

Lamplight Flames from Every House but You Don't See It

Lamplight flames from every house but you don't see it, blind one.
One day the lids will peel back from your eyes like deadly chains
    dropping off
and there will be nothing to say, hear or do, since He is alive, and He
    is also dead, and He'll never die again.

Since He lives in solitude the Yogis say his house is miles away;
He is next to you but you climb a palm tree seeking Him.   5
The Brahman priest goes house to house converting people;
he sets up a stone and worships it, when the spring of life is right
    there!
Kabir says: I can't tell you how sweet He is, better than Yoga and
    telling beads and all the pleasures of virtue and sin.

TRANSLATED BY TONY BARNSTONE

The Moon Shines inside My Body but My Eyes

The moon shines inside my body but my eyes
    are blind to it.
The moon is inside me and so is the sun.
The drum of eternity resounds within me, unstruck, but my ears don't
    hear it.

So long as you seek for *I* and *mine* your work will come to nothing;
to do heavenly work, murder your love of *I* and *mine*.   5
The real reason for work is to know;
when knowledge comes, give up your work.

The flower blossoms for the fruit; as the fruit swells the flower wilts.
The musk is in the deer, but the deer hunts for it outside, searching
    through the grass.

TRANSLATED BY TONY BARNSTONE

How Could Our Love Die?

How could our love die?
Like a lotus on the water I live for you.
I think only of you, like a Chakor bird astonished by the moon all
    night long.
This love ignited at the birth of time. It won't die when time dies.
Kabir says, my heart touching you is a river pouring into the sea.   5

TRANSLATED BY TONY BARNSTONE

Between the Conscious and the Unconscious

Between the conscious and the unconscious, the mind has put up a
    swing:
all earth creatures, even the supernovas, sway between these two trees,
and it never winds down.

Angels, animals, humans, insects by the million, also the wheeling sun
    and moon;
ages go by, and it goes on.   5

Everything is swinging: heaven, earth, water, fire,
and the secret one slowly growing a body.
Kabir saw that for fifteen seconds, and it made him a servant for life.

TRANSLATED BY ROBERT BLY

I Have Been Thinking of the Difference

I have been thinking of the difference
between water
and the waves on it. Rising,
water's still water, falling back,
it is water, will you give me a hint   5
how to tell them apart?

Because someone has made up the word
"wave," do I have to distinguish it
from water?

There is a Secret One inside us;   10
the planets in all the galaxies
pass through his hands like beads.

That is a string of beads one should look at with luminous eyes.

TRANSLATED BY ROBERT BLY

Are You Looking for Me?

Are you looking for me? I am in the next seat. My shoulder is against
    yours.
You will not find me in stupas, not in Indian shrine rooms, nor in
    synagogues, nor in cathedrals:
not in masses, nor kirtans, not in legs winding around your own neck,
    nor in eating nothing but vegetables.
When you really look for me, you will see me instantly—
you will find me in the tiniest house of time.   5
Kabir says: Student, tell me, what is God?
He is the breath inside the breath.

TRANSLATED BY ROBERT BLY

■ Mirabai (1498–1573) *Hindi* (poems)

TRANSLATED BY WILLIS BARNSTONE AND USHA NILSSON

The songs of Mirabai belong to a large oral tradition of song, a folk tradition of more than five thousand songs that can be heard from the lips of
professional singers and common folk alike across India, though as few as
three or four hundred are considered authentic. A similar fog surrounds
the details of Mirabai's life, which is obscured in legend. Some doubt that a

historical Mirabai existed and say that she was, as some say of the Chinese sage Laozi, not a single person but a tradition. Even if she didn't exist, this defiant sexual mystic with her wry and simple ecstatic songs is a marvelous and necessary invention. It is said that Mirabai was born in Merta, in Rajasthan, northwest India, to a powerful clan and was raised in her grand-father's court. When she was eight, she was engaged to the son of the ruler of Mewar, an arranged betrothal for political purposes. At eighteen she married the young prince Raga Bojaraja and went to live in Chitor, the cap-ital city. Though her husband worshiped Kali, goddess of destruction, Mirabai kept her faith in Krishna. At the palace she gathered a circle of devotees, but after her husband's death her mother-in-law and royal brother-in-law disagreed with her beliefs, abused her, and even tried to poison her with a tainted glass of holy water. She responded in acerbic verse: "Rana, I know you gave me poison / but I came through / as gold left in a fire / emerges bright as a dozen suns." When the poison failed, they gave her a fruit basket containing a poisonous serpent. In a last attempt, they made her lie on a bed of iron spikes.

Mirabai fled the palace and lived as a *sadhu,* a wandering holy beggar, dancing and singing her songs of love. She lived in places sacred to Krishna, eventually becoming a temple poet. Her extremely erotic religious poems are primarily addressed to Krishna, her dark-skinned lover whom she addresses as Hari, Girdhar, Shyam (dark one), or the cowherd, and she speaks in the voice of Radha (Krishna's mythic beloved). After the death of Mirabai's husband, Krishna became her heavenly prince, her "true hus-band." In her poems, she waits for him; she meets him in the darkness, in dream, in ecstasy; and she agonizes like Radha at his infidelities. Mirabai is thought to have died in Dwarka, but her songs are sung daily in the streets and temples of India.

FURTHER READING: Alston, A. J. *The Devotional Poems of Mirabai,* 1980. Nilsson, Usha. *Mira Bai,* 1970. Panvey, S. M., and Norman Zeide. *Poems from Mirabai,* 1964. Sethi, V. K. *Mira, the Divine Lover,* 1979.

Mira Is Dancing with Bells Tied

Mira is dancing with bells tied
on her ankles.
People say Mira has gone mad.

Her mother-in-law is upset
at the ruined family honor.

The king sends her a cup of poison.
Laughing, she drinks it
for her drink is Hari's beautiful face.

5

She has offered her body and her soul
at Hari's feet.   *10*
She drinks the honey of her vision.
Only he
is her ultimate protector.

Rana, I Know You Gave Me Poison

Rana, I know you gave me poison
but I came through
as gold left in a fire
emerges bright as a dozen suns.
Opinion and family name   *5*
I throw away like water.
You should hide, Rana.
I am a powerless mad woman.
Krishna's arrow in my heart
destroys my reason.   *10*
I hug the lotus feet of holy men,
give them body and soul.
Mira's lord knows she is his servant.

My Love Is in My House

My love is in my house,
I watched the road for years
but never saw him.
I put out the worship plate,
gave away gems.   *5*
After this, he sent word.
My dark lover has come,
joy is on my limbs.
Hari is an ocean,
my eyes touch him.   *10*
Mira is an ocean of joy.
She takes him inside.

I Don't Sleep. All Night

I don't sleep. All night
I am watching for my love.
Friends offer

wise words.
I reject them. *5*
Without him I can't rest,
but my heart is not angry.
My limbs are weak,
my lips call to him.
This pain of separation *10*
cannot be understood.
I am like the rainbird calling for clouds,
like fish craving water.
Mira is lost,
her senses are dead. *15*

My Pitcher Crashes on the Ground

My pitcher crashes on the ground.
I am stunned.
His beauty maddens me. Father, mother, brother
and sister
all say nice words. Come home, *5*
forget him.
But that dark dancer inhabits me.
His love is light all through my body.
Let them say I am lost.
The secret. Girdhar knows. *10*

You Broke My Bracelet

You broke my bracelet
when we made love.
In the morning my mother-in-law
will see it, and give me
hell. *5*
Morning always comes like lightning
for lovers
after their night.
I won't get up and leave.
The night was wonder I spent *10*
with you.
You filled me.
I came.

Day and Night

Day and night
I am obsessed with one thought.
You.
Shall I walk away from you?
I couldn't take it. I couldn't stay   5
alive.
Day after day
I climb up to the watchtower of my palace
and there in the turret
I scan the roads coming into the city.   10
Empty night. I despair.
The world is illusion.
Love for family is mere words.
Your lotus feet
is where I am.   15

The Modern Period

(Nineteenth and Twentieth Centuries)

■ Ghalib (Asadullah Khan Ghalib) (1797–1869) *Urdu* (poems)

TRANSLATED BY TONY BARNSTONE

Asadullah Khan Ghalib, known by his pen name Ghalib, was born in Agra in 1797. His father and uncle died when he was very young, so he lived with his mother's family with few father figures about. His education may have been at the hands of a tutor from Iran, a Zoroastrian who had converted to Islam, named Mulla Abdussamad Harmuzd. Around 1810, Ghalib married into a noble, cultivated family and moved to Delhi, where he lived for the remainder of his life, with the exception of a two-year stay in Calcutta. He began writing poetry in his childhood, when he was as young as seven or eight, and his first collection, written in Urdu, was compiled when he was twenty-four. For the rest of his career, however, he wrote for the most part in Persian. In addition to his poetic gifts, he is considered to be a great prose stylist, known for his eloquent letters. The Mughal king Bahadur Shah Zafar became his patron, and Ghalib wrote Urdu poetry (which Zafar favored over Persian) and the first part of a Persian history of the Mughal dynasty for him. Ghalib's letters were published late in his life and helped establish colloquial speech as the basis of prose literature. His poetry is romantic and mystical, and the lover who gives him so much trouble is often equated with God. Like that of the great Persian poet Hafiz, the style of Ghalib's poems is the rhymed, formal ghazal, in which the poet addresses himself by name in the final couplet. His poems are characterized by great wit, puns, and a mystical, erotic imagery so passionate as to veer at times into the surreal.

FURTHER READING: Ahmad, Aijaz. *Ghazals of Ghalib,* 1971; Jafri, Sardar, and Qurrat-ulain Hyder. *Ghalib and His Poetry,* 1970; Russell, R., and K. Islam. *Ghalib: Life and Letters,* 1969; Mujeeb, M. *Ghalib,* 1969.

Even Dew on a Red Poppy Means Something

Even dew on a red poppy means something.
It covers the scar on your vicious heart.

The dove is a claw of ash, the nightingale a coop of color.
What is the shriek of my charred heart to that?

Beside the lust for flame the flame is ash;   5
the heart withers as it loses heart.

I only say love is jail because you've locked me in.
My hand won't stray with this boulder on it.

Sun who lights the world, warm us too.
A strange time has touched us like a shadow.   10

She Considers Acting Sweet for Once

She considers acting sweet for once
but knows how she's hurt me and shies away.

She's short with me when I go on too long about love.
I should shut up; I even bore myself.

She's grown wary and I'm weak.   5
My tongue dies, and she won't ask.

I've got to keep it together. Damn!
What was I saying?

Here it is: even if she lifts her veil
I can't stand to look at her.   10

Her Stride Is an Arrow from a Taut Bow

Her stride is an arrow from a taut bow;
how can I open up that heart?

I say a word, she bites off my tongue:
"Shut up, *I'm* talking," she says.

Listen to me drivel.   5
God, I hope no one understands.

Even Alexander was fooled by Khizer,
so who should I believe in?

Ghalib! The world is dead.
Why even bother to complain?   10

At the Party I Have No Shame

At the party I have no shame;
I just sit here, though the fingers point.

I pawn my worn robe and prayer rug for wine;
it's been too long since we drank together.

Let me interrogate the earth. I'd say, *Miser!*   5
Why do you give back nothing?

With new friends she has a new habit:
she'll kiss you before you beg.

She's not a stone, not cruel;
she keeps some promises because she forgets.   10

Your Other Lover Flaunts Your Letter

Your other lover flaunts your letter
so he can brag about it.

You're so delicate and tenderly made, I want you to say
Hold me. Yet my hands flinch from your perfection.

Death is certain as my need to live;   5
I call you, certain you won't come.

I don't know whose vision this is.
A veil too thick for me to part.

Ghalib! Love is flame feeding on flame.
I can't light it. I can't put it out.   *10*

Look at Me! I Envy Myself, I'm So Lucky

Look at me! I envy myself, I'm so lucky.
Am I tough enough to bear her beauty?

Fears flare but I surrender my cracked heart:
the wine's so hot the glass is melting.

My God! How can she say *Behave yourself*?   *5*
Her shyness makes her shy away in shame

but passion won't let me shut up:
I'm so hot I can't stop for breath.

Asad! My shadow escapes from me like smoke.
My soul is fire. Nothing can stand this heat.   *10*

Think of Those Faces Mixed with Dust

Think of those faces mixed with dust.
Few of them show up again as roses or tulips.

The stars who form the Daughters of the Bier were veiled in sun.
What was in your hearts? At night you walked out naked.

A man whose arm is draped with your hair   *5*
can sleep peacefully. He owns the night.

We believe in one God. We break old patterns.
When our tribes died out they blended into faith.

Ghalib wept like this. Your city too
will be a brambled wilderness.   *10*

Each Step Opens More Distance to You

Each step opens more distance to you
as the desert flees with my own feet.

This searing heart so lights my desolate night
that your shadow eludes like wafting smoke.

Blistered feet decorate the desert of my lunacy.   *5*
A luminous string of blood pearls.

For you the goblet's colors leap through a hundred dances.
I catch this vision in a single astounded eye,

Asad! and from my burning eye a fire trickles
and glares on a garden of dirt and parched leaves.   *10*

■ Rabindranath Tagore (1861–1941)
Bengali (poems)

TRANSLATED BY WILLIAM RADICE

Nobel Prize–winning poet Rabindranath Tagore is the most famous of
Bengali writers. He was born in Calcutta in 1861 to a wealthy, aristocratic
family and was raised in an artistic and cultured environment. He was a
prolific and talented writer who threw his energies into many fields. In addition to writing one hundred books of poems, he wrote fiction and was a
painter and an innovative songwriter. He wrote many essays, travel diaries, a
book of popular science, satires, farces, and musical and dance dramas and
was deeply involved in the questions of social and agricultural policy. At
seventeen, he became recognized for writing love poems about the love of
Radha and Krishna in the style of the medieval Vaishnava poets (see, for example, Chandidas, in this volume). Like the great fiction writer Premchand, Tagore was deeply involved in the nationalist movement of his time
and was, in fact, a friend of Mahatma Gandhi; like Gandhi, he was devoted
to peace and denounced violence in any cause, even that of nationalism.
He was knighted in 1915, but after a British massacre in Amritsar led by
General Reginald Dyer, Tagore returned his knighthood in protest.

Tagore was a mystical, philosophical poet, deeply affected by his reading of the Upanishads, of the Isa Upanishad in particular. This mysticism
can be seen throughout his work and is responsible for the popularity of
his most widely read book, *Gitanjali* (1912), for which William Butler Yeats
wrote an introduction. His work was deeply influenced by the Bengali and
Sanskrit traditions.

Tagore won the Nobel Prize in Literature in 1913. In addition to
Gitanjali, other well-known works include *The Gardener* (1913), *Songs of Kabir*
(1915), *Fireflies* (1928), *Sheaves* (1932), and the play *The Post Office;* collections
of his work in English include *A Tagore Reader* (1966), *Collected Poems and Plays*
(1937), *The Housewarming and Other Selected Writings* (1965), *The Religion of
Man* (1930), and *Three Plays* (*Mukta-Dhara, Natire Puja, Chandalika*) (1950).

FURTHER READING: Bowes, Pratima. *Some Songs and Poems from Rabindranath Tagore,*
1985. Chakravarty, Amiya, ed. *A Tagore Reader,* 1961. Ghose, Sisirkumar. *The Later Poems
of Tagore,* 1961. Kripalani, Krishna. *Rabindranath Tagore: A Biography,* 1962. Radice,
William, tr. *Selected Poems: Rabindranath Tagore,* 1985. Robinson, Andrew. *The Art of Rabindranath Tagore.* Foreword by Satyajit Ray, 1989. Tagore, Rabindranath. *Angel of Surplus: Some Essays and Addresses on Aesthetics.* Edited by Sisirkumar Ghose, 1978.

The Sick-Bed

When I woke up this morning
There was a rose in my flower-vase:
The question came to me—
The power that brought you through cyclic time
To final beauty,   5
Dodging at every turn
The torment of ugly incompleteness,
Is it blind, is it abstracted,
Does it, like a world-denying *sannyasi*,
Make no distinction between beauty and the opposite of beauty?   10
Is it merely rational,
Merely physical,
Lacking in sensibility?
There are some who argue
That grace and ugliness take equal seats   15
At the court of Creation,
That neither is refused entry
By the guards.
As a poet I cannot enter such arguments—
I can only gaze at the universe   20
In its full, true form,
At the millions of stars in the sky
Carrying their huge harmonious beauty—
Never breaking their rhythm
Or losing their tune,   25
Never deranged
And never stumbling—
I can only gaze and see, in the sky,
The spreading layers
Of a vast, radiant, petalled rose.   30

Recovery

Every day in the early morning this faithful dog
Sits quietly beside my chair
For as long as I do not acknowledge his presence
By the touch of my hand.
The moment he receives this small recognition,   5
Waves of happiness leap through his body.
In the inarticulate animal world
Only this creature
Has pierced through good and bad and seen

Complete man,   *10*
Has seen him for whom
Life may be joyfully given,
That object of a free outpouring of love
Whose consciousness points the way
To the realm of infinite consciousness.   *15*
When I see that dumb heart
Revealing its own humility
Through total self-surrender,
I feel unequal to the worth
His simple perception has found in the nature of man.   *20*
The wistful anxiety in his mute gaze
Understands something he cannot explain:
It directs me to the true meaning of man in the universe.

On My Birthday

Today I imagine the words of countless
Languages to be suddenly fetterless—
After long incarceration
In the fortress of grammar, suddenly up in rebellion.
Maddened by the stamp-stamping   *5*
Of unmitigated regimented drilling.
They have jumped the constraints of sentence
To seek free expression in a world rid of intelligence,
Snapping the chains of sense in sarcasm
And ridicule of literary decorum.   *10*
Liberated thus, their queer
Postures and cries appeal only to the ear.
They say, 'We who were born of the gusty tuning
Of the earth's first outbreathing
Came into our own as soon as the blood's beat   *15*
Impelled man's mindless vitality to break into dance in his throat.
We swelled his infant voice with the babble
Of the world's first poem, the original prattle
Of existence. We are kin to the wild torrents
That pour from the mountains to announce   *20*
The month of Śrāban: we bring to human habitations
Nature's incantations—'
The festive sound of leaves rustling in forests,
The sound that measures the rhythm of approaching tempests,
The great night-ending sound of day-break—   *25*
From these sound-fields man has captured words, curbed them like a
    breakneck

Stallion in complex webs of order
To enable him to pass on his messages to the distant lands of the
     future.
By riding words that are bridled and reined
Man has quickened   *30*
The pace of time's slow clocks:
The speed of his reason has cut through material blocks,
Explored recalcitrant mysteries;
With word-armies
Drawn into battle-lines he resists the perpetual assault of imbecility.   *35*
But sometimes they slip like robbers into realms of fantasy,
Float on ebbing waters
Of sleep, free of barriers,
Lashing any sort of flotsam and jetsam into metre.
From them, the free-roving mind fashions   *40*
Artistic creations
Of a kind that do not conform to an orderly
Universe—whose threads are tenuous, loose, arbitrary,
Like a dozen puppies brawling,
Scrambling at each other's necks to no purpose or meaning: *45*
Each bites another—
They squeal and yelp blue murder,
But their bites and yelps carry no true import of enmity,
Their violence is bombast, empty fury.
In my mind I imagine words thus shot of their meaning,   *50*
Hordes of them running amuck all day,
As if in the sky there were nonsense nursery syllables booming—
Horselum, bridelum, ridelum, into the fray.

■ Mahatma Gandhi (Mohandas Karamchand Gandhi) (1869–1948) *English* (prose)

Mohandas Karamchand Gandhi (called Mahatma, or "Great Soul") is probably the most famous person to come out of modern India. Born in Porbandar, he was educated in India and London, passing the bar exam in London in 1889. He practiced law in India for a few years, but in 1893 he went to South Africa where his law practice flourished and where he used his new prominence in the Indian community to organize it against anti-Indian discrimination. While in South Africa, he gave up Western ways for Hindu ideals of asceticism, giving up material possessions and wearing the garb of an ascetic—loincloth and shawl. Using a strategy of civil disobedience, he forced an agreement from the South African government that alleviated anti-Indian discrimination.

In 1915, Gandhi returned to India, then under British colonial rule, where he carried on activities in favor of Indian self-rule and labor and agrarian reform and became a central figure in the Indian National Congress through the 1920s and early 1930s. He remained a tireless campaigner for reform, and although he was jailed for his activities in 1930 and 1942, Gandhi was central to the postwar meetings that led to India's independence. The violence between Hindus and Muslims that followed independence and has been a fact of life in India until today led Gandhi to fast in protest and to tour violent areas, attempting to broker peace. His attempts at mediation led to his murder on January 30, 1948, in New Delhi, by a Hindu extremist angered by Gandhi's concern for the Muslims.

The concept of civil disobedience was first codified in modern times by Henry David Thoreau in his 1849 essay "Civil Disobedience" (written about his overnight stay in a New England jail for refusing to pay taxes in protest over the Mexican War), but Gandhi put the method to lifelong use. Others, such as Martin Luther King, Jr., have followed his example. Today, Gandhi's method of passive resistance, civil disobedience, and nonviolence has been adopted by civil rights activists and political dissenters throughout the world.

FURTHER READING: Ashe, Geoffrey. *Gandhi: A Study in Revolution,* 1968. Gandhi, Mohandas Karamchand. *All Men Are Brothers: Life and Thoughts of Mahatma Gandhi as Told in His Own Words.* Edited by Krishna Kripalani, 1959, 1969; *An Autobiography: The Story of My Experiments with Truth.* Translated from the Gujarati by Mahadev Desai, 1954; *Satyagraha: Non-violent Resistance.* Edited by Bharatan Kumarappa, 1951, 1983. Nanda, Jawaharlal. *Mahatma Gandhi: A Biography,* 1958.

from Indian Home Rule

Passive Resistance

READER: Is there any historical evidence as to the success of what you have called soul-force or truth-force? No instance seems to have happened of any nation having risen through soul-force. I still think that the evildoers will not cease doing evil without physical punishment.

EDITOR: The poet Tulsidas has said: "Of religion, pity, or love, is the root, as egotism of the body. Therefore, we should not abandon pity so long as we are alive." This appears to me to be a scientific truth. I believe in it as much as I believe in two and two being four. The force of love is the same as the force of the soul or truth. We have evidence of its working at every step. The universe would disappear without the existence of that force. But you ask for historical evidence. It is, therefore, necessary to know what history means. The Gujarati equivalent means: "It so happened." If that is the meaning of history, it is possible to give copious evidence. But, if it means the doings of kings and emperors, there can be no evidence of soul-force or passive resistance in such history. You cannot expect silver ore in a tin mine. History, as we know it, is a record of the wars of the world, and so there is a proverb among Englishmen that a nation which has no history, that is, no wars, is a happy nation. How kings played, how they became enemies of one another, how they murdered one another, is found accurately recorded in history, and if this were all that had happened in the world, it would have been ended long ago. If the story of the universe had commenced with wars, not a man would have been found alive today. Those people who have been warred against have disappeared as, for instance, the natives of Australia of whom hardly a man was left alive by the intruders. Mark, please, that these natives did not use soul-force in self-defense, and it does not require much foresight to know that the Australians will share the same fate as their victims. "Those that take the sword shall perish by the sword." With us the proverb is that professional swimmers will find a watery grave.

The fact that there are so many men still alive in the world shows that it is based not on the force of arms but on the force of truth or love. Therefore, the greatest and most unimpeachable evidence of the success of this force is to be found in the fact that, in spite of the wars of the world, it still lives on.

Thousands, indeed tens of thousands, depend for their existence on a very active working of this force. Little quarrels of millions of families in their daily lives disappear before the exercise of this force. Hundreds of nations live in peace. History does not and cannot take note of this fact. History is really a record of every interruption of the even working of the force of love or of the soul. Two brothers quarrel; one of them repents and re-awakens the love that was lying dormant in him; the two again begin to live in peace; nobody takes note of this. But if the two brothers, through the intervention of solicitors or some other reason, take up arms or go to law—which is another form of the exhibition of brute force—their doings would be immediately noticed in the press, they would be the talk of their neighbors and would probably go down to history. And what is true of families and communities is true of nations. There is no reason to believe that there is one law for families and another for nations. History, then, is a record of an interruption of the course of nature. Soul-force, being natural, is not noted in history.

READER: According to what you say, it is plain that instances of this kind of passive resistance are not to be found in history. It is necessary to understand this passive resistance more fully. It will be better, therefore, if you enlarge upon it.

EDITOR: Passive resistance is a method of securing rights by personal suffering; it is the reverse of resistance by arms. When I refuse to do a thing that is repugnant to my conscience, I use soul-force. For instance, the Government of the day has passed a law which is applicable to me. I do not like it. If by using violence I force the Government to repeal the law, I am employing what may be termed body-force. If I do not obey the law and accept the penalty for its breach, I use soul-force. It involves sacrifice of self.

Everybody admits that sacrifice of self is infinitely superior to sacrifice of others. Moreover, if this kind of force is used in a cause that is unjust, only the person using it suffers. He does not make others suffer for his mistakes. Men have before now done many things which were subsequently found to have been wrong. No man can claim that he is absolutely in the right or that a particular thing is wrong because he thinks so, but it is wrong for him so long as that is his deliberate judgment. It is therefore meet that he should not do that which he knows to be wrong, and suffer the consequence whatever it may be. This is the key to the use of soul-force.

READER: You would then disregard laws — this is rank disloyalty. We have always been considered a law-abiding nation. You seem to be going even beyond the extremists. They say that we must obey the laws that have been passed, but that if the laws be bad, we must drive out the law-givers even by force.

EDITOR: Whether I go beyond them or whether I do not is a matter of no consequence to either of us. We simply want to find out what is right and to act accordingly. The real meaning of the statement that we are a law-abiding nation is that we are passive resisters. When we do not like certain laws, we do not break the heads of law-givers but we suffer and do not submit to the laws. That we should obey laws whether good or bad is a new-fangled notion. There was no such thing in former days. The people disregarded those laws they did not like and suffered the penalties for their breach. It is contrary to our manhood if we obey laws repugnant to our conscience. Such teaching is opposed to religion and means slavery. If the Government were to ask us to go about without any clothing, should we do so? If I were a passive resister, I would say to them that I would have nothing to do with their law. But we have so forgotten ourselves and become so compliant that we do not mind any degrading law.

A man who has realized his manhood, who fears only God, will fear no one else. Man-made laws are not necessarily binding on him. Even the Government does not expect any such thing from us. They do not say: "You must do such and such a thing," but they say: "If you do not do it, we will punish you." We are sunk so low that we fancy that it is our duty and our religion to do what the law lays down. If man will only realize that it is unmanly to obey laws that are unjust, no man's tyranny will enslave him. This is the key to self-rule or home-rule.

It is a superstition and ungodly thing to believe that an act of a majority binds a minority. Many examples can be given in which acts of majorities will be found to have been wrong and those of minorities to have been right. All reforms owe their origin to the initiation of minorities in opposition to majorities. If among a band of robbers a knowledge of robbing is obligatory, is a pious man to accept the obligation? So long as the superstition that men should obey unjust laws exists, so long will their slavery exist. And a passive resister alone can remove such a superstition.

To use brute-force, to use gunpowder, is contrary to passive resistance, for it means that we want our opponent to do by force that which we desire but he does not. And if such a use of force is justifiable, surely he is entitled to do likewise by us. And so we should never come to an agreement. We may simply fancy, like the blind horse moving in a circle round a mill, that we are making progress. Those who believe that they are not bound to obey laws which are repugnant to their conscience have only the remedy of passive resistance open to them. Any other must lead to disaster.

READER: From what you say I deduce that passive resistance is a splendid weapon of the weak, but that when they are strong they may take up arms.

EDITOR: This is a gross ignorance. Passive resistance, that is, soul-force, is matchless. It is superior to the force of arms. How, then, can it be considered only a weapon of the weak? Physical-force men are strangers to the courage that is requisite in a passive resister. Do you believe that a coward can ever disobey a law that he dislikes? Extremists are considered to be advocates of brute force. Why do they, then, talk about obeying laws? I do not blame them. They can say nothing else. When they succeed in driving out the English and they themselves become governors, they will want you and me to obey their laws. And that is a fitting thing for their constitution. But a passive resister will say he will not obey a law that is against his conscience, even though he may be blown to pieces at the mouth of a cannon.

What do you think? Wherein is courage required—in blowing others to pieces from behind a cannon, or with a smiling face to approach a cannon and be blown to pieces? Who is the true warrior—he who keeps death always as a bosom-friend, or he who controls the death of others? Believe me that a man devoid of courage and manhood can never be a passive resister.

This, however, I will admit: that even a man weak in body is capable of offering this resistance. One man can offer it just as well as millions. Both men and women can indulge in it. It does not require the training of an army; it needs no jiu-jitsu. Control over the mind is alone necessary, and when that is attained, man is free like the king of the forest and his very glance withers the enemy.

Passive resistance is an all-sided sword, it can be used anyhow; it blesses him who uses it and him against whom it is used. Without drawing a drop of blood it produces far-reaching results. It never rusts and cannot be stolen. Competition between passive resisters does not exhaust. The sword of passive resistance does not require a scabbard. It is strange indeed that you should consider such a weapon to be a weapon merely of the weak. . . .

READER: From what you say, then, it would appear that it is not a small thing to become a passive resister, and, if that is so, I should like you to explain how a man may become one.

EDITOR: To become a passive resister is easy enough but it is also equally difficult. I have known a lad of fourteen years become a passive resister; I have known also sick people do likewise; and I have also known physically strong and otherwise happy people unable to take up passive resistance. After a great deal of experience it seems to me that those who want to become passive resisters for the service of the country have to observe perfect chastity, adopt poverty, follow truth, and cultivate fearlessness.

Chastity is one of the greatest disciplines without which the mind cannot attain requisite firmness. A man who is unchaste loses stamina, becomes emasculated and cowardly. He whose mind is given over to animal passions is not capable of any great effort. . . .

Just as there is necessity for chastity, so is there for poverty. Pecuniary ambition and passive resistance cannot go well together. Those who have money are not expected to throw it away, but they are expected to be indifferent about it. They must be prepared to lose every penny rather than give up passive resistance.

Passive resistance has been described in the course of our discussion as truth-force. Truth, therefore, has necessarily to be followed and that at any cost. In this connection, academic questions such as whether a man may not lie in order to save a life, etc., arise, but these questions occur only to those who wish to justify lying. Those who want to follow truth every time are not placed in such a quandary; and if they are, they are still saved from a false position.

Passive resistance cannot proceed a step without fearlessness. Those alone can follow the path of passive resistance who are free from fear, whether as to their possessions, false honor, their relatives, the government, bodily injuries or death.

These observances are not to be abandoned in the belief that they are difficult. Nature has implanted in the human breast ability to cope with any difficulty or suffering that may come to man unprovoked. These qualities are worth having, even for those who do not wish to serve the country. Let there be no mistake, as those who want to train themselves in the use of arms are also obliged to have these qualities more or less. Everybody does not become a warrior for the wish. A would-be warrior will have to observe chastity and to be satisfied with poverty as his lot. A warrior without fearlessness cannot be conceived of. It may be thought that he would not need to be exactly truthful, but that quality follows real fearlessness. When a man abandons truth, he does so owing to fear in some shape or form. The above four attributes, then, need not frighten anyone. It may be as well here to note that a physical-force man has to have many other useless qualities which a passive resister never needs. And you will find that whatever extra effort a swordsman needs is due to lack of fearlessness. If he is an embodiment of the latter, the sword will drop from his hand that very moment. He does not need its support. One who is free from hatred requires no sword. A man with a stick suddenly came face to face with a lion and instinctively raised his weapon in self-defense. The man saw that he had only prated about fearlessness when there was none in him. That moment he dropped the stick and found himself free from all fear.

■ Sarat Chandra Chatterjee (1876–1938)
Bengali (story)

TRANSLATED BY S. SINHA

Bengali fiction writer Sarat Chandra Chatterjee ranks with Rabindranath Tagore and Bankim Chandra Chatterjee as one of the most important Bengali writers of the modern era. Though born a Brahman like Tagore and the earlier Chatterjee, he lived for much of his life in extreme poverty, and the acute sense of social injustice and the struggle simply to survive that permeates his stories derives from his own life experience. He also shows a deep sympathy for women in his writing, studying the question of women's rights and writing several essays about them, most famously "What Price Woman?," which has been described as an "impassioned, yet closely reasoned plea for the recognition of woman's right of self-determination and the moral and spiritual value of her personality."[1] Chatterjee is said to have roamed far afield in India as a Hindu *sannyasi,* and later as a Buddhist monk. Though he had no formal education, he began writing in his late twenties and became so successful that his works were translated into all the major Indian languages. He wrote twelve novels and many short stories; his fiction has been made into a number of films. "Drought" is considered among Chatterjee's very best stories.

FURTHER READING: Chatterjee, Sarat Chandra. *Drought and Other Stories.* Translated by Sasadhar Sinha, 1970.

Drought

The village was called Kashipur. It was a small village, but its *Zamindar*[1] was smaller still. Yet his tenants dared not stand up to him. He was so ruthless.

It was the birthday of his youngest son. It was noon. Tarkaratna, the priest, was on his way home from the landlord's house, where he had been offering prayers. It was nearing the end of May, but not a patch of cloud could be seen in the sky. The rainless firmament poured fire.

At the end of the field, beside the road, there stood the house of Gafur, the weaver. Now that the mud walls were in ruins, the courtyard touched the public highway, and the inner privacy was thrown on the mercy of the passers-by.

---

1. Sarat Chandra Chatterjee. *Drought and Other Stories.* Translated by Sasadhar Sinha. New Delhi: Sahitya Akademi, 1970, p. 8.

---

1. An official in charge of collecting land taxes. Also, a landholder.

"Hey! Gafur! Is anybody in?" called out Tarkaratna, standing in the shade of a tree by the roadside.

"What do you want? Father is down with fever," answered Gafur's little daughter, aged ten, appearing at the door.

"Fever! Call the scoundrel!"

The noise brought Gafur out, shivering with fever. A bull was tied to the old acacia that leaned against the broken wall.

"What do I see there?" demanded Tarkaratna, indicating the bull. "Do you realise that this is a Hindu village and the landlord himself a Brahmin?"[2] His face was crimson with indignation and the heat of the sun. It was to be expected that his words should be hot and harsh. But Gafur simply looked at him, unable to follow the import of his words.

"Well," said Tarkaratna, "I saw it tied there in the morning and it's still there. If the bull dies, your master will flay you alive! He is no ordinary Brahmin!"

"What shall I do, Father? I'm helpless. I have had fever for the last few days. I can't take him out to graze. I feel so ill."

"Can't you let him graze by himself?"

"Where shall I let him go, Father? People haven't threshed all their paddy yet. It's still lying in the fields. The straw hasn't been gathered. Everything is burnt to cinders—there isn't a blade of grass anywhere. How can I let him loose, Father? He might start poking his nose into somebody's paddy or eating somebody's straw."

Tarkaratna softened a little. "But you can at least tie him in the shade somewhere and give him a bundle of straw or two to munch. Hasn't your daughter cooked rice? Why not give him a tub of boiled rice water? Let him drink it."

Gafur made no reply. He looked helplessly at Tarkaratna, and a deep sigh escaped him.

"I see; you haven't even got that much? What have you done with your share of straw? I suppose you have gone and sold it to satisfy your belly? Not saved even one bundle for the bull! How callous you are!"

At this cruel accusation Gafur seemed to lose the power of speech. "This year I was to have received my share of straw," said Gafur slowly after a moment's hesitation, "but the master kept it all on account of my last year's rent. 'Sir, you are our lord and master,' I implored, falling at his feet. 'Where am I to go if I leave your domain? Let me have at least a little straw. There's no straw on my roof, and we have only one hut in which we two—father and daughter—live. We'll patch the roof with palm leaves and manage this rainy weather, somehow, but what will happen to our Mahesh without food?'

---

2. The first of the four Hindu classes, Brahmins (also "Brahmans") teach the Vedas and officiate at religious rites.

"Indeed! So you're fond enough of the bull to call him Mahesh! This is a joke."[3]

But his sarcasm did not reach Gafur. "But the master took no pity on me," he went on. "He gave me paddy to last only two months. My share of straw was added to his own stock—Mahesh didn't have even a wisp of it."

"Well, don't you owe him money?" said Tarkaratna, unmoved. "Why shouldn't you have to pay? Do you expect the landlord to support you?"

"But what am I to pay him with? We till four bighas[4] of land for him, but the paddy has dried up in the fields during the droughts in the last two years. My daughter and I have not even enough to eat. Look at the hut! When it rains, I spend the night with my daughter huddled in one corner—we can't even stretch our legs. Look at Mahesh! You can count his ribs. Do lend me a bit of hay for him so that he can have something to eat for a day or two." And Gafur sank down on the ground at the Brahmin's feet.

"No, no! Move aside! Let me go home, it's getting late." Tarkaratna made a movement as though to depart, smiling. "Good God! He seems to brandish his horns at me! Will he hurt?" he cried out with fright and anger, stepping hurriedly back from the bull.

Gafur staggered to his feet. "He wants to eat a handful," he said, indicating the wet bundle of rice and fruit in Tarkaratna's hand.

"Wants to eat? Indeed! Like master, like animal. Hasn't even a bit of straw to eat and must have rice and fruit. Take him away and tie him somewhere else! What horns! He will gore somebody to death one of these days." Edging a little, the priest made a quick exit.

Looking away from him, Gafur silently watched Mahesh, whose two deep, brown eyes were full of pain and hunger. "Didn't even give a handful," he muttered, patting the bull's neck and back. "You are my son, Mahesh," he whispered to him. "You have grown old and served us for eight years. I can't even give you enough to eat—but you know how much I love you, don't you?"

Mahesh only stretched out his neck and closed his eyes with pleasure.

"Tell me," went on Gafur, "how can I keep you alive in this dreadful year? If I let you loose, you will start eating other people's paddy or munching their banana leaves. What can I do with you? You have no strength left in your body—nobody wants you. They ask me to sell you at the cattle market. . . ." At the very idea his eyes filled with tears again. Wiping his tears on the back of his hand and looking this way and that, he fetched a tiny bunch of discolored old straw from behind the hut. "Eat it quickly, my child, otherwise . . ." he said, softly, placing it before Mahesh.

"Father . . ."

---

3. Another name for the god Shiva.

4. A unit of land measurement, now obsolete; about three-fourths of an acre.

"What is it?"

"Come and eat," answered Gafur's daughter, looking out of the door. "Why, have you again given Mahesh straw from the roof?"

He had feared as much. "It's old straw—it was rotting away," he answered, ashamed.

"I heard you pulling it, father."

"No, darling, it wasn't exactly . . ."

"But you know, father, the wall will crumble . . ."

Gafur was silent. He had nothing left but this hut. Who knew better than he that unless he was careful it would not last another rainy season. And yet what good was it really?

"Wash your hands and come and eat. I have served your food," said the little girl.

"Give me the rice water; let me feed him."

"There is none, father—it has dried up in the pot."

Nearly a week had passed. Gafur was sitting in the yard, sick of body and anxious. Mahesh had not returned since the day before.

He himself was helpless. Amina had been looking for the bull everywhere from early morning. The evening shadows were already falling when she came home. "Have you heard, father? Manik Ghose has sent Mahesh to the police pen," she said.

"Nonsense!"

"Yes, father, it's true. His servant said to me, 'Tell your father to look for the bull at Dariapur. . . .'"

"What did he do?"

"He entered their garden, father."

Gafur made no answer.

"At the end of three days, they say, the police will sell him at the cattle market."

"Let them," answered Gafur.

Amina did not know what the "cattle market" meant. She had often noticed her father grow restless whenever it was mentioned in connection with Mahesh, but today he went out without saying another word.

Under the cover of night, Gafur secretly came round to Banshi's shop.

"Uncle, you'll have to lend me a rupee," said he, putting down a brass plate under the seat. Banshi was well acquainted with this object. In the last two years he had lent a rupee at least five times on this security. He made no objection today either.

The next morning Mahesh was seen at his usual place again. An elderly Mohammedan was examining him with very sharp eyes. Not far away, on one side, Gafur sat on the ground, all hunched up. The examination over, the old man untied a ten-rupee note from a corner of his shawl, and, smoothing it again and again, said: "Here, take this. I shan't take anything off. I'm paying the full price."

Stretching his hand, Gafur took the money, but remained silent. As the two men who came with the old man were about to take the rope round the animal's neck, he suddenly stood bolt upright. "Don't touch that rope, I tell you. Be careful, I warn you!" he cried out hoarsely.

They were taken aback. "Why?" asked the old man in surprise.

"There's no why to it. He's my property—I shall not sell him; it's my pleasure," he answered in the same tone, and threw the note away.

"But you accepted the deposit yesterday," all three said in a chorus.

"Take this back," he answered, flinging the two rupees across to them.

Gafur begged for rice water from the neighbors and fed Mahesh. Patting him on the head and horns, he whispered vague sounds of endearment to him.

It was about the middle of June. Nobody who has not looked at an Indian summer sky would realize how terrible, how unrelenting, the heat can be. Not a trace of mercy anywhere! Today even the thought that some day this aspect of the sky will change, that it will become overcast with soft, vapor-laden clouds is impossible. It seemed as though the whole blazing sky would go on burning day after day endlessly, to the end of time.

Gafur returned home at noon. He was not used to working as a hired laborer, and it was only four or five days since his temperature had gone down. His body was still weak and tired. He had gone out to seek work, but in vain. He had had no success. Hungry, thirsty, tired, everything was dark before his eyes. "Is the food ready, Amina dear?" he called out from the courtyard.

Without answering, his daughter quietly came out and stood leaning against the wall.

"Is the food ready?" Gafur repeated without receiving an answer.

"What do you say? No? Why?"

"There's no rice, father."

"No rice? Why didn't you tell me in the morning?"

"Why, I told you last night."

" 'I told you last night,' " mimicked Gafur. "How am I to remember what you told me last night?" His anger grew more and more violent at the sound of his own voice. "Of course, there's no rice!" he growled, with his face more distorted than ever. "What does it matter to you whether your father eats or not? But the young lady must have her three meals! In the future I shall lock up the rice when I go out. Give me some water to drink—I'm dying of thirst. . . . So you haven't any water, either!"

Amina remained standing with bowed head as before. Realizing that there was not even a drop of water in the house, he lost all self-control. Rushing at her, he slapped her face noisily. "Wretched girl! What do you do all day? So many people die—why don't you?"

The girl did not utter a word. She took the empty earthen pitcher and went out into the afternoon sun, quietly wiping her silent tears.

The moment she was out of sight, her father was overwhelmed with remorse. He alone knew how he had brought up that motherless girl. He knew that this affectionate, dutiful quiet daughter of his was not to blame. They had never had enough to eat even while their little store of rice lasted. It was impossible to eat three times a day. Nor was he unaware of the reason for the absence of water. The two or three tanks in the village had all dried up. The little water that there was still in the private tank of Shibu Babu was not for the public. A few holes had been dug at the bottom of the other tanks, but there was such crowding and jostling for a little water that this chit of a girl could not even approach them. She stood for hours on end and, after much begging, if somebody took pity on her, she returned home with a little water. He knew all this. Perhaps there was no water today or nobody had found time to take pity on her. Something of the sort must have happened, he thought, and his own eyes, too, filled with tears.

"Gafur! Are you in?" somebody cried out from the yard. The landlord's messenger had arrived.

"Yes, I'm in. Why?" answered Gafur bitterly.

"Master has sent for you. Come."

"I haven't had any food yet. I will come later," said Gafur.

Such impudence seemed intolerable to the messenger. "It's master's order to drag you to him and give you a good thrashing," he roared, calling the man ugly names.

Gafur lost self-control for the second time. "We are nobody's slave," he replied, returning similar compliments. "We pay rent to live here. I will not go."

But in this world it is not only futile for the small to appeal to authority, it is dangerous as well. Fortunately the tiny voice seldom reaches big ears or who knows what might happen? When Gafur returned home from the landlord's and quietly lay down, his face and eyes were swollen. The chief cause of so much suffering was Mahesh. When Gafur left home that morning, Mahesh broke loose from his tether, and, entering the grounds of the landlord, had eaten up flowers and upset the corn drying in the sun. When finally they tried to catch him, he had hurt the landlord's youngest daughter and had escaped. This was not the first time this had happened, but Gafur was forgiven because he was poor. If he had come round, and, as on other occasions, begged for the landlord's forgiveness, he would probably have been forgiven, but instead he had claimed that he paid rent, and that he was nobody's slave. This was too much for Shibu Babu, the *Zamindar*, to swallow. Gafur had borne the beatings and tortures without protest. At home, too, he lay in a corner without a word. Hunger and thirst he had forgotten, but his heart was burning within him like the sun outside. He had kept no count of how time passed.

He was suddenly shaken out of his listlessness by a shriek of a girl. She was prostrate on the ground. The pitcher which she had been carrying tumbled over, and Mahesh was sucking up the water as it flowed onto the earth. Gafur was completely out of his mind. Without waiting another moment he seized his plowhead he had left yesterday for repair, and with both hands struck it violently on the bent head of Mahesh. Once only Mahesh attempted to raise his head, but immediately his starving, lean body sagged to the ground. A few drops of blood from his ears rolled down. His whole body shook once or twice and then, stretching the fore and hind legs as far as they would reach, Mahesh fell dead. "What have you done, father? Our Mahesh is dead!" Amina burst out weeping.

Gafur did not move nor answer her. He remained staring without blinking at a pair of motionless, beady, black eyes.

Before two hours were out the tanners living at the end of the village came crowding in and carried off Mahesh on a bamboo pole. Shuddering at the sight of the shining knives in their hands, Gafur closed his eyes but did not speak.

The neighbors informed him that the landlord had sent for Tarkaratna to ask for his advice. How would Gafur pay for the penance which the killing of a sacred animal demanded?

Gafur made no reply to these remarks, but remained squatting with his chin resting on his knees.

"Amina, dear, come, let's go," said Gafur, rousing his daughter at the dead of night.

She had fallen asleep in the yard. "Where, father?" she asked, rubbing her eyes.

"To work at the jute mill at Fulbere," said the father.

The girl looked at him incredulously. Through all his misery he had declined to go to Fulbere. "No religion, no respect, no privacy for women-folk there," she had often heard him say.

"Hurry up, my child; we have a long way to go," said Gafur.

Amina was going to collect the drinking bowl and her father's brass plate. "Leave them alone, darling. They'll pay for the penance for Mahesh," said Gafur.

In the dead of night Gafur set out, holding his daughter by the hand. He had nobody to call his own in the village. He had nothing to say to anybody. Crossing the yard, when he reached the acacia, he stopped stock-still and burst out crying loudly. "Allah," he said, raising his face towards the star-spangled black sky, "punish me as much as you like—Mahesh died with thirst on his lips. Nobody left even the tiniest bit of land for him to feed on. Please never forgive the landlord his sin, who never let him eat the grass nor drink the water you have given." They set out for the jute mill.

■ Premchand (1880–1936) *Hindi* (story)

TRANSLATED BY DAVID RUBIN

Premchand is the literary pseudonym of Dhanpat Rai Srivastava, who was probably the finest writer in Hindi and in Urdu. He was a pioneer writer of serious, realistic fiction, comparable to the work of Émile Zola or Charles Dickens. He was born to a lower-middle-class family near Benares in 1880 and grew up hearing both Hindi and Urdu. He was educated in Persian and Urdu, and Urdu was the language he began writing in at the start of his career. In 1914, he switched to Hindi, and versions of his stories, often in different forms, appear in both languages. He continued writing many works in Urdu throughout his life, but he believed that through Hindi he could reach a wider audience.

Premchand knew poverty as a child, and his parents died before he was twenty. He had little income and experienced poor health for the better part of his life, and most of his fame came after his death. In 1907, his first collection of short stories was banned for its nationalism, causing him to take on a pseudonym. Premchand was a strong advocate of the Independence movement, a follower of Gandhi, politically, and Tolstoy, esthetically. His work also shows the influence of Karl Marx, George Eliot, Charles Dickens, Anton Chekhov, and Maxim Gorky. His stories are extraordinary in the sympathy and realism with which they portray the village life of people of all castes, but most of all the Untouchables and the desperately poor. His work includes fourteen novels and more than three hundred short stories; he also wrote many essays, editorials, screenplays, and plays. Two of his stories, "The Chess Player" and "Deliverance," have been made into films by India's premier filmmaker Satyajit Ray, and "The Shroud" has been made into a Telegu film by Bengali director Mrinal Sen.

FURTHER READING: Premchand. *Deliverance and Other Stories.* Translated from the Hindi by David Rubin, 1969, 1988; *Twenty-four Stories by Premchand.* Translated by Nandini Nopany and P. Lal, 1980.

The Shroud

Father and son sat in silence at the door of their hut before a burnt-out fire and inside Budhiya, the son's young wife, lay fainting in the throes of childbirth. From time to time such an agonizing cry came out of her that their hearts skipped a beat. It was a winter night, all was silent, and the whole village was obliterated in the darkness.

Ghisu said, 'It looks as though she won't make it. You spent the whole day running around—just go in and have a look.'

Annoyed, Madhav said, 'If she's going to die why doesn't she get it over with? What can I do by looking?'

'You're pretty hard-hearted, aren't you? You live at your ease with somebody all year and then you don't give a damn about her.'

'But I couldn't stand looking at her writhing and thrashing.'

They were a family of Untouchable[1] leather-workers and had a bad name throughout the whole village. If Ghisu worked one day he'd take

---

1. The lowest class of people, itself comprised of many subclasses, whose touch was considered unclean by the higher caste Hindus. They are now called Scheduled Castes and discrimination against them was abolished in 1955.

three off. Madhav was such a loafer that whenever he worked for a half hour he'd stop and smoke his pipe for an hour. So they couldn't get work anywhere. If there was even a handful of grain in the house then the two of them swore off work. After a couple of days fasting Ghisu would climb up a tree and break off branches for firewood and Madhav would bring it to the market to sell. And so long as they had any of the money they got for it they'd both wander around in idleness. There was no shortage of heavy work in the village. It was a village of farmers and there were any number of chores for a hard-working man. But whenever you called these two you had to be satisfied with paying them both for doing one man's work between them. If the two of them had been wandering ascetics there would have been absolutely no need for them to practice. This was their nature. A strange life theirs was! They owned nothing except for some clay pots; a few torn rags was all that covered their nakedness. They were free of worldly cares! They were loaded with debts, people abused them, beat them, but they didn't suffer. People would loan them a little something even though they were so poor there was no hope of getting it back. At the time of the potato and pea harvest they would go into other people's fields and dig up potatoes and gather peas and roast them or they'd pick sugarcane to suck at night. Ghisu had reached the age of sixty living this hand-to-mouth existence, and like a good son Madhav was following in his father's footsteps in every way, and if anything he was adding lustre to his father's fame. The two of them were sitting before the fire now roasting potatoes they'd dug up in some field. Ghisu's wife had died a long time ago. Madhav had been married last year. Since his wife had come she'd established order in the family and kept those two good-for-nothings' bellies filled. And since her arrival they'd become more sluggish than ever. In fact, they'd begun to let it go to their heads. If someone sent for them to do a job, they'd bare-facedly ask for twice the wages. This same woman was dying today in child-birth and it was as though they were only waiting for her to die so they could go to sleep in peace and quiet.

Ghisu took a potato and while he peeled it said, 'Go and look, see how she is. She must be possessed by some ghost, what else? But the village exorcist wants a rupee for a visit.'

Madhav was afraid that if he went into the hut Ghisu would do away with most of the potatoes. He said, 'I'm scared to go in there.'

'What are you afraid of? I'll be right here.'

'Then why don't you go and look?'

'When my woman died I didn't stir from her side for three days. And then she'd be ashamed if I saw her bare like that when I've never even seen her face before. Won't she be worried about her modesty? If she sees me she won't feel free to thrash around.'

'I've been thinking, if there's a baby what's going to happen? There's nothing we're supposed to have in the house — ginger, sugar, oil.'

'Everything's going to be all right, God will provide. The very people who wouldn't even give us a pice[2] before will send for us tomorrow and give us rupees. I had nine kids and there was never a thing in the house but somehow or other the Lord got us through.'

In a society where the condition of people who toiled day and night was not much better than theirs and where, on the other hand, those who knew how to profit from the weaknesses of the peasants were infinitely richer, it's no wonder they felt like this. We could even say that Ghisu was much smarter than the peasants and instead of being one of the horde of empty-headed toilers he'd found a place for himself in the disreputable society of idle gossip-mongers. Only he didn't have the ability to stick to the rules and code of such idlers. So while others of his crowd had made themselves chiefs and bosses of the village, the whole community pointed at him in contempt. Nevertheless, there was the consolation that although he was miserably poor at least he didn't have to do the back-breaking labour the farmers did, and other people weren't able to take unfair advantage of his simplicity and lack of ambition.

They ate the potatoes piping hot. Since yesterday they'd eaten nothing and they didn't have the patience to let them cool. Several times they burned their tongues. When they were peeled the outside of the potatoes didn't seem very hot but as soon as they bit into them the inside burned their palates, tongues and throats. Rather than keep these burning coals in their mouths it was a lot safer to drop them down into their bellies, where there was plenty of equipment to cool them. So they swallowed them quickly, even though the attempt brought tears to their eyes.

At this moment Ghisu recalled the Thakur's wedding, which he'd attended twenty years before. The way the feast had gratified him was something to remember all his life, and the memory was still vivid today. He said, 'I won't forget that feast. Since then I've never seen food like it or filled my belly so well. The bride's people crammed everybody with *puris*, everybody! Bigshots and nobodies all ate *puris* fried in real *ghee*.[3] Relishes and curds with spices, three kinds of dried vegetables, a tasty curry, sweets — how can I describe how delicious that food was? There was nothing to hold you back, you just asked for anything you wanted and as much as you wanted. We ate so much that nobody had any room left for water. The people serving just kept on handing out hot, round, mouth-watering savouries on leaves. And we'd say, 'Stop, you mustn't,' and put our hands over the plates to stop them but they kept right on handing it out. And when everybody had rinsed his mouth we got *paan* and cardamom too. But how could I take any *paan?* I couldn't even stand up. I just went and lay down in my blanket right away. That's how generous that Thakur was!'

---

2. A monetary unit equal to one-quarter of a rupee.

3. *Puris* are flat, circular pieces of fried bread. *Ghee* is clarified butter.

Relishing the banquet in his imagination Madhav said, 'Nobody feeds us like that now.'

'Who'd feed us like that today? That was another age. Now everybody thinks about saving his money. Don't spend for weddings, don't spend for funerals! I ask you, if they keep on hoarding the wealth they've squeezed out of the poor, where are they going to put it? But they keep on hoarding. When it comes to spending any money they say they have to economize.'

'You must have eaten a good twenty *puris*?'

'I ate more than twenty.'

'I would have eaten fifty!'

'I couldn't have eaten any less than fifty. I was a husky lad in those days. You're not half so big.'

After finishing the potatoes they drank some water and right there in front of the fire they wrapped themselves up in their *dhotis*[4] and pulling up their knees they fell asleep—just like two enormous coiled pythons.

And Budhiya was still moaning.

* * *

In the morning Madhav went inside the hut and saw that his wife had turned cold. Flies were buzzing around her mouth. Her stony eyes stared upwards. Her whole body was covered with dust. The child had died in her womb.

Madhav ran to get Ghisu. Then they both began to moan wildly and beat their chests. When they heard the wailing the neighbours came running and according to the old tradition began to console the bereaved.

But there was not much time for moaning and chest-beating. There was the worry about a shroud and wood for the pyre. The money in the house had disappeared like carrion in a kite's nest.

Father and son went weeping to the village *zamindar*.[5] He hated the sight of the two of them and several times he'd thrashed them with his own hands for stealing or for not coming to do the work they'd promised to do. He asked, 'What is it, little Ghisu, what are you crying about? You don't show yourself much these days. It seems as though you don't want to live in this village.'

Ghisu bowed his head all the way to the ground, his eyes full of tears, and said, 'Excellency, an awful thing's happened to me. Madhav's woman passed away last night. She was in agony the whole time. The two of us never once left her side. We did whatever we could, gave her medicine— but to make a long story short, she gave us the slip. And now there's nobody left even to give us a piece of bread, master. We're ruined! My house has been destroyed! I'm your slave—except for you now who is there to see that she's given a decent funeral? Whatever we had we spent on medicine.

---

4. A *dhoti* is the loincloth worn by Hindu men.

5. A land-tax official, or, more generally, a landholder with an official capacity.

If your excellency is merciful, then she'll have a good funeral. Whose door can we go to except yours?

The *zamindar* was soft-hearted. But to be kind to Ghisu was like trying to dye a black blanket. He was tempted to say, 'Get out and don't come back! When we send for you, you don't show up but today when you're in a jam you come and flatter me. You're a sponging bastard!' But this was not the occasion for anger or scolding. Exasperated, he took out a couple of rupees and threw them on the ground. But he didn't utter a word of consolation. He didn't even look at Ghisu. It was as though he'd shoved a load off his head.

When the *zamindar* had given two rupees how could the shopkeepers and moneylenders of the village refuse? Ghisu knew how to trumpet the *zamindar*'s name around. Somebody gave him a couple of *annas*,[6] somebody else four. Within an hour Ghisu had harvested a tidy sum of five rupees. He got grain at one place, wood from somewhere else. And at noon Ghisu and Madhav went to the market to get a shroud. There were people already cutting the bamboo to make a litter for the corpse.

The tender-hearted women of the village came and looked at the dead woman, shed a few tears over her forlorn state and went away.

✳   ✳   ✳

When they reached the market Ghisu said, 'We have enough wood to burn her up completely, haven't we, Madhav?'

'Yes, there's plenty of wood, now we need the shroud.'

'That's right, come along and we'll pick up a cheap one.'

'Of course, what else? By the time we move the corpse it will be night—who can see a shroud at night?'

'What a rotten custom it is that somebody who didn't even have rags to cover herself while she was alive has to have a new shroud when she dies!'

'The shroud just burns right up with the body.'

'And what's left? If we'd had these five rupees before then we could have got some medicine.'

Each of them guessed what was in the other's mind. They went on wandering through the market, stopping at one cloth-merchant's shop after another. They looked at different kinds of cloth, silk and cotton, but nothing met with their approval. This went on until evening. Then the two of them, by some divine inspiration or other, found themselves in front of a liquor shop, and as though according to a previous agreement they went inside. For a little while they stood there, hesitant. Then Ghisu went up to where the tavernkeeper sat and said, 'Sahuji, give us a bottle too.'

Then some snacks arrived, fried fish was brought and they sat on the verandah and tranquilly began to drink.

---

6. An *anna* is a copper coin formerly used in India and Pakistan.

After drinking several cups in a row they began to feel tipsy. Ghisu said, 'What's the point of throwing a shroud over her? In the end it just burns up. She can't take anything with her.'

Madhav looked toward heaven and said, as though calling on the gods to witness his innocence, 'It's the way things are done in the world, otherwise why would people throw thousands of rupees away on Brahmans? Who can tell if anybody gets it in the next world or not?'

'The bigshots have lots of money to squander so let them squander it, but what have we got to squander?'

'But how will you explain it to people? Won't they ask, "Where's the shroud?"'

Ghisu laughed. 'So what? We'll say the money fell out of the knot in our *dhotis* and we looked and looked but couldn't find it. They won't believe it but they'll give the money again.'

Madhav laughed too over this unexpected stroke of luck. He said, 'She was good to us, that poor girl—even dying she got us fine things to eat and drink.'

They'd gone through more than half a bottle. Ghisu ordered four pounds of puris. Then relish, pickle, livers. There was a shop right across from the tavern. Madhav brought everything back in a trice on a couple of leaf-platters. He'd spent one and a half rupees; only a few pice were left.

The two of them sat eating their puris in the lordly manner of tigers enjoying their kill in the jungle. They felt neither fear of being called to account nor concern for a bad reputation. They had overcome those sensibilities long before.

Ghisu said philosophically, 'If our souls are content won't it be credited to her in heaven as a good deed?'

Respectfully Madhav bowed his head and confirmed, 'Absolutely will! Lord, you know all secrets. Bring her to paradise—we bless her from our hearts . . . the way we've eaten today we've never eaten before in our whole lives.'

A moment later a doubt rose in his mind. He said, 'What about us, are we going to get there some day too?'

Ghisu gave no answer to this artless question. He didn't want to dampen his pleasure by thinking about the other world.

'But if she asks us there, "Why didn't you people give me a shroud?" What will you say?'

'That's a stupid question!'

'But surely she'll ask!'

'How do you know she won't get a shroud? Do you think I'm such a jackass? Have I been wasting my time in this world for sixty years? She'll have a shroud and a good one too.'

Madhav was not convinced. He said, 'Who'll give it? You've eaten up all the money. But she'll ask me. I was the one who put the cinnabar in her hair at the wedding.'

Getting angry, Ghisu said, 'I tell you she'll have a shroud, aren't you listening?'

'But why don't you tell me who's going to give it?'

'The same people who gave before will give the money again—well, not the money this time but the stuff we need.'

As the darkness spread and the stars began to glitter the gaiety of the tavern also increased steadily. People sang, bragged, embraced their companions, lifted the jug to the lips of friends. All was intoxication, the very air was tipsy. Anybody who came in got drunk in an instant from just a few drops, the air of the place turned their heads more than the liquor. The sufferings of their lives drew them all there and after a little while they were no longer aware if they were alive or dead, not alive or not dead.

And father and son went on slopping it up with zest. Everyone was staring at them. How lucky the two of them were, they had a whole bottle between themselves.

When he was crammed full Madhav handed the leftover puris on a leaf to a beggar who was standing watching them with famished eyes. And for the first time in his life he experienced the pride, the happiness and the pleasure of giving.

Ghisu said, 'Take it, eat it and say a blessing—the one who earned it is—well, she's dead. But surely your blessing will reach her. Bless her from your heart, that food's the wages for very hard labour.'

Madhav looked heavenward again and said, 'She'll go to heaven, *Dada*, she'll be a queen in heaven.'

Ghisu stood up and as though bathing in waves of bliss he said, 'Yes, son, she'll go to heaven. She didn't torment anybody, she didn't oppress anybody. At the moment she died she fulfilled the deepest wish of all our lives. If she doesn't go to heaven then will those big fat people go who rob the poor with both hands and swim in the Ganges and offer holy water in the temples to wash away their sins?'

Their mood of credulity suddenly changed. Volatility is the special characteristic of drunkenness. Now was the turn for grief and despair.

'But *Dada*,' Madhav said, 'the poor girl suffered so much in this life! How much pain she had when she died.'

He put his hands over his eyes and began to cry, he burst into sobs.

Ghisu consoled him. 'Why weep, son? Be glad she's slipped out of this maze of illusion and left the whole mess behind her. She was very lucky to escape the bonds of the world's illusion so quickly.'

And the two of them stood up and began to sing.

'Deceitful world, why do you dazzle us with your eyes?
Deceitful world!'

The eyes of all the drunkards were glued on them and the two of them became inebriated in their hearts. Then they started to dance, they jumped and sprang, fell back, twisted, they gesticulated, they mimed their feelings, and finally they collapsed dead drunk right there.

▪ Jibanananda Das (1899 – 1954)
Bangladesh (poem)

TRANSLATED BY CHINDANANDA DAS GUPTA

Jibanananda Das was born in Barisal, East Bengal (now Bangladesh) in 1899, where, in his early years, he was educated at home because his father disapproved of formal schooling. He graduated from the University of Calcutta, taking a master's degree in English literature, and taught English literature in Calcutta City College and at Barisal. He was killed in 1954 in a Calcutta streetcar accident. His *Selected Poems* was awarded the highest honor of the Indian National Academy of Letters after his death. His other books include *Fallen Feathers* (1928), *Gray Manuscript* (1936), *The Great Earth* (1944), and *Darkness of the Seven Stars* (1948). He was a lyrical poet, a sensitive practitioner of "pure poetry." Donald Junkins writes of his work: "The mellifluous and dreamlike poems of Jibanananda Das celebrate the senses, yet they express a biting, ironic view of the world. Jibanananda's sounds are liquid, his landscapes reverie-like, and his vision detached; it is as if we are reading the poems through softly lighted glass."[1]

Grass

This dawning fills the earth
    With soft green light like tender lemon leaves;
Grass as green as the unripe pomelo[1] — such a fragrance —
    The does tear it with their teeth!
I, too, crave this grass-fragrance like green wine;
    I drink glass after glass.
I stroke the body of the grass — I smooth it eye to eye;
    My feathers on the wings of the grass
I am born as grass amid grass from some deep mother-grass,   5
    I descend from the sweet darkness of her body.

---

1. Donald Junkins, ed. *The Contemporary World Poets.* (New York: Harcourt Brace Jovanovich, 1976),17.

1. *Pomelo:* largest known citrus fruit; pear-shaped with coarse, dry flesh.

▪ R. K. Narayan (1906–) *English* (story)

R. K. Narayan was one of nine children born in Madras in South India to a high-caste family of Brahmans. His father was a schoolmaster, and from an early age Narayan wished to be a writer. After taking a B.A. at Maharaja College in Mysore, he married in 1934 but lost his wife after only five years.

Narayan writes in English, though his native language is Tamil, and many of his tales are set in the fictional town of Malgudi, in South India, a town that resembles the places of his childhood. Through his friendship with Graham Greene, his work was introduced to the West, and he has since become the most celebrated fiction writer to come out of modern India. In the introduction to *Under the Banyan Tree,* Narayan writes that "all theories of writing are bogus. . . . A story comes in being for some unknown reason and anyhow." However, he does say that "at one time I found material for my stories in the open air, market-place, and streets of Mysore . . . [and in] the sheer pleasure of watching people." He has written more than a dozen novels, five collections of short stories, and in addition to retelling India's legends in *Gods, Demons and Others,* he has abridged and retold the great Sanskrit epics in two volumes: *The Ramayana* and *The Mahabharata.* He has also written a volume of memoirs, *My Days.* Some of his novels include *Swami and Friends* (1935), *The Bachelor of Arts* (1937), *The Dark Room* (1938), *The Financial Expert* (1952), *Waiting for the Mahatma* (1955), *The Guide* (1958)—which received the National Prize of the Indian Literary Academy, India's highest literary honor—and *A Tiger for Malgudi* (1983). In recognition of many years of distinguished writing, he received an honorary Doctor of Literature degree at Leeds in 1967.

FURTHER READING: Beatina, Mary. *Narayan: A Study in Transcendence,* 1994. Goyal, Bhagwat S., ed. *R.K. Narayan's India: Myth and Reality,* 1993. Kain, Geoffrey, ed. *R.K. Narayan: Contemporary Critical Perspectives,* 1993. Pousse, Michel. *R.K. Narayan: A Painter of Modern India,* 1995. Walsh, William. *R.K. Narayan: A Critical Appreciation,* 1983.

Forty-five a Month

Shanta could not stay in her class any longer. She had done clay-modelling, music, drill, a bit of alphabets and numbers and was now cutting coloured paper. She would have to cut till the bell rang and the teacher said, "Now you may all go home," or "Put away the scissors and take up your alphabets—" Shanta was impatient to know the time. She asked her friend sitting next to her, "Is it five now?"

"Maybe," she replied.

"Or is it six?"

"I don't think so," her friend replied, "because night comes at six."

"Do you think it is five?"

"Yes."

"Oh, I must go. My father will be back at home now. He has asked me to be ready at five. He is taking me to the cinema this evening. I must go home." She threw down her scissors and ran up to the teacher. "Madam, I must go home."

"Why, Shanta Bai?"

"Because it is five o'clock now."

"Who told you it was five?"

"Kamala."

"It is not five now. It is—do you see the clock there? Tell me what the time is. I taught you to read the clock the other day." Shanta stood gazing at the clock in the hall, counted the figures laboriously and declared, "It is nine o'clock."

The teacher called the other girls and said, "Who will tell me the time from that clock?" Several of them concurred with Shanta and said it was nine o'clock, till the teacher said, "You are seeing only the long hand. See the short one, where is it?"

"Two and a half."

"So what is the time?"

"Two and a half."

"It is two forty-five, understand? Now you may all go to your seats—" Shanta returned to the teacher in about ten minutes and asked, "Is it five, madam, because I have to be ready at five. Otherwise my father will be very angry with me. He asked me to return home early."

"At what time?"

"Now." The teacher gave her permission to leave, and Shanta picked up her books and dashed out of the class with a cry of joy. She ran home, threw her books on the floor and shouted, "Mother, Mother," and Mother came running from the next house, where she had gone to chat with her friends.

Mother asked, "Why are you back so early?"

"Has Father come home?" Shanta asked. She would not take her coffee or tiffin[1] but insisted on being dressed first. She opened the trunk and insisted on wearing the thinnest frock and knickers, while her mother wanted to dress her in a long skirt and thick coat for the evening. Shanta picked out a gorgeous ribbon from a cardboard soap box in which she kept pencils, ribbons and chalk bits. There was a heated argument between mother and daughter over the dress, and finally Mother had to give in. Shanta put on her favourite pink frock, braided her hair and flaunted a green ribbon

---

1. Midday snack.

on her pigtail. She powdered her face and pressed a vermilion mark on her forehead. She said, "Now Father will say what a nice girl I am because I'm ready. Aren't you also coming, Mother?"

"Not today."

Shanta stood at the little gate looking down the street.

Mother said, "Father will come only after five; don't stand in the sun. It is only four o'clock."

The sun was disappearing behind the house on the opposite row, and Shanta knew that presently it would be dark. She ran in to her mother and asked, "Why hasn't Father come home yet, Mother?"

"How can I know? He is perhaps held up in the office."

Shanta made a wry face. "I don't like these people in the office. They are bad people—"

She went back to the gate and stood looking out. Her mother shouted from inside, "Come in, Shanta. It is getting dark, don't stand there." But Shanta would not go in. She stood at the gate and a wild idea came into her head. Why should she not go to the office and call out Father and then go to the cinema? She wondered where his office might be. She had no notion. She had seen her father take the turn at the end of the street every day. If one went there, perhaps one went automatically to Father's office. She threw a glance about to see if Mother was anywhere and moved down the street.

It was twilight. Everyone going about looked gigantic, walls of houses appeared very high and cycles and carriages looked as though they would bear down on her. She walked on the very edge of the road. Soon the lamps were twinkling, and the passers-by looked like shadows. She had taken two turns and did not know where she was. She sat down on the edge of the road biting her nails. She wondered how she was to reach home. A servant employed in the next house was passing along, and she picked herself up and stood before him.

"Oh, what are you doing here all alone?" he asked. She replied, "I don't know. I came here. Will you take me to our house?" She followed him and was soon back in her house.

Venkat Rao, Shanta's father, was about to start for his office that morning when a *jutka*[2] passed along the street distributing cinema handbills. Shanta dashed to the street and picked up a handbill. She held it up and asked, "Father, will you take me to the cinema today?" He felt unhappy at the question. Here was the child growing up without having any of the amenities and the simple pleasures of life. He had hardly taken her twice to the cinema. He had no time for the child. While children of her age in other houses had all the dolls, dresses and outings that they wanted, this

---

2. A two-wheeled horse-drawn carriage.

child was growing up all alone and like a barbarian more or less. He felt furious with his office. For forty rupees[3] a month they seemed to have purchased him outright.

He reproached himself for neglecting his wife and child—even the wife could have her own circle of friends and so on: she was after all a grown-up, but what about the child? What a drab, colourless existence was hers! Every day they kept him at the office till seven or eight in the evening, and when he came home the child was asleep. Even on Sundays they wanted him at the office. Why did they think he had no personal life, a life of his own? They gave him hardly any time to take the child to the park or the pictures. He was going to show them that they weren't to toy with him. Yes, he was prepared even to quarrel with his manager if necessary.

He said with resolve, "I will take you to the cinema this evening. Be ready at five."

"Really! Mother!" Shanta shouted. Mother came out of the kitchen.

"Father is taking me to a cinema in the evening."

Shanta's mother smiled cynically. "Don't make false promises to the child—" Venkat Rao glared at her. "Don't talk nonsense. You think you are the only person who keeps promises—"

He told Shanta, "Be ready at five, and I will come and take you positively. If you are not ready, I will be very angry with you."

He walked to his office full of resolve. He would do his normal work and get out at five. If they started any old tricks of theirs, he was going to tell the boss, "Here is my resignation. My child's happiness is more important to me than these horrible papers of yours."

All day the usual stream of papers flowed onto his table and off it. He scrutinized, signed and drafted. He was corrected, admonished and insulted. He had a break of only five minutes in the afternoon for his coffee.

When the office clock struck five and the other clerks were leaving, he went up to the manager and said, "May I go, sir?" The manager looked up from his paper. "You!" It was unthinkable that the cash and account section should be closing at five. "How can you go?"

"I have some urgent private business, sir," he said, smothering the lines he had been rehearsing since the morning: "Herewith my resignation." He visualized Shanta standing at the door, dressed and palpitating with eagerness.

"There shouldn't be anything more urgent than the office work; go back to your seat. You know how many hours I work?" asked the manager. The manager came to the office three hours before opening time and stayed nearly three hours after closing, even on Sundays. The clerks commented among themselves, "His wife must be whipping him whenever he is seen at home; that is why the old owl seems so fond of his office."

---

3. A rupee is an Indian unit of money.

"Did you trace the source of that ten-eight difference?" asked the manager.

"I shall have to examine two hundred vouchers. I thought we might do it tomorrow."

"No, no, this won't do. You must rectify it immediately."

Venkat Rao mumbled, "Yes, sir," and slunk back to his seat. The clock showed 5:30. Now it meant two hours of excruciating search among vouchers. All the rest of the office had gone. Only he and another clerk in his section were working, and of course, the manager was there. Venkat Rao was furious. His mind was made up. He wasn't a slave who had sold himself for forty rupees outright. He could make that money easily; and if he couldn't, it would be more honourable to die of starvation.

He took a sheet of paper and wrote: "Herewith my resignation. If you people think you have bought me body and soul for forty rupees, you are mistaken. I think it would be far better for me and my family to die of starvation than slave for this petty forty rupees on which you have kept me for years and years. I suppose you have not the slightest notion of giving me an increment. You give yourselves heavy slices frequently, and I don't see why you shouldn't think of us occasionally. In any case it doesn't interest me now, since this is my resignation. If I and my family perish of starvation, may our ghosts come and haunt you all your life—" He folded the letter, put it in an envelope, sealed the flap and addressed it to the manager. He left his seat and stood before the manager. The manager mechanically received the letter and put it on his pad.

"Venkat Rao," said the manager, "I'm sure you will be glad to hear this news. Our officer discussed the question of increments today, and I've recommended you for an increment of five rupees. Orders are not yet passed, so keep this to yourself for the present." Venkat Rao put out his hand, snatched the envelope from the pad and hastily slipped it in his pocket.

"What is that letter?"

"I have applied for a little casual leave, sir, but I think . . ."

"You can't get any leave for at least a fortnight to come."

"Yes, sir. I realize that. That is why I am withdrawing my application, sir."

"Very well, Have you traced that mistake?"

"I'm scrutinizing the vouchers, sir. I will find it out within an hour. . . ."

It was nine o'clock when he went home. Shanta was already asleep. Her mother said, "She wouldn't even change her frock, thinking that any moment you might be coming and taking her out. She hardly ate any food; and wouldn't lie down for fear of crumpling her dress. . . ."

Venkat Rao's heart bled when he saw his child sleeping in her pink frock, hair combed and face powdered, dressed and ready to be taken out. "Why should I not take her to the night show?" He shook her gently and called, "Shanta, Shanta." Shanta kicked her legs and cried, irritated at being disturbed. Mother whispered, "Don't wake her," and patted her back to sleep.

Venkat Rao watched the child for a moment. "I don't know if it is going to be possible for me to take her out at all—you see, they are giving me an increment—" he wailed.

■ Faiz Ahmed Faiz (1911–1984) *Urdu* (poems)

TRANSLATED BY NAOMI LAZARD

Pakistani poet Faiz Ahmed Faiz was editor of *The Pakistani Times* for many years and was awarded the Lenin Peace Prize in 1970. In 1979, he became editor of *Lotus,* a third-world literary magazine. He was certainly the best-known Pakistani poet of his day, and when he participated in poetry contests, up to fifty thousand people would gather to listen. Many of his poems have been set to music by established musicians. Faiz was born in 1911 in Sialkot, studied in Lahore, took a lectureship at Amritsar, and was involved with the Indian labor movement. In World War II, he served in the British Indian Army, and in the postwar period, he used his position at *The Pakistani Times* to speak out for social justice. In 1951, his outspokenness landed him in trouble with the authorities, who arrested him and put him on trial for his life. He was sentenced to four years in prison, one of three stays in the penitentiary, where he often suffered solitary confinement.

In his poetry, he often uses traditional meters, and his ghazals on love draw on a deep Urdu tradition; his political sufferings also inform his poetry. He died in 1984.

FURTHER READING: Kiernan, V. G., tr. *Poems by Faiz,* 1962. Lazard, Naomi, tr. *The True Subject: Selected Poems of Faiz Ahmed Faiz,* 1988. Sucha, Sain, tr. *Memory: Poetry of Faiz Ahmed Faiz,* 1987.

Before You Came

Before you came things were just what they were:
the road precisely a road, the horizon fixed,
the limit of what could be seen;
a glass of wine no more than a glass of wine.

Then the world took on the tints of my heart;   5
magnolia-petaled happiness of seeing you,
slate the color that fell
when I was fed up with everything.

With your advent roses burst into flame;
you were the author of dried-up leaves,   10

the dust, poison, blood.
You colored the night black.

As for the sky, the road, the cup of wine:
one was my tear-drenched shirt,
the other an aching nerve;   *15*
the third a mirror that never reflected the same thing.

This was all before you left me.

Now you have come back. Stay.
This time things will fall into place again;
the road can be the road,   *20*
the sky, sky;
the glass of wine, as it should be, the glass of wine.

Prison Meeting

This night is the tree of pain,
          greater than you or me,
greater because in its thicket of branches
a thousand candle-bearing stars have lost their way.
In this tree's shadow another thousand moons
have wept the last of their light.   *5*
This night is hell's own black
yet the darkness flares with your beauty.
It is a golden stream; a river of blood
flows back on its nether side.

This night is the tree of pain,   *10*
          vaster than you or me.
The tree lets go of a few pale leaves
that fall upon your hair, an incarnation of roses.
From its dew some moments of silence
          send rain onto your brow;
it forms a pearly diadem.
This tree is the essence of black;   *15*
its branches break my heart
but I pull them out, arrow after arrow.
These will be my weapons.

Morning of the grief-stricken, the heart-broken,
is not somewhere in the future; it is here   *20*
the shafts of pain have flowered into dawn's coral streaks.
It is here the murderous blade of grief
is changed into sparks, light ray against light ray.
This grief whose ashes burn in the rosebush of your arms;

this fruit garnered from the tree of pain 25
is my faith which is larger than any pain!
This morning that is on its way more
      bounteous than any night!

■ Ruth Prawer Jhabvala (1927–)
English (story)

Ruth Prawer Jhabvala was born in Cologne, Germany, to a Polish-Jewish family and moved to England in 1939. She went to Queen Mary College of London University, earning a master's degree; she married C. S. H. Jhabvala in 1951, and they moved to Delhi. Her work reflects the makeup of contemporary Indian society, dealing often with women's issues and, at times, with the attitudes and roles of the expatriate community. This story, "Picnic with Moonlight and Mangoes," comes from her book *How I Became a Holy Mother, and Other Stories* (1976). In addition to three other short story collections, Jhabvala has published *Out of India: Selected Stories* (1986) and many novels. She has been awarded England's Booker Prize and a MacArthur Foundation Award, in addition to other prestigious awards. She also wrote the screenplay for the Academy Award–winning movie *A Room with a View.*

FURTHER READING: Gooneratne, Yasmine. *Silence, Exile, and Cunning: The Fiction of Ruth Prawer Jhabvala,* 1983.

Picnic with Moonlight and Mangoes

Unfortunately the town in which Sri Prakash lived was a small one so that everyone knew what had happened to him. At first he did not go out at all, on account of feeling so ashamed; but, as the weeks dragged on, sitting at home became very dreary. He also began to realize that, with thinking and solitude, he was probably exaggerating the effect of his misfortune on other people. Misfortune could befall anyone, any time; there was really no need to be ashamed. So one morning when his home seemed particularly depressing he made up his mind to pay a visit to the coffee house. He left while his wife was having her bath—he told her he was going, he shouted it through the bathroom door, and if she did not hear above the running water that was obviously not his fault.

So when he came home and she asked him where he had been, he could say 'I *told* you' with a perfectly good conscience. He was glad of that because he could see she had been worried about him. While she served him his food, he did his best to reassure her. He told her how pleased they had all been to see him in the coffee house. Even the waiter had been pleased and had brought his usual order without having to be told. His wife said nothing but went on patiently serving him. Then he began somewhat to exaggerate the heartiness of the welcome he had received. He said things which, though not strictly true, had a good effect — not so much on her (she continued silently to serve him) as on himself. By the time he had finished eating and talking, he was perfectly reassured as to what had happened that morning. The little cloud of unease with which he had come home was dispelled. He realized now that no one had looked at him queerly, and that there had been no undertones in their 'Just see who is here.' It was only his over-sensitive nature that had made it seem like that.

He had always had a very sensitive nature: a poet's temperament. He was proud of it, but there was no denying that it had been the cause of many troubles to him — including the present one. The facts of the case were these: Sri Prakash, a gazetted government officer, had been suspended from his post in the State Ministry of Telecommunication while an inquiry was instituted regarding certain accusations against him. These were based on the words of a man who was a drunkard, a liar, and a convicted perjurer. His name was Goel and he was the father of a Miss Nimmi. Miss Nimmi had come to Sri Prakash to inquire about a possible vacancy as typist in his office. Sri Prakash had sincerely tried to help the girl, calling her for interviews several times, and the result of his good intentions had been that she had complained of his misbehaviour towards her. The father, after visiting Sri Prakash both in his office and at home and finding him not the man to yield to blackmail and extortion, had carried the complaint to Sri Prakash's superiors in the department. From there on events had taken their course. Naturally it was all extremely unpleasant for Sri Prakash — a family man, a husband and father of three respectably married daughters — but, as he was always telling his wife, he had no doubts that in the end truth and justice would prevail.

She never made any comment when he said that. She was by nature a silent woman: silent and virtuous. How virtuous! She was the ideal of all a mother and wife should be. He thanked God that he had it in him to appreciate her character. He worshipped her. He often told her so, and told everyone else too — his daughters, people in the office, sometimes even complete strangers (for instance, once a man he had shared a rickshaw with). Also how he was ready to tear himself into a thousand pieces, or lie down in the middle of the main bazaar by the clock tower and let all who came trample on him with their feet if by such an action he could save her one moment's anxiety. In this present misfortune there was of course a lot of anxiety. There was not only the moral hardship but also the practical one of having his salary held in arrears while the inquiry took its course. Already they had spent whatever his wife had managed to lay by and had had to sell the one or two pieces of jewelry that still remained from her dowry.

Now they were dependent for their household expenses on whatever their sons-in-law could contribute. It was a humiliating position for a proud man, but what was to be done? There was no alternative, he could not allow his wife to starve. But when his daughters came to the house and untied the money from the ends of their saris to give to their mother, he could not restrain his tears from flowing. His daughters were not as sympathetic towards him as his wife. They made no attempts to comfort him but looked at him in a way that made him feel worse. Then he would leave them and go to lie down on his bed. His daughters stayed for a while, but he did not come out again. He could hear them talking to their mother, and sometimes he heard sounds like the mother weeping. These sounds were unbearable to him, and he had to cover his head with the pillow so as not to hear them.

$$* \quad * \quad *$$

After that first visit to the coffee house, he continued to go every day. It was good to meet his friends again. He had always loved company. In the past, when he was still king in his own office, people had dropped in on him there all day long. At eleven o'clock they had all adjourned to the coffee house where they had drunk many cups of coffee and smoked many cigarettes and talked on many subjects. He had talked the most, and everyone had listened to and applauded him. But nowadays everything was changed. It was not only that he could not afford to drink coffee or pay for his own cigarettes: other things too were not as they had been. He himself was not as he had been. He had always been so gay and made jokes at which everyone laughed. Once he had jumped up on the table and had executed a dance there. He had stamped his feet and made ankle-bell noises with his tongue. And how they had laughed, standing around him in a circle—his friends and other customers, even the waiters: they had clapped their hands and spurred him on till he had jumped from the table—hands extended like a diver—and landed amid cheers and laughter in the arms held out to catch him.

Although nothing like that happened now, he continued to visit the coffee house regularly every morning; soon he was going regularly every evening too. There was usually a large party of friends, but one evening when he went there was no one—only a waiter flicking around with his dirty cloth, and a silent old widower, a regular customer, eating vegetable cutlets. The waiter was surly—he always had been, even in the days when Sri Prakash had still been able to hand out tips—and it was only after repeated inquiries that he condescended to say that, didn't Sri Prakash know? Hadn't they told him? They had all gone to Moti Bagh for a moonlight picnic with mangoes. Sri Prakash slapped his forehead, pretending he had known about it but had forgotten. It was an unconvincing performance and the waiter sneered, but Sri Prakash could not worry about that now. He had to concentrate on getting himself out of the coffee house without showing how he was feeling.

He walked in the street by himself. It was evening, there was a lot of traffic and the shops were full. Hawkers with trays bumped in and out of the crowds on the sidewalks. On one side the sky was melting in a rush of orange while on the other the evening star sparkled, alone and aloof, like a jewel made of ice. Exquisite hour — hour of high thoughts and romantic feelings! It had always been so for Sri Prakash and was so still. Only where was he to go, who was there to share with him the longing for beauty that flooded his heart?

'Oh-ho, oh-ho! Just see who is here!'

Someone had bumped against him in the crowd, now stood and held his arms in a gesture of affectionate greeting. It was the last person Sri Prakash would have wished to meet: Goel, the father of Miss Nimmi, his accuser, his enemy, the cause of his ruin and tears. Goel seemed genuinely delighted by this meeting; he continued to hold Sri Prakash by the arms and even squeezed them to show his pleasure. Sri Prakash jerked himself free and hurried away. The other followed him; he protested at this unfriendliness, demanded to know its cause. He claimed a misunderstanding. He followed Sri Prakash so close that he trod on his heels. Then Sri Prakash stood still and turned round.

'Forgive me,' said Goel. He meant for treading on his heels; he even made the traditional self-humbling gesture of one seeking forgiveness. They stood facing each other. They were about the same height — both were short and plump, though Goel was flabbier. Like Sri Prakash, he also was bald as a ball.

Sri Prakash could hardly believe his ears: Goel was asking him to come home with him. He insisted, he said he had some bottles of country liquor at home, and what good luck that he should have run into Sri Prakash just at this moment when he had been wondering what good friend he could invite to come and share them with him? When Sri Prakash indignantly refused, tried to walk on, Goel held on to him. 'Why not?' he insisted. 'Where else will you go?'

Then Sri Prakash remembered where everyone else had gone. The moonlight picnic at Moti Bagh was an annual outing. The procedure was always the same: the friends hired a bus and, together with their baskets of mangoes and crates of local whisky, had themselves driven out to Moti Bagh. They sang boisterous songs all the way. At Moti Bagh they cut up some of the mangoes and sucked the juice out of others. Their mouths became sticky and sweet and this taste might have become unpleasant if they had not kept washing it out with the whisky. They became very rowdy. They waited for the moon to rise. When it did, their mood changed. Moti Bagh was a famous beauty spot, an abandoned and half-ruined palace built by a seventeenth-century prince at the height of his own glory and that of his dynasty. When the moon shone on it, it became spectral, a marble ghost that evoked thoughts of the passing of all earthly things. Poems were recited, sad songs sung; a few tears flowed. Someone played the flute — as a matter of fact, this was Sri Prakash who had always taken a prominent part in these outings. But this year they had gone without him.

Goel did not live in a very nice part of town. The bazaar, though once quite prosperous, now catered mainly for poorer people; the rooms on top of the shops had been converted into one-night hotels. Goel's house, which was in a network of alleys leading off from this bazaar, would have been difficult to find for anyone unfamiliar with the geography of the locality. The geography of his house was also quite intricate, as every available bit of space—in the courtyard, galleries, and on staircase landings—had been partitioned between different tenants. Goel and his daughter Miss Nimmi had one long narrow room to themselves; they had strung a piece of string halfway across to serve as both clothes-line and partition. At first Sri Prakash thought the room was empty, but after they had been there for some time Goel shouted 'Oy!' When he received no answer, he pushed aside the pieces of clothing hanging from the string and revealed Miss Nimmi lying fast asleep on a mat on the floor.

Goel had to shout several times before she woke up. Then she rose from the mat—very slowly, as if struggling up from the depths of a sea of sleep—and sat there, blinking. Her sari had slipped from her breasts, but she did not notice. She also did not notice that they had a visitor. She was always slow in everything, slow and heavy. Her father had to shout, 'Don't you see who has come!' She blinked a few more times, and then very, very slowly she smiled and very, very slowly she lifted the sari to cover her breasts.

Goel told her to find two glasses. She got up and rummaged around the room. After a time she said there was only one. Sri Prakash said it didn't matter, he had to go anyway; he said he was in a hurry, he had to catch a bus for Moti Bagh where his friends awaited him. He got up but his host pressed him down again, asking what was the point of going now, why not stay here, they would have a good time together. 'Look,' Goel said, 'I've got money.' He emptied out his pockets and he did have money—a wad of bank notes, God knew where they had come from. He let Sri Prakash look his fill at them before putting them back. He said let's go to Badshahbad, we'll take the liquor and mangoes and we'll have a moonlight picnic of our own. He got very excited by this idea. Sri Prakash said neither yes nor no. Goel told Miss Nimmi to change into something nice, and she disappeared behind the clothes-line and got busy there. Sri Prakash did not look in that direction, but the room was saturated by her the way a store room in which ripe apples are kept becomes saturated by their savour and smell.

Badshahbad was not as far off as Moti Bagh—in fact, it was just at the outskirts of town and could be reached very quickly. It too was a deserted pleasure palace but had been built two centuries later than the one at Moti Bagh and as a rather gaudy imitation of it. However, now in the dark it looked just the same. The surrounding silence and emptiness, the smell of dust, the occasional jackal cry were also the same. At first Sri Prakash felt rather depressed, but his mood changed after he had drunk some of Goel's liquor. Goel was determined to have a good time, and Miss Nimmi, though silent, also seemed to be enjoying herself. She was cutting up the mangoes and eating rather a lot of them. The three of them sat in the dark, waiting for the moon to rise.

Goel fell into a reminiscent mood. He began to recall all the wonderful things he had done in his life: how he had sold a second-hand imported car for Rs.50,000, and once he had arranged false passports for a whole party of Sikh carpenters. All these activities had brought in fat commissions for himself—amply deserved, because everything had been achieved only through his good contacts. That was his greatest asset in life—his contacts, all the important people he had access to. He ticked them off on his fingers: the Under Secretary to the Welfare Ministry, the Deputy Minister of Mines and Fuel, all the top officers in the income tax department . . . He challenged Sri Prakash, he said: 'Name any big name, go as high as you like, and see if I don't know him.'

Sri Prakash got excited, he cried: 'My goodness! Big names—big people—whenever there was anything to be done, everyone said, "Ask Sri Prakash, he knows everyone, he has them all in his pocket." Once there was a function to felicitate our departmental Secretary on his promotion. The principal organizers came to me and said, "Sri Prakash, we need a VIP to grace the occasion." I replied, "I will get you the Chief Minister himself, just wait and see." And I did. I went to him, I said, "Sir, kindly give us the honour of your presence," and he replied, "Certainly, Sri Prakash, with pleasure." There and then he told his secretary to make a note of the appointment.'

'When I go into the Secretariat building,' Goel said, 'the peons stand up and salute. I don't bother with appointments. The personal assistant opens the big shot's door and says, "Sir, Goel has come." They know I don't come with empty hands. I slip it under their papers, no word spoken, they don't notice, I don't notice. The figures are all fixed, no need to haggle: 1000 to an Under Secretary, 2000 to a Deputy. Each has his price.'

Goel smiled and drank. Sri Prakash also drank. The liquor, illicitly distilled, had a foul and acrid taste. Sri Prakash remembered reading in the papers quite recently how a whole colony of labourers had been wiped out through drinking illicit country liquor. Nothing could be done for them, it had rotted them through and through.

Goel said: 'Let alone the Secretaries, there are also the Ministers to be taken care of. Some of them are very costly. Naturally, their term is short, no one can tell what will happen at the next elections. So their mouths are always wide open. You must be knowing Dev Kishan—'

'Dev Kishan!' Sri Prakash cried. 'He and I are like that! Like that!' He held up two fingers, pressed close together.

'There was some work in his Ministry, it was rather a tricky job and I was called in. I went to his house and came straight to the point. "Dev Kishan Sahib," I said—'

Sri Prakash suddenly lost his temper: 'Dev Kishan is not this type at all!' When Goel sniggered, he became more excited: 'A person like you would not understand a person like him at all. And I don't believe you went to his house—'

'Come with me right now!' Goel shouted. 'We will go together to his house and then you will see how he receives me—'

'Not Dev Kishan!' Sri Prakash shouted back. 'Someone else—not he—'

'He! The same!'

Although they were both shouting at the tops of their voices, Miss Nimmi went on placidly sucking mangoes. Probably the subject was of no interest to her; probably also she was used to people getting excited while drinking.

'As a matter of fact,' Goel sneered, 'shall I let you into a secret—his mouth is open wider than anyone's, they call him The Pit because he can never get enough, your Dev Kishan.'

'I don't believe you,' Sri Prakash said again, though not so fervently now. He really had no particular interest in defending this man. It was only that the mention of his name had called up a rather painful memory.

When his troubles had first begun, Sri Prakash had run around from one influential person to another. Most people would not receive him, and he had had to content himself with sitting waiting in their outer offices and putting his case to such of their clerical staff as would listen. Dev Kishan, however, was one of the few people who *had* received him. Sri Prakash had been ushered into his ministerial office which had two air-conditioners and an inscribed portrait of the President of India. Dev Kishan had sat behind an enormous desk, but he had not asked Sri Prakash to take the chair opposite. He had not looked at Sri Prakash either but had fixed his gaze above his head. Sri Prakash wanted to plead, to explain—he had come ready to do so—if necessary go down on his knees, but instead he sat quite still while Dev Kishan told him that a departmental inquiry must be allowed to proceed according to rule. Then Sri Prakash had quietly departed, passing through the outer office with his head lowered and with nothing to say for himself whatsoever. He had not spoken for a long while afterwards. He kept thinking—he was still thinking—of the way Dev Kishan had looked above his head. His eyes had seemed to be gazing far beyond Sri Prakash, deep into state matters, and Sri Prakash had felt like a fly that had accidentally got in and deserved to be swatted.

Goel did not want to quarrel any more. He had come on a picnic, he had spent money on liquor and mangoes and the hiring of a horse carriage to bring them here. He expected a good time in return. He refilled their glasses while remembering other outings he had enjoyed in the past. He told Sri Prakash of the time he and some friends had consumed one dozen bottles of liquor at a sitting and had become very merry. He nudged Sri Prakash and said, 'Girls were also brought.' He said this in a low voice, so that Miss Nimmi would not hear, and brought his face close to Sri Prakash. Sri Prakash felt a desire to throw the contents of his glass into this face. He imagined that the liquor contained acid and what would happen. He was filled with such strong emotion that something, some release was necessary: but instead of throwing the liquor in his host's face, he emptied it on the ground in a childishly angry gesture. Goel gave a cry of astonishment, Miss Nimmi stopped halfway in the sucking of a mango.

Just then the moon rose. The palace trembled into view and stood there melting in moonlight. Sri Prakash left his companions and went towards it as one drawn towards a mirage. It did not disappear as he approached, but it did turn out to be locked. He peered through the glass doors and could just make out the sleeping form of a watchman curled up on the floor. The interior was lit only by the palest beams filtering in from outside. By day there were too many curlicued arches and coloured chandeliers, too many plaster leaves and scrolls: but now in the moonlight everything looked as it should. Overcome by its beauty and other sensations, Sri Prakash sat down on the steps and wept. He had his face buried in his hands and could not stop.

After a while Goel joined him. He sat beside him on the steps. Goel began to talk about the passing away of all earthly things, the death of kings and pariah dogs alike. He waved his hand towards the abandoned pleasure palace, he said, 'Where are they all, where have they gone?' Although these reflections were perfectly acceptable—probably at this very moment Sri Prakash's friends were making the same ones at their picnic in Moti Bagh—nevertheless, coming from Goel, Sri Prakash did not want to hear them. He felt Goel had no right to them. What did he know of philosophy and history—indeed of anything except drinking and bribery? Sri Prakash lifted his head; irritation had dried his tears.

He said, 'Do you know what the Nawab Sahib Ghalib Hasan said when they came to tell him the enemy was at the gate?'

Goel did not know—he knew nothing—he hardly knew who the Nawab Sahib Ghalib Hasan was. To cover his ignorance, he waved his hand again and repeated, 'Where are they all, where have they gone?'

Sri Prakash began to instruct him. He knew a lot about the Nawab who had always been one of his heroes. Abandoning the palace at Moti Bagh, the Nawab had built himself this costly new palace here at Badshahbad and filled it with his favourites. There had been poets and musicians and dancing girls, cooks and wine tasters, a French barber, an Irish cavalry officer; also a menagerie which included a lion and an octopus. The Nawab himself wrote poetry which he read aloud to his courtiers and to the girls who massaged his feet and scented them. It was during such a session that messengers had come to tell him the enemy was at the gate. He had answered by reciting these verses which Sri Prakash now quoted to Goel: '*When in her arms, what is the drum of war? the sword of battle? nay, even the ancient whistle of bony-headed Death?*'

'Ah!' said Goel, laying his hand on his chest to show how deeply he was affected.

Quite pleased with this reaction, Sri Prakash repeated the quotation. Then he quoted more verses written by the Nawab. Goel turned out to be an appreciative listener. He swayed his head and sometimes shouted out loud in applause the way connoisseurs shout when a musician plays a note, a dancer executes a step showing more than human skill. Sri Prakash began rather to enjoy himself. It had been a long time since anyone had cared to listen to him reciting poetry. His wife and daughters—he had always regretted it—had no taste for poetry at all; not for music either, which he loved so much.

But then Goel made a mistake. Overcome by appreciation, he repeated a line that Sri Prakash had just quoted to him: '*O rose of my love, where have your petals fallen?*' But Goel's voice, which was vulgar and drunken, degraded these beautiful words. Suddenly Sri Prakash turned on him. He called him all the insulting names he could think of such as liar, swindler, blackmailer, and drunkard. Goel continued to sit there placidly, even nodding once or twice as if he agreed. Perhaps he was too drunk to hear or care; or perhaps he had been called these names so often that he had learned to accept them. But this passive attitude was frustrating for Sri Prakash; he ran out of insults and fell silent.

After a while he said, 'Why did you do it? For myself I don't care—but what about my wife and family? Why should their lives be ruined? Tell me that.'

Goel had no answer except a murmur of sympathy. As if grateful for this sympathy, Sri Prakash began to tell him moving incidents from his married life. They all illustrated the fact that his wife was an angel, a saint. The more Sri Prakash knew her the more he marvelled. In her he had studied all womanhood and had come to the conclusion that women are goddesses at whose feet men must fall down and worship. He himself had got into the habit of doing so quite often. Not now so much any more—his spirits were too low, he felt himself unworthy—but in the past when things were still well with him. Then he would come home from a late night outing with friends to find her nodding in the kitchen, waiting for him to serve him his meal. He would be overcome with love and admiration for her. With a cry that startled her from her sleep, he would fall down at her feet and lift the hem of her garment to press it to his lips. Although she tried to make him rise, he would not do so; he wanted to stay down there to make it clear how humble he was in relation to her greatness. Then she undressed him right there where he lay on the floor and tried to get him to bed. Sometimes she had to lift him up in her arms—he had always been a small man—and he loved that, he lay in her arms with his eyes shut and felt himself a child enfolded in its mother's love. 'Mother,' he would murmur in ecstasy, as she staggered with him to the bed.

Goel had fallen asleep. Sri Prakash was sorry, for although he did not esteem Goel as a person, he felt the need of someone to talk to. Not only about his wife; there were many other subjects, many thoughts he longed to share. It was like that with him sometimes. His heart was so full, so weighted with feeling, that he longed to fling it somewhere — to someone — or, failing someone, up to the moon that was so still and looked down at him from heaven. But there *was* someone; there was Miss Nimmi. She had remained where they had left her by the basket of mangoes and the bottles. She had finished eating mangoes. She did not seem to mind being left alone nor did she seem impatient to go home but just content to wait till they were ready. She sat with her hands folded and looked in front of her at the bare and dusty earth.

This patient pose was characteristic of her. It was the way she had sat in Sri Prakash's office when she had come to ask him for a job. That was why he had kept telling her to come back: to have the pleasure of seeing her in his office, ready to wait for as long as he wanted. She had reminded him of a chicken sitting plump and cooked on a dish on a table. By the third day he had begun to call her his little chicken. 'Fall to!' he would suddenly cry and make the motion of someone who grabbed from a dish and fell to eating. Of course she hadn't known what he meant, but she had smiled all the same.

'Fall to!' he cried now, as he joined her on the ground among the empty bottles. And now too she smiled. Like the palace floating behind her, she was transformed and made beautiful by moonlight. It veiled her rather coarse features and her skin pitted by an attack of smallpox in childhood.

He moved up close to her. Her breasts, as warm as they were plump, came swelling out of her bodice, and he put his hand on them: but respectfully, almost with awe, so that there was no harm in her leaving it there. 'Where is Papa?' she asked.

'Asleep. You need not worry.'

Very gently and delicately he stroked her breasts. Then he kissed her mouth, tasting the mango there. She let all this be done to her. It had been the same in his office — she had always kept quite still, only occasionally glancing over her shoulder to make sure no one was coming. She did the same now, glanced towards her father.

'You need not worry,' Sri Prakash said again. 'He has drunk a lot. He won't wake up.'

'He *is* waking up.'

They both looked towards Goel left alone in front of the palace. He was trying to stretch himself out more comfortably along the steps, but instead he rolled down them. It was not far, and the ground seemed to receive him softly; he did not move but remained lying there.

'Is he all right?' Miss Nimmi asked.

'Of course he is all right. What could happen to *him*?' Sri Prakash spoke bitterly. He took his hand away from her; his mood was spoiled. He said, 'Why did you let him do it to me? What harm have I done to him? Or to you? Answer.'

She had no answer. There was none, he knew. She could not say that he had harmed her, had done anything bad. Was it bad to love a person? To adore and worship the way he had done? Those moments in his office had been pure, and his feelings as sacred as if he were visiting a shrine to place flowers there at the feet of the goddess.

'Why?' he asked again. 'What did I do to you?'

'That is what Papa kept asking: "What did he do to you?" When I said you did nothing, he got very angry. He kept asking questions, he would not stop. Sometimes he woke me up at night to ask.'

Sri Prakash pressed his face into her neck. 'What sort of questions?' he murmured from out of there.

'He asked, "Where did he put his hand?" When I couldn't remember, he asked, "Here?" So I had to say yes. Because you did.'

'Yes,' he murmured. 'Yes I did.' And he did it again, and she let him.

She said, 'Papa shouted and screamed. He hit his head against the wall. But it wasn't only that—there were other things. He was going through a lot of other troubles at that time. Two men kept coming. They told him he would have to go to jail again. Papa is very frightened of going to jail. When he was there before, he came out *so* thin.' She showed how with her finger. 'He lost fifty pounds in there.'

Sri Prakash remembered Goel's demented state in those days. He had come to him many times, threatening, demanding money; he had looked like a madman, and Sri Prakash—still sitting secure behind his desk then, safe in his office—had treated him like one. 'Go to hell,' he had told him. 'Do what you like.' And the last time he had said that, Goel had pounded the desk between them and thrust his face forward into Sri Prakash's: 'Then you will see!' he had screamed. 'You will see and learn!' He had really looked like a madman—even with foam at his mouth. Sri Prakash had felt uneasy but nevertheless had laughed in the other's face and blown a smoke ring.

Miss Nimmi said, 'I was very frightened. Papa was in a terrible mood. He said he would teach you a lesson you would not forget. He said, "Why should I be the only person in this world to suffer blows and kicks? Let someone else also have a few of these." But afterwards those two men stopped coming, and then Papa was much better. He was cheerful again and brought me a present, a little mirror like a heart. And then he was sorry about you. He tried to go to your office again, to change his report, but they said it was too late. I cried when he came back and told me that.'

'You cried? You cried for me?' Sri Prakash was moved.

'Yes, and Papa also was sad for you.'

Goel was still lying at the foot of the steps where he had rolled down. Sri Prakash did not feel unkindly towards him—on the contrary, he even felt quite sorry for him. But his greatest wish with regard to him at the moment was that he would go on sleeping. Sri Prakash did not want to be disturbed in his private conversation with Miss Nimmi. In his mind he prayed for sufficient time, that they might not be interrupted by her father.

'I cried so much that Papa did everything he could to make me feel better. He brought me more presents—sweets and a piece of cloth. When still I went on crying, he said, "What is to be done? It is his fate."'

'He is right,' Sri Prakash said. He too spoke only to soothe her. He did not want Miss Nimmi to be upset in any way. He just wanted her to be as she always was and to keep still so that he could adore her to his heart's content. He raised the hem of her sari to his lips, the way he did to his wife; and he also murmured 'Goddess' to her the way he did to his wife—worshipping all women in her, their goodness and beauty.

■ Bharati Mukherjee (1942–) *English* (story)

Bharati Mukherjee is certainly among the finest of the twentieth-century Indian fiction writers. Her stories and novels specialize in depicting the fates and trials of immigrants from India, the Philippines, or elsewhere, and her Jewish or Tamil or Hindu protagonists all share the perspective of the outsider looking in—the immigrant to whom the Statue of Liberty turns out to be surrounded by high fences outside and is cheaply commercialized inside. A protagonist of Mukherjee's becomes, as in her story of that name, a "middleman," caught between cultures. The tension between cultural identity and assimilation is central to her work. Mukherjee was born in Calcutta and was educated in India before coming to the United States to do graduate work at the University of Iowa. She is married to writer Clark Blaise; has taught creative writing at Columbia, New York University, and Queens College; and currently teaches in the English department at University of California, Berkeley, where she has been named distinguished professor. Her books include *The Tiger's Daughter* (1971), *Wife* (1975), *Days and Nights in Calcutta* (1977), *Darkness* (1985), *The Middleman and Other Stories* (1988), *Jasmine* (1989), and *The Holder of the World* (1993).

FURTHER READING: Nelson, Emmanuel S. *Bharati Mukherjee: Critical Perspectives,* 1993.

Buried Lives

One March midafternoon in Trincomalee, Sri Lanka, Mr. N. K. S. Venkatesan, a forty-nine-year-old school-teacher who should have been inside a St. Joseph's Collegiate classroom explicating Arnold's "The Buried Life" found himself instead at a barricaded intersection, axe in hand and shouting rude slogans at a truckload of soldiers.

Mr. Venkatesan was not a political man. In his neighborhood he was the only householder who hadn't contributed, not even a rupee, to the Tamil Boys' Sporting Association, which everyone knew wasn't a cricket club so much as a recruiting center for the Liberation Tigers. And at St. Joe's, he hadn't signed the staff petition abhorring the arrest at a peaceful anti-Buddhist demonstration of Dr. Pillai, the mathematics teacher. Venkatesan had rather enjoyed talking about fractals with Dr. Pillai, but he disapproved of men with family responsibilities sticking their heads between billy clubs as though they were still fighting the British for independence.

Fractals claimed to predict, mathematically, chaos and apparent randomness. Such an endeavor, if possible, struck Mr. Venkatesan as a virtually holy quest, closer to the spirit of religion than of science. What had once been Ceylon was now Sri Lanka.

Mr. Venkatesan, like Dr. Pillai, had a large family to look after: he had parents, one set of grandparents, an aunt who hadn't been quite right in the head since four of her five boys had signed up with the Tigers, and three much younger, unmarried sisters. They lived with him in a three-room flat above a variety store. It was to protect his youngest sister (a large, docile girl who, before she got herself mixed up with the Sporting Association, used to embroider napkin-and-tablecloth sets and sell them to a middleman for export to fancy shops in Canada) that he was marching that afternoon with two hundred baby-faced protesters.

Axe under arm—he held the weapon as he might an umbrella—Mr. Venkatesan and his sister and a frail boy with a bushy moustache on whom his sister appeared to have a crush, drifted past looted stores and charred vehicles. In the center of the intersection, a middle-aged leader in camouflage fatigues and a black beret stood on the roof of a van without tires, and was about to set fire to the national flag with what looked to Mr. Venkatesan very much like a Zippo lighter.

"Sir, you have to get in the mood," said his sister's boyfriend. The moustache entirely covered his mouth. Mr. Venkatesan had the uncanny sensation of being addressed by a thatch of undulating bristles. "You have to let yourself go, sir."

This wasn't advice; this was admonition. Around Mr. Venkatesan swirled dozens of hyperkinetic boys in white shirts, holding bricks. Fat girls in summer frocks held placards aloft. His sister sucked on an ice cream bar. Every protester seemed to twinkle with fun. He didn't know how to have fun, that was the trouble. Even as an adolescent he'd battened down all passion; while other students had slipped love notes into expectant palms, he'd studied, he'd passed exams. Dutifulness had turned him into a pariah.

"Don't think you chaps invented civil disobedience!"

He lectured the boyfriend on how his generation—meaning that technically, he'd been alive though hardly self-conscious—had cowed the British Empire. The truth was that the one time the police had raided the Venkatesans' flat—he'd been four, but he'd been taught anti-British phrases like "the salt march" and "*satyagraba*"[1] by a cousin ten years older—he

---

1. A term for Mahatma Gandhi's policy of nonviolent resistance as a means to effect political reform.

had saluted the superintendent smartly even as constables squeezed his cousin's wrists into handcuffs. That cousin was now in San Jose, California, minting lakhs and lakhs of dollars in computer software.

The boyfriend, still smiling awkwardly, moved away from Mr. Venkatesan's sister. His buddies, Tigers in berets, were clustered around a vendor of spicy fritters.

"Wait!" the sister pleaded, her face puffy with held-back tears.

"What do you see in that callow, good-for-nothing bloke?" Mr. Venkatesan asked.

"Please, please leave me alone," his sister screamed. "Please let me do what I want."

What if *he* were to do what he wanted! Twenty years ago when he'd had the chance, he should have applied for a Commonwealth Scholarship. He should have immured himself in a leafy dormitory in Oxford. Now it was too late. He'd have studied law. Maybe he'd have married an English girl and loitered abroad. But both parents had died, his sisters were mere toddlers, and he was obliged to take the lowest, meanest teaching job in the city.

"I want to die," his sister sobbed beside him.

"Shut up, you foolish girl."

The ferocity of her passion for the worthless boy, who was, just then, biting into a greasy potato fritter, shocked him. He had patronized her when she had been a plain, pliant girl squinting at embroidered birds and flowers. But now something harsh and womanly seemed to be happening inside her.

"Forget those chaps. They're nothing but trouble-makers." To impress her, he tapped a foot to the beat of a slogan bellowing out of loudspeakers.

Though soldiers were starting to hustle demonstrators into double-parked paddy wagons, the intersection had taken on the gaudiness of a village fair. A white-haired vendor darted from police jeep to jeep hawking peanuts in paper cones. Boys who had drunk too much tea or soda relieved themselves freely into poster-clogged gutters. A dozen feet up the road a house-wife with a baby on her hip lobbed stones into storefronts. A band of beggars staggered out of an electronics store with a radio and a television. No reason not to get in the mood.

"Blood for blood," he shouted, timidly at first. "Blood begets blood."

"Begets?" the man beside him asked. "What's that supposed to mean?" In his plastic sandals and cheap drawstring pajamas, the man looked like a coolie or laborer.

He turned to his sister for commiseration. What could she expect him to have in common with a mob of uneducated men like that? But she'd left him behind. He saw her, crouched for flight like a giant ornament on the hood of an old-fashioned car, the March wind stiffly splaying her sari and long hair behind her.

"Get down from that car!" he cried. But the crowd, swirling, separated him from her. He felt powerless; he could no longer watch over her, keep her out of the reach of night sticks. From on top of the hood she taunted policemen, and not just policemen but everybody—shopgirls and beggars and ochre-robed monks—as though she wasn't just a girl with a crush on a Tiger but a monster out of one's most splenetic nightmares.

Months later, in a boardinghouse in Hamburg, Mr. Venkatesan couldn't help thinking about the flock of young monks pressed together behind a police barricade that eventful afternoon. He owed his freedom to the monks because, in spite of their tonsure scars and their vows of stoicism, that afternoon they'd behaved like any other hot-headed Sri Lankan adolescents. If the monks hadn't chased his sister and knocked her off the pale blue hood of the car, Mr. Venkatesan would have stayed on in Sri Lanka, in Trinco, in St. Joe's teaching the same poems year after year, a permanent prisoner.

What the monks did was unforgivable. Robes plucked knee-high and celibate lips plumped up in vengeful chant, they pulled a girl by the hair, and they slapped and spat and kicked with vigor worthy of newly initiated Tigers.

It could have been another girl, somebody else's younger sister. Without thinking, Mr. Venkatesan rotated a shoulder, swung an arm, readied his mind to inflict serious harm.

It should never have happened. The axe looped clumsily over the heads of demonstrators and policemen and fell, like a captured kite, into the hands of a Home Guards officer. There was blood, thick and purplish, spreading in jagged stains on the man's white uniform. The crowd wheeled violently. The drivers of paddy wagons laid panicky fingers on their horns. Veils of tear gas blinded enemies and friends. Mr. Venkatesan, crying and choking, ducked into a store and listened to the thwack of batons. When his vision eased, he staggered, still on automatic pilot, down side streets and broke through garden hedges all the way to St. Joseph's unguarded backdoor.

In the men's room off the Teacher's Common Room he held his face, hot with guilt, under a rusty, hissing faucet until Father van der Haagen, the Latin and Scriptures teacher, came out of a stall.

"You don't look too well. Sleepless night, eh?" the Jesuit joked. "You need to get married, Venkatesan. Bad habits can't always satisfy you."

Mr. Venkatesan laughed dutifully. All of Father van der Haagen's jokes had to do with masturbation. He didn't say anything about having deserted his sister. He didn't say anything about having maimed, maybe murdered, a Home Guards officer. "Who can afford a wife on what the school pays?" he joked back. Then he hurried off to his classroom.

Though he was over a half-hour late, his students were still seated meekly at their desks.

"Good afternoon, sir." Boys in monogrammed shirts and rice-starched shorts shuffled to standing positions.

"Sit!" the schoolmaster commanded. Without taking his eyes off the students, he opened his desk and let his hand locate *A Treasury of the Most*

Dulcet Verses Written in the English Language, which he had helped the headmaster to edit though only the headmaster's name appeared on the book.

Matthew Arnold was Venkatesan's favorite poet. Mr. Venkatesan had talked the Head into including four Arnold poems. The verses picked by the Head hadn't been "dulcet" at all, and one hundred and three pages of the total of one hundred and seventy-four had been given over to upstart Trinco versifiers' martial ballads.

Mr. Venkatesan would have nursed a greater bitterness against the Head if the man hadn't vanished, mysteriously, soon after their acrimonious coediting job.

One winter Friday the headmaster had set out for his nightly after-dinner walk, and he hadn't come back. The Common Room gossip was that he had been kidnapped by a paramilitary group. But Miss Philomena, the female teacher who was by tradition permitted the use of the Head's private bathroom, claimed the man had drowned in the Atlantic Ocean trying to sneak into Canada in a boat that ferried, for a wicked fee, illegal aliens. Stashed in the bathroom's air vent (through which sparrows sometimes flew in and bothered her), she'd spotted, she said, an oilcloth pouch stuffed with foreign cash and fake passports.

In the Teacher's Common Room, where Miss Philomena was not popular, her story was discounted. But at the Pillais's home, the men teachers had gotten together and toasted the Head with hoarded bottles of whiskey and sung many rounds of "For He's a Jolly Good Fellow," sometimes substituting "smart" for "good." By the time Mr. Venkatesan had been dropped home by Father van der Haagen, who owned a motorcycle, night had bleached itself into rainy dawn. It had been the only all-nighter of Mr. Venkatesan's life and the only time he might have been accused of drunkenness.

The memory of how good the rain had felt came back to him now as he glanced through the first stanza of the assigned Arnold poem. What was the function of poetry if not to improve the petty, cautious minds of evasive children? What was the duty of the teacher if not to inspire?

He cleared his throat, and began to read aloud in a voice trained in elocution.

> Light flows our war of mocking words, and yet,
> Behold, with tears mine eyes are wet!
> I feel a nameless sadness o'er me roll.
> Yes, yes, we know that we can jest,
> We know, we know that we can smile!
> But there's a something in this breast,
> To which thy light words bring no rest,
> And thy gay smiles no anodyne.
> Give me thy hand, and hush awhile,
> And turn those limpid eyes on mine,
> And let me read there, love! thy inmost soul.

"Sir," a plump boy in the front row whispered as Venkatesan finally stopped for breath.

"What is it now?" snapped Venkatesan. In his new mood Arnold had touched him with fresh intensity, and he hated the boy for deflating illusion. "If you are wanting to know a synonym for 'anodyne,' then look it up in the *Oxford Dictionary*. You are a lazy donkey wanting me to feed you with a silver spoon. All of you, you are all lazy donkeys."

"No, sir." The boy persisted in spoiling the mood.

It was then that Venkatesan took in the boy's sweaty face and hair. Even the eyes were fat and sweaty.

"Behold, sir," the boy said. He dabbed his eyelids with the limp tip of his school tie. "Mine eyes, too, are wet."

"You are a silly donkey," Venkatesan yelled. "You are a beast of burden. You deserve the abuse that you get. It is you emotional types who are selling this country down the river."

The class snickered, unsure what Mr. Venkatesan wanted of them. The boy let go of his tie and wept openly. Mr. Venkatesan hated himself. Here was a kindred soul, a fellow lover of Matthew Arnold, and what had he done other than indulge in gratuitous cruelty? He blamed the times. He blamed Sri Lanka.

It was as much this classroom incident as the fear of arrest for his part in what turned out to be an out-of-control demonstration that made Mr. Venkatesan look into emigrating. At first, he explored legal channels. He wasted a month's salary bribing arrogant junior-level clerks in four consulates—he was willing to settle almost anywhere except in the Gulf Emirates—but every country he could see himself being happy and fulfilled in turned him down.

So all through the summer he consoled himself with reading novels. Adventure stories in which fearless young Britons—sailors, soldiers, missionaries—whacked wildernesses into submission. From lending libraries in the city, he checked out books that were so old that they had to be trussed with twine. On the flyleaf of each book, in fading ink, was an inscription by a dead or retired British tea planter. Like the blond heroes of the novels, the colonials must have come to Ceylon chasing dreams of perfect futures. He, too, must sail dark, stormy oceans.

In August, at the close of a staff meeting, Miss Philomena announced coyly that she was leaving the island. A friend in Kalamazoo, Michigan, had agreed to sponsor her as a "domestic."

"It is a ploy only, man," Miss Philomena explained. "In the autumn, I am signing up for post-graduate studies in a prestigious educational institution."

"You are cleaning toilets and whatnot just like a servant girl? Is the meaning of 'domestic' not the same as 'servant'?"

Mr. Venkatesan joined the others in teasing Miss Philomena, but late that night he wrote away to eight American universities for applications. He took great care with the cover letters, which always began with "Dear Respected Sir" and ended with "Humbly but eagerly awaiting your response." He tried to put down in the allotted blanks what it felt like to be born so heartbreakingly far from New York or London. *On this small dead-end island, I feel I am a shadow-man, a nothing. I feel I'm a stranger in my own room. What consoles me is reading. I sink my teeth into fiction by great Englishmen such as G. A. Henty and A. E. W. Mason. I live my life through their imagined lives. And when I put their works down at dawn I ask myself, Hath not a Tamil eyes, heart, ears, nose, throat, to adapt the words of the greatest Briton. Yes, I am a Tamil. If you prick me, do I not bleed? If you tickle me, do I not laugh? Then, if I dream, will you not give me a chance, respected Sir, as only you can?*

In a second paragraph he politely but firmly indicated the size of scholarship he would require, and indicated the size of apartment he (and his sisters) would require. He preferred close proximity to campus, since he did not intend to drive.

But sometime in late April, the school's porter brought him, rubber-banded together, eight letters of rejection.

"I am worthless," Mr. Venkatesan moaned in front of the porter. "I am a donkey."

The porter offered him aspirins. "You are unwell, sahib."

The schoolteacher swallowed the tablets, but as soon as the servant left, he snatched a confiscated Zippo lighter from his desk and burned the rejections.

When he got home, his sister's suitor was on the balcony, painting placards, and though he meant to say nothing to the youth, meant to admit no flaw, no defeat, his body betrayed him with shudders and moans.

"Racism!" the youth spat as he painted over a spelling error that, even in his grief, Mr. Venkatesan couldn't help pointing out. "Racism is what's slamming the door in your face, man! You got to improvise your weapons!"

Perhaps the boy was not a totally unworthy suitor. He let the exclamations play in his head, and soon the rejections, and the anxiety that he might be stuck on the futureless island fired him up instead of depressing him. Most nights he lay in bed fully dressed—the police always raided at dawn—and thought up a hundred illegal but feasible ways to outwit immigration officials.

The least wild schemes he talked over with Father van der Haagen. Long ago and in another country, Father van der Haagen had surely given in to similar seductions. The Jesuit usually hooted, "So you want to rot in a freezing, foreign jail? You want your lovely sisters to walk the streets and come to harm?" But, always, the expatriate ended these chats with his boyhood memories of skating on frozen Belgian rivers and ponds. Mr. Venkatesan felt he could visualize snow, but not a whole river so iced up that it was as solid as a grand trunk highway. In his dreams, the Tamil schoolteacher crisscrossed national boundaries on skates that felt as soft and comforting as cushions.

In August his sister's suitor got himself stupidly involved in a prison break. The sister came to Mr. Venkatesan weeping. She had stuffed clothes and her sewing basket into a camouflage satchel. She was going into the northern hills, she said. The Tigers could count on the tea pickers.

"No way," Mr. Venkatesan exploded. When he was safely in America's heartland, with his own wife and car and all accoutrements of New World hearth and home, he wanted to think of his Trinco family (to whom he meant to remit generous monthly sums) as being happy under one roof, too. "You are not going to live with hooligan types in jungles."

"If you lock me in my room, I'll call the police. I'll tell them who threw the axe at the rally."

"Is that what they teach you in guerrilla camps? To turn on your family?" he demanded.

The sister wept loudly into her sari. It was a pretty lilac sari, and he remembered having bought it for her seventeenth birthday. On her feet were fragile lilac slippers. He couldn't picture her scrambling up terraced slopes of tea estates in that pretty get-up. "Nobody has to teach me," she retorted.

In her lilac sari, and with the white fragrant flower wreath in her hair, she didn't look like a blackmailer. It was the times. She, her boyfriend, he himself, were all fate's victims.

He gave in. He made her promise, though, that in the hills she would marry her suitor. She touched his feet with her forehead in the traditional farewell. He heard a scooter start up below. So the guerrilla had been waiting. She'd meant to leave home, with or without his permission. She'd freed herself of family duties and bonds.

Above the motor scooter's sputter, the grateful boyfriend shouted, "Sir, I will put you in touch with a man. Listen to him and he will deliver you." Then the dust cloud of destiny swallowed up the guerrilla bride-to-be and groom.

The go-between turned out to be a clubfooted and cauliflower-eared middle-aged man. The combination of deformities, no doubt congenital, had nevertheless earned him a reputation for ferocity and an indifference to inflicted suffering. He appeared on the front porch early one Saturday afternoon. He didn't come straight to the point. For the first half-hour he said very little and concentrated instead on the sweet almond-stuffed turnovers that the Venkatesan family had shaped and fried all day for a religious festival they'd be attending later that afternoon.

"You have, perhaps, some news for me?" Mr. Venkatesan asked shyly as he watched the man help himself to a chilled glass of mango fool. "Some important information, no?"

"Excuse me, sir," the man protested. "I know that you are a teacher and that therefore you are in the business of improving the mind of man. But forthrightness is not always a virtue. Especially in these troubled times."

The man's furtiveness was infectious, and Mr. Venkatesan, without thinking, thinned his voice to a hiss. "You are going over my options with me, no?"

"Options!" the man sneered. Then he took out a foreign-looking newspaper from a shopping bag. On a back page of the paper was a picture of three dour sahibs fishing for lobster. "You get my meaning, sir? They have beautiful coves in Nova Scotia. They have beautiful people in the Canadian Maritimes."

On cushiony skates and with clean, cool winds buoying him from behind, Mr. Venkatesan glided all the way into Halifax, dodging posses of border police. He married a girl with red, dimpled cheeks, and all winter she made love to him under a goose-down quilt. Summers he set lobster traps. Editors of quarterlies begged to see his poetry.

"Beautiful people, Canadians," he agreed.

"Not like the damn Americans!" The go-between masticated sternly. "They are sending over soldiers of fortune and suchlike to crush us."

Mr. Venkatesan, wise in ways of middlemen, asked, "This means you're not having a pipeline to America?"

The agent dipped into a bowl of stale fried banana chips.

"No matter. The time has come for me to leave."

The next day, Sunday, the man came back to find out how much Mr. Venkatesan might be willing to pay for a fake passport/airline tickets/safe houses en route package deal. Mr. Venkatesan named a figure.

"So you are not really anxious to exit?" the man said.

Mr. Venkatesan revised his figure. He revised the figure three more times before the go-between would do anything more human than sigh at him.

He was being taken by a mean, mocking man who preyed on others' dreams. He was allowing himself to be cheated. But sometime that spring the wish to get away—to flee abroad and seize the good life as had his San Jose cousin—had deepened into sickness. So he was blowing his life's savings on this malady. So what?

The man made many more trips. And on each trip, as Mr. Venkatesan sat the man down on the best rattan chair on the balcony, through the half-open door that led into the hallway he saw the women in his family gather in jittery knots. They knew he was about to forsake them.

Every brave beginning, in these cramped little islands, masked a secret betrayal. To himself, Mr. Venkatesan would always be a sinner.

Mr. Venkatesan threw himself into the planning. He didn't trust the man with the cauliflower ears. Routes, circuitous enough to fool border guards, had to be figured out. He could fly to Frankfurt via Malta, for instance, then hole up in a ship's cargo hold for the long, bouncy passage on Canadian seas. Or he could take the more predictable (and therefore, cheaper but with more surveillance) detours through the Gulf Emirates.

The go-between or travel agent took his time. Fake travel documents and work permits had to be printed up. Costs, commissions, bribes had to be calculated. On each visit, the man helped himself to a double peg of Mr. Venkatesan's whiskey.

In early September, three weeks after Mr. Venkatesan had paid in full for a roundabout one-way ticket to Hamburg and for a passport impressive with fake visas, the travel agent stowed him in the damp, smelly bottom of a fisherman's dinghy and had him ferried across the Palk Strait to Tuticorin in the palm-green tip of mainland India.

Tuticorin was the town Mr. Venkatesan's ancestors had left to find their fortunes in Ceylon's tea-covered northern hills. The irony struck him with such force that he rocked and tipped the dinghy, and had to be fished out of the sea.

The Friends of the Tigers were waiting in a palm grove for him. He saw their flashlights and smelled their coffee. They gave him a dry change of clothes, and though both the shirt and the jacket were frayed, they were stylishly cut. His reputation as an intellectual and killer (he hoped it wasn't true) of a Buddhist policeman had preceded him. He let them talk; it was not Venkatesan the schoolmaster they were praising, but some mad invention. Where he was silent from confusion and fatigue, they read cunning and intensity. He was happy to put himself in their hands; he thought of them as fate's helpers, dispatched to see him through his malady. That night one of them made up a sleeping mat for him in the back room of his shuttered grocery store. After that they passed him from back room to back room. He spent pleasant afternoons with them drinking sweet, frothy coffee and listening to them plan to derail trains or blow up bus depots. They read his frown as skepticism and redoubled their vehemence. He himself had no interest in destruction, but he listened to them politely.

When it was safe to move on, the Friends wrote out useful addresses in Frankfurt, London, Toronto, Miami. "Stay out of refugee centers," they advised. But an old man with broken dentures who had been deported out of Hamburg the year before filled him in on which refugee centers in which cities had the cleanest beds, just in case he was caught by the wily German police. "I shan't forget any of you," Mr. Venkatesan said as two Friends saw him off at the train station. The train took him to Madras; in Madras he changed trains for Delhi where he boarded an Aeroflot flight for Tashkent. From Tashkent he flew to Moscow. He would like to have told the story of his life to his two seat mates—already the break from family and from St. Joe's seemed the stuff of adventure novels—but they were two huge and grim Uzbeks with bushels of apricots and pears wedged on the floor, under the seat, and on their laps. The cabin was noisier than the Jaffna local bus with squawking chickens and drunken farmers. He communed instead with Arnold and Keats. In Moscow the airport officials didn't bother to look too closely at his visa stamps, and he made it to Berlin feeling cocky.

At Schönefeld Airport, three rough-looking Tamil men he'd not have given the time of day to back home in Trinco grappled his bags away from him as soon as he'd cleared customs. "This is only a piss stop for you, you lucky bastard," one of them said. "You get to go on to real places while hard-working fuckers like us get stuck in this hellhole."

He had never heard such language. Up until a week ago, he would have denied the Tamil language even possessed such words. The man's coarseness shocked Mr. Venkatesan, but this was not the moment to walk away from accomplices.

The expatriate Tamils took him, by bus, to a tenement building—he saw only Asians and Africans in the lobby—and locked him from the outside in a one-room flat on the top floor. An Algerian they did business with, they said, would truck him over the border into Hamburg. He was not to look out the window. He was not to open the door, not even if someone yelled, "Fire!" They'd be back at night, and they'd bring him beer and rolls.

Mr. Venkatesan made a slow show of getting money out of his trouser pocket—he didn't have any East German money, only rupees and the Canadian dollars he'd bought on the black market from the travel agent in Trinco—but the Tamils stopped him. "Our treat," they said. "You can return the hospitality when we make it to Canada."

Late in the evening the three men, stumbling drunk and jolly, let themselves back into the room that smelled of stale, male smells. The Algerian had come through. They were celebrating. They had forgotten the bread but remembered the beer.

That night, which was his only night in East Germany, Mr. Venkatesan got giggly drunk. And so it was that he entered the free world with a hangover. In a narrow, green mountain pass, trying not to throw up, he said goodbye to his Algerian chauffeur and how-do-you-do to a Ghanaian-born Berliner who didn't cut the engine of his BMW during the furtive transfer.

He was in Europe. Finally. The hangover made him sentimental. Back in Trinco the day must have deepened into dusk. In the skid of tires, he heard the weeping of parents, aunts, sisters. He had looked after them as long as he could. He had done for himself what he should have done ten years before. Now he wanted to walk where Shelley had walked. He wanted to lie down where consumptive Keats had lain and listened to his nightingale sing of truth and beauty. He stretched out in the back seat. When Mr. Venkatesan next opened his eyes, the BMW was parked in front of a refugee center in Hamburg.

"End of trip," the black Berliner announced in jerky English. "Auf Wiedersehen."[2]

Mr. Venkatesan protested that he was not a refugee. "I am paid up in full to Canada. You are supposed to put me in touch with a ship's captain."

The black man snickered, then heaved Mr. Venkatesan's two shiny new bags out on the street. "Goodbye. *Danke*."[3]

Mr. Venkatesan got out of the private taxi.

"Need a cheap hotel? Need a lawyer to stay deportation orders?"

A very dark, pudgy man flashed a calling card in his face. The man looked Tamil, but not anxious like a refugee. His suit was too expensive. Even his shirt was made of some white-on-white fancy material, though his cuffs and collar were somewhat soiled.

Mr. Venkatesan felt exhilarated. Here was another of fate's angels come to minister him out of his malady.

---

2. Farewell.

3. Thank you.

"The name is Rammi. G. Rammi, Esquire. One-time meanest goddamn solicitor in Paramaribo, Suriname. I am putting myself at your service."

He allowed the angel to guide him into a *rijstafel*[4] place and feed him for free.

Mr. Venkatesan ate greedily while the angel, in a voice as uplifting as harp music, instructed him on the most prudent conduct for undocumented transients. By the end of the meal, he'd agreed to pay Rammi's cousin, a widow, a flat fee for boarding him for as long as it took Rammi to locate a ship's captain whose business was ferrying furtive cargoes.

Rammi's cousin, Queenie, lived in a row house by the docks. Rammi had the cabdriver let them off a block and a half from Queenie's. He seemed to think cabdrivers were undercover immigration cops, and he didn't want a poor young widow bringing up a kid on dole getting in trouble for her charity.

Though Queenie had been telephoned ahead from a pay phone, she was dressed in nothing more formal than a kimono when she opened her slightly warped front door and let the men in. The kimono was the color of parrots in sunlight and reminded Mr. Venkatesan of his last carefree years, creeping up on and capturing parrots with his bare hands. In that glossy green kimono, Queenie the landlady shocked him with her beauty. Her sash was missing, and she clenched the garment together at the waist with a slender, nervous fist. Her smooth gold limbs, her high-bouncing bosom, even the stockingless arch of her instep had about them so tempting a careless sensuality that it made his head swim.

"I put your friend in Room 3A," Queenie said. "3B is less crowded but I had to put the sick Turk in it." She yelled something in German which Mr. Venkatesan didn't understand, and a girl of eight or nine came teetering out of the kitchen in adult-sized high heels. She asked the girl some urgent questions. The girl said no to all of them with shakes of her braided head.

"We don't want the fellow dying on us," Rammi said. Then they said something more in a Caribbean patois that Mr. Venkatesan didn't catch. "God knows we don't want complications." He picked up the two bags and started up the stairs.

3A was a smallish attic room blue with unventilated smoke, fitted with two sets of three-tier bunks. There were no closets, no cupboards, and on the bunk that Rammi pointed out as his, no bed linen. Four young men of indistinguishable nationality—Asia and Africa were their continents—were playing cards and drinking beer.

"Okay, 'bye," Rammi said. He was off to scout ship captains.

When Rammi left, despite the company, Mr. Venkatesan felt depressed, lonely. He didn't try to get to know where the men were from and where they were headed which was how he'd broken the ice in back room dormitories in

---

4. A dish from Indonesia, originally, in which a variety of foods are served with rice.

Tuticorin. One man spat into a brass spittoon. What did he have in common with these transients except the waiting?

By using his bags as a stepladder, he was able to clamber up to his allotted top bunk. For a while he sat on the bed. The men angled their heads so they could still stare at him. He lay down on the mattress. The rough ticking material of the pillow chafed him. He sat up again. He took his jacket and pants off and hung them from the foot rail. He slipped his wallet, his passport, his cloth bag stuffed with foreign cash, his new watch—a farewell present from Father van der Haagen—between the pillow and the mattress. He was not about to trust his cell mates. A little after the noon hour all four men got dressed in gaudy clothes and went out in a group. Mr. Venkatesan finally closed his eyes. A parrot flew into his dream. Mr. Venkatesan thrilled to the feathery feel of its bosom. He woke up only when Queenie's little girl charged into the room and ordered him down for lunch. She didn't seem upset about his being in underwear. She leaped onto the middle bunk in the tier across the room and told him to hurry so the food wouldn't have to be rewarmed. He thought he saw the flash of a man's watch in her hand.

Queenie had made him a simple lunch of lentil soup and potato croquettes, and by the time he got down to the kitchen it was no longer warm. Still he liked the spiciness of the croquettes and the ketchup was a tasty European brand and not the watery stuff served back home.

She said she'd already eaten, but she sat down with a lager and watched him eat. With her he had no trouble talking. He told her about St. Joe's and Father van der Haagen. He told her about his family, leaving out the part about his sister running wild in the hills with hooligans, and got her to talk about her family too.

Queenie's grandfather had been born in a Sinhalese village the name of which he hadn't cared to pass on—he'd referred to it only as "hellhole"—and from which he'd run away at age seventeen to come as an indentured laborer to the Caribbean. He'd worked sugar cane fields in British Guiana until he'd lost a thumb. Then he'd moved to Suriname and worked as an office boy in a coconut oil processing plant, and wooed and won the only daughter of the proprietor, an expatriate Tamil like him who, during the War, had made a fortune off the Americans.

He tried to find out about her husband, but she'd say nothing other than that he'd been, in her words, "a romantic moron," and that he'd hated the hot sun, the flat lands, the coconut palms, the bush, her family, her family's oil factory. He'd dreamed, she said, of living like a European.

"You make me remember things I thought I'd forgotten." She flicked her lips with her tongue until they shone.

"You make me think of doing things I've never done." He gripped the edge of the kitchen table. He had trouble breathing. "Until dinnertime," he said. Then he panted back up to his prison.

But Mr. Venkatesan didn't see Queenie for dinner. She sent word through the girl that she had a guest—a legitimate guest, a tourist from Lübeck, not an illegal transient—that evening. He felt no rage at being dumped. A man without papers accepts last-minute humiliations. He called Rammi from the pay phone in the hall.

That night Mr. Venkatesan had fun. Hamburg was not at all the staid city of burghers that Father van der Haagen had evoked for him in those last restless days of waiting in the Teacher's Common Room. Hamburg was a carnival. That night, with Rammi as his initiator into fun, he smoked his first joint and said, after much prodding, "*sehr schön*"[5] to a skinny girl with a Mohawk haircut.

The tourist from Lübeck had been given the one nice room. Queenie's daughter had shown Mr. Venkatesan the room while the man was checking in. It was on the first floor and had a double bed with a duvet so thick you wanted to sink into it. The windows were covered with *two* sets of curtains. The room even had its own sink. He hadn't seen the man from Lübeck, only heard him on the stairs and in the hall on his way to and from the lavatory walking with an authoritative, native-born German tread. Queenie hadn't instructed him to stay out of sight. Secretiveness he'd learned from his bunk mates. They could move with great stealth. Mr. Venkatesan was beginning to feel like a character in Anne Frank's diary. The men in 3A stopped wearing shoes indoors so as not to be heard pacing by the tourist from Lübeck.

The tourist went out a lot. Sometimes a car came for him. From the Tourist Office, Mr. Venkatesan imagined. How nice it would be to tour the city, take a boat trip! Meantime he had to eat his meals upstairs. That was the sad part. Otherwise he felt he had never been so happy.

Every morning as soon as he got the chance he called Rammi, though he was no longer keen for Rammi to find a crooked captain. He called because he didn't want Rammi to catch on that he was feeling whatever it was that he was feeling for Queenie. Like Rammi, he didn't want complications. What he did was remind Rammi that he wouldn't go into the hold of a ship that dumped its cargo into the Atlantic. He told Rammi that both in Trinco and in Tuticorin he'd heard stories of drowned Tamils.

Mr. Venkatesan's roommates stopped going out for meals. They paid Queenie's girl to buy them cold meats and oranges from the corner store. The only thing they risked going out for was liquor. He gathered from fragments of conversation that they were all sailors, from Indonesia and Nigeria, who'd jumped ship in Hamburg harbor. Whenever they went out, he could count on the girl prowling the attic room. He let her prowl. It was almost like having Queenie in the room.

---

5. Very beautiful.

There was only one worry. The girl lifted things—small things—from under pillows. Sometimes she played under the beds where he and the other men stored their suitcases, and he heard lids swish open or closed. He didn't think the things she stole were worth stealing. He'd seen her take a handful of pfennigs from a jacket pocket once, and another time envelopes with brilliant stamps from places like Turkey and Oman. What she seemed to like best to pilfer were lozenges, even the medicated kind for sore throat. It was as if covetousness came upon her, out of the blue, making her pupils twitch and glow.

He didn't mind the loss to his roommates. But he worried that they'd get her in trouble by sending her to the store. He would have to stop her. He would have to scold her as a father might or should without messing things up with Queenie.

One morning Queenie showed up in 3A herself. "I have good news," she whispered. Two of the four men were still in bed. Mr. Venkatesan could tell they hated having a grown woman in their room. "Rammi should have word for you tonight. I'm meeting him to find out more." The morning light, streaming in through a cracked stained-glass panel in the window, put such a heavenly sheen on her face that Mr. Venkatesan blurted out in front of his roommates, "I love you, I love you."

Queenie laughed. "Hush," she said. "You're not there yet. You don't want to wake up our Teuton. I need the legitimate business too."

It seemed to Mr. Venkatesan like an invitation. He followed her down into the front hall in his night clothes. In Tamil movies heroes in his position would have been wearing brocade smoking jackets. It didn't matter. He had made his declaration. Now fate would have to sink the crooked captain and his boat.

Queenie fussed with a pink, plastic clip in her hair. She knotted and re-knotted the wispy silk square around her throat. She tapped the longest fingernail he'd ever seen on the butterfly buckle of her belt. She was teasing him. She was promising he wouldn't really have to go. He wanted to stay, Anne Frank or not.

"Tonight should be a champagne night," she grinned. He saw the tensing of a dainty calf muscle as she straightened a stocking. "I'll see to coffee," she said.

Upstairs the man from Lübeck had hot water running in the bathroom sink. The pipes moaned. It was best to hide out in the kitchen until the man was back in his own room. Mr. Venkatesan joined Queenie's daughter at the dinette table. She had lozenges spread out on the tablecloth, like a sun spiked with long rays. She didn't look like a thief. She looked like a child he might have fathered if he'd married the bride his mother had picked for him in the days he'd still been considered a good catch. He hadn't married. Something dire had shown up in the conjunction of their horoscopes.

What if, just what if, what had seemed disastrous to the astrologer at the time had really been fate's way of reserving him for a better family with Queenie and this child in Hamburg?

"I'll sell you some," the child said. "I have English toffees too."

"Where?" He wanted to see her whole loot.

She ducked and brought out an old milk bottle from under the table. He saw the toffees in their red and blue wrapping papers. He saw a Muslim's worry beads. Some things in the bottle were shiny—he made out two rings among the keys and coins and coat buttons. There were two ID cards in the bottle. She reached for the cards. She had to have stolen one of the cards from a man in Room 3A. In the ID picture, which was amateurishly doctored, the roommate looked like a playboy sheikh, and not at all like a refugee without travel papers. He grabbed the roommate's card from her. It wouldn't hurt to have the fellow in his debt. The other card belonged to a very blond, very German man.

The child was shrewd. "I didn't steal anything," she snapped. "I don't know how the stuff got in that jar."

She tossed the blond man's ID to him to get rid of it, and he caught it as he had paper flowers, silk squares, and stunned rabbits hurled to front-row boys by magicians on fete days in his kindergarten. He had loved the magicians. They alone had given him what he'd wanted.

As in dreams, the burly blond man materialized out of thin air and blocked the doorway. The man had on a touristy shirt and short pants, but he didn't have the slack gait of a vacationer. He had to be the man who lived in the nice upstairs room, the man who slept under the cozy *duvet*, who brushed his teeth in a clean, pink sink he didn't have to share, the man from whom transients like Mr. Venkatesan himself had to hide out. This man yelled something nasty in German to Queenie's daughter. The child cowered.

The man yelled again. Mr. Venkatesan started to back away. Minute by minute the man ballooned with rage.

"No *deutsch*," Mr. Venkatesan mumbled.

"You filthy swine," the man shouted in English. "We don't want you making filthy our Germany." He threw five passports down on the kitchen table and spat on the top one. "The girl, she stole something from each of you scums," he hooted.

Mr. Venkatesan recognized his in the heap of travel documents. The child must have stolen it. The child must have filched it from under his pillow while he'd slept. She was a child possessed with covetousness. Now, because of her sick covetousness, he would rot in jail. He yanked the girl by her braids and shook her. The girl made her body go limp, taking away all pleasure in hate and revenge. The tourist from Lübeck ignored the screaming child. He got on the pay phone, the one Mr. Venkatesan called Rammi on every morning. Mr. Venkatesan heard the word "*Polizei!*" He was almost fifty. By fifty a man ought to stop running. Maybe what seemed accidental now—Queenie's daughter's kleptomania blowing away his plans for escape—wasn't accidental. He remembered what had consoled Dr. Pillai at the time of his arrest. Fractals. Nothing was random, the math teacher used to say. Nothing, not even the curliness of a coastline and the fluffiness of a cloud.

Mr. Venkatesan thought about the swoops and darts of his fate. He had started out as a teacher and a solid citizen and ended up as a lusty criminal. He visualized fate now as a buzzard. He could hear the whir of fleshy wings. It hopped off a burning car in the middle of a Trinco intersection.

Then, suddenly, Queenie the beauteous, the deliverer of radiant dreams, burst through the door of the kitchen. "Leave him alone!" she yelled to the man from Lübeck. "You're harassing my fiancé! He's a future German citizen. He will become my husband!"

■ Salman Rushdie (1947–   ) *English* (novel)

Before the Ayatollah Khomeini of Iran proclaimed a death sentence on Salman Rushdie on the fifteenth of February, 1989, Rushdie was the rising star of twentieth-century Indian writers, recipient of the Booker Prize for his earlier novel *Midnight's Children* and of an $850,000 advance from Viking Books for the novel that became *The Satanic Verses*. *The Satanic Verses* had been published in September 1988 and prior to Khomeini's proclamation had already been banned in India and South Africa and had been the subject of book burnings in Yorkshire, England, and the instigation for riots across India and Pakistan. The question of how offensive *The Satanic Verses* really is to Islam continues to be debated. Early critics admitted to damning Rushdie without ever reading his book. Syed Shahabuddin, for example, writes: "I have not read it, nor do I intend to. I do not have to wade through a filthy drain to know what filth is" (*Times of India*, 13 October 1988). Later, more careful critics found the portraiture of Muhammed and his followers degrading and objected, among other things, to the suggestion that Rushdie's Persian namesake, Salman al-Farsi, the first Persian convert to Islam, was a transcriber of the Quran who willfully changed passages (thus undermining the idea that the Quran contains the unadulterated words of Allah). After 1989, Rushdie was a fugitive with a price of several million dollars on his head and was under constant police protection; asassins attacked his Italian translator and killed his Japanese translator. Writers the world over, from James Michener to Günter Grass, expressed their solidarity with Rushdie, while the voices of Islam continued to excoriate him and deny him pardon. In between are voices such as that of Edward Said, who speaks out against censorship and violence, while asking: "Why must a Muslim, who could be defending and sympathetically interpreting us, now represent us so roughly, so expertly and so disrespectfully to an audience already primed to excoriate our traditions, reality, history, religion, language, and origin?"[1] Rushdie's own apology has not been efficacious; the Ayatollah's response was "Even if Salman Rushdie repents and becomes the most pious man of time, it is incumbent on every Muslim to employ everything he has got, his life and his wealth, to send him to hell" (*Irna Iranian News Agency,* 19 February 1989). The death sentence has since been lifted.

Salman Rushdie was born in 1947 in Bombay to a Muslim family who spoke both English and Urdu. He was educated at an English mission school, at Rugby, and at King's College, Cambridge, where he studied history. An important childhood influence was *The Thousand and One Nights,* and the structural and imaginative debt of his novels to this great repository of Indian and Middle Eastern wit and narrative is profound. In college, he set out to become a writer and wrote *Grimus* (1975) while working in advertising. His other novels include *Midnight's Children* (1980), *Shame* (1983), *The Satanic Verses* (1988), and *Haroun and the Sea of Stories* (1990).

"The Perforated Sheet" is the first chapter of Rushdie's celebrated novel *Midnight's Children.* In this selection, Rushdie's high-spirited, hilarious, mythic, and multivalent prose style can be seen; he achieves a level of wordplay and sheer creative bravado matched by few fiction writers— Vladimir Nabokov and John Barthes come to mind. Even in so short a selection, the characteristic Rushdie techniques can be seen: the narratives within narratives; the quibbling, self-revising, self-doubting narrator whose interjections create theatrical asides and foreshadowings of future events; and the interpenetration of past, present, and future in the narrative flow. Rushdie writes a kind of Indian Magical Realism, in which folklore, myth, and Quranic allegory coexist with intimately and tenderly portrayed characters, and high rhetoric blends with the vernacular. Though he uses postmodern literary techniques, Rushdie is at heart a modernist writer, whose writing is always at some level an allegory about writing (thus, "The Perforated Sheet" has meanings beyond the white bedsheet to which it refers). Like his protagonist, Rushdie has been "handcuffed to history," and in *Midnight's Children* we see him already exploring the conjunctions of Eastern and Western perspectives that landed him in hot water with *The Satanic Verses.* Like Bharati Mukherjee's "middleman," Rushdie's doctor (caught between Muslim faith and Western materialism) is a "half-and-halfer," with one foot in each culture.

FURTHER READING: Appignanesi, Lisa, and Sara Maitland, eds. *The Rushdie File,* 1989. Cohn-Sherbok, Dan, ed. *The Salman Rushdie Controversy in Interreligious Perspective,* 1990. Ruthven, Malise. *A Satanic Affair: Salman Rushdie and the Rage of Islam,* 1990.

---

1. Lisa Appignanesi, and Sara Maitland, eds. *The Rushdie File* (London: Fourth Estate, 1989), 176.

The Perforated Sheet, from **Midnight's Children**

I was born in the city of Bombay . . . once upon a time. No, that won't do, there's no getting away from the date: I was born in Doctor Narlikar's Nursing Home on August 15th, 1947. And the time? The time matters, too. Well then: at night. No, it's important to be more . . . On the stroke of midnight, as a matter of fact. Clock-hands joined palms in respectful greeting as I came. Oh, spell it out, spell it out: at the precise instant of India's arrival at independence, I tumbled forth into the world. There were gasps. And, outside the window, fireworks and crowds. A few seconds later, my father broke his big toe; but his accident was a mere trifle when set beside what had befallen me in that benighted moment, because thanks to the occult tyrannies of those blandly saluting clocks I had been mysteriously handcuffed to history, my destinies indissolubly chained to those of my country. For the next three decades, there was to be no escape. Soothsayers had prophesied me, newspapers celebrated my arrival, politicos ratified my authenticity. I was left entirely without a say in the matter. I, Saleem Sinai, later variously called Snotnose, Stainface, Baldy, Sniffer, Buddha and even Piece-of-the-Moon, had become heavily embroiled in Fate—at the best of times a dangerous sort of involvement. And I couldn't even wipe my own nose at the time.

Now, however, time (having no further use for me) is running out. I will soon be thirty-one years old. Perhaps. If my crumbling, over-used body permits. But I have no hope of saving my life, nor can I count on having even a thousand nights and a night. I must work fast, faster than Scheherazade, if I am to end up meaning—yes, meaning—something. I admit it: above all things, I fear absurdity.

And there are so many stories to tell, too many, such an excess of intertwined lives events miracles places rumours, so dense a commingling of the improbable and the mundane! I have been a swallower of lives; and to know me, just the one of me, you'll have to swallow the lot as well. Consumed multitudes are jostling and shoving inside me; and guided only by the memory of a large white bedsheet with a roughly circular hole some seven inches in diameter cut into the centre, clutching at the dream of that holey, mutilated square of linen, which is my talisman, my open-sesame, I must commence the business of remaking my life from the point at which it really began, some thirty-two years before anything as obvious, as *present*, as my clock-ridden, crime-stained birth.

(The sheet, incidentally, is stained too, with three drops of old, faded redness. As the Quran tells us: *Recite, in the name of the Lord thy Creator, who created Man from clots of blood.*)

One Kashmiri morning in the early spring of 1915, my grandfather Aadam Aziz hit his nose against a frost-hardened tussock of earth while attempting to pray. Three drops of blood plopped out of his left nostril, hardened instantly in the brittle air and lay before his eyes on the prayer-mat, transformed into rubies. Lurching back until he knelt with his head once more upright, he found that the tears which had sprung to his eyes had solidified, too; and at that moment, as he brushed diamonds contemptuously from his lashes, he resolved never again to kiss earth for any god or man. This decision, however, made a hole in him, a vacancy in a vital inner chamber, leaving him vulnerable to women and history. Unaware of this at first, despite his recently completed medical training, he stood up, rolled the prayer-mat into a thick cheroot, and holding it under his right arm surveyed the valley through clear, diamond-free eyes.

The world was new again. After a winter's gestation in its eggshell of ice, the valley had beaked its way out into the open, moist and yellow. The new grass bided its time underground; the mountains were retreating to their hill-stations for the warm season. (In the winter, when the valley shrank under the ice, the mountains closed in and snarled like angry jaws around the city on the lake.)

In those days the radio mast had not been built and the temple of Sankara Acharya, a little black blister on a khaki hill, still dominated the streets and lake of Srinagar. In those days there was no army camp at the lakeside, no endless snakes of camouflaged trucks and jeeps clogged the narrow mountain roads, no soldiers hid behind the crests of the mountains past Baramulla and Gulmarg. In those days travellers were not shot as spies if they took photographs of bridges, and apart from the Englishmen's houseboats on the lake, the valley had hardly changed since the Mughal Empire, for all its springtime renewals; but my grandfather's eyes—which were, like the rest of him, twenty-five years old—saw things differently . . . and his nose had started to itch.

To reveal the secret of my grandfather's altered vision: he had spent five years, five springs, away from home. (The tussock of earth, crucial though its presence was as it crouched under a chance wrinkle of the prayer-mat, was at bottom no more than a catalyst.) Now, returning, he saw through travelled eyes. Instead of the beauty of the tiny valley circled by giant teeth, he noticed the narrowness, the proximity of the horizon; and felt sad, to be at home and feel so utterly enclosed. He also felt—inexplicably—as though the old place resented his educated, stethoscoped return. Beneath the winter ice, it had been coldly neutral, but now there was no doubt: the years in Germany had returned him to a hostile environment. Many years later, when the hole inside him had been clogged up with hate, and he came to sacrifice himself at the shrine of the black stone god in the temple on the hill, he would try and recall his childhood springs in Paradise, the way it was before travel and tussocks and army tanks messed everything up.

On the morning when the valley, gloved in a prayer-mat, punched him on the nose, he had been trying, absurdly, to pretend that nothing had changed. So he had risen in the bitter cold of four-fifteen, washed himself in the prescribed fashion, dressed and put on his father's astrakhan cap; after which he had carried the rolled cheroot of the prayer-mat into the small lakeside garden in front of their old dark house and unrolled it over the waiting tussock. The ground felt deceptively soft under his feet and made him simultaneously uncertain and unwary. 'In the Name of God, the Compassionate, the Merciful . . .'—the exordium, spoken with hands joined before him like a book, comforted a part of him, made another, larger part feel uneasy—' . . . Praise be to Allah, Lord of the Creation . . .'—but now Heidelberg invaded his head; here was Ingrid, briefly his Ingrid, her face scorning him for this Mecca-turned parroting; here, their friends Oskar and Ilse Lubin the anarchists, mocking his prayer with their anti-ideologies—' . . . The Compassionate, the Merciful, King of the Last Judgment! . . .'—Heidelberg, in which, along with medicine and politics, he learned that India—like radium—had been 'discovered' by the Europeans; even Oskar was filled with admiration for Vasco da Gama, and this was what finally separated Aadam Aziz from his friends, this belief of theirs that he was somehow the invention of their ancestors—' . . . You alone we worship, and to You alone we pray for help . . .'—so here he was, despite their presence in his head, attempting to re-unite himself with an earlier self which ignored their influence but knew everything it ought to have known, about submission for example, about what he was doing now, as his hands, guided by old memories, fluttered upwards, thumbs pressed to ears, fingers spread, as he sank to his knees—' . . . Guide us to the straight path, The path of those whom You have favoured . . .'—But it was no good, he was caught in a strange middle ground, trapped between belief and disbelief, and this was only a charade after all—' . . . Not of those who have incurred Your wrath, Nor of those who have gone astray.' My grandfather bent his forehead towards the earth. Forward he bent, and the earth, prayer-mat-covered, curved up towards him. And now it was the tussock's time. At one and the same time a rebuke from Ilse-Oskar-Ingrid-Heidelberg as well as valley-and-God, it smote him upon the point of the nose. Three drops fell. There were rubies and diamonds. And my grandfather, lurching upright, made a resolve. Stood. Rolled cheroot. Stared across the lake. And was knocked forever into that middle place, unable to worship a God in whose existence he could not wholly disbelieve. Permanent alteration: a hole.

The young, newly-qualified Doctor Aadam Aziz stood facing the springtime lake, sniffing the whiffs of change; while his back (which was extremely straight) was turned upon yet more changes. His father had had a stroke in his absence abroad, and his mother had kept it a secret. His mother's voice, whispering stoically: '. . . *Because your studies were too important, son.*' This mother, who had spent her life housebound, in purdah, had suddenly found enormous strength and gone out to run the small gemstone business (turquoises, rubies, diamonds) which had put Aadam through medical college, with the help of a scholarship; so he returned to find the seemingly immutable order of his family turned upside down, his mother going out to work while his father sat hidden behind the veil which the stroke had dropped over his brain . . . in a wooden chair, in a darkened room, he sat and made bird-noises. Thirty different species of birds visited him and sat on the sill outside his shuttered window conversing about this and that. He seemed happy enough.

(. . . And already I can see the repetitions beginning; because didn't my grandmother also find enormous . . . and the stroke, too, was not the only . . . and the Brass Monkey had her birds . . . the curse begins already, and we haven't even got to the noses yet!)

The lake was no longer frozen over. The thaw had come rapidly, as usual; many of the small boats, the shikaras, had been caught napping, which was also normal. But while these sluggards slept on, on dry land, snoring peacefully beside their owners, the oldest boat was up at the crack as old folk often are, and was therefore the first craft to move across the unfrozen lake. Tai's shikara . . . this, too, was customary.

Watch how the old boatman, Tai, makes good time through the misty water, standing stooped over at the back of his craft! How his oar, a wooden heart on a yellow stick, drives jerkily through the weeds! In these parts he's considered very odd because he rows standing up . . . among other reasons. Tai, bringing an urgent summons to Doctor Aziz, is about to set history in motion . . . while Aadam, looking down into the water, recalls what Tai taught him years ago: 'The ice is always waiting, Aadam baba, just under the water's skin.' Aadam's eyes are a clear blue, the astonishing blue of mountain sky, which has a habit of dripping into the pupils of Kashmiri men; they have not forgotten how to look. They see—there! like the skeleton of a ghost, just beneath the surface of Lake Dal!—the delicate tracery, the intricate crisscross of colourless lines, the cold waiting veins of the future. His German years, which have blurred so much else, haven't deprived him of the gift of seeing. Tai's gift. He looks up, sees the approaching V of Tai's boat, waves a greeting. Tai's arm rises—but this is a command. 'Wait!' My grandfather waits; and during this hiatus, as he experiences the last peace of his life, a muddy, ominous sort of peace, I had better get round to describing him.

Keeping out of my voice the natural envy of the ugly man for the strikingly impressive, I record that Doctor Aziz was a tall man. Pressed flat against a wall of his family home, he measured twenty-five bricks (a brick for each year of his life), or just over six foot two. A strong man also. His beard was thick and red—and annoyed his mother, who said only Hajis, men who had made the pilgrimage to Mecca, should grow red beards. His hair, however, was rather darker. His sky-eyes you know about. Ingrid had said, 'They went mad with the colours when they made your face.' But the central feature of my grandfather's anatomy was neither colour nor height, neither strength of arm nor straightness of back. There it was, reflected in the water, undulating like a mad plantain in the centre of his face . . . Aadam Aziz, waiting for Tai, watches his rippling nose. It would have dominated less dramatic faces than his easily; even on him, it is what one sees first and remembers longest. 'A cyranose,' Ilse Lubin said, and

Oskar added, 'A proboscissimus.' Ingrid announced, 'You could cross a river on that nose.' (Its bridge was wide.)

My grandfather's nose: nostrils flaring, curvaceous as dancers. Between them swells the nose's triumphal arch, first up and out, then down and under, sweeping in to his upper lip with a superb and at present red-tipped flick. An easy nose to hit a tussock with. I wish to place on record my gratitude to this mighty organ—if not for it, who would ever have believed me to be truly my mother's son, my grandfather's grandson?—this colossal apparatus which was to be my birthright, too. Doctor Aziz's nose—comparable only to the trunk of the elephant-headed god Ganesh—established incontrovertibly his right to be a patriarch. It was Tai who taught him that, too. When young Aadam was barely past puberty the dilapidated boatman said, 'That's a nose to start a family on, my princeling. There'd be no mistaking whose brood they were. Mughal Emperors would have given their right hands for noses like that one. There are dynasties waiting inside it,'— and here Tai lapsed into coarseness—'like snot.'

On Aadam Aziz, the nose assumed a patriarchal aspect. On my mother, it looked noble and a little long-suffering; on my aunt Emerald, snobbish; on my aunt Alia, intellectual; on my uncle Hanif it was the organ of an unsuccessful genius; my uncle Mustapha made it a second-rater's sniffer; the Brass Monkey escaped it completely; but on me—on me, it was something else again. But I mustn't reveal all my secrets at once.

(Tai is getting nearer. He, who revealed the power of the nose, and who is now bringing my grandfather the message which will catapult him into his future, is stroking his shikara through the early morning lake . . .)

Nobody could remember when Tai had been young. He had been plying this same boat, standing in the same hunched position, across the Dal and Nageen Lakes . . . forever. As far as anyone knew. He lived somewhere in the insanitary bowels of the old wooden-house quarter and his wife grew lotus roots and other curious vegetables on one of the many 'floating gardens' lilting on the surface of the spring and summer water. Tai himself cheerily admitted he had no idea of his age. Neither did his wife—he was, she said, already leathery when they married. His face was a sculpture of wind on water: ripples made of hide. He had two golden teeth and no others. In the town, he had few friends. Few boatmen or traders invited him to share a hookah when he floated past the shikara moorings or one of the lakes' many ramshackle, waterside provision-stores and tea-shops.

The general opinion of Tai had been voiced long ago by Aadam Aziz's father the gemstone merchant: 'His brain fell out with his teeth.' (But now old Aziz sahib sat lost in bird tweets while Tai simply, grandly, continued.) It was an impression the boatman fostered by his chatter, which was fantastic, grandiloquent and ceaseless, and as often as not addressed only to himself. Sound carries over water, and the lake people giggled at his monologues; but with undertones of awe, and even fear. Awe, because the old halfwit knew the lakes and hills better than any of his detractors; fear, because of his claim to an antiquity so immense it defied numbering, and moreover hung so lightly round his chicken's neck that it hadn't prevented him from winning a highly desirable wife and fathering four sons upon her . . . and a few more, the story went, on other lakeside wives. The young bucks at the shikara moorings were convinced he had a pile of money hidden away somewhere—a hoard, perhaps, of priceless golden teeth, rattling in a sack like walnuts. Years later, when Uncle Puffs tried to sell me his daughter by offering to have her teeth drawn and replaced in gold, I thought of Tai's forgotten treasure . . . and, as a child, Aadam Aziz had loved him.

He made his living as a simple ferryman, despite all the rumours of wealth, taking hay and goats and vegetables and wood across the lakes for cash; people, too. When he was running his taxi-service he erected a pavilion in the centre of the shikara, a gay affair of flowered-patterned curtains and canopy, with cushions to match; and deodorised his boat with incense. The sight of Tai's shikara approaching, curtains flying, had always been for Doctor Aziz one of the defining images of the coming of spring. Soon the English sahibs would arrive and Tai would ferry them to the Shalimar Gardens and the King's Spring, chattering and pointy and stooped. He was the living antithesis of Oskar-Ilse-Ingrid's belief in the inevitability of change . . . a quirky, enduring familiar spirit of the valley. A watery Caliban, rather too fond of cheap Kashmiri brandy.

Memory of my blue bedroom wall: on which, next to the P. M.'s letter, the Boy Raleigh hung for many years, gazing rapturously at an old fisherman in what looked like a red dhoti, who sat on—what?—driftwood?—and pointed out to sea as he told his fishy tales . . . and the Boy Aadam, my grandfather-to-be, fell in love with the boatman Tai precisely because of the endless verbiage which made others think him cracked. It was magical talk, words pouring from him like fools' money, past his two gold teeth, laced with hiccups and brandy, soaring up to the most remote Himalayas of the past, then swooping shrewdly on some present detail, Aadam's nose for instance, to vivisect its meaning like a mouse. This friendship had plunged Aadam into hot water with great regularity. (Boiling water. Literally. While his mother said, 'We'll kill that boatman's bugs if it kills you.') But still the old soliloquist would dawdle in his boat at the garden's lakeside toes and Aziz would sit at his feet until voices summoned him indoors to be lectured on Tai's filthiness and warned about the pillaging armies of germs his mother envisaged leaping from that hospitably ancient body on to her son's starched white loose-pajamas. But always Aadam returned to the water's edge to scan the mists for the ragged reprobate's hunched-up frame steering its magical boat through the enchanted waters of the morning.

'But how old are you really, Taiji?' (Doctor Aziz, adult, redbearded, slanting towards the future, remembers the day he asked the unaskable question.) For an instant, silence, noisier than a waterfall. The monologue, interrupted. Slap of oar in water. He was riding in the shikara with Tai, squatting amongst goats, on a pile of straw, in full knowledge of the stick and bathtub waiting for him at home. He had come for stories—and with one question had silenced the storyteller.

'No, tell, Taiji, how old, *truly?*' And now a brandy bottle, materialising from nowhere: cheap liquor from the folds of the great warm chugha-coat. Then a shudder, a belch, a glare. Glint of gold. And—at last!—speech. 'How old? You ask how old, you little wet-head, you nosey . . .' Tai, forecasting the fisherman on my wall, pointed at the mountains. 'So old, nakkoo!' Aadam, the nakkoo, the nosey one, followed his pointing finger. 'I have watched the mountains being born; I have seen Emperors die. Listen. Listen, nakkoo . . .'—the brandy bottle again, followed by brandy-voice, and words more intoxicating than booze—' . . . I saw that Isa, that Christ, when he came to Kashmir. Smile, smile, it is your history I am keeping in my head. Once it was set down in old lost books. Once I knew where there was a grave with pierced feet carved on the tombstone, which bled once a year. Even my memory is going now; but I know, although I can't read.' Illiteracy, dismissed with a flourish; literature crumbled beneath the rage of his sweeping hand. Which sweeps again to chugha-pocket, to brandy bottle, to lips chapped with cold. Tai always had woman's lips. 'Nakkoo, listen, listen. I have seen plenty. Yara, you should've seen that Isa when he came, beard down to his balls, bald as an egg on his head. He was old and fagged-out but he knew his manners. "You first, Taiji," he'd say, and "Please to sit"; always a respectful tongue, he never called me crackpot, never called me *tu* either. Always *aap*. Polite, see? And what an appetite! Such a hunger, I would catch my ears in fright. Saint or devil, I swear he could eat a whole kid in one go. And so what? I told him, eat, fill your hole, a man comes to Kashmir to enjoy life, or to end it, or both. His work was finished. He just came up here to live it up a little.' Mesmerized by this brandied portrait of a bald, gluttonous Christ, Aziz listened, later repeating every word to the consternation of his parents, who dealt in stones and had no time for 'gas.'

'Oh, you don't believe?'—licking his sore lips with a grin, knowing it to be the reverse of the truth; 'Your attention is wandering?'—again, he knew how furiously Aziz was hanging on his words. 'Maybe the straw is pricking your behind, hey? Oh, I'm so sorry, babaji, not to provide for you silk cushions with gold brocade-work-cushions such as the Emperor Jehangir sat upon! You think of the Emperor Jehangir as a gardener only, no doubt,' Tai accused my grandfather, 'because he built Shalimar. Stupid! What do you know? His name meant Encompasser of the Earth. Is that a gardener's name? God knows what they teach you boys these days. Whereas I' . . . puffing up a little here . . . 'I knew his precise weight, to the tola! Ask me how many maunds, how many seers! When he was happy he got heavier and in Kashmir he was heaviest of all. I used to carry his litter . . . no, no, look, you don't believe again, that big cucumber in your face is waggling like the little one in your pajamas! So, come on, come on, ask me questions! Give examination! Ask how many times the leather thongs wound round the handles of the litter—the answer is thirty-one. Ask me what was the Emperor's dying word—I tell you it was "Kashmir." He had bad breath and a good heart. Who do you think I am? Some common ignorant lying pie-dog? Go, get out of the boat now, your nose makes it too heavy to row; also your father is waiting to beat my gas out of you, and your mother to boil off your skin.'

In the brandy bottle of the boatman Tai I see, foretold, my own father's possession by djinns . . . and there will be another bald foreigner . . . and Tai's gas prophesies another kind, which was the consolation of my grand-mother's old age, and taught her stories, too . . . and pie-dogs aren't far away . . . Enough. I'm frightening myself.

Despite beating and boiling, Aadam Aziz floated with Tai in his shikara, again and again, amid goats hay flowers furniture lotus-roots, though never with the English sahibs, and heard again and again the miraculous answers to that single terrifying question: 'But Taiji, how old are you, *honestly?*'

From Tai, Aadam learned the secrets of the lake—where you could swim without being pulled down by weeds; the eleven varieties of water-snake; where the frogs spawned; how to cook a lotus-root; and where the three English women had drowned a few years back. 'There is a tribe of fer-inghee women who come to this water to drown,' Tai said. 'Sometimes they know it, sometimes they don't, but I know the minute I smell them. They hide under the water from God knows what or who—but they can't hide from me, baba!' Tai's laugh, emerging to infect Aadam—a huge, booming laugh that seemed macabre when it crashed out of that old, withered body, but which was so natural in my giant grandfather that nobody knew, in later times, that it wasn't really his (my uncle Hanif inherited this laugh; so until he died, a piece of Tai lived in Bombay). And, also from Tai, my grandfa-ther heard about noses.

Tai tapped his left nostril. 'You know what this is, nakkoo? It's the place where the outside world meets the world inside you. If they don't get on, you feel it here. Then you rub your nose with embarrassment to make the itch go away. A nose like that, little idiot, is a great gift. I say: trust it. When it warns you, look out or you'll be finished. Follow your nose and you'll go far.' He cleared his throat; his eyes rolled away into the mountains of the past. Aziz settled back on the straw. 'I knew one officer once—in the army of that Iskandar the Great. Never mind his name. He had a vegetable just like yours hanging between his eyes. When the army halted near Gandhara, he fell in love with some local floozy. At once his nose itched like crazy. He scratched it, but that was useless. He inhaled vapours from crushed boiled eucalyptus leaves. Still no good, baba! The itching sent him wild; but the damn fool dug in his heels and stayed with his little witch when the army went home. He became—what?—a stupid thing, neither this nor that, a half-and-halfer with a nagging wife and an itch in the nose, and in the end he pushed his sword into his stomach. What do you think of that?'

. . . Doctor Aziz in 1915, whom rubies and diamonds have turned into a half-and-halfer, remembers this story as Tai enters hailing distance. His nose is itching still. He scratches, shrugs, tosses his head; and then Tai shouts.

'Ohé! Doctor Sahib! Ghani the landowner's daughter is sick.'

The message, delivered curtly, shouted unceremoniously across the surface of the lake although boatman and pupil have not met for half a decade, mouthed by woman's lips that are not smiling in long-time-no-see greeting, sends time into a speeding, whirligig, blurry fluster of excitement . . .

. . . 'Just think, son,' Aadam's mother is saying as she sips fresh lime water, reclining on a takht in an attitude of resigned exhaustion, 'how life does turn out. For so many years even my ankles were a secret, and now I must be stared at by strange persons who are not even family members.'

. . . While Ghani the landowner stands beneath a large oil painting of Diana the Huntress, framed in squiggly gold. He wears thick dark glasses and his famous poisonous smile, and discusses art. 'I purchased it from an Englishman down on his luck, Doctor Sahib. Five hundred rupees only — and I did not trouble to beat him down. What are five hundred chips? You see, I am a lover of culture.'

. . . 'See, my son,' Aadam's mother is saying as he begins to examine her, 'what a mother will not do for her child. Look how I suffer. You are a doctor . . . feel these rashes, these blotchy bits, understand that my head aches morning noon and night. Refill my glass, child.'

. . . But the young Doctor has entered the throes of a most unhippocratic excitement at the boatman's cry, and shouts, 'I'm coming just now! Just let me bring my things!' The shikara's prow touches the garden's hem. Aadam is rushing indoors, prayer-mat rolled like cheroot under one arm, blue eyes blinking in the sudden interior gloom; he has placed the cheroot on a high shelf on top of stacked copies of *Vorwärts* and Lenin's *What Is To Be Done?* and other pamphlets, dusty echoes of his half-faded German life; he is pulling out, from under his bed, a second-hand leather case which his mother called his 'doctori-attaché', and as he swings it and himself upwards and runs from the room, the word HEIDELBERG is briefly visible, burned into the leather on the bottom of the bag. A landowner's daughter is good news indeed to a doctor with a career to make, even if she is ill. No: *because* she is ill.

. . . While I sit like an empty pickle jar in a pool of Anglepoised light, visited by this vision of my grandfather sixty-three years ago, which demands to be recorded, filling my nostrils with the acrid stench of his mother's embarrassment which has brought her out in boils, with the vinegary force of Aadam Aziz's determination to establish a practice so successful that she'll never have to return to the gemstone-shop, with the blind mustiness of a big shadowy house in which the young Doctor stands, ill-at-ease, before a painting of a plain girl with lively eyes and a stag transfixed behind her on the horizon, speared by a dart from her bow. Most of what matters in our lives takes place in our absence: but I seem to have found from somewhere the trick of filling in the gaps in my knowledge, so that everything is in my head, down to the last detail, such as the way the mist seemed to slant across the early morning air . . . everything, and not just the few clues one stumbles across, for instance by opening an old tin trunk which should have remained cobwebby and closed.

. . . Aadam refills his mother's glass and continues, worriedly, to examine her. 'Put some cream on these rashes and blotches, Amma. For the headache, there are pills. The boils must be lanced. But maybe if you wore purdah when you sat in the store . . . so that no disrespectful eyes could . . . such complaints often begin in the mind . . .'

. . . Slap of oar in water. Plop of spittle in lake. Tai clears his throat and mutters angrily, 'A fine business. A wet-head nakkoo child goes away before he's learned one damn thing and he comes back a big doctor sahib with a big bag full of foreign machines, and he's still as silly as an owl. I swear: a too bad business.'

. . . Doctor Aziz is shifting uneasily, from foot to foot, under the influence of the landowner's smile, in whose presence it is not possible to feel relaxed; and is waiting for some tic of reaction to his own extraordinary appearance. He has grown accustomed to these involuntary twitches of surprise at his size, his face of many colours, his nose . . . but Ghani makes no sign, and the young Doctor resolves, in return, not to let his uneasiness show. He stops shifting his weight. They face each other, each suppressing (or so it seems) his view of the other, establishing the basis of their future relationship. And now Ghani alters, changing from art-lover to tough-guy. 'This is a big chance for you, young man,' he says. Aziz's eyes have strayed to Diana. Wide expanses of her blemished pink skin are visible.

. . . His mother is moaning, shaking her head. 'No, what do you know, child, you have become a big-shot doctor but the gemstone business is different. Who would buy a turquoise from a woman hidden inside a black hood? It is a question of establishing trust. So they must look at me; and I must get pains and boils. Go, go, don't worry your head about your poor mother.'

. . . 'Big shot,' Tai is spitting into the lake, 'big bag, big shot. Pah! We haven't got enough bags at home that you must bring back that thing made of a pig's skin that makes one unclean just by looking at it? And inside, God knows what all.' Doctor Aziz, seated amongst flowery curtains and the smell of incense, has his thoughts wrenched away from the patient waiting across the lake. Tai's bitter monologue breaks into his consciousness, creating a sense of dull shock, a smell like a casualty ward overpowering the incense . . . the old man is clearly furious about something, possessed by an incomprehensible rage that appears to be directed at his erstwhile acolyte, or, more precisely and oddly, at his bag. Doctor Aziz attempts to make small talk . . . 'Your wife is well? Do they still talk about your bag of golden teeth?' . . . tries to remake an old friendship; but Tai is in full flight now, a stream of invective pouring out of him. The Heidelberg bag quakes under the torrent of abuse. 'Sistersleeping pigskin bag from Abroad full of foreigners' tricks. Big-shot bag. Now if a man breaks an arm that bag will not let the bonesetter bind it in leaves. Now a man must let his wife lie beside that bag and watch knives come and cut her open. A fine business, what these foreigners put in our young men's heads. I swear: it is a too-bad thing. That bag should fry in Hell with the testicles of the ungodly.'

. . . Ghani the landowner snaps his braces with his thumbs. 'A big chance, yes indeed. They are saying good things about you in town. Good medical training. Good . . . good enough . . . family. And now our own lady doctor is sick so you get your opportunity. That woman, always sick these days, too old, I am thinking, and not up in the latest developments also, what-what? I say: physician heal thyself. And I tell you this: I am wholly objective in my business relations. Feelings, love, I keep for my family only. If a person is not doing a first-class job for me, out she goes! You understand me? So: my daughter Naseem is not well. You will treat her excellently. Remember I have friends; and ill-health strikes high and low alike.'

. . . 'Do you still pickle water-snakes in brandy to give you virility, Taiji? Do you still like to eat lotus-root without any spices?' Hesitant questions, brushed aside by the torrent of Tai's fury. Doctor Aziz begins to diagnose. To the ferryman, the bag represents Abroad; it is the alien thing, the invader, progress. And yes, it has indeed taken possession of the young Doctor's mind; and yes, it contains knives, and cures for cholera and malaria and smallpox; and yes, it sits between doctor and boatman, and has made them antagonists. Doctor Aziz begins to fight, against sadness, and against Tai's anger, which is beginning to infect him, to become his own, which erupts only rarely, but comes, when it does come, unheralded in a roar from his deepest places, laying waste everything in sight; and then vanishes, leaving him wondering why everyone is so upset . . . They are approaching Ghani's house. A bearer awaits the shikara, standing with clasped hands on a little wooden jetty. Aziz fixes his mind on the job in hand.

. . . 'Has your usual doctor agreed to my visit, Ghani Sahib?' . . . Again, a hesitant question is brushed lightly aside. The landowner says, 'Oh, she will agree. Now follow me, please.'

. . . The bearer is waiting on the jetty. Holding the shikara steady as Aadam Aziz climbs out, bag in hand. And now, at last, Tai speaks directly to my grandfather. Scorn in his face, Tai asks, 'Tell me this, Doctor Sahib: have you got in that bag made of dead pigs one of those machines that foreign doctors use to smell with?' Aadam shakes his head, not understanding. Tai's voice gathers new layers of disgust. 'You know, sir, a thing like an elephant's trunk.' Aziz, seeing what he means, replies: 'A stethoscope? Naturally.' Tai pushes the shikara off from the jetty. Spits. Begins to row away. 'I knew it,' he says, 'You will use such a machine now, instead of your own big nose.'

My grandfather does not trouble to explain that a stethoscope is more like a pair of ears than a nose. He is stifling his own irritation, the resentful anger of a cast-off child; and besides, there is a patient waiting. Time settles down and concentrates on the importance of the moment.

The house was opulent but badly lit. Ghani was a widower and the servants clearly took advantage. There were cobwebs in corners and layers of dust on ledges. They walked down a long corridor; one of the doors was ajar and through it Aziz saw a room in a state of violent disorder. This glimpse, connected with a glint of light in Ghani's dark glasses, suddenly informed Aziz that the landowner was blind. This aggravated his sense of unease: a blind man who claimed to appreciate European paintings? He was, also, impressed, because Ghani hadn't bumped into anything . . . they halted outside a thick teak door. Ghani said, 'Wait here two moments', and went into the room behind the door.

In later years, Doctor Aadam Aziz swore that during those two moments of solitude in the gloomy spidery corridors of the landowner's mansion he was gripped by an almost uncontrollable desire to turn and run away as fast as his legs would carry him. Unnerved by the enigma of the blind art-lover, his insides filled with tiny scrabbling insects as a result of the insidious venom of Tai's mutterings, his nostrils itching to the point of convincing him that he had somehow contracted venereal disease, he felt his feet begin slowly, as though. encased in boots of lead, to turn; felt blood pounding in his temples; and was seized by so powerful a sensation of standing upon a point of no return that he very nearly wet his German woollen trousers. He began, without knowing it, to blush furiously; and at this point his mother appeared before him, seated on the floor before a low desk, a rash spreading like a blush across her face as she held a turquoise up to the light. His mother's face had acquired all the scorn of the boatman Tai. 'Go, go, run,' she told him in Tai's voice, 'Don't worry about your poor old mother.' Doctor Aziz found himself stammering, 'What a useless son you've got, Amma; can't you see there's a hole in the middle of me the size of a melon?' His mother smiled a pained smile. 'You always were a heartless boy,' she sighed, and then turned into a lizard on the wall of the corridor and stuck her tongue out at him. Doctor Aziz stopped feeling dizzy, became unsure that he'd actually spoken aloud, wondered what he'd meant by that business about the hole, found that his feet were no longer trying to escape, and realized that he was being watched. A woman with the biceps of a wrestler was staring at him, beckoning him to follow her into the room. The state of her sari told him that she was a servant; but she was not servile. 'You look green as a fish,' she said. 'You young doctors. You come into a strange house and your liver turns to jelly. Come, Doctor Sahib, they are waiting for you.' Clutching his bag a fraction too tightly, he followed her through the dark teak door.

. . . Into a spacious bedchamber that was as ill-lit as the rest of the house; although here there were shafts of dusty sunlight seeping in through a fanlight high on one wall. These fusty rays illuminated a scene as remarkable as anything the Doctor had ever witnessed: a tableau of such surpassing strangeness that his feet began to twitch towards the door once again. Two more women, also built like professional wrestlers, stood stiffly in the light, each holding one corner of an enormous white bedsheet, their arms raised high above their heads so that the sheet hung between them like a curtain. Mr Ghani welled up out of the murk surrounding the sunlit sheet and permitted the nonplussed Aadam to stare stupidly at the peculiar tableau for perhaps half a minute, at the end of which, and before a word had been spoken, the Doctor made a discovery:

In the very centre of the sheet, a hole had been cut, a crude circle about seven inches in diameter.

'Close the door, ayah,' Ghani instructed the first of the lady wrestlers, and then, turning to Aziz, became confidential. 'This town contains many good-for-nothings who have on occasion tried to climb into my daughter's room. She needs,' he nodded at the three musclebound women, 'protectors.'

Aziz was still looking at the perforated sheet. Ghani said, 'All right, come on, you will examine my Naseem right now. *Pronto.*'

My grandfather peered around the room. 'But where is she, Ghani Sahib?' he blurted out finally. The lady wrestlers adopted supercilious expressions and, it seemed to him, tightened their musculatures, just in case he intended to try something fancy.

'Ah, I see your confusion,' Ghani said, his poisonous smile broadening, 'You Europe-returned chappies forget certain things. Doctor Sahib, my daughter is a decent girl, it goes without saying. She does not flaunt her body under the noses of strange men. You will understand that you cannot be permitted to see her, no, not in any circumstances; accordingly I have required her to be positioned behind that sheet. She stands there, like a good girl.'

A frantic note had crept into Doctor Aziz's voice, 'Ghani Sahib, tell me how I am to examine her without looking at her?' Ghani smiled on.

'You will kindly specify which portion of my daughter it is necessary to inspect. I will then issue her with my instructions to place the required segment against that hole which you see there. And so, in this fashion the thing may be achieved.'

'But what, in any event, does the lady complain of?'—my grandfather, despairingly. To which Mr Ghani, his eyes rising upwards in their sockets, his smile twisting into a grimace of grief, replied: 'The poor child! She has a terrible, a too dreadful stomach-ache.'

'In that case,' Doctor Aziz said with some restraint, 'will she show me her stomach, please.'

2

China

■

INTRODUCTION

China is the world's most populous nation, with more than 1.2 billion people, about a fifth of the world's inhabitants. It is dominated by a majority population of Han Chinese, but it contains many minority groups, including the Mongols, the Uigurs, the Hui, the Miao, the Koreans, the Tibetans, the Yi, and the Chuang. Since the second millennium B.C., Chinese civilization has patterned itself into a series of empires that flourished, weakened, and were overthrown—often by peasant revolts or barbarian invaders from the north—and then reestablished in a different form, often by invaders who assimilated Chinese culture and administration. Despite political upheavals, China has produced superb literary works through three millennia. Like Greece in the West, China's civilization—its culture, inventions, and spirit—has profoundly affected neighboring countries since ancient times, especially its extraordinary literature. Its poetry, at times ornate, at times chastely plain, at times deeply personal, even confessional, at times purely objective, is its major literary genre. In the twentieth century, classical Chinese poetry has been translated into European languages, where its conversational, intimate, and imagistic pastoral modes have permeated and changed the course of Western poetry, especially that in the United States and France.

The Shang dynasty (c. 1523–1027 B.C.) is the first kingdom documented in Chinese history, though it is traditionally thought to have been the successor to an earlier kingdom called the Xia dynasty. China's ancient tradition of writing originated in the Shang dynasty. Antecedents of modern characters have been found in divinitory rites inscribed on ox bones, tortoise shells, and bronze vessels that go back to 1400 B.C. The sophistication of this system of writing suggests an even earlier origin. Ancient Chinese books were written on strips of bamboo, then on silk from the second century B.C. to the second century A.D., when paper was invented. Printing on fixed wooden blocks was developed during the Tang dynasty (616–906) and on moveable blocks in the eleventh century, four centuries before printing emerged in the West. The fact that Chinese script was originally pictographic, though with phonetic values, helped it to spread across the huge expanse of China, where it aided communication between people speaking radically different dialects.

In 1027 B.C., the Shang dynasty was overthrown by the king of Zhou, a small dependent nation in the west of Shang territory. During the Zhou dynasty (c. 1027–221 B.C.), the doctrine that the Chinese king was exercising a "Mandate of Heaven" in his rule developed. This later became an extremely important doctrine both to justify imperial rule and to explain the fall of an empire (should an emperor prove corrupt or weak, Heaven would remove its mandate). During this period, the great philosophers Confucius and Mencius produced their major works on ethics, and *The Book of Songs,* the earliest anthology of Chinese poetry and one of the Confucian classics, was collected. Legend says *The Book of Songs* was edited by Confucius himself from a larger, earlier corpus (thus it is sometimes known as *The Confucian Odes*). It was also in the first millennium B.C. that the other texts that were to make up the core of the Confucian classics were composed, including *The Book of Changes, The Book of Rights, The Book of History,* and *The Spring and Autumn Annals.*

The changing canon of the Confucian classics (which has at various times numbered as few as five and as many as thirteen books) has been the basis for the Chinese educational system from the second century B.C. to the early decades of the twentieth century. A thorough grounding in the moral precepts, historical examples, divinitory rights, and poetry contained in the classics was the essential preparation for a person pursuing an administrative career. The roots of the Chinese civil service system go back to the first imperial dynasty, the Qin dynasty (221–207 B.C.), ruled over by Emperor Qin Shi Huang Di, who brought the fragmented and warring states of China under one rule. This "first emperor" of China is notorious for decreeing that all books deemed threatening to the new order be burned. However, he also built the Great Wall and presided over a short-lived empire, the predecessor of a series of dynasties that—despite invasions from the north, peasant revolts, and periods of fragmentation—were to unite Chinese culture into a two-thousand-year tradition. It is perhaps most important that he created a system of political and social promotion based on ability versus nobility. Later, in the Sui dynasty (589–607), this system was augmented with a system of standardized examinations that applicants must pass for promotion. Though applicants of greater wealth had a distinct advantage (having had access to greater educational opportunities), the Chinese civil service system, which existed in various forms for more than two thousand years, has been the world's most successful and long-lived system of more-or-less egalitarian social promotion and was the basis for the British civil service system. Through this system there developed a literate class of scholar officials who had mastered the same essential knowledge, giving Chinese civilization a coherence and continuity that belie its political history of fragmentation, foreign invasion, civil war, and the rise and fall of dynasties.

This same commonality of knowledge has lent a somewhat insular aspect to Chinese literature, seen in the high use of literary allusion. A Confucian respect for the past has also fostered a Chinese esthetic of virtuoso performance within handed-down forms and genres. Strong reverence for tradition has led to periods of literary stagnation at times, but it is balanced by a counter-Confucian Chinese tradition of the innovative outsider. In the words of a commentator in *Poets' Jade Splinters,* a Song dynasty compilation of literary critiques, "The first taboo in writing is to walk behind others."

During the Zhou dynasty, two perhaps mythical men, Laozi and Zhuangzi, are said to have written paradoxical and mystical texts that were to become the core of the Daoist tradition. An ancient counterpoint to Confucian duty, morality, and politics was set down around the third century B.C. in these basic texts, the *Dao de Jing* and the *Zhuangzi.* Daoism celebrates whimsy, spontaneity, paradox, and a supreme good that is metaphysical (as opposed to the Confucian moral good). With its disdain for duty, power, and politics, Daoism is an ancient counter-tradition that has been central to the developing character of China.

Buddhism has been a third important philosophical and religious tradition in China. Both Theravada and Mahayana Buddhism came to China from Indian and central Asia around the second century A.D. At first Buddhism's influence was small, but its philosophy of the suffering in and impermanence of the mundane world caught on in the fourth century as China suffered war, invasion, and political and economic turbulence. Inevitably, Chinese Buddhists came to write their own compositions, some of which became scriptures for various Chinese Buddhist sects. Buddhist influence on literature owes much to the development of Chan (which in Japanese becomes Zen), a school that came to accept poetry as a form of religious expression. Great Chinese Buddhist poets include Han Shan and Wang Wei; great Japanese Buddhist writers include Saigyo, Kenko, Basho, and Ryokan. It should be understood that despite doctrinal differences, Buddhism and Daoism were mutually influential in China, and it was not uncommon for a poet such as Wang Wei to look back with equal reverence to his Daoist predecessor Tao Yuanming (365–427) and to the revered Indian lay Buddhist Vimalakirti.

Since poetry has been the mainstream of literary expression in Chinese literature, it is often afforded great powers of influence in the Chinese critical tradition, as in the "Great Preface" to *The Book of Songs.* The preface states that poetry is a Confucian rectifier that sets the proper relationships between spouses, establishes respect and loyalty for the old, strengthens human ties, ameliorates civilizations, and excises bad customs. Poetry is even afforded Daoist cosmic powers in texts such as Lu Ji's *The Art of Writing:* "With heaven and earth contained in your head/nothing escapes the pen in your hand."

Chinese metrics are based on the number of characters per line, each character being one phonetic syllable. Rhyme and rhythm have aesthetic value and also the semantic function of dividing and organizing units of meaning (especially important, since Chinese poetry was unpunctuated until modern times). These formal ways of organizing meaning also help the reader to decipher the text. As the Chinese poet was a renaissance man or woman, skilled in diverse arts, Chinese poetry is a total art, often chanted or set to music, or calligraphically inscribed on paintings, screens, fans, or stone. In contrast to poetry in phonetic alphabets, Chinese poetics is built upon characters. Chinese characters, though popularly thought of in the West as wholly pictographic, are a combination of pictographic, phonetic, and ideographic elements. In part, a Chinese character, like the Arabic numeral, conveys meaning rather than sound, which has permitted it to be used by diversely pronounced dialects from all centuries, and even to be adopted into Korean and Japanese. In addition to simple pictographic and ideographic and phonetic characters, more complex characters developed through the combination of these elements: hence the sun and moon characters when combined make up the character for brightness (*ming*). At times, the visual and ideographic elements in the characters allow the poet to create radical condensation of meaning, to pun, to create ironies, and to convey pictures and ideas largely unavailable to poets restricted to phonetic alphabets. In the West, only the highly experimental visual poetics of Guillaume Apollinaire's *Calligrammes,* the typographical forays of the Dada poets, the shaped poems of George Herbert and his medieval precursors, and the picture poems of contemporary Concrete poets attempt to merge image and meaning in a comparable fashion.

Qu Yuan (third century B.C.) was the first Chinese poet whose name we know. His works are collected in the second most ancient collection of Chinese poetry, *The Songs of Chu,* and are celebrated for their Confucian dedication to duty and creation of a subjective and suffering persona, who bewails his personal condition. The Han dynasty (206 B.C.–A.D. 220) is notable for its rhyme-prose (*fu*), a form of mixed prose and poetry, and for the folk ballads (*yuefu*) gathered by the Music Bureau. The great poet of the Six Dynasties period (220–589) was Tao Yuanming (365 or 372–427), whose poems of paradisal country retreat from the scholar-official's career make him China's Thoreau and a model for later poets. The golden age of Chinese poetry was the Tang dynasty (618–907). Its three major poets were the stylistic master and Confucian social commentator Du Fu (712–770), the Daoist romantic drunkard Li Bai (701–762), and the Daoist-Buddhist nature poet Wang Wei (701–761). The Tang also produced a corpus of poetry by extraordinary women poets, including Yu

Xuanji (c. 843–868) and Xue Tao (768–831), as well as masterpieces in the Chinese short story, a minor form until then.

China's dynasties were continually threatened by invaders from the north, and, in the Song dynasty (960–1279), an invasion of the Manchurian Jurchens conquered northern China. In the Song dynasty, *ci* poems, a form of poetry set to melodies from central Asia, became extremely popular, and master poets emerged, including Ouyang Xiu (1007–1072), Su Dongpo (1036–1101), and Li Qingzhao (1084–c. 1151), among others. In the thirteenth century, Genghis Khan's Mongols invaded China and captured the north in 1234. In 1279, under Genghis Khan's grandson Kublai Khan, the Mongols overran the south, where the Southern Song dynasty had been stubbornly holding out. The succeeding Yuan dynasty (1280–1367) was ruled by Mongols, who incorporated much of the Chinese administrative system into their rule. During the Yuan dynasty, drama containing poetry flourished. During the Ming (1368–1644) and Qing (1644–1911) dynasties, the novel became prominent, with great works such as the fantastic, picaresque voyages of *Monkey,* the martial epic of *Three Kingdoms,* the erotic classic *The Golden Lotus,* and the dynastic epic *Dream of the Red Chamber.* The Qing dynasty was yet another period in which China was ruled by northern invaders, this time by the Manchus, a Manchurian tribe descended from the Jurchens.

The modern era was marked by humiliating interactions with Western and Eastern colonial powers. In the nineteenth century, China was forced to surrender Hong Kong to the British; open itself to trade, unequal treaties, and the importation of opium; and also allow the establishment of foreign zones in Shanghai, which were under extraterritorial administration. The Chinese imperial system fell in 1911 to a revolution that established a republic in China under the rule of Sun Yatsen. There followed a pattern of incursions from Japan that culminated in the occupation of Manchuria in 1931 and the invasion of China in 1937. Mao Zedong began his revolution in 1926, and after twenty-three years of civil war, on October 1, 1949, a new dynasty began in Beijing under Communist rule. During these turbulent times prior to the Communist revolution, the Chinese literati system was abolished, and Chinese intellectuals turned increasingly to Western models in their poetry, essays, and fiction. Some adopted a romantic/modernist estheticism, while others, like Lu Xun (1881–1936), wrote short stories with a radical agenda.

With Communist rule came a new era in China and for Chinese writers. At his *Talks at the Yenan Forum on Literature and Art,* Mao Zedong set out the basis for acceptable literature under Marxism: art and literature are for the masses, should be about them as well, and have the purpose of "producing works that awaken the masses, fire them with enthusiasm, and impel them to unite and struggle to transform the environment." This doctrine paralleled the strictures placed upon writing in 1932 by the Union of Soviet Writers, which proclaimed Socialist Realism as a compulsory literary practice. However, in China this doctrine produced little work of lasting value, and literature went into an eclipse for decades. In successive political moments, the Anti-Rightist Campaign (1957) and the Cultural Revolution (1966–1976), writers, artists, and intellectuals suffered severe governmental repression. After the death of Mao in 1976, the arts in China began to flourish again, along with a nascent Democracy Movement that many writers were associated with in its various incarnations. In recent years, waves of repression and censorship culminated in the Tiananmen Square massacre in 1989, in which the army was called in to disperse Democracy Movement protestors, hundreds of whom were killed. Many Chinese writers have gone into exile since then.

Zhou Dynasty

(1027–221 B.C.)

■ The Book of Songs (c. 600 B.C.) (poems)

The Book of Songs is the earliest anthology of Chinese poetry and the thematic and formal source of the Chinese poetic tradition. The Chinese name for *The Book of Songs* is the *Shi Jing,* and the term *shi* (the general term for poetry, like the Japanese *waka*) derives from its name. Legend has it that its three hundred and five anonymous poems were compiled by Confucius (551–479 B.C.) from an earlier manuscript of around three thousand songs. The assertion that Confucius was the compiler is questionable, but certainly the anthology was extant in Confucius' time, and it seems likely that the anthology was collected between 1100 and 600 B.C. Confucius refers to *The Book of Songs* in the *Analects,* and it was part of the curriculum of his disciples; it is counted among the Confucian classics that form the basis of Confucian education. The collection was banned in the third century B.C., along with the other Confucian classics during the Qin dynasty's "burning of the books," but it was reconstructed during the Han dynasty, and the recension that is most complete derives from this time. *The Book of Songs* contains three basic categories of song: folk songs and ballads, court songs, and songs to accompany ritual dancing and the rites of ancestor worship. Like the Sanskrit Vedas, these songs provide a window onto the simple and beautiful life of an ancient time. Heroes and ancestors are praised; love is made; war is waged; farmers sing to their crops; people complain about their taxes; and moral categories are set forth in stark and powerful forms. Though these poems are songs, the music has been lost. Some of them have been revised from folksong roots by court musicians, rhymed, and arranged into stanzas.

FURTHER READING: Karlgren, Bernhard. *The Book of Odes,* 1950. Legge, James. *The Chinese Classics,* Vol. 3, 1960. McNaughton, William. *The Book of Songs,* 1971. Pound, Ezra. *The Classic Anthology as Defined by Confucius,* 1954. Waley, Arthur. *The Book of Songs,* 1937. Wang, C. H. *The Bell and the Drum: Shih Ching as Formulaic Poetry in an Oral Tradition,* 1974.

In the Wilds Is a Dead River-Deer

In the wilds is a dead river-deer
wrapped in white rushes.
A lady yearned for spring
and a fine man seduced her.

In the woods are clusters of bushes   5
and in the wilds a dead river-deer
wrapped in white rushes.
There was a lady fine as jade.

Oh! Slow down, don't be so rough,
let go of my girdle's sash.   10
Shhh! You'll make the dog bark.

TRANSLATED BY TONY BARNSTONE AND CHOU PING

Fruit Plummets from the Plum Tree

Fruit plummets from the plum tree
but seven of ten plums remain;
you gentlemen who would court me,
come on a lucky day.

Fruit plummets from the plum tree   5
but three of ten plums still remain;
you men who want to court me,
come now, today is a lucky day!

Fruit plummets from the plum tree.
You can fill up your baskets.   10

Gentlemen if you want to court me,
just say the word.

TRANSLATED BY TONY BARNSTONE AND CHOU PING

White Moonrise

The white rising moon
is your bright beauty
binding me in spells
till my heart's devoured.

The light moon soars   5
resplendent like my lady,
binding me in light chains
till my heart's devoured.

Moon in white glory,
you are the beautiful one   10
who delicately wounds me
till my heart's devoured.

TRANSLATED BY TONY BARNSTONE AND WILLIS BARNSTONE

Ripe Millet[1]

Rows and rows of ripe millet,
the sorghum sprouts,
and I take long slow walks
with a shaking, shaken heart.
My friends say   5
"His heart is hurting"
but strangers wonder
"What can he be looking for?"

---

1. According to the "Preface" of *The Book of Songs,* the poet is a minister of the Eastern Zhou dynasty (770–256 B.C.). He comes to the capital city of the earlier Western Zhou dynasty (tenth century–771 B.C.) and finds all the temples are destroyed and the royal palace is replaced by rows and rows of millet. Moved by time's ravages, he improvises this poem.

O far far blue heaven
what makes me feel this way?   *10*

Rows and rows of ripe millet,
the sorghum is in spike,
and I take long slow walks
with a drunken heart.
My friends say   *15*
"His heart is hurting"
but strangers wonder
"What can he be looking for?"
O far far blue heaven
what makes me feel this way?   *20*

Rows and rows of ripe millet,
the sorghum is all grain,
and I take long slow walks
with a choking heart.
My friends say   *25*
"His heart is hurting"
but strangers wonder
"What can he be looking for?"
O far far blue heaven
what makes me feel this way?   *30*

TRANSLATED BY TONY BARNSTONE AND CHOU PING

There Are Tall Weeds in the Fields

There are tall weeds in the fields
with glistening dew drops.
Here comes a beautiful girl
with eyes like clear water.
We meet here by chance—   *5*
just as I wished.

Here are tall weeds in the fields
with sparking dew drops.
There comes a beautiful girl,
graceful as her eyes.   *10*
We meet here by chance—
let's find a place and hide.

TRANSLATED BY TONY BARNSTONE AND CHOU PING

When the Gourd Has Dried Leaves[1]

When the gourd has dried leaves,
you can wade the deep river.
Keep your clothes on if the water's deep;
hitch up your dress when it's shallow.

The river is rising,   5
pheasants are chirping.
The water is just half a wheel deep,
and the hen is chirping for the cock.

Wild geese are trilling,
the rising sun starts dawn.   10
If you want to marry me,
come before the river is frozen.

The ferry-man is gesturing,
other people are going, but not me,
other people are going, but not me,   15
I'm waiting for you.

TRANSLATED BY TONY BARNSTONE AND CHOU PING

All the Grasslands Are Yellow

All the grasslands are yellow
and all the days we march
and all the men are conscripts
sent off in four directions.

All the grasslands are black   5
and all the men like widowers.
So much grief! Are soldiers
not men like other men?

We aren't bison! We aren't tigers
crossing the wilderness,   10
but our sorrows
roam from dawn till dusk.

Hairy tailed foxes slink
through the dark grass

---

1. The ancient Chinese used to tie gourds around their waists as a safety device when wading across a river.

as we ride tall chariots   *15*
along the wide rutted roads.

TRANSLATED BY TONY BARNSTONE AND CHOU PING

◼ Confucius (c. 551–479 B.C.) (philosophy)

TRANSLATED BY RAYMOND DAWSON

Confucius is a distant romanization of the Chinese name Kong and the appellation Fuzi, meaning "master" (thus Confucius = Master Kong). Definite evidence about the life of Confucius is scant and legends abound, so modern scholars have tried to detect the man through internal evidence in *The Analects* (a collection of his dialogues and utterances probably recorded by his disciples after his death). Confucius was born in humble circumstances in what is today Shandong province, in the feudal state of Lu, at a time of incessant warfare among the Chinese states. The Zhou dynasty had broken into warring factions, and Confucius sought to restore the lost peace and to guide governments in how to rule fairly and well; he proposed a system of conduct for all people based on an ultimate principle of *ren,* or humanism, goodness. This humanism is to be expressed through etiquette and ritual, or *li;* a government based on such moral principles and order will be reflected in the behavior of its populace. Underlings should be loyal to their rulers, yet critical of them when they part from the Way (*Dao*), and people should behave with empathy for one another: "Do not inflict on others what you yourself would not wish done to you." One should practice self-control and respect for ancestors and behave correctly to family, with a sense of deep filial respect. Family relations function as a microcosm of those of the state.

Confucius had a dream of an ideal society, with virtuous, hardworking people ruled over by incorruptible, wise, and benevolent officials—a system of order and mutual respect. His vision had as profound an effect on Chinese government and ethics as the laws of Manu did on India, as the ancient legal code of the Babylonian king Hammurabi did on the Judeo-Christian tradition, or Plato's dialogic vision on Western civilization. A distinguishing feature of his philosophy is that religion has no part in it, though his thought was later distorted to incorporate supernatural elements and to support tyrannical governments. Confucius never achieved the sort of important position he coveted, despite years of wandering China to spread his ideas and to convince rulers to accept his reforms; but his disciples did, and they spread his thought so successfully that a Confucian education became the essential preparation for entry into the Chinese scholar bureaucracy. *The Analects* of Confucius is only one of a number of Confucian classics, whose memorization was the moral and intellectual grounding of the Confucian path of study. The classics include such texts as *The Book of Songs* and *The Book of Changes,* and their total number varies between five and thirteen, depending on what source and dynasty is studied. In the first century A.D., a practice began of offering sacrifices and veneration in shrines devoted to Confucius, a practice that has continued through this century. It has been eclipsed at times by other systems of order and religion and was banned in 213 B.C. by the first Qin emperor. But the Confucian canon was reconstructed by Emperor Wu in 136 B.C., and at several times in Chinese history, it became a state religion.

FURTHER READING: Creel, H. G. *Confucius: The Man and the Myth,* 1951. Dawson, Raymond, tr. *Confucius: The Analects,* 1993. Hall, D. L., and R. T. Ames. *Thinking through Confucius,* 1987. Lau, D.C., tr. *Confucius: The Analects,* 1979. Waley, Arthur, tr. *The Analects of Confucius,* 1938.

from *The Analects*

Book 1

2. Master You[1] said: 'Few indeed are those who are naturally filial towards their parents and dutiful towards their elder brothers but are fond of opposing their superiors; and it never happens that those who do not like opposing their superiors are fond of creating civil disorder.[2] The gentleman concerns himself with the root; and if the root is firmly planted, the Way grows. Filial piety and fraternal duty—surely they are the roots of humaneness.'

3. The Master said: 'Clever words and a plausible appearance have seldom turned out to be humane.'

6. The Master said: 'Young men should be filial when at home and respectful to elders when away from home. They should be earnest and trustworthy. Although they should love the multitude far and wide, they should be intimate only with the humane. If they have any energy to spare after so doing, they should use it to study "culture".'

11. The Master said: 'When his father is alive, you observe a man's intentions. It is when the father is dead that you observe the man's actions. If

---

1. You Ruo is generally referred to as Master You, and he makes his own pronouncements instead of merely putting questions to Master Kong. Clearly he was a teacher in the Confucian tradition.

2. This sentence is an expression of what later became the standard Confucian view that the political virtues of obedience and loyalty are family virtues writ large.

for three years he makes no change from the ways of his father, he may be called filial.'

16. The Master said: 'One does not worry about the fact that other people do not appreciate one. One worries about not appreciating other people.'

Book 2

2. The Master said: 'The *Songs* number three hundred, but I will cover their meaning with a single quotation: "Let there be no depravity in your thoughts."'[3]

3. The Master said: 'If you lead them by means of government and keep order among them by means of punishments, the people are without conscience in evading them. If you lead them by means of virtue and keep order among them by means of ritual, they have a conscience and moreover will submit.'

11. The Master said: 'If by keeping the old warm one can provide understanding of the new, one is fit to be a teacher.'

12. The Master said: 'A gentleman does not behave as an implement.'[4]

17. The Master said: 'You,[5] shall I teach you about understanding something? When you understand something, to recognize that you understand it; but when you do not understand something, to recognize that you do not understand it—that is understanding.'

19. Duke Ai[6] asked: 'What action does one take so that the people will be obedient?' Master Kong replied saying: 'If you promote the straight and set them above the crooked, then the people will be obedient. If you promote the crooked and set them above the straight, then the people will not be obedient.'

---

3. The *Songs* are *The Book of Songs,* one of the Confucian classics [Editor].

4. This important saying puts in a nutshell the belief that the gentleman's training should not be confined to particular skills so that he may become the tool or implement of others. It must instead develop his moral qualities and powers of leadership. Thus in the later Empire the traditional Chinese education for government service was concerned with the study of Confucian writings rather than with the acquisition of techniques.

5. The personal name of the well-known disciple Zilu, whose character shines clearly through this motley collection of sayings and anecdotes. He was an extrovert man of action and not very fond of learning. Often the exchanges between Zilu and Master Kong, brief though they are, shed an amusing light on the character of Zilu and the Master's attitude towards him.

6. Ruler of Lu between 494 and 468 [B.C.]. The actual power was in the hands of the Three Families, so presumably this was said when he was planning to try to regain power.

22. The Master said: 'If someone is untrustworthy in spite of being a man, I do not know what he will do. If carriages have no means of yoking horses to them, how are they ever made to go?'

Book 4

5. The Master said: 'Riches and honours—these are what men desire, but if this is not achieved in accordance with the appropriate principles, one does not cling to them. Poverty and obscurity—these are what men hate, but if this is not achieved in accordance with the appropriate principles, one does not avoid them. If a gentleman abandons humaneness, how does he make a reputation? The gentleman never shuns humaneness even for the time it takes to finish a meal. If his progress is hasty, it is bound to arise from this; and if his progress is unsteady, it is bound to arise from this.'

8. The Master said: 'If one has heard the Way in the morning, it is all right to die in the evening.'

14. The Master said: 'One is not worried about not holding position; one is worried about how one may fit oneself for appointment. One is not worried that nobody knows one; one seeks to become fit to be known.'

16. The Master said: 'The gentleman is familiar with what is right, just as the small man is familiar with profit.'

17. The Master said: 'When you come across a superior person, think of being equal to him. When you come across an inferior person, turn inwards and examine yourself.'

18. The Master said: 'In serving father and mother, one remonstrates gently. If one sees that they are intent on not following advice, one continues to be respectful and does not show disobedience; and even if one finds it burdensome, one does not feel resentful.'

23. The Master said: 'There are few indeed who fail in something through exercising restraint.'

24. The Master said: 'The gentleman wishes to be slow in speech but prompt in action.'

25. The Master said: 'Virtue is not solitary. It is bound to have neighbours.'

Book 5

1. The Master said of Gongye Chang that he might be given a wife for, although he had been put in prison, this was not through any crime of his. He gave him his own daughter in marriage.

9. The Master said to Zigong[7]: 'Out of You and Hui which is the better?' He replied: 'How dare I even have a look at Hui? Hui is the sort of person who, by hearing one thing, understands ten; but I am the sort of person who, by hearing one thing, understands two.' The Master said: 'You are not as good as he is. Both you and I are not as good as he is.'

12. Zigong said: 'If I do not want others to inflict something on me, I also want to avoid inflicting it on others.' The Master said: 'Si, this is not a point you have yet reached.'

20. Ji Wen Zi thought three times before acting. When the Master heard of this, he said: 'Twice will do.'

24. The Master said: 'Who says that Weisheng Gao[8] was upright? Someone begged vinegar from him and he begged it from his neighbour and handed it over.'

Book 6

11. The Master said: 'A man of quality indeed was Hui! He lived in a squalid alley with a tiny bowlful of rice to eat and a ladleful of water to drink. Other men would not endure such hardships, but Hui did not let his happiness be affected. A man of quality indeed was Hui!'

23. The Master said: 'The wise delight in water, but the humane delight in mountains. For although the wise are active, the humane are at rest. And although the wise will find joy, the humane will have long life.'

Book 7

19. The Duke of She asked Zilu about Master Kong. Zilu did not reply. The Master said: 'Why did you not just say that he is the sort of person who gets so worked up that he forgets to eat, is so happy that he forgets anxieties, and is not aware that old age will come.'

---

7. Zigong was one of Confucius' best-known disciples. He is also referred to as Si . . . [Editor].

8. He was so insistent on keeping his promises that, having said he would meet his girlfriend in the dried-up bed of a stream, he drowned because the water rose before she turned up; but Master Kong had apparently heard something less flattering about him.

37. The Master said: 'The gentleman is calm and peaceful; the small man is always emotional.'

38. The Master was genial and yet strict, imposing and yet not intimidating, courteous and yet at ease.

Book 8

8. The Master said: 'One is roused by the Songs, established by ritual, and perfected by music.'

9. The Master said: 'The people may be made to follow something, but may not be made to understand it.'

21. The Master said: 'In Yu it seems there is no fault as far as I am concerned. Although he ate and drank abstemiously, he displayed the utmost devotion[9] towards the ghosts and spirits. Although normally he wore poor garments, he displayed the utmost elegance in his sacrificial robes and headdress. He lived in humble dwellings, but devoted all his energies to drains and ditches. In Yu it seems there is no fault as far as I am concerned.'

Book 9

2. A villager from Daxiang said: 'Great indeed is Master Kong, but despite his broad learning there is nothing for which he has made a reputation.' When the Master heard this, he told his disciples: 'What do I take up? Do I take up charioteering?[10] Or do I take up archery? I take up charioteering.'

11. Yan Hui, sighing heavily, said: 'The more I look up to it,[11] the higher it is; the more I penetrate it, the harder it becomes; I see it ahead of me and suddenly it is behind. Our Master skilfully lures people on step by step. He broadens me with culture and restrains me with ritual. If I wanted to stop, I could not; and when I have exhausted all my talents, it seems as if there is something which he has established profoundly; but even though I long to pursue it, I have no way of doing so at all.'

14. The Master wished to dwell among the nine wild tribes of the East. Someone said: 'They are uncivilized, so what will you do about that?'

---

9. In supplying plentiful sacrificial food in contrast with his own personal abstemiousness.

10. A sarcastic response to the failure to appreciate that the gentleman is a generalist rather than a specialist.

11. Master Kong's teaching. This is a classic account of the disciples' admiration.

The Master said: 'If a gentleman dwelt among them, what lack of civility would they show?'

18. The Master said: 'I have never come across anyone who admires virtue as much as he admires sexual attraction.'

26. The Master said: 'The three armies can be robbed of their commander, but an ordinary person cannot be robbed of his purpose.'

Book 10

11. When the stables caught fire the Master, on returning from court, said: 'Did anyone get hurt?' He did not ask about the horses.

Book 11

9. When Yan Hui[12] died, the Master said: 'Alas, Heaven has bereaved me, Heaven has bereaved me!'

10. When Yan Hui died, the Master became distressed as he bewailed him. His followers said: 'Master, you have become distressed.' 'Have I?' he said. 'Well, if that man is not to be the object of my distress, then for whom am I to be distressed?'

Book 12

2. Zhonggong[13] asked about humaneness. The Master said: 'When you are away from home, behave as if receiving an important guest. Employ the people as if you were officiating at a great sacrifice. Do not impose on others what you would not like yourself. Then there will be no resentment against you, either in the state or in the family.' Zhonggong said: 'Although I am not clever, I beg to put this advice into practice.'

3. Sima Niu[14] asked about humaneness. The Master said: 'The humane person is hesitant in his speech.' He said: 'Hesitant in his speech! Is that all that is meant by humaneness?' The Master said: 'To do it is difficult, so in speaking about it can one avoid being hesitant?'

7. Zigong asked about government. The Master said: 'If there is enough food and if there are enough weapons, the people will put their trust in

---

12. Yan Hui was Confucius' favorite disciple [Editor].

13. Zhonggong (alias Ran Yong) was a disciple [Editor].

14. Sima Niu was a disciple [Editor].

it.' Zigong said: 'Suppose you definitely had no alternative but to give up one of these three, which would you relinquish first?' The Master said: 'I would give up weapons.' Zigong said: 'Suppose you definitely had no alternative but to give up one of the remaining two, which would you relinquish first?' The Master said: 'I would give up food. From of old death has come to all men, but a people will not stand if it lacks trust.'

8. Ji Zicheng said: 'A gentleman is merely the stuff he is made of. Why take account of culture?' Zigong said: 'It is a pity you said that, sir, about the gentleman, since a team of four horses will not catch up with the tongue. Culture is just as important as the stuff one is made of, and the stuff one is made of is just as important as culture. The skin of a tiger or leopard is no different from the skin of a dog or a sheep.'

17. Ji Kang Zi[15] asked Master Kong about government. Master Kong replied: 'To govern means to correct. If you take the lead by being correct, who will dare not to be corrected?'

19. Ji Kang Zi asked Master Kong about government, saying: 'Suppose I were to kill those who lack the Way in order to advance those who have the Way, how would that be?' Master Kong replied: 'You are running the government, so what is the point of killing? If you desire good, the people will be good. The nature of the gentleman is as the wind, and the nature of the small man is as the grass. When the wind blows over the grass it always bends.'

22. Fan Chi[16] asked about humaneness. The Master said: 'It is to love others.' He asked about understanding. The Master said: 'It is to understand others.' Fan Chi had not yet fathomed his meaning, so the Master said: 'If one raises the straight and puts them above the crooked one can make the crooked become straight.'

Book 13

3. Zilu said: 'If the Lord of Wei were waiting for you to run the government, what would you give priority to?' The Master said: 'What is necessary is to rectify names, is it not?' Zilu said: 'If this were to take place, it would surely be an aberration of yours. Why should they be rectified?' The Master said: 'How uncivilized you are. With regard to what he does not understand the gentleman is surely somewhat reluctant to offer an

---

15. Ji Kang Zi was the head of one of the powerful three families who ousted the rulers of Lu, Confucius' home state [Editor].

16. A disciple.

opinion. If names are not rectified, then words are not appropriate. If words are not appropriate, then deeds are not accomplished. If deeds are not accomplished, then the rites and music do not flourish. If the rites and music do not flourish, then punishments do not hit the mark. If punishments do not hit the mark, then the people have nowhere to put hand or foot. So when a gentleman names something, the name can definitely be used in speech; and when he says something, it can definitely be put into practice. In his utterances the gentleman is definitely not casual about anything.'

5. The Master said: 'A man may know by heart the three hundred *Songs*, but if he is given a post in government and cannot successfully carry out his duties, and if he is sent to far places and cannot react to the circumstances as he finds them, then even if he has learnt to recite many of them, of what use is this to him?'

11. The Master said: '"If good men ran a state for a hundred years, they might therefore vanquish cruelty and abolish killing." How true is this saying!'

15. Duke Ding[17] asked if there was a single saying with which one might make a state prosperous. Master Kong replied: 'A saying cannot be quite like that. But there is a saying among men which runs "to be a ruler is difficult and to be a subject is not easy." If one understands that to be a ruler is difficult, then does this not come close to making a state prosperous through one saying?' He said: 'Is there a single saying with which one might ruin a state?' Master Kong replied: 'A saying cannot be quite like that. But there is a saying among men which runs "I have no pleasure in being a ruler, except that nobody opposes me with his words." As far as his good points are concerned, it is surely good, isn't it, that nobody opposes him? But as far as his bad points are concerned, if nobody opposes him, is this not close to ruining a state with a single saying?'

18. The Duke of She told Master Kong: 'In my locality there is a certain paragon, for when his father stole a sheep, he, the son, bore witness against him.' Master Kong said: 'In my locality those who are upright are different from this. Fathers cover up for their sons[18] and sons cover up for their fathers. Uprightness is to be found in this.'

---

17. The Duke of Lu.

18. This encapsulates the Chinese regard for the importance of the family as compared with the state. Informing against parents in antiquity, as more recently in the Cultural Revolution, represents the antithesis of Confucian values.

Book 14

22. Zilu asked about serving a ruler. The Master said: 'It means don't be deceitful. But do stand up to him.'

27. The Master said: 'The gentleman is ashamed that his words have outstripped his deeds.'

30. The Master said: 'One does not worry about the fact that other people do not appreciate one. One worries about the fact that one is incapable.'

34. Someone said: 'What about "Repay hostility with kindness"?' The Master said: 'How then do you repay kindness? Repay hostility with uprightness and repay kindness with kindness.'

35. The Master said: 'Nobody understands me, do they?' Zigong said: 'Why is it that none of them understands you?' The Master said: 'I do not feel resentful towards Heaven and I do not put blame on men. But although my studies are of lowly things they reach up above, and the one that understands me will be Heaven, will it not?'

41. The Master said: 'If their superior loves the rites,[19] the people will be easy to command.'

43. Yuan Rang was waiting in an oafish manner. The Master said: 'When he was young he was not deferential, so when he grew up nothing was passed on by him, and now he is an old man he does not die—this seems terrible.' And he struck his shins with a stick.

Book 15

2. When they were in Chen they suffered an interruption in the supply of provisions, so the followers became ill and nobody was capable of getting up. Feeling aggrieved, Zilu addressed the Master. 'Does suffering exist even for the gentleman?' he said. The Master said: 'The gentleman remains firm in the face of suffering, but if the small man suffers, he is carried away on a flood of excess.'

8. The Master said: 'Not to talk with people although they can be talked with is to waste people. To talk with people although they can't be talked with is to waste words. A man of understanding does not waste people, but he also does not waste words.'

---

19. Refers to religious practice, but ritual also suggests a sense of reverence toward life.

12. The Master said: 'If a man avoids thinking about distant matters he will certainly have worries close at hand.'

21. The Master said: 'What the gentleman seeks in himself the small man seeks in others.'

23. The Master said: 'Gentlemen do not promote someone because of what he says, and do not reject what is said because of who said it.'

24. Zigong asked: 'Is there a single word such that one could practise it throughout one's life?' The Master said: 'Reciprocity perhaps? Do not inflict on others what you yourself would not wish done to you.'

30. The Master said: 'If one commits an error and does not reform, this is what is meant by an error.'

35. The Master said: 'The people's connection with humaneness is more important than water or fire. As for water and fire, I have come across people who have died through stepping on them, but I have never come across people who have died through stepping on humaneness.'

Book 16

7. Master Kong said: 'There are three things which the gentleman guards against: in the time of his youth, when his vital powers have not yet settled down, he is on his guard in matters of sex; when he reaches the prime of life and his vital powers have just attained consistency, he is on his guard in matters of contention; and when he becomes old and his vital powers have declined, he is on his guard in matters of acquisition.'

8. Master Kong said: 'There are three things which the gentleman holds in awe: he is in awe of the decree of Heaven, he is in awe of great men, and he is in awe of the words of sages. The small man, being unaware of the decree of Heaven, is not in awe of it. He is rude to great men and ridicules the words of sages.'

Book 17

2. The Master said: 'Only the most intelligent and the most stupid do not change.'

6. When Bi Xi sent for him, the Master wanted to go. Zilu said: 'Master, I once heard the following from you: "If someone in his own person does those things which are not good, the gentleman does not enter his domain." Bi Xi is carrying out a rebellion using Zhongmou as his base, so what is the point of your going there?' The Master said: 'Yes, I have said such a thing, but is it not said that "hard indeed is that which is not worn

thin by grinding" and "white indeed is that which will not turn black from dyeing"? Surely I am not just a bitter gourd![20] How can I hang there and not be eaten?'

8. The Master said: 'My young friends, why do none of you study the *Songs*? The *Songs* may help one to be stimulated, to observe, to be sociable, and to express grievances. One uses them at home to serve one's father, and one uses them in distant places to serve one's ruler. One also gains much knowledge concerning the names of birds and beasts and plants and trees.'

   The Master said to Boyu: 'Have you done the *Zhounan* and *Shaonan*?[21] If although one is a man one has not done the *Zhounan* and *Shaonan*, surely it is like standing with one's face to the wall?'

13. The Master said: 'Is it really possible to serve one's ruler alongside vulgar persons? For while they have not yet obtained something, they are worried about obtaining it; and when they have obtained it, they are worried about losing it. And if they are worried about losing it, there are no lengths to which they will not go.'

23. The Master said: 'Only women[22] and small men seem difficult to look after. If you keep them close, they become insubordinate; but if you keep them at a distance, they become resentful.'

Book 19

21. Zigong said: 'The errors of the gentleman are like eclipses of the sun and moon. When he errs everyone observes him; and when he makes a correction, everyone looks up to him.'

■ Laozi (Lao Tzu) (c. Fourth to Third Centuries B.C.) (poems/philosophy)

TRANSLATED BY GIA-FU FENG AND JANE ENGLISH

Laozi was the legendary author of the *Dao De Jing*, a collection of prose and verse wisdom literature that is considered the seminal and essential work of Daoism. Yet about Laozi and the *Dao De Jing* mysteries abound. It is

---

20. A potent symbol of Master Kong's frustration at not obtaining employment. This time the employment would have been in the state of Jin rather than in his native state of Lu. The sayings about grinding and dyeing are meant to indicate the Master's incorruptibility.

21. First two books of the *Book of Songs*.

22. Commentators of course attempt to soften the misogyny.

by no means certain that a historical personage named Laozi ever existed. The title *Dao De Jing* (*Classic of the Way and Its Power*) is a later name for the collection that originally was called simply *Laozi*. Since Laozi also means "old man," and there is evidence of a body of wisdom literature whose various book titles all translate as "elder" or "old man," it may be that this collection is the lone survivor of this lost genre. It may be that the *Dao De Jing* is an anthology of sayings by diverse authors linked by common themes or the work of one author augmented by later redactors. The traditional Laozi is said to have been an older contemporary of Confucius (551–479 B.C.) who instructed the younger sage in the rites, but this story seems not to have circulated until the third century B.C. It is now thought that the text dates from no earlier than the third or fourth centuries B.C. In the first century B.C., the famous historian Sima Qian recounted the Confucius encounter and other stories about Laozi, which he gathered from sources now lost. The story about Laozi's writing the *Dao De Jing* follows:

> Laozi cultivated the way and virtue, and his teachings aimed at self-effacement. He lived in Zhou for a long time, but seeing its decline he departed; when he reached the Pass, the Keeper there was pleased and said to him, "As you are about to leave the world behind, could you write a book for my sake?" As a result, Laozi wrote a work in two books, setting out the meaning of the way and virtue in some five thousand characters, and then departed. None knew where he went to in the end.[1]

The book itself has more than the five thousand characters mentioned by Sima Qian and is divided into eighty-one chapters in two sections. Unlike the *Zhuangzi,* the *Dao De Jing* is not a work of anecdotes and parables; it is a general, didactic work of great poetic beauty, mystery, and ambiguity. Central to the work and to Daoism is the concept of the *Dao,* which means the way, method, or reason.[2] The Dao is ineffable—it can't be captured in words; it is as small as the essential nature of the smallest thing and as large as the entire universe. The term *De* means "virtue" and refers to the nature of a thing—its inherent virtue and energy. The term *Jing* means "classic," and thus the title of the book translates as *The Classic of the Dao and the De.* The Dao in this work is seen as the source of the world, as everything and, at the same time, nothing. It is fluid, weak, and passive, yet it conquers all and is the source of all action. Its nature is paradoxical because it is so large that it contains both ends of all oppositions. The Dao is also a contemplative method for understanding oneself and for merging with the Dao. Different interpreters see it either as a method of survival through passive resistance written in a time of great insecurity and turmoil or as a more mystical treatise. In any case, a number of passages treat the proper behavior of citizen and ruler and suggest that true self-interest lies in selflessness

---

1. D. C. Lau, tr. *Lao Tzu: Tao Te Ching* (Harmondsworth: Penguin, 1963), 9. The Wade-Giles transliteration of this quotation has been changed to the Pinyin system.

2. In the translation that follows, "Dao" is transliterated as "Tao."

(thus, the ruler must humble himself before the people in order to rule, follow in order to lead).

Like Confucianism, Daoism took on magical elements as it developed, and the longevity of the follower of the Dao (who would live longer in turbulent times) was interpreted as physical immortality. Daoism resembled Western alchemy in its quest for the secret of immortality and, later, came in part to blend with Buddhism. Throughout Chinese literature and intellectual history, Daoism has been a liberating counterbalance to the dogmatic order of Confucianism. The *Dao De Jing* has been translated into English dozens of times, with varying degrees of success. At one end of the spectrum are scholarly, authoritative, and informative translations, which are inconsistently successful as poetry; at the other end of the spectrum are poetic interpretations, or modern imitations, which are good literature throughout but in which this ancient text is radically modernized. In searching for a compromise, we have settled on a lesser-known translation that attempts to be as true as possible to an original text that is notoriously ambiguous, while reflecting in lucid English its mysteriousness and literary qualities.

FURTHER READING: Chan, Wing-tsit, tr. *The Way of Lao Tzu*, 1963. Feng, Gia-fu, and Jane English, trs. *Lao Tsu: Tao Te Ching*, 1972. Lau, D. C., tr. *Lao Tzu: Tao Te Ching*, 1963. Waley, Arthur. *The Way and Its Power*, 1934. Wu, John C. H., tr. *Tao Teh Ching*, 1961.

from *The Dao De Jing*

One

The Tao that can be told is not the eternal Tao.
The name that can be named is not the eternal name.
The nameless is the beginning of heaven and earth.
The named is the mother of ten thousand things.
Ever desireless, one can see the mystery.   5
Ever desiring, one can see the manifestations.
These two spring from the same source but differ in name; this
    appears as darkness.
Darkness within darkness.
The gate to all mystery.

Four

The Tao is an empty vessel; it is used, but never filled.
Oh, unfathomable source of ten thousand things!
Blunt the sharpness,
Untangle the knot,

Soften the glare,   *5*
Merge with dust.
Oh, hidden deep but ever present!
I do not know from whence it comes.
It is the forefather of the emperors.

Eleven

Thirty spokes share the wheel's hub;
It is the center hole that makes it useful.
Shape clay into a vessel;
It is the space within that makes it useful.
Cut doors and windows for a room;   *5*
It is the holes which make it useful.
Therefore profit comes from what is there;
Usefulness from what is not there.

Sixteen

Empty yourself of everything.
Let the mind rest at peace.
The ten thousand things rise and fall while the Self watches their
    return.
They grow and flourish and then return to the source.
Returning to the source is stillness, which is the way of nature.   *5*
The way of nature is unchanging.
Knowing constancy is insight.
Not knowing constancy leads to disaster.
Knowing constancy, the mind is open.
With an open mind, you will be openhearted.   *10*
Being openhearted, you will act royally.
Being royal, you will attain the divine.
Being divine, you will be at one with the Tao.
Being at one with the Tao is eternal.
And though the body dies, the Tao will never pass away.   *15*

Twenty-two

Yield and overcome;
Bend and be straight;
Empty and be full;
Wear out and be new;
Have little and gain;   *5*
Have much and be confused.

Therefore wise men embrace the one
And set an example to all.
Not putting on a display,
They shine forth.   *10*

Not justifying themselves,
They are distinguished.
Not boasting,
They receive recognition.
Not bragging,   *15*
They never falter.
They do not quarrel,
So no one quarrels with them.
Therefore the ancients say, "Yield and overcome."
Is that an empty saying?   *20*
Be really whole,
And all things will come to you.

Thirty

Whenever you advise a ruler in the way of Tao,
Counsel him not to use force to conquer the universe.
For this would only cause resistance.
Thorn bushes spring up wherever the army has passed.
Lean years follow in the wake of a great war.   *5*
Just do what needs to be done.
Never take advantage of power.

Achieve results,
But never glory in them.
Achieve results,   *10*
But never boast.
Achieve results,
But never be proud.
Achieve results,
Because this is the natural way.   *15*
Achieve results,
But not through violence.

Force is followed by loss of strength.
This is not the way of Tao.
That which goes against the Tao comes to an early end.   *20*

Thirty-three

Knowing others is wisdom;
Knowing the self is enlightenment.
Mastering others requires force;
Mastering the self needs strength.

He who knows he has enough is rich.   *5*
Perseverance is a sign of will power.
He who stays where he is endures.
To die but not to perish is to be eternally present.

Forty-three

The softest thing in the universe
Overcomes the hardest thing in the universe.
That without substance can enter where there is no room.
Hence I know the value of non-action.

Teaching without words and work without doing   5
Are understood by very few.

Forty-seven

Without going outside, you may know the whole world.
Without looking through the window, you may see the ways of heaven.
The farther you go, the less you know.

Thus the sage knows without traveling;
He sees without looking;   5
He works without doing.

Forty-nine

The sage has no mind of his own.
He is aware of the needs of others.

I am good to people who are good.
I am also good to people who are not good.
Because Virtue is goodness.   5
I have faith in people who are faithful.
I also have faith in people who are not faithful.
Because Virtue is faithfulness.

The sage is shy and humble—to the world he seems confusing.
Men look to him and listen.   10
He behaves like a little child.

Fifty-five

He who is filled with Virtue is like a newborn child.
Wasps and serpents will not sting him;
Wild beasts will not pounce upon him;
He will not be attacked by birds of prey.
His bones are soft, his muscles weak,   5
But his grip is firm.
He has not experienced the union of man and woman, but is whole.
His manhood is strong.
He screams all day without becoming hoarse.
This is perfect harmony.   10

Knowing harmony is constancy.
Knowing constancy is enlightenment.

It is not wise to rush about.
Controlling the breath causes strain.
If too much energy is used, exhaustion follows.   15
This is not the way of Tao.
Whatever is contrary to Tao will not last long

Sixty-one

A great country is like low land.
It is the meeting ground of the universe,
The mother of the universe.

The female overcomes the male with stillness,
Lying low in stillness.   5

Therefore if a great country gives way to a smaller country,
It will conquer the smaller country.
And if a small country submits to a great country,
It can conquer the great country.
Therefore those who would conquer must yield,   10
And those who conquer do so because they yield.

A great nation needs more people;
A small country needs to serve.
Each gets what it wants.
It is fitting for a great nation to yield.   15

Seventy-six

A man is born gentle and weak.
At his death he is hard and stiff.
Green plants are tender and filled with sap.
At their death they are withered and dry.

Therefore the stiff and unbending is the disciple of death.   5
The gentle and yielding is the disciple of life.

Thus an army without flexibility never wins a battle.
A tree that is unbending is easily broken.

The hard and strong will fall.
The soft and weak will overcome.   10

Seventy-eight

Under heaven nothing is more soft and yielding than water.
Yet for attacking the solid and strong, nothing is better;
It has no equal.
The weak can overcome the strong;
The supple can overcome the stiff.   5
Under heaven everyone knows this,
Yet no one puts it into practice.

Therefore the sage says:
> He who takes upon himself the humiliation of the people is fit
> to rule them.
> He who takes upon himself the country's disasters deserves to be   *10*
> king of the universe.

The truth often sounds paradoxical.

▪ Zhuangzi (Chuang Tzu) (c. 369–286 B.C.) (philosophy)

TRANSLATED BY BURTON WATSON

Daoist philosopher Zhuangzi is a shadow behind the work that bears his name. Little is known of his life, except that a man named Zhuangzi (Master Zhuang) lived in the fourth century B.C., in what is now Henan province. Early in life he was a petty official in "the lacquer garden" of Meng, but for most of his life he scorned officialdom, preferring to be his own man. The great historian Sima Qian remarks that he had vast knowledge and that he wrote a long work explaining Laozi's teachings and attacking the doctrine of the early philosophers Confucius (551–479 B.C.) and Mo Tzu (470–391 B.C.?). Zhuangzi is the most important interpreter of Daoism, and his unconventional spirit had only sarcasm for stultifying rituals and hierarchies. The Dao is the unity beneath all things, and the person who sees this soon finds, like William Blake, that true marriage lies in contraries. Zhuangzi was able to look at the things of the world with a sense of relativism; therefore, since tall equals short and here equals there, if the true reality is seen to be beneath the surface, "There is nothing in the world bigger than the tip of an autumn hair, and Mount T'ai is little. No one has lived longer than a dead child, and [long lived] P'eng-tsu died young." Though the Dao is absolute, it is not unchanging; in fact, its very nature is flux. A comparison with Buddhism, in which the defining characteristic of the absolute is its freedom from flux, is informative.

Instead of presenting a system of ethical and social reform like other philosophers of his time, Zhuangzi celebrated spontaneity and the cultivation of an inner emptiness that allowed one to merge with the Dao. Human problems are created by human categories; the way out of them is not through changing the world but through changing the way you understand the world. Death and life are mere manifestations of the Dao and thus they are changes in form but not changes in essence. Therefore, we should free ourselves from fear of death and from attachment to life's worries: "How do I know that loving life is not a delusion? How do I know that in hating death I am not like a man who, having left home in his youth, has forgotten the way back?" This freedom is the primary benefit that Zhuangzi tries to give his readers, usually through dazzling rhetoric, humor, nonsense phrases, and paradoxes designed to shock us out of our preconceptions. Like Tang dynasty poet Wang Wei in his most Daoist poems, Zhuangzi celebrates inaction, even laziness, as opposed to a life of struggle for gain and a character dominated by desire. By following the Way of Daoism, one may even gain magical powers and immortality. As is the case with so many of the world's mystics, history has elided the life and left us the thought. But behind these fresh and ancient words, one can intuit a peculiar mind, like the Dao inscribed within the things of the world. In the end, it is hard to know whether the Zhuangzi text had only one author, but it is tempting to think of a man named Zhuangzi, a free spirit, unbounded and mystical, wry and just a bit crazed.

FURTHER READING: Kaltenmark, Max. *Lao Tzu and Taoism.* Translated by Roger Greaves, 1965. Watson, Burton, tr. *Chuang Tzu: Basic Writings,* 1964; tr. *Records of the Grand Historian of China,* 1961.

from *The Zhuangzi*

Great understanding is broad and unhurried; little understanding is cramped and busy. Great words are clear and limpid; little words are shrill and quarrelsome. In sleep, men's spirits go visiting; in waking hours, their bodies hustle. With everything they meet they become entangled. Day after day they use their minds in strife, sometimes grandiose, sometimes sly, sometimes petty. Their little fears are mean and trembly; their great fears are stunned and overwhelming. They bound off like an arrow or a crossbow pellet, certain that they are the arbiters of right and wrong. They cling to their position as though they had sworn before the gods, sure that they are holding on to victory. They fade like fall and winter—such is the way they dwindle day by day. They drown in what they do—you cannot make them turn back. They grow dark, as though sealed with seals—such are the excesses of their old age. And when their minds draw near to death, nothing can restore them to the light.

Joy, anger, grief, delight, worry, regret, fickleness, inflexibility, modesty, willfulness, candor, insolence—music from empty holes, mushrooms springing up in dampness, day and night replacing each other before us, and no one knows where they sprout from. Let it be! Let it be! [It is enough that] morning and evening we have them, and they are the means by which we live. Without them we would not exist; without us they would have nothing to take hold of. This comes close to the matter. But I do not know what makes them the way they are. It would seem as though they have some True Master, and yet I find no trace of him. He can act—that is certain. Yet I cannot see his form. He has identity but no form.

The hundred joints, the nine openings, the six organs, all come together and exist here [as my body]. But which part should I feel closest to?
I should delight in all parts, you say? But there must be one I ought to favor
more. If not, are they all of them mere servants? But if they are all servants,
then how can they keep order among themselves? Or do they take turns
being lord and servant? It would seem as though there must be some True
Lord among them. But whether I succeed in discovering his identity or not,
it neither adds to nor detracts from his Truth.

Once a man receives this fixed bodily form, he holds on to it, waiting
for the end. Sometimes clashing with things, sometimes bending before
them, he runs his course like a galloping steed, and nothing can stop him.
Is he not pathetic? Sweating and laboring to the end of his days and never
seeing his accomplishment, utterly exhausting himself and never knowing
where to look for rest—can you help pitying him? I'm not dead yet! he
says, but what good is that? His body decays, his mind follows it—can you
deny that this is a great sorrow? Man's life has always been a muddle like
this. How could I be the only muddled one, and other men not muddled?

*   *   *

Words are not just wind. Words have something to say. But if what
they have to say is not fixed, then do they really say something? Or do they
say nothing? People suppose that words are different from the peeps of
baby birds, but is there any difference, or isn't there? What does the Way
rely upon,[1] that we have true and false? What do words rely upon, that we
have right and wrong? How can the Way go away and not exist? How can
words exist and not be acceptable? When the Way relies on little accomplishments and words rely on vain show, then we have the rights and wrongs of
the Confucians and the Mo-ists. What one calls right the other calls wrong;
what one calls wrong the other calls right. But if we want to right their
wrongs and wrong their rights, then the best thing to use is clarity.

Everything has its "that," everything has its "this." From the point of
view of "that" you cannot see it, but through understanding you can know
it. So I say, "that" comes out of "this" and "this" depends on "that"—which
is to say that "this" and "that" give birth to each other. But where there is
birth there must be death; where there is death there must be birth. Where
there is acceptability there must be unacceptability; where there is unacceptability there must be acceptability. Where there is recognition of right
there must be recognition of wrong; where there is recognition of wrong
there must be recognition of right. Therefore the sage does not proceed in
such a way, but illuminates all in the light of Heaven.[2] He too recognizes a
"this," but a "this" which is also "that," a "that" which is also "this." His
"that" has both a right and a wrong in it; his "this" too has both a right and

---

1. Following the interpretation of Chang Ping-lin. The older interpretation of yin here and in
the following sentences is, "What is the Way hidden by," etc.

2. [The Chinese word translated here as "Heaven" is] *T'ien,* which for Chuang Tzu means Nature or the Way.

a wrong in it. So, in fact, does he still have a "this" and "that"? Or does he in fact no longer have a "this" and "that"? A state in which "this" and "that" no longer find their opposites is called the hinge of the Way. When the hinge is fitted into the socket, it can respond endlessly. Its right then is a single endlessness and its wrong too is a single endlessness. So I say, the best thing to use is clarity.

To use an attribute to show that attributes are not attributes is not as good as using a nonattribute to show that attributes are not attributes. To use a horse to show that a horse is not a horse is not as good as using a non-horse to show that a horse is not a horse,[3] Heaven and earth are one attribute; the ten thousand things are one horse.

What is acceptable we call acceptable; what is unacceptable we call unacceptable. A road is made by people walking on it; things are so because they are called so. What makes them so? Making them so makes them so. What makes them not so? Making them not so makes them not so. Things all must have that which is so; things all must have that which is acceptable. There is nothing that is not so, nothing that is not acceptable.

For this reason, whether you point to a little stalk or a great pillar, a leper or the beautiful Hsi-shih, things ribald and shady or things grotesque and strange, the Way makes them all into one. Their dividedness is their completeness; their completeness is their impairment. No thing is either complete or impaired, but all are made into one again. Only the man of far-reaching vision knows how to make them into one. So he has no use [for categories], but relegates all to the constant. The constant is the useful; the useful is the passable; the passable is the successful; and with success, all is accomplished. He relies upon this alone, relies upon it and does not know he is doing so. This is called the Way.

But to wear out your brain trying to make things into one without realizing that they are all the same—this is called "three in the morning." What do I mean by "three in the morning"? When the monkey trainer was handing out acorns, he said, "You get three in the morning and four at night." This made all the monkeys furious. "Well, then," he said, "you get four in the morning and three at night." The monkeys were all delighted. There was no change in the reality behind the words, and yet the monkeys responded with joy and anger. Let them, if they want to. So the sage harmonizes with both right and wrong and rests in Heaven the Equalizer. This is called walking two roads.

*   *   *

Now I am going to make a statement here. I don't know whether it fits into the category of other people's statements or not. But whether it fits

---

3. A reference to the statements of the logician Kung-sun Lung, "A white horse is not a horse" and "Attributes are not attributes in and of themselves."

into their category or whether it doesn't, it obviously fits into some category. So in that respect it is no different from their statements. However, let me try making my statement.

There is a beginning. There is a not yet beginning to be a beginning. There is a not yet beginning to be a not yet beginning to be a beginning. There is being. There is nonbeing. There is a not yet beginning to be nonbeing. There is a not yet beginning to be a not yet beginning to be nonbeing. Suddenly there is being and nonbeing. But between this being and nonbeing, I don't really know which is being and which is nonbeing. Now I have just said something. But I don't know whether what I have said has really said something or whether it hasn't said something.

There is nothing in the world bigger than the tip of an autumn hair, and Mount T'ai is little. No one has lived longer than a dead child, and P'eng-tsu died young.[4] Heaven and earth were born at the same time I was, and the ten thousand things are one with me.

We have already become one, so how can I say anything? But I have just said that we are one, so how can I not be saying something? The one and what I said about it make two, and two and the original one make three. If we go on this way, then even the cleverest mathematician can't tell where we'll end, much less an ordinary man. If by moving from nonbeing to being we get to three, how far will we get if we move from being to being? Better not to move, but to let things be!

* * *

How do I know that loving life is not a delusion? How do I know that in hating death I am not like a man who, having left home in his youth, has forgotten the way back?

Lady Li was the daughter of the border guard of Ai.[5] When she was first taken captive and brought to the state of Chin, she wept until her tears drenched the collar of her robe. But later, when she went to live in the palace of the ruler, shared his couch with him, and ate the delicious meats of his table, she wondered why she had ever wept. How do I know that the dead do not wonder why they ever longed for life?

He who dreams of drinking wine may weep when morning comes; he who dreams of weeping may in the morning go off to hunt. While he is dreaming he does not know it is a dream, and in his dream he may even try to interpret a dream. Only after he wakes does he know it was a dream. And someday there will be a great awakening when we know that this is all a great dream. Yet the stupid believe they are awake, busily and brightly assuming they understand things, calling this man ruler, that one herdsman—how dense! Confucius and you are both dreaming! And when

---

4. The strands of animal fur were believed to grow particularly fine in autumn: hence "the tip of an autumn hair" is a cliché for something extremely tiny. P'eng-tsu was the Chinese Methuselah.

5. She was taken by Duke Hsien of Chin in 671 B.C., and later became his consort.

I say you are dreaming, I am dreaming, too. Words like these will be labeled the Supreme Swindle. Yet, after ten thousand generations, a great sage may appear who will know their meaning, and it will still be as though he appeared with astonishing speed.

Suppose you and I have had an argument. If you have beaten me instead of my beating you, then are you necessarily right and am I necessarily wrong? If I have beaten you instead of your beating me, then am I necessarily right and are you necessarily wrong? Is one of us right and the other wrong? Are both of us right or are both of us wrong? If you and I don't know the answer, then other people are bound to be even more in the dark. Whom shall we get to decide what is right? Shall we get someone who agrees with you to decide? But if he already agrees with you, how can he decide fairly? Shall we get someone who agrees with me? But if he already agrees with me, how can he decide? Shall we get someone who disagrees with both of us? But if he already disagrees with both of us, how can he decide? Shall we get someone who agrees with both of us? But if he already agrees with both of us, how can he decide? Obviously, then, neither you nor I nor anyone else can know the answer. Shall we wait for still another person?

But waiting for one shifting voice [to pass judgment on] another is the same as waiting for none of them.[6] Harmonize them all with the Heavenly Equality, leave them to their endless changes, and so live out your years. What do I mean by harmonizing them with the Heavenly Equality? Right is not right; so is not so. If right were really right, it would differ so clearly from not right that there would be no need for argument. If so were really so, it would differ so clearly from not so that there would be no need for argument. Forget the years; forget distinctions. Leap into the boundless and make it your home!

* * *

Once Chuang Chou[7] dreamt he was a butterfly, a butterfly flitting and fluttering around, happy with himself and doing as he pleased. He didn't know he was Chuang Chou. Suddenly he woke up and there he was, solid and unmistakable Chuang Chou. But he didn't know if he was Chuang Chou who had dreamt he was a butterfly, or a butterfly dreaming he was Chuang Chou. Between Chuang Chou and a butterfly there must be some distinction! This is called the Transformation of Things.

* * *

You hide your boat in the ravine and your fish net[8] in the swamp and tell yourself that they will be safe. But in the middle of the night a strong man shoulders them and carries them off, and in your stupidity you don't know why it happened. You think you do right to hide little things in big

---

6. I follow the rearrangement of the text suggested by Lü Hui-ch'ing. But the text of this whole paragraph leaves much to be desired and the translation is tentative.

7. Another name for Chuang Tzu (Zhuanzi) [Editor].

8. Following the interpretation of Yü Yuen.

ones, and yet they get away from you. But if you were to hide the world in the world, so that nothing could get away, this would be the final reality of the constancy of things.

✳ ✳ ✳

Master Ssu, Master Yü, Master Li, and Master Lai were all four talking together. "Who can look upon inaction as his head, on life as his back, and on death as his rump?" they said. "Who knows that life and death, existence and annihilation, are all a single body? I will be his friend!"

The four men looked at each other and smiled. There was no disagreement in their hearts and so the four of them became friends.

All at once Master Yü fell ill. Master Ssu went to ask how he was. "Amazing!" said Master Yü. "The Creator is making me all crookedly like this! My back sticks up like a hunchback and my vital organs are on top of me. My chin is hidden in my navel, my shoulders are up above my head, and my pigtail points at the sky. It must be some dislocation of the yin and yang!"

Yet he seemed calm at heart and unconcerned. Dragging himself haltingly to the well, he looked at his reflection and said, "My, my! So the Creator is making me all crookedly like this!"

"Do you resent it?" asked Master Ssu.

"Why no, what would I resent? If the process continues, perhaps in time he'll transform my left arm into a rooster. In that case I'll keep watch on the night. Or perhaps in time he'll transform my right arm into a crossbow pellet and I'll shoot down an owl for roasting. Or perhaps in time he'll transform my buttocks into cartwheels. Then, with my spirit for a horse, I'll climb up and go for a ride. What need will I ever have for a carriage again?

"I received life because the time had come; I will lose it because the order of things passes on. Be content with this time and dwell in this order and then neither sorrow nor joy can touch you. In ancient times this was called the 'freeing of the bound.' There are those who cannot free themselves, because they are bound by things. But nothing can ever win against Heaven — that's the way it's always been. What would I have to resent?"

✳ ✳ ✳

Yen Hui said, "I'm improving!"

Confucius said, "What do you mean by that?"

"I've forgotten benevolence and righteousness!"

"That's good. But you still haven't got it."

Another day, the two met again and Yen Hui said, "I'm improving!"

"What do you mean by that?"

"I've forgotten rites and music!"

"That's good. But you still haven't got it."

Another day, the two met again and Yen Hui said, "I'm improving!"

"What do you mean by that?"

"I can sit down and forget everything!"

Confucius looked very startled and said, "What do you mean, sit down and forget everything?"

Yen Hui said, "I smash up my limbs and body, drive out perception and intellect, cast off form, do away with understanding, and make myself identical with the Great Thoroughfare. This is what I mean by sitting down and forgetting everything."

Confucius said, "If you're identical with it, you must have no more likes! If you've been transformed, you must have no more constancy! So you really are a worthy man after all![9] With your permission, I'd like to become your follower."

* * *

Do not be an embodier of fame; do not be a storehouse of schemes; do not be an undertaker of projects; do not be a proprietor of wisdom. Embody to the fullest what has no end and wander where there is no trail. Hold on to all that you have received from Heaven but do not think you have gotten anything. Be empty, that is all. The Perfect Man uses his mind like a mirror—going after nothing, welcoming nothing, responding but not storing. Therefore he can win out over things and not hurt himself.

* * *

Once, when Chuang Tzu was fishing in the P'u River, the king of Ch'u sent two officials to go and announce to him: "I would like to trouble you with the administration of my realm."

Chuang Tzu held on to the fishing pole and, without turning his head, said, "I have heard that there is a sacred tortoise in Ch'u that has been dead for three thousand years. The king keeps it wrapped in cloth and boxed, and stores it in the ancestral temple. Now would this tortoise rather be dead and have its bones left behind and honored? Or would it rather be alive and dragging its tail in the mud?"

"It would rather be alive and dragging its tail in the mud," said the two officials.

Chuang Tzu said, "Go away! I'll drag my tail in the mud!"

* * *

Hui Tzu said to Chuang Tzu, "Your words are useless!"

Chuang Tzu said, "A man has to understand the useless before you can talk to him about the useful. The earth is certainly vast and broad, though a man uses no more of it than the area he puts his feet on. If, however, you were to dig away all the earth from around his feet until you reached the Yellow Springs,[10] then would the man still be able to make use of it?"

"No, it would be useless," said Hui Tzu.

"It is obvious, then," said Chuang Tzu, "that the useless has its use."

* * *

---

9. Chuang Tzu probably intends a humorous reference to the words of Confucius in Analects VI, 9: "The Master said, 'What a worthy man was Hui!'"

10. The underworld.

The fish trap exists because of the fish; once you've gotten the fish, you can forget the trap. The rabbit snare exists because of the rabbit; once you've gotten the rabbit, you can forget the snare. Words exist because of meaning; once you've gotten the meaning, you can forget the words. Where can I find a man who has forgotten words so I can have a word with him?

■ The Songs of Chu [attributed to Qu Yuan (Ch'ü Yüan), 322–295 B.C.?] (poem)

TRANSLATED BY DAVID HAWKES

The Songs of Chu is the second great anthology of Chinese poetry. These works come from the kingdom of Chu, a southern state located in the central valley of the Yangtze River; *The Songs of Chu* are thus often considered representative of a southern style of poetry, versus the northern style of *The Book of Songs*. The two collections have formal elements in common, however, and modern scholars question the adequateness of the northern/ southern dichotomy. Most of the anthology's poems are attributed to Qu Yuan (c. 322–295 B.C.?), the first Chinese poet whom we know by name, but the anthology itself reached its final form only in the second century A.D. It seems unlikely that Qu Yuan composed all the works attributed to him. We know little about the historical Qu Yuan, except that he belonged to the royal house of Chu and served in the court of King Huai (reigned 328–229 B.C.). As a result of slander from a jealous colleague, Qu fell from the king's graces and was said to have written the important poem "Encountering Sorrow" to show his faithfulness and remonstrate with the king. Qu Yuan was supposed to have repeatedly warned the king against the aggressions of the state of Qin, but he was ignored, and the king was captured by Qin. After the king's death in captivity abroad, his son was inaugurated, but he proved as gullible and flawed a king as his father. He banished Qu Yuan to the far south where Qu Yuan drowned himself in the Miluo River in protest. Eventually, the state of Chu was swallowed up by Qin. Qu Yuan is widely admired as an early figure of the honest retainer who dares to criticize his superiors, along the Confucian model, and his death is the subject of the yearly Dragon Boat Festival in China.

If *The Book of Songs* consists primarily of poems in a lyric mode, *The Songs of Chu* are longer narratives, more dramatic in nature. In addition to the extended narrative poem "Encountering Sorrow," the collection includes a set of shamanistic ritual songs in which the shaman sexually joins with the deity (the "Nine Songs"); the "Heavenly Questions," a riddling, gnomic series of questions about the origin of the cosmos, mythology, and Chinese history; "Far Journey," a celestial voyage that bears resemblance to "Encountering Sorrow"; the "Nine Arguments," attributed to Song Yu (fourth–third centuries B.C.), a series of poems that is the origin of later evocations of the melancholy associated with autumn, such as Ouyang Xiu's "The Autumn Sound" or Meng Jiao's "Autumn Meditations" in this volume; "The Fisherman," a dialogue in which a fisherman advises Qu Yuan not to abandon office and commit suicide; and a series of three poems, two of them shamanistic in nature, that are summons to the soul, or to a virtuous gentleman to come out of retirement.

FURTHER READING: Hawkes, David, tr. *Ch'u Tz'u: The Songs of the South, an Ancient Chinese Anthology*, 1959. Waley, Arthur. *The Nine Songs: A Study of Shamanism in Ancient China*, 1955. Yang, Hsien-yi, and Gladys Yang, trs. *Ch'u Tz'u: Li Sao and Other Poems of Chu Yuan*, 1955.

The Fisherman

When Ch'ü Yüan was banished,
He wandered along the river's banks, or walked at the marsh's edge,
    singing as he went,
His expression was dejected, and his features emaciated.
A fisherman caught sight of him.
'Are you not the Lord of the Three Gates?'[1] said the fisherman. 'What   *5*
    has brought you to this pass?'
'Because all the world is muddy and I alone am clear,' said Ch'ü Yüan,
'And because all men are drunk and I alone am sober,
'I have been sent into exile.'
'The Wise Man is not chained to material circumstances,' said the
    fisherman, 'but can move as the world moves.
'If all the world is muddy, why not help them to stir up the mud and   *10*
    beat up the waves?
'And if all men are drunk, why not sup their dregs and swill their lees?
'Why get yourself exiled because of your deep thoughts and your fine
    aspirations?'
Ch'ü Yüan replied, 'I have heard it said:
'"He who has just washed his hair should brush his hat; and he who
    has just bathed should shake his clothes."
'How can I submit my spotless purity to the dirt of others?   *15*
'I would rather cast myself into the waters of the river and be buried
    in the bowels of fishes,
'Than hide my shining light in the dark and dust of the world.'
The fisherman, with a faint smile, struck his paddle in the water and
    made off.

---

1. The title is otherwise unknown. Wang I thought that Ch'ü Yüan held it as Registrar of the three royal clans of Ch'u—Chao, Ch'ü, and Ching.

And as he went he sang: 'When the Ts'ang-lang's waters are clear, I
    can wash my hat-strings in them;
'When the Ts'ang-lang's waters are muddy, I can wash my feet in
    them.'[2]   *20*
With that, he was gone, and did not speak again.

Han Dynasty

(206 B.C.–A.D. 220)

■ Liu Xijun (Liu Hsi-chün) (Late Second Century B.C.) (poem)

TRANSLATED BY TONY BARNSTONE AND CHOU PING

Around 107 B.C., Liu Xijun, a Chinese princess from the Han royal family, was married for political reasons to the chief of the Wusun tribe, a nomadic band to the northwest of China. When she arrived, she found her new husband to be aged and decrepit. They would see each other once in six months or a year, and they could not communicate because they had no common language. This song is attributed to her.

Lament

My family married me off
to the King of the Wusun,
and I live in an alien land
a million miles from nowhere.
My house is a tent.   *5*
My walls are of felt.
Raw flesh is all I eat,
with horse milk to drink.
I always think of home

---

2. This song is also found in the *Book of Mencius*. Tasselled hat-strings were a badge of official
rank. The meaning is that you should seek official employment in good times and retire gracefully when the times are troubled. The Fisherman thinks Ch'ü Yüan is taking things too seriously and should make less fuss about his principles.

and my heart stings.
O to be a yellow snow-goose
floating home again!

10

■ Anonymous Folk Songs from the Music Bureau (120 B.C.)

TRANSLATED BY TONY BARNSTONE AND CHOU PING

The *Yuefu* refers to the Music Bureau, which was set up around 120 B.C. by Emperor Wu of the Han dynasty and abolished in 6 B.C. by Emperor Ai. At the time of its dissolution, it employed eight hundred and twenty-nine people. Its function was to collect songs by the common people, in part as a way of judging their reactions to the imperial government. The Music Bureau employees also performed rites and created sacrificial music. The collected songs came to be called *yuefu* songs, and this term designated a type of poem written in imitation of *yuefu* themes throughout the history of Chinese poetry. As in the songs of *The Book of Songs*, the popular themes of the folksongs have proven to be more enduring and affecting than the ritual hymns or the eulogies in praise of the dynasty. Though the majority of the poems fall into regular lines, there are poems of irregular meter. The Tang dynasty "new Music Bureau" songs of Bo Juyi and Yuan Zhen deviate from *yuefu* form and content, seeking formal freedoms and, often, satirizing the abuses of the ruling classes.

FURTHER READING: Watson, Burton. *The Columbia Book of Chinese Poetry: From Early Times to the Thirteenth Century,* 1984.

The East Gate

I stride out the East Gate
and don't look back.
The next moment I'm in our doorway,
about to break down.
There's no rice in our pot.
I see hangers but no clothes.
So I draw my sword and again head out the East Gate!
My wife grabs me by the shirt and sobs
"I'm not like other wives. I could care less for gold and rank.

5

I'm happy to eat gruel if I'm with you.   *10*
Look up! The sky is a stormy ocean.
Look down! See your small son's yellow face?
To go now is wrong."
"Bah!" I say,
"I'm going now   *15*
before it's too late.
We can barely survive as it is
and white hairs are raining from my head."

A Sad Tune

I sing a sad song when I want to weep,
gaze far off when I want to go home.
I miss my old place.
Inside me, a dense mesh of grief.
But there's no one to go back to,   *5*
no boat across that river.
This heart is bursting but my tongue is dead.
My guts are twisting like a wagon wheel.

■ Fu Xuan (Fu Hsüan) (A.D. 217–278) (poem)

TRANSLATED BY TONY BARNSTONE AND WILLIS BARNSTONE

Fu Xuan was a poet who wrote primarily in the Music Bureau style of poetry. Sixty-three of his poems survive. Apparently, he was an extraordinarily prolific writer, but most of his work has been lost. Despite being impoverished and orphaned as a child, he became rich and famous, largely because of his literary genius. It is common in the Chinese tradition for male writers to write in a female persona. In these poems, the author usually wears the mask of a particular female character, a vain ambitious woman, a noveau riche, a ceremonial goddess, or simply a wife separated from her spouse. It is rare, however, for the male poet to write with the compelling and enlightened sympathy for the maltreatment of women in general shown by Fu Xuan. The devaluation of women in Chinese society rests in part on economics, and these attitudes are likely to be shared by women as well as men. As one woman from today's Sichuan province puts it: "Girls are no use. They can't inherit your house or your property. You struggle all your life, but who gets your house in the end? Your daughters all marry out and belong to someone else."[1] Such attitudes are deeply root-ed in Chinese culture. The female hero of a Six Dynasties folk tale states: "My unhappy parents have six daughters but no son . . . so they have no real descendant. . . . Since we cannot work to support them, but are simply a burden to them and no use at all, the sooner we die the better."[2] The cru-elest manifestation of such attitudes is in the rash of female infanticide that has developed due to China's "One family, one child" population control policy.

To Be a Woman

It is bitter to be a woman,
the cheapest thing on earth.
A boy stands commanding in the doorway
like a god descended from the sky.
His heart hazards the four seas,   5
thousands of miles of wind and dust,
but no one laughs when a girl is born.
The family doesn't cherish her.
When she's a woman she hides in back rooms,
scared to look a man in the face.   10
They cry when she leaves home to marry—
a brief rain, then mere clouds.
Head bowed she tries to compose her face,
her white teeth stabbing red lips.
She bows and kneels endlessly,   15
even before concubines and servants.
If their love is strong as two stars
she is like a sunflower in the sun,
but when their hearts are water and fire
a hundred evils descend on her.   20
The years change her jade face
and her lord will find new lovers.
Who were close like body and shadow
will be remote as Chinese and Mongols.
Sometimes even Chinese and Mongols meet   25
but they'll be far as polar stars.

---

1. W. J. F. Jenner and Delia Davin, eds., *Chinese Lives: An Oral History of Contemporary China* (New York: Pantheon Books, 1987), 130.

2. Jianing Chen, *The Core of Chinese Fiction* (Beijing: New World Press, 1990), 24.

Six Dynasties Period

(A.D. 220–589)

■ Lu Ji (Lu Chi) (A.D. 261–303)
(literary criticism in rhyme-prose)

TRANSLATED BY TONY BARNSTONE AND CHOU PING

Lu Ji was born in Huading in 261 to a great military family, and he also became a distinguished general and literary scholar. He lived through a turbulent time, in which warring states vied for control of a splintered country, and he ended badly, executed on trumped-up charges of treason after losing a major battle. He was a prolific writer, but his only major work was a rhyme-prose piece of literary criticism titled *The Art of Writing* (*Wen Fu*). The influence of this relatively short piece on Chinese literary thought cannot be overestimated, but its value is not merely critical—it is also an excellent exemplar of the concepts it discusses. In *The Art of Writing*, Lu Ji treats the writer's preparation to write, which is described as a kind of Daoist vision quest through internal space and through the literary past, and he treats the process that rises out of this internal journey, believing that the writers' words should match their internal impulse, the way a face changes to express emotion. He also presents a catalogue of styles and genres, gives writing tips, and describes common errors into which writers fall. He describes the sources of inspiration and of writer's block, and he discusses the complex relation between originality and reverence for great writers of the past: "To learn writing from classics is like carving an axe handle with an axe—the model is right in your hand." His cosmic view of the writing process is mirrored by his faith in the universal power of literature: "It can save teetering governments and weak armies; / it gives voice to the dying wind of human virtue." *The Art of Writing* is written in "rhyme-prose" (*fu*), a form characterized by rhymed verse interspersed with prose passages and by a pairing of lines into rhetorical parallelism, rather like Western poetry's use of chiasmus. Lu Ji's verse essay is commonly compared with Alexander Pope's *Essay on Poetry* (and with Pope's model, the *Ars Poetica* of Horace) as a great example of literary criticism in verse; the comparison takes on particular relevance when one compares the balanced rhetoric of Pope's rhymed heroic couplets with Lu Ji's parallelism. With characteristic humility, Lu Ji doubts his own ability to get at the essence of writing ("this art can't be captured by the finest words"), and there will always be something ineffable about the writing process, as the world's creative writing teachers can testify; but in this superlative effort, Lu Ji has created a masterpiece.

FURTHER READING: Birch, Cyril, ed. *Anthology of Chinese Literature, From Earliest Times to the Fourteenth Century,* 1965. Bishop, John L., ed. *Studies in Chinese Literature,* 1965. Hamill, Sam, tr. *Wen Fu: The Art of Writing,* 1987. Owen, Stephen, ed. and tr. *Readings in Chinese Literary Thought,* 1992. Barnstone, Tony, and Chou Ping, eds. and trs. *The Art of Writing: Teachings of the Chinese Masters,* 1996.

The Art of Writing

Preface

After reading many talented writers, I have gained insights into the writing craft. The ways that words and expressions ignite meaning, varied as they are, can be analyzed and critiqued for their beauty and style. Through my own efforts I know how hard it is to write, since I always worry that my ideas fail to express their subject and my words are even further removed from insufficient ideas. The problem is easy to understand; the solution is more difficult. So I started writing this rhymed essay to comment on elegant classics and talk about how strong and weak points find their way into our writings. Someday, I hope, I will be able to capture these subtle secrets in words. To learn writing from classics is like carving an axe handle with an axe—the model is right in your hand, but the spontaneous skills needed to carve a new creation are often beyond words. What can be said, however, is verbalized in what follows.

1. The Impulse

A poet stands between heaven and earth
and watches the dark mystery.
To nourish myself I read the classics.
I sigh as the four seasons spin by
and the swarm of living things kindles many thoughts.   *5*
In rough autumn it hurts to see leaves stripped away,
but how tender the soft sprigs in budding spring.
Morning frost is awe in my heart,
my ambition floats with high clouds,
I devote songs to ancestors   *10*
and sing the clean fragrance of their virtue.
I roam the classics, a forest of treasures,
and love their elegant balance of style and substance.
Inspired, I lay down the book I was reading
and let words pour out from my brush.   *15*

2. Meditation

At first I close my eyes. I hear nothing.
In interior space I search everywhere.
My spirit gallops to the earth's eight borders
and wings to the top of the sky.
Soon, misty and brightening like the sun about to dawn,   *20*
ideas coalesce and images ignite images.
When I drink the wine of words
and chew flowers from the Six Books,[1]
I swim freely in the celestial river
and dive into the sea's abyss.   *25*
Sometimes words come hard—they resist me
till I pluck them from deep water like hooked fish;
sometimes they are birds soaring out of a cloud
that fall right into place, shot with arrows,
and I harvest lines neglected for a hundred generations,   *30*
rhymes unheard for a thousand years.
I won't touch a flower already in morning bloom
but quicken the unopened evening buds.
In a blink I see today and the past,
put out my hand and touch all the seas.   *35*

3. Process

Search for the words and sphere of thought,
then seek the proper order;
release their shining forms
and tap images to hear how they sing.
Now leaves grow along a branching thought.   *40*
Now trace a current to its source.
Bring the hidden into light
or form the complex from simplicity.
Animals shake at the tiger's changing pattern
and birds ripple off when a dragon is seen;   *45*
some words belong together
and others don't join, like jagged teeth,
but when you're clear and calm
your spirit finds true words.
With heaven and earth contained in your head   *50*
nothing escapes the pen in your hand.
It's hard to get started at first,

---

1. The Confucian Classics.

painful like talking with cracked lips,
but words will flow with ink in the end.
Essence holds content as the trunk lifts the tree;   55
language is patterned into branches, leaves and fruit.
Now words and content match
like your mood and face—
smile when you're happy
or sigh when your heart hurts.   60
Sometimes you can improvise easily.
Sometimes you only bite the brush and think.

4. The Joy of Words

Writing is joy
so saints and scholars all pursue it.
A writer makes new life in the void,   65
knocks on silence to make a sound,
binds space and time on a sheet of silk
and pours out a river from an inch-sized heart.
As words give birth to words
and thoughts arouse deeper thoughts,   70
they smell like flowers giving off scent,
spread like green leaves in spring,
a long wind comes, whirls into a tornado of ideas
and clouds rise from the writing-brush forest.

5. The Many Styles

But styles are diverse;   75
there is no absolute standard for anything,
and since things keep changing all the time
how to nail down the perfect description?
Control of language shows an author's skills;
craftsmanship comes when rhetoric pays concept's bill.   80
Writing is a struggle between presence and absence.
Wade through the shallows, and if it's deep, swim.
It is all right to abandon compass and square
if you are a mirror held up to real shapes.
To seduce the eye use a florid style,   85
but to please the mind be precise.
Still, a full description can't be confined;
discourse blooms when it goes beyond words.

6. Genres

Poetry (*shi*) is a bright web of sensuous emotion.
The rhymed essay (*fu*) is clear and coherent as an exposition;   90
stele inscriptions (*bei*) are refined and faithful to detail;
an elegy (*lei*) is a painful tangle of sorrow;
inscriptions (*ming*) are gentle and succinct, but deep in meaning;
didactic compositions (*zhen*) jolt you through powerful logic;
odes (*song*) are gentle in tone and graceful in style;   95
explanatory essays (*lun*) are accurate and convincing;
memorandums to the king (*zou*) should be proper and clear,
written debates (*shuo*) should dazzle with eloquence.
Though there are so many different genres
they all oppose deviance and license   100
and insist you present your argument
with not one wasted word.

7. The Music of Words

Like shifting forms in the world
literature takes on many shapes and styles
as the poet crafts ideas   105
into elegant language.
Let the five tones be used in turn
like five colors in harmony,[2]
and though they vanish and reappear inconstantly
and though it seems a hard path to climb   110
if you know the basic laws of order and change
your thoughts like a river will flow in channels.
But if your words misfire
it's like grabbing the tail to lead the head:
clear writing turns to mud   115
like painting yellow on a base of black.

8. Revision

A sentence may contradict what comes before
or trespass on what follows.
Sometimes the idea is good but words fail,
and fine words may make no sense.   120

---

2. Perhaps an early gesture toward metrical regulation based on the four tones of classical Chinese. The traditional primary colors in China included white, black, red, yellow, and blue/green.

In such cases it is wise to set the two apart
since they harm each other when put together.
It is delicate to judge which idea or word works better—
a difference finer than a wheat ear's hairs.
Weigh each word on a scale; 125
use a measuring cord to make your cuts.

9. The Riding Crop

Sometimes your writing is a lush web of fine thoughts
that undercut each other and muffle the theme.
When you reach the pole there's nowhere else to go—
more becomes less if you try to improve what's done. 130
A powerful phrase at the crucial point
will whip the piece like a horse and make it gallop;
though all the other words are in place
they wait for the crop to run a good race.
A whip is always more help than harm; 135
stop revising when you've got it right.

10. Making It New

Perhaps thoughts and words blend
into a lucid beauty, a lush growth;
they flame like a bright brocade,
poignant as a string orchestra. 140
But if you fail to make it new
you can only repeat the past.
Even when your own heart is your loom
someone may have woven that textile before,
and to be honorable and keep integrity 145
you must disown it despite your love.

11. Ordinary and Sublime

Flowering forth, a tall rice ear
stands proudly above the mass,
a shape eluding its shadow,
its sound refusing echoes. 150
The best line is a towering crag.
It won't be woven into an ordinary song.
The mind can't find a match for it
but casts about, unwilling to give up.

After all, jade veins make a mountain shimmer,   *155*
pearls in water make the river seductive,
green kingfishers give life
even to the ragged thornbushes,
and classic and folk songs
blend into a fine contrast.   *160*

12. A One-String Harp

When an author composes too short a poem,
it trails off with a lonely feeling
like looking down at solitude with no friends
or peering into the vast sky, disconnected.
One string on a harp is crisp and sweet   *165*
but sings without resonance and harmony.

13. Harmony

Trust your words to jangling sounds
and their beauty will lose its luster.
When the ugly and beautiful mix in one body
the good quality will be stained.   *170*
When pipes play too fast for the dancers,
they chase each other without harmony.

14. Heart

When natural reason is sacrificed for strangeness—
an absurd and empty quest for trifles—
words are numb and loveless   *175*
like drifting souls who can never go home.
It's like plucking a thin string near the bridge:
you make harmonies without heart.

15. Dignity

When you race madly after a choral medley,
seduced by cheap and gaudy sounds,   *180*
your flashy poem caters to the vulgar taste
like the rowdy notes of a common tune.
The erotic songs of Fanglu and Shangjian
have base appeal but no grace.

16. Over-Restraint

But if your poem is too pure and graceful   *185*
and free from wild excess,
it's blander than the aftertaste of a spiceless broth,
thinner than ghostly harmonics from a temple lute.
One singer plus a three-person chorus
is elegant but without allure.   *190*

17. Forming Form

Tailor the poem to be plump or slender,
look it over and consider the form.
Make changes when they're apt,
sensitive to the subtle difference they make.
Sometimes raw language conveys clever ideas   *195*
and light words carry weighty truth.
Sometimes you wear old clothes yet make them new
or discover clarity in the murk.
Sometimes you see it all in a flash,
sometimes it takes a lot of work.   *200*
Be like a dancer arcing her long sleeves to music
or a singer improvising to the strings;
like the craft of master wheelwright Bian,[3]
this art can't be captured by the finest words.

18. The Well-Wrought Urn

My heart respects conventional rules   *205*
and laws of composition.
I recall the great works of old masters
and see how my contemporaries have failed—
poems from the depth of a wise heart
may be laughed at by those who are blind.   *210*
Poems fine as jade filigree and coral
are common as beans on the plain,
endless like air in the world's great bellows,
eternal as the universe;
they grow everywhere   *215*

---

3. Zhuangzi tells of an encounter between wheelwright Bian and Duke Huan of Chi. Bian told the duke that his craft contained a subtle, incommunicable essence, which he could not put into words in order to pass on the trade to his son. Words are shadows of life, half-expressions. Therefore, Bian concluded, the "words of the sage" that the duke had been reading were "nothing but dregs."

but my small hands hold only a few.
My water jar is often empty. It worries me.
I make myself sick trying to expand my pieces.
I limp along with short poems
and patch up my songs with common notes.   *220*
I'm never happy with what I've done,
so how can my heart be satisfied?
Tap my work: I fear it clunks like a dusty earthen bowl
and I'm shamed by the song of musical jade.

19. Inspiration

As to the flash of inspiration   *225*
and traffic laws on writing's path—
what comes can't be stopped,
what leaves will not be restrained.
It hides like fire in a coal
then flares into a shout.   *230*
When instinct is swift as a horse
no tangle of thoughts will hold it back:
a thought wind rises in your chest,
a river of words pours out from your mouth,
and so many burgeoning leaves sprout   *235*
on the silk from your brush,
that colors brim out of your eyes
and music echoes in your ears.

20. Writer's Block

But when the six emotions[4] are stagnant,
the will travels yet the spirit stays put—   *240*
a petrified and withered tree,
hollow and dry as a dead river.
Then you must excavate your own soul,
search yourself till your spirit is refreshed.
But the mind gets darker and darker   *245*
and you must pull ideas like silk from a cocoon.
Sometimes you labor hard and build regrets—
then dash off a flawless gem.
Though this thing comes out of me,
I can't master it with strength.   *250*

---

4. Sorrow, joy, hate, love, pleasure, anger. The list is changeable, and at times a seventh emotion, desire, is added.

I often stroke my empty chest and sigh:
what blocks and what opens this road?

21. The Power of a Poem

The function of literature is
to express the nature of nature.
It can't be barred as it travels space   *255*
and boats across a hundred million years.
Gazing to the fore, it forms models for people to come;
looking aft, meditates on symbols of the ancients.
It can save teetering governments and weak armies;
it gives voice to the dying wind of human virtue.   *260*
No matter how far, this road will take you there;
it will express the subtlest point.
It waters the heart like clouds and rain,
and shifts form like a changeable spirit.
Inscribed on metal and stone it spreads virtue.   *265*
Flowing with pipes and strings, each day the word is new.

■ Tao Qian (T'ao Ch'ien) (A.D. 365 or 372–427) (poems and prose)

Daoist poet Tao Qian is also known as Tao Yuanming (T'ao Yüan-ming). He is equally famous for his prose "Preface to the Poem on the Peach Blossom Spring" and for his remarkable poems celebrating a return to nature and an epicurean love of wine. He lived in a time of great political instability known as the Six Dynasties period (A.D. 222–589), and his work expresses the anxiety and weariness that this time produced. He went through a succession of official posts, working as a military advisor and a magistrate, but he was unsatisfied with this life and retired to the country where he lived out his remaining years as a farmer. His work reflects this life: he is primarily known as a poet of nature, China's first great landscape poet. In his work opposition develops between nature's purity and simplicity (exemplified by his own self-representation as a farmer-sage) and the "dusty" world of the court and the marketplace: "After all those years like a beast in a cage / I've come back to the soil again." Like Thoreau in his beanfield for the American literary tradition, Tao Qian came to represent for later Chinese poets the quintessential model of the official who has escaped "the world's net" for a life closer to spiritual values. Countless later poets (notably Wang Wei) echo his lines when they write about the country life. In his own time, however, he was not appreciated. The dominant mode of poetry in his day was flowery and artificial. The great poets of the Tang and Song dynasties, however, came to treasure Tao's poetry for its measured simplicity, its lack of adornment, and its conscious use of common words. Around one hundred thirty of his poems survive.

FURTHER READING: Acker, William. *T'ao the Hermit: Sixty Poems by T'ao Ch'ien,* 1952. Chang, Lily Pao-hu, and Marjorie Sinclair. *The Poems of T'ao Ch'ien,* 1953. Davis, A. R. *T'ao Yuan-ming,* 1984. Hightower, James Robert. *The Poetry of T'ao Ch'ien,* 1970. Hinton, David, tr. *The Selected Poems of T'ao Ch'ien,* 1993.

Return to My Country Home

1.

When young I couldn't bear the common taste;
I loved the mountains and the peaks.
Yet I fell into the world's net
and wasted thirteen years.
But trapped birds long for their old woods   *5*
and fish in the pool still need deep waters
so I'm breaking earth in the south field,
returning to the country to live simply,
with just ten acres
and a thatch roof over some rooms.   *10*
Elm and willow shade the back eaves,
rows of peach and plum trees by the front hall.
A distant village lost in haze,
smoke twines from neighbors' houses.
From deep in the lanes, dogs bark,   *15*
a cock chuckles high up in a mulberry.
No dust or clutter within my courtyard door,
just empty rooms and time to spare.
After all those years like a beast in a cage
I've come back to the soil again.   *20*

2.

No social events in the fields,
no carriage wheels whir through these back roads.
Bright sun, but I close my cane door
and empty myself in my empty rooms.

Sometimes I meet the peasants   *5*
going here and there in palm-leaf raincoats,
but we speak of nothing
except how the crops are doing.

Each day my hemp and mulberries grow taller
and my land gets wider every day   *10*
but any day the frost or hail
could beat it flat as a field of weeds.

3.

So long away from these mountains and lakes,
today I'm wild with pleasure in the fields.
Now nephews and nieces hold my hands
as we part brush and enter the wild ruin of a town.

We search through hills and gravemounds   *5*
and the lingering signs of ancient folk,
scattered wells and traces of their hearths,
rotten stumps of bamboo and mulberry groves.

I ask a man who is gathering wood here
"What happened to all these people?"   *10*
The woodsman turns to me and says
"They're dead, that's all, there's not one left!"

In thirty years, at court or market, all things change.
I know now these are not empty words,
that we live among shadows and ghosts   *15*
and return at last to nothingness.

TRANSLATED BY TONY BARNSTONE AND CHOU PING

Poem from the Series "Drinking Wine"

I built my hut near people
yet never hear carriage or horse.
"How can that be?" you ask.
Since my heart is a wilderness the world fades.
Gathering chrysanthemum by the east hedge,   *5*
my lazy eyes meet South Mountain.
Mountain air is clean at twilight
as birds soar homeward wing to wing.
Beneath these things a revelation hides
but it dies on the tongue when I try to speak.   *10*

TRANSLATED BY TONY BARNSTONE AND CHOU PING

Preface to the Poem on the Peach Blossom Spring

TRANSLATED BY BURTON WATSON

During the T'ai-yüan era (376–397) of the Chin dynasty, there was a man of Wu-ling who caught fish for a living. Once he was making his way up a valley stream and had lost track of how far he had gone when he suddenly came upon a forest of peach trees in bloom. For several hundred paces on either bank of the stream there were no other trees to be seen, but fragrant grasses, fresh and beautiful, and falling petals whirling all around.

The fisherman, astonished at such a sight, pushed ahead, hoping to see what lay beyond the forest. Where the forest ended there was a spring that fed the stream, and beyond that a hill. The hill had a small opening in it, from which there seemed to come a gleam of light. Abandoning his boat, the fisherman went through the opening. At first it was very narrow, with barely room for a person to pass, but after he had gone twenty or thirty paces, it suddenly opened out and he could see clearly.

A plain stretched before him, broad and flat, with houses and sheds dotting it, and rich fields, pretty ponds, and mulberry and bamboo around them. Paths ran north and south, east and west across the fields, and chickens and dogs could be heard from farm to farm. The men and women who passed back and forth in the midst, sowing and tilling the fields, were all dressed just like any other people, and from white-haired elders to youngsters with their hair unbound, everyone seemed carefree and happy.

The people, seeing the fisherman, were greatly startled and asked where he had come from. When he had answered all their questions, they invited him to return with them to their home, where they set out wine and killed a chicken to prepare a meal.

As soon as the others in the village heard of his arrival, they all came to greet him. They told him that some generations in the past their people had fled from the troubled times of the Ch'in dynasty (221–207 B.C.) and had come with their wives and children and fellow villagers to this faraway place. They had never ventured out into the world again, and hence in time had come to be completely cut off from other people. They asked him what dynasty was ruling at present—they had not even heard of the Han dynasty, to say nothing of the Wei and Chin dynasties that succeeded it. The fisherman replied to each of their questions to the best of his knowledge, and everyone sighed with wonder.

The other villagers invited the fisherman to visit their homes as well, each setting out wine and food for him. Thus he remained for several days before taking his leave. One of the villagers said to him, "I trust you won't tell the people on the outside about this."

After the fisherman had made his way out of the place, he found his boat and followed the route he had taken earlier, taking care to note the places that he passed. When he reached the prefectural town, he went to call on the governor and reported what had happened. The governor immediately dispatched men to go with him to look for the place, but though he tried to locate the spots that he had taken note of earlier, in the end he became confused and could not find the way again.

Liu Tzu-chi of Nan-yang, a gentleman-recluse of lofty ideals, heard the story and began delightedly making plans to go there, but before he could carry them out, he fell sick and died. Since then there have been no more "seekers of the ford."[1]

Tang Dynasty

(618–907)

■ Wang Wei (701–761) (poems)

TRANSLATED BY TONY BARNSTONE, WILLIS BARNSTONE, AND XU HAIXIN

Wang Wei is considered to be one of a triad (with Du Fu and Li Bai) of the greatest poets of the Tang dynasty, the most fertile period for Chinese literature. He was equally famous as a landscape painter and was the founder of the Southern school of landscape painters. He was a talented musician as well. The central conflict in Wang Wei's life was between his career as a successful official and his devotion to Daoism and Chan Buddhism. Born Wang Mojie, he took the courtesy name Wei; the two names together (Wei Mojie) make up the Chinese transliteration of the Buddhist saint Vimalakirti, who affirmed the lay practice of Buddhism. Many of his poems express his desire to retreat from the "dusty, busy" world of the court to his estate at Wang River, and his poems often allude to Tao Qian (365–427), whose own hermetic retreat was a model for future poets. Wang Wei's famous series of poems, the Wang River sequence, is set at his estate, and these almost purely objective landscape descriptions are subtly infused with a Buddhist consciousness or, more accurately, lack of consciousness. Of all Chinese poets, Wang Wei is the one who comes closest to

---

1. An allusion to *Analects* XVIII, 6, in which Confucius sends one of his disciples to inquire about a fording place across a river. Here, of course, the phrase refers to seekers of the utopian land of the Peach Blossom Spring.

Zhuangzi's description of the perfect man: "Be empty, that is all. The Perfect Man uses his mind like a mirror—going after nothing, welcoming nothing, responding but not storing." So one of his most famous poems begins with "the empty mountain" as the landscape symbol for the annihilation of consciousness: "Nobody in sight on the empty mountain." Yet Wang Wei always keeps one foot in the real world, and with simplicity, an accurate eye, and piercing social judgment, he portrays the military, the court, the rebellious Daoist drunkard, and the lonely rooms of women whose husbands are fighting on the northern frontier. His poems work with few words, often treating traditional themes, yet the mind behind these words is so fresh and authentic that each simple line takes on the quality of originality, of having been uttered on the first morning of speech. So he has been called, like the Spanish poet Antonio Machado (1875–1939), the poet of few words, the poet of silence. His poems are often described as spoken paintings, his paintings as silent poems. As Robert Payne observes, he "can evoke a whole landscape in a single line."[1]

Wang Wei was born in what is today Shanxi province, and he passed the Imperial Examinations in 721. He had a series of appointments of increasing importance in Changan, the Tang dynasty capital, from Assistant Director of the Imperial Music Office to Right Assistant Director of the Department of State Affairs, his most important post, which he attained in 759. Early in his career, he was sent into a brief exile to the provinces for a minor indiscretion and turned to the tradition of exile poetry, which Li Bai and Du Fu were also to practice, and in which he was to excel. In 756, the Tartar general An Lushan led a rebellion that captured Changan, and Wang Wei was imprisoned in a temple, where he attempted suicide, but later he was sent to Luoyang and forced to serve in the rebels' puppet government. When the rebellion was put down, Wang Wei's life was in danger because of his collaboration, but because he had written a poem while imprisoned denouncing the dismemberment of a court musician who refused to play for the rebels at Frozen Emerald Pond, Emperor Suzong restored him to his former office. Wang Wei never did give up the world of the court for religious practice. His vacillation, however, makes him humanly fallible, and the conflict between his desire to be without desire and his worldly career is central to his most touching poems.

FURTHER READING: Barnstone, Tony, Willis Barnstone, and Xu Haixin, trs. *Laughing Lost in the Mountains: Poems of Wang Wei*, 1992. Chang, Yin-nan, and Lewis C. Walmsley, trs. *Poems of Wang Wei*, 1958. Robinson, G. W., tr. *Poems of Wang Wei*, 1973. Yip, Wai-lim, tr. *Hiding the Universe: Poems by Wang Wei*, 1972. Yu, Pauline, tr. *The Poetry of Wang Wei: New Translations and Commentary*, 1980.

---

1. Robert Payne, ed., *The White Pony* (New York: Mentor, 1947), 151.

My Cottage at Deep South Mountain

In my middle years I love the Tao
and by Deep South Mountain I make my home.
When happy I go alone into the mountains.
Only I understand this joy.
I walk until the water ends, and sit   5
waiting for the hour when clouds rise.
If I happen to meet an old woodcutter,
I chat with him, laughing and lost to time.

Sketching Things

Slender clouds. On the pavilion a small rain.
Noon, but I'm too lazy to open the far cloister.
I sit looking at moss so green
my clothes are soaked with color.

Climbing the City Tower North of the River

Wells and alleys lead me to the rocky hills.
From a traveler's pavilion up in clouds and haze
I watch the sun fall—far from this high city—
into blue mountains mirrored by distant water.
Fire on the shore where a lonely boat is anchored.   5
Fishermen and evening birds go home.
Dusk comes to the silent expanse of heaven and earth
and my heart is calm like this wide river.

About Old Age, in Answer to a Poem by Subprefect Zhang

In old age I ask for peace
and don't care about things of this world.
I've found no good way to live
and brood about getting lost in my old forests.
The wind blowing in the pines loosens my belt,   5
the mountain moon is my lamp while I tinkle my lute. You ask,
how do you succeed or fail in life?
A fisherman's song is deep in the river.

Deer Park

Nobody in sight on the empty mountain
but human voices are heard far off.
Low sun slips deep in the forest
and lights the green hanging moss.

Luan Family Rapids

In the windy hiss of autumn rain
shallow water fumbles over stones.
Waves dance and fall on each other:
a white egret startles up, then drops.

House Hidden in the Bamboo Grove

Sitting alone in the dark bamboo,
I play my lute and whistle song.
Deep in the wood no one knows
the bright moon is shining on me.

Magnolia Basin

On branch tips the hibiscus bloom.
The mountains show off red calices.
Nobody. A silent cottage in the valley.
One by one flowers open, then fall.

To My Cousin Qiu, Military Supply Official

When young I knew only the surface of things
and studied eagerly for fame and power.
I heard tales of marvelous years on horseback
and suffered from being no wiser than others.
Honestly, I didn't rely on empty words;
I tried several official posts.
But to be a clerk—always fearing punishment
for going against the times—is joyless.

5

In clear winter I see remote mountains
with dark green frozen in drifted snow.   *10*
Bright peaks beyond the eastern forest
tell me to abandon this world.
Cousin, like Huilian[1] your taste is pure.
You once talked of living beyond mere dust.
I saw no rush to take your hand and go—   *15*
but how the years have thundered away!

Missing Her Husband on an Autumn Night[2]

1.

Ting, ting. Leaking water.[3] Night has no end.
Far far light clouds and a moon wet with dew.
Fall makes hidden insects cry all night long.
I haven't sent your winter clothes; may flying frost not come.

2.

Cassia shadows begin to cover the moon.[4] More dew.   *5*
My silks are thin but I haven't changed my dress.
Far into the night I play a silver harp, eagerly.
My heart is afraid of empty rooms I don't dare go into.

Seeing Zu Off at Qizhou

Only just now we met and laughed
yet here I'm crying to see you off.
In the prayer tent we are broken.
The dead city intensifies our grief.
Coldly the remote mountains are clean.   *5*
Dusk comes. The long river races by.

---

1. Xie Huilian (397–433) was the valued cousin of the famous Northern and Southern Dynasties poet Xie Lingyun (385–433). Huilian was a talented young man who began to write at the age of ten. Later poets often referred to him when praising their cousins or brothers.

2. This poem is written from the point of view of a woman whose husband is at the frontier.

3. The leaking water refers to the dripping of a waterclock.

4. According to an old legend there is a cassia tree on the moon, 5,000 feet high, and a man called Wu Gang chops the tree as a punishment for seeking immortality. The tree grows whole again after each ax blow.

You undo the rope, are already gone.
I stand for a long time, looking.

Things in a Spring Garden

Last night's rain makes me sail in my wooden shoes.
I put on my shabby robe against the spring cold.
As I spade open each plot, white water spreads.
Red peach flowers protrude from the willow trees.
On the lawn I play chess, and by a small wood   5
dip out water with my pole and pail.
I could take a small deerskin table
and hide in the high grass of sunset.

Escaping with the Hermit Zhang Yin

My brother Zhang has five carts of books.
A hermit, he reads endlessly.
Whenever he soaks his brush with ink he surpasses the sage of grass
      calligraphy.
When he writes a poem it makes a classical verse seem like a
      throwaway.
Behind closed doors under Two Chamber Mountains,   5
he's been a hermit for more than ten years.
He looks like a wild man
pausing with fishermen.
Autumn wind brings desolation.
Five Willows seem taller as their leaves drop.   10
Seeing all this I hope to leave the peopled world.
Across the water in my small cottage
at year's end I take your hand.
You and I, we are the only ones alive.

Song of Peach Tree Spring[5]

My fishing boat sails the river. I love spring in the mountains.
Peach blossoms crowd the river on both banks as far as sight.
Sitting in the boat, I look at red trees and forget how far I've come.
Drifting to the green river's end, I see no one.

---

5. Wang Wei's poem is modeled on an earlier one by Tao Qian (365–427). See Tao Qian's
"Preface to the Poem on the Peach Blossom Spring." This mythical, timeless Taoist paradise is
the quintessential Chinese utopia.

Hidden paths winding into the mountain's mouth.   5
Suddenly the hills open into a plain
and I see a distant mingling of trees and clouds.
Then coming near I make out houses, bamboo groves and flowers
where woodcutters still have names from Han times
and people wear Qin dynasty clothing.   10
They used to live where I do, at Wuling Spring,
but now they cultivate rice and gardens beyond the real world.

Clarity of the moon brings quiet to windows under the pines.
Chickens and dogs riot when sun rises out of clouds.
Shocked to see an outsider, the crowd sticks to me,   15
competing to drag me to their homes and ask about their native
        places.
At daybreak in the alleys they sweep flowers from their doorways.
By dusk woodcutters and fishermen return, floating in on the waves.

They came here to escape the chaotic world.
Deathless now, they have no hunger to return.   20
Amid these gorges, what do they know of the world?
In our illusion we see only empty clouds and mountain.
I don't know that paradise is hard to find,
and my heart of dust still longs for home.

Leaving it all, I can't guess how many mountains and waters lie behind   25
        me,
and am haunted by an obsession to return.
I was sure I could find my way back, the secret paths again.
How could I know the mountains and ravines would change?
I remember only going deep into the hills.
At times the green river touched cloud forests.   30
With spring, peach blossom water is everywhere,
but I never find that holy source again.

Suffering from Heat[6]

The red sun bakes earth and heaven
where fire clouds are shaped like mountains.
Grass and woods are scorched and wilting.
The rivers and lakes have all dried up.
Even my light silk clothes feel heavy   5
and dense foliage gives thin shade.

---

6. See also "The Fire Sermon" from the Maha-Vagga.

The bamboo mat is too hot to lie on,
I dry off, soaking my towel with sweat.
I think of escaping from the universe
to be a hermit in a vastness   *10*
where a long wind comes from infinity
and rivers and seas wash away my turbulence.
When I see my body holding me here
I know my heart is not enlightened.
Abruptly I enter a gate of sweet dew   *15*
where there is a medicine to cool me.

Questioning a Dream

Don't be fooled. Why bother with the shallow joys of favor or worry
    about rejection?
Why flounder in the sea helping others, or being abandoned?
Where can you dig up a Yellow Emperor[7] or Confucius to consult
    with?
How do you know your body isn't a dream?

■ Li Bai (Li Pai) (701–762) (poems)

TRANSLATED BY WILLIS BARNSTONE, TONY BARNSTONE, AND CHOU PING

Li Bai is probably the best-known Chinese poet in the West and with Du
Fu is considered the finest poet of the Tang dynasty. He has attracted the
best translators and has influenced several generations of American poets,
from Ezra Pound to James Wright. Yet among Western readers there is considerable confusion surrounding his name. He is best known in English as
Li Po, though he is also called Li Pai, Li T'ai-po, and Li T'ai-pai, all of these
being Wade-Giles transliterations of his Chinese names; for each of these
names there is a new English version, according to the now-accepted Pinyin
transliteration system (Li Bo, Li Bai, Li Tai-bo, and Li Tai-bai). To add to
the confusion, Ezra Pound, in *Cathay,* his famous sequence of Chinese
poems in translation, refers to him as Rihaku, a transliteration of the Japanese pronunciation of his name.

The facts of Li Bai's life come to us through a similar veil of contradictions and legends. Where he was born is unknown—and there are those

---

7. A wise, mythical emperor.

who say he was of Turkic origin — but it seems he was probably born in Central Asia and was raised in Sichuan province. His brashness and bravado are characteristic of a tradition of poets from this region, including the great Song poet Su Dongpo. He claimed he was related to the Imperial family, though this claim is likely to be spurious. Perhaps he wandered as a Daoist hermit in his teens; certainly, Daoist fantasy permeates his work. He left his home in 725 and wandered through the Yangtze River Valley, hoping to gain recognition of his talents, though he was alone among the great Tang poets in never taking the Imperial Examinations. He married the first of his four wives during this period. In 742, he was summoned to the capital at Changan, modern Xian, and was appointed to the Hanlin Academy by Emperor Xuanzong. During his time in the capital, he became close friends with Du Fu, who addresses a number of poems to him. Within a few years, he was expelled from the court (apparently for insulting the emperor's favorite eunuch) and made to leave Changan, and he began presenting himself as an unappreciated genius, or as one friend named him "a banished immortal." In 755, the An Lushan rebellion took place, in which a Turkish general led his group of Chinese border armies against the emperor. Li Bai was forced to leave Hunan for the South, where he entered the service of the Prince of Yun, sixteenth son of the Emperor, who led a secondary revolt. Eventually, Li was arrested for treason, sent into exile, and was later given amnesty. He continued his wanderings in the Yangtze Valley, seeking patrons, until his death at sixty-two.

About one thousand poems attributed to Li Bai have come down to us, though some of them were probably written by imitators. While most of the poems were occasional poems (poems written for specific occasions), others incorporated wild journeys, Sichuan colloquial speech, and dramatic monologues, such as his famous "A Song of Zhanggan Village." Perhaps the most remarkable subject for his poems, however, was himself. He portrays himself as a neglected genius; a drunk; a wanderer through Daoist metaphysical adventures; and a lover of moon, friends, and women. His colloquial speech and confessional celebration of his own sensual flamboyance and fallible self made him the best loved and most imitated Chinese poet in English and helped to establish a conversational, intimate tone in modern American poetry. Ezra Pound's *Cathay* put him at the center of the revolution in modern verse. All these qualities plus an extraordinary lucidity of image made him extremely popular in China as well, in his day and today. A number of his poems are in the Han dynasty *yuefu* form, which allowed him to indulge in radically irregular lines that gave his imagination free play. He was an influential figure in the Chinese cult of spontaneity, which emphasized the poet's genius in extemporizing a poem: "Inspiration hot, each stroke of my pen shakes the five mountains." Among the many legends about Li Bai, the most enduring is the account of his death. Like Ishmael in the crow's nest, wanting to penetrate the illusory world that he saw reflected in the water, Li Bai was said to be so drunk in a boat that he fell overboard and drowned, trying to embrace the moon reflected in the water. Since the "man in the moon" is a woman in Chinese myth, the legend of Li's death takes on an erotic meaning, mixing thanatos and eros. As in *Moby Dick,* to "strike through the mask" and see the face of truth is to embrace death.

FURTHER READING: Cooper, Arthur. *Li Po and Tu Fu,* 1973. Hamill, Sam. *Banished Immortal: Visions of Li T'ai-po,* 1987. Pound, Ezra. *Cathay,* 1915. Seaton, J. P., and James Cryer. *Bright Moon, Perching Bird,* 1987. Waley, Arthur. *The Poetry and Career of Li Po,* 1950.

A Song of Zhanggan Village

My hair was still cut straight across my forehead
and I was playing, pulling up flowers by the front door,
when you rode up on a bamboo horse
and danced round the bench, monkeying with the green plums.
And we lived together in the village of Zhanggan,   5
two small people without hate or suspicion.
At fourteen I became your wife,
so bashful I never laughed.
I lowered my head and faced the dark wall.
You called me a thousand times but I couldn't look at you.   10
At fifteen my tortured brow calmed
and I wanted to be with you like ashes in dust.
I'd die waiting for you, embracing a pillar,
so why must I climb the widows' tower?
At sixteen you left   15
for Qutang Gorge where floodwaters crush against Yanyu Rock
and I haven't touched you for five months.
Now I hear monkeys screeching into the sky
and mosses drown the place by our door
where your feet sank in the earth when you left,   20
moss so deep I can't sweep it away.
It's a windy autumn. The leaves are falling early.
In the eighth month butterflies dart in pairs
through high grass in the west garden.
They hurt my heart.   25
I grow older, my face ruddy with pain.
If you are coming down through the Three Gorges
please write me

and I will come out to meet you
even as far as Long Wind Sands.   *30*

Grievance at the Jade Stairs

The jade steps are whitening with dew.
My gauze stockings are soaked. It's so late.
I let down the crystal blind
and watch the glass clear autumn moon.

Drinking Alone by Moonlight

A pot of wine in the flower garden,
but no friends to drink with me.
So I raise my cup to the bright moon
and to my shadow, which makes us three,
but the moon won't drink   *5*
and my shadow just creeps about my heels.
Yet in your company, moon and shadow,
I have a wild time till spring dies out.
I sing and the moon shudders.
My shadow staggers when I dance.   *10*
We have our fun while I can stand
then drift apart when I fall asleep.
Let's share this empty journey often
and meet again in the milky river of stars.

Drunk All Day

To live in this world is to have a big dream;
why punish myself by working?
So I'm drunk all day.
I flop by the front door, dead to the world.
On waking, I peer at the garden   *5*
where a bird sings among the flowers
and wonder what season it is.
I think I hear him call "mango birds sing in spring wind."
I'm overcome and almost sigh.
But no, I pour another cup of wine,   *10*

sing at the top of my lungs and wait for the bright moon.
When my song dies out, I forget.

Song on Bringing in the Wine

Can't you see the Yellow River
pours down directly from heaven?
It sprints all the way to the ocean
and never comes back.
Can't you see the clear hall mirror   5
is melancholy with our gray hair?
In the morning our braids are black silk.
In the evening they are snow.
When happy, be happy all the way,
never abandoning your gold cup   10
empty to face the moon alone.
Heaven gave me talent. It means something.
Born with genius, a failure now, I will succeed.
Although I waste a thousand ounces of gold
they will come back.   15
We butcher cows, cook lambs,
for a wild feast, and must drink
three hundred cups at a time.
Friends Chengfuze and Danqiuchen,
bring in the wine   20
and keep your mouths full.
I'll sing for you. I'll turn
your ears. Bells and drums,
good dishes and jade are worth
nothing. What I want   25
is to be drunk, day and night,
and never again sober up.
The ancient saints and sages are forgotten.
Only the fame of great drunks
goes from generation to generation.   30
In the Temple of Perfect Peace
Prince Cheng once gave a mad party,
serving ten thousand pots of wine.
Long ago. Tonight, let no one
say I am too poor to supply   35
vats of alcohol. I'll find
my prize horse and fur coat
and ask my boy to sell them
for fine wine. Friends, we drink

till the centuries of the sorrow   *40*
of our existence dissolve.

Questioning in the Mountains

You ask me why I live in the jade mountains.
I smile, unanswering. My heart is calm.
Peach petals float on the water, never come back.
There is a heaven and earth beyond
       the crowded town below.

Song

The whole forest is a blur
woven by fog.
Cold mountain is color of melancholy,
mauve.
Twilight comes into a tall house.   *5*
Someone is unhappy upstairs.
Standing on the jade steps,
a woman is wasting time, nothing to do.
Birds wing off for home
but what road can take me there?   *10*
Pavilion after pavilion join far, far, far.

Seeing Meng Haoran Off

From Yellow Crane Tower you sail
the river west as mist flowers bloom.
A solitary sail, far shadow, green mountains at the empty end of vision.
And now, just the Yangtze river touching the sky.

Seeing a Friend Off

Blue mountains past the north wall,
White water snaking eastward.
Here we say goodbye for the last time.
You will fade like a hayseed blowing ten thousand miles away.

Floating clouds are the way of the wanderer.   5
The sun sets like the hearts of old friends.
We wave goodbye as you leave. Horses neigh and neigh.

Saying Goodbye to Song Zhiti

Clear as empty sky, the Chu River
meanders to the far blue sea.
Soon there will be a thousand miles between us.
All feelings distill to this cup of wine.
The cuckoo chants the sunny day;   5
monkeys on the river banks are howling evening wind.
All my life I haven't wept
but I weep here, unable to stop.

Brooding in the Still Night

Bright moonlight before my bed;
I think at first the floor has frost.
I look up to the mountain moon,
then bow my head in a dream of home.

Hearing a Flute on a Spring Night in Luoyang

Whose jade flute secretly flies in the night?
Spring wind scatters sound all over Luoyang.
The midnight flute keens a farewell song, "Snap the Willow Branch."
Thinking of my old home and garden, I break.

River Song

Magnolia oars. A spicewood boat.
Jade flutes and gold pipes fill the air at bow and stern.
We have a thousand jugs of tart wine
and singing girls who drift with us on the waves.
Like a Taoist immortal floating off on a yellow crane,   5
my wandering mind empties and soars with white gulls.
Qu Yuan's poems hang overhead with sun and moon

but the Chu king's palace is an empty mountain.
Inspired, each stroke of my brush shakes the five mountains.
The poem done, I laugh proudly over the hermit's land.   *10*
If fame and money could last forever
the Han River would flow backward.

I Listen to Jun, a Monk from Shu, Play His Lute

The Shu monk carries a green silk lute
west down Omei Mountain
and each sweep of his hand
is the song of a thousand pines in the valley.
Flowing water cleans my wanderer's heart   *5*
and the sound lingers like a frosty bell
till I forget the mountain soaking in green dusk,
autumn clouds darkly folding in.

Song of the North Wind

The fire dragon lives at Ice Gate
and light comes from its eyes at night,
yet why no sun or moon to light us here?
We have only the north wind howling furiously out of heaven.
On Yen Mountain snowflakes are as big as a floor mat   *5*
and every flake drops on us.
The woman of Yo Zhou in December
stops singing and laughing. Her eyebrows tighten.
Lounging against the door she watches people pass by
and remembers her husband at the north frontier   *10*
and the miserable cold.
When he left he took his sword to guard the border.
He left his tiger-striped quiver at home,
with its white-feathered arrows, now coated
with dust on which spiders spin their traps.   *15*
The arrows remain, useless. Her husband is dead
from the war. He won't return.
The widow won't look at the arrows.
Finally, it's too much, and she burns them to ashes.
Easier to block the Yellow River with a few handfuls of sand,   *20*
than to scissor away her iron grief
here in the north wind, the rain, the snow.

Hunting Song

Frontier sons are lifelong illiterates
who know only how to hunt big game and brag about being tough
    guys.
They feed their Mongolian ponies white grass
to make them plump and strong in the autumn.
They race proudly on their horses chasing the sun's shadows.   5
They brush snow off with the crack of a gold whip.
Half drunk, they call their falcon and wander far off to hunt.
They stretch their bows like a full moon and never miss.
One whistling arrow flies and two gray cranes fall.
The desert spectators step back in dread.   10
These virile heroes shake the sands.
Confucian scholars are no match for them.
What good is it to lock one's doors and read books till one is gray?

Missing the East Mountains

It's long since I've gone to the East Mountains.
How many seasons have the tiny roses bloomed?
White clouds—unblown—fall apart.
In whose court has the bright moon dropped?

Summer Day in the Mountains

Lazy today. I wave my white feather fan.
Then I strip naked in the green forest,
untie my hatband and hang it on a stone wall.
Pine wind sprinkles my bare head.

Having a Good Time by Myself

Facing wine, not aware it's getting dark,
I've been sitting so long my gown brims over
    with petals.
Drunk, I rise to follow the moon in the brook
long after birds and people have gone home.

Sent Far Off

This room was all flowers when my beauty was here.
Now gone, only an empty bed.
The embroidered quilt is folded up. I can't sleep.
Three years gone, yet I still smell her fragrance.
Why doesn't the fragrance dissipate?   5
Why doesn't my beauty come back?
I miss her until yellow leaves drop
and white dawn moisture soaks the green moss.

■ Du Fu (Tu Fu) (712–770) (poems)

If there is one undisputed genius of Chinese poetry it is Du Fu. The
Daoist Li Bai was more popular, the Buddhist Wang Wei was sublimely simple and more intimate with nature, but the Confucian Du Fu had extraordinary thematic range and was a master and innovator of all the verse
forms of his time. During his lifetime, he never achieved fame as a poet and
thought himself a failure in his worldly career. Perhaps only a third of his
poems survive due to his long obscurity; his poems appear in no anthology
earlier than one dated one hundred thirty years after his death, and it was-
n't until the eleventh century that he was recognized as a preeminent poet.
His highly allusive, symbolic complexity and resonant ambiguity is at times
less accessible than the immediacy and bravado of Li Bai. Yet there is a suddenness and pathos in much of his verse, which creates a persona no less
constructed than Wang Wei's reluctant official and would-be hermit or Li
Bai's blithely drunken Daoist adventurer. Most of what we know of his life is
recorded in his poems, but there are dangers to reading his poems as history and autobiography. By the time he was in his twenties, he was referring
to his long white hair—in the persona of the Confucian elder. As Sam
Hamill notes, "It was natural that many a poet would adopt the persona of
the 'long white-haired' and old man—this lent a younger poet an authority
of tone and diction he might never aspire to otherwise."[1] Du Fu is sometimes called the "poet of history" because his poems record the turbulent
times of the decline of the Tang dynasty and constitute in part a Confucian
societal critique of the suffering of the poor and the corruption of officials.
He also records his own sufferings, exile, and falls from grace, as well as the

---

1. Sam Hamill, tr., *Facing the Snow: Visions of Tu Fu* (New York: White Pine Press, 1988),
unpaged.

death of his son by starvation, but some critics have suggested that the poems on these themes are exaggerated in the service of self-dramatization.

Du Fu was born to a prominent but declining family of scholar-officials, perhaps from modern-day Henan province, though he referred to himself as a native of Duling, the ancestral home of the Du clan. In the Six Dynasties period, his ancestors were in the service of the southern courts; his grandfather, Du Shenyan, was an important poet of the early Tang dynasty, and a more remote ancestor, Du Yu (222–284), was a famed Confucianist and military man. In spite of family connections, Du Fu had difficulty achieving patronage and/or governmental postings, and twice failed the Imperial Examinations, in 735 and 747. He was a restless traveler, and the poems of this early period show him to be a young man given to revelry, military and hunting arts, painting, and music. In 744, he met Li Bai, and the basis was formed for one of the world's most-famed literary friendships; the two poets devote a number of poems to each other. In 751, he passed a special examination that he finagled through submitting rhyme-prose works directly to the emperor, but it was not until 755 that he was offered a post—a rather humilating posting in the provinces—which he rejected, accepting instead the patronage of the heir apparent. In the winter of that year, however, the An Lushan rebellion broke out, and the emperor fled to Sichuan and abdicated; the heir apparent became the new emperor in Gansu province. Meanwhile, the rebels seized the capital, and Du Fu, attempting to join the new emperor in the distant northwest, was captured by the rebels. He was detained for a year but managed to escape; and after traveling in disguise through the occupied territory, he joined the emperor's court in the position of Reminder. He was arrested soon after for his outspokenness in defending a friend, a general who had failed to win a battle, but he was pardoned and exiled to a low posting in Huazhou. He quit his job there and moved to Chengdu, where he and his family depended upon the kindness of friends and relatives and moved again and again to avoid banditry and rebellions.

In spite of this instability, his poems show a serenity during this period, particularly those years from 760–762, when he lived in a "thatched hut" provided by a patron and friend named Yan Yu, who hired him in the years that followed as a military advisor. After Yan's death in 765, Du Fu left Chengdu, traveling down the Yangtze River, finding patrons, and dreaming of a return to Changan, which was prevented by invasions from Tibet. He spent his final three years traveling on a boat, detained in sickness, and finally winding down to his death as he journeyed down the Yangtze, apparently accepting the withering of his life: "It's a release to feel my spirit fade;/Let sorrow come when it may" (from "Written While Traveling on a Boat, Ill and Fevered").

FURTHER READING: Cooper, Arthur, tr. *Li Po and Tu Fu*, 1973. Hamill, Sam, tr. *Facing the Snow: Visions of Tu Fu*, 1980. Hawkes, David, tr. *A Little Primer of Tu Fu*, 1967. Hinton, David, tr. *The Selected Poems of Tu Fu*, 1988. Hung, William, tr. *Tu Fu: China's*

Greatest Poet, 1952. Rexroth, Kenneth, tr. *One Hundred Poems from the Chinese*, 1971. Seaton, J. P., and James Cryer, trs. *Li Po and Tu Fu: Bright Moon, Perching Bird*, 1987.

Facing Snow

Battles, sobbing, many new ghosts.
An old man, I sadly chant poems.
Wild clouds lower and touch the thin evening.
Fast snow dances in swirling wind.
A ladle abandoned, no green wine in the cask.   5
Fire still seems to redden the empty stove.
No news, the provinces are cut off.
With one finger I write my sorrows in the air.

TRANSLATED BY TONY BARNSTONE AND CHOU PING

Broken Lines

River so blue the birds seem to whiten.
Flowers almost flame on the green mountainside.
Spring is dying yet again.
Will I ever go home?

TRANSLATED BY TONY BARNSTONE AND CHOU PING

A Hundred Worries

I remember I had a child heart at fifteen,
healthy as a brown calf running wild.
In August, when pears and dates ripened in the courtyard
I'd climb the trees a thousand times a day.
All at once I am fifty,   5
and I sit and lie around more than I walk or stand.
I force smiles and small talk to please my patrons,
but a hundred worries tangle my emotions.
Coming home to the same four empty walls,
I see this grief mirrored in my old wife's glance.   10
My sons don't treat their father with respect.
They greet me by the door with angry screams for rice.

TRANSLATED BY TONY BARNSTONE AND CHOU PING

To Wei Ba

In this life we never meet,
orbiting far like polar stars,
so what evening is this
where I can share your candlelight?
Youth is just a few slim hours,   5
and now our hair and sideburns are gray.
Last time I came, half our old friends were ghosts.
I moaned in shock, my guts on fire.
How could I know that after twenty years
I'd enter your hall again?   10
When we parted you were unmarried.
Now your sons and daughters form a line,
sweetly show respect for their father's friend
and ask me where I'm from.
With their questions still flying,   15
you send them for wine and plates,
for spring chives fresh cut in the evening rain
and rice steamed in with yellow millet.
"How hard it is for us to meet!" You cry,
and one toast grows to ten.   20
After ten cups I'm still not drunk,
just warmed by our old friendship.
Tomorrow mountains will come between us,
and we'll be lost in the world like mist.

TRANSLATED BY TONY BARNSTONE AND CHOU PING

Dreaming of Li Bai

I've swallowed sobs for the lost dead,
but this live separation is chronic grief.
From the malarial south of the river
no news comes of the exiled traveler,
but you visit my dream, old friend,   5
knowing I ache for you.
Are you are a ghost?
No way to tell with the long road between us.
Your spirit comes through green maple woods
slips home past darkening border fortresses.   10
You are caught in the law's net,
so how can your spirit have wings?
The sinking moon pours onto the rafters

and your face glows in my mind.
The water is deep, the waves are wide.   *15*
Don't let the dragons snatch you!

TRANSLATED BY TONY BARNSTONE AND CHOU PING

A Painted Falcon

Wind and frost swirl from white silk
where a magnificent black hawk is painted.
His shoulders poised as he seeks for hares,
glancing sidelong with a Hun's angry blue eyes.
Grasp the gleaming leash and collar,   *5*
whistle him down from his bar,
and he'll strike the common birds
spattering the plain with blood and feathers.

TRANSLATED BY TONY BARNSTONE AND CHOU PING

New Moon

Narrow rays from the first slice of moon
slant from the quavering edge of the dark orb,
which barely crests the ancient fortress,
wallowing in the surf of evening clouds.
The river of stars is one eternal color.   *5*
Empty cold pours through the mountain pass.
The front courtyard is white dew
and chrysanthemums secretly drenched with dark.

TRANSLATED BY TONY BARNSTONE AND CHOU PING

Spring Night Happy about Rain

The good rain knows when to fall.
It comes when spring blossoms.

It steals in on the wind, submerged in night,
moistening all things gently without sound.

Black wilderness, black paths, black clouds;   5
only a torch on a river boat sparks.

At dawn I see all things red and wet,
and flowers drown the City of Brocade.1

TRANSLATED BY TONY BARNSTONE AND CHOU PING

River Village

The clear river curves to embrace the village.
Everything is relaxed here in long summer.
Swallows come and go as they like in the hall,
gulls are necking in the water.   5
My old wife is drawing a Go board on paper,
my little son is hammering a needle into a fishing hook.
As long as old friends give me daily supplies,
what else could my humble body desire?

TRANSLATED BY TONY BARNSTONE AND CHOU PING

Moonlit Night[2]

In Fuzhou tonight there's a moon
my wife can only watch alone.
Far off, I brood over my small children
who don't even remember Changan.   5

Her satin hair dampening in fragrant mist,
jade arms chilled by clear moonlight,
when will we lean together between empty curtains,
beaming as tear tracks dry on our faces?

TRANSLATED BY TONY BARNSTONE AND CHOU PING

---

1. A poetic epithet for the city of Chengdu in Sichuan Province.
2. Written while captive in Changan, separated from his family.

Ballad of the War Wagons

Carts grumble and rattle
and horses whinny and neigh
as the conscripts pass, bows and quivers strapped to their
    waists.
Parents, wives and children run to see them off
till dust-clouds drown the bridge south of Changan.   5
Tugging at soldiers' clothes, they wail and throw themselves in the
    way,
their wails rising into the clouds.

On the roadside a passerby asks what's happening.
The soldiers only say "We're called up often,
some went North at fifteen to guard the Yellow River   10
and still at forty are farming frontier settlements out West.
We left so young the village chief wrapped our turbans for us;
we came back white-haired but now we're off to fortify the
    frontier!
The men there have shed a salt ocean of blood,
but the warlike Emperor still lusts for empire.   15
My lord, haven't you heard how in two hundred districts east of
    China's mountains
countless villages grow just weeds and thorns?
Even if a stout wife tries to plough and hoe,
east to west the crops grow wild over broken terraces.
Qin soldiers are fierce warriors,   20
so we are driven forth like chickens or dogs.

You, sir, can ask questions
but conscripts don't dare complain.
This winter
they haven't released the Guanxi troops   25
but officials still press for the land tax.
Land tax! How are we to pay that?
The truth is it's a sour thing to have sons.
Better to have a daughter—
at least she can marry a neighbor.   30
Our sons lie unburied in the grass.
My lord, have you seen the Blue Sea's shore
where the old white bones lie ungathered?
New ghosts keen and old ghosts weep
jiu, jiu, like twittering birds as rain sifts from the bleak sky.   35

TRANSLATED BY TONY BARNSTONE AND CHOU PING

P'eng-ya Road

I remember fleeing the rebels
through dangerous northern canyons,

the midnight moon shining bright
on narrow P'eng-ya Road.

So poor we went on foot,   5
we were embarrassed meeting strangers.

A few birds sang in the valleys,
but we met no one ever returning.

My daughter was so starved she bit me,
she screamed her painful hunger.   10

I clamped her mouth shut tight,
fearful of wolves and tigers.

She struggled hard against me,
she cried and cried.

My son was sympathetic   15
and searched the wilds for food.

Then five days of heavy rain arrived,
and we trudged through freezing mud.

We had no coats, no shelter,
we were dressed in cold, wet clothes.   20

Struggling, struggling, we made
but a mile or two each day.

We ate wild fruits and berries,
and branches made our roof.

Mornings we slogged through water,   25
evenings we searched for smoke on the skyline.

We stopped at a marsh
to prepare our climb to the pass,

and met a Mr. Sun
whose standards are high as clouds.   30

We came through the dark
and lamps were lit, gates opening before us.

Servants brought warm water
so we could bathe our aching feet.

They hung paper banners   35
in our honor.

Mrs. Sun came out with all her children.
They wept for our condition.

My children slept, exhausted,
until we roused them with food.   *40*

Our host took a vow
he'd always remain my brother.

His home was made our home,
to provide for every comfort.

Who could imagine in such troubled times   *45*
he'd bare his heart and soul?

A year has passed since that fated night.
The Barbarians still wage war.

If I had the wings of the wild goose,
I'd fly to be at his side.   *50*

TRANSLATED BY SAM HAMILL

Gazing in Springtime

The empire is shattered but rivers and peaks remain.
In spring wild grass and trees drown the city.

A time so bad, even the flowers rain tears.
I hate this separation, yet birds startle my heart.

The signal fires have burned three months;   *5*
I'd give ten thousand gold coins for one letter.

I scratch my head and my white hair thins
till it can't even hold a pin.

TRANSLATED BY TONY BARNSTONE AND CHOU PING

Thoughts While Night Traveling

Slender wind shifting the shore's fine grass.
Lonely at night below my boat's tall mast.
Stars hang low as the vast plain broadens,
the swaying moon makes the great river race.
How can poems make me known?   *5*
I'm old and sick, my career over.

Drifting, just drifting. What kind of man am I?
A lone gull floating between earth and sky.

TRANSLATED BY TONY BARNSTONE AND CHOU PING

Broken Boat

All my life I've had my heart set on going off
to the land of the lakes—the boat was built for it,
and long ago too. That I used to row
every day on the creek that runs by my rail gate
is beside the point. But then came the mutiny,   5
and in my panic I fled far away, where
my only concern was to get back here
to these familiar hills.
The neighbors are all gone now,
and everywhere the wild bamboo   10
sprouts and spreads and grows tall.
No more rapping its sides as I sing—
it's spent the whole autumn underwater.
All I can do now is watch the other travelers—
birds sailing off in their westward flights,   15
and even the river, embarrassing me
by moving off eastward so easily.
Well, I could dig up the old one,
and a new one's easy enough to buy,
but it's really the running away that troubles me—   20
this recent escape and so many before—
that even in this simple cottage
a man cannot stay put long.

TRANSLATED BY STEPHEN OWEN

■ Meng Jiao (Meng Chiao) (751–814) (poems)

TRANSLATED BY JAMES A. WILSON

Meng Jiao was the oldest and among the best of the circle of writers who gathered around the great prose master Han Yu in the last decade of the eighth century. He met Han Yu in Changan in 791, but though Han Yu passed the Imperial Examinations in 792, Meng Jiao failed, as he did again in 793. He finally passed in 796 but did not receive a position for four years, and even then it was a humiliatingly insignificant post in the provinces. He even lost this post within a few years and settled in Luoyang, where he lived for the rest of his life dependent on patrons and friends. Around five hundred of his poems survive, most of them in the "old style" verse (*gu shi*). Though Meng Jiao was popular enough in his own time, his reputation went into a tailspin some centuries after his death, because of his brash, disturbing, and jarring verse, which seemed to lack grace and decorum. In fact, it wouldn't be an exaggeration to say that his verse has inspired not so much neglect as active hatred, even in such distinguished readers as Su Shi (Su Dongpo), who states baldly in his two poems "On Reading Meng Jiao's Poetry" that "[he] hate[s] Meng Jiao's poems," which sound to him like a "cold cicada wail":

> My first impression is of eating little fishes—
> What you get's not worth the trouble;
> Or of boiling tiny mud crabs
> And ending up with some empty claws.
> (tr. Burton Watson)

There is no doubt that Su Dongpo is a master of the literary put-down, and, after all, Meng Jiao's poems *do* come across as shrill, self-obsessed, and self-pitying—yet in this lies much of his interest. The glaze of decorous objectivity that is so beautiful in much of Chinese poetry is scraped off in his poems, revealing a didactic would-be Confucian moralist who ends up writing startling, ghostly, and elegiac poems about his own sorrows and idiosyncracies. The series of "Autumn Meditations" from which the following poems come is among his best work. Written late in life, it portrays the poet as despised and sick with illness and self-doubt, and the whole piece is shot through with the elegiac sound of autumn (shang), which Ouyang Xiu writes about later in his marvelous piece "The Autumn Sound." If it seems strange to celebrate so fallible a figure, consider his own words: "these sour moans / are also finished verse."

FURTHER READING: Owen, Stephen. *The Poetry of Meng Chiao and Han Yu,* 1975.

from *Autumn Meditations*

1.

moonlight edges
past the door

like a sword's
inevitable flight

my old bones   *5*
can't move for fear

my sick strength
sinks even more

insects complain
as they lust for what glitters   *10*

birds try to nest
in the fire of stars

widows caress
their last white hairs

orphans weep   *15*
for no end to their pain

all the vain years
float farther off

my will to follow
falls with the night   *20*

3.

the frost air
invades my sick bones

I'm so old
my frame forms ice

rotted hairs   *5*
stab me in the dark

cold aches
can't be fought off

my violent cries
wing me toward light   *10*

a wild power
battles with my crutch

until I collapse
too gaunt to hold up

my gut hungry   *15*
and my heart brought to ruin

fools on all sides
would have me take drugs

from their words
it's clear I'm despised   *20*

let my ears buzz
let my choked soul open

let me recall
how there's no end to merit

in full sunlight   *25*
I see what sores remain

bound by dark
I hear the knots of flies

their aim
is unerring   *30*

one feeds
at my freshest scab

yet while you gorge
on hidden poisons

I bear with   *35*
the life I have left

your frozen flights
won't take you far

winter will wear
on your hearts   *40*

birth and death
possess a season

cold and heat
soon turn on each other

I raise up   *45*
to thank the grand master of fates

who granted me
mine when I asked

■ Han Yu (Han Yü) (768–824) (poem)

TRANSLATED BY TONY BARNSTONE AND CHOU PING

Han Yu was born in 768 in Nanyang, Henan province, to a literary family. He is considered to be among China's finest prose writers, second only to Sima Qian, and he is the first among the Eight Great Prose Masters of the Tang and Song. His father died when he was two, and he was raised in the family of his older brother, Han Hui. He taught himself to read and write and was a student of philosophical writings and of Confucianist thought. His family moved to Changan in 774 but was banished to southern China in 777 because of his association with disgraced minister Yuan Zai. Han Hui died in 781, leaving the family in poverty, and they returned north around 784. In 792, after four attempts, Han Yu passed the Imperial Examinations, and a few years later he went into the service of the military governor of Bianzhou, and later of the military governor of Xuzhou. Finally, in 802, he obtained a post as instructor at the Imperial University, a job that he held periodically, between other postings and several periods of exile; ultimately, he was made rector of the university. After a number of other distinguished posts in the government, he died at the age of 56 in Changan.

Han Yu was a Confucian thinker and was deeply opposed to Buddhism, which was then popular in the court. In fact, he came close to being executed in 819 for sending a letter to the emperor in which he denounced "the elaborate preparations being made by the state to receive the Buddha's fingerbone, which he called 'a filthy object' and which he said should be 'handed over to the proper officials for destruction by water and fire to eradicate forever its origin.'"[1] He believed that literature and ethics were intertwined, and he led a revolution in prose style against the formal ornamentation then popular. He championed instead *gu wen* (old style prose), which was characterized by simplicity, logic, and an emphasis on apt and exact expression. He was the center of a group of prose writers who adopted this style, a group that included Meng Jiao, whose poetry Han Yu appreciated. Other writers included in this anthology who adopted this style are Ouyang Xiu and Su Shi (Su Dongpo). While Han Yu's lasting reputation lies as a prose innovator, he was also a fine poet.

FURTHER READING: Owen, Stephen. *The Poetry of Meng Chiao and Han Yu,* 1975. Watson, Burton. *The Columbia Book of Chinese Poetry: From Early Times to the Thirteenth Century,* 1984.

Mountain Rocks[1]

Ragged mountain rocks efface the path.
Twilight comes to the temple where bats hover.
Outside the hall I sit on steps and gaze at torrential new rain.

---

1. Liu, Wu-chi, Liu *An Introduction to Chinese Literature* (Bloomington:Indiana University Press, 1973), 126.

---

1. Han Yu's poems are often satirically anti-Buddhist, as in his poem "The Girl of Mt. Hua," which depicts Daoists and Buddhists abandoning their temples at the sight of a beautiful young woman. In this poem, however, he abandons his famous hatred of Buddhism and celebrates the natural simplicity of a Buddhist mountain retreat.

Banana leaves are wide, the cape jasmine is fat.
A monk tells me the ancient Buddhist frescos are good 5
and holds a torch to show me, but I can barely see.
I lie quiet in night so deep even insects are silent.
From behind a rise the clear moon enters my door.

In the dawn I am alone and lose myself,
wandering up and down in mountain mist. 10
Then colors dazzle me: mountain red, green stream,
and a pine so big, ten people linking hands can't encircle it.
Bare feet on slick rock as I wade upstream.
Water sounds—shhhh, shhhh. Wind inflates my shirt.
A life like this is the best. 15
Why put your teeth on the bit and let people rein you in?
O friends,
how can we grow old without returning here?

■ Xue Tao (Hsüeh T'ao) (768–831) (poems)

Xue Tao was well respected as a poet during the Tang dynasty. She was born either in the Tang capital Zhangan or in Chengdu, present-day Sichuan province, when her father, a minor government official, was posted there. A story about her childhood, perhaps apocryphal, suggests that she was able to write complex poems by the age of seven or eight. She may have gained some literary education from her father, but he died before she had come to marriageable age, and she ended up being a very successful courtesan (one of the few paths for women in Tang dynasty China in which conversation and artistic talent were encouraged). After Wei Gao, the military governor, became her literary patron, her reputation was widespread. She seems to have had an affair with another famous literary figure, Yuan Zhen. Late in life she went to live in seclusion and put on the habit of a Taoist churchwoman.

FURTHER READING: Larsen, Jeanne, tr. *Brocade River Poems: Selected Works of the Tang Dynasty Courtesan Xue Tao,* 1987.

Spring-Gazing Song

Blossoms crowd the branches: too beautiful to endure.
Thinking of you, I break into bloom again.
One morning soon, my tears will mist the mirror.
I see the future, and I will not see.

TRANSLATED BY CAROLYN KIZER

Seeing a Friend Off

The waterland spreads with reeds and night frost.
Cold moon and mountains are bluish pale.
Who says we'll be thousands of miles apart?
My dream can travel to the farthest border pass.

TRANSLATED BY TONY BARNSTONE AND CHOU PING

■ Li Gongzuo (Li Kung-tso) (c. 770–c. 848) (story)

TRANSLATED BY CHOU PING

Li Gongzuo was one of the finest Tang dynasty writers of literary-language stories. He came from what is today Gansu province but seems to have lived primarily in central and southern China. He may have been distantly related to the Imperial family, and after passing his examinations, he had a career as a low-ranking administrator. Only four of his stories survived, but two of them are classics. "Xie Xiaoe" is an early detective story, often anthologized, whereas "The Governor of Southern-Bough" is an expansion of Shen Jiji's famous tale "The World inside a Pillow." Like Zhuangzi's parable of the man who dreamed he was a butterfly, this story has become a famous Chinese touchstone about the illusory nature of life and the equivalence of life and dream.

FURTHER READING: Wang, Chi-chen, tr. *Traditional Chinese Tales,* 1944. Wong, Elizabeth Te-chen, tr. *Ladies of the Tang: 22 Classical Chinese Stories,* 1961. *The Dragon King's Daughter. Ten Tang Dynasty Stories,* 1954.

The Governor of Southern-Bough

Chunyu Fen from Dongping was a chivalrous man roaming in the Wu and Chu areas. Indulging in alcohol and a quick temper, unconstrained by rules and concerns in life, he threw away an enormous portion of his family wealth to support other gallant and brave men. As he had training in martial arts, he was once appointed a subordinate general in the Huinan Army, but because he offended the marshal by losing his temper after too many a drink, he was reprimanded and dismissed. After that he started drifting again and became even more careless in his way of life. He made the wine bottle his profession.

His ancestral home was about three miles away to the east of the Guangling (now Yangzhou) city. To the south of his house, there was a giant ancient locust tree with thick boughs and long branches, providing a green shade of several *mu*.[1] Chunyu Fen and his gallant friends would drink wildly under this tree every day.

One day in the ninth month in the seventh year of the Zhenyuan reign (A.D. 791), Chunyu Fen drank too much and got sick. Two friends at the table held his arms and helped him return home. They let him rest in the east corridor outside the main hall, saying, "Have a nap. We'll feed the horses and wash our feet, and we'll leave when you are better." Chunyu Fen removed his headpiece and rested his head on the pillow. In a state of half consciousness, he seemed to have a dream. He saw two messengers in purple who knelt before him, saying, "The king of the Hui'an Kingdom sent us to deliver his invitation to you." Without knowing what he was doing, Chunyu got off the bed and smoothed up his clothing, and followed the two messengers to the gate. There was a black-painted carriage pulled by four horses with an entourage of seven to eight attendants. They helped him to get on the carriage and they went through the gate, heading straight to the hole under the giant locust tree.

The messengers drove the carriage directly into the hole. Chunyu Fen was very much surprised and yet dared not to ask. Suddenly he saw mountains and rivers, clouds and sky, vegetation and roads, though they were all quite different from those in the human world. After traveling for about a dozen miles, a city wall appeared in the distance. Carriages and pedestrians were coming and going endlessly. Attendants standing on both sides of the carriage were announcing their arrival in harsh voices and pedestrians were trying to make way for them as soon as they could. Then they entered a big city with red gates and tall towers. Four golden characters on the gate tower read "Great Huian Kingdom." The gate guards saluted them in a hurry and ran to pass on the news of their coming. Soon a messenger on horseback came with an announcement, "The king's order—the royal son-in-law has traveled a long distance. Take a rest in the Donghua Guest House first." After saying that, he led the way.

After a while, they came to a gate with doors wide open, and Chunyu Fen stepped down from the carriage and went in. He saw painted banisters, sculptured pillars, rows of beautiful flowers and exotic fruits in the courtyard and, upon entering the hall, he saw to his delight chairs and tables, seat cushions, curtains, wine and dishes ready to serve. Suddenly he heard a voice announcing, "The Right Prime Minister is coming," and Chunyu Fen went down the stairs to wait for him respectfully. A man in a purple gown with an ivory court-tablet walked to him rapidly. They exchanged

---

1. *Mu* is a unit of land in Chinese, equal to 0.0667 hectares.

greetings in most polite and appropriate ways. "Our majesty," the Right Prime Minister said, "welcomes you to our out-of-the-way kingdom and plans to marry you to our princess." "How could a humble person like me hope for this?" Chunyu Fen answered. The Right Prime Minister invited Chunyu Fen to visit the king together with him.

After about a hundred steps, they passed through a red-painted gate. With spears, halberds, long and short axes displayed, hundreds of guards on either side of the passage stepped back to let them pass. Among them Chunyu Fen spotted a friend, Zhou Bian, who used to be one of his wine-drinking companions. Chunyu Fen was secretly happy about this, though he dared not walk up to him to talk. The Right Prime Minister led him to the main hall, where the guards looked grave and formidable. This must be the king's palace, he thought. Sitting on the throne was a tall and serious-looking man, dressed up in a white silk robe and a red crown. Chunyu Fen was shivering in fear and did not look up. The guards on either side asked him to kneel down.

"Some time ago," the king said, "we heard from your father that he would not turn down our small kingdom's proposal, and thus let my second daughter Yaofang marry you and serve you." Chunyu Fen continued to kowtow and didn't dare to say a single word. The king continued, "You stay in the guest house for the time being, and we will arrange the wedding next." Then there was a royal edict, ordering the Right Prime Minister to accompany Chunyu Fen to the guest house. Chunyu Fen kept wondering how this marriage had come about. His father was a general stationed on the border and was lost somewhere there in a foreign land. No one knew if he was still alive or not. Is it possible that his father's negotiations with the northern barbarians had led to all this? Chunyu Fen was utterly confused.

That night, everything needed in the wedding was well prepared: the four wedding gifts—lambs, wild swans, coins and silk—impressive guards of honor, girl singers and bands, food and candles, carriages and horses. Besides there were a bevy of girls, who were called Bright-sun, Green-stream, Super-immortal, Lower-immortal and the like, and each of them had hundreds of attendants. Those girls all wore emerald-phoenix bonnets, capes decorated with golden clouds and colorful jewelry and gold hairpins that dazzled the eye. They were strolling about and having fun. When they arrived at the guest house, they all competed in teasing Chunyu Fen. Charming and seductive, they rendered Chunyu Fen speechless with their wit and eloquence.

One of the girls said to Chunyu Fen, "One day on the third day in the third month I went to the Zen-wisdom Temple with Madame Linzhi to watch Youyan doing the Brahman dance in the India Courtyard. With other girls I sat on a stone couch under the northern window. At that time you were a lad and you got off your bamboo horse to watch. Teasing and flirting, all by yourself you approached us by force. Qiongyin and I tied a knot with a red handkerchief and hung it on a bamboo branch. How could you forget all that? Also, once on the sixteenth in the seventh month, I met Shangzhenzi in the Xiaogan Temple and we listened to Master Qixuan's interpretation of the Guanyin Scripture. I donated two gold phoenix hairpins at the lecture and Shangzhenzi donated a box made of rhino horn. You were also present among the audience at that time. You asked for Master Qixuan's permission and had a closer look at the hairpins and the box, sighing again and again with amazement and marveling at them for a long time. Then you turned around and looked at us, saying "Such beautiful girls and such beautiful things do not belong to the human world." For a while you tried to find out our names, then you asked where we lived, but I ignored your questions. With your eyes nailed on me all the time, you looked in love. Haven't you been missing me at all?" Chunyu Fen replied with two lines from the *Book of Songs,* "Hidden deep in my heart, never forgotten for a single day." The girls responded, "How can one imagine that we are relatives now!"

Then three men dressed up in impressive hats and sashes came to salute Chunyu Fen, saying "We are here by the king's order to be the royal son-in-law's best men." One of them was Chunyu Fen's friend, so Chunyu Fen pointed at him and asked, "Aren't you Tian Zihua from Pingyi?" The man answered, "Right." Chunyu Fen walked up to him and held his hands, and they talked for a long while. Then Chunyu Fen asked, "How come you are living here?" Tian Zihua answered, "I was roaming about and fortunately came into favor with the Right Prime Minister Duan, who is the Marquis of Wucheng, and thanks to him I settled down here." Chunyu Fen asked again, "Zhou Bian is also here, do you know him?" Zihua answered "Zhou Bian is an important figure here. He is the Chief of Criminal Investigation with a lot of power and influence. He protected me on several occasions." They talked and laughed, feeling very happy. Before long, a spoken message was relayed to them, "Now the royal son-in-law may enter." The three best men handed him a sword, jade ornaments, hat and clothes and asked Chunyu Fen to change. Zihua said, "What a surprise to witness your magnificent wedding here today! Don't forget me."

Now dozens of beautiful girls started to play various kinds of exotic music. The sound was sweet and clear while the melodies were slow and slightly melancholy. Such music was never heard in the human world. Dozens of others were holding candles to lead the way. On both sides golden and emerald curtains were carried. Colorful and shining, they extended for about a mile. Chunyu Fen sat straight in a carriage, feeling both dizzy and nervous. Tian Zihua tried to tell him jokes and make him relax. The group of girls and relatives all got into their phoenix-wings carriage and followed them. They reached a gate with a sign, "Xiuyi Palace."

The bevy of immortal girls was already lined up on both sides and asked Chunyu Fen to get off the carriage. The rituals and procedures in the wedding process were exactly the same as those in the human world. When the fans and head-cover were removed, Gold Branch Princess's face was revealed. Though just fourteen or fifteen years old, she was as beautiful as a fairy. The token-exchange rituals were really impressive.

After their marriage, the couple fell deeper in love day by day while Chunyu Fen became more and more glorious and influential in social life. His carriages and banquets for entertaining guests were only second to the king's in importance and scale.

One day, the king ordered Chunyu Fen and officials to summon up troops, and they went on a royal hunt at Tortoise Mountain in the west of the kingdom. The mountains there were tall and magnificent, the lakes vast and deep, the forest thick and grass green. All kinds of animals and birds made their home there. They hunted many animals and returned to the city after evening.

Chunyu Fen said to the king, "On my wedding day, your majesty said that it was according to my father's wishes. I remember that my father was stationed at the border to assist the generals there and he was defeated and lost in a foreign country. There was no communication between us for seventeen or eighteen years. If your majesty knows where he is, please let me go visit him." The king immediately answered, "Your father is defending the territory in the north; we have been in touch all the time. You can write a letter to inform him; there is no need to visit him personally." Chunyu Fen asked his wife to prepare presents, and together with the letter he had them sent to his father. A few days later, a reply came. Chunyu Fen scrutinized the letter and found written there the old man's life story, along with words of love and instruction, and the memories and emotions he remembered from the past. His father asked about the relatives—who were still in this world and who were already gone—and he also asked what was established in the hometown and what had been abandoned. Then he bemoaned the long distance that made communication between them almost impossible. His sad words conveyed a sense of depression. But he would not allow Chunyu Fen to visit him, saying, "It is going to be in the year of Dingchou that we shall meet." Chunyu Fen looked at the letter and couldn't help sobbing.

One day, his wife asked Chunyu Fen, "Why don't you want to run an office?" Chunyu Fen replied, "I'm so used to this kind of relaxed life that I know nothing about administration." His wife said, "You take the position and I'll assist you." So his wife talked to the king. Several days later, the king told Chunyu Fen, "The Southern Bough State in my kingdom doesn't have good administration. The governor is now removed from his position and I want to make use of your great talent. Please accept this appointment. You can go with my daughter." Chunyu Fen accepted the appointment very politely. The king issued an edict to relevant officials to prepare for the new governor's journey. Gold, jade, silk, trunks, maids and servants, carriages and horses were allocated and lined up at the end of the main street, so the princess could take them with her after the seeing-off ceremony. Chunyu Fen was only a roaming chivalrous man when he was young and he had never dreamed about anything like this. Now he was extremely happy and he submitted a memorial to the king.

"I, your humble servant, an insignificant son from a general's family, have no real talent and skills. When given too much responsibility, I might ruin the court's administration. I feel worried that with the reins in my hand, I will cause upheavals through poor governance. Therefore, now I hope to search for talented and virtuous personnel to make up for my shortcomings. Your humble servant feels that the Chief of Criminal Investigation, Zhou Bian from Yingchuan, is loyal, honest and straightforward and he maintains the law strictly with no selfish motives, thus he would make a very good assistant. Besides, Tian Zihua from Pingyi, an intellectual with no official position yet, is a cautious man with great integrity. He has a keen sense for the changes in the world and knows very clearly about the essence of moral education. Those two persons and I have been friends for over ten years and thus I know their talent well and I can trust them with my administrative work. I humbly request that Zhou Bian be appointed the Chief of Law in the Southern Bough State and Tian Zihua the Chief of Agriculture in the Southern Bough State. This way I can make achievements in administration while national laws and regulations will be maintained in good order."

The king made the appointments according to the memorial.

That night, the king and the queen held a seeing-off banquet in the southern part of the city. The king said to Chunyu Fen, "The Southern Bough is a big state in our kingdom. The land is fertile with abundant local products and the population is big with a strong disposition. It takes caring policies to run that state well. Now with the assistance of Zhou and Tian, I hope you'll work hard and live up to the kingdom's expectation."

The queen said to the princess, "Mr. Chunyu Fen is a staunch man with a passion for drink, and on top of that he is young. The art of being a good wife is to be tender and obedient. If you can deal with him well, I'll feel relieved. Though the Southern Bough State is not too far away from the capital, we will no longer see each other in the morning and evening every day. Now we have to part and I can't help crying."

Chunyu Fen and the princess respectfully saluted the king and queen and set off to the south. They sat in the carriage protected by guards on horseback, laughing and talking all the way, feeling elated.

Several days later, they arrived at the Southern Bough State. All the officials and clerks, Buddhist and Daoist monks, elders from local gentry, bands, carriages, armed guards and horses with bells came to welcome them. Crowds and the sound of drums and bells extended for about a dozen miles. The city wall, the lookouts and the towers all looked very magnificent and seemed to exude happiness. When they were passing through the gate, they saw a big horizontal sign hanging overhead, "Capital of Southern Bough State." There were rows of red-painted lattice windows, and gates with weapons displayed on the outside. They all looked solemn and profound.

The moment Chunyu Fen stepped out of his carriage he started investigating the local customs and tried to lessen the suffering of the people there. He trusted his administrative work to Zhou Bian and Tian Zihua and thus did a good job in governing the state. In the twenty years of his service, moral education became far reaching in the area, the local people not only sang praises of him, building a monument to record his achievements, but also built a temple for him when he was still alive. With great appreciation for his talent, the king bestowed him land and titles of nobility and made him an equal to the rank of prime minister. Step by step, Zhou Bian and Tian Zihua were promoted to high ranks for their achievement in administration. In those years, Chunyu Fen had five sons and two daughters. The sons were all given official positions by means of the official hereditary benefits, the daughters all got engaged with sons related to the royal family. Their glory and wealth were so overwhelming that for a time no one was Chunyu Fen's match.

One year, however, a nation called the Sandalwood Vines came to invade the Southern Bough State. The king ordered Chunyu Fen to train his officers and soldiers and get ready to resist the intruders. Chunyu Fen submitted a memorial, recommending Zhou Bian as the leader of 30,000 soldiers so as to stop the coming enemy at Yrotai City. But Zhou Bian depended too much on his own valor and overlooked the enemy's strength, and he was completely defeated. Zhou Bian managed to escape alone on horseback, having lost his armor, and returned to the city at midnight. The enemy collected all the military supplies and armor before they returned to their own country.

Chunyu Fen threw Zhou Bian in jail and asked for punishment from the king, but the king pardoned him. It was in that same month that Zhou Bian, the Chief of Criminal Investigation, died of a vicious ulcer in his back. Then Chunyu Fen's wife, the Gold Bough Princess, became sick and also died in about ten days. Chunyu Fen submitted his resignation so as to accompany the princess's hearse back to the capital. The king approved it. Tian Zihua, the Chief of Agriculture, was appointed the acting governor.

Chunyu Fen cried aloud in his sadness and that signaled the departure of the princess's body back to the capital. Guards of Honor escorted the procession, men and women all wailed by the roadside, people and clerks arranged tables of wine and food for sacrifice. Those who held on to the carriage or blocked the road to stop Chunyu Fen from leaving them were too many to be counted.

When they finally arrived at the capital, the king and the queen dressed in white were also standing on the outskirt of the city, weeping and waiting for the hearse to come home. A posthumous title, "Shunyi Princess," was bestowed on the princess. Escorted by guards of honor and bands, draped in a royal cover, the princess's coffin was buried at the

Coiling-Dragon Mountain, about three miles away to the east of the capital. In the same month, Rongxin, the son of the ex-Chief of Criminal Investigation Zhou Bian also accompanied his father's coffin back to the capital.

Chunyu Fen, as the governor of a big state for a long time, had made extensive friends among the officials in the capital and all the aristocratic families were on good terms with him. Since coming back to the capital on resignation, he had no restraints in associating with people and entertaining friends, and his influence grew day by day until even the king grew suspicious of him. Just then someone submitted a memorial, "Unusual changes are observed in the heavenly bodies, forecasting a big disaster in the country: the capital has to be moved, the ancestor's temple will be destroyed. The event will be provoked by outsiders, though its cause can be located inside the innermost walls." The public opinion was that Chunyu Fen had overstepped boundaries and caused this omen from the heavens. Therefore the king took away Chunyu Fen's guards, banned his association with friends and put him under house arrest.

Chunyu Fen was proud of the fact that as a governor in a big state for many years he had never made any administrative mistake. Now that he had to put up with groundless complaints and defamation, he was very unhappy. The king also understood how he felt, and therefore said to him, "We've been family for over twenty years. Unfortunately my daughter died too young and could not live to her old age together with you. We are really sad about this." The queen added that she wanted to have the grandchildren nurtured in the palace. Then the king said to Chunyu Fen, "You've been away from your hometown for so long, it's time that you returned there to visit your relatives. You can leave my grandchildren here, don't worry about them. Three years later, I will welcome you back." Chunyu Fen replied, "This is my home. Where do you want me to return?" The king laughed, saying, "You were from the human world, your home is not here." When the king said this, it was as if Chunyu were being awakened from a dream, and he fell into a confusion through which pierced clear memories of his former life. He couldn't help weeping and asked for permission to go home. The king ordered guards to escort him. Chunyu Fen kowtowed again and took his departure. Once again he saw the same two messengers in purple and followed them.

Outside the main gate, the carriage waiting there was very shabby; his attendants, servants and carrriage driver were not there at all. He sighed deeply in surprise. After getting on the carriage and running for a few miles, they went out of the city. He looked around and recognized the road along which he had came from the east and saw the same rivers, mountains and fields. Only the two messengers were no longer that impressive. Chunyu Fen felt even more unhappy and asked them. "When will we get to Guangling?" The two messengers were singing, and they ignored his questioning for a long time, though one eventually snapped, "Soon."

After a while, the carriage came out of a hole. Chunyu Fen saw the streets in his hometown, exactly the same as many years ago. He felt sad and tears started to drop. The two messengers helped him to get off the carriage and enter his own house. After walking up the steps, Chunyu Fen saw his own body lying in the eastern corridor outside the main hall. He was really frightened and didn't dare to approach himself. The two messengers yelled his name loudly for a few times, and he suddenly woke up as if he never had slept. He saw the servants sweeping the courtyard and two friends were washing their feet, sitting on the couch. The evening sun was still lingering on the western wall; the wine left in the goblet still looked almost brimming by the east window. Things go fast in a dream—as if one whole lifetime had elapsed!

Chunyu Fen marveled at what had happened and sighed. Then he called his two friends and told them about his dream. They were astonished. They followed Chunyu Fen to the outside and found the big hole under the locust tree. Chunyu Fen pointed at the hole and said, "I went through this hole in my dream." The two friends thought it must be some fox or tree ghost haunting this place. They summoned servants with axes and chopped off the swollen parts of the tree trunk as well as the brush and branches to search for the innermost part of the hole. They dug for more than ten yards and suddenly found a big opening, spacious enough to contain a bed. Soil was accumulated there in the shape of walls, towers and palace with bushels of ants hiding there. Right in the middle there was a small cinnabar-colored platform, occupied by two giant ants. They had white wings and red heads, and were a little bit more than three inches long. Protected by several dozen large ants, no ants could get close to them. They must have been the king and the queen. So this was the capital of the Huian Kingdom.

Then they found another opening. It led straight up to the southern bough for about forty yards. The tunnel went zigzag inside the tree. There were also city walls and small towers with swarms of ants living there. That must be the Southern Bough State where Chunyu Fen served as the governor. In addition, there was another hole, extending twenty yards to the west with a big low opening in the middle in the shape of a basement. There was a rotten tortoise there, its shell as big as a bushel container. Soaked in accumulated rain, grass was growing rampantly, almost covering the tortoise shell. This must have been Tortoise Mountain where Chunyu Fen went hunting. Then they found another hole, about ten yards on the east, with old tree roots entangled together like snakes and dragons. There was a mound in the middle about a yard tall—that must be the princess' tomb.

Chunyu Fen recalled all those days and sighed with deep feeling. He found that everything here was exactly as he saw in his dream. He did not want his friends to destroy it and ordered the servants to cover it up as it was. That night, a big storm came suddenly. The next morning when they went back there to check, all the ants had moved to some unknown place. It matched the earlier prediction, ". . . a big disaster in the country: the capital has to be moved." Now the omen had come true.

Then Chunyu Fen recalled the invasion initiated by the Nation of Sandalwood Vine and thus asked his two friends to help him search for it. At one place five hundred yards away to the east of the residence, there was a dried mountain stream with a big Sandalwood tree covered by vines, and its shade was so thick that it blocked out the sun. By the tree there was a hole with swarms of ants hiding in it. Wasn't this the Nation of Sandalwood Vine?

O, if the ant's intelligence and spiritual power are beyond human understanding, how about those big animals hiding in the mountains?

At that time, Chunyu Fen's wine friends Zhou Bian and Tian Zihua both lived in the Liuhe county and they were out of touch with Chunyu Fen for about ten days. Immediately Chunyu Fen sent servants to visit them and learned that Zhou Bian had died of an acute disease while Tian Zihua was also sick in bed. Chunyu Fen realized then both the emptiness of being a governor in the Southern Bough State and the ephemerality of human life. Therefore he was converted to Daoism and became abstinent from both sex and wine. Three years later in the year of Dingchou, he died at home at the age of forty-seven, exactly as his father's letter said in the dream.

The present author Gong Zuo was traveling from Wu to Luoyang in the eighth month in autumn in the eighteenth year of Zhenyuan reign (802). With his boat moored by the Hui river, he met with Chunyu Fen by chance. He asked Chunyu Fen about that dream and investigated the actual places many times and wrote this biographical sketch to entertain those who are nosy for anecdotes. Though this story relates to the supernatural and involves things not found in the canons, I hope it can admonish those who obtain official positions and luxurious life by dishonest means. For generations of gentlemen to come, please be aware of the fact that promotions are accidental, like that in the Southern Bough, and please don't be too proud about your fame and position. Li Zhao, ex-advisor to military affairs in Huazhou wrote the following lines as a comment on this story:

> The highest pay and position,
> the most powerful in the capital,
> but in the eyes that can see through—
> humans and ants are just the same.

■ Bo Juyi (Po Chü-i) (772–846) (poems)

Bo Juyi was born in Henan to a poor family of scholars. He took the Imperial Examinations at age twenty-seven and dreamed, with his friend Yuan Zhen, of being a reformer; but his career as an official was less than illustrious, and his attempts to criticize incidents of injustice only caused him to be banished from the capital (Changan) in 815. He was the Prefect of Hangzhou (822–825) and then of Suzhou (825–827) but finally retired from political life, which he found ultimately to be a disappointment, and turned to Buddhism. As a writer, however, he fared somewhat better. He was popular in his lifetime, and his poems were known by peasants and court ladies alike. He was very popular in Japan: a number of his poems found their way into *The Tale of Genji,* he was the subject of a *noh* play, and he has even become a sort of Shinto deity. More than twenty-eight hundred of his poems survive, as he was careful to preserve his work; in 815, he sent his writings to Yuan Zhen, who edited and compiled them into an edition of his collected work in 824–825. His poems show an interest in recording his times and his private life alike and often reveal an empathy with the poor that belies the heights of his own career. They are often written in a deliberately plain style, and some poems are written in imitation of the folk songs collected by the Music Bureau (*yuefu* poems) in the second century B.C. Arthur Waley notes that according to a popular account, Bo Juyi used to read his poems to an old peasant woman and would change any line that she could not understand. There is a benevolent directed intelligence in his poems that comes through the refractions of culture and translation and makes us feel the powerful presence of this poet who died more than a thousand years ago.

FURTHER READING: Levi, Howard S. *Translations from Po Chu-i's Collected Works,* 1971. Waley, Arthur. *The Life and Times of Po Chu-i,* 1949; *Translations from the Chinese,* 1971.

Night Rain

Chirp of an early cricket. Silence.
The lamp dies then flares up again.
Night must be raining outside the window:
plink, plunk on the banana leaves.

TRANSLATED BY TONY BARNSTONE AND CHOU PING

The Old Charcoal Seller

The old charcoal seller
chops wood and makes charcoal at South Mountain.
With a face full of dust and soot,
his hair is grey and his fingers all black.
How much can he make from selling charcoal?
Just enough to clothe his body and feed his mouth.
His clothes are very thin.
but he wishes it colder to keep charcoal prices high.
It snowed one foot outside the city during the night,

5

and he drove his charcoal cart through frozen ruts at dawn.   *10*
Now the sun is high, the ox is tired and the man hungry;
they take a rest in the mud outside the South Gate.
Who are those two men galloping near on horseback?
—Messengers in white shirt and yellow gown.
They read a document in the name of the emperor   *15*
and turn the cart around, yell at the ox to head north.
A cartful of charcoal weighs about a ton,
but the palace messengers make the old man give it up
for just half a roll of red gauze and a piece of damask silk
they leave tied around the ox's head.   *20*

TRANSLATED BY TONY BARNSTONE AND CHOU PING

Watching the Reapers

Farmers have few slow months
and the fifth one is double busy.
Southern wind rises at night.
and the wheatfields yellow.
Women carry food on shoulder,   *5*
kids bring water along.
They go together to feed their men
who are working at the South Hill
with feet burned by hot soil,
backs scorched by the bright and flaming sky.   *10*
But they are too exhausted to feel the heat
and don't want the long summer days to end.

There is a poor woman nearby,
carrying her son in her arm.
She gleans wheat ears with her right hand,   *15*
a broken basket hanging on her left elbow.
She looks up and tells me
a story that twists my heart:
all their harvest is gone to pay for the land rent,
she picks these ears to fill hungry stomachs.   *20*
What achievement, what virtue, have I
that I need not labor like a farmer?
I have an income of three hundred bushels,
and a surplus of food at the end of year.
I am ashamed, and these thoughts   *25*
nag at me for the rest of the day.

TRANSLATED BY TONY BARNSTONE AND CHOU PING

At the End of Spring

To Yüan Chen.[1]

> The flower of the pear-tree gathers and turns to fruit;
> The swallows' eggs have hatched into young birds.
> When the Seasons' changes thus confront the mind
> What comfort can the Doctrine of Tao give?
> It will teach me to watch the days and months fly   5
> Without grieving that Youth slips away;
> If the Fleeting World is but a long dream,
> It does not matter whether one is young or old.
> But ever since the day that my friend left my side
> And has lived an exile in the City of Chiang-ling,   10
> There is one wish I cannot quite destroy:
> That from time to time we may chance to meet again.

TRANSLATED BY ARTHUR WALEY

On His Baldness

> At dawn I sighed to see my hairs fall;
> At dusk I sighed to see my hairs fall.
> For I dreaded the time when the last lock should go . . .
> They are all gone and I do not mind at all!
> I have done with that cumbrous washing and getting dry;   5
> My tiresome comb for ever is laid aside.
> Best of all, when the weather is hot and wet,
> To have no top-knot weighing down on one's head!
> I put aside my dusty conical cap;
> And loose my collar-fringe.   10
> In a silver jar I have stored a cold stream;
> On my bald pate I trickle a ladle-full.
> Like one baptized with the Water of Buddha's Law,
> I sit and receive this cool, cleansing joy.
> Now I know why the priest who seeks Repose   15
> Frees his heart by first shaving his head.

TRANSLATED BY ARTHUR WALEY

---

1. Bo Juyi's great friend.

Light Furs, Fat Horses

> A show of arrogant spirit fills the road;
> a glitter of saddles and horses lights up the dust.
> I ask who these people are—
> trusted servants of the ruler, I'm told.
> The vermilion sashes are all high-ranking courtiers;   5
> the purple ribbons are probably generals.
> Proudly they repair to the regimental feast,
> their galloping horses passing like clouds.
> Tankards and wine cups brim with nine kinds of spirits;
> from water and land, an array of eight delicacies.   10
> For fruit they break open Tung-t'ing oranges,
> for fish salad, carve up scaly bounty from T'ien-ch'ih.
> Stuffed with food, they rest content in heart;
> livened by wine, their mood grows merrier than ever.
> This year there's a drought south of the Yangtze.   15
> In Ch'ü-chou, people are eating people.

TRANSLATED BY BURTON WATSON

■ Liu Zongyuan (Liu Tsung-yüan) (773–819) (poems, fable, and essay)

Liu Zongyuan was one of the finest prose writers of the Tang dynasty and was one of only two Tang dynasty writers included among the Eight Great Prose Masters of the Tang and Song. He was a friend of Han Yu, and one of the followers of the "ancient style" prose movement, which emphasized clarity and utility over ornament in prose writing. He was also a relatively minor poet. He was born and raised in Changan, the capital of the Tang dynasty. After a highly successful early career in civil government, he was reassigned to a post in the provinces (in Yongzhou, Hunan province) after the abdication of Emperor Shunzong in 805. A decade later, he was banished even farther away, to modern Guangxi. His works in exile are considered to be his finest. The writings done in the capital were bureaucratic in nature, and he considered them primarily a means to advance his career; in exile, however, he wrote a number of delightful didactic pieces, showing a Neo-Confucian synthesis of both Daoism and Buddhism (unlike Han Yu, Liu Zongyuan was not adverse to the wave of Buddhism that was then sweeping across China). He is particularly known for his allegorical writings and for his fables, which like Aesop's fables often are tales about animals. "The Donkey of Guizhou" fits into this category. "The Snake-Catcher" is one of his finest pieces, a satire about the hardships of excessive taxation.

His poem "River Snow" is considered a prime example of the extreme condensation of meaning valued in Chinese poetry and has been the subject of numerous landscape paintings. It is a terrifically imagistic poem; the twenty characters of the poem create a whole landscape, sketch an intimate scene, and suggest a chill ineffable solitude. There is also a Buddhist element to the poem, and Liu Zongyuan's old man becomes like Wallace Stevens's "Snow Man," with a "mind of winter":

> For the listener, who listens in the snow,
> And, nothing himself, beholds
> Nothing that is not there and the nothing that is.

FURTHER READING: Liu, Shih Shun. *Chinese Classical Prose: The Eight Masters of the T'ang-Sung Period,* 1979.

River Snow

A thousand mountains. Flying birds vanish.
Ten thousand paths. Human traces erased.
One boat, bamboo hat, bark cape—an old man.
Alone with his hook. Cold river. Snow.

TRANSLATED BY TONY BARNSTONE AND CHOU PING

Song of an Evening River

A ray of setting sun paves the water,
half the river is emerald, half the river ruby.
I love the third night in the ninth month—
dewdrops turn into pearls, the moon into a bow.

TRANSLATED BY TONY BARNSTONE AND CHOU PING

The Donkey of Guizhou

There were no donkeys in Guizhou until an eccentric transported one there by boat. After its arrival, no one could find a use for it and so they let the donkey loose in the foothills of the mountains.

A tiger spotted the donkey and found it so large and strange that he thought it must surely be supernatural. Hiding in the woods, the tiger watched the donkey, creeping somewhat closer, but keeping a healthy respect for the unknown animal.

One day, the donkey brayed, and the tiger was so scared that it ran far away, thinking that the donkey was going to swallow it up. But after pacing back and forth, eyeing the donkey, the tiger began to wonder if this creature were really so frightful.

By and by, the tiger got used to the donkey's voice, and once again approached the donkey, first from front, and then from the rear, still not daring to attack. But the tiger kept coming closer and closer, dashing in, charging, shoving, and jostling the donkey roughly. Eventually, the donkey could not control its anger any more and kicked the tiger. The tiger was overjoyed, saying "So, that's all it has got." Leaping upon the donkey, the tiger sank its teeth in, tearing open its throat and devouring all its flesh, before going on his way.

What a tragedy! The donkey's large body *appeared* powerful, and its loud voice *sounded* fierce. If the donkey hadn't shown its meager skills, the tiger, violent as it was, would still be in doubt and fear, lacking the courage to attack. Now look at the poor donkey!

TRANSLATED BY CHOU PING

The Snake-Catcher

In the wilderness of Yongzhou, there was a kind of extraordinary snake, black with white patterns, that could kill even weeds and trees with a touch. No person has ever recovered from its bite. However, if one can catch it and air-dry it, as an ingredient in Chinese medicine it can cure leprosy, palsy, and boils, and removes dead tissues and tumors. For this reason, the court physician began collecting the snakes from the people in the name of the emperor. Every year, two such snakes were to be submitted, and those who caught them were exempt from land rent and taxes. And so the people in Yongzhou started to compete in catching the snakes.

The family of one Mr. Jiang has been exclusively in this business for three generations now. When I asked him about it, Jiang's answer was, "My grandfather died from this; so did my father. Now I've been catching snakes for twelve years and have been on the edge of death many times." He looked terribly morose when saying these words. I felt sorry for him and said, "Do you hate this job? I'll tell the people in charge to let you pay land rent instead. How about that?"

Hearing this, Jiang seemed to be seized by an even deeper sadness, and began to weep, saying "You feel sorry for me and so you want to help me survive? But the misfortune of having this task is not as bad as paying my land tax. If I hadn't been doing this, I'd have been in worse misery long ago. For three generations my family have been living in this area, altogether about sixty years now. During these decades, our neighbors' lives have been getting harder and harder. They have exhausted what the land can produce, spent up all the family's income. Weeping, they have had to move on, suffering hunger and thirst, the difficulties of the road. Exposed to wind and rain, struggling through winter and summer, they breathe in plagued air and often die with their bodies entangled together. Of the families of my grandfather's generation, not even one out of ten still exists; of my father's generation, only two or three out of ten are still here; in my generation, more than half the families who were here twelve years ago are gone. They have either died out or moved to other places. I am still here because I am a snake-catcher. When those vicious tax-collectors come to our village, they shout and yell from the east to the west, rousting people from north to south. People scream in fear, and even the dogs and hens are disturbed. Every night I get up slowly to check if my snakes are still there in the jar. Only then, relaxing, can I fall back into sleep again. I carefully feed those two snakes and submit them at the required date. After that I calmly enjoy what my field can produce and in this way I'll live till my last tooth falls out. Though twice in a year I run the risk of losing my life, for the rest of the year I have peace and happiness and don't suffer every day like my neighbors. Even if I die right now from catching the snake, I have still survived so many villagers here. Of what can I complain?"

Hearing this, I grew even sadder. Confucius said, "Tyranny is fiercer than a tiger." I used to doubt this saying, but after hearing Jiang's story I've come to believe it. Alas, who knew that the land rent and taxes could be even more poisonous than a snake? That's why I've written this essay; I wait for those whose job is to investigate the people's complaints to get the message.

TRANSLATED BY CHOU PING

■ Yuan Zhen (Yüan Chen) (779–831) (poem)

Yuan Zhen, known by the epithet Yuan the Genius, was among the most brilliant poets and statesmen of the Tang dynasty. He was born in Changan to a family descended from the royal house that ruled northern China during the Northern Wei dynasty in the fifth and sixth centuries. A brilliant scholar, he passed the examinations in the category of "clarification of the classics" when he was fourteen, and, when he was twenty-four, he passed the "highly selective" examination, which landed him an appointment in the Imperial library with Bo Juyi, the poet who was to be his lifelong friend. Several years later, he passed the final palace examination, monitored by the emperor, and gained the highest score, resulting in a position close to the emperor. Like his friend Bo, Yuan dreamed of being a reformer, a dream that was to result in a series of banishments. He did, however, help to create a poetic movement, termed "the new music bureau songs" movement, which attempted to recapture the formal freedoms and the simplicity of diction of the *yuefu* form of the Han dynasty and to use poetry for the serious ends of social reform. His tale "The Story of Ying-Ying" is among the best-known love stories in China.

FURTHER READING: Ma, Y. W., and Joseph S. M. Lau, eds. *Traditional Chinese Stories,* 1978.

When Told Bai Juyi Was Demoted and Sent to Jiangzhou

A dying lamp's low flame tosses the shadows.
This evening I was told you were demoted to Jiujiang.
I was so startled I sat up in my final sickbed.
Dark wind is blowing rain into cold windows.

TRANSLATED BY TONY BARNSTONE AND CHOU PING

■ Sikong Tu (Ssu-k'ung T'u) (837–908) (poems, literary criticism)

TRANSLATED BY TONY BARNSTONE AND CHOU PING

Tang dynasty poet Sikong Tu's "The Twenty-four Styles of Poetry" was an influential attempt to sketch out and embody the common genres of classical Chinese poetry. Though the poems in this series set out to define basic categories, they are so notoriously obscure (each line having been interpreted in fantastically different ways by later commentators) as to achieve the opposite effect. Yet, as Stephen Owen has noted, Sikong Tu's mode is impressionistic, and though there is often great controversy about the meaning of any particular line, there is "remarkable agreement about the general point being made for each category."[1] Tu, a minor official from Shanxi, was celebrated as a poet and a critic; he was deeply influenced first by the Confucian and later by the Taoist and Buddhist traditions. He starved himself to death in protest when the Tang Dynasty was overthrown.

FURTHER READING: Giles, Herbert Allen. *A History of Chinese Literature,* 1967. Owen, Stephen. *Readings in Chinese Literary Thought,* 1992. Yang, Xiangyi, and Gladys Yang. *Poetry and Prose of the Tang and Song,* 1984. Barnstone, Tony, and Chou Ping, eds. and trs. *The Art of Writing: Teachings of the Chinese Masters,* 1996.

---

1. See his discussion in Stephen Owen, *Readings in Chinese Literary Thought.* Cambridge, MA: Council on East Asian Studies/Harvard University Press, 1992, pp. 299–357.

from **The Twenty-four Styles of Poetry**

The Implicit Style

Without a single word
the essence is conveyed.
Without speaking of misery
a passionate sadness comes through.

It's true, someone hidden controls the world;   5
with that being you sink or float.
This style's like straining full-bodied wine
or like a flower near bloom retreating into bud.

It is dust in timeless open space,
is flowing, foaming, sea spume,   10
shallow or deep, cohering, dispersing.
One out of a thousand contains all thousand.

The Carefree and Wild Style

Abide by your nature,
honest and unrestrained.
Whatever you pick up makes you rich
when candor is your friend.

Build your hut below a pine,   5
toss off your hat and read a poem.
You know if it's morning or evening
but have no idea what dynasty it is.

Do what fits your whim.
Why bother to achieve?   10
If you free your nature
you'll have this style.

The Lucid and Rare Style

Through bright and slender pines
shivering ripples flow.
Sunlit snow covers the strand.
Across the water, a fishing boat.

A pleasant person, jadelike,   5
in clogs, seeks hidden landscapes,
strolling, then pausing,
as the sky's empty blue goes on and on.

This spirit is ancient and rare
but so limpid it can't be held—   10

like moonlight at dawn,
a hint of autumn in the air.

The Flowing Style

It takes in like a water mill
and turns like a pearl marble.
It is beyond words
and these are clumsy metaphors.

Earth spins on a hidden axis   5
and the universe rolls slowly around its hub.
If you search out the origin
you'll find a corresponding motion.

Climb high into spiritual light.
Then dive deep into dark nothing.   10
All things for thousands of years
are caught up in the flow.

■ Yu Xuanji (Yü Hsüan-chi) (c. 843–868) (poems)

TRANSLATED BY GEOFFREY WATERS

Yu Xuanji is among the finest women poets of the Tang dynasty. Only fifty of her poems are extant, but these few reveal a passionate persona, mourning absent lovers, letting her feelings out in nature, all in an exquisite and imaginative language scarcely surpassed in her time. She was born in the Tang capital of Changan (modern-day Xian), where she was a sophisticated courtesan, the concubine of a government official who abandoned her after taking her to the south of China. She managed to return to the capital where she lived in extreme poverty, which may have led her at the end of her brief life to become a Daoist nun. She lived a pious life, yet, in her quarters at the Convent of Gathered Blessings, continued to receive her lovers, a double role that may be stranger to Western eyes than it was in her time. When she was twenty-four, she was executed on the charge of murdering her maid in jealousy over one of her callers. It is thought that these charges were trumped up, and the very detail with which the account is given belies its veracity.

FURTHER READING: Barnstone, Aliki, and Willis Barnstone, eds. *A Book of Women Poets from Antiquity to Now,* 1980.

To Tzu-an

Parting, a thousand cups won't wash away the sorrow.
Separation is a hundred knots I can't untie.

After a thaw, orchids bloom, spring returns,
Willows catch on pleasure boats again.

We meet and part, like the clouds, never fixed.   5
I've learned that love is like the river.

We won't meet again this spring,
But I can't rest yet, winesick in Jade Tower.

Letting My Feelings Out

Relaxed, nothing to do,
I travel alone in dancing light:

Clouds break, moon on water,
Adrift in a loosed boat.

I hear a lute from Hsiao Liang Temple,   5
A song from Yü Liang's Tower.

Clumps of bamboo are my companions
And stones my friends.

Swallows and sparrows follow me,
I need no silver nor gold.   10

I fill the cup with the green spring wine;
Under the moon, subtle music.

By the clear pond around my steps
I pull my hairpin out and let the bright stream flow.

In bed reading,   15
Half-drunk, I get up and comb my hair.

■ Li Yu (Li Yü) (936–978) (poems)

Li Yu was the last emperor of the Southern Tang dynasty, whose capital was Nanjing. He is also known as Li Houzhu— *houzhu* means "last ruler." He ascended to the throne in 961 but was destined to rule only fourteen years. In 975, he was taken prisoner when the House of Song conquered his realm. He was carried north to the Song capital, Kaifeng. After years of imprisonment, the Song emperor sent him a glass of poisoned wine on his birthday. He died, forty-one years old. Li Yu seems to have been much better at the business of culture than he was at running his empire. He was a noted painter, musician, and calligrapher, and under his reign the Southern Tang became an important cultural center. He is considered the first important innovator in the *ci* (*tz'u* in Wade-Giles transliteration) form of poetry, which was to be the form in which much of the best poetry of the Song dynasty was written. Whereas the form had previously counted as its prime subject matter love of nature and romantic love, in Li Yu's hands, the form was expanded to include meditations upon great philosophical themes — the impermanence of life and the vanity of human wishes. He also made the form startlingly personal. His best poems mourn the death of his first wife in 964 and bitterly lament his imprisonment.

FURTHER READING: Liu, Yih-ling, and Shahid Suhrawardy. *Poems of Lee Hou-chu,* 1948.

To the Tune of "A Bushel of Pearls"

Morning makeup is almost done —
a few more light touches on the lips.
Revealing the tip of a lilac tongue,
she sings transparently clear,
her mouth just parting, like a cherry.

5

Charming how her wide silk sleeve turns crimson wet
after sweeping across sweet wine in a deep goblet.
She is fragile, seductive, lying aslant an embroidered bed —
after chewing on her red hair-string,
with a laugh she spits it on her man.

10

TRANSLATED BY TONY BARNSTONE AND CHOU PING

To the Tune of "Lost Battle"

My family's kingdom lasted forty years —
three thousand *li* of mountains and rivers.
In phoenix pavilions and dragon towers built up to heaven,
among jade trees and branches like spring mist and vines,
how could I know anything about wars?

But since being captured and enslaved,   5
my waist has shriveled,
my hair turned gray.
I was most lost the day we parted at the Temple of Ancestors:
the imperial orchestra was playing farewell songs
while I stood in tears facing my palace girls.
                                                                                                                         10

TRANSLATED BY TONY BARNSTONE AND CHOU PING

To the Tune of "Beauty Yu"

Will spring blooms and autumn moon never end?
These memories are too much.
Last night east wind pierced my narrow tower again,
and I saw lost kingdoms in the clean bright moon.

The carved railings and jade steps must still be there,
though lovely faces must have aged.   5
How much sorrow do I feel?
Like riverwater in spring it flows to the east.

TRANSLATED BY TONY BARNSTONE AND CHOU PING

To the Tune of "Crows Cawing at Night"

Alone I ascended West Tower in silence
while the moon appeared like a hook.
Cool fall was locked in the maple garden, calm and quiet.

This thing can't be cut,   5
it gets more messy trying to straighten it out.
A melancholy departure,
there's a raw feeling in my heart.

TRANSLATED BY BRENDAN CONNELL AND MARTY JIANG

To the Tune of "Encountering Joy"

Charming blossoms in the grove say goodbye to crimsoning spring.
They are gone too soon.
It can't be helped, since cold rain comes in the morning and wind at
    night.

She's crying; rouge melts with tears.
I'm drunk with her asking me to stay,   5
"When will you be back?"
It's natural that the river keeps flowing east,
and men always feel regret.

TRANSLATED BY BRENDAN CONNELL AND MARTY JIANG

Song Dynasty

(960–1279)

■ Mei Yaochen (Mei Yao-ch'en) (1002–1060) (poem)

TRANSLATED BY KENNETH ROXROTH

Mei Yaochen was an official-scholar of the early Song dynasty whose poems helped initiate a new realism in the poetry of his age. He was a life-long friend of the poet Ouyang Xiu, but he never attained the career success of his famous companion. He did not pass the Imperial Examinations until he was forty-nine, and his career was marked by assignments in the provinces, alternating with periods in the capital. Twenty-eight hundred of his poems survive in an edition edited by Ouyang Xiu. His early poems often are marked by social criticism based on a Neo-Confucianism that sought to reform the military and civil services; these poems tended to be written in "old style" verse (*gu shi*). He was also a distinctly personal poet, who wrote about the loss of his first wife and baby son in 1044 and about the death of a baby daughter a few years later. His poems are colloquial and confessional and strive for a simplicity of speech that suggests meanings beyond the words themselves.

FURTHER READING: Chaves, Jonathan. *Mei Yao-ch'en and the Development of Early Sung Poetry*, 1976.

Sorrow[1]

Heaven took my wife. Now it
Has also taken my son.
My eyes are not allowed a
Dry season. It is too much
For my heart. I long for death.   5
When the rain falls and enters
The earth, when a pearl drops into
The depth of the sea, you can
Dive in the sea and find the
Pearl, you can dig in the earth   10
And find the water. But no one
Has ever come back from the
Underground Springs. Once gone, life
Is over for good. My chest
Tightens against me. I have   15
No one to turn to. Nothing,
Not even a shadow in a mirror.

■ Ouyang Xiu (Ou-yang Hsiu) (1007–1072) (poems, rhyme-prose)

Ouyang Xiu is considered to be a prime example of the Chinese ideal of the multifaceted scholar-official, equivalent to the Western ideal of the Renaissance man. He was raised by his widowed mother in great poverty in an isolated region of what is today Hubei. He studied on his own and with the help of his mother for the Imperial Examinations, which were important credentials for government service, a road that was opened to him by the rise of printing early in the Song dynasty. While studying, he was strongly influenced by the works of Han Yu, whose works had been largely forgotten by this time. He passed the Imperial Examinations in 1030 and embarked on a lifelong and quite successful career as an official in Luoyang, though he found himself twice exiled during his career.

He is the author of a famous history, *The New History of the Tang,* and the compiler of *The New History of the Five Dynasties,* and he wrote an influential set of commentaries on historical inscriptions titled *Postscripts to Collected*

---

1. He seems to have lost all his family. Here begin several poems of loss. Although they echo the Emperor Wu of Han and many others they are none the less poignant and remind one of the later sepulchral epigrams of the Greek Anthology.

Ancient Inscriptions. He is also the author of a set of commentaries on poetics titled *Mr. One-six's Talks on Poetics.* (Mr. One-six was a pen name referring to his desire to be always in the presence of his wine, chess set, library, zither, and archaeological collection.) This compilation was the first treatise in the aphoristic *shi-hua* form (see *Poets' Jade Dust* later in this section for examples of the form). Ouyang Xiu is esteemed as a prose master whose essays have clean and simple language and fluid argumentation; he helped lead a movement away from ornamental prose styles to a simpler style of "ancient prose," a traditionalist movement that had as its aim a Confucian moral regeneration. His melancholy essay "The Autumn Sound" is among his most famous; compare it with Meng Jiao's series of sad "Autumn Meditations," which also meditate on autumn sorrow.

His poetry is also marvelous, and he was instrumental in raising the *ci* form of poetry (poems written to fit popular songs) into a widespread and important Song poetic style. His plain style and use of colloquial expressions made his poetry accessible to larger audiences and helped preserve its freshness for audiences today. Like Andrew Marvell, he was a sensualist who is known for his *carpe diem* poems: "You cannot hold it . . . / Pretty girls grow old . . . / No flowers to be plucked / from empty bough." Late in life he gave himself the title "The Old Drunkard." He was also an individualist, both in his approach to writing and in his interpretations of the classics; translator J. P. Seaton sees this individualism as an outgrowth of his self-education. As a politician, he was known for his Confucian ethics. A man with many talents, he is not easily summed up in a brief headnote.

FURTHER READING: Egan, Richard C. *The Literary Works of Ou-yang Hsiu,* 1984. Liu, James T. C. *Ou-yang Hsiu, An Eleventh Century Neo-Confucianist,* 1967. Seaton, J. P. *Love and Time: The Poems of Ou-yang Hsiu,* 1989.

You Cannot Hold It

You cannot hold it . . .
Pretty girls grow old
and indolent; there is an end to spring.
When breeze is warm and moon so fine,
if you can manage yellow gold, buy smiles.   5
Nurture the tender blossoms there, don't wait.
No flowers to be plucked
from empty bough.

TRANSLATED BY J. P. SEATON

The Autumn Sound[1]

One night as I, Ou-yang Tzu, was reading I suddenly heard a sound far away towards the southwest. I listened with apprehension and said, "It is strange!" At first it sounded like the murmuring of the rain or the rustling of the wind; suddenly it burst into the galloping of horses and the splashing of waves, as though a mountain torrent were roaring in the startled night and a thunderstorm were howling in the air. What it struck tinkled and chinked like the breaking of metals and stones. It also seemed like a muffled march of soldiers, each with a bit in his mouth [to keep the soldiers in silence], hurriedly advancing to the attack; no bugles were heard, only the tramp of men and horses.

"What noise is that?" I said to my boy servant. "Go out and see."

"The moon and stars are brightly shining," the boy replied. "The Celestial River is up in the sky. Nowhere is there any noise of men; the noise comes from the trees."

"Alas, what a pity!" said I. "This is the autumn sound. How is it that autumn comes?

"The autumn phenomena are thus: Its color is gray and dull, as the sky is blue and the sun is brilliant; its air is chilly and shivering, as the blasts pierce our body; its meaning is desolate and solitary, as the hills are abandoned and the streams sink low. Therefore its sound is sad and mournful, and yet it shouts with forces. All the rich luxuriance of the green prospers, and all the fine foliage of the trees presents a beautiful scene. However, as the autumn approaches, the green turns pale and trees decay. This is the destroying force of the autumn that sweeps away all the foliage and luxuriance.

"For autumn is the season for criminal execution, and so its time is darkness as a symbol of destruction; its appropriate element is 'metal,'[2]—this is what is called the essential principle of the universe. It always makes death its chief purpose. This is how Nature governs all: as spring is the epoch of growth, so autumn is the epoch of maturity. Therefore in music, its sound is *shang*,[3] a sad sound, and its note is *yi*,[4] a dying note. Shang is sorrow: that which is old must be sad. Yi is death: that which passes maturity must die.

---

1. This is a *fu*, a piece of descriptive poetic prose interspersed with verse. The lines are all irregular as in prose, but are punctuated with rhymes to enhance the beauty of recital. Both the artificiality of the Han *fu* and the frivolity of later lyrical *fu* are avoided in this beautiful piece.

2. The five elements—water, fire, wood, metal, and earth—are the active agents that produce and overcome each other in an endless cycle, upon which the whole scheme of the mystic school of Chinese philosophy is based.

3. The ancient Chinese scale of notation consists of five sounds, known as *kung, shang, chiap, chi,* and *yü.*

4. The Chinese scale originally consisted of nine notes. A twelve-note scale was later developed, and flats or sharps were used as needed.

"Ah! Plants and trees fade away in their due season, even though they have no feelings. But man is an animal and is the divinest of all things. Hundreds of cares wreck his heart, and thousands of tasks wear out his body. What affects his mind will shake his vitality. How much greater is the strain when a man strives to attain what is beyond his ability and worries himself to achieve what is beyond his intelligence. It is no wonder that his rosy cheeks turn pale and that his black hair turns white. How can a man whose frame is not made of metal and stone outlast the plants and trees? Just think a while: who steals away his strength? Why should man accuse the autumn sound?"

The boy made no answer. He was fast asleep. No soul could be heard but that of the cricket chirping its response to my mournful sigh!

TRANSLATED BY CH'U CHAI AND WINBERG CHAI

■ Su Dongpo (Su Tung-p'o) (1036–1101) (poems, rhyme-prose)

Su Dongpo (also known as Su Shi) was born in Sichuan province in Meishan to an illustrious family of officials and distinguished scholars. He, his brother, and his father were considered to be among the finest prose masters of both the Tang and Song dynasties and were known as the Three Sus. He took the Imperial Examinations in 1057 and was noticed by the powerful tastemaker, politician, poet, and chief examiner Ouyang Xiu, who became his patron. Like Ouyang, Su Dongpo was a Renaissance man, who in addition to having a political career was an innovator in and master of poetry, prose, calligraphy, and painting. He was among the founders of the important Southern Song style of painting. He believed that poems and paintings should be as spontaneous as running water, yet rooted in an objective rendering of emotions in the world. Around twenty-four hundred of his poems in the *shi* form survive, along with three hundred fifty *ci* form poems. These latter are poems derived from song forms, and like Ouyang, Su was important in expanding this genre's use and possibilities. His political career, like that of his patron, was vicissitudinous, involving demotions, twelve periods of exile, and even three months in prison primarily because of his opposition to the powerful reformer Wang Anshi. During an exile in Huangzhou, Su Shi began calling himself Su Dongpo (Eastern Slope), which was the name of his farm. His poems are informed by a knowledge of Daoism and Chan (Zen) Buddhism, and like that earlier mystical farmer-poet Tao Qian, contented on his farm, he retired from the political world. His personality shines clearly through his poems; he was a personal poet who recorded the pain of his separations in exile and of his baby son's death, his joy in a simple walk in the countryside, and the pleasures of a good cup of wine. He is known for the exuberance he brings to writing and is even credited with being the founder of a school of heroic abandonment in writing. The poem "Inscription for Gold Mountain Temple," included here, belongs to a tradition of Chinese concrete poetry (word games and shaped poems), which is virtually unknown in the West. In Chinese this beautiful poem can be read forwards and backwards, producing two descriptions of the temple: from night to day and from day to night. In the interest of giving a readable version, we have done two English translations: from beginning to end and from end to beginning, changing prepositions, articles, and verb forms to make each poem natural, yet retaining the order of the basic elements.

FURTHER READING: Le Gros Clark, C. D. *The Prose Poetry of Su Tung P'o*, 1935. Lin, Yutang. *The Gay Genius: The Life and Times of Su Tungpo*, 1947. Watson, Burton. *Su Tung-p'o: Selections from a Sung Dynasty Poet*, 1965.

Inscription for Gold Mountain Temple (I)[1]

Tides follow hidden waves. The snow mountain tilts.
Distant fishing boats are hooking the moonlight.
A bridge faces the temple gate. The pine path is narrow.
By the doorsill is the fountain's eye where stone ripples transparently.

Far, far green trees — the river sky is dawning.   5
Cloudy, cloudy scarlet afterglow. The sea is sun bright.
View of the distance: four horizons of clouds join the water.
Blue peaks are a thousand dots. A few weightless gulls.

TRANSLATED BY TONY BARNSTONE AND CHOU PING

Inscription for Gold Mountain Temple (II)

Gulls are weightless, a few dots. A thousand peaks are blue.
Water joins the clouds' edges in four distant views.
Bright day. Sea glows with scarlet clouds on clouds.
Dawning sky and river trees are green, and far, far.

Transparent ripples from the stone eye: fountain by the doorsill.   5
A narrow path and pine gate where the temple faces the bridge.

---

1. Some scholars question the attribution of this poem to Su Dongpo.

A bright moon hooks boats. Fishing waters are distant.
A tilted mountain is a snow wave, secretly following tides.

TRANSLATED BY TONY BARNSTONE AND CHOU PING

Written on the North Tower Wall after Snow

In yellow dusk the slender rain still falls,
but the calm night comes windless and harsh.

My bedclothes feel like splashed water.
I don't know the courtyard is buried in salt.

Light dampens the study curtains before dawn.   5
With cold sound, half a moon falls from the painted eaves.

As I sweep the north tower I see Horse Ear Peak
buried except for two tips.

TRANSLATED BY TONY BARNSTONE AND CHOU PING

Written in Response to Ziyou's Poem about Days in Mianchi[2]

A life touches on places
like a swan alighting on muddy snow—
accidental claw tracks left in the slush
before it soars east or west into the random air.

The old monk is dead, interred beneath the new pagoda,   5
and on ruined walls the poems we brushed are illegible.
Do you still remember the rugged path,
the endless road, our tired bodies, how our lame donkey brayed?

TRANSLATED BY TONY BARNSTONE AND CHOU PING

---

2. In earlier years, Su Shi and his brother had traveled together through this region. Their horses had died, and so they were riding on donkeys. They stayed at the temple in Mianchi and wrote poems on the wall.

Boating at Night on West Lake

Wild rice stems endless on the vast lake.
Night-blooming lotus perfumes the wind and dew.
Gradually the light of a far temple appears.
When the moon goes black, I watch the lake gleam.

TRANSLATED BY TONY BARNSTONE AND CHOU PING

Brushed on the Wall of Xilin Temple

From the side it is a range; straight on, a peak.
Far, near, high, low, it never looks the same.
I can't see Mount Lu's true face
because I'm on the mountain.

TRANSLATED BY TONY BARNSTONE AND CHOU PING

Because of a Typhoon I Stayed at Gold Mountain for Two Days

Up in the tower a bell is talking to itself.
The typhoon will wash out the ferry by tomorrow.
Dawn comes with white waves dashing dark rocks
and shooting through my window like deflected arrows.   5
A dragon boat of a hundred tons couldn't cross this river
but a fishing boat dances there like a tossed leaf.
It makes me think, why rush to the city?
I'll laugh at such fury of snakes and dragons,
stay aimlessly till the servants start to wonder   10
—with this kind of storm, my family won't mind.
I look for my friend, monk Qianshan. He's alone,
meditating past midnight and listening for the breakfast drum.3

TRANSLATED BY TONY BARNSTONE AND CHOU PING

---

3. Literally, the "porridge drum," the wooden board that when beaten announces that the porridge breakfast is served.

The Red Cliff

On the day of full moon in the seventh month in autumn, 1082, I sailed with some friends to Red Cliff in a boat. A cool, laconic wind blew in but didn't bother to stir up any waves. While raising a winecup to toast, I recited a poem about the brilliant moon and sang out a stanza from the *Book of Songs* about a beauty.

Before long, the moon rose over the east mountain, lingering between the Big Dipper and the Cowherd. Dewy mist was floating across the river, and the glittering water seemed to blend into the sky. Giving free rein to the small, reed-like boat, we drifted among vast fields of water, as if gliding on air, not knowing where we would stop, and it seemed we would fly right out of this world and stand in space, like winged immortals.

So we went on drinking and having a good time, singing songs while beating time on the boat's sides. The song went like this:

> Our cassia oars
> and magnolia paddles
> cut into the moon
> and slice its flowing light.
> My heart is like this great expanse,
> longing for my lover
> in another corner of the sky.

One of the guests, who was good at playing the vertical bamboo flute, spontaneously accompanied the song with his instrument. The sound was low and melancholy as if someone tortured by love was murmuring out secret affection, punctuated by sobs and complaints. Like a whiff of everlasting smoke the melody lingered on. The music was so touching that it could make a dragon dance at the bottom of an abyss, or make a widow weep in a drifting boat.

I was saddened by the music, and after straightening up my gown and sitting upright, I asked my friend, "Why did you make it so sad?"

He replied, "'Under a bright moon and sparse stars, ravens and magpies fly east.' Aren't those lines by Cao Cao? Xiakou is to the west, and Wuchang is over there to the east. See the mountains and the river winding around each other, and the trees so dark green? Isn't this the place where Cao was trapped by General Zhou? Cao had just taken the city of Jinzhou, and set out down the river east to Jiangling. The boats jostled for hundreds of miles, and his banners and flags blocked out the sky. Pouring a libation into the river, Cao Mengde improvised those lines with a long spear in his hands. He was without doubt the greatest hero of his time. But where is he now?

"As for you and me, we simply fish in the river or chop firewood by the river banks. We find company in fish and shrimp, and make friends with elk and deer. We sail in a leaf-like boat and we pour wine from a gourd to toast each other. But our lives are as brief as those of insects, and we are small and insignificant as a grain of sand in the ocean! So we are sad—we are sad because our lives are so short while the Yangtze River runs on forever. We dream about flying in the sky with immortals and embracing the moon's longevity. But I know this is not easily attained, and thus sadness flew out of my bamboo flute."

I asked, "Do you really know the river and the moon? The water flows away, like this, and yet it never actually leaves; the moon up there waxes and wanes, and yet it remains the same. If you watch them from the perspective of change, the sky and the earth seem to wheel through change endlessly; but if you observe from the perspective of changelessness, both we and the world are inexhaustible. So what is there to be envied?

"Everything in the sky and the earth has its proper owner, and I won't take a single hair of anything that does not belong to me. Still, the clear wind along the river, which becomes music in our ears, or the moon in the mountains, which fills our eyes with beautiful colors, are free for the taking, and they are inexhaustible. This is the creator's everlasting treasure, placed here for us to enjoy."

Now my friend seemed happy. He smiled, and we washed our wine cups to toast again. When at last all the dishes and fruits were finished, the cups and plates piled up in disorder, we lay down to sleep in the boat, unaware that dawn was starting to brighten the east.

TRANSLATED BY TONY BARNSTONE AND CHOU PING

■ Li Qingzhao (Li Ch'ing-chao) (1084–c. 1151) (poems)

TRANSLATED BY TONY BARNSTONE AND CHOU PING

Li Qingzhao is China's finest woman poet. She was born in what is today Qinan, Shandong Province, to a gifted literary family, and her own talent was recognized in her teens. In 1101, she married happily to Zhao Mingzheng, the son of a powerful politician who shared her tastes for literature, painting, and calligraphy, and who soon embarked on a career as an official himself. When China went through the tumultuous transition from the Northern to the Southern Song dynasties, Li Qingzhao's husband's career was cut short, and they devoted themselves to art collecting and cataloging. An invasion of the Qin Tatars in 1127 sent Li Qingzhao fleeing from the capital with just a few belongings at a time when her husband had left for Nanking to attend his mother's funeral. She traveled across China for months, finally joining her husband in Nanking, where he was now mayor.

Just two years later, her husband died en route to a new posting, and Li Qingzhao drifted across China, settling at last in Linan (modern Hangzhou), where she was briefly married to a minor military official. Her poems are the best evidence of her life, showing the sorrow she went through over separations from her husband and over his death and sketching her life as a society woman. Only about fifty poems have survived from her six volumes of verse.

FURTHER READING: Rexroth, Kenneth, and Ling Chung, trs. *Li Ch'ing-Chao: Complete Poems,* 1979.

To the Tune of "Intoxicated in the Shade of Flowers"

Slight mist, the clouds are fat. This endless day is torture.
Lucky Dragon incense dissolves in the gold animal.
It's Autumn Festival, a good season,
but by midnight the chill will pierce
my jade pillow and thin silk curtains.   5

I drink wine by the east fence in yellow dusk
and a secret fragrance fills my sleeves.
Do not say my spirit isn't frayed.
The west wind tangles in the curtains.
I am thinner than a yellow flower.   10

To the Tune of "One Blossoming Sprig of Plum"

The scent of red lotus fades and my jade mat is cold as autumn.
Gently I loosen my silk robe
and enter the magnolia boat alone.
Who has sent an embroidered letter via clouds?
Wild geese form a character in the sky: *return.*   5
The west tower fills with moon.

Blossoms drift and water flows where it will,
but my heart is still sick,
split between this place and where you are.
I can't kill this desire.   10
Even when my eyebrows relax,
my heart flares up again.

To the Tune of "Spring at Wu Ling"[1]

The wind fades. Dropped blossoms perfume the earth.
At the end of the day, I'm too lazy to comb my hair.
His things remain, but he is gone, and the world is dead.
I try to speak but choke in tears.

I hear that spring is lovely at Twin Brook.   5
I'd row there in a light craft
but fear my grasshopper boat
is too small to carry this grief.

To the Tune of "Silk Washing Brook"

I don't need deep cups of thick amber wine.
My feelings will warm before I drown in drink.
Already sparse bells are answering the night wind.

Lucky Dragon incense fades as my soul-dream breaks.
From my loose hair drops a soft gold hairpin;   5
I wake alone and watch the red candle die.

To the Tune of "Dream Song"

I'll never forget sunset at Brook Pavilion —
drunk with beauty, we lost our way.
When the ecstasy faded, we turned our boat home,
but it was late and we strayed into a place deep
        with lotus flowers
and rowed hard, so hard   5
the whole shore erupted with herons and gulls.

To the Tune of "Dream Song"

Sharp wind last night, and sparse raindrops.
Thick sleep hasn't eased this hangover.
I want to ask the servant rolling up the blinds
has the flowering begonia blossomed?
Do you know?   5

---

1. Written after her husband's death.

Do you know?
Are the green leaves fat? The thin flowers red?

▪ Poets' Jade Dust (compiled before 1244) (aphorisms/literary criticism)

TRANSLATED BY TONY BARNSTONE AND CHOU PING

Poets' Jade Dust is an extraordinary Song dynasty collection of aphoristic prescriptions for writers, humorous anecdotes about poetry and poets, epigrammatic commentaries, and rules for composing literature. Its form is called *shi hua* (meaning "poetry-speech"), and it was defined and popularized in the Song dynasty. *Poets' Jade Dust* is considered to be among the finest of such collections (some critics call it the best). It was compiled by Wei Qingzhi, a native of Fuzhou City, Fujian province. His dates are unknown and very little is known of his life. He was said to be very talented, but apparently he was not interested in the path of the scholar-official. We also know that he was a great lover of chrysanthemum bushes — so great that he planted a thousand of them! The book consists of twenty volumes, and since the preface by Huang Sheng is dated 1244, it must have been compiled before then.

Shi hua is a form of literary jottings that had predecessors in the Tang dynasty and earlier but was not an identifiable genre until the great Song dynasty statesman, historian, antiquarian, and poet Ouyang Xiu (1007–1072) published twenty-eight literary notes in a collection later called *Liuyi Shi Hua (Mr. Six-one's Shi Hua)*, though its original title was probably simply *Shi Hua*. At its best, the genre combines biting, incisive comments about poetic craft with a casual tone, a wry wit, and interesting anecdotes. From the time of the Southern Song onward, however, *shi hua* became more and more systematic, and the randomness of the collections gave way to increasingly ordered compilations. Noted sinologist Stephen Owen notes that this led to a loss of the "original color" and charm of the form, and he comments:

> The trend toward systematization in some Southern Sung *shih-hua* should be understood in the context of the popularization of literary studies in the later Southern Sung and early Yüan. The Northern Sung intellectuals cultivated an appearance of ease; sophisticated discussion of poetry was supposed to be a pastime. In the Southern Sung, we find the beginnings of a mass audience, seeking advice on composition from the masters and guidance in judgment. The printing industry of Hang-chou fed the desires of the urban bourgeoisie to participate in elite culture by the transformation of *shih-hua* into poetic education.[1]

---

1. Stephen Owen, *Readings in Chinese Literary Thought* (Cambridge, MA: Council on East Asian Studies/Harvard University Press, 1992), 360–361. (Owen is using the Wade-Giles system of transliteration, in which *shi hua* is rendered *shih-hua*.)

Poets' Jade Dust is a systematic anthology of *shi hua* that fit into this popularization of the genre.

FURTHER READING: Barnstone, Tony, and Chou Ping, eds. and trs. *The Art of Writing: Teachings of the Chinese Masters,* 1996. Owen, Stephen. *Readings in Chinese Literary Thought,* 1992.

from The Preface by Huang Sheng

Comments on poetry are like doctors' prescriptions: if they are not accurate they are useless, as a bad prescription has no medical value. So, only a good doctor can judge if the prescription is effective or not and only a good poet can know if the comments are right or not. This compilation is no easy job.

Burning Poetry

from Notes by Song Zijing

Whenever I see my old work I want to burn the poems I hate. Mei Yaochen congratulates me: "You have made progress."

Don't Walk behind Others

from Notes by Song Zijing

For your work to pass through the generations you must have your own distinctive style. If you always use a compass to draw a circle and a ruler to draw a square you will always remain a slave. As the ancients say: you can't build a house inside a house. Lu Ji says: avoid the morning flower in full blossom and gather instead evening buds which are not yet open. Han Yu says: all clichés must go; this is the essence of prose. *The Book of the Hermit Fisherman of Zhao River* comments that this is also true of poetry. If you just repeat clichés and imitate old works without any change or original ideas, how can you become a famous poet? Huang Luzhi writes that if you follow someone you will always be behind. The first taboo in writing is to walk behind others.

Don't Beat the Ducks

from The Hermit's Comments on Poetry

Lu Shilong, the governor of Xuan State, used to enjoy caning the women registered as courtesans, the "Government Prostitutes" who served the officials. These singing girls all tried to escape, but they couldn't get away from him. Then, a Hangzhou courtesan arrived in Xuan State. Because of her beauty and talent Shilong grew very fond of her, and wouldn't allow her to depart. One day a local courtesan committed a minor offence, and when Shilong was about to cane her again, she pleaded in tears, "I don't want to deny my guilt. I'm just afraid that this beating will make the lady from Hangzhou scared." So Shilong pardoned her and let her depart. Because of this incident, Mei Yaochen wrote the following poem:

> Don't beat the ducks!
> You will scare the swan.
> The swan that lands on the pond's north shore
> is not an old bald bird on a lonely islet.
> Even the bald bird wants to fly off
> so wouldn't a swan with her long wings?

Enlightenment

from Lui's Rules for Schoolchildren

If you write with enlightenment your work will naturally be better than your contemporaries.' Inspiration enters at the border between hard work and laziness. In this way Zhang Changshi, watching Madame Gong Sun doing a sword dance was suddenly enlightened about the art of calligraphy. Zhang's heart had been so focused on his calligraphy that when he saw this dance he gained insight into the heights of his own art. Someone else watching the sword dance would consider it irrelevant. This is true for both calligraphy and for writing.

Ways to Kill a Landscape

from Xiqing Comments on Poetry

Yi Shan [another name for the Tang poet Li Shangyin] wrote many miscellaneous pieces, then divided them into more than ten different categories. One humorous category was called "Ways to Kill a Landscape." Here are some examples: 1. Wash your feet in a clear spring. 2. Dry your loincloth upon the flowers. 3. Build your house against a mountain. 4. Burn your zither to cook a crane. 5. Drink tea in front of the flowers. 6. Scream underneath a pine tree. When An Yuanxian, the Prime Minister, was dismissed from office, he spent his time enjoying mountain spring water and wine, and wrote the following poem, thinking of this category:

> The new tea leaves on Qi Mountain are green like mist
> and I boil mountain spring water in porcelain pots.
> I don't go to the human world to kill the landscape,
> I only have my wine and get drunk in front of flowers.

Be Specific

from **The Eye of Poetry**

Good poetry stands out from other poems. If poets write on the same subject this becomes clear when you compare their work. When I traveled along the road to Sichuan and stopped at Zhoubi Station I recalled two famous lines by Shi Manqing:

> In my mind water flows into the distance.
> Outside my sorrow the old mountains are still green.

Although people like these two lines, to me it seems they could describe almost any place, even though they were written about this station.

Convey the Idea, Not the Name

from **Forbidden Meat**

Su Dongpo says: Good painters paint the spirit, not the form. Good poets convey the idea, not the name. Here is a poem by him:

> Comparing a painting to the object
> is how a child judges paintings.
> If you think your poem is the last word on a subject
> it shows you're not a poet.

Simple and Wonderful

from **Quotations by Tang Zixi**

A Tang poet writes:

> A mountain monk doesn't know how to count the years.
> When one leaf falls he knows it's autumn.

Compare these lines with Tao Yuanming's lines:

> Even without a calendar
> the four seasons make a year.

We feel the Tang poet's lines try too hard. In the Preface to "Peach Blossom Spring" Tao says "They don't know the Han Dynasty, let alone Wei and Jin."[1] We can see how simple and wonderful his lines are.

Lines Should Not Be Redundant (1)

from Comments on Poetry by Coi Kuanfu

Poets between the Jin Dynasty and the Song Dynasty wrote many good lines, but they often used two lines to say the same thing. Here are two examples:

> The new lotus trembles as fish play.
> Petals fall when birds scatter.

> Cicada cries quiet the forest.
> Bird calls darken the mountains.

Lines like this are not bad; the problem is redundancy.

Lines Should Not Be Redundant (2)

from Notes by Sheng Kuo

Looking at the examples given above, Wang Anshi suggested to replace the line "Bird calls darken the mountains" with "The wind stops but petals still drop"; in this way the first line suggests motion within stillness and the next line creates stillness within motion.

---

1. "Peach Blossom Spring" is a tale about a fisherman who lost his way and sailed into a peach grove where he lost all sense of time and found a lost land where people had been cut off from the outside since the Qin Dynasty (221–207 B.C.). Once he left to go back home again he could never find his way back to this idyllic place. This is the quintessential Chinese tale of a lost utopia.

The Elliptical Method

from **The Cold Study**

When Zheng Gu writes a poem about falling leaves he doesn't mention them directly, yet people can infer the subject matter from his poem:

> It's hard for returning ants to find their holes,
> easy for birds to see their nests.
> The monk is never sick of them covering the porch
> but a layman will find one of them too much.

The Disease of Unintentional Similarity

from **East Window Notes**

When Cheng Shimeng was the governor of Hongzhou he built a meditation room at his residence. He loved this room so much that he went there every day, and he inscribed these two lines on a stone:

> No matter how busy, I come here once a day.
> I often come at midnight carrying a lantern.

Li Yuangui saw this inscription and laughed, saying, "This is a poem about going to the toilet!"

Three Ways to Steal

from **Varieties in a Poetic Garden**

There are three kinds of plagiarism in poetry writing. The clumsiest thief steals the words. Cheng Ju's line "The light of sun and moon is heavenly virtue" is from Fu Changyu's line "The light of sun and moon is transparent." The second kind of plagiarist steals the idea. Consider Shen Chenqi's lines:

> The remains of summer flee from a small pond.
> Coolness returns to the tips of tall trees first.

Now consider the original lines by Liu Hun:

> Ripples arise in the pool.
> Autumn comes to tall poplar trees.

The third type of theft doesn't leave much trace. Wang Changlin's lines go:

> With two carp in my hand
> I watch wild geese fall into distance.

The original lines by Qi Kang are:

> My eyes see off migrating cranes.
> Holding up my zither, I wave.

Clichés Must Go

from The Eye of Poetry

A friend came to me with a poem that began "Coldness in November . . . ," so I asked him, "Have you noticed how Du Fu uses the names of the months in his poems? For example, 'The waves swell in March.' Here March is used because it is early for large waves to be seen. Another example is 'June comes with cold wind and cold sun.' June is used because such late coldness is unusual. But many of us write lines like 'Coldness in November . . .' when we should avoid such obvious expressions."

Dexterity in a Single Word

from The Book of the Hermit Fisherman of Zhao River

In each line there should be a key word that will act like a magic pill or a Midas touch to make the line work. For example Meng Haoran writes:

> Thin clouds dilute the sky's silver river.[2]
> Scattered raindrops tap on leaves of the parasol tree.

The key words in these two lines are "dilute" and "tap"; without them these lines wouldn't be good. Mr. Chen once purchased a collection of Du Fu's poetry in which many characters were missing.[3] For example here is a line in which the last character was absent:

---

2. The Milky Way.

3. The second part of this commentary also appears in Ouyang Xiu's *Mr. Six-one's Comments on Poetry*.

The weightless body of a bird

Mr. Chen asked his guests to complete the line. People suggested "shoots by" or "lands" or "soars" or "descends" but no one could agree on the best word. Later, Mr. Chen got a better version of Du Fu's poems and found the line actually reads "The weightless body of a bird flickers by." Mr. Chen sighed and admitted that Du Fu's original word was much better.

Plain and Natural

from Sunny Autumn Rhymed Language

First master elegance, and then strive for the plain style. Nowadays many people write clumsy, facile poems and flatter themselves that they've mastered the plain style. I can't help laughing at this. Poets know that simplicity is difficult. There are poems that illustrate the rigor the plain style demands:

> Today as in ancient times
> it's hard to write a simple poem.
> —Mei Yaochen[4]

> The lotus flower rises from clear water,
> naturally without ornament.
> —Li Bai

Plain and natural lines are best.

Some Lines by Tao Yuanming

from Notes from Fu's Study

> Gathering chrysanthemum by the east hedge
> my lazy eyes meet South Mountain.

Su Dongpo says that those who don't comprehend poetry want to change these lines by Tao Yuanming, turning the word "meet" into "watch." This is trading jade for garbage. Bo Juyi tried to emulate Tao's lines like so:

---

4. Mei Yaochen, like Tao Yuanming, is considered an exemplary plain-style poet; but his work, unlike that of Tao Yuanming, comes in for some criticism. Mei An, for example, writes, "Mei Yaochen's poetry is not plain, it's dry."

> Occasionally I pour a cup of wine,
> sitting and watching Southeast Mountain.

I think this is a very poor imitation.[5]

Read More and Write More

Su Dongpo

The secret of writing lies in reading more and writing more. Many writers worry about writing too little, yet they are too lazy to read. Whenever they write a poem they want it to be the best one around, but it's almost impossible for such writers to achieve this. By constantly writing you will learn to diagnose faults and diseases in what you write, and you won't have to wait for others to point them out.

Epigrammatically Succinct Lines

from Wang Zhifang's Comments on Poetry

There was a poet named Guo Xiangzhen who became famous because of a line written by Mei Yaochen about him: "At the quarry in the moonlight I heard the banished immortal again." These lines suggest that Guo is Li Bai's reincarnation [since "Banished Immortal" was Li's nickname]. The best known lines by Guo Xiangzhen are these:

> Endless flight of birds across the blue evening sky.
> Wind in the reeds when the fisherman stops singing.

When Su Dongpo was Prefect of Qiantang, Guo Xiangzhen visited him and showed him a scroll of his poems. Then he gave a reading in which his voice was so loud it shook up his audience. Afterward he asked Su Dongpo, "What do you think of my poems?" Su Dongpo replied, "One hundred percent good." Flattered and surprised Guo asked, "Really? In what way?" Su answered, "Seventy percent oration and thirty percent poetry!"

---

5. These famous lines by Tao Yuanming are cherished for the way they suggest the joining of the poet with nature through the lack of active looking; the poet encounters the mountain naturally as he looks up as if running into a friend. Bo Juyi, on the other hand, is actively watching his mountain; this suggests a distance from nature.

Push or Knock

from Notes of Xiang Su

When the monk Jia Dao came to Luoyang, monks were forbidden to leave the monastery after noon. Jia Dao wrote a sad poem about this and Han Yu liked the poem so much he helped him get permission to become a layman. The story of their famous meeting follows.

When Jia Dao was concentrating on his poems he would often run into important people without being aware of it. One day, riding his donkey, he was thinking about these lines:

> Birds return to their nests in trees by the pond.
> A monk is knocking at a door by moonlight.

He couldn't decide whether to replace the word "knocking" with "pushing," so he was making wild gestures on his donkey, acting out first a knock and then a push. While doing this he encountered the procession of the Mayor, Han Yu, and neglected to give way. Arrested by the bodyguards, and brought before Han Yu, he was asked to explain his actions. He explained how he was trying to decide between these two words. Han Yu considered this for a long time, and said at last, " 'Knocking' is better." They became fast friends after that.[6]

The Boat over the Moon

from Notes from Jinshi Hall

A Korean diplomat was traveling in a boat across the sea, and he started to improvise a poem:

> Waterfowl float and dive.
> Mountain clouds part and blend.

The poet Jia Dao, hearing this, pretended to be an oarsman, and completed the poem:

> Oars cut through the sky in the waves.
> The boat skates over the moon in the water.

The Korean diplomat exclaimed "Excellent! Really good!" And after that he never talked about poetry again.[7]

---

6. This is a famous story, so famous that even today when Chinese writers have to decide between alternate words they ask, " 'Push' or 'knock'?"

7. The Korean diplomat was ashamed to be bested poetically by someone he thought to be a common oarsman.

Yuan Dynasty

(1280–1367)

■ Ma Zhiyuan (Ma Chih-yüan) (c. 1260–1334) (poems)

Yuan dynasty playwright and poet Ma Zhiyuan is best known for his masterly play *Autumn in the Han Palace,* in which prose passages alternate with *qu* poems. He also wrote *san qu* poems—*qu* poems written independent of a play. *Qu* and *san qu* poems are, like *ci* poems, written in set patterns of rhyme and tonal sequence and are characterized by lines of varying length, but they tend to be even more colloquial in their speech. From his poems, we know that Ma was a government official for some time and that in middle age he resigned his position to spend the remainder of his life writing poems and plays. The poems selected here show his dual attitude toward nature. On the one hand, like Tao Qian, he desires to retire from public life and to be at peace in the wilderness, chasing a butterfly (an allusion to a famous parable by Zhuangzi) through his dream. On the other hand, he knows that the law of nature is change, and his poems evoke the pathos of mutability and nature's sure eating away of works thrown up in human hubris.

FURTHER READING: Chaves, Jonathan, tr., ed. *The Columbia Book of Later Chinese Poetry: Yuan, Ming, and Ch'ing Dynasties (1297–1911),* 1986. Keene, Donald. "Autumn in the Palace of Han," in Birch, Cyril, ed. *Anthology of Chinese Literature from the Early Times to the Fourteenth Century,* 1965. Liu, Jung-en, tr. *Six Yuan Plays,* 1972.

Autumn Thoughts to the Tune of "Sky-Clear Sand"

Withered vines, old trees, ravens at dusk.
A small bridge, a flowing brook, a cottage.
Ancient roads, west wind, and a lean horse.
The evening sun dies west.
A broken man at the sky's edge.

5

TRANSLATED BY TONY BARNSTONE AND CHOU PING

Autumn Thoughts to the Tune of "Sailing at Night"

1.

One hundred years of light and dark is like a butterfly dream.
Looking back at the past, I can't help sighing.
Today spring comes,
tomorrow blossoms fade.
Hurry up and drink—the night is old, the lamp is going out.   *5*

2.

Think of the Qin palace, the Han tombs,
turned to withered weeds, cow pastures.
Otherwise, fishermen and woodcutters wouldn't chatter here.
Even if broken tombstones still lie across tangled graves,
it's hard to tell a snake from a dragon in the worn inscriptions.   *5*

3.

After the "fox trace" and "hare hole" battle strategies,
how many heroes survive?
The kingdoms of Wei or Jin are like the waist of a tripod,
snapped in half.

4.

Before my eyes the red sun slants west,
fast as a cart racing downhill.
When dawn comes in the clear mirror my hair has turned white.
I might as well say goodbye to my shoes when climbing into bed!
Don't laugh at a turtledove's clumsy nest—   *5*
sometimes the fool just plays the fool.

5.

Now that fame and money are spent,
I have no worries about right and wrong.
Red dust no longer gathers at my front gate.
Green shade of trees is nice on the cornices.
Blue mountains patch gaps in the wall   *5*
of my thatched cottage, my bamboo fence.

6.

When crickets chant I sleep well, as if ironed to the bed.
When roosters crow all things start swirling endlessly.

When will the fight for money and fame ever end?
Packed ants circling and circling in battle formations,
a chaos of swarming, spinning bees making honey,   *5*
pushing and buzzing like flies fighting for blood.

Duke Fei of Green Wilderness Hall,
County Prefect Tao of the White Lotus Society,
these were people who loved the coming of autumn.
When dew forms, I pick yellow day-lilies.   *10*
With frost, I cook purple crabs.
I mull wine over a fire of red leaves.

The life of a man is over after a few cups.
There will only be so many Festivals of Climbing.
I'm going to tell my wily houseboy: *15*
if anyone sends for me, even Beihai himself,
say that my name is East Fence, and I'm too drunk to come.

TRANSLATED BY TONY BARNSTONE AND CHOU PING

To the Tune of "Thinking about Nature"

A day is forever in the slow village to the west.
In the tedium, the first cicada buzzes,
sunflowers are poised
to open, and bees invade the morning.   *5*
Unconscious on my pillow, I chase a butterfly through my dream.

TRANSLATED BY TONY BARNSTONE AND WILLIS BARNSTONE

Autumn Moon on the Tung T'ing Lake, to the Tune of "Shou Yang"

Clouds block the moon,

Wind clatters the bells.

Each multiplies

     my sadness.

So,   *5*

    to pour my heart out

        on paper,

I went to turn up the wick

    with a sigh

so profound   *10*
        it blew out the flame.

TRANSLATED BY G. GACH AND C. H. KWOCK

■ Shi Naian (Shih Nai-an) and Luo Guanzhong (Lo Kuan-chung) (Late Fourteenth Century) (novel)

TRANSLATED BY SIDNEY SHAPIRO

Outlaws of the Marsh is a novel almost certainly composed by many hands, in spite of its highly questionable attribution to Shi Naian and Luo Guanzhong, both of whom probably flourished in the fourteenth century. These attributions are highly popular but discounted by serious scholars, and it seems likely that the novel evolved organically out of popular accounts of the heroic exploits of a group of outlaws led by Song Jiang during the Northern Song period. These stories have held much the same position in the Chinese popular imagination that Robin Hood's valiant outlaws of Sherwood Forest have held in English. The transmission of the text remains among the thorniest of all textual problems in Chinese literature, obscured by politics, legend, and the novel's own evolutionary nature. Many recensions exist, from a 71-chapter version to one of 124 chapters. In addition, there are three major sequels and a body of plays and historical accounts that the novel must in part have derived from. It has been celebrated in poems and paintings, by professional storytellers, and even by contemporary Chinese American writer Frank Chin, in his novel *Donald Duk*. It seems likely that there was a historical Song Jiang who led a bandit group, surrendered to the government, and subsequently fought in its service to put down rebellions (in the novel there are 108 outlaw heroes, many of whom achieve remarkable depth of characterization). The novel is picaresque, and both individual chapters and larger sections easily stand on their own. In the hilarious chapter presented here, the hero Lu Da, who has become an outlaw by killing a rapacious butcher for attempting to swindle the Jin family, makes a fuss while hiding out as a Buddhist monk.

FURTHER READING: Buck, Pearl S., tr. *All Men Are Brothers,* 1933. Jackson, J. H., tr. *Water Margin,* 1937. Shapiro, Sidney, tr. *Outlaws of the Marsh,* 1981.

from Outlaws of the Marsh

Chapter 2

SAGACIOUS LU PUTS MOUNT WUTAI IN AN UPROAR

After leaving Weizhou, Lu Da hurried pellmell east and west, passing through several prefectural towns. With him it was a case of:

> Any food when you're hungry,
> When you're cold rags save life;
> Any road when you're frightened,
> When you're poor any wife.

He dashed about in a panic, with no idea where to go.

After many days of wandering, he arrived in Yanmen, a county seat in the prefecture of Daizhou. It was a bustling town with many people and thriving markets. Carts and horses filled the streets, which were lined by shops conducting trade and commerce of every type. Although only a county seat, it was more prosperous than a prefectural capital.

On a street corner he saw a crowd gathered in front of a proclamation. Someone was reading it aloud. Illiterate himself, he pushed forward to listen. This is what he heard:

> *By order of the military commander of Taiyuan, this county hereby publishes the following notice from Weizhou: Wanted — the killer of Butcher Zheng. Name — Lu Da, former major in the Weizhou garrison command. Any man who conceals him or gives him food and shelter shall be deemed equally guilty. Whoever arrests and brings him forward, or offers information leading to his arrest, shall receive a reward of one thousand strings of cash. . . .*

As Lu Da stood listening, someone threw his arms around him from behind and cried: "What are you doing here, brother Zhang?" He pulled Lu Da away from the street corner.

Lu Da turned to see who was hustling him away. It was none other than Old Jin from the Weizhou tavern, the man he had rescued. The old fellow didn't stop pulling till they reached an isolated spot. Then he said:

"You're too rash, benefactor. That notice offers a thousand strings of cash for your capture. How could you stand there looking at it? If I hadn't spotted you, you might have been nabbed by the police. Your age, description and place of origin are all there."

"To tell you the truth, when I went to the foot of the Zhuangyuan Bridge that day to see Zheng the butcher about your affair, I killed the churl with three blows of the fist, and had to flee. I've been knocking about for forty or fifty days now, and just happened to wander into this town. I thought you were returning to the Eastern Capital. What are you doing here?"

"After you saved me, benefactor, I found a cart. Originally I intended to go back to the Eastern Capital, but I was afraid that rogue would catch up and you wouldn't be around to rescue us. So I changed my mind and headed north. On the road I met an old neighbor from the capital who was coming here on business. He took me and my daughter along. He was good enough to find her a match. She's now the mistress of a wealthy man, Squire Zhao. The squire has provided her with a house. Thanks to you, benefactor, we now have plenty to eat and wear. My daughter has often spoken to the squire of your kindness. He is also fond of jousting. He's said many times he'd like to meet you, but that was never possible before. You must come and stay with us a few days. We can talk about what you should do next."

Lu Da and Old Jin walked less than half a *li* when they came to the door of a house. The old man pushed aside the bamboo curtain and called: "Daughter, our benefactor is here."

The girl emerged, neatly made up and attractively dressed. She begged Lu Da to be seated in the center of the room. Then, as if offering votive candles, she kowtowed before him six times. "If you hadn't rescued us, benefactor," she said, "we'd never possess what we have today." She invited him upstairs to the parlor.

"Don't bother," said Lu Da. "I must be going."

"Now that you're here, benefactor, of course we can't let you leave," said the old man. He took Lu Da's staff and bundles and ushered him up the stairs. To his daughter he said: "Keep our benefactor company. I'll arrange about dinner."

"Don't go to a lot of trouble," said Lu Da. "Anything will do."

"Even if I gave my life I could never repay your benevolence," said Old Jin. "A little simple food — it's not worth mentioning."

The three drank till almost nightfall. Suddenly they heard a commotion outside. Lu Da opened the window and looked. Some twenty to thirty men, all armed with staves, were gathered in front of the house. "Bring him down," they were shouting. A gentleman on a horse cried: "Don't let the rascal get away!"

Lu Da realized that he was in danger. He snatched up a stool and started down the stairs. Old Jin, waving his hands, rushed down ahead of him, exclaiming: "Nobody move!" He ran over to the man on horseback and said a few words. The mounted gentleman laughed. He ordered his band to disperse.

When the men had gone, the gentleman got off his horse and entered the house. Old Jin asked Lu Da to come down. The gentleman bowed as Lu Da descended the stairs.

"'Meeting a man of fame is better than just hearing his name.' Please accept my homage, righteous Major."

"Who is this gentleman?" Lu Da asked Old Jin. "We don't know each other. Why should he be so respectful?"

"This is Squire Zhao, my daughter's lord. Someone told him that a young man I had brought to his house was upstairs, drinking. So he got some of his vassals and came to fight. When I explained, he sent them away."

"So that was it," said Lu Da. "You could hardly blame him."

Squire Zhao invited Lu Da to the upper chamber. Old Jin reset the table, and once more prepared food and drink. Zhao ushered the major to the seat of honor. Lu Da refused.

"How could I presume?"

"A small mark of my respect. I have heard much of the major's heroism. What great good fortune that I could meet you today."

"Though I'm just a crude fellow who's committed a capital offence, the squire doesn't scorn my lowliness and is willing to make my acquaintance. If there's any way I can be of service, you have only to speak."

Squire Zhao was very pleased. He asked all about the fight with Zheng the butcher. They talked of this and that, discussed jousting with arms, and drank far into the night. Then everyone retired.

The following morning Zhao said: "I'm afraid this place isn't very safe. Why not come and stay at my manor a while?"

"Where is it?" asked Lu Da.

"A little over ten *li* from here, near a village called Seven Treasures."

"All right."

Lu Da stayed at the manor for six or seven days. He and the squire were chatting in the study one day when Old Jin hastily entered. He looked to see that no one else was around, then said to Lu Da: "You mustn't think me overly cautious, benefactor. But ever since the night the squire and his vassals raised such a row in the street because you were drinking upstairs, people have been suspicious. Word has spread that you were there. Yesterday three or four policemen were questioning the neighbors. I'm worried that they'll come here and arrest you. It would be awful if anything should happen to you, benefactor."

"In that case," said Lu Da, "I'd better be on my way."

"Things might turn out badly if I kept you here, Major," the squire admitted. "Yet if I don't, I'll lose a lot of face. I have another idea. It's foolproof and will give you complete protection. But maybe you won't be willing."

"I'm a man with a death penalty waiting for him. I'll do anything to find refuge."

"That's fine. Where the Wenshu Buddha used to meditate on Mount Wutai, some thirty-odd *li* from here, a monastery was erected. They have nearly seven hundred monks. The abbot is my friend. My ancestors were patrons of the monastery and contributed to its upkeep. I have promised to sponsor a novice, and have bought a blank certificate, but have not yet found a suitable man. If you agree to join the Buddhist order, Major, I'll pay all expenses. Would you be willing to shave off your hair and become a monk?"

Lu Da thought to himself: "Who could I go to for protection if I were to leave here today? I'd better accept his offer." Aloud he said: "I'll become a monk if you sponsor me, Squire. I rely entirely on your kindness."

And so it was decided. That night, clothing, expense money and silks were prepared. Everyone rose early the next morning. Lu Da and the squire set out for Mount Wutai, accompanied by vassals carrying the gifts and luggage. They reached the foot of the mountain before mid-morning. Squire Zhao and Lu Da went up in sedan-chairs, sending a vassal on ahead to announce them.

At the monastery gate, they found the deacon and supervisor waiting to welcome them. They got out of their sedan-chairs and rested in a small pavilion while the abbot was notified. He soon emerged with his assistant and the elder. Squire Zhao and Lu Da hurried forward and bowed. The abbot placed the palms of his hands together before his chest in Buddhist greeting.

"It's good of you to travel this long distance, patron," he said.

"There is a small matter I'd like to trouble you about," said the squire.

"Please come into the abbey and have some tea."

Lu Da followed Squire Zhao to the hall. The abbot invited the squire to take the seat for guests. Lu Da sat down on a couch facing the abbot. The squire leaned over and whispered to him: "You're here to become a monk. How can you sit opposite the abbot?"

"I didn't know," said Lu Da. He rose and stood beside Squire Zhao.

The elder, the prior, the abbot's assistant, the supervisor, the deacon, the reception monk, and the scribe arranged themselves in two rows, according to rank, on the east and west sides of the hall.

Zhao's vassals left the sedan-chairs in a suitable place and carried into the hall several boxes which they laid before the abbot.

"Why have you brought gifts again?" asked the abbot. "You've already made so many donations."

"Only a few small things," replied Squire Zhao. "They don't merit any thanks."

Some lay brothers and novices took them away.

Squire Zhao stood up. "I have something to ask of you, Great Abbot. It has long been my desire to sponsor a new member for this monastery. Although I have had the certificate ready for some time, until today I have not been able to do so. This cousin here is named Lu. He formerly was a military officer, but because of many difficulties he wants to have done with mundane affairs and become a monk. I earnestly hope Your Eminence will exercise mercy and compassion and, as a favor to me, accept this man into your order. I will pay all expenses. I shall be very happy if you consent."

"Gladly," said the abbot. "This will add lustre to our monastery. Please have some tea."

A novice served tea. After all had drunk, he removed the cups. The abbot consulted with the elder and the prior on the ceremony for receiving Lu Da into the order, then instructed the supervisor and deacon to prepare a vegetarian meal.

"That man hasn't the makings of a monk," the elder said to the other monks, privately. "See what fierce eyes he has!"

"Get them out of here a while," they requested the Receiver of Guests. "We want to talk to the abbot."

The reception monk invited Squire Zhao and Lu Da to rest in the visitors' hostel. They departed, and the elder and the others approached the abbot.

"That new applicant is a savage-looking brute," they said. "If we accept him, he's sure to cause trouble."

"He's a cousin of Squire Zhao, our patron. How can we refuse? Hold your doubts while I look into the matter." The abbot lit a stick of incense and sat cross-legged on a couch. Muttering an incantation, he went into a trance. By the time the incense was consumed, he returned.

"You can go ahead with the ordination," said the abbot. "This man represents a star in Heaven. His heart is honest. Even though his appearance is savage and his life has been troubled, he will eventually become purified and attain sainthood. None of you is his equal. Mark my words. Let no one dissent."

"The abbot is only covering up his faults," the elder said to the others. "But we'll have to do as he says. We can only advise. If he won't listen, that's up to him."

Squire Zhao and the others were invited to dine in the abbey. When they had finished, the supervisor presented a list of what Lu Da would need as a monk—special shoes, clothing, hat, cape and kneeling cushion. The squire gave some silver and asked that the monastery buy the necessary materials and make them up.

A day or two later all was ready. The abbot selected a propitious day and hour, and ordered that the bells be rung and the drums beaten. Everyone assembled in the preaching hall. Draped in their capes, nearly six hundred monks placed the palms of their hands together in an obeisance to the abbot sitting on his dais, then separated into two groups. Squire Zhao, bearing gifts of silver ingots and fine cloth and carrying a stick of incense, approached the dais and bowed.

The purpose of the ceremony was announced. A novice led Lu Da to the abbot's dais. The prior told him to remove his hat, divided his hair into nine parts and knotted them. The barber shaved them all off. He reached with his razor for Lu Da's beard.

"Leave me that, at least," the major exclaimed.

The monks couldn't repress their laughter.

"Hear me," the abbot said sternly from his dais. "Leave not a single blade of grass, let the six roots of desire be torn out. All must be shaven clean away, lest they manifest themselves again," he intoned. "Off with it," he ordered.

The barber quickly finished the job. Presenting the certificate to the abbot, the elder requested him to select a name by which Lu Da should be known in the Buddhist order.

"A spark from the soul is worth more than a thousand pieces of gold," the abbot chanted. "Our Buddhist Way is great and wide. Let him be called Sagacious."

The scribe filled out the certificate and handed it to Sagacious Lu. At the abbot's direction he was given his monk's garments and told to put them on. Then he was led to the dais. The abbot placed his hand on Lu's head and instructed him in the rules of conduct.

"Take refuge in Buddha, the Law and the Monastic Order. These are the three refuges. Do not kill, steal, fornicate, drink or lie. These are the five precepts."

Lu Da didn't know he was supposed to answer "I shall" to each of the first three and "I shall not" to each of the last five.

"I'll remember," he said.

Everyone laughed.

Squire Zhao invited all present into the assembly hall where he burned incense and offered a vegetarian feast to the Buddhist gods. He gave gifts to every member of the monastery staff, high or low. The deacon introduced Sagacious to various members of the monastery, then conducted him to the rear building where the monks meditated. Nothing further happened that night.

The next day, Squire Zhao decided to leave. He said goodbye to the abbot, who tried in vain to keep him. After breakfast, all the monks went with him as far as the monastery gate. Squire Zhao placed his palms together and said, "Abbot, teachers, be compassionate. My young cousin Lu is a crude, direct fellow. If he forgets his manners or says anything offensive or breaks any rules, please forgive him, as a favor to me."

"Don't worry, Squire," said the abbot. "I shall teach him gradually to recite the prayers and scriptures, perform services, and practise meditation."

"In the days to come I will show my gratitude," promised the squire. He called Lu over to a pine tree and spoke to him in a low voice: "Your life must be different from now on, brother. Be restrained in all things, under no circumstances be proud. Otherwise, it will be hard for us to see each other again. Take good care of yourself. I'll send you warm clothing from time to time."

"No need to tell me, brother," said Lu. "I'll behave."

The squire took his leave of the abbot and the monks, got into his sedan-chair and set off down the mountain for home. His vassals followed, carrying the other, now empty, sedan-chair and boxes. The abbot and the monks returned to the monastery.

When Lu got back to the meditation room, he threw himself down on his bed and went to sleep. The monks meditating on either side shook him into wakefulness.

"You can't do that," they said. "Now that you're a monk, you're supposed to learn how to sit and meditate."

"If I want to sleep, what's it to you?" Lu demanded.

"Evil!" exclaimed the monks.

"What's this talk about eels? It's turtles I like to eat."

"Oh, bitter!"

"There's nothing bitter about them. Turtle belly is fat and sweet. They make very good eating."

The monks gave up. They let him sleep.

The next day they wanted to complain to the abbot. But the elder advised against it. He said: "The abbot is only covering up his faults when he says he will attain sainthood and that none of us is his equal. But there's nothing we can do about it. Just don't bother with him."

The monks went back. Since no one reprimanded him, Sagacious sprawled out on his bed every night and slept snoring thunderously. When he had to relieve himself he made a terrible racket getting up. He pissed and crapped behind one of the halls. His filth was all over the place.

The abbot's assistant reported the matter. "That Lu has no manners. He's not in the least like a man who's left the material world. How can we keep a fellow like that in the monastery?"

"Nonsense," retorted the abbot. "Don't forget our donor's request. Sagacious will change later on."

No one dared argue.

And so, Sagacious Lu remained in the monastery on Mount Wutai. Before he knew it, four or five months had passed. It was early winter and Lu's mind, which had been quiescent for a long time, began to stir. One clear day he put on his black cloth cassock, fastened his raven-dark girdle, changed into monk's shoes, and strode from the monastery.

Halfway down the mountain he halted to rest in a pavilion. He sat down on a low "goose neck" bench and said to himself with a curse: "In the old days I had good meat and drink every day. But now that I'm a monk I'm shrivelling up from starvation. Squire Zhao hasn't sent me anything to eat for a long time. My mouth is absolutely tasteless. If only I could get some wine."

He saw in the distance a man carrying two covered buckets on a shoulder-pole. A ladle in his hand, the man trudged up the slope singing this song:

Before Mount Nine Li an old battlefield lies,
There cowherds find ancient spears and knives,

As a breeze stirs the waters of the Wu River broad,
We recall Lady Yu's farewell to her lord.

Lu watched him approach. The man entered the pavilion and put down his load.

"Hey, fellow, what have you got in those buckets?" Lu asked.

"Good wine."

"How much a bucket?"

"Are you serious, monk, or are you just kidding?"

"Why should I kid you?"

"This wine is for the monastery's cooks, janitors, sedan-chair carriers, caretakers, and field laborers—no one else. The abbot has warned me that if I sell to a monk he'll take back the money and house the monastery loaned me for my winery. I don't dare sell you any of this."

"You really won't?"

"Not if you kill me!"

"I won't kill you, but I will buy some of your wine."

The man didn't like the look of things. He picked up his carrying-pole and started to walk away. Lu dashed out of the pavilion after him, seized the pole with both hands, and kicked the fellow in the groin. The man clapped both hands to his injured parts and dropped to a squatting position. He couldn't straighten up for some time.

Sagacious Lu carried both buckets to the pavilion. He picked the ladle off the ground, removed the covers, and began drinking. Before long, one of the buckets was empty.

"Come around to the monastery tomorrow and I'll pay you," he said.

The man had just recovered from his pain. If the abbot found out, it would mean an end to his livelihood. How could he seek payment from Lu at the monastery? Swallowing his anger, he separated the remaining wine into two half-buckets. Then he shouldered the load, took the ladle and flew down the mountain.

Lu sat in the pavilion a long time. The wine had gone to his head. He left the pavilion, sat down beneath a pine tree and again rested for quite a spell. The wine was taking increasing effect. He pulled his arms out of his cassock and tied the empty sleeves around his waist. His tattooed back bare, he strode up the mountain, swinging his arms.

The monastery gate-keepers had been watching him from afar. They came forward when he approached and barred his way with their split bamboo staves.

"You're supposed to be a disciple of Buddha," they barked. "How dare you come here in this besotted condition? You must be blind. Haven't you seen the notice? Any monk who breaks the rules and drinks gets forty blows of the split bamboo and is expelled from the monastery. Any gate-keeper who lets a drunken man enter gets ten blows. Go back down the mountain, quickly, if you want to save yourself a beating."

In the first place, Lu was a new monk, in the second, his temper hadn't changed. Glaring, he shouted: "Mother-screwing thieves! So you want to beat me? I'll smash you!"

The situation looked bad. One of the gate-keepers sped back inside and reported to the supervisor, while the other tried to keep Sagacious out with his staff. Lu flipped it aside and gave him a staggering slap in the face. As the man struggled to recover, Lu followed with a punch that knocked him groaning to the ground.

"I'll let you off this time, varlet," said Sagacious. He walked unsteadily into the monastery.

The supervisor had summoned the caretakers, cooks, janitors and sedan-chair carriers—nearly thirty men. Now, armed with staves, they poured out of the western cloister and rushed to meet Lu. The ex-major strode towards them with a thunderous roar. They didn't know he had been an army officer. He sprang at them so fiercely they fled in confusion into the sutra hall and closed the latticed door. Sagacious charged up the steps. With one punch and one kick he smashed the door open. The trapped men raised their staves and came out fighting.

The abbot, who had been notified by the supervisor, hurried to the scene with four or five attendants.

"Sagacious," he shouted, "I forbid you to misbehave."

Lu was drunk, but he recognized the abbot. He cast aside his staff, advanced and greeted him.

"I had a couple of bowls of wine, but I did nothing to provoke these fellows," said Sagacious. "They came with a gang and attacked me."

"If you have any respect for me," said the abbot, "you'll go to your quarters at once and sleep it off. We'll talk about this tomorrow."

"It's only my respect for you that stops me from lambasting those scabby donkeys!"

The abbot told his assistant to help Lu to the monks' hall. He collapsed on his bed and slept, snoring loudly.

A crowd of monks surrounded the abbot. "We told you so," they said. "Now you see what's happened? How can we keep a wildcat like that in our monastery? He upsets our pure way of life."

"It's true he's a bit unruly," the abbot admitted, "but he'll become a saint later on. At present, we can do nothing. We must forgive him, for the sake of our donor, Squire Zhao. I'll give him a good lecture tomorrow, and that will be the end of it."

The monks laughed coldly. "Our abbot isn't very bright," they said among themselves. All retired to their respective abodes.

The next morning the abbot sent his assistant to the monks' quarters to summon Sagacious Lu. He was still asleep. The assistant waited while he got up and put on his cassock. Suddenly, Lu dashed out, barefoot. The surprised assistant followed. He found Lu pissing behind the temple. The assistant couldn't help laughing. He waited till Lu had finished, then said:

"The abbot wants to see you."

Lu went with him to the cleric's room.

"Although you originally were a military man," said the abbot, "I ordained you because of Squire Zhao's sponsorship. I instructed you: Do not kill, steal, fornicate, drink or lie. These are the five precepts by which all monks are bound. First of all, no monk is allowed to drink. But yesterday evening you came back drunk and beat up the gate-keepers, broke the vermilion latticed door of the sutra hall and drove out the cooks and janitors, shouting and yelling all the while. How could you behave so disgracefully?"

Lu knelt before him. "I'll never do such things again."

"You're a monk now," the abbot continued. "How could you violate our rule against drinking and upset our pure way of life? If it weren't for the sake of your sponsor Squire Zhao I'd expel you from the monastery. Don't you ever act like that again."

Lu placed his palms together. "I wouldn't dare," he asserted fervently.

The abbot ordered breakfast for him and, with many kindly words, exhorted him to reform. He gave Lu a cassock of fine cloth and a pair of monk's shoes, and told him to return to his quarters.

Topers should never drink their fill. "Wine can spur action, or ruin everything," as the old saying goes. If drinking makes the timid brave, what does it do to the bold and impetuous?

For three or four months after his drunken riot Lu didn't venture to leave the monastery. Then one day the weather suddenly turned warm. It was the second lunar month. Lu came out of his quarters, strolled through the monastery gate and stood gazing in admiration at the beauty of Mount Wutai. From the foot of the mountain the breeze brought the sound of the clanging of metal. Sagacious returned to his quarters, got some silver and put it inside his cassock near his chest. Then he ambled down the slope.

He passed through an archway inscribed with the words: "Wutai, a Blessed Place." Before him he saw a market town of six or seven hundred families. Meat, vegetables, wine and flour were on sale.

"What am I waiting for?" Lu said to himself. "If I had known there was a place like this, instead of snatching that fellow's bucket I would have come down and bought my own wine. I've been holding back so long that it hurts. Let's see what sort of food they have on sale here."

Again he heard the clang of metal.

Next to a building with the sign "Father and Son Inn" was an ironsmith's shop. The sound was coming from there. Lu walked over. Three men were beating iron.

"Got any good steel, master smith?" he asked the eldest of them.

The man was a little frightened at the sight of Lu's face, with newly sprouted bristles sticking out wildly all over. He ceased his hammering and said: "Please have a seat, Reverend. What kind of work do you want done?"

"I need a Buddhist staff and a monk's knife. Do you have any first-rate metal?"

"I do indeed. How heavy a staff and knife do you want? We'll make them according to your requirements."

"The staff should be a hundred catties."

"Much too heavy," the smith laughed. "I could make it for you, but you'd never be able to wield it. Even Guan Gong's[1] halberd wasn't more than eighty-one catties!"

"I'm every bit as good as Guan Gong," Sagacious burst out impatiently. "He was only a man, too."

"I mean well, Reverend. Even forty-five catties would be very heavy."

"You say Guan Gong's halberd was eighty-one catties? Make me a staff of that weight, then."

"Too thick, Reverend. It would look ugly, and be clumsy to use. Take my advice, let me make you a sixty-two catty Buddhist staff of burnished metal. Of course, if it's too heavy, don't blame me. For the knife, as I said, we don't need any specifications. I'll use the best steel."

"How much for the two?"

"We don't bargain. You can have them at rock-bottom—five ounces of silver for both."

"It's a deal. If you do a good job, I'll give you more."

The smith accepted the silver. "We'll start right away."

"I have some small change here. Come out and have a bowl of wine with me."

"Excuse me, Reverend. I must get on with my work. I can't keep you company."

Sagacious Lu left the ironsmith's. Before he had gone thirty paces, he saw a wine shop banner sticking out from the eaves of a house. He raised the hanging door screen, entered the shop, sat down, and pounded on the table.

"Bring wine," he shouted.

The proprietor came up to him. "Forgive me, Reverend. My shop and investment money all are borrowed from the monastery. The abbot has a rule for us tavern keepers. If any of us sells wine to a monk, he takes back the money and drives us out of our premises. Don't hold it against me."

"All I want is a little wine. I won't say I bought it here."

"Impossible. Please try some place else. I'm sorry."

Lu rose to his feet. "If another place serves me, I'll have something to say to you later!"

He left the wine shop and walked on. Soon he saw another wine flag suspended over a doorway. He went in, sat down and called:

"Wine, host. Be quick."

"How can you be so ignorant, Reverend?" the tavern keeper demanded. "You must know the abbot's rules. Do you want to ruin me?"

Sagacious insisted on being served, but the tavern keeper was adamant. Lu had no choice but to leave. He went to four or five more wine shops. All refused to serve him.

"If I don't think of something, I'll never get any wine," he said to himself. At the far end of the market-place he saw amid blossoming apricot trees a small house from which a bundle of broom straw was hanging. He

---

1. Guan Gong, a famous general of the Three Kingdoms period (220–280).

came closer and found it was a little wine shop. Lu went in and sat down by the window.

"Host," he called, "bring wine for a wandering monk."

The rustic owner came over and scrutinized him. "Where are you from, Reverend?"

"I'm a travelling monk who's just passing through. I want some wine."

"If you're from the Mount Wutai monastery, I'm not allowed to sell you any."

"I'm not. Now bring on the wine."

Lu's appearance and manner of speaking struck the rustic owner as odd. "How much do you want?"

"Never mind about that. Just keep bringing it by the bowlful."

Lu consumed ten big bowls of wine. "Have you any meat?" he asked. "I want a platter."

"I had some beef earlier in the day," said the proprietor, "but it's all sold out."

Sagacious caught a whiff of the fragrance of cooking meat. He went into the yard and found a dog boiling in an earthenware pot by the compound wall.

"You've got dog meat," he said. "Why won't you sell me any?"

"I thought as a monk you wouldn't eat it, so I didn't ask."

"I've plenty of money here." Lu pulled out some silver and handed it over. "Bring me half."

The proprietor cut off half the dog carcass and placed it on the table with a small dish of garlic sauce. Lu tore into it delightedly with both hands. At the same time he consumed another ten bowls of wine. He found the wine very agreeable and kept calling for more. The shop owner was dumbfounded.

"That's enough, monk," he urged.

Lu glared at him. "I'm paying for what I drink. Who's asking you to interfere?"

"How much more do you want?"

"Bring me another bucketful."

The host had no choice but to comply. Before long, Sagacious had downed this, too. A dog's leg that he hadn't finished he put inside his cassock.

"Hold on to the extra silver," he said as he was leaving. "I'll be back for more tomorrow."

The frightened proprietor could only helplessly gape. He watched as Lu headed towards Mount Wutai.

Halfway up the slope, Lu sat down in the pavilion and rested. The wine began to take effect. Leaping up, he cried: "I haven't had a good workout in a long time. I'm getting stiff and creaky in the joints. What I need is a little exercise."

Lu came out of the pavilion. He gripped the end of each sleeve in the opposite hand and swung his arms vigorously up and down, left and right, with increasing force. One arm accidentally struck against a post of the pavilion. There was a loud crack as the post snapped. Half the pavilion collapsed.

Two gate-keepers heard the noise and climbed to a high vantage point for a look. They saw Lu staggering up the slope.

"Woe," they exclaimed. "That brute is soused again!"

They closed the gate and barred it. Peering through a crack, they watched Lu advance. When he found the gate locked, he drummed on it with his fists. But the gate-keepers didn't dare let him in.

Lu pounded a while, in vain. Suddenly he noticed a Buddhist guardian idol on the left side of the gate.

"Hey, you big worthless fellow," Lu shouted. "Instead of helping me knock on the gate, you raise your fist and try to scare me! I'm not afraid of you!"

He jumped on the pedestal and ripped up the railing as easily as pulling scallions. Grabbing a broken post, he flailed it against the idol's leg, bringing down a shower of gilt and plaster.

"Woe," cried the gate-keepers. They ran to inform the abbot.

Lu paused, then turned and observed the guardian idol on the right.

"How dare you open your big mouth and laugh at me?" he yelled. He leaped on the pedestal and struck the idol's leg two hard blows. The figure toppled to the ground with a thunderous crash.

Lu laughed uproariously, holding the broken post in his hand.

When the gate-keepers notified the abbot he merely said: "Don't provoke him. Go back to your gate."

At that moment, the elder, the supervisor, the deacon, and other responsible monks entered the hall. "That wildcat is very drunk," they said. "He's wrecked the mid-slope pavilion and the guardian idols at the gate. How can we put up with this?"

"Since ancient times it's been known that 'Even a king shuns a drunkard.' All the more necessary for me to avoid them," replied the abbot. "If he's broken idols, we'll ask his sponsor Squire Zhao to make us new ones. Zhao can repair the pavilion too. Let Sagacious do as he wishes."

"Those guardian idols are the lords of the gate," the monks protested. "You can't change them around just like that."

"Never mind the gate idols," retorted the abbot. "Even if they were the idols of the leading Buddhas themselves that were destroyed, there'd be nothing we could do about it. Stay out of his way. Didn't you see how savage he was the other day?"

"What a muddle-headed abbot," the monks muttered as they left the hall. "Don't open that gate," they instructed the gate-keepers. "Just stand inside and listen."

"If you mother-screwing scabby donkeys don't let me in," bellowed Sagacious, "I'll set fire to this stinking monastery and burn it down!"

"Remove the bar and let the beast in," the monks hastily called to the gate-keepers. "If we don't, he's really liable to do it!"

The gate-keepers tiptoed up to the gate, pulled the bolt, then flew back and hid themselves. The other monks scattered.

Lu pushed hard against the gate with both hands. Unexpectedly, it gave way, and he stumbled in and fell flat on his face. He crawled to his feet, rubbed his head, and hurried to his quarters.

He pushed aside the door curtain and plunged into the meditation room. The monks, who were sitting cross-legged on their pallets, looked up, startled. They immediately lowered their heads. On reaching his own pallet, Sagacious noisily vomited. The stench was frightful. "Virtue be praised," cried the monks, holding their noses.

Lu clambered onto his pallet and opened his cassock and girdle, ripping them in the process. The dog's leg dropped to the floor. "Good," said Sagacious. "I was just getting hungry." He picked it up and began to eat.

The monks hid their faces behind their sleeves. Those nearest him stayed as far out of his way as possible. Lu tore off a piece of dog meat and offered it to the monk on his left.

"Try it," he recommended.

The man pressed his sleeve ends tightly against his lips.

"Don't you want any?" asked Lu. He shoved the meat at the man on his right. The fellow tried to slip off his pallet and escape, but Sagacious seized him by the ear and crammed the meat into his mouth.

Four or five monks on the opposite side of the room jumped up and hurried over. They pleaded with Lu to desist. He flung aside his dog's haunch and drummed his knuckles on their shaven pates. The whole meditation room was thrown into an uproar. Monks got their cassocks and bowls from the closets and quickly left. There was a general exodus. The elder couldn't stop them.

Cheerfully, Sagacious fought his way out. Most of the monks fled to the cloisters. This time the supervisor and deacon didn't notify the abbot, but summoned all the monks on duty, including every caretaker, cook, janitor and sedan-chair carrier they could muster—nearly two hundred men in all. These bound their heads with bandannas, armed themselves with clubs and staves, and marched on the monks' hall.

Lu let out a roar when he saw them. Not having any weapon he ran into the meditation room, knocked over the altar table in the front of the idol of Buddha, tore off two of the table legs, and charged out again.

He came at the attackers so fiercely that they hastily retreated to the cloisters. Sagacious advanced, flourishing his table legs. His adversaries closed in on him from both sides. Lu was furious. He feinted east and struck west, he feinted south and thumped north. Only those furthest away escaped his cudgels.

Right to the door of the preaching hall the battle raged. Then the voice of the abbot rang out: "Sagacious, stop that fighting! You, too, you monks!"

The attackers had suffered several dozen injured. They were glad to fall back when the abbot appeared. Lu threw down his table legs.

"Abbot, help me," he cried. By now he was eight-tenths sober.

"Sagacious, you're giving me too much trouble," said the cleric. "The last time you got drunk and raised a rumpus I wrote your sponsor Squire Zhao about it and he sent a letter of apology. Now you've disgraced yourself again, upset our pure way of life, wrecked the pavilion and damaged two idols. All this we can overlook. But you drove the monks from the meditation room, and that's a major crime. Wenshu Buddha meditated where our monastery stands today. For centuries these hallowed grounds have known only tranquillity and the fragrance of incense. It's no place for a dirty fellow like you. The next few days, you stay with me in the abbot's hall. I'll arrange for you to be transferred elsewhere."

The former major went with the abbot to his residence. The cleric told the supervisor to send the monks back to their meditations. Those who had been injured were to go and rest. Sagacious spent the night in the abbot's hall.

The next morning the abbot consulted with the elder. They decided to give Lu some money and send him on. But first it was necessary to notify Squire Zhao. The abbot wrote a letter and dispatched it to his manor with two messengers, who were instructed to wait for his reply.

Zhao was quite upset by the abbot's missive. In his answer he hailed the cleric respectfully and said: "I will pay for the repair of the broken gate guardians and the pavilion. Lu must go wherever the abbot sends him."

The abbot then directed his assistant to prepare a black cloth cassock, a pair of monk's shoes, and ten ounces of silver, and to summon Lu.

"Sagacious," said the abbot, "the last time you got drunk and made a disturbance in the monks' hall, you didn't know any better. This time you got drunk again, broke the guardian idols, wrecked the pavilion, and caused a riot in the hall of meditation. That's a serious crime. You've also injured many of our monks. Our monastery is a peaceful place. Your conduct is very bad. As a courtesy to Squire Zhao I'm giving you a letter of introduction to another place where you can stay. It's impossible for us to keep you here. In the Eastern Capital a Buddhist brother of mine, called the Lucid Teacher, is the abbot of the Great Xiangguo Monastery. Take this letter to him and ask him to find you a job. Last night I had a vision and composed a four-line prophetic verse to guide your destiny. You must remember these words."

Kneeling before him, Lu said: "I'd like to hear the prophecy."

The abbot intoned: "Take action in the forest, prosper in the mountains, flourish amid the waters, but halt at the river."

Sagacious kowtowed to the abbot nine times, shouldered his knapsack, tied bundles round his waist, and placed the letter in a pocket. He bid farewell to the abbot and the monks, left Mount Wutai, put up in the inn next door to the ironsmith and waited for his staff and sword. The monks were glad to be rid of him. The abbot told the lay brothers to clean up the wreckage of the guardian idols and the pavilion. A few days later Squire Zhao brought some money personally and had the idols and pavilion repaired.

Ming Dynasty

(1368–1644)

■ Wu Chengen (Wu Ch'eng-en)
(c. 1500–1582) (novel)

TRANSLATED BY ARTHUR WALEY

Monkey is a rambunctious, adventurous, satirical jaunt, a novel of the late Ming dynasty that recounts the story of the sage Xuanzang (596–664), also known as Tripitaka, after the "triple basket"—a great repository of Buddhist literature (see "Theravada Buddhist Texts" [the Tipitaka] in the section on Indian literature). This monk's seventeen-year journey to India to bring back Buddhist scriptures to China had been the subject of a number of plays, folktales, and other accounts; and Wu Chengen, the supposed author of *Monkey*, draws upon and elaborates on this tradition to make a novel of a hundred chapters. For more than three centuries, the author was thought to be Qiu Changchun (fl. 1220), who was an advisor to Genghis Khan. Now the scholar Hu Shi has documented that Wu Chengen, a minor official, writer, and poet of the Ming dynasty was most likely the author. He probably wrote *Monkey* in his later years, and a preface he wrote to a now lost collection of short stories gives a clue to his motivation: "I was very fond of strange stories when I was a child. In my village-school days, I used to buy stealthily the popular novels and historical recitals. Fearing that my father and my teacher might punish me for this and rob me of these treasures, I carefully hid them in secret places where I could enjoy them unmolested." Wu Chengen goes on to say that he dreamed of writing his own "Book of Monsters," and it was probably an adult version of his childhood fear of censure that caused him to distribute the novel anonymously.

In part, *Monkey* is an allegorical journey of the spirit, like *Pilgrim's Progress;* in part, it is a broad satire of government, religion, and society; and, in part, it is a wild romantic fantasy. The central character in the novel is not really Tripitaka, but a powerful, magical trickster of a monkey who is his companion and is allegorically interpreted as representing the mind. Another companion is Pigsy, a half-pig and half-human creature, who represents sensuality, laziness, gluttony—all the pleasures and faults of the body. Tripitaka is by no means a perfect, ideal character; he is fearful, foolish, selfish, and fallible, a series of traits that often lands him in hot water with demons who want to eat his flesh and thus gain immortality. He represents the average person. A third companion, Sandy, is a rather ill-defined representation of earnestness. A white horse who had been a dragon prince also aids Tripitaka on his journey. The first part of the book deals almost exclusively with Monkey, his origin, his acquisition of Daoist magic, and his wild adventures, and culminates with his epic battle with the forces of Heaven and his subjugation by the Buddha. He is imprisoned in a mountain for five hundred years and is released at last to use his considerable powers in the service of the Buddha, who wants to bring previously unknown texts of Mahayana Buddhism to China. The majority of the book (chapters 13 to 97) deals with the journey itself, and the book ends with the voyagers having an audience with the Buddha, returning to China with the scriptures, and achieving their final apotheosis. The novel's mixing of high seriousness and farce, adventure and mysticism has made it among the most popular of the traditional Chinese novels, while the apt dialogue, vernacular prose, and around seven hundred cleanly integrated poems make it a stylistic and narrative tour de force.

FURTHER READING: Waley, Arthur, tr. *Monkey*, 1942; *The Real Tripitaka and Other Pieces*, 1952. Yu, Anthony C., tr. *Journey to the West*, 4 vols., 1977–1983.

from **Monkey**

Chapter I

There was a rock that since the creation of the world had been worked upon by the pure essences of Heaven and the fine savours of Earth, the vigour of sunshine and the grace of moonlight, till at last it became magically pregnant and one day split open, giving birth to a stone egg, about as big as a playing ball. Fructified by the wind it developed into a stone monkey, complete with every organ and limb. At once this monkey learned to climb and run; but its first act was to make a bow towards each of the four quarters. As it did so, a steely light darted from this monkey's eyes and flashed as far as the Palace of the Pole Star. This shaft of light astonished the Jade Emperor as he sat in the Cloud Palace of the Golden Gates, in the Treasure Hall of the Holy Mists, surrounded by his fairy Ministers. Seeing this strange light flashing, he ordered Thousand-league Eye and Down-the-wind Ears to open the gate of the Southern Heaven and look out. At his bidding these two captains went out to the gate and looked so sharply and listened so well that presently they were able to report, 'This steely light comes from the borders of the small country of Ao-lai, that lies to the east of the Holy Continent, from the Mountain of Flowers and Fruit. On this mountain is a magic rock, which gave birth to an egg. This egg changed into a stone monkey, and when he made his bow to the four quarters a steely light flashed from his eyes with a beam that reached the Palace of the Pole Star. But now he is taking a drink, and the light is growing dim.'

The Jade Emperor condescended to take an indulgent view. 'These creatures in the world below,' he said, 'were compounded of the essence of heaven and earth, and nothing that goes on there should surprise us.' That monkey walked, ran, leapt and bounded over the hills, feeding on grasses and shrubs, drinking from streams and springs, gathering the mountain flowers, looking for fruits. Wolf, panther and tiger were his companions, the deer and civet were his friends, gibbons and baboons his kindred. At night he lodged under cliffs of rock, by day he wandered among the peaks and caves. One very hot morning, after playing in the shade of some pine-trees, he and the other monkeys went to bathe in a mountain stream. See how those waters bounce and tumble like rolling melons!

There is an old saying, 'Birds have their bird language, beasts have their beast talk.' The monkeys said, 'We none of us know where this stream comes from. As we have nothing to do this morning, wouldn't it be fun to follow it up to its source?' With a whoop of joy, dragging their sons and carrying their daughters, calling out to younger brother and to elder brother, the whole troupe rushed along the streamside and scrambled up the steep places, till they reached the source of the stream. They found themselves standing before the curtain of a great waterfall.

All the monkeys clapped their hands and cried aloud, 'Lovely water, lovely water! To think that it starts far off in some cavern below the base of the mountain, and flows all the way to the Great Sea! If any of us were bold enough to pierce that curtain, get to where the water comes from and re-turn unharmed, we would make him our king!' Three times the call went out, when suddenly one of them leapt from among the throng and an-swered the challenge in a loud voice. It was the Stone Monkey. 'I will go,' he cried, 'I will go!' Look at him! He screws up his eyes and crouches; then at one bound he jumps straight through the waterfall. When he opened his eyes and looked about him, he found that where he had landed there was no water. A great bridge stretched in front of him, shining and glinting. When he looked closely at it, he saw that it was made all of burnished iron. The water under it flowed through a hole in the rock, filling in all the space under the arch. Monkey climbed up on to the bridge and, spying as he went, saw something that looked just like a house. There were stone seats and stone couches, and tables with stone bowls and cups. He skipped back to the hump of the bridge and saw that on the cliff there was an inscription in large square writing which said, 'This cave of the Water Curtain in the blessed land of the Mountain of Flowers and Fruit leads to Heaven.' Mon-key was beside himself with delight. He rushed back and again crouched, shut his eyes and jumped through the curtain of water.

'A great stroke of luck,' he cried, 'A great stroke of luck!' 'What is it like on the other side?' asked the monkeys, crowding round him. 'Is the water very deep?' 'There is no water,' said the Stone Monkey. 'There is an iron bridge, and at the side of it a heaven-sent place to live in.' 'What made you think it would do to live in?' asked the monkeys. 'The water,' said the Stone Monkey, 'flows out of a hole in the rock, filling in the space under the bridge. At the side of the bridge are flowers and trees, and there is a chamber of stone. Inside are stone tables, stone cups, stone dishes, stone couches, stone seats. We could really be very comfortable there. There is plenty of room for hundreds and thousands of us, young and old. Let us all go and live there; we shall be splendidly sheltered in every weather.' 'You go first and show us how!' cried the monkeys, in great delight. Once more he closed his eyes and was through at one bound. 'Come along, all of you!' he cried. The bolder of them jumped at once; the more timid stretched out their heads and then drew them back, scratched their ears, rubbed their cheeks, and then with a great shout the whole mob leapt forward. Soon they were all seizing dishes and snatching cups, scrambling to the hearth or fighting for the beds, dragging things along or shifting them about, behaving indeed as monkeys with their mischievous nature might be expected to do, never quiet for an instant, till at last they were thoroughly worn out. The Stone Monkey took his seat at the head of them and said, 'Gentlemen! "With one whose word cannot be trusted there is nothing to be done!"[1] You promised that any of us who managed to get through the waterfall and back again, should be your king. I have not only come and gone and come again, but also found you a comfortable place to sleep, put you in the enviable position of being householders. Why do you not bow down to me as your king?'

Thus reminded, the monkeys all pressed together the palms of their hands and prostrated themselves, drawn up in a line according to age and standing, and bowing humbly they cried, 'Great king, a thousand years!' After this the Stone Monkey discarded his old name and became king, with the title 'Handsome Monkey King.' He appointed various monkeys, gibbons and baboons to be his ministers and officers. By day they wandered about the Mountain of Flowers and Fruit; at night they slept in the Cave of the Water Curtain. They lived in perfect sympathy and accord, not mingling with bird or beast, in perfect independence and entire happiness.

The Monkey King had enjoyed this artless existence for several hundred years when one day, at a feast in which all the monkeys took part, the king suddenly felt very sad and burst into tears. His subjects at once ranged themselves in front of him and bowed down, saying, 'Why is your Majesty so sad?' 'At present,' said the king, 'I have no cause for unhappiness. But I have a misgiving about the future, which troubles me sorely.' 'Your Majesty is very hard to please,' said the monkeys, laughing. 'Every day we have happy meetings on fairy mountains, in blessed spots, in ancient caves, on holy islands. We are not subject to the Unicorn or Phoenix, nor to the restraints of any human king. Such freedom is an immeasurable blessing.

---

1. *Analects* of Confucius, II. 22.

What can it be that causes you this sad misgiving?' 'It is true,' said the Monkey King, 'that to-day I am not answerable to the law of any human king, nor need I fear the menace of any beast or bird. But the time will come when I shall grow old and weak. Yama, King of Death, is secretly waiting to destroy me. Is there no way by which, instead of being born again on earth, I might live forever among the people of the sky?'

When the monkeys heard this they covered their faces with their hands and wept, each thinking of his own mortality. But look! From among the ranks there springs out one monkey commoner, who cries in a loud voice 'If that is what troubles your Majesty, it shows that religion has taken hold upon your heart. There are indeed, among all creatures, three kinds that are not subject to Yama, King of Death.' 'And do you know which they are?' asked the Monkey King. 'Buddhas, Immortals and Sages,' he said. 'These three are exempt from the Turning of the Wheel, from birth and destruction. They are eternal as Heaven and Earth, as the hills and streams.' 'Where are they to be found?' asked the Monkey King. 'Here on the common earth,' said the monkey, 'in ancient caves among enchanted hills.'

The king was delighted with this news. 'To-morrow,' he said, 'I shall say good-bye to you, go down the mountain, wander like a cloud to the corners of the sea, far away to the end of the world, till I have found these three kinds of Immortal. From them I will learn how to be young forever and escape the doom of death.' This determination it was that led him to leap clear of the toils of Re-incarnation and turned him at last into the Great Monkey Sage, equal of Heaven. The monkeys clapped their hands and cried aloud, 'Splendid! Splendid! To-morrow we will scour the hills for fruits and berries and hold a great farewell banquet in honour of our king.'

Next day they duly went to gather peaches and rare fruits, mountain herbs, yellow-sperm, tubers, orchids, strange plants and flowers of every sort, and set out the stone tables and benches, laid out fairy meats and drinks. They put the Monkey King at the head of the table, and ranged themselves according to their age and rank. The pledge-cup passed from hand to hand; they made their offerings to him of flowers and fruit. All day long they drank, and next day their king rose early and said, 'Little ones, cut some pine-wood for me and make me a raft; then find a tall bamboo for a pole, and put together a few fruits and such like. I am going to start.' He got on to the raft all alone and pushed off with all his might, speeding away and away, straight out to sea, till favoured by a following wind he arrived at the borders of the Southern World. Fate indeed had favoured him; for days on end, ever since he set foot on the raft, a strong southeast wind blew and carried him at last to the north-western bank, which is indeed the frontier of the Southern World. He tested the water with his pole and found that it was shallow; so he left the raft and climbed ashore. On the beach were people fishing, shooting wild geese, scooping oysters, draining salt. He ran up to them and for fun began to perform queer antics which frightened them so much that they dropped their baskets and nets and ran for their lives. One of them, who stood his ground, Monkey caught hold of, and ripping off his clothes, found out how to wear them himself, and so dressed up went prancing through towns and cities, in market and bazaar, imitating the people's manners and talk. All the while his heart was set only on finding the Immortals and learning from them the secret of eternal youth. But he found the men of the world all engrossed in the quest of profit or fame; there was not one who had any care for the end that was in store for him. So Monkey went looking for the way of Immortality, but found no chance of meeting it. For eight or nine years he went from city to city and town to town till suddenly he came to the Western Ocean. He was sure that beyond this ocean there would certainly be Immortals, and he made for himself a raft like the one he had before. He floated on over the Western Ocean till he came to the Western Continent, where he went ashore, and when he had looked about for some time, he suddenly saw a very high and beautiful mountain, thickly wooded at the base. He had no fear of wolves, tigers or panthers, and made his way up to the very top. He was looking about him when he suddenly heard a man's voice coming from deep amid the woods. He hurried towards the spot and listened intently. It was someone singing, and these were the words that he caught:

> I hatch no plot, I scheme no scheme;
> Fame and shame are one to me,
> A simple life prolongs my days.
> Those I meet upon my way
> Are Immortals, one and all,
> Who from their quiet seats expound
> The Scriptures of the Yellow Court.

When Monkey heard these words he was very pleased. 'There must then be Immortals somewhere hereabouts,' he said. He sprang deep into the forest and looking carefully saw that the singer was a woodman, who was cutting brushwood. 'Reverend Immortal,' said Monkey, coming forward, 'your disciple raises his hands.' The woodman was so astonished that he dropped his axe. 'You have made a mistake,' he said, turning and answering the salutation, 'I am only a shabby, hungry woodcutter. What makes you address me as an "Immortal"?' 'If you are not an Immortal,' said Monkey, 'why did you talk of yourself as though you were one?' 'What did I say,' asked the woodcutter, 'that sounded as though I were an Immortal?' 'When I came to the edge of the wood,' said Monkey, 'I heard you singing "Those I meet upon my way are Immortals, one and all, who from their quiet seats expound the Scriptures of the Yellow Court." Those scriptures are secret, Taoist texts. What can you be but an Immortal?' 'I won't deceive you,' said the woodcutter. 'That song was indeed taught to me by an Immortal, who lives not very far from my hut. He saw that I have to work hard for my living and have a lot of troubles; so he told me when I was worried by anything to say to myself the words of that song. This, he said, would comfort me and get me out of my difficulties. Just now I was upset about something and so I was singing that song. I had no idea that you were listening.'

'If the Immortal lives close by,' said Monkey, 'how is it that you have not become his disciple? Wouldn't it have been as well to learn from him how never to grow old?' 'I have a hard life of it,' said the woodcutter. 'When I was eight or nine I lost my father. I had no brothers and sisters, and it fell upon me alone to support my widowed mother. There was nothing for it but to work hard early and late. Now my mother is old and I dare not leave her. The garden is neglected, we have not enough either to eat or wear. The most I can do is to cut two bundles of firewood, carry them to market and with the penny or two that I get buy a few handfuls of rice which I cook myself and serve to my aged mother. I have no time to go and learn magic.' 'From what you tell me,' said Monkey, 'I can see that you are a good and devoted son, and your piety will certainly be rewarded. All I ask of you is that you will show me where the Immortal lives; for I should very much like to visit him.'

'It is quite close,' said the woodcutter. 'This mountain is called the Holy Terrace Mountain, and on it is a cave called the Cave of the Slanting Moon and Three Stars. In that cave lives an Immortal called the Patriarch Subodhi. In his time he has had innumerable disciples, and at this moment there are some thirty or forty of them studying with him. You have only to follow that small path southwards for eight or nine leagues,[2] and you will come to his home.' 'Honoured brother,' said Monkey, drawing the woodcutter towards him, 'come with me, and if I profit by the visit I will not forget that you guided me.' 'It takes a lot to make some people understand,' said the woodcutter. 'I've just been telling you why I can't go. If I went with you, what would become of my work? Who would give my old mother her food? I must go on cutting my wood, and you must find your way alone.'

When Monkey heard this, he saw nothing for it but to say goodbye. He left the wood, found the path, went uphill for some seven or eight leagues and sure enough found a cave-dwelling. But the door was locked. All was quiet, and there was no sign of anyone being about. Suddenly he turned his head and saw on top of the cliff a stone slab about thirty feet high and eight feet wide. On it was an inscription in large letters saying, 'Cave of the Slanting Moon and Three Stars on the Mountain of the Holy Terrace.' 'People here,' said Monkey, 'are certainly very truthful. There really is such a mountain, and such a cave!' He looked about for a while, but did not venture to knock at the door. Instead he jumped up into a pine-tree and began eating the pine-seed and playing among the branches. After a time he heard someone call; the door of the cave opened and a fairy boy of great beauty came out, in appearance utterly unlike the common lads that he had seen till now. The boy shouted, 'Who is making a disturbance out there?' Monkey leapt down from his tree, and coming forward said with a bow, 'Fairy boy, I am a pupil who has come to study Immortality. I should not dream of making a disturbance.' '*You* a pupil!' said the boy laughing.

---

2. A league was 360 steps.

'To be sure,' said Monkey. 'My master is lecturing,' said the boy. 'But before he gave out his theme he told me to go to the door and if anyone came asking for instruction, I was to look after him. I suppose he meant you.' 'Of course he meant me,' said Monkey. 'Follow me this way,' said the boy. Monkey tidied himself and followed the boy into the cave. Huge chambers opened out before them, they went on from room to room, through lofty halls and innumerable cloisters and retreats, till they came to a platform of green jade, upon which was seated the Patriarch Subodhi, with thirty lesser Immortals assembled before him. Monkey at once prostrated himself and bumped his head three times upon the ground, murmuring, 'Master, master! As pupil to teacher I pay you my humble respects.' 'Where do you come from?' asked the Patriarch. 'First tell me your country and name, and then pay your respects again.' 'I am from the Water Curtain Cave,' said Monkey, 'on the Mountain of Fruit and Flowers in the country of Ao-lai.' 'Go away!' shouted the Patriarch. 'I know the people there. They're a tricky, humbugging set. It's no good one of them supposing he's going to achieve Enlightenment.' Monkey, kowtowing violently, hastened to say, 'There's no trickery about this; it's just the plain truth I'm telling you.' 'If you claim that you're telling the truth,' said the Patriarch, 'how is it that you say you came from Ao-lai? Between there and here there are two oceans and the whole of the Southern Continent. How did you get here?' 'I floated over the oceans and wandered over the lands for ten years and more,' said Monkey, 'till at last I reached here.' 'Oh well,' said the Patriarch, 'I suppose if you came by easy stages, it's not altogether impossible. But tell me, what is your *hsing*?'[3] 'I never show *hsing*,' said Monkey. 'If I am abused, I am not at all annoyed. If I am hit, I am not angry; but on the contrary, twice more polite than before. All my life I have never shown hsing.'

'I don't mean that kind of hsing,' said the Patriarch. 'I mean what was your family, what surname had they?' 'I had no family,' said Monkey, 'neither father nor mother.' 'Oh indeed!' said the Patriarch. 'Perhaps you grew on a tree!' 'Not exactly,' said Monkey. 'I came out of a stone. There was a magic stone on the Mountain of Flowers and Fruit. When its time came, it burst open and I came out.'

'We shall have to see about giving you a school-name,' said the Patriarch. 'We have twelve words that we use in these names, according to the grade of the pupil. You are in the tenth grade.' 'What are the twelve words?' asked Monkey. 'They are Wide, Big, Wise, Clever, True, Conforming, Nature, Ocean, Lively, Aware, Perfect and Illumined. As you belong to the tenth grade, the word Aware must come in your name. How about Aware-of-Vacuity?' 'Splendid!' said Monkey, laughing. 'From now onwards let me be called Aware-of-Vacuity.'

So that was his name in religion. And if you do not know whether in the end, equipped with this name, he managed to obtain enlightenment or not, listen while it is explained to you in the next chapter.

---

3. There is a pun on *hsing*, 'surname' and *hsing*, 'temper.'

Chapter II

Monkey was so pleased with his new name that he skipped up and down in front of the Patriarch, bowing to express his gratitude. Subodhi then ordered his pupils to take Monkey to the outer rooms and teach him how to sprinkle and dust, answer properly when spoken to, how to come in, go out, and go round. Then he bowed to his fellow-pupils and went out into the corridor, where he made himself a sleeping place. Early next morning he and the others practised the correct mode of speech and bearing, studied the Scriptures, discussed doctrine, practised writing, burnt incense. And in this same way he passed day after day, spending his leisure in sweeping the floor, hoeing the garden, growing flowers and tending trees, getting firewood and lighting the fire, drawing water and carrying it in buckets. Everything he needed was provided for him. And so he lived in the cave, while time slipped by, for six or seven years. One day the Patriarch, seated in state, summoned all his pupils and began a lecture on the Great Way. Monkey was so delighted by what he heard that he tweaked his ears and rubbed his cheeks; his brow flowered and his eyes laughed. He could not stop his hands from dancing, his feet from stamping. Suddenly the Patriarch caught sight of him and shouted, 'What is the use of your being here if, instead of listening to my lecture, you jump and dance like a maniac?' 'I am listening with all my might,' said Monkey. 'But you were saying such wonderful things that I could not contain myself for joy. That is why I may, for all I know, have been hopping and jumping. Don't be angry with me.' 'So you recognize the profundity of what I am saying?' said the Patriarch. 'How long, pray, have you been in the cave?' 'It may seem rather silly,' said Monkey, 'but really I don't know how long. All I can remember is that when I was sent to get firewood, I went up the mountain behind the cave, and there I found a whole slope covered with peach-trees. I have eaten my fill of those peaches seven times.' 'It is called the Hill of Bright Peach Blossom,' said the Patriarch. 'If you have eaten there seven times, I suppose you have been here seven years. What sort of wisdom are you now hoping to learn from me?' 'I leave that to you,' said Monkey. 'Any sort of wisdom—it's all one to me.'

'There are three hundred and sixty schools of wisdom,' said the Patriarch, 'and all of them lead to Self-attainment. Which school do you want to study?' 'Just as you think best,' said Monkey. 'I am all attention.' 'Well, how about Art?' said the Patriarch. 'Would you like me to teach you that?' 'What sort of wisdom is that?' asked Monkey. 'You would be able to summon fairies and ride the Phoenix,' said the Patriarch, 'divine by shuffling the yarrow-stalks and know how to avoid disaster and pursue good fortune.' 'But should I live forever?' asked Monkey. 'Certainly not,' said the Patriarch. 'Then that's no good to me,' said Monkey. 'How about natural philosophy?' said the Patriarch. 'What is that about?' asked Monkey. 'It means the teaching of Confucius,' said the Patriarch, 'and of Buddha and Lao Tzu, of the Dualists and Mo Tzu and the Doctors of Medicine; reading scriptures, saying prayers, learning how to have adepts and sages at your beck and call.' 'But should I live forever?' asked Monkey. 'If that's what you are thinking about,' said the Patriarch, 'I am afraid philosophy is no better than a prop in the wall.' 'Master,' said Monkey, 'I am a plain, simple man, and I don't understand that sort of patter. What do you mean by a prop in the wall?' 'When men are building a room,' said the Patriarch, 'and want it to stand firm, they put a pillar to prop up the walls. But one day the roof falls in and the pillar rots.' 'That doesn't sound much like long life,' said Monkey. 'I'm not going to learn philosophy!' 'How about Quietism?' asked the Patriarch. 'What does that consist of?' asked Monkey. 'Low diet,' said the Patriarch, 'inactivity, meditation, restraint of word and deed, yoga practised prostrate or standing.' 'But should I live forever?' asked Monkey. 'The results of Quietism,' said the Patriarch, 'are no better than unbaked clay in the kiln.' 'You've got a very poor memory,' said Monkey. 'Didn't I tell you just now that I don't understand that sort of patter? What do you mean by unbaked clay in the kiln?' 'The bricks and tiles,' said the Patriarch, 'may be waiting, all shaped and ready, in the kiln; but if they have not yet been fired, there will come a day when heavy rain falls and they are washed away.' 'That does not promise well for the future,' said Monkey. 'I don't think I'll bother about Quietism.'

'You might try exercises,' said the Patriarch. 'What do you mean by that?' asked Monkey. 'Various forms of activity,' said the Patriarch, 'such as the exercises called "Gathering the Yin and patching the Yang," "Drawing the Bow and Treading the Catapult," "Rubbing the Navel to pass breath." Then there are alchemical practices such as the Magical Explosion, Burning the Reeds and Striking the Tripod, Promoting Red Lead, Melting the Autumn Stone, and Drinking Bride's Milk.' 'Would these make me live forever?' asked Monkey. 'To hope for that,' said the Patriarch, 'would be like trying to fish the moon out of the water.' 'There you go again!' said Monkey. 'What pray do you mean by fishing the moon out of the water?' 'When the moon is in the sky,' said the Patriarch, 'it is reflected in the water. It looks just like a real thing, but if you try to catch hold of it, you find it is only an illusion.' 'That does not sound much good,' said Monkey; 'I shan't learn exercises.' 'Tut!' cried the Patriarch, and coming down from the platform, he caught hold of the knuckle-rapper and pointed it at Monkey, saying, 'You wretched simian! You won't learn this and you won't learn that! I should like to know what it is you do want.' And so saying he struck Monkey over the head three times. Then he folded his hands behind his back and strode off into the inner room, dismissing his audience and locking the door behind him. The pupils all turned indignantly upon Monkey. 'You villainous ape,' they shouted at him, 'do you think that is the way to behave? The Master offers to teach you, and instead of accepting thankfully, you begin arguing with him. Now he's thoroughly offended and goodness knows when he'll come back.' They were all very angry and poured abuse on him; but Monkey was not in the least upset, and merely replied by a broad grin. The truth of the matter was, he understood the language of secret signs. That was why he did not take up the quarrel or attempt to argue. He knew that the Master, by striking him three times, was giving him an appointment at the third watch; and by going off with his hands folded behind his back, meant that Monkey was to look for him in the inner apartments. The locking of the door meant that he was to come round by the back door and would then receive instruction.

The rest of the day he frolicked with the other pupils in front of the cave, impatiently awaiting the night. As soon as dusk came, like the others, he went to his sleeping place. He closed his eyes and pretended to be asleep, breathing softly and regularly. In the mountains there is no watchman to beat the watches or call the hours. The best Monkey could do was to count his incoming and outgoing breaths. When he reckoned that it must be about the hour of the Rat (11 p.m.–1 a.m.) he got up very quietly and slipped on his clothes, softly opened the front door, left his companions and went round to the back door. Sure enough, it was only half shut. 'The Master certainly means to give me instruction,' said Monkey to himself. 'That is why he left the door open.' So he crept in and went straight to the Master's bed. Finding him curled up and lying with his face to the wall, Monkey dared not wake him, and knelt down beside the bed. Presently the Patriarch woke, stretched out his legs and murmured to himself:

> Hard, very hard!
> The Way is most secret.
> Never handle the Golden Elixir as though it were a mere toy!
> He who to unworthy ears entrusts the dark truths
> To no purpose works his jaws and talks his tongue dry.

'Master, I've been kneeling here for some time,' said Monkey, when he saw the Patriarch was awake. 'You wretched Monkey,' said Subodhi, who on recognizing his voice pulled off the bed-clothes and sat up. 'Why aren't you asleep in your own quarters, instead of coming round behind to mine?' 'At the lecture to-day,' said Monkey, 'you ordered me to come for instruction at the third watch, by way of the back gate. That is why I ventured to come straight to your bed.' The Patriarch was delighted. He thought to himself 'This fellow must really be, as he says, a natural product of Heaven and Earth. Otherwise he would never have understood my secret signs.' 'We are alone together,' said Monkey, 'there is no one to overhear us. Take pity upon me and teach me the way of Long Life. I shall never forget your kindness.' 'You show a disposition,' said the Patriarch. 'You understood my secret signs. Come close and listen carefully. I am going to reveal to you the Secret of Long Life.' Monkey beat his head on the floor to show his gratitude, washed his ears and attended closely, kneeling beside the bed. The Patriarch then recited:

> To spare and tend the vital powers, this and nothing else
> Is sum and total of all magic, secret and profane.
> All is comprised in these three, Spirit, Breath and Soul;
> Guard them closely, screen them well; let there be no leak.

Store them within the frame;
That is all that can be learnt, and all that can be taught.
I would have you mark the tortoise and snake, locked in tight
    embrace.
Locked in tight embrace, the vital powers are strong;
Even in the midst of fierce flames the Golden Lotus may be planted,
The Five Elements compounded and transposed, and put to new use.
When that is done, be which you please, Buddha or Immortal.

By these words Monkey's whole nature was shaken to the foundations. He carefully committed them to memory; then humbly thanked the Patriarch, and went out again by the back door.

A pale light was just coming into the eastern sky. He retraced his steps, softly opened the front door and returned to his sleeping place, purposely making a rustling noise with his bed-clothes. 'Get up!' he cried. 'There is light in the sky.' His fellow pupils were fast asleep, and had no idea that Monkey had received Illumination.

Time passed swiftly, and three years later the Patriarch again mounted his jewelled seat and preached to his assembled followers. His subject was the parables and scholastic problems of the Zen Sect, and his theme, the tegument of outer appearances. Suddenly he broke off and asked, 'Where is the disciple Aware-of-Vacuity?' Monkey knelt down before him and answered 'Here!' 'What have you been studying all this time?' asked the Patriarch. 'Recently,' said Monkey, 'my spiritual nature has been very much in the ascendant, and my fundamental sources of power are gradually strengthening.' 'In that case,' said the Patriarch, 'all you need learn is how to ward off the Three Calamities.' 'There must be some mistake,' said Monkey in dismay. 'I understood that the secrets I have learnt would make me live forever and protect me from fire, water and every kind of disease. What is this about three calamities?' 'What you have learnt,' said the Patriarch, 'will preserve your youthful appearance and increase the length of your life; but after five hundred years Heaven will send down lightning which will finish you off, unless you have the sagacity to avoid it. After another five hundred years Heaven will send down a fire that will devour you. This fire is of a peculiar kind. It is neither common fire, nor celestial fire, but springs up from within and consumes the vitals, reducing the whole frame to ashes, and making a vanity of all your thousand years of self-perfection. But even should you escape this, in another five hundred years, a wind will come and blow upon you. Not the east wind, the south wind, the west wind or the north wind; not flower wind, or willow wind, pine wind or bamboo wind. It blows from below, enters the bowels, passes the midriff and issues at the Nine Apertures. It melts bone and flesh, so that the whole body dissolves. These three calamities you must be able to avoid.' When Monkey heard this, his hair stood on end, and prostrating himself he said, 'I beseech you, have pity upon me, and teach me how to avoid these calamities.

I shall never forget your kindness.' 'There would be no difficulty about that,' said the Patriarch, 'if it were not for your peculiarities.' 'I have a round head sticking up to Heaven and square feet treading Earth,' said Monkey. 'I have nine apertures, four limbs, five upper and six lower internal organs, just like other people.' 'You are like other men in most respects,' said the Patriarch, 'but you have much less jowl.' For monkeys have hollow cheeks and pointed nozzles. Monkey felt his face with his hand and laughed saying, 'Master, I have my debits, but don't forget my assets. I have my pouch, and that must be credited to my account, as something that ordinary humans haven't got.' 'True enough,' said the Patriarch. 'There are two methods of escape. Which would you like to learn? There is the trick of the Heavenly Ladle, which involves thirty-six kinds of transformation, and the trick of the Earthly Conclusion, which involves seventy-two kinds of transformation.' 'Seventy-two sounds better value,' said Monkey. 'Come here then,' said the Patriarch, 'and I will teach you the formula.' He then whispered a magic formula into Monkey's ear. That Monkey King was uncommonly quick at taking things in. He at once began practising the formula, and after a little self-discipline he mastered all the seventy-two transformations, whole and complete. One day when master and disciples were in front of the cave, admiring the evening view, the Patriarch said, 'Monkey, how is that business going?' 'Thanks to your kindness,' said Monkey, 'I have been extremely successful. In addition to the transformations I can already fly.' 'Let's see you do it,' said the Patriarch. Monkey put his feet together, leapt about sixty feet into the air, and riding the clouds for a few minutes dropped in front of the Patriarch. He did not get more than three leagues in the whole of his flight. 'Master,' he said, 'that surely is cloud-soaring?' 'I should be more inclined to call it cloud-crawling,' said the Patriarch laughing. 'The old saying runs, "An Immortal wanders in the morning to the Northern Sea, and the same evening he is in Ts'ang-wu." To take as long as you did to go a mere league or two hardly counts even as cloud-crawling.' 'What is meant by that saying about the Northern Sea and Ts'ang-wu?' asked Monkey. 'A real cloud-soarer,' said the Patriarch, 'can start early in the morning from the Northern Sea, cross the Eastern Sea, the Western Sea and the Southern Sea, and land again at Ts'ang-wu. Ts'ang-wu means Ling-ling, in the Northern Sea. To do the round of all four seas in one day is true cloud-soaring.' 'It sounds very difficult,' said Monkey. 'Nothing in the world is difficult,' said the Patriarch, 'it is only our own thoughts that make things seem so.' 'Master,' said Monkey, prostrating himself, 'You may as well make a good job of me. While you're about it, do me a real kindness and teach me the art of cloud-soaring. I shall never forget how much I owe to you.' 'When the Immortals go cloud-soaring,' said the Patriarch, 'they sit cross-legged and rise straight from that position. You do nothing of the kind. I saw you just now put your feet together and jump. I must really take this opportunity of teaching you how to do it properly. You shall learn the Cloud Trapeze.' He then taught him the magic formula, saying, 'Make the pass, recite the spell, clench your fists, and one leap will carry you head over heels a hundred and eight thousand leagues.'

When the other pupils heard this, they all tittered, saying, 'Monkey is in luck. If he learns this trick, he will be able to carry dispatches, deliver letters, take round circulars—one way or another he will always be able to pick up a living!'

It was now late. Master and pupils all went to their quarters; but Monkey spent all night practising the Cloud Trapeze, and by the time day came he had completely mastered it, and could wander through space where he would.

One summer day when the disciples had for some time been studying their tasks under a pine-tree, one of them said, 'Monkey, what can you have done in a former incarnation to merit that the Master should the other day have whispered in your ear the secret formula for avoiding the Three Calamities? Have you mastered all those transformations?' 'To tell you the truth,' said Monkey, 'although of course I am much indebted to the Master for his instruction, I have also been working very hard day and night on my own, and I can now do them all.' 'Wouldn't this be a good opportunity,' said one of the pupils, 'to give us a little demonstration?' When Monkey heard this, he was all on his mettle to display his powers. 'Give me my subject,' he said. 'What am I to change into?' 'How about a pine-tree?' they said. He made a magic pass, recited a spell, shook himself, and changed into a pine-tree.

The disciples clapped and burst into loud applause. 'Bravo, Monkey, bravo,' they cried. There was such a din that the Patriarch came running out with his staff trailing after him. 'Who's making all this noise?' he asked. The disciples at once controlled themselves, smoothed down their dresses and came meekly forward. Monkey changed himself back into his true form and slipped in among the crowd, saying, 'Reverend Master, we are doing our lessons out here. I assure you there was no noise in particular.' 'You were all bawling,' said the Patriarch angrily. 'It didn't sound in the least like people studying. I want to know what you were doing here, shouting and laughing.' 'To tell the truth,' said someone, 'Monkey was showing us a transformation just for fun. We told him to change into a pine-tree, and he did it so well that we were all applauding him. That was the noise you heard. I hope you will forgive us.' 'Go away, all of you!' the Patriarch shouted. 'And you, Monkey, come here! What were you doing, playing with your spiritual powers, turning into—what was it? A pine-tree? Did you think I taught you in order that you might show off in front of other people? If you saw someone else turn into a tree, wouldn't you at once ask how it was done? If others see you doing it, aren't they certain to ask you? If you are frightened to refuse, you will give the secret away; and if you refuse, you're very likely to be roughly handled. You're putting yourself in grave danger.' 'I'm terribly sorry,' said Monkey. 'I won't punish you,' said the Patriarch, 'but you can't stay here.' Monkey burst into tears. 'Where am I to go to?' he asked. 'Back to where you came from, I should suppose,' said the

Patriarch. 'You don't mean back to the Cave of the Water Curtain in Ao-lai!' said Monkey. 'Yes,' said the Patriarch, 'go back as quickly as you can, if you value your life. One thing is certain in any case; you can't stay here.' 'May I point out,' said Monkey, 'that I have been away from home for twenty years and should be very glad to see my monkey-subjects once more. But I can't consent to go till I have repaid you for all your kindness.' 'I have no desire to be repaid,' said the Patriarch. 'All I ask is that if you get into trouble, you should keep my name out of it.' Monkey saw that it was no use arguing. He bowed to the Patriarch, and took leave of his companions. 'Wherever you go,' said the Patriarch, 'I'm convinced you'll come to no good. So remember, when you get into trouble, I absolutely forbid you to say that you are my disciple. If you give a hint of any such thing I shall flay you alive, break all your bones, and banish your soul to the Place of Ninefold Darkness, where it will remain for ten thousand aeons.' 'I certainly won't venture to say a word about you,' promised Monkey. 'I'll say I found it all out for myself.' So saying he bade farewell, turned away, and making the magic pass rode off on his cloud trapeze, straight to the Eastern Sea. In a very little while he reached the Mountain of Flowers and Fruit, where he lowered his cloud, and was picking his way, when he heard a sound of cranes calling and monkeys crying. 'Little ones,' he shouted, 'I have come back.' At once from every cranny in the cliff, from bushes and trees, great monkeys and small leapt out with cries of 'Long live our king!' Then they all pressed round Monkey, kowtowing and saying, 'Great King, you're very absent-minded! Why did you go away for so long, leaving us all in the lurch, panting for your return, as a starving man for food and drink? For some time past a demon has been ill-using us. He has seized our cave, though we fought desperately, and now he has robbed us of all our possessions and carried off many of our children, so that we have to be on the watch all the time and get no sleep day or night. It's lucky you've come now, for if you had waited another year or two, you'd have found us and everything here-abouts in another's hands.' 'What demon can dare commit such crimes?' cried Monkey. 'Tell me all about it and I will avenge you.' 'Your majesty,' they said, 'he is called the Demon of Havoc, and he lives due north from here.' 'How far off?' asked Monkey. 'He comes like a cloud,' they said, 'and goes like a mist, like wind or rain, thunder or lightning. We do not know how far away he lives.' 'Well, don't worry,' said Monkey. 'Just go on playing around, while I go and look for him.' Dear Monkey King! He sprang into the sky straight northwards and soon saw in front of him a high and very rugged mountain. He was admiring the scenery, when he suddenly heard voices. Going a little way down the hill, he found a cave in front of which several small imps were jumping and dancing. When they saw Monkey, they ran away. 'Stop!' he called, 'I've got a message for you to take. Say that the master of the Water Curtain Cave is here. The Demon of Havoc, or whatever he is called, who lives here, has been ill-treating my little ones and I have come on purpose to settle matters with him.' They rushed into the cave and cried out, 'Great King, a terrible thing has happened!' 'What's the matter?' said the demon. 'Outside the cave,' they said, 'there is a monkey-headed creature who says he is the owner of the Water Curtain Cave. He says you have been ill-using his people and he has come on purpose to settle matters with you.' 'Ha, ha,' laughed the demon. 'I have often heard those monkeys say that their king had gone away to learn religion. This means that he's come back again. What does he look like and how is he armed?' 'He carries no weapon at all,' they said. 'He goes bare-headed, wears a red dress, with a yellow sash, and black shoes—neither priest nor layman nor quite like a Taoist. He's waiting naked-handed outside the gate.' 'Bring me my whole accoutrement,' cried the demon. The small imps at once fetched his arms. The demon put on his helmet and breastplate, grasped his sword, and going to the gate with the little imps, cried in a loud voice, 'Where's the owner of the Water Curtain Cave?' 'What's the use of having such large eyes,' shouted Monkey, 'if you can't see old Monkey?' Catching sight of him the demon burst out laughing. 'You're not a foot high or as much as thirty years old. You have no weapon in your hand! How dare you strut about talking of settling accounts with me?' 'Cursed demon,' said Monkey. 'After all, you have no eyes in your head! You say I am small, not seeing that I can make myself as tall as I please. You say I am unarmed, not knowing that these two hands of mine could drag the moon from the ends of Heaven. Stand your ground, and eat old Monkey's fist!' So saying he leapt into the air and aimed a blow at the demon's face. The demon parried the blow with his hand. 'You such a pigmy and I so tall!' said the demon. 'You using your fists and I my sword—No! If I were to slay you with my sword I should make myself ridiculous. I am going to throw away my sword and use my naked fists.' 'Very good,' said Monkey. 'Now, my fine fellow, come on!' The demon relaxed his guard and struck. Monkey closed with him, and the two of them pommelled and kicked, blow for blow. A long reach is not so firm and sure as a short one. Monkey jabbed the demon in the lower ribs, pounded him in the chest, and gave him such a heavy drubbing that at last the demon stood back, and picking up his great flat sword, slashed at Monkey's head. But Monkey stepped swiftly aside, and the blow missed its mark. Seeing that the demon was becoming savage, Monkey now used the method called Body Outside the Body. He plucked out a handful of hairs, bit them into small pieces and then spat them out into the air, crying 'Change!' The fragments of hair changed into several hundred small monkeys, all pressing round in a throng. For you must know that when anyone becomes an Immortal, he can project his soul, change his shape and perform all kinds of miracles. Monkey, since his Illumination, could change every one of the eighty-four thousand hairs of his body into whatever he chose. The little monkeys he had now created were so nimble that no sword could touch them or spear wound them. See how they leap forward and jump back, crowd round the demon, some hugging, some pulling, some jabbing at his chest, some swarming up his legs. They kicked him, beat him, pommelled his eyes, pinched his nose, and while they were all at it, Monkey slipped up and snatched away the Demon's sword. Then pushing through the throng of small monkeys, he raised the sword and brought it down with such tremendous force upon the demon's skull, that he clove it in twain. He and the little monkeys then rushed into the cave and made a quick end of the imps, great and small. He then said a spell, which caused the small monkeys to change back into hairs. These he put back where they had come from; but there were still some small monkeys left—those that the Demon had carried off from the Cave of the Water Curtain. 'How did you get here?' he asked. There were about thirty or forty of them, and they all said with tears in their eyes, 'After your Majesty went away to become an Immortal, we were pestered by this creature for two years. In the end he carried us all off, and he stole all the fittings from our cave. He took all the stone dishes and the stone cups.' 'Collect everything that belongs to us and bring it with you,' said Monkey. They then set fire to the cave and burnt everything in it. 'Now follow me!' said Monkey. 'When we were brought here,' they said, 'we only felt a great wind rushing past, which whirled us to this place. We didn't know which way we were coming. So how are we to find the way home?' 'He brought you here by magic,' said Monkey. 'But what matter? I am now up to all that sort of thing, and if he could do it, I can. Shut your eyes, all of you, and don't be frightened.' He then recited a spell which produced a fierce wind. Suddenly it dropped, and Monkey shouted, 'You may look now!' The monkeys found that they were standing on firm ground quite close to their home. In high delight they all followed a familiar path back to the door of their cave. They and those who had been left behind all pressed into the cave, and lined up according to their ranks and age, and did homage to their king, and prepared a great banquet of welcome. When they asked how the demon had been subdued and the monkeys rescued, he told them the whole story; upon which they burst into shouts of applause. 'We little thought,' they said, 'that when your Majesty left us, you would learn such arts as this!' 'After I parted from you,' said Monkey, 'I went across many oceans to the land of Jambudvipa, where I learnt human ways, and how to wear clothes and shoes. I wandered restless as a cloud for eight or nine years, but nowhere could I find Enlightenment. At last after crossing yet another ocean, I was lucky enough to meet an old Patriarch who taught me the secret of eternal life.' 'What an incredible piece of luck!' the monkeys said, all congratulating him. 'Little ones,' said Monkey, 'I have another bit of good news for you. Your king has got a name-in-religion. I am called Aware-of-Vacuity.' They all clapped loudly, and presently went to get date-wine and grape-wine and fairy flowers and fruit, which they offered to Monkey. Everyone was in the highest spirits. If you do not know what the upshot was and how he fared now that he was back in his old home, you must listen to what is related in the next chapter.

Qing Dynasty

(1644–1911)

▪ Pu Songling (Pu Sung-ling) (1640–1715) (story)

TRANSLATED BY YANG XIANYI AND GLADYS YANG

Pu Songling is the finest story writer of the early Qing dynasty. He came from what is today Shandong, was a failed scholar who was unable to pass the provincial examination, had a career as a personal secretary, and later became a tutor for a family of local gentry. He is best known for his collection of fantastic stories titled *Strange Stories from the Leisure Studio,* which consisted of folk stories and legends he culled from his extensive contact with the common people. He elaborated on and retold these stories, wrote many stories himself, and derived other tales in the collection from previous written sources. He is noted for his development of dialogue, a technique still nascent in earlier Chinese fiction, and is celebrated for the realism of his characters, in spite of the healthy dose of the supernatural that runs throughout the tales. Many of the stories deal with immortals, ghosts, fox spirits, transformations, supernatural love, and horror, but, despite his interest in the fantastic, many of his tales have serious social content.

FURTHER READING: Giles, Herbert A., tr. *Strange Stories from a Chinese Studio,* 1880. Lu, Yunzhong, et al., trs. *Strange Tales of Liaozhai,* 1988. Yang, Xianyi, and Gladys Yang, eds. *Selected Tales of Liaozhai,* 1981.

The Cricket

During the reign of Xuan De, cricket fights were popular at court and a levy of crickets was exacted every year. Now these insects were scarce in the province of Shaanxi, but the magistrate of Huayin—to get into the good books of the governor—presented a cricket which proved a remarkable fighter. So much so that his county was commanded to present crickets regularly and the magistrate ordered his bailiffs to produce them. Then young fellows in town began to keep good crickets and demand high prices for them, while the crafty bailiffs seized this chance to make money. Thus each cricket they collected was the ruin of several households.

Now in this town lived a scholar named Cheng Ming, who had failed repeatedly in the district examination. This slow-witted pedant was appointed
beadle on the recommendation of the crooked bailiff and could not evade
this service hard as he tried. In less than a year his small patrimony was exhausted. Then came another levy of crickets. Cheng dared not extort
money from the country folk but neither could he pay the sum himself. At
his wit's end, he longed to die.

"What good would dying do?" demanded his wife. "You had better go
out and look for a cricket yourself. There is just one chance in ten thousand that you may catch one."

Cheng agreed. With a bamboo tube and wire cage he searched from
dawn till dusk among ruins and waste land, peering under rocks and exploring crevices, leaving no stone unturned—but all in vain. The two or
three crickets he caught were poor specimens which did not come up to
standard. The magistrate set him a time limit and beat him when he failed,
till in little more than ten days he had received some hundred strokes and
his legs were so covered with sores that he could not continue his search.
Tossing painfully on his bed, his one thought was to die.

Then to their village came a hump-backed diviner who could tell fortunes by consulting spirits. Cheng's wife, taking money, went to ask his advice.
She found his gate thronged with pink, blooming girls and white-haired old
women. Entering, she saw a curtain before the inner room, with incense on a
table in front of it. Those come to ask their fortune burned incense in the tripod and kowtowed. The diviner prayed beside them, staring into space, but
though his lips moved no one knew what it was he said and all listened respectfully. Finally a slip of paper was tossed from the inner room with the answer to the question asked—an answer which invariably proved correct.

Cheng's wife put her money on the table, burned incense and kowtowed like the other women. Presently the curtain moved and a piece of
paper fluttered to the ground. Instead of writing it had a painting of a
building like a temple with a small hill behind covered with rocks of every
shape and overgrown with thorns. A cricket was crouching there while beside it a toad was making ready to spring. She had no idea what this meant,
but the cricket at least had some connection with their problem. Accordingly she folded the paper and took it home to her husband.

Cheng wondered. "Is this supposed to show me where I should look for
a cricket?"

On examining the picture closely, he recognized Great Buddha
Monastery east of the village. So taking the paper with him, he struggled
along with the help of a stick to the back of the monastery. There he found
an old grave overgrown with brambles. Skirting this, he saw that the stones
lying scattered around were exactly like the painting. He pricked up his
ears and limped slowly through the brambles, but he might just as well have
been looking for a needle or a grain of mustard-seed. Though he strained
every nerve he found nothing. As he was groping around, a toad hopped
into sight. Cheng gave a start and hurried after it. The toad slipped into the

undergrowth and, following it, he saw a cricket at the root of a bramble. He snatched at it but the cricket leapt into a crevice in a rock and would not come out though he prodded it with a straw. Not till he poured water on it, did it emerge. It seemed a fine specimen and he picked it up. Seen close to it, it had a large body and long tail, dark neck and golden wings, and he was a happy man as he carried it home in the cage to delight his household, who considered it more precious than the rarest jade. The cricket was kept in a pot and fed upon white crab's flesh and the yellow kernel of chestnuts, tended with loving care till such time as the magistrate should ask for it.

Now Cheng had a son of nine, who uncovered this pot on the sly while his father was out. At once the cricket jumped out and sprang about so nimbly that he could not catch it. Finally the boy grabbed it, but in doing so tore off a leg and crushed it so that the next moment it died. The frightened child ran crying to his mother. When she heard what had happened she turned as pale as death.

"You wicked boy!" she cried. "You'll catch it when your father comes home!"

Her son went off in tears. Soon Cheng came back and when he heard his wife's story he felt as if he had been turned to ice. In a passion he searched for his son, who was nowhere to be found until at last they discovered his body in the well. Then anger turned to sorrow. Cheng cried out in anguish and longed to kill himself. Husband and wife sat with their faces to the wall in their thatched and smokeless cottage in silent despair. As the sun began to set he prepared to bury the boy, but upon touching the child found there was still breath in him. Overjoyed, he laid the small body on the couch and towards the middle of the night the child came round. Cheng and his wife began to breathe again, but their son remained in a trance with drooping eyelids. The sight of the empty cricket cage brought back Cheng's grief, but he dared not scold the child now. He did not close his eyes all night, and as the sun rose in the east he was still lying in stark despair when a cricket chirped outside the door. He rose in amazement to look, and sure enough there was a cricket. He clutched at it, but it chirped and hopped away. He put his hands over it but to no avail: when he turned up his palms the cricket escaped again. So he chased it up and down till it disappeared round the corner of the wall, and while searching for it he discovered another cricket on the wall. But this was a little, dark red insect, not to be compared with the first. Deciding that it was too small to be worth catching, Cheng looked round again for the one he had lost. At once the small cricket hopped from the wall to his sleeve, and he saw it resembled a mole-cricket with speckled wings, a square head and long legs—it might be a good one. So he was glad to keep it.

Cheng meant to present this cricket to the yamen, but fearing that it might not do he decided first to give it a trial fight. Now a young fellow in that village had a cricket called Crab Blue which had beaten every other insect it fought, and its owner wanted such an exorbitant price for it that it had remained on his hands. This man called on Cheng and laughed to see his cricket, producing his own for comparison. At the sight of this large, handsome insect, Cheng felt even more diffident and dared not offer a fight. The young man, however, insisted on a match; and since his poor cricket was useless in any case Cheng thought he might as well sacrifice it for a laugh. So the two combatants were put in one basin, where the small one crouched motionless as a stick of wood. The young man laughed heartily and prodded it with a pig's bristle, but still it made no move. At that he laughed louder and louder until at last the cricket was roused to fury. It hurled itself at its opponent, attacking savagely. In an instant it had leapt forward with bristling tail and seized the other by the neck. The horrified young man made haste to separate the two contestants, while the little cricket chirped proudly as if to announce its victory to its master. Cheng was glorying in this sight when a cock bore down on the cricket and pecked at it. Cheng gave a cry, rooted to the ground in horror; but luckily the cock missed the small cricket which leapt a foot or more away. The cock gave chase, the cricket was under its claws. Cheng, unable to intervene, stamped his foot and turned pale. But the next thing he knew the cock was flapping its wings and craning its neck—his cricket had fastened its teeth in the cock's comb. Amazed and exultant, he put the cricket back in its cage.

Later Cheng presented this cricket to the magistrate, who abused him angrily for producing one so small. Refusing to believe Cheng's account of the little creature's exploits, the magistrate pitted it against some other crickets and it defeated them all. He tried it with a cock, and again it turned out exactly as Cheng had said. Then the magistrate rewarded Cheng and presented this cricket to the governor, who put it in a golden cage and sent it joyfully to the emperor with a detailed report of its prowess.

In his palace the emperor tried the cricket with Butterfly, Praying Mantis, Yolita, Green Forehead and many other champions, but none was a match for it. And he prized it even more highly when he found that it would dance in time to music. In high good humour, he rewarded the governor with fine steeds and silk garments. And the governor, not forgetting where the cricket came from, within a short time commended the magistrate for outstanding merit. The magistrate, pleased in his turn, exempted Cheng from his duties and ordered the local examiner to see that he passed the next examination.

A year later Cheng's son was restored to his senses. He said, "I dreamed I was a cricket, a quick, good fighter. Now I have woken up."

The governor also rewarded Cheng so handsomely that within a few years he owned vast estates, whole streets of houses and countless flocks and herds. When he went abroad, his furs and carriage were more splendid than a noble's.

The recorder of these marvels comments: The emperor may do a thing once and forget it afterwards, but those who carry out his orders make this a general rule. Then when officials are greedy for profit and their underlings are bullies, men are driven to sell their wives and children. This shows that since each step an emperor takes is fraught with consequence for his subjects it behooves him to be very careful. This man Cheng, first impoverished by rapacious officials, grew so rich thanks to a cricket that he went about in magnificent carriages and furs. He could never have dreamed of such good fortune when he was a beadle and was being beaten! Because Heaven wished to reward an honest man, the governor and magistrate also benefited from the cricket. It is true, as the ancients said: "When a man becomes immortal and soars to heaven, his chickens and dog attain immortality too."

■ Yuan Mei (Yüan Mei) (1716–1798) (poems)

TRANSLATED BY J. P. SEATON

Qing dynasty writer Yuan Mei was born to a wealthy family. He took the civil service examinations at an early age and was appointed to office at twenty-four. While in office at Jiangnan, he developed a plot of land into a gardened estate that was famed for its architecture and landscaping. He retired at forty and spent his remaining years in literary and artistic pursuits. In addition to poems, he wrote a collection of ghost stories titled *What the Sage Didn't Discuss* (a reference to Confucius' avoidance of the supernatural in his discourses) and a number of essays. His *Comments on Poetry from the Sui Garden* is a major compilation of poetry criticism. Though he often strikes a philosophical note, he is certainly one of the most personable of Chinese poets, not adverse to humor, sympathetic with the poor, bearing a strong resemblance to the Tang poet Bo Juyi.

FURTHER READING: Chaves, Jonathan. *The Columbia Book of Later Chinese Poetry: Yuan, Ming, and Ch'ing Dynasties (1279–1911),* 1986. Waley Arthur. *Yuan Mei: Eighteenth Century Chinese Poet,* 1956.

Four Zen Poems

1. Just Done

A month alone behind closed doors:
forgotten books remembered, clear again.
Poems come, like water to the pool,
welling,
      up and out,
from perfect silence.

2. P'u-t'o Temple

A temple hidden, treasured
            in the mountain's cleft.
Pines, bamboo
        such a subtle flavor:
The ancient Buddha sits there, wordless,
The welling source speaks for him.

3. Motto

When I meet a monk
        I do bow politely.
When I see a Buddha
        I don't.
If I bow to a Buddha
        the Buddha won't know.
But I honor a monk:
            he's here now
        apparently, or, at least,
        he seems to be.

4. Near Hao-pa

(I saw in the mist a little village of a few tiled roofs, and joyfully ad-
    mired it.)

There's a stream, and there's bamboo,
        there's mulberry, and hemp.
        Mist-hid, clouded hamlet,
        a mild, a tranquil place.
        Just a few tilled acres.
        Just a few tiled roofs.
        How many lives would I
            have to live, to get
                that simple?

5

▪ Li Ruzhen (Li Ju-chen) (c. 1763–c. 1830) (novel)

TRANSLATED BY LIN TAI-YI

Those familiar with the work of Chinese American storyteller Maxine
Hong Kingston may recognize the story recounted in this selection from
the novel *Flowers in the Mirror* by Qing dynasty writer Li Ruzhen. A version of
it was told to Kingston by her mother as a folktale and reworked into the

first tale in her book of story-essays, *China Men. Flowers in the Mirror* is often compared to Jonathan Swift's *Gulliver's Travels*. The most celebrated section of the novel is a wild and fantastic series of voyages to strange lands undertaken by Tang Ao, a scholar who wants to become a Daoist hermit, and his brother-in-law Merchant Lin. Among other places the travelers find themselves are the Country of Sexless People, the Country of Intestineless People, the Country of Flaming People, the Country of Black-Bottomed People, and, in this episode, the Country of Women. As is often the case with fiction that takes you to exotic locations, the real target of the story is much closer to home. *Flowers in the Mirror* can even be regarded as an early feminist novel, in which footbinding is satirized as equivalent to shaving "off pieces of the nose to make it smaller" (a prophetic commentary on modern nose jobs?), and in the ideal Daoist fairyland of Little Penglai, there is an imperial examination especially for women. The feminist irony of the excerpt included here speaks for itself.

Li Ruzhen was born in Hebei province in Taxing in 1763. He was a failed scholar, much like his hero Tang Ao, who could pass the Imperial Examinations (which were the meal-ticket for scholars) only at the county level. For twenty years he lived with his brother who was an official in the salt bureau in Jiangsu province. In a later appointment, he was an assistant to a Hunan province magistrate in charge of building dikes along the Yellow River. In addition to his knowledge of literature, Li was an expert in astrology, medicine, mathematics, music, calligraphy, gardening, painting, and various parlor and board games. In this ironic passage, the most exquisite torture for the traveler Merchant Lin is to be treated in the way women were commonly treated. Readers interested in western parallels to this tale may wish to look at Charlotte Perkins Gilman's early feminist novel *Herland* and at the Log of Christopher Columbus.

FURTHER READING: Lin, Tai-yi, tr. *Flowers in the Mirror,* 1966.

from **Flowers in the Mirror**

When Tang Ao heard that they had arrived at the Country of Women, he thought that the country was populated entirely by women, and was afraid to go ashore. But Old Tuo said, 'Not at all! There are men as well as women, only they call men women, and women men. The men wear the skirts and take care of the home, while the women wear hats and trousers and manage affairs outside. If it were a country populated solely by women, I doubt that even Brother Lin here would dare to venture ashore, although he knows he always makes a good profit from sales here!'

'If the men dress like women, do they use cosmetics and bind their feet?' asked Tang Ao.

'Of course they do!' cried Lin, and took from his pocket a list of the merchandise he was going to sell, which consisted of huge quantities of rouge, face powder, combs and other women's notions. 'Lucky I wasn't born in this country,' he said. 'Catch me mincing around on bound feet!'

When Tang Ao asked why he had not put down the price of the merchandise, Lin said, 'The people here, no matter rich or poor, from the "King" down to the simplest peasant, are all mad about cosmetics. I'll charge them what I can. I shall have no difficulty selling the whole consignment to rich families in two or three days.'

Beaming at the prospect of making a good profit, Lin went on shore with his list.

Tang Ao and Old Tuo decided to go and see the city. The people walking on the streets were small of stature, and rather slim, and although dressed in men's clothes, were beardless and spoke with women's voices, and walked with willowy steps.

'Look at them!' said Old Tuo. 'They are perfectly normal-looking women. Isn't it a shame for them to dress like men?'

'Wait a minute,' said Tang Ao. 'Maybe when they see us, they think, "Look at them, isn't it a shame that they dress like women"?'

'You're right. "Whatever one is accustomed to always seems natural," as the ancients say. But I wonder what the men are like?'

Old Tuo discreetly called Tang Ao's attention to a middle-aged woman, who was sitting in front of her doorstep, sewing on a shoe. Her hair was braided and coiled smoothly on top of her head, and decorated with pearls and jade. She was wearing long gold loops of earrings with precious stones in them, and wore a long mauve gown with an onion-green shirt underneath, from which peeped the toes of tiny feet shod in red silk shoes. With long, tapering fingers, the woman was doing embroidery. She had beautiful eyes and was carefully powdered and rouged, but when she lifted her head, they saw that her lip was covered by a thick moustache.

Tang Ao and Old Tuo could not help laughing out loud.

The 'woman' looked up and said, 'What are you laughing at, lassies?'

The voice sounded as deep and hoarse as a cracked gong. Tang Ao was so startled that he took to his heels and ran.

But the 'woman' shouted after them. 'You must be women, since you have whiskers on your faces. Why are you wearing men's clothes and pretending to be men? Aren't you ashamed of yourselves! I know you dress like this because you want to mingle with the men, you cheap hussies! Take a look at yourselves in the mirror. Have you forgotten that you are women? It's lucky for you you only met up with me! If it had been somebody else who had caught you casting those sneaky glances, you would have been beaten almost to death!'

'This is the first time I have ever had such an experience,' muttered Tang Ao. 'But I suspect Brother Lin will receive better treatment at their hands.'

'Why?' said Old Tuo.

'Well, he is very fair, and since he lost his beard at the Country of Flaming People, he may be mistaken by these people for a real woman. But come to think of it, isn't it worrying?'

As they walked further on, they saw some 'women' on the streets as well as 'men'. Some were carrying babies in their arms, and others leading children by the hand. All the 'women' walked on dainty bound feet, and in crowded places, acted shy, as if they were embarrassed to be seen. Some of the younger ones were beardless, and upon careful study, Tang Ao discovered that some of the aging or middle-aged 'women' shaved their lips and chins in order to appear younger.

The two returned to the junk before Merchant Lin. But when the latter did not come back at supper time, and it was past the second drum, Mistress Lu began to be worried. Tang Ao and Old Tuo went on shore with lanterns to look for him, but discovered that the city gates were shut for the night.

The next day, they went to look again, but found not a trace of Lin. On the third day, some sailors went with them, but still they could not find him.

When a few days had passed, it seemed as if Merchant Lin had vanished, like a rock sinking to the bottom of the sea. Mistress Lu and Pleasant wailed with grief. Tang Ao and Old Tuo went to make inquiries every day.

They could not know that Merchant Lin had been told by one of his customers that the 'King's uncle' wanted to buy some of his goods. Following instructions, he went to the 'Royal Uncle's' Residence in the Palace, and handed his list of merchandise to the gate-keeper. Soon the gatekeeper came back and said that it was just what the 'King' was looking for for his 'concubines' and 'maids,' and asked Lin to be shown into the inner apartments.

The attendant led Merchant Lin through guarded doors and winding paths until he was at the door of the inner apartments, where a guard told him, 'Please wait here, madam. I shall go in and inquire what the royal wishes are.' She took Lin's list, and after a short time, returned and said, 'But madam hasn't put any prices on her list. How much do you charge for a picul of rouge? How much is a picul of perfumed powder? And hair lotion? And hair ribbons?'

Lin told her the prices, and the guard went in and came out again and asked, 'How much is a box of jade ornaments, madam? And your velvet flowers? How much is a box of your fragrant beads? And what about the combs?'

Merchant Lin told her and the guard again went to report, and came back and said, 'The King has been choosing imperial concubines and wants to buy some of your goods for them. He invites you to go inside, since you come from the Kingdom on Earth and we are friendly allies. However, madam must behave with courtesy and respect when she is in the presence of His Majesty.'

Merchant Lin followed the guard inside, and was soon in the presence of the 'King.' After making a deep bow, he saw that she was a woman of some thirty years old, with a beautiful face, fair skin and cherry-red lips. Around her there stood many palace 'maids.'

The 'King' spoke to Lin in a light voice, holding the list of articles in her slender hands, and looking at him with interest as he answered her questions.

'I wonder what she is staring at me like this for,' Merchant Lin thought to himself. 'Hasn't she ever seen a man from the Kingdom on Earth before?'

After a while, he heard her say that she was keeping the list of goods, and ordered palace 'maids' to prepare a feast and wine for the 'woman' from the Kingdom on Earth.

In a little time, Merchant Lin was ushered to a room upstairs, where victuals of many kinds awaited him. As he ate, however, he heard a great deal of noise downstairs. Several palace 'maids' ran upstairs soon, and calling him 'Your Highness,' kowtowed to him and congratulated him. Before he knew what was happening, Merchant Lin was being stripped completely bare by the maids and led to a perfumed bath. Against the powerful arms of these maids, he could scarcely struggle. Soon he found himself being anointed, perfumed, powdered and rouged, and dressed in a skirt. His big feet were bound up in strips of cloth and socks, and his hair was combed into an elaborate braid over his head and decorated with pins. These male 'maids' thrust bracelets on his arms and rings on his fingers, and put a phoenix headdress on his head. They tied a jade green sash around his waist and put an embroidered cape around his shoulders.

Then they led him to a bed and asked him to sit down.

Merchant Lin thought that he must be drunk, or dreaming, and began to tremble. He asked the maids what was happening, and was told that he had been chosen by the 'King' to be the Imperial Consort, and that a propitious day would be chosen for him to enter the 'King's' chambers.

Before he could utter a word, another group of maids, all tall and strong and wearing beards, came in. One was holding a threaded needle. 'We are ordered to pierce your ears,' he said as the other four 'maids' grabbed Lin by the arms and legs. The white-bearded one seized Lin's right ear, and after rubbing the lobe a little, drove the needle through it.

'Ooh!' Merchant Lin screamed.

The maid seized the other ear, and likewise drove the needle through it. As Lin screamed with pain, powdered lead was smeared on his earlobes and a pair of 'eight-precious' earrings was hung from the holes.

Having finished what they came to do, the maids retreated, and a black-bearded fellow came in with a bolt of white silk. Kneeling down before him, the fellow said, 'I am ordered to bind Your Highness's feet.'

Two other maids seized Lin's feet as the black-bearded one sat down on a low stool, and began to rip the silk into ribbons. Seizing Lin's right foot, he set it upon his knee, and sprinkled white alum powder between the toes and the grooves of the foot. He squeezed the toes tightly together, bent them down so that the whole foot was shaped like an arch, and took a length of white silk and bound it tightly around it twice. One of the others sewed the ribbon together in small stitches. Again the silk went around the foot, and again, it was sewn up.

Merchant Lin felt as though his feet were burning, and wave after wave of pain rose to his heart. When he could stand it no longer, he let out his voice and began to cry. The 'maids' hastily made a pair of soft-soled red shoes, and these they put on both his feet.

'Please, kind brothers, go and tell Her Majesty that I'm a married man,' Lin begged. 'How can I become her Consort? As for my feet, please liberate them. They have enjoyed the kind of freedom which scholars who are not interested in official careers enjoy! How can you bind them? Please tell your "King" to let me go. I shall be grateful, and my wife will be very grateful.'

But the maids said, 'The King said that you are to enter his chambers as soon as your feet are bound. It is no time for talk of this kind.'

When it was dark, a table was laid for him with mountains of meat and oceans of wine. But Merchant Lin only nibbled, and told the 'maids' they could have the rest.

Still sitting on the bed, and with his feet aching terribly, he decided to lie down in his clothes for a rest.

At once a middle-aged 'maid' came up to him and said, 'Please, will you wash before you retire?'

No sooner was this said than a succession of maids came in with candles, basins of water and spittoon, dressing table, boxes of ointment, face powder, towels, silk handkerchiefs, and surrounded him. Lin had to submit to the motions of washing in front of them all. But after he had washed his face, a maid wanted to put some cream on it again.

Merchant Lin stoutly refused.

'But night time is the best time to treat the skin,' the white-bearded maid said, 'This powder has a lot of musk in it. It will make your skin fragrant, although I dare say it is fair enough already. If you use it regularly your skin will not only seem like white jade, but will give off a natural fragrance of its own. And the more fragrant it is, the fairer it will become, and the more lovely to behold, and the more lovable you will be. You'll see how good it is after you have used it regularly.'

But Lin refused firmly, and the maids said, 'If you are so stubborn, we will have to report this, and let Matron deal with you tomorrow.'

Then they left him alone. But Lin's feet hurt so much that he could not sleep a wink. He tore at the ribbons with all his might, and after a great struggle succeeded in tearing them off. He stretched out his ten toes again, and luxuriating in their exquisite freedom, finally fell asleep.

The next morning, however, when the black-bearded maid discovered that he had torn off his foot-bandages, he immediately reported it to the 'King,' who ordered that Lin should be punished by receiving twenty strokes of the bamboo from the 'Matron.' Accordingly, a white-bearded 'Matron' came in with a stick of bamboo about eight feet long, and when the others had stripped him and held him down, raised the stick and began to strike Lin's bottom and legs.

Before five strokes had been delivered, Lin's tender skin was bleeding, and the Matron did not have the heart to go on. 'Look at her skin! Have you ever seen such white and tender and lovable skin? Why, I think indeed her looks are comparable to Pan An and Sung Yu!' the Matron thought to himself. 'But what am I doing, comparing her bottom and not her face to them? Is that a compliment?'

The foot-binding mind came and asked Lin if he would behave from now on.

'Yes, I'll behave,' Lin replied, and they stopped beating him. They wiped the blood from his wounds, and special ointment was sent by the 'King' and ginseng soup was given him to drink.

Merchant Lin drank the soup, and fell on the bed for a rest. But the 'King' had given orders that his feet must be bound again, and that he should be taught to walk on them. So with one maid supporting him on each side, Merchant Lin was marched up and down the room all day on his bound feet. When he lay down to sleep that night, he could not close his eyes for the excruciating pain.

But from now on, he was never left alone again. Maids took turns to sit with him. Merchant Lin knew that he was no longer in command of his destiny.

Before two weeks were over, Lin's feet had begun to assume a permanently arched form, and his toes begun to rot. Daily medical ablutions were given to them, and the pain persisted.

'I should have thought that Brother-in-law and Old Tuo would have come to my rescue by now,' he thought one day as he was being led up and down his room. 'I have endured all I can! I'd be better off dead!'

He sat down on the edge of the bed, and began to tear off his embroidered shoes and silk bandages. 'Go tell your "King" to put me to death at once, or let my feet loose,' he told the Matron.

But when he returned, the Matron said, 'The King said that if you don't obey his orders, you are to be hung upside down from the beam of the house.'

'Then do it quickly! The quicker the better!' said Lin, impatient to have an end put to his agony.

Accordingly, they tied a rope around his feet and hung him upside down from the beam. Merchant Lin saw stars before his eyes. Sweat poured out of his body, and his legs became numb. He closed his eyes and waited for death to come to the rescue. But it did not come. At last he could stand it no longer, and began to scream like a pig being led to slaughter.

The order was given to cut him down.

From now on, Lin was completely in the power of the maids. Wanting to complete the task their 'King' had assigned them as soon as possible, they tied the bandages around his feet tighter than ever. Several times, Lin thought of committing suicide, but with people watching him constantly, he had not a chance.

In due course, his feet lost much of their original shape. Blood and flesh were squeezed into a pulp and then little remained of his feet but dry bones and skin, shrunk, indeed, to a dainty size. Responding to daily anointing, his hair became shiny and smooth, and his body, after repeated ablutions of perfumed water, began to look very attractive indeed. His eyebrows were plucked to resemble a new moon. With blood-red lipstick and powder adorning his face, and jade and pearl adorning his coiffure and ears, Merchant Lin assumed, at last, a not unappealing appearance.

The 'King' sent someone to watch his progress every day. One day, the Matron announced that the task of foot-binding had been completed. When the 'King' herself came upstairs to have a look, she saw a Lin whose face was like a peach blossom, whose eyes were like autumn lakes, whose eyebrows suggested the lines of distant hills, and who stood before her in a willowy stance.

She was delighted. 'What a beauty!' she thought to herself. 'If I hadn't seen her hidden possibilities beneath her ridiculous man's costume, her beauty might never have come to light!'

She took a pearl bracelet and put it on Merchant Lin's wrist, and the 'maids' persuaded him to sink down on his knees and give thanks. The 'King' pulled him up and made him sit down beside her, and began to fondle his hands and smell them and look appreciatively at his dainty feet.

Lin went red with shame.

Extremely pleased, the 'King' decided that Lin should enter her chambers the very next day. When Merchant Lin heard this, he saw his last hopes vanish. He was not even able to walk without someone to help him, and spent the whole night thinking about his wife and shedding tears.

In the morning, the 'maids' came especially early to shave off the fine hairs from his face, and to powder him and comb him in preparation for his wedding. Supported by a pair of red embroidered high heeled shoes, his longer-than-ordinary 'golden lotuses' became not obtrusively large. He wore a bridal crown and gown, and with jewels dangling and waves of perfume issuing from his person, was if not notably beautiful, at least a rather charming 'bride.'

■ Cao Xueqin (Ts'ao Hsüeh-chin) (c. 1715–1763) and Gao E (Kao E) (c. 1740–1815) (novel)

Dream of the Red Chamber, also known as *Story of the Stone,* is the masterpiece of Chinese realist fiction. It seems to have been written by Cao Xueqin, an impoverished descendant of a distinguished family of naturalized Manchus. His grandfather Cao Yin (1658–1712) had been the protege of

Emperor Kangxi, but the family fell out of favor and had most of its property confiscated. Cao Xueqin had a classical education and was a teacher in a school for the children of the nobility. He retired to the Western Hills, outside Beijing, and devoted his final years to literature. He is thought to have written the first eighty chapters of the novel, which circulated after his death under the title *Story of the Stone;* the last forty chapters were probably written by Gao E, a later writer of lesser talent. The debate about these final forty chapters, which Gao claimed were based on a fragmentary original conclusion to the novel, is bitter and involved and has divided the vast field of literary studies that has grown up around the novel (called Redology).

On one level, the story centers on the frustrated love of protagonist Jia Bao-yu (Precious Jade) for his cousin Lin Dai-yu (Black Jade), complicated by the attractions of another cousin Xue Bao-chai (Precious Virtue), whom Bao-yu is tricked into marrying, while Dai-yu at the moment of the marriage dies of a bitter illness. Bao-yu is the scion of the decadent but prosperous Jia family, whose decline through its own moral bankruptcy constitutes another major movement of the novel. Much of the novel is set at the Jia estate, whose two houses are linked by a pleasure garden. Bao-yu is born with a piece of jade in his mouth, and he is the incarnation of the Divine Luminescent Stone-in-Waiting (the stone of the title), as Dai-yu is the incarnation of a plant that the stone nurtures into life. The stone is brought to the earth to live by a Buddhist monk and a Daoist priest. After the disastrous death of Dai-yu, the monk and priest take Bao-yu off to a religious life. For the body of the novel, however, the stone, incarnated as Bao-yu, ignores the wisdom of the religious path, losing himself instead in sensuality. This is an extremely limited account of the novel's range; there are 423 characters, many of whom are brought into three dimensions, and the novel as a whole is a tapestry of Chinese life, speech, customs, and behavior at all levels. In this excerpt, Lin Dai-yu, sick and fevered, has a dream about her absent lover, the psychological significance of which will be clear to the reader.

FURTHER READING: Hawkes, David, and John Minford, trs. *The Story of the Stone,* 5 vols., 1979–1987. McHugh, Florence, and Isabel McHugh, trs. *The Dream of the Red Chamber,* 1958. Wang, Chi-cheng, tr. *Dream of the Red Chamber,* [1929] 1958. Yang, Hsien-yi, and Gladys Yang, trs. *A Dream of Red Mansions,* 3 vols., 1978–1980.

Dream of the Red Chamber

from *Chapter 82*

TRANSLATED BY JOHN MINFORD

That evening, when Dai-yu went into her side-room to undress for the night, she caught sight of the lychees again. They reminded her of the old woman's visit, and revived the pain she had felt at her tactless gossiping.

Dusk was falling, and in the stillness a thousand gloomy thoughts seemed to close in and oppress her mind.

'My health is so poor . . . And time's running out. I know Bao-yu loves me more than anyone else. But Grannie and Aunt Wang still haven't mentioned it! If only my parents had settled it for us while they were still alive . . . But suppose they had? What if they had married me to someone else? Who could ever compare with Bao-yu? Perhaps I'm better off like this after all! At least I've still some hope.'

Like the rope on a pulley her secret hopes and fears spun up and down, tangling themselves tighter and tighter round her heart. Finally, with a sigh and a few tears, she lay down in her clothes, weary and depressed.

She became vaguely aware of one of the junior maids coming in and saying:

'Miss Lin, Mr Jia Yu-cun is outside and wants to see you.'

'What could he want?' thought Dai-yu to herself. 'I'm not a regular student of his. I'm not even a boy. He just happened to coach me when I was a little girl. Anyway, all the times he's come to see Uncle Zheng he's never once asked after me, so why should I have to see him now?'

She told the maid to convey her respects and thank Mr Yu-cun for calling, but to say that poor health obliged her to stay in bed.

'But Miss,' said the maid, 'I think he's come to congratulate you, and some people have come to take you to Nanking.'

As she was speaking, a group incuding Xi-feng, Lady Xing, Lady Wang and Bao-chai advanced into the room and announced cheerfully:

'Congratulations my dear! And bon voyage!'

'What do you mean?' asked Dai-yu in great confusion.

'Come on now.' It was Xi-feng who replied. 'You needn't try and pretend you haven't heard the news. Your father's been promoted to Grain Intendant for Hupeh Province and has made a second and highly satisfactory marriage. He doesn't think it right that you should be left here on your own, and has asked Yu-cun to act as go-between. You're engaged to be married to a relation of your new stepmother's, a widower himself I believe. They've sent some servants to fetch you home. You'll probably be married straight away. It's all your stepmother's idea. In case you're not properly taken care of on the voyage, she has asked your cousin Lian to accompany you.'

Xi-feng's words made Dai-yu break out in a cold sweat. She now had a feeling that her father was still alive. She began to panic, and said defiantly:

'It's not true! It's all a trick of Xi-feng's!'

She saw Lady Xing give Lady Wang a meaningful look:

'She won't believe us. Come, we are wasting our time.'

'Aunt Wang! Aunt Xing! Don't go!' Dai-yu begged them, fighting back her tears. But she received no reply. They all gave her a curious smile, and then left together.

As she stood there and watched them go, panic seized her. She tried to speak, but the only sound that came was a strangled sobbing from the back of her throat. Then she looked about her and saw that somehow she had been transported to Grandmother Jia's apartment. In that same instant she thought to herself: 'Grannie's the only one that can save me now!' and fell at the old lady's feet, hugging her by the knees.

'Save me Grannie, *please!* I'd rather die than go away with them! That stepmother's not my real mother anyway. I just want to stay here with you!'

Grandmother Jia's face only registered a cold smile.

'This has nothing to do with me.'

'But what's to become of me, Grannie?' she sobbed.

'Being a man's second wife has its advantages,' Grandmother Jia replied. 'Think of the double dowry you'll have.'

'If I stay, I won't cause you any extra expense, I promise I won't. Oh please save me!'

'It's no use,' said Grandmother Jia. 'All girls marry and leave home. You're a child and don't understand these things. You can't live here for ever, you know.'

'I'll do anything to stay—I'll work for my keep, be a slave, anything! Only please don't let them take me away!'

This time Grandmother Jia made no reply. Dai-yu hugged her again and sobbed:

'Oh Grannie! You've always been so good to me, fussed over me so—how can you treat me like this in my hour of need! Don't you care about me any more? I may not be one of your real grandchildren, a true Jia like the others, but my mother was your own daughter, your own flesh and blood! For her sake have pity on me! Don't let me be taken away!'

With these last words she flung herself frantically upon Lady Jia, burying her head in her lap and sobbing violently.

'Faithful,' the old lady commanded, 'take Miss Dai-yu to her room to rest. She is wearing me out.'

There was no mistaking the finality in Grandmother Jia's voice. To Dai-yu, suicide now seemed the only course. She rose, and as she walked from the room her heart yearned for a mother of her own to turn to. All the affection shown her by grandmother, aunts and cousins alike, had now been exposed for what it was and had been all along—a sham. Suddenly she thought: 'Why haven't I seen Bao-yu today? *He* might still know of a way out.' And as the thought entered her mind, she looked up and sure enough, there, standing right in front of her, all laughter and smiles, was Bao-yu himself.

'My warmest congratulations, cuz!'

This was too much for Dai-yu. Her last vestige of maidenly reserve vanished. She clutched hold of him and cried out:

'Now I know how heartless and cruel you really are, Bao-yu!'

'No, you are wrong,' he replied. 'But if you have a husband to go to, then we must go our separate ways.'

Dai-yu listened in despair as this, her very last hope, was taken from her. Clinging to him helplessly, she gave a feverish cry:

'Oh Bao! I've no separate way to go! How could you say such a thing!'

'If you don't want to go, then stay here,' he replied calmly. 'You were originally engaged to me. That's why you came to live here. Has it never occurred to you how specially I've always treated you? Haven't you noticed?'

Suddenly, it all seemed clear. She really was engaged to Bao-yu after all. Of course she was! In an instant her despair changed to joy.

'*My* mind is made up once and forever! But you must give me the word. Am I to go? Or am I to stay?'

'I've told you, stay here with me. If you still don't trust me, look at my heart.'

With these words he took out a small knife and brought it down across his chest. Blood came spurting out. Terrified out of her wits, Dai-yu tried to staunch the flow with her hand crying out:

'How could you? You should have killed me first!'

'Don't worry,' said Bao-yu. 'I'm going to show you my heart.'

He fumbled about inside the gaping flesh, while Dai-yu, shaking convulsively, afraid someone might burst in on them at any moment, pressed him to her tightly and wept bitterly.

'Oh no!' said Bao-yu. 'It's not there anymore! My time has come!'

His eyes flickered and he fell with a dull thud to the floor. Dai-yu let out a piercing scream. She heard Nightingale calling her:

'Miss Lin! Miss Lin! You're having a nightmare! Wake up! Come along now, you must get undressed and go to sleep properly.'

Dai-yu turned over in her bed. So it had all been a nightmare. But she could still feel her throat choking, her heart was still pounding, the top of her pillow was drenched in sweat, and a tingly, icy sensation ran down her back and chilled her to the core.

'Mother and father died long ago. Bao-yu and I have never been engaged,' she thought to herself. 'What ever could have made me have such a dream?'

The scenes of her dream passed before her eyes again. She was on her own in the world, she reflected. Supposing Bao-yu really died—what then? The thought was enough to bring back all the pain and confusion. She began to weep, and tiny beads of sweat broke out down the length of her body. Finally she struggled up, took off her outer robe and told Nightingale to make the bed. She lay down again, and began turning restlessly from side to side, unable to get to sleep. She could hear the gentle sighing of the wind outside her window—or was it the drizzle falling softly on the roof? Once, the sound died away and she thought she could hear someone calling in the distance. But it was only Nightingale, who had already fallen asleep and was snoring in a corner of the room. With a great effort, Dai-yu struggled out of bed, wrapped the quilt around her and sat up. An icy draught from a crack in the casement soon sent her shivering back under the covers again. She was just beginning to doze off when the sparrows struck up their dawn-chorus from their nests in the bamboos. First light was gradually beginning to show through the shutters and paper window-panes.

Dai-yu was now wide awake again and started coughing. Nightingale awoke at once.

'Still awake, Miss? Coughing too—it sounds as if you've caught a chill. Why, it's almost light, it'll soon be morning! Please try and stop thinking so much, and rest. You need to sleep.'

'I want to sleep,' replied Dai-yu. 'But what's the good? I just can't. You go back to sleep anyway.' These last words were interrupted by another fit of coughing.

Nightingale was already distressed at her mistress's condition and had no inclination to go back to sleep. When she heard her coughing again, she hurried over to hold up the spittoon. By now it was dawn outside.

'Haven't you gone to sleep?' asked Dai-yu.

'Sleep?' replied Nightingale cheerfully. 'It's already daylight.'

'In that case, could you change the spittoon?'

'Certainly Miss.'

Leaving the full spittoon on a table in the outer room, Nightingale went promptly to fetch a fresh one, which she placed at the foot of the kang. Then, closing the door of the inner room carefully behind her and letting down the flower-patterned portière, she went out to wake Snow-goose, taking the full spittoon with her. When she came to empty it in the courtyard, and looked closer, she noticed to her horror some specks of blood in the phlegm.

'Goodness!' she blurted out. 'How awful!'

'What's the matter?' Dai-yu called out at once from inside.

'Oh nothing, Miss!'

Nightingale tried her best to cover up her blunder. 'The spittoon slipped in my hand and I nearly dropped it.'

'You didn't find anything odd in the phlegm?'

'Oh no, Miss.' A lump came into Nightingale's throat, and she could say no more. Tears came streaming down her cheeks.

Dai-yu had already noticed a sickly taste in her mouth, and her earlier suspicions were strengthened first by Nightingale's cry of alarm, and now by the unmistakable note of dismay in her voice.

'Come in,' she told Nightingale. 'It must be cold outside.'

'I'm coming, Miss.' She sounded more disconsolate than ever. Her tragic snuffly tone set Dai-yu shivering. The door opened and she walked in, still dabbing her eyes with a handkerchief.

'Come along now,' said Dai-yu. 'Crying so early in the morning?'

'Who's crying?' said Nightingale, doing her best to smile. 'It's so early and my eyes are a bit itchy, that's all. You were awake longer than ever last night, weren't you, Miss? I could hear you coughing half the night.'

'I know. The more I wanted to sleep, the wider awake I became.'

'You're not well, Miss. I think all this worrying is ruining your health. And good health is like the hill in the proverb:

Keep the hill green, keep the hill green.
And you'll never lack fuel for winter again.

Besides, everyone here cares for you so. Her Old Ladyship does, Her Lady-ship does, *everyone* does!'

How could Nightingale know that the mere mention of these homely names, intended to reassure and comfort, was enough to conjure up again the horror of the nightmare? Dai-yu felt her heart thumping, everything went black before her eyes, and she seemed on the point of fainting alto-gether. Nightingale quickly held out the spittoon while Snowgoose patted her lightly on the back. After a long while she coughed up another mouth-ful of phlegm. In it was a thick wriggling strand of dark red blood. The two maids were pale with fright. They stood supporting her, one on each side, until finally she slumped back, scarcely conscious. Nightingale, aware of the critical nature of her condition, looked at Snowgoose and made an urgent movement with her lips that clearly meant: 'Go and fetch some-one—quickly!'

The Modern Era

■ Lu Xun (Lu Hsün) (1881–1936) (story)

TRANSLATED BY YANG HSIEN-YI AND GLADYS YANG

Lu Xun is the pen name taken by Zhou Shuren, China's premier twentieth-century fiction writer. He is also considered a leading essayist of his time. When young, Lu Xun studied medicine in Japan but turned to lit-erature in 1906 after the Russo-Japanese war. In 1909 he returned to China and taught at the National Beijing University, among other schools, believ-ing that by his teaching and writing he could begin to effect changes on a China that he perceived as decadent and failing—views that caused him trouble with the government and that obliged him to leave Beijing to teach in Fukien and Canton. In 1927, he moved to Shanghai, giving up acade-mia, and turned full time to writing. In addition to his short stories and polemical essays, he is the author of a trailblazing history of Chinese fiction. He died on October 19, 1936, of tuberculosis in Shanghai.

His interest in reform led him to inscribe in his fiction a subtle political nervous system beneath the skin of words. Such political allegories can be strongly seen in his most famous tales, "A Madman's Diary" and "The True Story of Ah Q." The grotesquery and paranoia of "A Madman's Diary" will remind Western readers of Fyodor Dostoyevsky's *Notes from the Underground* and of Franz Kafka's *The Metamorphosis*. As in Kafka's tale, the narrator in this story has undergone a metamorphosis into something frightening and strange. The diarist has become possessed by the belief that the people of the town around him, the doctor, even his own brother, have taken to eating human flesh and plan to kill him and feast on his body. Is his belief paranoid fantasy, a fascinating window into the skewed mental processes of a madman? Or is it an allegorical representation of the moral vacuum of Chinese society, with consumption, competition, and exploitation of the poor represented as cannibalism, in which humanity becomes its own proper prey? Or, finally, is it in some way both at once, so that the particular form that his madness takes lies in a perception of human and universal truths to which "sane" society is blind?

FURTHER READING: Lee, Leo Ou-fan, ed. Lu Xun and His Legacy, 1985; Voices from the Iron House: A Study of Lu Xun, 1987. Lu, Hsun. The Complete Stories of Lu Xun. Translated by Yang Xianyi and Gladys Yang, 1981; Diary of a Madman and Other Stories. Translated by William A. Lyell, 1990; Lu Hsun: Complete Poems. A translation with introduction and annotation by David Y. Chen, 1988; Lu Xun, Selected Works. Translated by Yang Xianyi and Gladys Yang, 1980; Selected Stories of Lu Hsun. Translated by Yang Hsien-yi and Gladys Yang, 1977; Silent China; Selected Writings of Lu Xun. Edited and translated by Gladys Yang, 1973. Weiss, Ruth F. Lu Xun: A Chinese Writer for All Times, 1985.

A Madman's Diary

Two brothers, whose names I need not mention here, were both good friends of mine in high school; but after a separation of many years we gradually lost touch. Some time ago I happened to hear that one of them was seriously ill, and since I was going back to my old home I broke my journey to call on them. I saw only one, however, who told me that the invalid was his younger brother.

"I appreciate your coming such a long way to see us," he said, "but my brother recovered some time ago and has gone elsewhere to take up an official post." Then, laughing, he produced two volumes of his brother's diary, saying that from these the nature of his past illness could be seen, and that there was no harm in showing them to an old friend. I took the diary away, read it through, and found that he had suffered from a form of persecution complex. The writing was most confused and incoherent, and he had made many wild statements; moreover he had omitted to give any dates, so that only by the colour of the ink and the differences in the writing could one tell that it was not written at one time. Certain sections, however, were not altogether disconnected, and I have copied out a part to serve as a subject for medical research. I have not altered a single illogicality in the diary and have changed only the names, even though the people referred to are all country folk, unknown to the world and of no consequence. As for the title, it was chosen by the diarist himself after his recovery, and I did not change it.

I

Tonight the moon is very bright.

I have not seen it for over thirty years, so today when I saw it I felt in unusually high spirits. I begin to realize that during the past thirty-odd years I have been in the dark; but now I must be extremely careful. Otherwise why should that dog at the Chao house have looked at me twice?

I have reason for my fear.

II

Tonight there is no moon at all, I know that this bodes ill. This morning when I went out cautiously, Mr. Chao had a strange look in his eyes, as if he were afraid of me, as if he wanted to murder me. There were seven or eight others, who discussed me in a whisper. And they were afraid of my seeing them. All the people I passed were like that. The fiercest among them grinned at me; whereupon I shivered from head to foot, knowing that their preparations were complete.

I was not afraid, however, but continued on my way. A group of children in front were also discussing me, and the look in their eyes was just like that in Mr. Chao's while their faces too were ghastly pale. I wondered what grudge these children could have against me to make them behave like this. I could not help calling out: "Tell me!" But then they ran away.

I wonder what grudge Mr. Chao can have against me, what grudge the people on the road can have against me. I can think of nothing except that twenty years ago I trod on Mr. Ku Chiu's[1] accounts sheets for many years past, and Mr. Ku was very displeased. Although Mr. Chao does not know him, he must have heard talk of this and decided to avenge him, so he is conspiring against me with the people on the road. But then what of the children? At that time they were not yet born, so why should they eye me so strangely today, as if they were afraid of me, as if they wanted to murder me? This really frightens me, it is so bewildering and upsetting.

I know. They must have learned this from their parents!

III

I can't sleep at night. Everything requires careful consideration if one is to understand it.

Those people, some of whom have been pilloried by the magistrate, slapped in the face by the local gentry, had their wives taken away by

---

1. Ku Chiu means "Ancient Times." Lu Hsun had in mind the long history of feudal oppression in China.

bailiffs, or their parents driven to suicide by creditors, never looked as frightened and as fierce then as they did yesterday.

The most extraordinary thing was that woman on the street yesterday who spanked her son and said, "Little devil! I'd like to bite several mouthfuls out of you to work off my feelings!" Yet all the time she looked at me. I gave a start, unable to control myself; then all those green-faced, long-toothed people began to laugh derisively. Old Chen hurried forward and dragged me home.

He dragged me home. The folk at home all pretended not to know me; they had the same look in their eyes as all the others. When I went into the study, they locked the door outside as if cooping up a chicken or a duck. This incident left me even more bewildered.

A few days ago a tenant of ours from Wolf Cub Village came to report the failure of the crops, and told my elder brother that a notorious character in their village had been beaten to death; then some people had taken out his heart and liver, fried them in oil and eaten them, as a means of increasing their courage. When I interrupted, the tenant and my brother both stared at me. Only today have I realized that they had exactly the same look in their eyes as those people outside.

Just to think of it sets me shivering from the crown of my head to the soles of my feet.

They eat human beings, so they may eat me.

I see that woman's "bite several mouthfuls out of you," the laughter of those green-faced, long-toothed people and the tenant's story the other day are obviously secret signs. I realize all the poison in their speech, all the daggers in their laughter. Their teeth are white and glistening: they are all man-eaters.

It seems to me, although I am not a bad man, ever since I trod on Mr. Ku's accounts it has been touch-and-go. They seem to have secrets which I cannot guess, and once they are angry they will call anyone a bad character. I remember when my elder brother taught me to write compositions, no matter how good a man was, if I produced arguments to the contrary he would mark that passage to show his approval; while if I excused evil-doers, he would say: "Good for you, that shows originality." How can I possibly guess their secret thoughts—especially when they are ready to eat people?

Everything requires careful consideration if one is to understand it. In ancient times, as I recollect, people often ate human beings, but I am rather hazy about it. I tried to look this up, but my history has no chronology, and scrawled all over each page are the words: "Virtue and Morality." Since I could not sleep anyway, I read intently half the night, until I began to see words between the lines, the whole book being filled with the two words—"Eat people."

All these words written in the book, all the words spoken by our tenant, gaze at me strangely with an enigmatic smile.

I too am a man, and they want to eat me!

IV

In the morning I sat quietly for some time. Old Chen brought lunch in: one bowl of vegetables, one bowl of steamed fish. The eyes of the fish were white and hard, and its mouth was open just like those people who want to eat human beings. After a few mouthfuls I could not tell whether the slippery morsels were fish or human flesh, so I brought it all up.

I said, "Old Chen, tell my brother that I feel quite suffocated, and want to have a stroll in the garden." Old Chen said nothing but went out, and presently he came back and opened the gate.

I did not move, but watched to see how they would treat me, feeling certain that they would not let me go. Sure enough! My elder brother came slowly out, leading an old man. There was a murderous gleam in his eyes, and fearing that I would see it he lowered his head, stealing glances at me from the side of his spectacles.

"You seem to be very well today," said my brother.

"Yes," said I.

"I have invited Mr. Ho here today," said my brother, "to examine you."

"All right," said I. Actually I knew quite well that this old man was the executioner in disguise! He simply used the pretext of feeling my pulse to see how fat I was; for by so doing he would receive a share of my flesh. Still I was not afraid. Although I do not eat men, my courage is greater than theirs. I held out my two fists, to see what he would do. The old man sat down, closed his eyes, fumbled for some time and remained still for some time; then he opened his shifty eyes and said, "Don't let your imagination run away with you. Rest quietly for a few days, and you will be all right."

Don't let your imagination run away with you! Rest quietly for a few days! When I have grown fat, naturally they will have more to eat; but what good will it do me, or how can it be "all right"? All these people wanting to eat human flesh and at the same time stealthily trying to keep up appearances, not daring to act promptly, really made me nearly die of laughter. I could not help roaring with laughter, I was so amused. I knew that in this laughter were courage and integrity. Both the old man and my brother turned pale, awed by my courage and integrity.

But just because I am brave they are the more eager to eat me, in order to acquire some of my courage. The old man went out of the gate, but before he had gone far he said to my brother in a low voice, "To be eaten at once!" And my brother nodded. So you are in it too! This stupendous discovery, although it came as a shock, is yet no more than I had expected: the accomplice in eating me is my elder brother!

The eater of human flesh is my elder brother!

I am the younger brother of an eater of human flesh!

I myself will be eaten by others, but none the less I am the younger brother of an eater of human flesh!

V

These few days I have been thinking again: suppose that old man were not an executioner in disguise, but a real doctor; he would be none the less an eater of human flesh. In that book on herbs, written by his predecessor Li Shih-chen,[2] it is clearly stated that men's flesh can be boiled and eaten; so can he still say that he does not eat men?

As for my elder brother, I have also good reason to suspect him. When he was teaching me, he said with his own lips, "People exchange their sons to eat." And once in discussing a bad man, he said that not only did he deserve to be killed, he should "have his flesh eaten and his hide slept on."[3] I was still young then, and my heart beat faster for some time, he was not at all surprised by the story that our tenant from Wolf Cub Village told us the other day about eating a man's heart and liver, but kept nodding his head. He is evidently just as cruel as before. Since it is possible to "exchange sons to eat," then anything can be exchanged, anyone can be eaten. In the past I simply listened to his explanations, and let it go at that; now I know that when he explained it to me, not only was there human fat at the corner of his lips, but his whole heart was set on eating men.

VI

Pitch dark. I don't know whether it is day or night. The Chao family dog has started barking again.

The fierceness of a lion, the timidity of a rabbit, the craftiness of a fox. . . .

VII

I know their way; they are not willing to kill anyone outright, nor do they dare, for fear of the consequences. Instead they have banded together and set traps everywhere, to force me to kill myself. The behaviour of the men and women in the street a few days ago, and my elder brother's attitude these last few days, make it quite obvious. What they like best is for a man to take off his belt, and hang himself from a beam; for then they can enjoy their heart's desire without being blamed for murder. Naturally that

---

2. A famous pharmacologist (1518–1593), author of *Ben-cao-gang-mu,* the *Materia Medica.*

3. These are quotations from the old classic *Zuo Zhuan.*

sets them roaring with delighted laughter. On the other hand, if a man is frightened or worried to death, although that makes him rather thin, they still nod in approval.

They only eat dead flesh! I remember reading somewhere of a hideous beast, with an ugly look in its eye, called "hyena" which often eats dead flesh. Even the largest bones it grinds into fragments and swallows: the mere thought of this is enough to terrify one. Hyenas are related to wolves, and wolves belong to the canine species. The other day the dog in the Chao house looked at me several times; obviously it is in the plot too and has become their accomplice. The old man's eyes were cast down, but that did not deceive me!

The most deplorable is my elder brother. He is also a man, so why is he not afraid, why is he plotting with others to eat me? Is it that when one is used to it he no longer thinks it a crime? Or is it that he has hardened his heart to do something he knows is wrong?

In cursing man-eaters, I shall start with my brother, and in dissuading man-eaters, I shall start with him too.

VIII

Actually, such arguments should have convinced them long ago. . . .

Suddenly someone came in. He was only about twenty years old and I did not see his features very clearly. His face was wreathed in smiles, but when he nodded to me his smile did not seem genuine. I asked him: "Is it right to eat human beings?"

Still smiling, he replied, "When there is no famine how can one eat human beings?"

I realized at once, he was one of them; but still I summoned up courage to repeat my question:

"Is it right?"

"What makes you ask such a thing? You really are . . . fond of a joke. . . . It is very fine today."

"It is fine, and the moon is very bright. But I want to ask you: Is it right?"

He looked disconcerted, and muttered: "No. . . ."

"No? Then why do they still do it?"

"What are you talking about?"

"What am I talking about? They are eating men now in Wolf Cub Village, and you can see it written all over the books, in fresh red ink."

His expression changed, and he grew ghastly pale. "It may be so," he said, staring at me. "It has always been like that. . . ."

"Is it right because it has always been like that?"

"I refuse to discuss these things with you. Anyway, you shouldn't talk about it. Whoever talks about it is in the wrong!"

I leaped up and opened my eyes wide, but the man had vanished. I was soaked with perspiration. He was much younger than my elder brother, but even so he was in it. He must have been taught by his parents. And I am afraid he has already taught his son: that is why even the children look at me so fiercely.

IX

Wanting to eat men, at the same time afraid of being eaten themselves, they all look at each other with the deepest suspicion. . . .

How comfortable life would be for them if they could rid themselves of such obsessions and go to work, walk, eat and sleep at ease. They have only this one step to take. Yet fathers and sons, husbands and wives, brothers, friends, teachers and students, sworn enemies and even strangers, have all joined in this conspiracy, discouraging and preventing each other from taking this step.

X

Early this morning I went to look for my elder brother. He was standing outside the hall door looking at the sky, when I walked up behind him, stood between him and the door, and with exceptional poise and politeness said to him:

"Brother, I have something to say to you."

"Well, what is it?" he asked, quickly turning towards me and nodding.

"It is very little, but I find it difficult to say. Brother, probably all primitive people ate a little human flesh to begin with. Later, because their outlook changed, some of them stopped, and because they tried to be good they changed into men, changed into real men. But some are still eating — just like reptiles. Some have changed into fish, birds, monkeys and finally men; but some do not try to be good and remain reptiles still. When those who eat men compare themselves with those who do not, how ashamed they must be. Probably much more ashamed than the reptiles are before monkeys.

"In ancient times Yi Ya boiled his son for Chieh and Chou to eat; that is the old story.[4] But actually since the creation of heaven and earth by Pan Ku men have been eating each other, from the time of Yi Ya's son to the

---

4. According to ancient records, Yi Ya cooked his son and presented him to Duke Huan of Chi who reigned from 685 to 643 B.C. Chieh and Chou were tyrants of an earlier age. The madman has made a mistake here.

time of Hsu Hsi-lin,[5] and from the time of Hsu Hsi-lin down to the man caught in Wolf Cub Village. Last year they executed a criminal in the city, and a consumptive soaked a piece of bread in his blood and sucked it.

"They want to eat me, and of course you can do nothing about it single-handed; but why should you join them? As man-eaters they are capable of anything. If they eat me, they can eat you as well; members of the same group can still eat each other. But if you will just change your ways immediately, then everyone will have peace. Although this has been going on since time immemorial, today we could make a special effort to be good, and say this is not to be done! I'm sure you can say so, brother. The other day when the tenant wanted the rent reduced, you said it couldn't be done."

At first he only smiled cynically, then a murderous gleam came into his eyes, and when I spoke of their secret his face turned pale. Outside the gate stood a group of people, including Mr. Chao and his dog, all craning their necks to peer in. I could not see all their faces, for they seemed to be masked in cloths; some of them looked pale and ghastly still, concealing their laughter. I knew they were one band, all eaters of human flesh. But I also knew that they did not all think alike by any means. Some of them thought that since it had always been so, men should be eaten. Some of them knew that they should not eat men, but still wanted to; and they were afraid people might discover their secret; thus when they heard me they became angry, but they still smiled their cynical, tight-lipped smile.

Suddenly my brother looked furious, and shouted in a loud voice:

"Get out of here, all of you! What is the point of looking at a madman?"

Then I realized part of their cunning. They would never be willing to change their stand, and their plans were all laid; they had stigmatized me as a madman. In future when I was eaten, not only would there be no trouble, but people would probably be grateful to them. When our tenant spoke of the villagers eating a bad character, it was exactly the same device. This is their old trick.

Old Chen came in too, in a great temper, but they could not stop my mouth, I had to speak to those people:

"You should change, change from the bottom of your hearts!" I said. "You must know that in the future there will be no place for man-eaters in the world.

"If you don't change, you may all be eaten by each other. Although so many are born, they will be wiped out by the real men, just like wolves killed by hunters. Just like reptiles!"

Old Chen drove everybody away. My brother had disappeared. Old Chen advised me to go back to my room. The room was pitch dark. The

---

5. A revolutionary at the end of the Ching dynasty (1644–1911), Hsu Hsi-lin was executed in 1907 for assassinating a Ching official. His heart and liver were eaten.

beams and rafters shook above my head. After shaking for some time they grew larger. They piled on top of me.

The weight was so great, I could not move. They meant that I should die. I knew that the weight was false, so I struggled out, covered in perspiration. But I had to say:

"You should change at once, change from the bottom of your hearts! You must know that in the future there will be no place for man-eaters in the world. . . ."

XI

The sun does not shine, the door is not opened, every day two meals.

I took up my chopsticks, then thought of my elder brother; I know now how my little sister died: it was all through him. My sister was only five at the time. I can still remember how lovable and pathetic she looked. Mother cried and cried, but he begged her not to cry, probably because he had eaten her himself, and so her crying made him feel ashamed. If he had any sense of shame. . . .

My sister was eaten by my brother, but I don't know whether mother realized it or not.

I think mother must have known, but when she cried she did not say so outright, probably because she thought it proper too. I remember when I was four or five years old, sitting in the cool of the hall, my brother told me that if a man's parents were ill, he should cut off a piece of his flesh and boil it for them if he wanted to be considered a good son; and mother did not contradict him. If one piece could be eaten, obviously so could the whole. And yet just to think of the mourning then still makes my heart bleed; that is the extraordinary thing about it!

XII

I can't bear to think of it.

I have only just realized that I have been living all these years in a place where for four thousand years they have been eating human flesh. My brother had just taken over the charge of the house when our sister died, and he may well have used her flesh in our rice and dishes, making us eat it unwittingly.

It is possible that I ate several pieces of my sister's flesh unwittingly, and now it is my turn. . . .

How can a man like myself, after four thousand years of man-eating history—even though I knew nothing about it at first—ever hope to face real men?

XIII

Perhaps there are still children who have not eaten men? Save the children. . . .

■ Mao Zedong (Mao Tse-tung) (1893–1976) (poems)

TRANSLATED BY WILLIS BARNSTONE AND KO CHING-PO

To Westerners, whose own association of poetry with government belongs to the long-distant era of the literate and literary courtier, the fact that the most powerful revolutionary and politician of twentieth-century China is also among its finest modern poets may seem stranger than it does to the Chinese. Mao Zedong was born in Shaoshan, Hunan province, in 1893 to a family of well-off peasants. He worked on his father's farm, attended schools, and from 1913–1918 was educated in Zhangsha at the First Provincial Normal School, where he encountered revolutionary writings. He worked in Beijing in a library in the winter of 1918–1919 and was strongly influenced by Li Dazhao and Chen Duxiu, who were to become Communist leaders. Mao was present in Shanghai in 1921, at the founding of the Chinese Communist Party, and he was engaged in the 1927 peasant uprisings in Hunan. He spent several years with the Communist guerrillas in Jiangxi and other border areas; and after Nationalist armies forced the Communists to flee on the disastrous Long March of 1934, Mao became the supreme leader of the party. Eventually he led the Communists to victory, and after the founding of the People's Republic of China in 1949, he became its chairman. In spite of challenges from within and without the party, Mao remained China's most important politician until his death in 1976, after which party moderates, under the leadership of Deng Xiaoping, took over from Mao's political coterie, the Gang of Four.

In his 1942 "Talks at the Yenan Forum on Literature and Art," Mao stated that literature is always political, that its true purpose should be to fire the masses with revolutionary fervor, to celebrate revolution and the people (not the subjective consciousness of the author), and that it should be judged on utilitarian grounds. Mao's comments were the basis for the Chinese development of Socialist Realist literature and were the authority upon which writers who did not fit the revolutionary model were criticized, censored, or worse. Mao's own poetry was written in classical forms, though he advised his readership not to emulate him in this. Its content is heroic, visionary, and revolutionary, and it dramatizes the historical events that led to the new Republic.

FURTHER READING: Barnstone, Willis, and Ko Ching-Po, trs. *The Poems of Mao Tse-tung*, 1972.

Loushan Pass

A hard west wind,
in the vast frozen air wild geese shriek to the morning moon,
frozen morning moon.
Horse hoofs shatter the air
and the bugle sobs.   5

The grim pass is like iron
yet today we will cross the summit in one step,
cross the summit.
Before us greenblue mountains are like the sea,
the dying sun like blood.   10

Snow

The scene is the north lands.
Thousands of li sealed in ice,
ten thousand li in blowing snow.
From the Long Wall I gaze inside and beyond
and see only vast tundra.   5
Up and down the Yellow River
the gurgling water is frozen.
Mountains dance like silver snakes,
hills gallop like wax bright elephants
trying to climb over the sky.   10
On days of sunlight
the planet teases us in her white dress and rouge.
Rivers and mountains are beautiful
and made heroes bow and compete to catch the girl—lovely earth.
Yet the emperors Shih Huang and Wu Ti   15
were barely able to write.
The first emperors of the Tang and Sung dynasties were crude.
Genghis Khan, man of his epoch
and favored by heaven,
knew only how to hunt the great eagle.   20
They are all gone.

Only today are we men of feeling.

The Gods

On the Death of His Wife Yang Kai-hui

I lost my proud poplar and you your willow.
As poplar and willow they soar straight up into the ninth heaven
and ask the prisoner of the moon, Wu Kang, what is there.
He offers them wine from the cassia tree.

The lonely lady on the moon, Chang O, spreads her vast sleeves   5
and dances for these good souls in the unending sky.
Down on earth a sudden report of the tiger's defeat.
Tears fly down from a great upturned bowl of rain.

Saying Good-bye to the God of Disease

Mauve waters and green mountains are nothing
when the great ancient doctor Hua To could not defeat a tiny worm.
A thousand villages collapsed, were choked with weeds, men were lost
    arrows.
Ghosts sang in the doorway of a few desolate houses.
Yet now in a day we leap around the earth   5
or explore a thousand Milky Ways.
And if the cowherd who lives on a star asks about the god of plagues,
tell him, happy or sad, the god is gone, washed away in the waters.

■ Wen Yiduo (Wen I-to) (1899–1946) (poem)

TRANSLATED BY ARTHUR SZE

Wen Yiduo was born in 1899 in Xishui, Hubei province, and was perhaps the finest poet of the Western-influenced Crescent School of poetry in
pre-revolution China. After a thorough traditional education in the
Chinese classics, he studied painting in Chicago, Colorado, and New York.
He had had exposure to Western literature in college, and this exposure
caused him to attempt writing poetry in the vernacular (until this time he
had written in traditional forms). While in America, he met Carl Sandburg,
Amy Lowell, and Harriet Monroe, editor of the distinguished and influential journal *Poetry,* which published so many of the American Modernist
poets. It was John Keats, however, who became his poetic model in this period. Wen's first book, *The Red Candle,* was published at this time. Wen was

disturbed by the racial discrimination he witnessed in American China-
towns, and he moved back to China, hoping to organize an intellectual re-
newal. Back in China, he dabbled in politics; helped found the influential
Crescent School of poets, which met in his apartment; and became a distinguished scholar, specializing in the study of *The Songs of Chu*. During this
period, he published his second and final volume, *Dead Waters*. His poetry is
vernacular, yet polished and formally rigorous; he makes it "dance in
chains," in Han Yu's phrase. On July 15, 1946, he was assassinated by hired
agents of the Guomindang (the nationalist party in China, which, after losing the civil war to the Communists in 1949, has maintained its power base
in Taiwan).

FURTHER READING: Payne, Robert, ed. *Contemporary Chinese Poetry*, 1947. Yeh,
Michelle, tr. *Anthology of Modern Chinese Poetry*, 1992.

Miracle

I never wanted the red of fire, the black at midnight
of the Peach Blossom Pool, the mournful melody of the *p'i p'a*,[1]

or the fragrance of roses. I never loved the stern
pride of the leopard, and no white dove ever had

the beauty I craved. I never wanted any of these things,   5
but their *crystallization*—a miracle ten thousand

times more rare than them all! But I am famished and harried.
I cannot go without nourishment: even if it is

dregs and chaff, I still have to beg for it. Heaven knows
I do not wish to be like this. I am by no means   10

so stubborn or stupid. I am simply tired of waiting,
tired of waiting for the miracle to arrive; and

I dare not starve. Ah, who doesn't know of how little worth
is a tree full of singing cicadas, a jug of turbid wine,

or smoky mountain peaks, bright ravines, stars   15
glittering in the empty sky? It is all so ordinary,

so inexorably dull, and it isn't worth our ecstatic joy,
our crying out the most moving names, or the

longing to cast gold letters and put them in a song.
I also affirm that to let tears come   20

---

1. See Tao Qian's "Preface to the Poem on the Peach Blossom Spring" and Wang Wei's treatment of the story in "Song of Peach Tree Spring."

at the song of an oriole is trivial, ridiculous,
and a waste of time. But who knows? I cannot be otherwise.

I am so famished and harried I take lamb's quarters
and wild hyssop for fine grain, —

         but there's no harm   25
in speaking clearly as long as the miracle appears.

Then at once I will cast off the ordinary. I will never
again gaze at a frosted leaf and dream of a spring blossom's

dazzle. I will not waste my strength, peel open
stones, and demand the warmth of white jade.   30

Give me one miracle, and I will never again whip ugliness,
and compel it to give up the meaning of its

opposite. Actually, I am weary of all this,
and these strained implications are hard to explain.

All I want is one clear word flashing like a Buddhist relic   35
with fierce light. I want it whole, complete,

shining in full face. I am by no means so stubborn
or stupid; but I cannot see a round fan without

seeing behind it an immortal face. So,
I will wait for as many incarnations as it takes—   40

since I've made a vow. I don't know how many
incarnations have already passed; but I'll wait

and wait, quietly, for the miracle to arrive.
That day must come! Let lightning strike me,

volcanoes destroy me. Let all hell rise up and crush me!   45
Am I terrified? No, no wind will blow out

the light in me. I only wish my cast-off body
would turn into ashes. And so what? That, that minutest

fraction of time is a minutest fraction of—
ah, an extraordinary gust, a divine and stellar hush   50

(sun, moon, and spin of all stars stopped,
time stopped too) — the most perfectly-round peace.

I hear the sound of the door pivoting: and with it
the rustling of a skirt. That is a miracle.

And in the space of a half-open gold door,   55
you are crowned with a circle of light!

■ Lao She (1899–1966) (story)

TRANSLATED BY DON J. COHN

Lao She is the pen name of Shu Qungchun, a Manchu who was born in Beijing in 1899. He was raised in poverty because of his father's early death, yet he managed to graduate from college, taking his degree in 1917 and going on to teach and start his career as a writer. In 1924, he taught in England at the School of Oriental and African Studies and wrote several novels. He returned to China, where he wrote his masterpiece, *Camel Xiangzi*, a novel that was translated into English in 1945 as *Rickshaw Boy*. The novel became a best-seller in English, but the satirical and pessimistic conclusion, which pleased neither the translator nor the Chinese critics, was changed into an improbable and romantic happy ending. Lao She was an organizer against the Japanese during World War II, and after the war he spent time in America, lecturing and writing. After the revolution succeeded in 1949, he returned to China and became a revolutionary writer, praising the new society. He died in 1966, during the Great Proletarian Cultural Revolution, perhaps murdered during this time of social turmoil. He is second only to Lu Xun as the finest Chinese fiction writer of the twentieth century and is noted for the light and humorous touch he brings to his fiction, even when he is waxing indignant against social injustice.

FURTHER READING: Chang, Jian-lih, tr. *A Translation of Lao She's "The Burning Train,"* 1988. Hu, Jieqing, ed. *The Crescent Moon and Other Stories*, 1990. James, Jean, tr. *Ma and Son: A Novel*, 1980. Kao, George, ed. *Two Writers and the Cultural Revolution: Lao She and Chen Jo-hsi*, 1980. Shi, Xiaoqing, tr. *Camel Xiangzi*, 1981. Xiong, Deni, tr. *Heavensent*, 1986.

Filling a Prescription

The Japanese troops were holding their regular target practice outside the Qihua Gate. As usual, the police guarding the gate were checking all the Chinese passing back and forth. Since the police were Chinese themselves, they were much more thorough and bold about guarding against Chinese spies than they were about the enemy; it was so much easier for them. Policemen were different from soldiers; they weren't responsible for foreign affairs.

Niu Ertou had unbuttoned both his short and long padded cotton jackets, and his blue cotton sash was tied loosely around his waist. Though this left a sizable portion of his bare chest exposed to the wind, he still felt hot; firstly, because he was walking very quickly; and secondly, because he was anxious and upset. His father had contracted a serious illness—the prescription cost more than a dollar! He lived nearly ten *li* from the Qihua Gate. The gate stood directly in front of him now; if he left the city immediately and took all the shortcuts he knew, he might make it home in time to let his father take his first dose by sunset. He sped up his pace; he was carrying the medicine in one hand and a rolled-up book in the other.

A large crowd stood in front of the gate, surrounded by the police. Ertou was in too much of a hurry to hang around and watch what was going on, and headed straight for the passageway which led through the broad gate tower.

"Where do you think you're going?" The sound of the policeman's voice echoed in the empty passageway.

Ertou was in too much of a hurry to figure out if this question was addressed to him or not, and kept on walking. Why, he wondered, was it so silent in the passageway?

"Hey, boy! I'm talking to you, you bastard. Get back here!" Someone grabbed Ertou by the arm.

"My father's waiting for me to bring him this medicine." Only then did Ertou realize that it was a policeman. "I didn't rob anybody!"

"Even if your grandfather wants to take his medicine, he also has to wait a little while." The policeman pushed Ertou towards the crowd.

Everyone there had their jackets unbuttoned. Ertou didn't have to waste his time on this, since his jackets were already unbuttoned. So he took the time to survey the scene. The people there were divided into three groups. Those dressed in silks and satins stood together in one spot; those wearing cotton gowns which weren't covered with mud made up a second group; and those dressed like Ertou formed a third. Though those in the first group had also unbuttoned their jackets, the policemen only gave them a cursory frisking and let them go. Ertou thought, "Doesn't look too bad. Fifteen minutes and I'll be on my way. I'll have to hurry when I get out of here." Things weren't going so smoothly for the men in the second group. Anyone with even the slightest bulge in their clothing had to be frisked twice. As the policemen worked their way through the crowd, they came to a man in his forties with a red nose, who refused to be searched.

"Get your supervisor over here!"

When the supervisor saw who it was, he said, "Oh it's you, Third Master. I'm sorry, I didn't notice you when you arrived. There's too much to do here; my hands are tied. I'm truly sorry." Without even a smile, the red-nosed man said, "You ought to get your eyes fixed. What a disgrace!" Rubbing his nose, he proceeded through the gate.

It seemed like hours before they got around to Ertou's group. "Take off your coats, my good men, you won't freeze to death," one of the policemen said with a laugh. "While you're at it, you can pick some of the lice out of the lining of my coat for me." This remark came from a man who might have been a ricksha puller. "Let's have no nonsense here; take 'em off and air 'em out." The policeman took another man's coat and shook it a few times. The coat's owner laughed and said, "The only thing I've got hidden in there is dirt." Upon hearing this wisecrack, the policeman threw the coat onto the ground. "Have a little more dirt, then."

There were only a few people left when it came to Ertou's turn. All those who had arrived after Ertou were placed in a separate group.

"What's that?" The policeman pointed to the object in his hand.

"Medicine."

"No, I mean the thing you've got rolled up there."

"It's a book I picked up in a public toilet."

"Let me see it."

The policeman glanced at the book's cover and noticed it was red. He handed it to the inspector. The inspector examined the book's cover as well and noticed it was red. Then he looked at Ertou. He flipped through the first few pages, but seemed to be unable to grasp the gist of it. Then, wetting his finger thoroughly with saliva, he flipped through another ten pages, paused for a moment, raised his head, looked at the gate tower, and glanced at Ertou again. "Take him inside," he said, and a policeman stepped forward.

Ertou instinctively took a step backwards. He knew he was in trouble now, but he didn't know why.

"My father's waiting for his medicine. I picked up this book in a public toilet."

Grabbing Ertou by the collar, the policeman said, "Listen to me, buddy. If you don't behave yourself, you're going to get your head bashed in."

"But my father's waiting for his medicine!" Though Ertou was anxious now, he didn't raise his voice. His vocal cords were immune to this sort of thing.

"Get him out of here!" The inspector's face was slightly pale; perhaps he thought Ertou was carrying a bomb on his person.

Being anxious was futile for Ertou at this point, but he couldn't stay there any longer. Suddenly tears welled up in his eyes.

The policeman took him into the station and whispered something to the sergeant on duty. The sergeant took the book and flipped through it.

The stoutly built sergeant was extremely polite. "What is your surname, huh?" He drew out the "huh" like an actor in a western-style comedy.

"Niu.[1] My name is Niu Ertou." His nose twitched as he answered.

"Hm, what village are you from, Ertou, huh?"

"Ten-*li* Village."

"Hm, Ten-*li* Village. That's outside the Qihua Gate." The sergeant nodded, extremely pleased with his superior knowledge of geography. "What were you doing in the city, hm?" His "hm" was even longer than his "huh."

"I was having a prescription filled, my father's sick." Tears were now rolling down his cheeks.

---

1. Niu means "ox."

"Whose father, huh? Speak up! It's a good thing I'm not very suspicious. Now, I want you to tell me the truth. Who gave you this book?"

"I picked it up in a public toilet."

"If you don't tell me the truth, I'm going to make things very difficult for you." The fat sergeant appeared fatter than he had ten minutes ago; perhaps this is what happened to him every time he got angry. "Young man, don't be as stubborn as an ox with me. If you tell the truth, I'll let you go. We're looking for the man who gave you this book, understand? Huh?"

"I swear to you, I picked it up in a toilet. I don't want it anymore. Just let me go!"

"I don't think you're going anywhere right now." The sergeant took one more look at the book and decided to retain Ertou for further interrogation.

Ertou was extremely upset now. "But sir, my father is waiting for his medicine."

"You mean there aren't any pharmacies outside the gate, so you had to come into the city to buy medicine? There must be some other reason." The sergeant was about to smile, but stopped himself. He felt extremely satisfied about his own profound wisdom.

"The doctor told me to have the prescription made up at the Huaidetang Pharmacy downtown. The medicine's better there. Sir, I beg you, let me go now. I don't want that book anymore. Is that alright?"

"No, that's not alright."

That night, they took Ertou to the Bureau of Public Security.

"Ru Yin" the writer and "Qing Yan" the literary critic were enemies, though the two of them had never met. Ru Yin earned his living by writing fiction while Qing Yan made a career out of writing criticism. When their works appeared in the magazines and newspapers, it was always Ru Yin who took the lead, with Qing Yan following close behind. No matter what Ru Yin wrote, Qing Yan always aimed the same poison arrow at him — "unsound thinking." Though this in no way affected the sale of his works, Ru Yin always felt that in the final accounting, the psychological victory belonged to Qing Yan. He didn't know whether or not the people who bought his cheap books smiled out of sympathy for him when they thought: "Who cares whether his thinking is sound or not; his stories make really entertaining reading." He hoped his readers didn't think this way and consoled himself by thinking, "Maybe there's somebody out there who really respects me." He was very much like a self-satisfied businessman. But whenever he received any fees or royalties for his writing, he imagined Qing Yan looking over his shoulder and saying, "Ahah! I see you've earned some money again! I guess that's one that got away. Just wait and see, I'm not finished with you yet!"

Once by coincidence their two photos appeared together in a magazine. This really piqued Ru Yin's imagination. In the picture, Qing Yan had a big head, long hair, protruding eyes and a pug nose like that of a Pekinese dog. The best thing you could say about him was that he looked like Socrates. It was this imaginary Socrates who very frequently haunted Ru Yin.

A number of malicious thoughts occurred to Ru Yin. Judging from his pen name alone—Qing Yan means "black swallow"—he had probably started out as an insignificant popular love story writer. But now that he had changed careers and was earning his living by condemning everything he read as "unsound thinking," it was just as well to ignore him. However, passive consolation is never quite as satisfactory as an active attack: the bullets of "unsound thinking" were still flying directly over his head.

Ru Yin wondered how he could set his thinking "straight"? The answer to this question could certainly not be found in Qing Yan's critical writings. There was one way in which Qing Yan didn't resemble Socrates: Socrates asked a lot of questions and was always full of answers; he often went around in circles, sometimes ending up lost inside his own arguments. But Qing Yan's style was to stand at the finish line of a 100 metre race, grab the slowest runner and slap him in the face. Ru Yin's only way out was to change the way he wrote. He read through a number of books which were supposed to be representative of "sound thinking"—though some of them had already been banned. He found them disappointing, since most of them were nothing more than anemic romances. He knew he could write much better than that.

He started to write in this style. He published a few pieces and waited eagerly for Qing Yan's response. But once again the response was: "Unsound thinking!"

When he made a careful comparison of his own work and that of the so-called orthodox writers, he noticed that they were written in entirely different languages: his were in Chinese, while theirs were written in some western-style Chinese. The content was also different: his stories were expressions of light and shade, sincerity and degradation, ideals and emotions; theirs were comedies laced through with "blood" and "death."

Despite this, Ru Yin's latest works ended up as "unsound thinking."

He wanted to play a joke on Qing Yan in order to shut him up once and for all. He started producing imitations of the so-called orthodox works, using foreign-style language and plots which though lively were far from realistic. He sent a number of them off to some magazines.

Strangely enough, every single story was returned to him. One in particular was accompanied by a polite letter from an editor:

> *In times like these, when there is no freedom of speech, the use of such words as red, yellow, blue, white and black could get us all wiped out. Nearly all the language in your story is of this type.*

Ru Yin couldn't stop laughing. So this was the way the world worked: words could really deceive people. Writers, readers, critics and censors all came from the same mould.

He now understood why Qing Yan only attacked him for his "unsound thinking" and said very little about the other aspects of his works: it was because he was scared. This was quite a fair assessment. Now more than ever, he wanted to play a trick on Qing Yan. With his own money, he printed up a short anthology of stories previously rejected by publishers. He addressed a copy to Qing Yan and sent it to him via the editorial office of a certain magazine; in this way Qing Yan would be sure to get it. Even though he had spent his own money, he felt this was a positive move. "I went out on my own and printed these stories; let's see if he has the courage to criticize them without rejecting them outright."

Qing Yan went to the editorial office of X Magazine to see if there was any "news" for him. He found three letters and a package waiting for him on his desk. He read the letters first and then opened the package. It was a book with a red cover—written by Ru Yin. Qing Yan smiled. He felt sorry for Ru Yin. All authors deserve sympathy to some degree. After breaking through the barriers erected by the editorial departments, they're inevitably subjected to the wrath of the critics. But never under any circumstances should a critic lower himself out of compassion for an author. Unfair criticism could put one in a very awkward position. This he knew very well; but truly fair criticism could have even more serious consequences. The general rule was that writing which lacked barbs couldn't be considered literary criticism.

Qing Yan was the sort of person who would never hurt a fly. But writing criticism was his way of earning a living, and most hatchet men performed their jobs in order to eat. He knew all of this, but he still played dumb. He also knew which publications didn't like which writers, and by keeping this in mind whenever he wrote anything, further secured his own position. You might say that he was a man without ideals; considering the overall situation, however, perhaps he could be forgiven for this. The truth was that he never intended to be at odds with Ru Yin, since he didn't enjoy being at odds with anyone; but criticism was criticism. If he could have come up with a more original phrase than "unsound thinking," he would have rejected those two words a long time ago, for he had no particular affection for them. But since he had nothing more novel or convincing at hand, he had to make do with them; it was as simple at that.

He had long wanted to meet Ru Yin, to sit down for a good talk with him and even to become his friend. If they couldn't meet, at least he could write him a letter urging him to take back his red book as soon as possible, since it was a dangerous thing. If Ru Yin wanted to carry this game any further, smoking cigarettes and fussing over pedantic stylistic changes were the least useful things he could do. It would be better for him to think up something new. No matter how you looked at it, writing and criticism were just two forms of pedantry. All the flattery and hostility which were so much a part of the literary life amounted to little more than a waste of paper and ink, and no one engaged in these activities would ever contribute a single new page to human history.

The history of literature and literary criticism was little more than the history of numerous individuals flattering themselves; if these subjects never existed, libraries would certainly be a lot less empty and dull.

With his nose raised, Qing Yan let out with a snort. Rolling up the book, he left the editorial office. When he reached the southern corner of the Four Eastern Archways, he felt the urge to relieve himself. He put the book down on the mud wall surrounding the public toilet in order to facilitate tucking up his long brocade gown. As he stood in the stall, blocking the doorway, someone approached him from behind. As he was eager to allow this stranger to take his turn, he quickly straightened his gown and walked out holding his breath.

He'd gone quite a long way before he remembered the book, but he decided not to go back and look for it. Without the book in hand, he could still write his review. Fortunately, he remembered the book's title and author.

Ertou had been in jail for two days now, but he still had no idea what that book was about. All he could remember was that it was thin and had a red cover. He was totally illiterate. The more he hated that little book, the more he worried about his father's illness; that dirty rotten book was killing his father. They continued interrogating him, but he always gave the same answer: "I picked it up in a public toilet." It was hard enough for him to imagine that someone had written the book in the first place. Couldn't he find anything better to do than write a book? All Ertou'd done was pick it up. When he had nothing else to do in the winter, he'd go around collecting dung in the same way. How was that any different from picking up a book?

"Who gave it to you?" They asked him this same question over and over again.

Ertou was twenty years old, but no one had ever given him a book. How on earth could books have anything to do with him? He couldn't very well tell a lie and say that Doggy Zhang or Blackie Li had given it to him; that would mean getting innocent people in trouble. The only authentic-sounding name he could think of was Meng Zhanyuan, the head of the village martial arts society. This name, like Huang Tianba or Zhao Zilong, who were characters in popular tales, seemed like something out of a book. But he couldn't get the head of the society involved in this affair. If Meng Zhanyuan weren't there during the annual spring pilgrimage to Miaofeng Mountain, there was no guarantee that the village team wouldn't be defeated by the team from Scholartree Village in the "Five-Tiger Cudgel" contest. But when he thought about his father's illness, he could no longer worry about this sort of thing. If he could only turn into a puff of smoke and escape through a crack in the door. That damned book! That goddamned dirty book! Maybe it contained the prescription for the bogey man's magic potion!

Another day went by. Ertou was sure his father was dead.

He had no medicine to take. Ertou was nowhere to be seen. This would be enough to drive his father mad. Concluding that his father was dead,

Ertou held his head in his hands. Tears began falling down his cheeks, and before long he started crying out loud despite himself.

When he stopped crying, he made up his mind to tell the policemen that Meng Zhanyuan had given him the book. This was the only name he could think of that sounded bookish enough. Neither "Doggy" nor "Blackie," not to mention "Little Seventy," seemed like appropriate names for people who gave books away.

But after giving it further consideration, he decided not to do it this way. It would be so unfair! He really and truly had picked up the book without thinking. Moreover, since he had found it in the city, Meng Zhanyuan couldn't possibly have given it to him. The facts didn't tally. His mind unresolved, Ertou's thoughts turned to his father's death. He could see all the members of his family wearing mourning dress, only he wasn't there. This was enough to drive anyone crazy!

That night, another man was put in Ertou's cell. He was young and well dressed, and had shackles around his ankles. Ertou's curiosity allowed him some respite from his worrying. Also, the sight of this cultivated man wearing shackles but displaying no sign of distress had a calming effect on him.

The new arrival was the first to speak. "What are you here for, my good man?"

"I picked up a book. Screw the ancestors of that damned book!" Ertou exploded with spite.

"What book was it?" The young man's eyes darkened slightly.

"A book with a red cover." That was all Ertou could remember. "I can't read."

"Oh!" the young man said, nodding his head.

Neither of them spoke. A few moments passed before Ertou broke the silence:

"What . . . are you here for?"

"I wrote a book!" the young man replied with a laugh.

"Oh, it was you who wrote that dirty rotten book."

Ertou had never met a person who could write books, but since this young man wrote books, he naturally assumed he was the one who had written the book with the red cover. He didn't know what to do now. He wanted to punch this writer in the nose, but there were too many policemen around. They'd already arrested him once, and he didn't want to make things any worse for himself. Having decided not to punch him, he now had no way of venting his anger. "You had nothing better to do, your hands got itchy, and so you wrote that dirty fuckin' book!" Ertou stared at the young man, gnashing his teeth.

The young man smiled mischievously. "But that book was written for your benefit."

Ertou couldn't restrain himself any longer. "I'll smack you one, you son of a bitch!" But he didn't lift a finger. Ertou was actually frightened of the young man, perhaps because his face, his manner, his youth and his clothing didn't quite match the shackles on his legs. He was very pale, but his skin was fine and smooth. His eyes were rather dull, and he was constantly smiling in a sort of an unnatural way. He was quite thin, and his narrow ankles were encumbered by those iron shackles! Ertou's fear arose from not knowing what kind of person this strange young man was.

The young man sat there smiling, and looked up at Ertou. "You can't read?"

Ertou sat there dumbly for a few moments, reluctant to answer, but he finally responded with a little grunt.

"Where did you find the book?"

"In a public toilet. Why does that matter?"

"Did they ask you about it?"

"None of your . . . !" Ertou swallowed the second half of his sentence. Besides his fear, he now felt somewhat suspicious of this young man.

"If you tell me, I'll help you get out of here." The young man's smile became more serious. He was thinking: "I wrote this dirty book for you, but you can't even read it. Isn't it my job to get you out of this mess?"

"They asked me who I got it from, but I didn't say anything."

"Let's say I tell them it was me that lost the book in the toilet. Wouldn't that solve all your problems?" By now the young man's smile looked rather silly.

"That would really be swell!" Ertou smiled. He hadn't smiled once in the last three days, so his lips remained sealed. "Shall we go talk to them now?"

"Not now. We had better wait till tomorrow when they start asking me questions."

"But my father's very sick. He may be dead by now!"

"First, tell me where you found that book."

"On the south side of the Four Eastern Archways, when I was taking a goddamned piss!" At that moment, Ertou felt something strange inside him. He could think of no way to describe this sensation properly; it was as if he were lost in the dark. He remembered one time several years ago when the locusts ate all the grain in the fields.

"Is this what you were wearing? What else did you have with you?"

"I was wearing the same outfit and I was carrying a package of medicine." Ertou began thinking of his father again.

Qing Yan returned home feeling very ill at ease. He couldn't get Ru Yin off his mind. Pacing back and forth in his room, he chuckled to himself; he still had to criticize Ru Yin's book. He could only write a short piece, since he'd lost the book. Writing literary criticism was second nature to him now, so he could easily broaden the scope of his attack and describe the binding or the cover; a literary critic was free to express his opinions on aesthetics. "If a book's red cover can symbolize the contents of a story, then this little juggling performance by Ru Yin is a cause for disappointment. For the book's cover, he has chosen thick, glossy red paper; as for the contents . . . well, the contents are full of unsound thinking." He went on from there and wrote seven or eight hundred words. In each and every sentence, he displayed his great authority. Criticism, after all, was a form of literature.

He was comfortably satisfied with the precision of his writing; it had always been more severe than his thinking. It was his writing that secured him his reputation. He felt he had been unfair to Ru Yin, but this was the way it had to be. When he met Ru Yin some day, a few words of explanation would suffice to clear up any misunderstanding.

If writers obtained their pleasure at the expense of fictitious characters, then literary critics obtained theirs at the expense of the authors they criticized. After making a few minor revisions, he dropped the article in the mailbox.

Two days later, Qing Yan's article appeared in the paper. Two days after that, he learned that Ru Yin had been arrested.

Qing Yan wasn't worried about the article he had written. Critics were rarely arrested on the grounds of sound thinking. But if that were the case, it would matter very little. Besides students who read fiction and enjoyed following the petty skirmishes fought regularly on the literary battlefield, was anyone aware that literary critics existed at all? Wasn't the whole writing business, after all, just a huge heap of rubbish? At the same time, though, Qing Yan was upset about Ru Yin. He knew there had to be something meaningful in all of this for him, though he didn't know what it was yet, and could only describe it in a negative way: this meaningful something had nothing to do with either sound or unsound thinking. Truth and nonsense are entirely different things. In other words, if an author wants to describe a soldier, it doesn't mean he has to join the army. Now he understood! The positive solution was to create a new page or two of history, not just write a few silly articles. This thought had occurred to him before, but now he was convinced it was true. Yet he still wanted to rescue Ru Yin, even though this wasn't very "meaningful" for him.

Two days later, Ertou said goodbye to Ru Yin.

When he got home, he learned that his father's burial had taken place two days before. Ertou swore that he'd never buy medicine in the city again.

■ Wang Meng (1934–) (story)

TRANSLATED BY QINGYUN WU

Born in Hebei province, Wang Meng became a Communist Party member before he was fourteen years old. In 1949, he went to Beijing, where he worked in the Communist Youth League and entered a party school and studied political theory. His first novel, *Spring Time Fever,* was published in 1953, when he was only nineteen, and he became a nationally prominent literary figure in 1956 when he published "The Young Newcomer in the Organization Department," a story mildly critical of bureaucracy. This story was politically criticized a year later during the 1957 Anti-Rightist

Campaign, a period of serious repression that directly followed a movement of political and literary liberalization, the Hundred Flowers Campaign. The slogan of that campaign had been "Let a hundred flowers bloom and a hundred schools of thought contend," but when the open debate that this campaign invited actually took place, the government cracked down and purged three hundred thousand intellectuals, among them Wang Meng. He was sent into internal exile in the countryside, where he worked as a manual laborer for the next five years. In 1963, after a brief reprieve during which he taught in Beijing, he was exiled again to Xinjiang province, where he worked with the Chinese Writers' Association. In 1965, at the inception of the Great Proletarian Cultural Revolution (a ten-year period of social repression ignited by Mao Zedong as a power play against moderate elements in the Communist Party), he was again assigned to manual labor.

A few years after the death of Mao in 1976 and the subsequent fall of the Gang of Four, Wang was reinstated as a professional writer in Beijing, publishing a number of modernist stories and the modernist novel *Bolshevik Salute*. In 1986, he was appointed Minister of Culture, but he was dismissed in 1989 during the purges that followed the massacre at Tiananmen Square. In his modernist experiments, Wang Meng uses techniques of fragmentation, stream of consciousness, and an increasing psychologizing and subjectivity in depiction of character—a marked departure from the straightforward narrative of the Socialist Realist fiction that dominated before the death of Mao. Mao, in his "Talks at Yenan Forum on Literature and Art," had asked writers to become a "cultural army" to "produce works that awakened the masses, fire them with enthusiasm and impel them to unite and struggle to transform their environment." Art was to be a utilitarian means toward revolution and the dissemination of revolutionary ideology; writers who focused more on aesthetics and themselves were "merely termites in the revolutionary ranks." Therefore, Wang Meng's work of the new period is revolutionary simply in its refusal to be revolutionary. He is the equivalent in fiction to the modernist poets who began writing in the late 1970s and who were criticized for their obscure (*meng long*) poetics. Wang's short story "Anecdotes of Minister Maimaiti" is a darkly humorous, picaresque set of chapters that parodies the revolutionary fervor of the Cultural Revolution from the point of view of a Uygur protagonist (the Turkik Uygurs reside in Xinjiang province).

FURTHER READING: Larson, Wendy, tr. *Bolshevik Salute: A Modernist Chinese Novel*, 1989. Liu, Xinwu. *Prize-Winning Stories from China*, 1978–1979, 1981.

Anecdotes of Minister Maimaiti: A Uygur Man's Black Humor

Six essential elements for sustaining life (in order of their importance): first, air; first, sunshine; first, water; first, food; first, friendship; first, humor.

Happiness comes when tears dry.

The sense of humor is the superiority complex of intelligence.

—*from* Ancient Philosophical Aphorisms *(not yet published)*

1. Why Was Minister Maimaiti as Young as an Evergreen?

May 6, 1979. The wind was gentle, the sun was warm, the willows showing the first hint of green. In the Dashizi Muslim Restaurant, I ran into Minister Maimaiti and his twin brother, Saimaiti, neither of whom I had seen for more than ten years. I looked first at Maimaiti:

> Although merciless time had carved mountains and rivers on his face
> His vitality radiated from a thick crown of glossy black hair,
> His ruddy face was as warm and cheering as bread hot from the oven
> and in his laughter hope and cynicism tussled like romping children.

I turned to his brother Saimaiti:

> His bony back quivered like a tightened bow.
> In his dull eyes shadows of death flickered.
> He always sighed before speaking as if his stomach ached.
> In his hand he ever clutched a little bottle of heart pills.

I was so shocked by the contrast, of course, that as soon as I had said "Salamu"[1] and finished greeting them, I asked, "What has happened to you two these last years?"

"I suffered from The Catastrophe . . ." Saimaiti replied.

Maimaiti added, "I also suffered from The Catastrophe . . ."

Saimaiti: "As soon as the Unprecedented Event occurred, I was called one of the 'Black Gang' and locked up . . ."

Maimaiti: "I was also seized and locked up . . ."

Saimaiti: "I was beaten . . ."

Maimaiti: "I was whipped . . ."

Saimaiti: "I climbed the mountains to carry stone . . ."

Maimaiti: "I went down into the earth to dig coal . . ."

Saimaiti: "When I was officially labeled an Active Counterrevolutionary Element, my wife divorced me . . ."

Maimaiti: "When I was publicly labeled a Three Antis Element (Anti-Party, Anti-people, Anti-socialism), my children's mother married another man . . ."

Ailaibailai![2] Six of one, half a dozen of the other. Like peas, the twins' experiences seemed indistinguishable. Confused by this counterpoint of

---

1. Uygur for "May you have a long life."
2. Xinjiang slang for "What nonsense."

woes, I couldn't help asking. "Since you both suffered the same fates, why does brother Maimaiti look so young and Saimaiti so ancient?"

With tears quivering in his eyes, Saimaiti moaned, sighed, and beat his sides with his fists.

Pointing at his smiling face, Maimaiti said, "He lacks *this,* you see? He still broods and suffers. But me, I never let a day pass without making a joke."

2. The Crime of Minister Maimaiti (Which Lays Bare the True Nature of the New-Style Wedding That Breaks Away from "The Four Olds")

In 1966 the tide of the Cultural Revolution was surging high. Yet the Uygur people of the remote countryside of Xinjiang Province could make no sense of it. The villagers didn't know who were their targets, or indeed why anyone should be attacked at all. They just did not know how to "make revolution." In fact, they did not even know why they should make revolution. They could only shrug their shoulders and say to each other in Uygur expression, "Haven't got any message yet."

Yet by this time the Uygur villagers were so accustomed to the Party's successive movements that they felt they were obliged to make some attempt, any attempt, however muddled it might be, as if they were drawing a tiger playfully by using a cat as a model. Therefore they criticized Deng Tuo, recited Chairman Mao's Quotations, killed pigeons, and burned the Koran. The teenagers were very excited by all of this because they got to do all those things that had previously been forbidden, while their more conservative elders, though nervous and alert, mostly remained silent.

"Change through class struggle!" That was the motto of the day. Maimaiti's uncle, Mu Ming, Party Secretary of the Fourth Brigade (which changed its name to the Struggle Brigade when the Cultural Revolution began), took the lead by shaving off his beautiful mustache and beard, throwing away his embroidered cap, and putting aside his long tunic, black corduroy trousers, and boots in favor of an imitation army uniform. With an imitation soldier's cap on his head, a red band bearing the words "Red Guard" on his arm, Liberation Rubber shoes on his feet, and a kindergarten-child's red satchel containing Mao's Red Book slung over one shoulder, Mu Ming, a brand-new man, appeared on the horizon.

At that time Mu Ming's eldest daughter, Tilakizi, was going to be married to Mulajidi, who not only was the most intelligent young man in the village but was also the newly elected Political Commissar of the Struggle Brigade. When the news got out, however, the Commune Secretary and the Work Team Leader from the central provincial office sent for Mu Ming, Mulajidi, and Tilakizi and sternly warned the young couple that they must firmly break with the "Four Olds" (old ideas, old culture, old customs, old traditions). Included among these "Olds" was the traditional Uygur wedding ceremony: there was to be no slaughtering of sheep, no drinking, no dancing, no wedding presents—and certainly no prayers or blessings. No, their own marriage would have to begin with a new-style proletarian wedding.

"What exactly is this new-style proletarian wedding?" Mu Ming asked, trying to look and sound as much like a Red Guard as possible.

"The ceremony will be as follows. First, all present will recite from the Quotations, in particular the Three Speeches. Second, you will invite the leaders of the province, county, and commune to give speeches. Finally, the young couple will bow three times to the portrait of Chairman Mao, once to the assembled leaders, and once to each other. That's it. Of course, there will be no dowry from either family. However, both sides may exchange copies of the Red Book, portraits of our esteemed Chairman, sickles, and manure forks. No entertainment is allowed. After the wedding, the groom will spend the wedding night watering crops, and the bride will make forty posters of the Chairman's Quotations, done in red and yellow paint on wooden boards. . . ."

Mu Ming was more than a little surprised to hear this. He had thought that shaving off his mustache and wearing his pseudo-Red Guard uniform would make him sufficiently revolutionary. Little did he know, however, that he still was 108,000 *li* from "carrying the revolution through to the end."

Mulajidi scowled and rolled his eyes. He had assumed that by being a political commissar he could just go through the motions of being a revolutionary, spouting slogans, avoiding physical labor, and yet nevertheless ending up with more work points than other villagers. Now he would be forced to act out a senseless charade on his own wedding night, one that no one but a sexless idiot would possibly consent to.

Tilakizi was all tears. As a girl grows older her desire becomes stronger, and Tilakizi had been thinking for months about those first sweet, shy, tender moments when she and Mulajidi could be alone together. But never had she imagined that her wedding would be like one of those political-education classes conducted by the militia.

Furious at their reaction, the Commune Secretary and the Team Leaders lambasted the father, daughter, and future son-in-law, then ordered Mu Ming to get to work at once spreading the political and ideological word among the youth. After the trio had departed, the Commune Secretary called the League Secretary, the Chairman of the Poor and Middle Peasants Association, the Chairwoman of the Women's Federation into their office. Their job, he explained to them, would be to monitor the trio to discover the true thoughts and feelings of each and then badger them into changing their minds.

By all appearances, this method seemed to be working. The new-style proletarian wedding was duly held. Leaders gave speeches, officials posed with the couple for photos, revolutionary songs such as "The East Is Red" and "The Helmsman on the Sea" were sung, and solemn passages like "holding a memorial meeting to express our sorrows" were read. This model wedding was then reported in bulletins, local newspapers, and county broadcasts. And to top it all off, Xinhua News Agency carried the word to the country at large.

Ten days later, Mu Ming's family held the real wedding. Sheep were slaughtered, silks were exchanged, and the bride and groom paid all the customary visits to relatives—it was a true Uygur wedding. Luckily, this underground wedding was not all that risky. In the first place, since the new-style proletarian wedding had already been publicized, it had served its purpose. In the second place, the Party officials were all too busy accusing one another of being capitalist roaders or else defending themselves from such attacks.

A Uygur man's beard grows very fast, so in ten days Mu Ming at least had a healthy stubble, if not the respectable growth that would bring a man universal prestige. As the saying goes, "Although the old man lost his horse, who knows that it might not turn out for the best." Mu Ming did not appear as a comic Red Guard at the real wedding. After the ceremony, the bride and groom were as inseparable as paint and wood.

Of course, Minister Maimaiti knew all about his cousin's wedding. He made an anecdote of it to tell his friends, concluding, "The advantage of the new-style proletarian wedding is that it postponed the real wedding long enough for my uncle to let his beard grow out. The disadvantage is that they had to spend fifty *yuan* more than their budget; since besides butchering sheep and buying wine for the real wedding, they had to buy watermelon seeds, candy, and cigarettes for the new-style wedding."

These were not times in which to make such mistakes, however. Everyone was accusing everyone else of all sorts of things, and Maimaiti himself was soon under examination for taking "The Black Line" in literature. When his remarks concerning the wedding were denounced as a rightist's attack on the Great Proletarian Cultural Revolution, Maimaiti was seized for questioning.

To protect his uncle and cousin, Maimaiti insisted that he had made up the entire story of the underground wedding. As a result, he had yet one more charge laid against him, that of "spreading rumors for sabotage and encouraging a return to capitalism." After being convicted, he was tightly sealed in a cowshed.

3. At Last Minister Maimaiti Becomes a Writer Recognized by the People

Now let us turn back the clock a bit. Maimaiti had always been a lover of books, even as a child. In 1958, because of his scholarship and sensitivity, he was selected to be the Provincial Minister of Literature and Arts. This gave him the opportunity to meet many famous writers and poets, which increased his love for literature still more and made him determined to become a writer himself. Therefore he wrote and wrote and wrote. And although his manuscripts were rejected time and again, he kept on writing. Finally a few of his short poems and prose pieces were published in literary magazines and in the popular press. Unfortunately, no one paid the slightest attention to any of them. Readers and critics alike were unanimous in ignoring him. Established writers yawned, while emerging writers left him unread. Every time he petitioned to join the writers union, he was turned down. Eventually he became bitter.

It was only when he was denounced as a member of the Black Gang and sent off to a prison farm that his fortunes changed, because he now was in the company of all the famous writers and poets he had previously admired and envied. At last, he was one of them.

On an April day in 1967, Maimaiti and his colleagues were working in a vineyard when they heard a terrible racket: drums thundering, bugles blowing, and Quotations being chanted in unison. Realizing that a band of "revolutionary warriors" was approaching, the intelligentsia scattered like startled animals in the jungle. Some dived into ditches; some hid behind bushes; others just lay flat among the army of the ants, hoping to avoid another confrontation with the Army of the Revolution.

Unfortunately, Maimaiti had a bad ear infection, and so he heard neither the Red Guards approaching nor his colleagues' shouts of warning. Besides, he had come to enjoy his work in the vineyards and was so absorbed in his digging that he did not even notice that anything unusual was happening. As a result, he alone was left to serve as a target. Before he knew it, the Red Guards had surrounded him. They glared at him. Here stood a dangerous enemy of the people. Their courage and commitment were about to be tested.

"Who are you?" the Red Guards snarled.

"One of the Black Gang, a Three Antis Element," Maimaiti replied meekly. He dropped his hands to his sides and tried to look as ashamed and repentant as possible.

"What were you before?"

"Minister of Literature and Arts."

"Aha! A capitalist roader. A man of the Black Line. What are your crimes, monster?"

"I attacked the breaking away from the 'Four Olds,' worthy comrades, and wrote some reactionary articles."

"Which articles? How many?"

"Well, let me see . . ." Excited to talk about his writing, Maimaiti forgot about his penitent pose. "The first one was about . . ." With extraordinary seriousness and meticulousness, he reported the exact content of all his published articles, including a news report of less than a hundred words.

"What else have you written?"

Maimaiti promptly reported all the manuscripts that had been killed by editors.

"Do you know Zhou Yang?"

"Yes, of course." Actually, Maimaiti only knew the name. In Uygur, the same word is used for "know personally" and "know by name." Naturally his answer was misinterpreted.

The young warriors were startled.

Thinking that this man must be a famous writer, a really dangerous enemy, they began shouting revolutionary slogans. "Crush the enemy under your feet! Knock him from his high seat! Revolution is guiltless; rebellion is reasonable!" and so on.

Soon they grew tired of mere words and began to transpose their ideas into action, of which Maimaiti was the recipient. He did his best to huddle up into a ball, for two reasons: one, to show his submissiveness and, two, to protect his intestines. At the same time he kept saying "Oh" and "Ouch" in a voice that was neither too loud nor too faint. This moderate moaning was a deliberate ploy, learned from experience. If a victim clenched his teeth and made no noise, the young warriors, thinking he was defying them, would only become more antagonized. If he yelled too much, however, they would interpret this as a protest against their actions and would also become more antagonized. Therefore, the wisest course was to moan piteously but in a carefully modulated tone. By the time they had finished with him, Maimaiti had been beaten black and blue. His gums and nostrils were bleeding. His eyes were swollen like walnuts. It would have taken a nutcracker to open them. His back, sides, legs, and belly were all covered with cuts and bruises. Nevertheless, his heart, liver, spleen, stomach, kidneys, and bladder had all escaped injury. His tactic had worked.

But although the young warriors had broken Maimaiti's body, they still felt that they had not yet touched his soul. So they wrote six big characters on his back with a big brush and smelly black ink, "Black Writer Maimaiti!" Then, in high spirits, the young revolutionary warriors marched off, singing a revolutionary song, away from one victory but onward to a greater one.

Some twenty minutes later, the other writers crawled out of their hiding places one by one. Some tried to help Maimaiti to his feet. Others tried to console him. Some sighed for him. Others blamed him for not heeding their warnings. But they all agreed that the trouble with Maimaiti was that he worked too hard and was too honest and naive to know that a wise man always keeps his eyes open to six ways and his ears listening in eight directions.

Pushing away all helping hands, Maimaiti stood up. Shivering, he spat the blood out of his mouth. Then, disregarding all his other injuries, he pointed to his back and asked what the young warriors had written there.

"Black Writer Mai-mai-ti!" they read in unison.

"Aha!" Maimaiti shouted. Because of all the blood in his mouth and the loosened teeth, his words weren't clear. Yet his excitement was beyond words.

"You don't recognize me as a writer. You never have. But see, the people, they've recognized me at last!"

The crowd burst out laughing. They laughed till tears of joy came to their eyes.

4. Romance in the Cowshed

The Black Gang at the prison farm had to fetch drinking water from a motor-driven pump two kilometers away. This task was so difficult that they arranged to take turns with it. But in that April of 1968, Maimaiti amazed everyone by volunteering to take over this task completely. The shoulder-pole and pails became his own property. At first they thought he was "learning from Lei Feng" and doing extra work in order to secure an earlier release, so they let him alone. But when this continued, someone finally got suspicious and asked him about it.

"Why do you go out of your way to do extra work? What are you up to?"

Maimaiti didn't try to hide his secret. In fact, it was with pride that Maimaiti declared, "Near the well lives a very pretty girl."

"A pretty girl?" The men of the Black Gang could hardly believe their ears.

"A pretty girl. More than a pretty girl." He began to declaim a poem he had written in her honor.

> Her beauty is both sun and moon but
> Shines with a lovelier light;
> Her shimmering hair reflects a halo of love.
> When I see her,
> My heart bursts into flame,
> My body turns to charcoal,
> And tears of love spill from my eyes.
> She is my love,
> My light, and all my joy.

When the men heard this, they were dumbfounded. Then they made up their minds to follow him. And although Maimaiti knew their intentions, he didn't seem to mind.

He didn't even seem to mind when his "pretty girl" was discovered to be a fifty-year-old woman with a baggy goiter, a cataract, and a bent back. The men of the Black Gang laughed uproariously, calling him a liar, an idiot, and so on. But to their surprise, Maimaiti just smiled to himself and waited for the commotion to die down.

Then, with patient irony, he said, "You fine writers and poets—how can you write? Where is your imagination? We've been here for twenty dry months. I would think that anyone in a flowered blouse and red scarf would be beautiful to any of us."

This time no one laughed, except Maimaiti, who simply went on smiling and laughing to himself.

5. Why Didn't Minister Maimaiti Shut the Door When He Slept at Night?

In the barracks where the Black Gang slept, Maimaiti's bed was nearest the door, and this was how all the trouble began. At bedtime, whenever someone closed the door, Maimaiti would open it again. This led his colleagues to attempt to explain to him the complexities of class struggle. Society wasn't yet perfect, and so there might be thieves around. Even though all the prisoners were members of the Black Gang, most were nevertheless wearing wristwatches. Many had money and grain coupons in their pockets.

"You fail to understand logic," Maimaiti told them with his usual indifference. "Thieves, robbers, and all other sorts of bad men are, after all, human beings. Is this not true? We, on the other hand, have been told that we are not human beings but incarnations of Satan. If men do not fear Satan, should Satan be afraid of men?"

Unfortunately, this was overheard by a guard. He at once called Maimaiti in for questioning.

The guard: "You've been spreading poisonous dissension among the prisoners, haven't you?"

Maimaiti: "I wouldn't dare."

The guard: "You're angry because you've been classified as monsters. You're full of resentment."

Maimaiti: "Oh, no. I'm absolutely content."

The guard: "You're a reactionary."

Maimaiti: "I certainly am an incarnation of Satan."

The guard: "You've always been a reactionary."

Maimaiti: "Yes indeed. I've always been an incarnation of Satan."

The guard: "Why are you such a reactionary?"

Maimaiti (lowering his head): "I was influenced by Liu Shaoqi."

The guard (upon hearing the name Liu Shaoqi relaxes somewhat, thinking that Maimaiti's political consciousness has been raised at least a little. Adopting a softer tone, he continues): "Confess honestly. The Party is always lenient with those who confess their crimes. If you confess your crimes, you can be remolded, and the sooner you are remolded, the sooner you can return to the ranks of the people!"

Maimaiti: "I am determined to turn myself from an incarnation of Satan into a man, and as quickly as I can."

The guard: "Then think carefully about what you have done. Don't think that you can hide any of your crimes from us. And don't try confessing the minor ones to cover up the serious ones. Confess the grave ones now, and we'll be much easier on you."

Maimaiti (lowering his head and wringing his hands as if he were undergoing a convulsive ideological inner struggle): "There is a crime . . . but no, it's too horrible to talk about."

The guard (his eyes lighting up): "Out with it! Out with it! Whatever it is, if you confess now, I can assure you that we won't pull the pigtails of your crime, won't parade you in a high paper hat, and won't club you like a dog."

Maimaiti (meekly): "It was I who started the First World War. And I'm ashamed to say that's not all. I started the Second World War as well. And now—oh—it's too horrible—I'm feeling the impulse to start a third."

The guard (hopelessly confused): "Er???"

6. The Return of Minister Maimaiti

Nothing that Maimaiti said or did caused him to be set free. But after the downfall of the Gang of Four, it was determined that Maimaiti had been persecuted unjustly, so he was not only released from the cowshed but also restored to his former position as Minister of Literature and Arts for Xinjiang Province. Upon his release, one of the first things he did was to seek out his uncle Mu Ming and his cousin-in-law Mulajidi to find out how they had fared during the Cultural Revolution.

He was amazed to learn that they had not only survived but that, because of him, they had prospered. Mulajidi, the Political Commissar of the Struggle Brigade, told the story.

When they learned from the newspaper that Minister Maimaiti had been arrested, the Struggle Brigade immediately held a large-scale criticism meeting to denounce him. As political commissar, Mulajidi had a special role in criticism meetings. It was he who led the villagers in denouncing the Tripartite Village, the February Countercurrent, capitalist roaders such as Liu, Deng, Tao, Peng, Luo, Lu, Yang, Wang, Guan, and Qi. The method of denouncing was very simple. Ten minutes before it was time for work, Mulajidi would call all the villagers together and read them the names of those to be denounced. (Actually, who's who didn't matter.) Then the villagers all waved their arms above their heads, shouting "down with . . . ," inserting the names from the blacklist as they were read off to them. There was a slight problem, however, since in the Uygur language "down with" sounds very much like "long live" and the villagers sometimes became confused, shouting "down with" when they were supposed to be shouting "long live" and vice versa. Nevertheless, the villagers were used to covering each other, and no one was reported for this. At any rate, as a result of these criticism meetings, Mulajidi's and Mu Ming's positions were secure. In fact, Maimaiti was to provide an even greater benefit for them.

During the summer of 1967, a red flag contest was held to see which brigade could harvest the most grain. The Struggle Brigade lagged behind the Vigilance Brigade in both quality and quantity of the harvest. So, fearing they would lose, Mulajidi decided to shift the contest to political grounds. He asked the leader of the Vigilance Brigade, "Have you denounced Liu Shaoqi?"

"Of course."

"Have you criticized Wu Han?"

"Certainly."

"Have you criticized Minister Maimaiti?"

"Ah . . . Who? Mai . . . who?" The leader of the Vigilance Brigade was obviously at a loss.

Thus the Struggle Brigade won the contest and kept the red flag.

When he heard this story, Minister Maimaiti laughed till the tears streamed down his face. Patting his cousin-in-law on the back, he said, "I never dreamed that I would become a requirement for winning the red flag."

Time passed, and Maimaiti, as Minister of Literature and Arts, was required to read all the new exposé literature about the suffering of intellectuals during the Cultural Revolution. "So many comic possibilities have turned sour under their pens," he complained and then set about writing a novel of his own about the Cultural Revolution. When he had finished, he asked a friend who taught Chinese at the Institute for Minority Nationalities to translate it into Chinese for him. Then he requested a leave of absence from his post and, using his own money, traveled all the way to Beijing to hand the manuscript personally to the editor-in-chief at the Chinese People's Literature Press.

Out of special concern for a minority writer, particularly one who was a minister, the editor-in-chief quickly got to work on it. When he was through, however, he had to point out to Maimaiti that the structure was too loose and episodic and that the tone and depiction of character were too playful. Moreover, he added, the book was superficial and seemed cynical as well. For all these reasons, the book could not be published.

Minister Maimaiti argued with him about this.

"The book has to be published, even if what you've said is true, because if people read this book, they won't commit suicide during future political movements—if there are any."

The editor was deeply moved by this because he himself had more than once considered suicide during those troubled years. Finally he said that he would keep the manuscript and reconsider it.

But he murmured to himself, "For the prevention of suicide . . . can I really give this as a reason for publishing the book? What will the other editors say?"

It was at the Dashizi Muslim Restaurant, where I mentioned meeting Maimaiti at the beginning of this story, that he told me about his problems with his manuscript. In fact, he asked me to talk to the editor-in-chief about it on his behalf.

"If you need to give the editor a few gifts, I have plenty of raisins and butter here," he added.

"I think the problem is your manuscript," I replied, trying to look stern. "If it's good, all presses will compete to publish it. Giving gifts to our editors, what nonsense. It's a question of quality."

"Quality indeed," he replied. "But who is to judge exactly what quality is? I'm beginning to wonder if people recognized me as a writer only when they beat me up and if I became the requirement for winning the red flag contest only when I was locked in a cowshed." His voice was quiet but not without a tinge of loneliness.

His words seemed to add yet a few more gray hairs to his brother Saimaiti's head.

But just then, the waiter came with our delicious food—fried meat, steamed meat, spiced meatballs, and sweet and sour ribs. Minister Maimaiti opened a bottle of Ancient City wine, filled his cup, and, holding his glass high, gave the following toast to me and to all his readers.

Ah, life! You may not be always sweet,
But you are never only bitter.
You may seem to drown a man,
Yet you flow forward, wider and wider.
Sometimes you seem stagnant and waveless,
Yet you are constantly changing in a profusion of colors.
In your ice is always fire.
In your sorrow always joy.
Prisons, knives, whips—
How can they hold life back?
Threats, slanders, lies—
Can they pull joy up by its root?
Do not weep, for tears disgust a man.
What is tragedy? A game, too affected.
Let's burst out laughing,
The power of laughter is the power of life!
Able to laugh, able to live.
Dare to laugh, dare to live.
Love laughter, love life.

At this, Minister Maimaiti drained his cup to the bottom.

■ Chen Rong (Ch'en Jung) (1936–) (story)

TRANSLATED BY CHUN-YE SHIH

Chen Rong was born in Hankow, at the junction of the Han and Yangtze Rivers, a city now incorporated into the larger metropolitan area of Wuhan. After the revolution in 1949, she left school and after a brief time working in a book shop joined the staff of the *Southwest Workers Daily*. In 1954, she moved to Beijing and studied Russian, working at a radio station as a translator. In 1964, after a stint in the countryside in Shanxi province, she returned to Beijing and began her career as a playwright and fiction writer. Her long story "At Middle Age" was made into a film directed by

Wang Qimin that won China's Best Film Award. "Regarding the Problem of Newborn Piglets in Winter" is a biting and absurd portrait of the rigid hierarchies and stultifying bureaucracy of contemporary China.

FURTHER READING: Yang, Gladys, ed. *Seven Contemporary Chinese Women Writers*, 1982.

Regarding the Problem of Newborn Piglets in Winter

1. "H'mm, Have You Considered . . . ?"

"Silent is the night over the military harbor . . ." On the color television screen gleamed the graceful white figure of Su Xiaoming singing in her low soft voice.

"Grandma, turn it louder," the six-year-old Babe issued a command from the large soft couch she was sprawled on.

"Loud enough!" Grandma nevertheless walked over and turned the volume up slightly.

Babe suddenly jumped up and knelt on the couch. "Grandpa, can you hear?" she cried over the back of the couch.

"Don't yell. Grandpa's resting."

"Let our sailors sleep in peace . . ." the song went on.

So Grandpa slept on.

Zhang Dingfan was resting; his eyes closed, his gray hair pillowed against the sofa back and his arm limp on the armrest. After a day's hard work his wrecked nerves found repose in the lull of his own snoring.

Suddenly, a wind blew up outside and the door and the window rattled. The green velveteen curtain gave a stir.

Zhang Dingfan turned his head and uttered a sound barely audible, "H'mm."

Madam Zhang, wife of the Secretary, rose to her feet and walked over to the door and the window for a quick inspection. Both were tightly shut. Then she touched the heater; it was toasty warm. Everything seemed to be in order so she fetched a light wool blanket from the bedroom and walked toward the Secretary. Just as she was about to cover him with the blanket, Zhang Dingfan sat up with a jerk and stopped her. He turned his face toward the door and called, "Little You."

Madam Zhang, startled for a second, piped up in unison, "Mr. You, Mr. You."

In reply, a young man in his thirties came in from the anteroom.

"Get me Chief Jiao of Agriculture and Forestry."

Mr. You stepped lightly toward the table in the corner. He turned the lamp on and dialed the telephone. After he was connected to the right party, he raised the receiver, turned round and said, "Comrade Dingfan."

Zhang Dingfan rose slowly and walked toward the telephone. He seated himself in a chair before he took the receiver in his hand.

"It's me" he coughed. "Looks like it's getting colder. H'mm . . ."

Quickly Madam Zhang turned the volume of the television set to the lowest. Poor Su Xiaoming suddenly became mute, her red lips gaping and closing soundlessly.

"Grandma, I can't hear, I can't hear," Babe protested.

"Don't fuss, Grandpa is working."

Work is sacred; Babe stopped shouting.

"H'mm, have you considered—this sudden change in temperature and the problem of piglets in the winter—h'mm, we'd better do something. No, no, not by memorandum. First, notify every district in the county by telephone. Proceed level by level this very night. Don't let any piglet die from the cold. Then you may follow up by memorandum. Work on the draft right away."

He hung up the telephone, "These people, just like counters on an abacus—they only move when you give them a push. How can we ever achieve the Four Modernizations?"

"All right—it's all right now that you've alerted them," Madam Zhang comforted him.

"Grandma," Babe couldn't wait any longer.

The volume was once again adjusted. The singer had disappeared. With the tinkling of electronic music and a sudden pop, eight modernized angels in their white tight-fitting costumes emerged on the color screen, dancing and twisting their slender waists.

"No, no, I want Su Xiaoming," Babe demanded, rolling in the sofa and kicking her feet in the air.

Zhang Dingfan bent down to pat his granddaughter's head and said cheerfully, "Why not this? The melody of youth. Very nice."

2. "We'll Have Wonton Tonight."

Every light was burning in Chief Jiao's office, the Municipal Department of Agriculture and Forestry.

The young cadre had just finished a memorandum: "Regarding the Problem of Newborn Piglets in Winter" which he had been working on all evening. Now he was presenting it to the Chief for approval.

"No good, don't write this way." Chief Jiao quickly looked over the document and threw it on the desk. "Now, in writing a memorandum, you must avoid empty, boastful and irrelevant expressions."

He picked up the manuscript again and pointed at it, "Look here, 'After the winter solstice comes the Prelude of Cold,' who doesn't know that? And here, 'The development of a pig farm is a matter of great importance in promoting food production, supplies of meat to urban people, and reserve funds for the Four Modernizations of our country.' This is empty talk. Needless to say, more pigs means more money and more food. You have to use your brains to draft a memorandum."

The young cadre was totally lost—staring, wordless.

"Come here, sit down. Let's discuss this. A few concrete suggestions should make this memo more practical."

Burning the midnight oil was Chief Jiao's forté. He arose from his seat vigorously, while the young cadre sat down and opened his notebook.

"Regarding newborn piglets in winter—the first problem is to protect them from the cold. Isn't that right? The condition of winterization, in general, is not sufficient. Some pig farms are equipped with straw mats and curtains etc., but most are without even this minimum protection. Such conditions are contradictory to the objective of protecting newborn piglets. So the first and most important issue here is adequate winterization, and toward that end we must adopt every feasible and effective means." Chief Jiao rambled on, pacing the floor to and fro. He rolled his eyes and thought of more to say.

"The problem of piglets in the winter is mainly that of cold and hunger. Cold is an external cause, whereas hunger, an internal one—insufficient feeding will cause decline in body temperature, which in turn will cause decrease in resistance. Therefore, the second point is to keep the little piglets well fed. That's right. Be sure to include this point—increase the proportion of dietary nutrition in pigs' feed."

Chief Jiao made sure that the young cadre had jotted down what he had just said before he came to the third point:

"Furthermore, include the disease prevention. By the way, what is the most common disease that threatens pigs in the winter? As I remember we issued a special memo to that effect last time. You may repeat it here: how to prevent the premature death of newborn piglets."

Chief Jiao walked over to the file bureau, opened the door and gleefully produced a document, "Here is a good paragraph you may copy from: 'Report promptly any case of illness to the local Veterinary Disease Prevention Division. Meantime, take proper measures in treating the infected pig, in accordance with the rules and regulations currently in effect. In case of failure to report, a severe measure of action will be taken and the rule of accountability applies to all.' Add something to the effect that it is important to carry out the objective of prevention."

With an ache in his writing hand and a sense of relief in his heart, the young cadre peered at the Chief's thick babbling lips and could not help admiring him.

"The fourth point, emphasize the importance of political enlightenment. I need not provide you with the exact wording here. Also mention the material reward. You know that helps. Now, how many points do we have now? Four? H'mm . . ."

Chief Jiao stopped pacing the floor. The young cadre closed his notebook.

"Wait a minute. Last but not least: each level of the Party Committee should take the initiative by establishing the NEWBORN-PIGLETS-IN-THE-WINTER

LEADERSHIP GROUP. Designate an assistant secretary to be in charge. Each related department should share the work responsibility. United we fight the problem. Report and follow up at regular intervals, and so on."

The young cadre bent down his head and wrote swiftly. One could hear the sound of his ball-point pen scratching the paper.

Chief Jiao stretched himself and heaved a deep breath. He cracked open his thick lips in a self-satisfied smile, "That's fine, now just add a little effort on your part—a bit of polishing up will do."

He looked at his watch. Eleven o'clock. "Let's go," he said while locking the desk drawer. "Time for our midnight snack. We'll have wonton tonight."

3. "There'll Be Words Aplenty in a Memorial Service."

The cigarette butts piled up like a mound inside the ashtray. A ring of ashes scattered around it. The smoke, rising steadily from the tray, swirled around the room like a fog, dense and gray.

Ma Mingpeng, the Secretary of the County Committee, was leaning against the desk, holding a cigarette with his smoke-stained fingers. His small wearied eyes blinked in his dark and sullen face. Two little pouches hung under his eyes.

Since coming to the office early this morning, he had not stepped away except twice to go to the dining hall. The Committee meeting took up the whole morning, and the Study Group the afternoon. The evening was first occupied by the conference of Leadership Groups from the Security Promotion Committee, followed by the report of "No-Office Project" on the issues of disputes between a county chemical factory and a Production Group. Now sitting in front of him was an old cadre looking for a job. Every word the cadre uttered smashed like a nail on his numb and fatigued nerves.

"Secretary Ma, many years have gone by since the collapse of the Gang of Four. I am still wandering about like a desolate ghost, not a sign of work. Others have got their positions back. Why is it so hard in my case?"

"You're an old comrade, I'll be candid with you. We're having problems inside the Committee: more people than work. Every department is already staffed with seven or eight chiefs. People are talking: too many cooks but no broth. Where can I place you?"

"I need to work, even a doorman's job will do."

"That's what you think. Well, I know old comrades like you are dedicated to the Revolution, not your own interests. But what could I do? You were already a cadre before the Cultural Revolution. The authorities will have to place you in a proper position. Comrade, don't worry . . ."

"How can I help it? I'm reaching sixty."

The telephone rang. Ma Mingpeng picked up the receiver.

"What? Emergency notice from the City Committee—piglets in the winter. Erh . . . erh . . . well, very well." Ma Mingpeng rolled his eyes; procedures one after another turned up in his mind which he issued over the telephone as rapidly as an electronic computer, "First, telephone all the communes tonight and relate the message of the City Committee. Urge them to comply and adopt appropriate means. Second, as soon as you receive the memorandum from the City Committee, pass it on to the Regular Committee. Third, notify the Regular Committee to add one more agenda on Thursday's meeting—the problem of piglets in the winter. Fourth, request the people from the Cattle Office to draft a supplementary notice based on the ideas of the City Committee and present it for further discussion at the regular meeting. Fifth, ask the Cattle Office to send someone over to inspect and collect material for a further report. A report to the City Committee should be scheduled in a few days."

Putting the receiver down, Ma Mingpeng touched his temple with his smoke-stained fingers and closed his puffy eyelids.

"All these years, what am I? How could I justify myself to the people? Secretary Ma, just think one day I might drop dead and not even a memorial service in my honor . . ."

Ma Mingpeng opened his eyes and said with a half smile, "Rest assured Comrade, there'll be words aplenty in a memorial service."

4. "The Peasants, They Can't Live without a Son."

"It's getting late. I say, let's call it a day. I've made up my mind today not to waste any more electricity. Go to bed early."

In the Commune Conference Room the fire in the fireplace had been out for a long time. Light from the smoking pipes and hand-rolled cigarettes flickered now and then and made the room cozy and seemingly warmer. Shen Guigeng, the Secretary of the Commune, was conferring with the cadres from the Production Group and Political Group.

"How many working units did you say have joined the System of Contract and Accountability? The Production Group reported fifty-seven units, which I think is a blown-up figure. Nowadays the emphasis is on truthful reports. We don't need to pad the figure."

No one said anything. The Production Group Leader made a mark on his papers.

"The Safety Training Class for truck drivers will begin day after tomorrow. But the majority of units have not yet handed in the enrollment list. This calls for our immediate attention. Three people died from accidents in one month. It's a matter of life and death, not to be overlooked. Will you, Chief Yu, take charge of this matter? Send someone to check tomorrow. Those drivers know nothing about safety regulations and some don't even have a driver's license. They race down the street like mad men. If we don't do something, our commune will soon become notorious."

Secretary Shen rubbed his bloodshot eyes and changed the subject to a few "trivial matters" such as forthcoming visitors to the commune. He then turned to ask the committee members, "Is there anything you wish to say?"

The plump Big Sister Gu, a member from Planned Parenthood, asked, "What are we to do when we report to the County Committee about the enforced birthrate? The goal is set for an increase of eight out of one thousand, but ours is way over eighteen."

"That's no good. Planned parenthood should be enforced. One more is too much."

"I know, but we can't make them do it. Our people from Planned Parenthood and doctors from the Public Health, they all dread going to the country. People point at their backs and curse them for doing such wicked things. Young wives scamper at the very sight of our white uniforms. The other day some woman hid in the closet for half a day, nearly died of suffocation."

"You should enlighten the masses."

"Enlighten them! How do you enlighten them? You just go and try. The peasants will tell you—without a son who would paint the house for me in the spring, harvest the grain for me in the autumn? These days, with the new bonus system, more labor means more money. Where would you be without manpower? They don't care if you restrict their rations, they want their son."

Secretary Shen sighed, "Ai, quite so. The peasants, they can't live without a son."

"What do you suggest we should do?"

"What to do, that's up to you. Why should we have Planned Parenthood if you ask me?"

Secretary Shen stood up, which meant the meeting was over. The roomful of people stretched and yawned and shuffled their respective chairs and stools. One after another they got up. At this moment Little Wang, the cadre of the Commune Office, entered the room.

"Secretary Shen, emergency telephone call from the County."

"Wait. Don't leave yet." Secretary Shen took the message from the cadre and looked at it. Then he said to Little Wang, "Telephone every group right away. Make sure they don't let any piglets die. Notify all of them tonight. If there is no answer by phone, you'll have to run over there. Every notice must be sent out before dawn."

Little Wang left. The roomful of people looked at one another and wondered why on earth the problem of piglets should become such a crisis.

"The County Committee telephoned to convey the message from the City Committee that we must deal with this issue of piglets in winter," Secretary Shen said as he seated himself again in his chair. "We'll have to discuss this problem and consume more electricity tonight. Let's see, all of you from the Production Group stay behind."

5. "Those City Girls . . ."

The television program had already finished some time ago but a few youngsters still remained in the office. They were talking, eating watermelon seeds and teasing Grandpa Cao.

"Hi, you, lift your feet, stop throwing seeds on the floor, don't you see I'm sweeping behind you as fast as I can?"

Grandpa Cao, holding a big broom, was sweeping the floor which was strewn with cigarette butts, watermelon seeds and dust. Panting hard, he looked fierce, as though he was about to chase them out.

"Ya. This is our Group, not your home," a youngster answered back.

"What? As long as I'm paid for doing the job, I'm in charge here. Hey, move your butt over to the fireplace, will you?"

The youngster swaggered over to the fireplace and spat out a few more watermelon seeds, "What do you know? Grandpa Cao is in charge here. Looking after a fourteen-inch black and white television set so he can just sit and watch it all day long."

"I watch television!" Grandpa Cao scoffed and glared. "Pooh, what a disgrace. Nowadays, good-looking girls strip themselves half naked. That's the kind of fashion for you. I bet those city girls wear no pants. If I had a daughter who exposes herself like that, I'd break her neck."

The youngsters cracked up so hard that they almost fell over.

"What's so funny? None of you has a streak of decency left. You all want to follow the ways of those city slickers."

"You're right. If I get a job in the city, what I'll do first is buy myself a pair of bell-bottomed jeans and a pair of sandals. Then I'll wear my hair long and put on a pair of toad-like dark glasses. When I come to see you, Grandpa Cao, you won't even recognize me."

"You, I could recognize you even if you were burned to ashes! You good-for-nothing."

"Ah, you're as good as treasures from an excavation."

"What?" Grandpa Cao was shuffling the chairs around after the sweeping. The phrase "treasures from an excavation" sounded alien to his ears.

"He said you ought to keep company with the Emperors from the Ming Tombs," another youth explained, winking.

"I'm not that fortunate."

The roar of laughter nearly drowned out the ring of the telephone. Only the youth standing near the phone heard it. He picked up the receiver, "Yes, you want Old Cao? What do you have to say? Just tell me."

The other party refused.

"Tell you! You'd better step aside quick," Grandpa Cao smiled proudly. He rubbed his hands on his pants before he solemnly took the receiver, "Hello, the Commune, it's me. Are you Comrade Wang, still up? Ah, about piglets. Nothing wrong. We're expecting two litters—so I heard from the Guos. Any time now—what? Don't let any die from the cold. If there's any trouble, just ask for me—fine, good-bye."

Grandpa Cao replaced the telephone and looked at the young men in the room, "I say, who'll send a message to the Village Cadre?"

The young men grimaced and shrugged.

"Not me, I wouldn't dare. This is important business from the Commune Office. I can't be responsible."

"Whoever is paid should do the job."

"Then I'd better step aside."

Grandpa Cao glared at them, put on his old lamb wool tunic and left for the trip to the Village Cadre.

6. "For the Sake of the Extra Five Dollars . . ."

The wife of Xu Quan, the Village Cadre, was awakened by the pounding on the door. "What on earth is the matter? Scaring people like this in the middle of the night," she muttered.

Xu Quan was sitting in the chair with his quilted coat over his shoulders. He fished out his tobacco box from his pocket and rolled a cigarette. He slowly answered his wife. "A notice from the Commune: don't let any piglets die from the cold . . ."

"That's worrying for nothing. The pigs are contracted to the Guo family who are capable and clever people. Why should they let any pig die? You just come back to bed and get some sleep."

"No, I'll have to check the pigs," Xu Quan stretched an arm into the coat sleeve, "I heard this evening they're expecting piglets tonight. If anything should happen, I'll be the first one to blame."

"Look at yourself—so 'positive,' all for the sake of the extra five dollars a month. You think of it as something special, but not me," she suddenly sat up, pulling the quilt over her and becoming very agitated, "If you're really so 'positive,' try and earn more for your family. Look at our neighbor Old Du. After a couple of long trips and some secret deals, he's earned at least several thousand already and they're building a five-room brick house now."

"I won't do anything illegal."

"Is it illegal to contract the work of the rice field? Good for those who did. The price of rice is going up, plus the price for good production; one family can easily earn up to seven or eight hundred dollars. Only you, fool, hooked by the official title, have stuck with poverty. You can burn your eyes out with envy."

"It's a good thing for people to earn more. The policy nowadays is to let people prosper. What are you griping about?"

"I'm not unscrupulous. I'm only talking about you. If you were clever, you'd have put our name in at the time of signing the contract."

"Put my name in? How do I find the time? Half of my days are taken up by meetings. I'm only busy and concerned with the good of the public."

"Tut, tut, not that nonsense again. As a cadre for more than ten years, what have you done for your family? We're all in for misery with you. The good of the public indeed! You've got the whole village against you."

"You're envious. Why don't you work in the rice field yourself? Nobody's stopping you. You want to get rich by doing nothing but staying in bed. No such luck."

He pushed open the door and stepped over the threshold.

"Put on your dog-skin hat. If you get a cold, I've no money to buy medicine." A black furry object flew toward him and landed on the crook of his elbow.

He put the hat on his head and turned around, "Just leave me alone."

7. "I'll Make Up Words to Suit Whatever Tune the Authority Picks."

In the pig-farm lights were shining brightly. Xu Quan called once before he lifted the cotton curtain. A rush of warm air greeted him.

He held his hands together and looked around. Mammy Guo's second daughter was squatting in front of the fireplace, making a fire. Mammy Guo, in a blue apron and with sleeves rolled up high, was lifting the lid of a pot in which the rice broth was cooking.

"Newborn piglets?"

"Yes, a litter of twelve, every one alive." Mammy Guo wiped off the perspiration from her forehead with her elbow. She was all smiles. She replaced the lid and wiped her hands on the apron. She then led the cadre inside.

On the warm kang, twelve tiny piglets huddled together in a bundle of round, plump and quavering bodies. A little humming noise came out from the bundle.

"Our pig farm is doing well this time," Xu Quan complimented her cheerfully.

"The group trusts us to do the job and lets us contract the pig farm. Of course, we want to do our very best. We need all the help we can get so I sent for my father from the next village."

Xu Quan saw an old man in the far corner of the room, squatting in front of a broken table and drinking wine by himself.

"Come on, have a cup," Mammy Guo brought out a wine cup.

"Ha, have you moved here with the pigs?" Xu Quan, laughing, squatted down.

"I'm worried if I'm away. It's really more convenient staying right here with the pigs, especially early mornings and late at night."

"Let's drink. What a day." The old man lifted his cup.

With a lightened heart and prompted by the warm hospitality, Xu Quan lifted his cup and finished the wine in a few gulps. A current of heat came over him. Just think, twelve piglets—Mammy Guo really knows what she's doing. He asked her about her past farm experience and her suggestions for the future.

"I just feed them—that's all. I can't read a single word; don't ask me about my experience," Mammy Guo said, quite pleased with herself.

Yes, what could she say? I have to make up my own report. H'mm—"To carry out the System of Accountability—if every member in the Commune shares the responsibility, the cadre can be assured of success,"—pretty good—but one sentence is not enough—this wine is not bad, must be at least sixty-five per cent alcohol, better than the one I bought last time—Mammy Guo is quite a capable woman, how she mobilizes everybody, old and young, the eighty-year-old father and the school-aged daughter—isn't this an "experience"? "Enlist all help, regardless of age or sex, in our care for the piglets"—sounds nice, but wait, how stupid can I get? This jingle is from the late fifties, no longer popular now. "Mass mobilization means massive achievement"—no good, you don't see such slogans on newspapers anymore. I have to use new expressions, such as "United in heart and spirit, we strive for the Four Modernizations"—that's better—one hears it broadcast eight times a day—but what category of modernization does Mammy Guo's work fit in?—I'd better stop drinking. Tomorrow I have to report to my superior—but what shall I say about "experience"? Pooh—never mind, when the time comes, I'll make up words to suit whatever tune the authority picks.

■ Bei Dao (Pei Tao) (1949–) (poems)

Bei Dao is the pen name of Zhao Zhenkai. He was born in 1949, in Beijing, and was a construction worker for some years during the Cultural Revolution. In 1979, during the period of literary and social unrest known as the Peking Spring, he started the famous underground literary magazine *Jintian (Today)* and soon became the leading poet of the 1980s and the most famous representative of Misty poetry, a poetry affected by Western Modernism, Symbolism, and Surrealism that came in for fierce criticism by the defenders of the old school Socialist Realist poetry that Mao had championed and prescribed. With the new acceptance of Chinese Modernism and the thaw in official censorship that came in the middle 1980s, he gained mainstream acceptance, editing an official magazine and becoming a member of the Chinese Writers' Association. During the summer 1989 Democracy Movement, he was overseas at a writer's conference and elected to remain in exile from China. His work has been widely translated and anthologized, and four collections of his poetry, *The August Sleepwalker* (1990), *Old Snow* (1991), *Forms of Distance* (1995), and *Landscape over Zero* (1996) are available from New Directions Press. His fiction collection is titled *Waves* (1986). He is currently living in California and teaching at the University of California, Irvine.

FURTHER READING: Barnstone, Tony, ed. *Out of the Howling Storm: The New Chinese Poetry,* 1993. Finkel, Donald, ed. *A Splintered Mirror: Chinese Poetry from the Democracy Movement,* 1991. Soong, Stephen C., and John Minford, eds. *Trees on the Mountain: An Anthology of New Chinese Writing,* 1984.

Sweet Tangerines

Sweet tangerines
flooded with sun sweet tangerines

let me move through your hearts
bearing burdens of love

sweet tangerines   5
rinds breaking with delicate rains

let me move through your hearts
worries turned to tears of relief

sweet tangerines
bitter nets keep each fleshy piece   10

let me move through your hearts
as I wander in the wreckage of dreams

sweet tangerines
flooded with sun sweet tangerines

TRANSLATED BY JAMES A. WILSON

Coming Home at Night

After braving the music of the air raid alarm
I hang my shadow on the hat-stand
take off the dog's eyes
(which I use for escape)
remove my false teeth (these final words)   5
and close my astute and experienced pocket watch
(that garrisoned heart)

The hours fall in the water one after the other
in my dreams like depth bombs
they explode   10

TRANSLATED BY BONNIE MCDOUGALL AND CHEN MAIPING

Night: Theme and Variations

Here is where the roads converge:
parallel light beams
like a long conversation suddenly broken,
the air stuffed with truck drivers' pungent smoke
and rude indistinct curses,   5
people in a line replaced with fences
Light leaking from a cracked door
is flicked to the roadside with cigarette butts
and trampled by quick feet
A billboard leans on an old man's lost stick,   10
about to walk away
A stone waterlily withered
in the fountain pool, a building deliberates collapse,
the rising moon suddenly strikes
a bell again and again   15
and the past reverberates within palace walls
Now the sundial turns and calibrates deviations,
waiting for the emperor's grand morning ceremony
Brocade dresses and ribbons toss up in the breeze
and brush away the dust on the stone steps   20
A shadow of a tramp slinks past the wall,
colorful neon lights glow for him
and all night keep him from sleep
A stray cat leaps onto a bench
to inspect the water's trembling mist of light   25
But a mercury lamp rudely opens window curtains
to peer at the privacy of others
disturbing lonely people and their dreams
Behind a small door
a hand quietly draws the catch   30
as if pulling a gun bolt

TRANSLATED BY TONY BARNSTONE AND NEWTON LIU

Beyond

A tempest in a teacup leads the marching sea.
Beyond the harbor, adrift on their sleepless bed,
the coupling levers make fast the chains of power.
Beyond the frame, a plaster figure wearing a classical smile
speaks from the manifold shadows of one day.   5
Beyond credulity, a race horse outruns death.

Implacably, the moon imprints its seal upon black happenings.
Beyond the story, a plastic tree is thrashing in the wind.
This dismal fare is our excuse for survival.

TRANSLATED BY DONALD FINKEL AND XUELIANG CHEN

■ Shu Ting (Shu T'ing) (1952–) (poem)

TRANSLATED BY CHOU PING

Shu Ting is the pen name of Gong Peiyu. Associated with the Misty school of poets, she was the leading woman poet in China in the 1980s. A southeast Fujian native, she was sent to the countryside during the Cultural Revolution before she graduated from junior high school. Then she worked in a cement factory and later a textile mill. In 1979, Shu published her first poem and in 1983 was asked to be a professional writer by the Chinese Writers' Association, Fujian Branch, of which she now is the deputy chairperson. Her collections of poetry include *Brigantines* (1982) and *Selected Lyrics of Shu Ting and Gu Cheng* (1985). She won the National Poetry Award in 1981 and 1983. Her work is deeply romantic in nature and must be understood as a reaction to the repression of romance in literature, film, song, and theatre during the decade-long Great Proletarian Cultural Revolution (1966–1976). Shu's tender, romantic poems sometimes do not play as well in English translation since modern and postmodern sensibilities have outmoded such sentiment, but her poems have a crystalline, lyrical strength that saves her from being saccharine and has made her the best-known contemporary Chinese woman poet in the West.

FURTHER READING: Barnstone, Tony, ed. *Out of the Howling Storm: The New Chinese Poetry*, 1993. Finkel, Donald, ed. *A Splintered Mirror: Chinese Poetry from the Democracy Movement*, 1991. Kizer, Carolyn. *Carrying Over: Poems from the Chinese, Urdu, Macedonian, Yiddish and French African*, 1988. Lin, Julia C. *Women of the Reed Plain: An Anthology of Contemporary Chinese Women's Poetry*, 1992. Soong, Stephen C., and John Minford, eds. *Trees on the Mountain: An Anthology of New Chinese Writing*, 1984. Yeh, Michelle, ed. *Anthology of Modern Chinese Poetry*, 1992.

Two or Three Incidents Recollected

A cup of wine overturned.
A stone path sails in moonlight.
Where the blue grass is flattened,
is an abandoned azalea.

The eucalyptus trees are swirling
and stars above teem into a kaleidoscope.

5

The rusty eyes of an anchor
mirror the dizzy sky.

Holding up a book to shade the candle
and with a finger in between the lips,   *10*
I sit in an eggshell quiet,
having a semi-transparent dream.

■ Liang Heng (1954–) and Judith Shapiro (1953–) (memoir, written in English)

Since the 1949 Communist Revolution, China has swung back and forth between periods of relative expression and repression. *Son of the Revolution* is a memoir that fits into the category of "Scar Literature," or literature recording the widespread repression of the decade-long Great Proletarian Cultural Revolution of 1966 to 1976. This literature poured out in the period after the death of Mao Zedong and the fall of the Gang of Four. Liang Heng's mother was a victim of the 1957 Anti-Rightist Campaign, a period of extreme repression that followed upon a brief welcoming of dissent during the 1956 Hundred Flowers campaign. In 1966, after years in which more moderate leaders had been gaining power, Chairman Mao launched another period of cultural struggle—the Cultural Revolution—as a ploy to regain his eroding power. During this period, China fell victim to roving Red Brigade youth bands who took the struggle against lingering remnants of the feudal past into their own hands, resorting often to torture, murder, ideological indoctrination, and even, according to a recent report, cannibalism. In Liang Heng's terrific memoir, written with his wife Judith Shapiro, he recounts how the pressures of this anarchistic period turned families against themselves, as the children are forced to criticize their father, and as Liang Heng himself is driven to the brink of suicide on trumped up charges. Liang Heng was born in Changsha in 1954 and graduated from Hunan Teachers College in 1981. After marrying Judith Shapiro, who taught American literature at the Teachers College, he came to the United States and earned a master's degree from Columbia University. *Son of the Revolution* was published by Vintage Books in 1984.

from *Son of the Revolution*

from *Chapter Five: The Smashed Temples*

While the criticism movement was getting started, college and middle-school students were forming the first Red Guard units. They were relatively conservative, protecting most of the Party leaders if only because those leaders were also the Red Guards' fathers and mothers. Fiercely proud of their "good" backgrounds—so much so that they would allow only students descended from the "Five Red Types" (Revolutionary cadres, Revolutionary martyrs, Revolutionary soldiers, workers, and poor and lower-middle peasants) to join them—these first Red Guards focused their attack on the so-called Five Black Types: landlords, rich peasants, counter-revolutionaries, "bad elements," and Rightists. Their slogan was, "If the father is a hero, the son is a brave man; if the father is a reactionary, the son is a bastard," thus settling the question of class standing for all eternity. The irony of the situation was that these sons and daughters of high-ranking cadres were creating a movement that would soon double back to attack their parents; they themselves would become the victims of their own Revolutionary fervor.

In Changsha, the initial group was called the "Red Defense Guards," and by an incredible fluke Liang Fang managed to become a member. Because there were so many cadres' children at the No. 1 Middle School, that school was among the first to become organized, and because Liang Fang took part in the organizing work, the issue of her Rightist parent was temporarily overlooked. She had finally achieved her long-coveted Revolutionary glory. She must have renounced our mother with extraordinary enthusiasm in order to pass muster.

Liang Fang rarely came home, of course. We got most of our news of her through Liang Wei-ping, who moved about a good deal and saw her through school activities. One day Liang Wei-ping returned in a state of great excitement. Liang Fang had told her that the Party Secretary of the No. 1 Middle School had denounced himself for betraying the Communists to the KMT before Liberation, and then had hanged himself in the cellar where he was being kept a prisoner. A real class enemy exposed! The other news was that a lot of students were preparing to go to Peking to report to Mao's wife, Jiang Qing, and the other members of the Cultural Revolution Directorate. There was an off-chance that they might be able to see Chairman Mao himself.

The August 18 *Hunan Daily* was a red-ink issue. It told of thousands of Red Guards gathering in Tian An Men Square, and Chairman Mao making an appearance and allowing a student to pin the Red Guard armband on his sleeve. Great numbers of middle-school and college students had been permitted to mount the tower and shake hands with him, and it was plain that a broad new movement had been launched.

We felt the first echoes in Changsha soon after. The representatives of the first Peking Red Guard group, the "United Action Committee," arrived from the capital bringing with them a first taste of the violence that would spread throughout China. They were staying at the luxurious government hotel near the Martyrs' Park when they got into a fight with one of the hotel workers, a boy whose grandfather had been a landlord before Liberation. I don't know the details of the argument but they nearly beat him to death with their wide leather belts.

What amazed me was the reaction of the Party Committees to this episode. There was a glass propaganda case by the front gate of the newspaper, which usually held exhibits on factory production, "little friends" dancing in nursery school, or instructive displays on the life of the model soldier Lei Feng. Now appeared photographs of the violence, hailed as "Revolutionary heroism." Changsha wasn't the first practice ground for this new breed of terrorism, of course, but the incident was the first most of us had heard of. Later, such events would become all too familiar.

After their visit, the local movement spread beyond the "Red Defense Guards," although membership was still restricted to the "Five Red Types." The groups usually chose their names from some poem or quotation from Chairman Mao, so we had the "Jinggang Mountain" group, the "East Is Red" group, the "Chase the Exhausted Enemy" group, the "Struggle with the Waves in the Middle of the Current" group, and many more. We got used to seeing the Red Guard costume—People's Liberation Army green pants and jacket, a wide leather belt, and the prized bright red armband. Liang Wei-ping wanted to join, but because of our mother she was told she could only work at school, which had been converted into a Red Guard hospitality station, a kind of inn for Red Guards from other provinces. She was crushed, but glad to be allowed to help at all. They kept her very busy boiling water and pushing desks around to make beds for all the guests.

The "Sixteen Articles" had stressed the need to criticize the "Four Olds"—old thought, old customs, old culture, and old morals—and this was the thrust of the Red Guards' first campaign. The immediate and most visible result was that the names of everything familiar changed overnight. Suddenly "Heaven and Heart Park" became "People's Park." "Cai E Road," named for a hero of the Revolution of 1911, became "Red Guard Road." The Northern Station where I had pushed carts for a day was now to be found on "Combat Revisionism Street," and a shop named after its pre-Liberation Capitalist proprietor became "The East Is Red Food Store." Changsha quickly acquired a "Red Guard Theater," a "Shaoshan Road," a "People's Road," and an "Oppose Imperialism Road."

All this was extremely confusing, especially for the old people, and everybody was always getting off at the wrong bus stop and getting lost. To make matters even worse, the ticket-sellers on the buses were too busy giving instructive readings from the Quotations of Chairman Mao between stops to have much time to help straighten out the mess. Of course, there were some people who never did get used to it, and to this day they live on the ghosts of streets whose names today's young people have never heard of. (Ten years later an old man asked me where Education Road was, but I had no idea there was such a street. Then he asked a nearby policeman, but he didn't know either. More and more people got involved, forming a circle around him and telling him that he was mistaken, that there was no such street. Finally he protested, "How could I be wrong? Changsha already had that street by the thirty-seventh year of the Republic of China!" Everybody burst out laughing; he was using the obsolete pre-Liberation system of counting years dating from the 1911 Revolution.)

People changed their own names, too. One of my classmates rejected his old name, Wen Jian-ping ("Wen Establish Peace"), in favor of Wen Zao-fan ("Wen Rebel"). My neighbor Li Lin ("Li Forest") called herself Li Zi-hong ("Li Red from Birth") to advertise her good background. Zao Cai-fa ("Zao Make Money") became Zao Wei-dong ("Zao Protect the East"). Another friend got rid of the "Chiang" in his name because it was the same as Chiang Kai-shek's.

So, there was a lot of excitement in the city, but at home it was very quiet. Father spent every evening at his writing, and Liang Wei-ping and I never felt much like talking. We were sitting silently like this, reading and writing, on the hot night that Liang Fang came home. I hadn't seen her in more than three weeks. She was a changed person.

She looked splendid, never better, strong and slim where her leather belt cinched in her waist. Her green army-style uniform with its cap of authority over her short braids gave her an air of fashion and confidence I had never seen in her before. She looked a real soldier, and I sat up straight and stared with big eyes, unsure whether or not she was really my sister. My desire for my own Red Guard uniform dated from that instant.

Father emerged when he heard voices and looked glad to see Liang Fang. "How have things been going?" he asked. "We haven't seen you in a long time."

"The situation is excellent," she answered in the language of Revolution. "We're washing away all the dirty water. But I never sleep. Every night we're out making search raids."

"What's a search raid?" I asked.

"You know, before you've been on a search raid you have no idea what's really going on in this society. People have been hiding all sorts of things. Counterrevolutionary materials, pre-Liberation Reactionary artworks, gold, jade, silver, jewelry—the trappings of Feudalism-Capitalism-Revisionism are everywhere."

My father looked surprised. "What do you care about those kinds of things?"

But Liang Fang was too involved in her story to answer. "We have a schedule to follow. Every night we go to a series of homes and go through every book, every page to see if there's any anti-Party material. It's an incredible amount of work. We have to check all the boxes and suitcases for false bottoms and sometimes pull up the floors to see if anything's been hidden underneath."

Liang Wei-ping brought her a basin of hot water and a towel to clean her face, and when she stood up to wash, her eye fell on a traditional painting of a horse by Xu Bei-hong. "What are you doing with *that?* Xu Bei-hong was denounced ages ago. You people are too careless." She went over to take it down, but Father's voice stopped her.

"What's wrong with it? That has nothing to do with any Capitalist-Revisionist line. Leave it be."

She said, "But you don't know what's been happening. It's not just a question of paintings, but of all the old things. Where do you think I've been all day? I was up on Yuelu Mountain with the Hunan University students trying to get rid of those old monuments and pavilions. And it wasn't an easy job, either. Half the stuff's made of stone. We had to use knives and axes to dig out the inscriptions. Stinking poetry of the Feudal Society! But it's all gone now, or boarded shut."

"Can we still go play there?" I asked.

"Well . . . ," she hesitated. "Maybe for now you'd better not; people might think you were there for the wrong reasons."

Father had found his voice. "How could you destroy the old poetry carved in the temples and pavilions? What kind of behavior is that?"

"What kind of behavior? Revolutionary action, that's what. The Hengyang District Red Guards have already destroyed all the temples on the Southern Peak of Heng Mountain. So much for the 'sacred mountain'!"

When I heard the words "Southern Peak" I remembered that Waipo had told me how people went to burn incense, setting out from their doorsteps and kneeling every few paces all the way to the mountaintop. If Waipo knew the temples were gone, what would she do? Who would light incense for her now?

"Who asked you to do those things?" Father demanded.

"Father," she answered with exaggerated patience. "You really don't understand the Cultural Revolution at all, do you? We have to get rid of the Four Olds. That includes everything old. Don't you even read your own newspaper? You'd better keep up with things or you'll be in trouble."

Father protested, "It's one thing to get rid of old customs and ideas, and another to go around smashing ancient temples."

"What good are they? They just trick people, make them superstitious. They're a bad influence on the young people."

"Who ever influenced you?" Father demanded. "No one in your whole life ever asked you to believe in any Buddhas."

Liang Fang didn't have an answer, which irritated her. "Well, anyway, they're all old things. Why aren't there Revolutionary poems, Chairman Mao's poems, statues of people's heroes, workers, peasants, and soldiers?"

Father despaired. "It's all over! China's old culture is being destroyed." He hit the table with his finger for emphasis. "Such precious historical treasures. All those symbols of China's ancient culture gone in only a few days. You've wronged your ancestors."

Liang Fang lost her temper. "No wonder people criticize you. You just keep following the Revisionist line and refuse to change, don't you?"

Father said angrily, "All right! I don't care, then. But I forbid you to touch that picture."

The quarrel ended on that note, as Father went into his inner room and closed the door. I couldn't figure out who was right, but I knew that Chairman Mao supported the Red Guards. So I said to Liang Fang, "Forget it, why don't you? It's hard for him to give up his ideas. Why don't we talk about something more pleasant?"

But Liang Fang was angry and didn't want to talk.

"I just came home to get a good night's sleep, anyway," she said. "What a family." She walked over, lay down on the larger bed, and was asleep almost immediately.

Chapter Six: Traveling Struggle

The search raids soon spread to the newspaper. It was a terrifying time, because every night we heard the sounds of loud knocks, things breaking, and children crying. Like every family with a member attacked in the posters, we knew the Red Guards would eventually come to our house, and we were constantly on edge. During the day we went to see the exhibits of confiscated goods; at night we lay dressed, sleeplessly waiting for our turn.

At eleven one night the knocks finally came, loud, sharp, and impatient. We sat up in bed automatically. Father emerged from the inside room and turned on the light. He motioned with his head for Liang Wei-ping to get the door.

There were seven or eight of them, all men or boys, and the small room seemed very crowded. Despite the heat they were all wearing white cloths over their mouths and noses, and dark clothes. The one who seemed to be the leader carried a long metal spring with a rubber tip. He struck it against the table top with a loud crack.

"Liang Shan!" he said. "Is there anything Feudalist-Capitalist-Revisionist in your house?"

Father stammered, "No, no. I had pictures of Liu Shao-qi but I turned them in to the Work Team. Nothing else."

"Father!" The man sliced at the table again.

Liang Wei-ping started to cry.

"What are you blubbering about? Cut it out. You and the boy, get over there in the corner."

We cowered there, trying to keep our sobs silent.

"What you must understand is that this is a Revolutionary action," the man announced. "Right?"

"Yes, yes, a Revolutionary action." I had never seen my father plead with anyone before. I had never seen him without his dignity.

"You welcome it, don't you! Say it!"

Something stuck in my father's throat.

"Shit. You've always been a liar!" Two Red Guards took him by each arm and grabbed his head, pushing it down so he was forced to kneel on the floor. They shook him by the hair so his glasses fell off, and when he groped for them they kicked his hands away. "Liar!"

The others were already starting to go through our things, some going into the other rooms for the books, others to the boxes. For several minutes there was silence except for the rustling of paper and the opening of boxes and drawers. Then one of them cried out.

"Quite a fox, isn't he? We said he was a liar!" The Red Guard had two Western ties and a Western-style jacket. "What's the meaning of this?"

"Ties," my father mumbled.

They kicked him. "Ties! Do you think we're children? Everyone knows these are ties. Capitalist ties. Or hadn't you heard?"

Father was pointing excitedly. "They were ordered through the newspaper. For some jobs. It wasn't my idea. For receptions and—" The spring slammed down on his hand and he cringed in pain.

"Who told you to point your finger? Think you can order people around still, don't you? Stinking intellectual!"

Liang Wei-ping cried, "How can you go hitting people that way? He can't even see properly."

"Shut up, little crossbreed, or we'll be hitting you next," snapped the Red Guard standing by the bureau. "Look at this! Fancy pants and sleeves with three buttons!"

From the other room came two Red Guards with armfuls of books. They dumped them unceremoniously on the floor near where Father was kneeling and went back for more. Tang poetry fell on top of histories, foreign novels on the Chinese Classics. Our house had always looked very neat and spare; I had never realized we had so many books.

After an hour they had finished going through everything. My comic books of the Classics had been added to the pile; the Xu Bei-hong horse had been crumpled and tossed on top. Everything we owned was in disorder on the floor, and even our pillows had been slit open with a knife. Father had been on his knees for a long time, and was trembling all over. The Red Guards were stuffing things into a large cloth bag when one of them got an idea for another game.

He put our large metal washbasin on the floor and built a little mound in it out of some of the finest books. He lit a match underneath and fanned it until the whole thing was aflame. Then he fed the fire, ripping the books in two one at a time and tossing them on. Father turned his head away. He didn't need his glasses to know what was on the pyre.

"What's the matter, Liang Shan? Light hurt your eyes?" The leading Red Guard held the metal spring out in front of him like a snake. "'A Revolutionary action.' Say it. 'It's a good fire.'"

Father was silent. I prayed he would speak.

"You shitting liar. Say it!" The man grabbed Father by the hair and twisted his head to make him look at the flames. "'It's a good fire!'"

My father's face looked very naked without his glasses, and the light from the fire shone on it and glistened in the tear lines on his cheeks. I could hardly hear him.

"A Revolutionary action," he whispered. "It's a good fire!"

They let him go; it was over. They shouldered the bag and filed out, the last putting our transistor radio into his pocket as he passed the table. We three couldn't find a word of comfort for each other; we just put things back in order in silence. The next day we discovered they had also helped themselves to Father's salary for that month.

The feeling of terror remained in our hearts for many days without fading. Then one evening when we were eating dinner, Liang Fang came home again. Somehow I didn't feel as glad to see her as usual.

Liang Wei-ping seemed to feel the same way. "Oh, you're back," she said, and continued eating. Maybe it was that Liang Fang was participating in the things that had hurt us so much. She must have sensed something, for she just got herself a bowl and sat down with us.

Then she noticed that the house was not the same. "What's wrong?" she demanded. "Has there been a search raid here or something?"

"There certainly has," Liang Wei-ping said. In great anger she told her what had happened that night, emphasizing the way the Red Guards had treated Father.

Finally Father interrupted coldly, "What's the point of talking about it? It's all 'Revolutionary action.'"

Father's sarcasm stung Liang Fang and she said defensively, "Father, I swear I would never do that type of thing. Whenever any of the boys in our group hit anyone, we girls always criticize them afterwards. And I would never take advantage of a search raid to fatten my own purse."

Even though she must have been terribly angry at Father because of the posters about him, it seemed she needed his understanding. And in spite of how hurt he had been, he still felt concerned for his daughter. "How have things been going lately?" he asked finally. "I'm always worried about you."

"Since the end of August there have been two Red Guard factions, and I'm in the real Rebel group now," she answered. "I quit the Red Defense Guards because they refused to attack the real seats of power, the Party leaders, and just wanted to denounce intellectuals. Also, they were getting more and more elitist. Finally the snobs asked everyone to get proof from their units that they had good backgrounds. So one day I came here to the newspaper . . . ," she paused and looked awkwardly at Father, embarrassed at not having stopped by the house. "At first the people in the office wouldn't give me anything because they said there was no precedent, and then I finally persuaded them. Well, it turned out that they wrote about Mother being a Rightist. I ended up throwing the paper into the outhouse, and I had to quit the group.

"But now I'm very happy, because there are even more people in our new Rebel group. Now I'm on my way to a cotton mill to drive out people with Conservative 'Protect the Emperor' viewpoints. We're going to organize the workers to seize power from the leadership. There'll be people going to all the units. I've heard it'll be mostly students from Hunan Teachers College coming here to the newspaper."

Father interrupted. "But which faction is right? It would be terrible if it turned out you were on the wrong side."

She laughed. "The Cultural Revolution Directorate in Peking supports us. The Conservative Red Guards are done for and some of their leaders are being arrested. They were wrong to try to make Revolution into a private club. Madame Jiang Qing criticized them for their elitism ages ago. The issue is the Party leaders themselves now. No one is immune anymore." She paused and picked up her bowl and started shoveling food in with her chopsticks.

When the meal was over, Father asked her whether she needed anything. "I don't need money," she answered. "I get eight *jiao* a day, plus four *liang* [one *liang* equals fifty grams] worth of rice coupons. All the Rebel groups get stipends now." She hesitated. "But I could really use a mosquito net."

This wasn't such a simple request. There were three beds, my father's in one room, one for me, and one for my sisters in the other. Each bed had a net, but this was no ordinary luxury. To get one you not only needed 40 *yuan*, nearly a month's salary, and scarce cotton coupons, but also a special mosquito net coupon. Father got the coupon for the new net on his bed only because of his marriage. But he was very generous. "Take mine," he said. "I'll use mosquito incense."

Liang Fang refused at first. "How can I take yours? I thought Liang Heng could sleep with you and I could take his."

"Take it, take it. If the Revolution needs it, I'll give it up gladly." This was the first joke Father had made in months. We all laughed together.

But after Liang Fang had left, he seemed worried again. This Cultural Revolution was getting more complicated. It was hard to keep track of who was right and who wrong. "One day you're black and then you're red and then you're black again," he said. "Children, whatever you do please remember to be careful what you say. Never give your opinion on anything, even if you're asked directly. Just believe Chairman Mao's words, they're the only thing that seems to be reliable anymore."

I remembered his words for many years. They were another lesson in self-protection in modern society. And events showed that a lot of other people had learned the same lessons as I.

The next day, students from the colleges on the West Bank of the Xiang River gathered in front of the *Hunan Daily* gateway. They had come to organize the Rebel group. Young reporters and workers from the printing and repair shops put up posters welcoming them, and the students lined up in formation, waving copies of the *Quotations of Chairman Mao* and shouting, "Learn from the *Hunan Daily's* Rebel group!" Then they marched in to the sounds of drums, red armbands reading "Chase the Exhausted Enemy" on every sleeve. All the old newspapermen left their desks, and it would be a full ten years before most of them returned. My father was among them. That day marked the end of his newspaper career.

But as Liang Fang had predicted, the arrival of the student Rebels coincided with a change in the focus of the attack, away from intellectuals like my father and toward the Party powerholders. Our old primary school was turned into a makeshift prison for about ten of the top political leaders, while their families were moved to a broken-down building near the newspaper compound's wall. Once I went to Gang Di's home and could hardly believe how the eight of them were living crammed into one tiny room. His mother and sister slept on a bed, but everyone else was sleeping on benches and chairs pushed together. And all thirteen-odd families shared one kitchen with a huge hole in its crumbling wall.

The family meetings held by the Work Team yielded to criticism meetings with attendance obligatory. There were all kinds, every day, big and small, but the one that made the deepest impression on me was the sort called "traveling struggle." It was a lot like the way the People's Liberation Army had dealt with the landlords after Liberation (I'd seen that in movies), but even more cruel.

The loudspeaker called us all outside, and in a few minutes I saw it coming. A group of Rebels were in the lead shouting "Down with the Capitalist Roaders" and "Long Live Chairman Mao Thought." Following them were about ten of the old "leading comrades" tied together on a long rope like beads on a string, their hands bound. They were wearing tall square-topped paper hats inscribed with phrases like I AM A BASTARD or I AM A FOOL, and around their necks were wooden signs with their names and crimes like FU KAI-XUN, CAPITALIST ROADER POWER USURPER or MENG SHU-DE, FILIAL GRANDSON OF THE LANDLORD CLASS. Those on the Editorial Committee had milder labels, such as DEVOTED ASSISTANT TO THE CAPITALIST ROADERS. Behind them, unbound, walked my father and some of the other intellectuals; they were less important, so their placards were light and made of paper, and they wore no hats. Still, they saddened me. They walked with their heads bowed low, carrying brass gongs, which they beat in time to the chanted slogans. As Father passed our doorway he bowed his head down even lower; he must have known I was watching him.

The Team walked very slowly, picking up more people with each building it passed. I followed at a distance, not wanting Father to see me, and I was astonished to hear a few low voices speaking in a very different spirit from that of the slogan shouters in front.

"Those placards must be terribly heavy," a woman's voice said.

"Some of those Rebels aren't such models of purity themselves," a man muttered. "Someone ought to investigate *their* backgrounds." The words comforted me even though I didn't know who had said them. Probably a family member like myself.

In a crowd, we passed the dining hall, the basketball court, the clinic, and all the dormitories, and went back past the primary school, finally reaching the auditorium on the fourth floor of the modern office building where we had had our Family Member meetings. There was a huge picture of Chairman Mao on the wall directly behind the platform, and the words BIG CRITICISM MEETING were written in huge characters on a hanging banner. On the side walls were more banners, with quotations from Chairman Mao and Rebel slogans. The Capitalist Roaders were already kneeling on the platform, their hands tied behind their backs with long ropes; the intellectuals "assisting" at the meeting were standing on each side with their heads bowed, facing inwards. Father was on the right toward the back, so I chose a seat on the far right beyond his line of vision.

First came a test for the intellectuals. Each in turn was ordered to recite one of the "Three Essays" by Chairman Mao, either "On Serving the People," "In Memory of Norman Bethune," or "The Foolish Old Man Who Moved the Mountain." If anyone made a mistake, he would have to kneel in apology before the picture of Chairman Mao until the end of the meeting. The test applied to the intellectuals alone; as a Rebel leader declared, "Capitalist Roaders don't have the right to recite the works of Chairman Mao."

Several people had their heads on the floor in humiliation when it came Father's turn, and my heart was in my mouth. They ordered him to recite "On Serving the People," and when he had said only two sentences, he abruptly stopped. I was nearly in tears. Suddenly all around me, I heard the next line whispered, as if people were reciting along with him, prompting him. Father adjusted his glasses for a moment. Then, in a strong clear voice, he recited the whole thing without stopping, supported by what I knew was his confident love for Chairman Mao.

When the Capitalist Roaders' turn came, they had to recite the big character posters attacking them. The meeting went on and on, and whenever someone stumbled there were cries of "Give him an airplane ride, give him an airplane ride!" At this the Rebels tossed the rope binding the man's arms behind him over a pipe at the top of the auditorium and hoisted him up in the air, letting him squirm in agony like a dragonfly with pinched wings.

Some of the family members couldn't bear it and left the auditorium in tears. Gang Di's older sister ran out with a loud sob, pulling Gang Di behind her, when their father was hauled aloft. It wasn't my father who was being tortured, but I couldn't bear it either, and followed them out. Luckily no one noticed, and we got away.

I had hardly reached home when Liang Wei-ping came in, panting for breath. I didn't want to talk, but she insisted on telling me about a big demonstration she'd seen on May First Road. Fifty or sixty open trucks had passed on their way to the execution ground in the eastern suburbs. "The woman who was going to be shot was in the first truck, standing there tied up with a handkerchief stuffed into her mouth and a huge bamboo sign on her back, which reached way over her head," my sister said, pacing excitedly. "There was a big red X on it, and below it said she was a KMT spy about to be executed! And on each side of her there were two Red Guards holding her by the back of the neck and pushing her head down." The same truck carried Reactionaries who had already confessed—some wore heavy iron placards that made them bend under the weight; others, less serious offenders, had wooden ones. And they all had gongs and were shouting things like "I am a counterrevolutionary, I am wrong" or "Thank you, Chairman Mao, for not making me die."

I couldn't bear to listen. It made me miserable. But she rattled on. "My classmates said they were probably all teachers, movie actors, old cadres, writers, and people like that. There were Rebels with bayonets in all the trucks. I never saw so many Red Guards before." Liang Wei-ping hadn't noticed that Father had come slowly up the stairs and was standing quietly in the doorway, listening. "Everybody was shouting slogans and the children were throwing rocks and sticks. One of them hit the KMT spy right in the head."

"Stop it," I finally broke in. "Don't talk about it anymore. Can't you see that Father's tired?"

Liang Wei-ping turned in embarrassed surprise and said, "Father, I didn't know you were home. I'll get some hot water for you."

While she was busy with the thermos and basin and towel, I led Father into his bedroom and fluffed up his pillow for him. Soon she came in with the steaming towel, and he rubbed his face and neck as if to wash away weeks of dirt. When he was finished he looked up wearily. "Well, Liang Wei-ping. It's a good thing you watched other people's 'traveling struggle' and not mine. You might not have found it so entertaining." He lay slowly back against the pillow and closed his eyes.

We shut the door softly behind us. As if she hated herself, Liang Wei-ping said, "I feel terrible, talking about those things in front of Father." She sat down on her bed and stared out the window for a long, long time.

Chapter Seventeen: Interrogation

Soon after Liang Wei-ping left, Father returned to his work on the Propaganda Team and I went back to school to begin the new semester. My sister's stories had influenced me, and I resolved to improve my relationship with the peasant children. This was relatively easy to do, for I understood them very well. I knew they were more afraid of ghosts than of anything else, and I used to impress them by nonchalantly visiting places they believed haunted. My classmates were already a little afraid of me because of my height and toughness; now they began to see me as some sort of hero.

What really kept me out of fights was the discovery of the boarded-up storeroom. It was a flat-roofed building near the basketball court, and an idle moment's investigation through the cracks in the door revealed that it was full of books, probably from the pre-Cultural Revolution school library. I hadn't read a good book since the Red Guards' search raid more than four years earlier, and my heart pounded. I quickly organized my handful of best friends, now including two peasant boys, and swore them to secrecy. Late that night, we pried off a few boards and climbed in. The acrid dust and mildew irritated our throats, and spiderwebs were everywhere; the books lay in broken piles, and the yellow paper bindings were sticky to the touch. But I felt as though we had entered paradise!

Someone had a flashlight, and we passed it about with shaking hands as we made our selections. We rationed ourselves, as we did when we stole sweet potatoes, for fear of being discovered. I chose a history of Europe and translations of Hegel's *Dialectics* and Flaubert's *Madame Bovary*. We replaced the boards carefully when we left.

It seemed there would be no end to our secret new pleasures. My life changed completely. I read with a passion I had felt for nothing else, keeping a diary about everything. The world of the imagination opened to me; I had new dreams and ambitions. My fellow thieves and I held discussions on literature and even began to write poetry, meeting on the windy riverbank but never feeling cold. We were a small literary society of fifteen-year-olds.

One day a classmate—I never found out who—took one of my poems from my desk and turned it in to a political cadre. It was a pessimistic poem, about my road of life leading nowhere. I was publicly criticized, and "dissatisfied with reality" was written in my file. Even that didn't quell my literary fervor. I simply began to turn it outward, writing letters to faraway friends and family like Little Li, who was still in Changsha because his parents had not yet been "liberated" from the study class. I developed quite an active correspondence, receiving answers to all my letters except those to Peng Ming. I imagined he must be too busy making Revolution to write.

Then one Saturday morning, classes were canceled for a special school-wide meeting. New slogans were up in the big classroom, all of them dealing with class struggle, so we knew something important was in the air.

The political work group was the section of the school Revolutionary Committee with the real power, and Liu Guo-rong, a graduate of the Hunan Teachers College's Politics Department, was the head of it. This was his meeting, and he strode to the podium as if girding himself for a performance.

It was a short meeting, but an exciting one. Liu's gold fillings sparkled in his expressive mouth, and a fine spray of saliva rained into the first rows at emphatic moments. A new movement was on, he told us, to round up the counterrevolutionary "May Sixteenth" conspirators.

"This nationwide secret organization has tried to attack our beloved Premier Zhou En-lai by sabotaging diplomatic relations with foreign countries," he bellowed. "They have a manifesto and a plan. Their activities are vicious. They use our postal system to spread their pernicious conspiracy everywhere." Liu paused, and we held our breaths. Finally he hissed, "We have a May Sixteenth conspirator right here in this room!"

Pandemonium broke as we chattered excitedly and craned our heads about hoping to identify the culprit. My mind raced down the list of my simple country teachers, but it seemed impossible that any of them should be involved in something so terrifying, so dangerous. Liu continued, "After the meeting, the counterrevolutionary will come to my office and surrender. I will put up five locked boxes throughout the school so that those of you who think they have spotted other counterrevolutionary activities can put in their reports. Don't worry, I am the only person with the keys. No one will know about your suspicions but you and me." He flashed his golden smile. "Meeting dismissed."

In the classroom, I held a whispered consultation with the members of my literary group and we decided to disband and return the stolen books that evening. Other classmates were checking their desks to make sure nothing had been planted there. Then I felt a hand on my shoulder. It was Teacher Deng, a member of the school Revolutionary Committee. "Liang Heng," he said, "Liu Guo-rong wants to see you."

I hurried behind him past my classmates' stares, shame burning me. A direct confrontation with Liu Guo-rong was too terrible to contemplate. I couldn't imagine what I had done.

The political work office held nothing but locked cabinets from floor to ceiling, the slogans on the walls, and some wooden chairs and a large desk. Liu sat behind this, smoking, a thick folder in front of him. He jerked his head toward an empty chair, and I sat down, trembling. Then he almost smiled.

"Did you forget to bring your ears with you this morning? You wanted a personal invitation?"

I flushed deeper in an agony of confusion.

"Well, you can still confess your activities as a May Sixteenth conspirator," said Liu, gesturing to a sheaf of blank papers on which I now noticed the heading "Confession" in big black characters.

My protests were useless. Liu shook his folder at me and claimed he knew everything, while I racked my brains for what the contents might be. Finally, he stood up and said, "You won't be leaving here until you've confessed, so you might as well begin now. Someone will bring you your lunch." I heard the key turn in the lock after him.

That morning the sounds of my classmates' voices rang in the corridors and I glued myself to the barred window hoping to catch a glimpse of a friend. I enumerated the possibilities over and over, rejecting them all: Could it be the books I had sent to Little Li in Changsha? Our literary group? The stolen sweet potatoes?

At noon, Teacher Deng came with food, and he whispered kindly to me, "You better confess, or heaven knows what will happen. The letter came from the Peking Public Security Bureau."

That explained it. Peng Ming must be in some kind of trouble. If I had come to the notice of Peking, things looked very bad for me indeed. But I recalled the content of my letters, and felt a bit calmer. I had done nothing but speak of our old friendship and ask Peng Ming if he could send me some materials on the arts; he was, after all, a composer.

Liu came back that afternoon to question me. His face was constantly changing, sometimes fierce, sometimes kind and smiling, until I felt numb and I wasn't really sure what was right anymore. On the one hand, he threatened me with jail; on the other, he promised me I could join the Communist Youth League if I only admitted my crime. "Your father came to the countryside with a black mark on his record, and before it's wiped clean you give him a counterrevolutionary son!" Liu said. "Think of the glory for your family if you tell the Party everything! Think how proud your father will be!"

At one point I mentioned Peng Ming's name. Liu lit up ecstatically. "Aha, you've confided the name of your counterrevolutionary contact to the Party! That's wonderful!" And he seized a piece of paper and, consulting his watch, noted down the exact moment of my "confession." Then he looked at me expectantly. "Go on."

I don't know how many times I explained the nature of my friendship with Peng Ming. I told Liu that we had been neighbors, that he had taken me with him on a New Long March. I explained that I had helped out in Peking, that his sister and my sister were classmates. But I insisted I knew nothing about any May Sixteenth conspiracy, nor that Peng Ming might have anything to do with counterrevolutionary activities. I didn't understand much of what was happening to me, but I thought I might as well die rather than confess something false that might be used against my friend.

In the late afternoon, Liu opened his folder and took out the letters I had written to Peking. I broke out in sweat then: I had never dreamed the Public Security Bureau could be so thorough.

"These letters were written in your own hand, right?" asked Liu.

"Of course," I responded. I described again the nature of my friendship with Peng Ming and my reasons for writing the letters.

Liu wasn't happy. "You're only a fifteen-year-old boy, and you dare take me for a three-year-old child," he said, rising and approaching me threateningly. He seized me at the base of the neck and squeezed. "Confess your counterrevolutionary plot!" he commanded.

It hurt so much I couldn't control my tears. "I've never heard of any May Sixteenth conspiracy." I sobbed. "I've told you everything I know."

And so it went, on and on in circles. They made me sleep there on the desk that night, and the next, and the next. Liu came to question me every afternoon, sometimes hitting me, sometimes flattering me and trying to bribe me with political favors. Teacher Deng brought me my meals, and was kind to me with cigarettes and information. I think what hurt me most during that time was the way my friends betrayed me.

Every time Liu came in, he had new "evidence" in his hand, reports pushed into the locked boxes by the people I had trusted most. The people I had defended in fights turned me in, the people with whom I had stolen food. My literary friends told of our book thefts and our poetry meetings; my homeroom teacher wrote about my "bad thought." And when I called out the window to my round-headed friend Little Wu, he looked frightened and hurried away. Every day I traced out the history of my relationship with Peng on the papers marked "Confession"; every day Liu took them away, muttering, "Another crime."

It was Teacher Deng who gave me the strength not to "confess" a lie. He explained that the letter from the Peking Security Bureau had asked only that I be investigated, not that I be arrested. Still, I knew that Liu would have me arrested if he could. It would be great Revolutionary glory if he could ferret out a big counterrevolutionary in his little country school, a great boost for his career. So every night I cried, torn between the desire not to hurt Peng Ming and the desire to protect Father from yet another disgrace.

On the fifth day, Liu didn't come until late in the day, and he had a plainclothes Public Security officer with him. "This is your last chance," he announced with satisfaction. "If you don't confess today, tomorrow you'll go to jail." Before my eyes, he went to a cabinet, unlocked it, and handed my file over to the officer.

That night, as I lay on my desk, I had no tears left. I had lived fifteen years, but I had no desire to live even one more. I had been the victim of political movements since the age of three, first through my mother, then through my father, and now through an absurd coincidence in my own affairs. Society hated me. It had turned me into an outcast and a thief. My stepmother disliked me and my father was a broken man. I even hated him for what he had done to our family.

I imagined the next day I would be brought to jail as a criminal, paraded through the streets as the peasants shouted, "Down with the counterrevolutionary!" My friends would be among them, throwing rocks and sticks, laughing at my shame, glad that now the country would be that much more secure than it had been before the criminal's arrest. Perhaps first there would be a public criticism meeting, a beating, a humiliation. . . .

The dusty dark lightbulb hanging several yards above me was still visible in the night. Suddenly, I realized that I could die. I could unscrew that lightbulb and put my hand there where the current flowed and I would be dead. I should never again be tormented by memories of Mother's humiliated and accepting face as Father cursed her for betraying the Party's faith in her; of Nai Nai's swollen cheeks as she lay in her black coffin; of Father kneeling before his burning books, praising the Party; of Liang Fang's feces-covered shoes as she came home to write her Thought Reports. I should never again hear the words "stinking intellectual's son," or lie on my stomach in the sweet potato fields; my throat wouldn't hurt anymore where Liu had squeezed it. I was amazed at the simplicity of it all.

The thought came quickly and I acted quickly. Standing on the table, I reached the bulb easily and it unscrewed smoothly into my hand. It was a lonely action, and I felt suddenly angry that it should be so. There should have been someone to help me do it, or someone to urge me not to. I reflected bitterly that after my death the mob would stone my body just as it would if I were alive, the difference being that now they would say that the counterrevolutionary had killed himself because of his crime. I would never be able to explain to Father that I wasn't guilty, and I remembered his old, sad face, weeping, telling himself to be patient and tolerant, that someday his question would be made clear. Another thought struck me with equal force: If I died, Peng Ming's enemies could invent my confession, and use it against him just as if I had penned it with my own hand.

The desire to live came strong then, stronger than the desire to die. I remember Father excitedly recording the peasant boy's folk song by torchlight, still a man of letters even in the midst of greatest trouble. I thought of Mother and Waipo, waiting for me in Changsha, and Liang Wei-ping sharing her rice *baba* among the peasants. The hoodlums had cared for me so well on the streets, and Teacher Luo had forgiven me so graciously for the caricatures I had drawn of him. There was so much good in this crazy world, but so much more that was impossible to understand.

Why should two good people like my parents be forced to divorce each other? Why should Liang Fang raise a machine gun against her fellow teenagers? Why did the peasants fear the cadres so terribly if they were representatives of our great Communist Party? Why were people so determined to make me and Peng Ming look like counterrevolutionaries when we wanted only to make a contribution to our country? Why had the Revolution given us all so little when we had sacrificed everything for it?

That night, I resolved that I would seek the answers to these questions. If I was to live, it would no longer be numbly and aimlessly. I would live bravely. I would not be like Father, denying the facts and fooling himself, nor like Pockmark Liu, disillusioned and cynical. I would go to prison, but I would study so that I could understand why my country had produced such tragedies.

The next morning, Liu arrived, but he was alone. "You can go," he said dourly.

It was no wonder I believed in fate, my life was just that crazy. I thought I must be dreaming again, but I didn't want to question my luck. I stumbled out, blinking in the bright light.

Later, I learned that the Central Committee in Peking had issued a document saying that too many people were being arrested on May Sixteenth conspiracy charges, and that in fact the conspiracy was not so big. Liu had to let me go. Still, the incident was by no means easily forgotten. My classmates shunned me, and Liu had his ways of having his revenge. In my file he wrote, "Corresponded with person with serious political questions," and when my class finished lower middle school that spring, I was the only one not allowed to proceed to upper middle school. The reason: "Complicated Thought."

■ Yang Lian (Yang Lien) (1955–) (poem)

TRANSLATED BY TONY BARNSTONE AND NEWTON LIU

Yang Lian, one of the original Misty poets, is currently living in New Zealand, teaching at the University of Auckland. He was born in Beijing, but during the Cultural Revolution, he was sent down to the countryside, where he began to write poetry. Collections of his poetry in English include *In Symmetry with Death* (Australian National University), *Masks and Crocodile* (University of Sydney), and *The Dead in Exile* (Tiananmen Publications). His collection of "proses" (poetic essays) will be published in Taiwan soon.

FURTHER READING: Barnstone, Tony, ed. *Out of the Howling Storm: The New Chinese Poetry,* 1993. Finkel, Donald, ed. *A Splintered Mirror: Chinese Poetry from the Democracy Movement,* 1991. Soong, Stephen C., and John Minford, eds. *Trees on the Mountain: An Anthology of New Chinese Writing,* 1984. Yeh, Michelle, ed. *Anthology of Modern Chinese Poetry,* 1992.

An Ancient Children's Tale

How should I savor these bright memories,
their glowing gold, shining jade, their tender radiance like silk
that washed over me at birth?
All around me were industrious hands, flourishing peonies, and
     elegant upturned eaves.
Banners, inscriptions, and the names of nobility were everywhere,   5
and so many temple halls where bright bells sang into my ears.
Then my shadow slipped over the fields and mountains, rivers and
     springtime
as all around my ancestors' cottages I sowed
towns and villages like stars of jade and gemstones.
Flames from the fire painted my face red; plowshares and pots   10
clattered out their bright music and poetry
which wove into the sky during festivals.
How should I savor these bright memories?
When I was young I gazed down at the world,
watching purple grapes, like the night, drift in from the west   15
and spill over in a busy street. Every drop of juice became a star

set into the bronze mirror where my glowing face looked back.
My heart blossomed like the earth or the ocean at daybreak
as camel bells and sails painted like frescos embarked
from where I was to faraway lands to clink the gold coin of the sun.   *20*

When I was born
I would laugh even at
the glazed and opulent palaces, at the bloody red
walls, and at the people rapt in luxurious dreams
for centuries in their incense-filled chambers.   *25*
I sang my pure song to them with passion,
but never stopped to think
why pearls and beads of sweat drain to the same place,
these rich tombs filled with emptiness,
or why in a trembling evening   *30*
a village girl should wander down to the river,
her eyes so clear and bright with grief.

In the end, smoking powder and fire erupted in the courtyard;
between endless mountains and the plain, horse hooves
came out of the north, and there was murder and wailing   *35*
and whirling flags and banners encircling me like magic clouds,
like the patched clothes of refugees.
I saw the torrential Yellow River
by moonlight unfolding into a silver white elegy
keening for history and silence.   *40*
Where are the familiar streets, people and sounds?
And where are the seven-leaved tree and new grass,
the river's song beneath a bridge of my dreams?
There is only the blood of an old man selling flowers clotting
    my soul,
only the burned houses, the rubble and ruins   *45*
gradually sinking into shifting sands
and turning into dreams, into a wasteland.

■ Ha Jin (Ha Chin) (1956–) (story, written in English)

Ha Jin was born in 1956 in Liaoning. The son of an army officer, he entered the People's Army early in the Cultural Revolution at a time when the schools were closed. He worked as a telegraph operator for some time, then went back to school, earning a B.A. and an M.A. After coming to the United States and taking his Ph.D. at Brandeis University in English and

American literature, he went to Emory University, where he is now a professor of English. His book of poems, *Between Silences: A Voice from China*, appeared from the University of Chicago Press in 1990. He won a Pushcart Prize for the story reprinted here. Like so many of his contemporaries, Ha Jin elected to remain in exile from China after the Tiananmen Square massacre of 1989. So he is in the unusual position of being a Chinese poet and fiction writer who works in English and now lives in America. As he writes in a letter: "Without question, I am a Chinese writer, not an American-Chinese poet, though I write in English. If this sounds absurd, the absurdity is historical rather than personal . . . since I can hardly publish anything in Chinese now." He now writes in English because "after June 1989 I realized that I could not return to China in the near future if I wanted to be a writer who has the freedom to write." This story, set on the Russian-Chinese border during the Cultural Revolution, dramatizes the conflict on a psychological border as well, that between raw human needs and strict ideological fetters. The narrator, who bears a striking resemblance to Herman Melville's Captain Vere in *Billy Budd,* is presented as sympathetic to the flawed protagonist but ultimately restricted by party bureaucracy and a tense border situation. In this story, Ha Jin shows a remarkable ironic ability, also evident in his poetry, to record history from the inside, from the point of view of its imperfect and often unsympathetic protagonists.

FURTHER READING: Barnstone, Tony, ed. *Out of the Howling Storm: The New Chinese Poetry,* 1993. Jin, Ha. *Between Silences: A Voice from China,* 1990; *Facing Shadows,* 1996; *Ocean of Words: Army Stories,* 1996; *Under the Red Flag: Stories,* 1997.

My Best Soldier

I couldn't believe it when I saw that the photo sent over by the Regimental Political Department was Liu Fu's. How clumsy he looked in it: a submachine gun slanted before his chest; above his army fur hat, in the right corner, stretched a line of characters, "Defend My Motherland"; his smile was still a country boy's, lacking the sternness of a soldier's face. He had been in my platoon for only about ten months. How could he, a new soldier, become a secret customer of Little White Fairy in Hutou Town so soon?

Our political instructor, the Party secretary of our company, interrupted my thought, "I've talked with him, and he admitted he had gone to that woman six times this year."

"Six times?" Again I was surprised. "He is new. How could he get to know her so quick?"

"I asked the same question." Instructor Chang tapped his cigarette lightly over an ashtray and raised his head, looking across the small room in which we were sitting. He wanted to make sure that the orderly was not in the next room. "I think there must have been a pimp, but Liu Fu insisted he got to know the Fairy by himself when he had his hair cut in her barbershop. Obviously he is a novice in this business. No old hand would leave his picture with that weasel."

"You're right." I remembered last year a bulletin issued by the Regimental Political Department had carried a report on this young woman. After being caught in bed with an officer, Little White Fairy was brought to the Regimental Headquarters, where she confessed many soldiers and officers had visited her. Once she had received six army men in a single night, but she didn't know any of their names. Each man gave her a two-*yuan* bill and then went to bed with her. That was all. Regimental Commissar Feng swore to have those men found out, for they must have belonged to our Fifth Regiment, the only army unit in Hutou. But those were old dogs and had never left any trace.

"You should talk to him." Secretary Chang exhaled a small cloud. "Comrade Wang Hu, your platoon has done everything well this year except this Liu Fu matter. Don't get lost in the training. Mind modeling is more important. You see whenever we slack a little in ideological education, problems will appear among our men."

"Secretary Chang, I'll talk to him immediately. From now on I will pay more attention to ideological education."

"Good."

It seemed he didn't want to talk more, so I stood up and took my leave. Outside, the snow had stopped and the north wind turned colder. On my way back to my platoon, I felt bad, wondering how to handle the case. I was upset by Liu Fu. What a shame. I had always considered him as a candidate for an important job. His squad leader, Li Yaoping, was going to be demobilized the next year, and I had planned to have Liu Fu take over the squad. To be fair, Liu was in every way an excellent soldier. He surpassed all of my men in hand-grenade throwing. He could throw a grenade seventy-two meters. In our last practice with live ammunition, he scored eighty-four points with nine shots, which was higher than everybody except me. I got eighty-six. If we had a contest with the other three platoons, I would surely place him as our first man.

Needless to say, I liked him, not only for his ability and skills but also for his personality. He was a big fellow, over a hundred and eighty centimeters tall and a little heavily built but very nimble. His wide eyes reminded me of a small pony in my home village. In a way, his square mouth and bushy brows made him resemble those ancient generals in Spring-Festival pictures. All the other soldiers liked him a lot too, and he had quite a few friends in our Ninth Company.

I can never forget how he became a figure of poetry. In the spring, when we sowed soybeans, I assigned the Third Squad to pull a plough, since we didn't have enough horses and oxen. On the first day the men were soaked with sweat and complained that it was animal's work. Though they sang some revolutionary songs and even pretended to be Japanese soldiers marching into a village, still there was no way of making the labor lighter. But the next day was different. Liu Fu and two other boys in the Third Squad appeared with bald heads. They said a bald head would make the sweating more endurable and the washing easier after the work. The atmosphere in the field came alive. The three shining round heads were wavering about like balloons at the front of the team. Everybody wanted to get some fun out of it. Because Liu Fu was taller and had a bigger head, he became the main butt. In a few hours a poem was made in his honor, and the soldiers in the field chanted:

> When Big Liu takes off his hat,
> The county magistrate shakes his head:
> "Such a vast piece of alkaline land,
> How can the grain yield reach the Plan!"

> When Big Liu takes off his hat,
> The hardware store is so glad:
> "With such a big shining bulb,
> How many customers can we attract!"

> When Big Liu takes off his hat,
> The saleswoman is scared out of breath:
> "Having sold condoms for so many years,
> I've never seen such a length and breadth!"

In a few days the whole company learned the doggerel. Big Liu was never offended by it. He even chanted it with others, but he would replace the name "Big Liu" with "Small Wang," "Old Meng," and some others. As his popularity grew he was welcomed everywhere in the company. A boy like him could be a very able leader of a squad or a platoon. This was why I had planned to promote him to squad leader the next year. But who could tell he was a "Flowery Fox."

Our Party secretary was right: there must have been a pimp. Hutou was over fifty *li* away from Mati Mountain where we garrisoned; at most Liu Fu had gone to the county town seven or eight times on Sundays. He had seen Little White Fairy six times? Almost every time he went there? It was impossible, unless at the very beginning somebody took him directly to that woman. I remembered Li Dong had gone with him for his first visit to the town, and the second time Zhao Yiming had accompanied him. Both of the older soldiers were pretty reliable; it was unlikely that they could be pimps. But to know a man's face is not to know his heart. I had to question Liu Fu about this.

Our talk did not take long. He looked crestfallen and ashamed, but he denied there had been somebody else involved and insisted to me that a good man must accept the consequences of his own actions.

In a way, I appreciated his only blaming himself for the whoring. If another man was found like him in my platoon, I would have trouble clearing our name. People would chuckle and say the First Platoon had a whoring gang. That would give Liu Fu himself a hard time too, because he would surely be treated by the other men as a sort of traitor.

But I did take this case seriously, for I had to stop it. We garrisoned the borderline to defend our country, and we must not lose our fighting spirit by chasing women. Unlike the Russians on the other side, we Chinese were revolutionary soldiers, and we must not rely on women to keep up our morale. Every Saturday night we saw from our watch tower the Russians having many college girls over in their barracks. They would sing and dance around bonfires, kiss and embrace one another in the open air, roll and fuck in the woods. They were barbarians and Revisionists, while we were Chinese and true Revolutionaries.

So I ordered Liu Fu to write out his self-criticism, examining the elements of bourgeois ideology in his brain and getting a clear understanding of the nature of his offence. He wept and begged me not to take disciplinary action against him. He was afraid his family would know it and he would carry the stain for the rest of his life. I told him that a disciplinary action would have to be taken, and that I was unable to help him with that. It was better to tell him the truth.

"So I'm done for?" His horsy eyes watched my mouth expectantly.

"Your case was sent down by the Regimental Political Department. You know, our company cannot interfere with a decision from above. Usually, an offender like you is punished with a disciplinary action, but this doesn't mean you will have to carry it for the rest of your life. It depends on your own behavior. Say, from now on if you behave well in every way, you may have it taken out of your file when you are demobilized."

He opened his big mouth, but he didn't say anything, as if he swallowed down some words that had been stuck in his throat. The word "demobilized" must have struck him hard, because a soldier like him from the countryside would work diligently in order to be promoted to officer's rank. It would be a misfortune for him to return to his poor home village, where no job waited for him, and without a job no girl would marry him. But with such a stigma in his record, Liu Fu's future in the army was fixed: he would never be an officer.

Two days later he turned in his self-criticism. On eight white sheets were lines of big scrawled words and a few ink stains. A country boy like him of course couldn't say extraordinary things. His language was plain, and many sentences were broken. The gist of his self-criticism was that he had not worked hard enough to purge the bourgeois ideology from his head and that he had contracted the disease of liberalism. The Seventh Rule for the Army stated clearly: "Nobody is allowed to take liberties with women," but he had forgotten Chairman Mao's instruction and violated the rule. He also had forgotten his duty as a soldier staying on the Northern Frontier:

when the enemies were sharpening their teeth and grinding their sabers at the borderline, he was indulging himself in sexual pleasure. He was unworthy of the nurture of the Party, unworthy of the Motherland's expectation, unworthy of his parents' efforts to raise him, unworthy of the gun that the people had entrusted to his hands, unworthy of his new green uniform.

I knew he was not a glib man, so I spared him the trouble of putting more self-scathing words in the writing. His attitude was sincere; this alone counted.

He looked a little comforted when I told him that I would try to persuade Secretary Chang to ask the Regimental Political Department to administer less severe punishment to him. "This is not over yet," I warned him, "but you mustn't take it as a heavy burden. Try to turn over a new leaf and work hard to make up for it."

He said he was grateful and would never forget my help.

Two weeks passed. We had not heard anything from the Political Department about the decision on Liu Fu's case. Neither the Party secretary nor the company commander ever requested an action. It would be unwise to do that, because the longer we waited the more lenient the punishment would be. Time would take away the interest and the urgency of the case. In fact, none of the company leaders would welcome a severe action against Liu Fu. Liu was their man; no good leader would like to see his own man being punished.

A month passed, and still nothing happened. Liu Fu seemed very patient and was quieter than before. To prevent him from being involved with Little White Fairy again, we kept him at Mati Mountain on weekends. We were also very strict about permitting other men, especially new soldiers, to visit Hutou Town.

One night it was my turn to make the round through all our sentry posts, checking the men on duty to make sure they wouldn't doze off. We had five posts, including the new one at the storehouse where we kept our food and a portion of our ammunition. I hated to do the supervision at midnight when you had to jump out of bed and pretend to be as awake as a cat. If you didn't look spirited in front of them, the men on duty would follow your example and make no effort to stay awake.

I went to the parking yard first, where our trucks and mortars stood, and caught the sentry smoking in the dark. I ordered him to put out his cigarette. The boy complained it was too cold and he couldn't keep his eyelids apart if he had nothing to do. I told him that everybody had to stand his hours on cold nights. Nobody but the Lord of Heaven was to blame for the cold. As for his sleepiness, he'd better bear in mind that we were merely four *li* away from the Russians. If he didn't stay alert, he put his own neck at risk. The Russians often sent over their agents to find out our sentry positions and deployment. They would get rid of a sentry if they found it necessary and convenient. So for his own safety, he'd better keep his eyes open and not show them where he was.

Then I went to the gate post and our headquarters. Everything was fine at these two places. I chatted with each of the men for a few minutes and gave them some roasted sunflower seeds. Then I left for the storehouse.

The post was empty there, so I waited inside the house, believing the sentry must have been urinating or emptying his bowels somewhere outside.

After ten minutes nobody showed up. I began to worry and was afraid something unusual might have happened. I couldn't shout to summon the sentry over. That was the last thing you would do at night, because it would wake up the whole company and the Russians might hear it as well. But I had to find out where the sentry hid himself. He must have been dozing away somewhere. There were no disordered footprints in the snow; it was unlikely that the sentry had been kidnapped or murdered. I picked up a line of footprints that looked new and followed it for a little distance. They were heading towards our stable. I raised my eyes and saw a dim light at the skylight on the stable's roof. Somebody must be there. What's he up to in the stable? Who is on duty? I looked at my luminous watch—1:30—and couldn't recall who was the sentry.

Getting close to the door, I heard some noise inside, so I hastened my steps. With my rifle I raised the cotton door-curtain a little to have a view inside and make sure no one was hiding behind the door waiting to knock me down.

It was Liu Fu! He was standing beside our gray mule, buckling the belt around his pants. His gun leaned against the long manger, and his fur hat hung on its muzzle. Beyond the mule stood a dozen horses asleep with downcast heads. So he is the sentry. The rascal, he's using the stable as a latrine. How luxurious, keeping his butt warm in here.

No. I noticed something unusual. Behind the gray mule's hindquarters was a bench. On the bench there were some particles of snow and some wet smudges. The beast! He has been screwing the mule! Looking at him, I found his sweating face distorted with an awkward but clear expression, as if saying to me: *I can't help it, please, I can't help it!*

I sprang at him and grabbed him by the front of his jacket. Though he was much bigger and stronger than myself, I felt he went limp in my hand. Of course, a spent beast. I started slapping his face and cursing, "You— mule fucker! You never give your cock a break! I'll geld you today and throw your itchy balls to the dogs!"

He didn't resist and merely moaned, as if my cursing and slapping made him feel better. He looked so ashamed. Not encountering any resistance I soon cooled down. You couldn't go on for long beating a man who didn't even raise his hands to defend himself. I let him go and ordered, "Back to the storehouse. We'll settle it tomorrow."

He picked up his gun, wiped away the tears on his cheeks with his hat, and went out quietly. In the stable all the animals were out of sleep now, their eyes open and their ears cocked up. One horse snorted.

I couldn't wait for tomorrow, and had Li Yaoping, his squad leader, woken up. We had to talk before I reported it to our Party secretary. I wanted to know more about Liu Fu. It was understandable if you screwed a girl in the town, since there was no woman in the mountain. But to screw a dumb animal like that, who could imagine it! It nauseated me.

Li was not completely awake when he came into my room. I gave him a cigarette and struck a match for him. "Sit down. I want to talk with you."

He sat on a stool and began smoking. "What do you want to talk about on a dark—" He looked at his watch. "It's already half past two in the morning."

"I want to talk about Liu Fu. Just now I found him in the stable fooling around with the gray mule." I wouldn't say "He screwed the mule," since I didn't see him do it. But I was sure of it, and Liu Fu himself did not deny it when I cursed and beat him. I was about to explain to Li what I meant.

"Oh no, you mean he did it again?" Li shook his freckled face.

"Yes. So you knew it already?"

"Ye—yes." He nodded.

"Why didn't you inform me of that before? Who gave you the right to hide it from me?" I was angry and would have yelled at him if some of my men were not sleeping in the adjacent room.

"He promised me that he would never do it again." Li looked worried. "I thought I should give him a chance."

"A chance? Didn't we give him one when he was caught with Little White Fairy?" I felt outraged. Apparently this thing had been going on in my platoon for quite a while, but I had never got a whiff of it. "Tell me, when did you see him do it and how many times."

"I saw him with the mule just once. It was last Saturday night. I saw him standing on a bench and hanging on the mule's hindquarters. I watched for a minute through the back window of the stable, then I coughed. He was scared and immediately fell off. When he saw me come in, he knelt down begging me to forgive him and not to tell on him. He looked so piteous, a big fellow like that, so I told him I wouldn't tell. But I did criticize him."

"What did you say? How did you criticize him, my comrade Squad Leader?" I felt it strange—he sounded as if he might sell his sister if he took pity on a man.

"I asked him why he had to screw the mule." Li looked rather cheerful.

"What a stupid question. How did he answer it?"

"He said, 'You know, Squad Leader, only—only mules don't foal. I promise, I'll never touch any—any of these mares.'" Li started tittering.

"What? It's absurd. You mean he thought he could get those mares with babies?"

"Yeah, yes!"

"What a silly fellow! So moral, he's afraid of being a father of horsy bastards." I couldn't help laughing, and Li's tittering turned into loud laughter too.

"Shhh—." I reminded him of the sleepers.

"I told him even the mule must not be 'touched,' and he promised not to do it again." Li winked at me.

"Old Li, you're an old fox."

"Don't be so hard on me, my platoon leader. To be fair, he is a good boy in every way except that he can't control his lust. I don't know why. If you say he has too much bourgeois stuff in his head, that won't fit. He is from a pure poor peasant family, a healthy seedling on a red root—"

"I don't want you to work out a theory, Old Li. I want to know how we should handle him now. This morning, in a few hours, I will report it to our Company Headquarters. What should we say and how should we say it?"

"Well, do you want to get rid of him or keep him?"

This was indeed the crucial question, but I didn't have an answer. Liu Fu was my best man and I would need him in the future. "What's your opinion then? At least, we must not cover it up this time." I realized that Old Li hadn't told on Liu Fu because he wanted to keep him in his squad.

"Certainly, he had his chance already. How about—"

The door burst open and somebody rushed in. It was Ma Pingli, our youngest boy, who was to stand the three-o'clock shift at the storehouse. "Platoon Leader, Liu Fu is not—not at the post." He took the fur cover off his nose, panting hard. "All the telephone wires are cut. We can't call anywhere."

"Did you go around and look for him?"

"Yes, everywhere."

"Where's his gun?"

"The gun is still there, in the post, but his person's gone."

"Hurry up! Bring over the horses!" I ordered. "We'll go get him."

Ma ran away to the stable. I glanced at Old Li. The look on his face showed he understood what was happening. "Take this with you." I handed him a semi-automatic rifle, which he accepted absentmindedly, and I picked up another one for myself. In uneasy silence, we went out waiting for Ma.

The horses sweated all over, climbing towards the borderline. I calculated that we would have enough time to stop him before he could get across. He had to climb a long way from the southern side of the mountain to avoid being spotted by our watch tower. But when we reached the Wusuli River, a line of fresh footprints stretched before us, winding across the snow-covered surface of the river, extending itself into the other side, and gradually losing its trail in the bluish whiteness of the vast Russian territory.

"The beast, stronger than a horse," I said. It was unimaginable that he could run so fast in the deep snow.

"He's there!" Ma Pingli pointed to a small slope partly covered by gray bushes.

Indeed, I saw a dark dot moving towards the edge of the thicket, which was about five hundred meters away from us. Impossible—surely he was too smart not to put on his white camouflage cape. I raised my binoculars, and saw him carrying a big stuffed gunnysack on his right shoulder and running desperately for the shelter of the bushes, a camouflage cape secured around his neck flapping behind him like a huge butterfly. I gave the binoculars to Old Li.

Li watched. "He's taking a sack of *Forwards* with him!" he said with amazement.

"He stole it from the kitchen. I saw the kitchen door broken," Ma reported. We all knew our cooks stored *Forwards,* the newspaper of Shenyang Military Region, in gunnysacks as kindling. We had been told not to toss the paper about, because the Russians tried to get every issue of it in Hong Kong and would pay more than ten dollars for it.

"The Russians may not need those back issues at all," I said. "They've already got them. They only want recent ones. He's dumb."

Suddenly a yellow light pierced the sky over the slope. The Russians' lookout tower must have spotted him; their Jeep was coming to pick him up.

Old Li and I looked at each other. We knew what we had to do. No time to waste. "We have no choice," I muttered, putting a sighting glass onto my rifle. "He has betrayed our country, and he is our enemy now."

I raised the rifle and aimed at him steadily. A burst of fire fixed him there. He collapsed in the distant snow, and the big sack fell off his shoulder and rolled down the slope.

"You got him!" Ma shouted.

"Yes, I got him. Let's go back."

We mounted on the saddles; the horses immediately galloped down the mountain. They were eager to get out of the cold wind and return to their stable.

All the way back, none of us said another word.

■ Chou Ping (1957–) (poem, written in English)

Chou Ping was born in Changsha City, Hunan province, in 1957. The Pinyin transliteration of his name is Zhou Ping, and the Wade-Giles transliteration is Chou P'ing, but he prefers "Chou Ping" to either transliteration. He writes poetry in both Chinese and English, and his poetry and translations of Chinese poetry into English have appeared in such American journals as the *Literary Review* and *Nimrod,* and a substantial selection of his work has appeared in *Out of the Howling Storm: The New Chinese Poetry* (Wesleyan, 1993). He has also co-translated a book of Chinese literary criticism titled *The Art of Writing: Teachings of the Chinese Masters* (Shambhala, 1996). In 1983, he studied English literature in the Advanced Teachers' Training Program at Beijing Foreign Language University, where he studied poetry with Willis Barnstone. It was at that time that he began writing his poems in English instead of Chinese, as part of his study of English language and literature; the practice stuck. He taught at Xiangtang Teachers' College, Hunan province, until fall 1991, when he enrolled in the graduate program in English at Indiana University in Bloomington. After completing his master's degree in English and a master's in fine arts in creative writing at Indiana, Chou Ping enrolled in the Ph.D. program in East Asian languages at Stanford University, where he completed yet another master's degree in Chinese and is at this writing completing his Ph.D. In a generation of poets who are often obscure or polemical, his poems are tender, funny, and whimsical, and peculiarly his own.

FURTHER READING: Barnstone, Tony, ed. *Out of the Howling Storm: The New Chinese Poetry,* 1993.

Ways of Looking at a Poet

1.

a wreck tossed upon a hazy shore
cursing the delicious banality
of being lost at a familiar place

2.

a newspaper wriggled up in wind
and waltzed around on a green lawn
it stumbled over its own shadow
and fell back in a conscious coma

3.

a raven in a vacant wood, winging
the black pages of the future

4.

a dressmaker's dummy sneaked into a street
looking for King Midas's hand

5.

an old man in rags bought a magnolia
to pin it on the flower girl's dress

6.

monotonous waves
irresistible countdown of life

7.

a sun skated across the ocean
feeling pretty dark inside

8.

an admirable punching sack, receiving
every blow with an appreciative bow

9.

a rage enclosed in a free balloon
moving up and down in darkness
desperately eager to pierce a hole
and wait for the immediate slow death

10.

a broken mirror
with godlike indifference
sleeping open-eyed

11.

the slewing arm of a trackless trolley
picking azure flowers from a dark canvas

12.

an ant climbs up the sky
in search of a thought

13.

a nose practicing saxophone at night

14.

a sweet noise
wrapping around one's neck
like a hot towel in summer

■ Tang Yaping (T'ang Ya-p'ing) (1962–) (poems)

TRANSLATED BY TONY BARNSTONE AND NEWTON LIU

Tang Yaping represents the new voice of women's poetry from China:
voraciously sexual, dark, and irreverent. She was born in 1962 in Sichuan

and graduated from Sichuan University as a philosophy major in 1983. She is currently working as an editor at the Guizhou television station in the southwest of China.

FURTHER READING: Barnstone, Tony, ed. *Out of the Howling Storm: The New Chinese Poetry,* 1993.

from *Black Desert (Suite)*

Black Nightgown

I fill a bottomless bottle with water and bathe my feet
Nights when it rains are most interesting
I've asked a man over to talk
Before he comes I do not think
—I pull down the purple sash and turn a pink wall-lamp on   5
My black nightgown does three rounds about the room
—then the door is knocked on three times
He comes in with a black umbrella
and opens it up on the floor in the middle of the room
We start to drink strong tea   10
Noble compliments pour like piped water
Sweet lies shine like bright stars
Gradually I lean back on the sofa
and with scholarly passion tell the story of an old maid
The god that was between us runs away   15
covering his ears and without one slipper
This evening of talk leaves me dizzy
When telling a story
the darker the night the better it is
and the heavier it rains the better   20

Black Rock

Looking for a man to torture her
a beauty with tiger teeth smiling
lives in the footprints of suicide
She's tough but she finds only despair
The empty earth, the blank sky,   5
are deep as you want them to be
This dead rock was also rock when alive,
had nothing to hate, nothing to love,
nothing to be loyal to, nothing to defect from
The more the sorrow, the more the joy   10
Let some inconceivable idea control everything

A hairy little bird has pecked away all stupid responsibility
A head refuses to let a dream enter
Circulating blood spills disaster everywhere
Now the forbidden fruit is full and ripe;   *15*
it will be seized without foreplay
Pregnant women's faces are everywhere
Freckles seem to butterfly off
The nightmare mystifies, but it thrills
You've got to convulse while alive   *20*

3

Japan

■

INTRODUCTION

Japan is a nation of islands lying off Asia's eastern seaboard, across the Sea of Japan from Korea, China, and Siberia. There are four major islands; the largest and most historically important is Honshu. Little is known about the early history of the Japanese people, though it is said that the empire was founded by Emperor Jimmu in 556 B.C., and after A.D. 57 there are occasional references to the Japanese in Chinese histories. By the first century A.D., the Japanese had long been exposed to Chinese culture, particularly through their neighbors the Koreans. Although much of Japan's history with Korea has been warlike, the early Japanese owe a great deal to Korea, and to Chinese culture, which reached Japan through the corridor of Korea. The Japanese also absorbed Koreans into their society, and in fact up to a third of the early Japanese nobility may have been of Korean descent. This proximity to the cultural influences of Korea and China, combined with long periods of government-mandated isolationism, has enabled the Japanese to develop an extraordinarily sophisticated culture. Japan's literary tradition rivals that of much larger nations and of cultures of much greater antiquity.

The early Japanese were an agricultural people ruled by a warrior aristocracy factioned into ancestral clans. Each was ruled by a warrior chieftain who was also the chief priest. The society was stratified into nobility, peasants, and slaves. In the third century A.D., the Yamato clan took hold of the area south of modern Kyoto, an agriculturally fertile region that afforded the Yamatos the economic and military strength to conquer a large number of other clans and establish the Yamato state. Under this rule, the conquered clans were forced to worship the Yamato sun-goddess deity and a pantheon of lesser gods, and out of this grew the native Japanese religion of Shinto, emphasizing ancestral worship and ritual cleanliness.

In A.D. 538, Buddhism was introduced to Japan when a Korean king gifted Buddhist scriptures and images to the Yamato court, thus beginning a long era of Buddhist influence in Japanese history. Buddhism has accompanied Japanese culture—its art, architecture, philosophy, poetry, fiction, and popular tales—from the time of the earliest Buddhist temples at the beginning of the seventh century A.D. Prince Shotoku (574–622) was the leader in recommending governmental reforms that would integrate Buddhist ethical thought and Confucian political philosophy into the Yamato administration. Beginning in 607, the prince was responsible for sending thousands of young Japanese to China to study under the tutelage of Tang dynasty administrators and Buddhist monks and artists. These students returned with fruitful ideas to Japan and in 654, twenty-two years after Shotoku's death, joined his proteges in overturning the Yamato government. One year later, the supporters of Shotoku's Chinese-Buddhist policies instituted the Taika Reforms, an attempt to transform Japan's political and bureaucratic system into a centralized structure modeled after the Tang Chinese empire. In 710, the city of Nara was founded, copied after Changan, the Tang dynasty capital, and became Japan's first capital city. From 710 to 794, known as the Nara era, Buddhist monasteries grew and flourished. As landowners, monks participated in the political process up to the level of the Imperial court. It was during this era that the earliest Japanese history, *Record of Ancient Matters* (712), was completed. This document was a dynastic and mythological record incorporating poetry.

In the second half of the eighth century, the *Manyoshu* was compiled. This anthology, whose name means "The Collection of Ten Thousand Leaves," is the largest and oldest collection of Japanese poetry, consisting of more than four thousand poems by people of all stations of life. Notable among these was Kakinomoto Hitomaro (died c. 708–715). He and the Tokugawa era writer Matsuo Basho (1644–1694) are considered Japan's finest poets. Poetry has always been the most esteemed form in Japanese literature and is commonly composed by people of all classes. For much of Japanese history, poetry was central to culture and literature: poetry contests were frequent; imperially sanctioned anthologies were regularly commissioned; and early readers often memorized these anthologies as well as the great anthologies of Chinese poetry. Poetry also commonly appears in Japanese fiction, theater, memoirs and histories, where it is the language of love, of emotions of all kinds, and of the gods. Much Japanese poetry is love poetry because poem exchanges were an essential aspect of courting rituals. Among the early poets of the *Manyoshu* are a number of talented women whose passionate personas in their poems of love anticipate later great women poets, such as Ono no Komachi (ninth century), Izumi Shikibu (c. 974–1034), and Yosano Akiko (1878–1942). Along with Sappho of Greece, Mirabai of India, and Li Qingzhao of China, Ono, Izumi, and Yosano are among the world's major erotic poets.

Ono and Izumi flourished in the era immediately following the Nara period, the Heian era (794–1185). The Heian is considered a period in which a true Japanese sensibility flowered, particularly in the arts and literature. The Imperial family in Nara had moved the capital city to Heian (modern Kyoto) after 770 when a Buddhist priest at Nara had unsuccessfully tried to take over the throne. This event spurred strong feelings against Buddhism and Chinese culture, resulting in a governmental injunction against relations with China in 838 and encouraging the development of uniquely Japanese architecture, painting, and literature.

The Japanese system of writing in Chinese characters (*kanji*) had been borrowed from the Chinese in the third and fourth centuries A.D. during the Yamato era. However, the ideographic nature of *kanji* did not fully express the nuances of the Japanese language, with its inflected verbs and honorific forms. This Chinese character scheme was augmented with two phonetic syllabaries in the eighth-century Heian period, finally rendering a Japanese writing system that allowed for the inflection of *kanji* characters through their juxtaposition with syllabic prefixes, suffixes, and particles. The improved system liberated Japanese writers to compose in their native syntax and stray from the confines of traditional Chinese literary forms and genres.

Although a number of Japanese literary genres owe their existence to the Chinese example, in their Japanese incarnation they are inevitably filtered through a different cultural, aesthetic, and linguistic sensibility. Further, basic linguistic differences between Japanese and Chinese limited imitation. In contrast to monosyllabic and tonal Chinese, Japanese is a polysyllabic tongue, without tones, and though they shared the same characters, the prosodies of each literature developed differently. Whereas Chinese poetry has metrical systems based on line length and tone and generally rhymes, Japanese poetry uses a syllabic measure, normally consisting of alternating lines of five and seven syllables, and rhyme is less frequent. In contrast to Japanese novels, which are often immensely long and episodic, Japanese poetry tends to be concentrated and runs toward the minimalist. It is even more condensed than the elegantly succinct poetry of China. Japan's poetry is comprised of brilliant images whose subtle connections create epiphanies of perception and emotion. Consider Yosa Buson's brief lines, "Red plum flowers/burn/on horse plop." This simple haiku is wisdom poetry, a Zen riddle. In joining fallen beauty and fallen excrement, the poem is a meditation on life's transience, on nature and natural functions. It startles us with immediacy, and when put aside the poem continues to enlighten and resonate. It should be added that there was also a Japanese tradition of writing poems in Chinese characters and forms.

In Japan, fiction had an earlier and more sophisticated development than in China, and diaries, books of random jottings, and travel literature, though anticipated in China, are particularly striking genres in Japan. In the Heian period, the new phonetic script was the domain of women, whereas Chinese characters were generally considered a masculine script. Two great works of aristocratic prose by Japanese women, written in the phonetic script, stand out in this period and are quintessentially Japanese in their literary achievement: *The Tale of Genji* by Murasaki Shikibu (978– c. 1014), considered by some scholars to be the world's first novel, with its exploration of psychological subjectivity and full use of dialogue; and *The Pillow Book* of Sei Shonagon (c. 966–1017), a collection of *zuihitsu*, or random thoughts and meditations.

During the Heian period, as they cultivated their graceful, erotic, intensely aesthetic lives of poetry, painting, fiction and the art of love, various court families fought for political power over the Imperial government. The aristocratic Fujiwara clan emerged as dominant. Meanwhile, in the countryside, the Japanese warrior code of *bushido* was gaining popularity, and in 1156, fueled by diminishing Imperial power and fighting between aristocratic clans, civil war broke out. The Taira and Minamoto clans were victorious over the emperor and Fujiwara clan, and eventually the Minamotos defeated the Taira and established the Kamakura shogunate (1185–1333).

Over the next seven centuries, the political rule of Japan fell into the hands of the *shoguns,* the military chief generals and feudal lords who controlled the samurai warriors. The Kamakura shogunate was succeeded by the Ashikaga shogunate (1336–1603) in a time known as the Muromachi period, and later by the Tokugawa shogunate (1603–1868). In the Kamakura and Muromachi periods, ideals of warfare and *bushido* were often treated in literature, as in the martial epic *Tale of the Heike* and in noh plays by Zeami Motokiyo (1363–1443) and others (though Zeami was certainly not limited to martial themes). The Kamakura era was also a period of great changes in Japanese Buddhism. Though many Buddhists considered this time "the age of the decline of dharma" because of the militarism and commercialism that had permeated monastic culture, Buddhism was reinvigorated by a new influx of Chinese ideas through Dogen (1200–1253), the founder of the Soto school of Japanese Zen Buddhism. In addition, Buddhists actively proselytized a form of lay Buddhism, adopting the earlier Tendai and Shingon schools of Buddhism into new popularizations and simplifications of Buddhist practice, called the Pure Land sect and the Lotus sect. All this ferment is reflected in the production of extraordinary Buddhist literature in the Kamakura period.

Japan has three main forms of drama: the puppet theater (*bunraku*), the noh play, and kabuki. The great names of Japanese drama are Zeami Motokiyo, whose noh plays represent the very highest examples of the form, and Chikamatsu Monzaemon (1653–1724), whose puppet and kabuki plays have caused him to be called the Shakespeare of Japan. Chikamatsu is typical of the authors of the Tokugawa era in his concern with representing ordinary life and ordinary people. This was also the time in which haiku developed as a serious literary form, championed by Matsuo Basho. This minimalist art honed psychological perceptions, social commentary, and startling depictions of nature into a mere seventeen syllables. It is a very personal, humorous, and accessible form, and it often learns high art from peasant life. As Basho writes: "Culture's beginnings:/from the heart of the country/rice-planting songs."

In the sixteenth century during the Muromachi period, Japan came into contact with Europeans. Christianity was introduced in 1549, and for close to a century there was a lively intercourse of cultural and trade relations with the Portuguese, Dutch, English, and Spanish. In 1603, Tokugawa Ieyasu became the first Tokugawa shogun and moved the capital city north to Edo (modern Tokyo). In 1639, during the reign of the Tokugawa shoguns, the nation entered a period of profound isolation, repressing Christianity, forbidding Japanese to travel overseas, and excluding all foreigners from the islands, with the exception of the Dutch, who were confined to Nagasaki. After a number of failed attempts by Russians, Europeans, and Americans to break into this closed society, this isolation was punctured in 1854 with the forced entry of Commodore Matthew Perry and a fleet of U.S. warships. In 1867, the last Tokugawa shogun resigned, ushering in the Meiji Restoration, in which Emperor Meiji (1852–1912) was restored to nominal power. In the Meiji period, Japan quickly changed, compelled into a knowledge of its own weakness by the unequal treaties it was obliged to sign. Within a few decades, Japan became industrially modernized, reestablished its military might, abolished feudalism, and converted itself into a modern state, complete with military conscription, compulsory education, a constitution, and an avid attempt to assimiliate the new science and technology.

In the twentieth century, Japanese nationalism led the nation to a series of imperialist invasions of countries throughout Asia—Korea, China, Formosa (modern Taiwan), Southeast Asia, the Philippines, and the Dutch East Indies. In World War II, Japan sided with the Axis powers Germany and Italy. Japanese participation in World War II was brought to an end within days of the dropping of two atomic bombs on the Japanese cities of Hiroshima and Nagasaki in August 1945 by the United States. Some two hundred thousand people, mostly civilians, were killed in the two explosions. Radiation poisoning condemned many others to a slow death or produced genetic defects in their descendents. It may also be said that Japanese imperialism and nationalism were mortally wounded in the blasts. After the war, the Japanese reinvented themselves as a peaceful nation focusing primarily on economic efforts.

Japanese literature went through a similar transformation from the nineteenth to the twentieth century. Translations of Western fiction and poetry proliferated in the late nineteenth century, and Western approaches to literature soon appeared in Japan. In poetry, though traditional verse forms continued to be written, they were radically adapted and modernized; and successive modern Western poetic movements—Romanticism, Symbolism, and Modernism—had their Japanese innovators and adherents. Novels began to reflect more than inner life and formally determined outer behavior expressed in an artificial literary language; now a more vernacular, naturalistic prose appeared that showed a new interest in social problems. The novel began to be esteemed for more than didactic purpose and moral lessons. Some writers reacted against the naturalist novel, choosing instead to adopt a detached aestheticism. In the twentieth century, a school of proletarian literature flourished briefly before it came under nationalist repression. In 1968, the novelist Kawabata Yasunari (1899–1972) won the Nobel Prize in literature, and in 1994 a second Japanese novelist, Oe Kenzaburo (1935–), also won the Nobel Prize.

Reactions to the Japanese defeat in World War II have pervaded modern Japanese literature. Oe's novels are saturated with a sense of loss, irony, and the grotesque. Tanikawa Shuntaro, who had witnessed the burnt corpses of neighbors while bicycling through Tokyo after it was fire-bombed in 1945, has reacted with renewed humanism and an idealistic faith that "life is possible" despite the worst horrors of human nature. Mishima Yukio, Japan's most famous modern writer, reacted with fierce nationalism, embracing the code of *bushido* and a worship of beauty and death, culminating in his own ritual suicide, performed after addressing the troops of a paramilitary army he had organized, hoping to achieve a coup d'état. Sakaki Nanao had been a radio operator in World War II and had tracked the B-29 that dropped the atom bomb on Nagasaki. He and his fellow soldiers were ordered by their superior officer to commit mass suicide. Only the emperor's voice on the radio ordering soldiers *not* to kill themselves saved them. Sakaki has responded to the devastations of the war with an antinationalism as fierce as Mishima's nationalism, and with Buddhist, ecological, and antinuclear activism. Like the "Lost Generation" in the West after World War I, Japanese writers wrote with a sense that the traditions of the past had been turned upside down after World War II, and that they were writing in a world that had been made a wasteland. Mishima's militant nationalism was an attempt to reclaim endangered Japanese traditions. A number of other postwar writers have positioned themselves, however, in the role of pacifist social critic and spiritual advisor, which, of course, is itself a traditional role for the Japanese poet, as seen in the Zen poetry of Saigyo, Ryokan, Muso Soseki, and others. The poetry of Tamura Ryuichi, for example, asserts that war—nuclear and conventional—is an apotheosis of the human will to destroy. The physical wasteland of postwar Japan, for Tamura, was a projection of a spiritual disease, a result of the false paradigms of *bushido*. All he wants, in the end, therefore is "on the tongues of gravediggers,/the taste of ice cream."

—Ayame Fukuda and the editor

Ancient Period

(to 794)

Poems from the *Manyoshu* (Collection of Ten Thousand Leaves)

INTRODUCTION

The *Manyoshu* is the earliest and greatest collection of Japanese poetry. It was compiled in the late eighth century A.D., during the Nara period, and it contains more than four thousand poems, from as early as the fourth century and as late as 759. The majority of the poems, however, were composed in the seventh and eighth centuries. Though there were probably a number of compilers, the final editor was Otomo Yakamochi. The *Manyoshu* is prized for the simplicity and purity of its poetry, as opposed to the more elegant and ornate styles that dominated in the later Imperial anthologies. The collection is divided into twenty books, but despite some grouping by author, chronology, source, subject, or mode, there is no overarching pattern of arrangement. It contains poems by diverse authors—from emperors to frontier guards—and its tone ranges from sublime to passionate to comic.

The collection is dominated by its 4,207 *tanka,* but it includes 265 *choka,* 62 *sedoka,* and a few poems in minor forms and in Chinese. Classical Japanese poetry, or *waka,* is based on the rhythm produced through lines of alternating numbers of syllables, generally an alternation between five and seven syllables. The *tanka,* meaning short poem, is a poem of five lines whose syllable count is 5/7/5/7/7. The *choka,* meaning long poem, is constructed of a varying number of 5/7 phrases capped with a 7/7 couplet; in the eighth century, the *choka* began to die out as the *tanka* took over. Often a *tanka* is attached to the end of a longer *choka* to crystalize the meaning (these envoys are called *hankas*). A *sedoka* consists of six lines in a rhythm of 5/7/7/5/7/7.

The *Manyoshu* holds the seminal position in Japanese literature that the *Greek Anthology* held in ancient Western literature (also containing approximately four thousand diverse poems) and that *The Book of Songs* holds for China. It is the source to which Japanese poets go again and again to revitalize their art. It represents the great literary flowering of Japan at a time when the Imperial system was cohering out of the clan coalitions of the ancient period, when large cities at Fujiwara and Nara were constructed, and when Japanese art was undergoing a similar flowering. Thus, it has provided the nation a historical as well as literary source of self-definition, to the point of nationalism, although in fact up to a third of the nobility were then Korean in origin and the cultural origins of Japan were rooted deeply in both Korea and China.

FURTHER READING: Levy, Ian Hideo, tr. *The Ten Thousand Leaves: A Translation of the "Manyoshu," Japan's Premier Anthology of Classical Poetry,* 1981. Shinkokai, Nippon Gakujutsu, tr. *The Manyoshu,* 1965. Yasuda, Kenneth, tr. *Land of the Reed Plains: Ancient Japanese Lyrics from the Manyoshu,* 1960. Wright, Harold, tr. *Ten Thousand Leaves: Love Poems from the Manyoshu,* 1979.

■ Empress Iwanohime (?–A.D. 347)

TRANSLATED BY AYAME FUKUDA

Iwanohime was the consort of Emperor Nintoku, the 16th Emperor. In A.D. 314, she was proclaimed empress, and she died in A.D. 347. Her poems are among the earliest examples of the Japanese love poem tradition.

Missing Emperor Nintoku (Four Poems)

The Days Lengthen

The days lengthen
as you travel.
Should I search the mountains
for you or wait
and wait?   5

I Would Rather Die

I would rather
lie down and die
pillowed on the rocks
of a crooked mountain
than want you this much.   5

I Will Wait For You

I will wait for you
as long as I live,
until my lingering black locks
are laced with frost.

Will My Desire Fade

Will my desire fade
in this autumn field
as morning mists slip
through stalks of rice
and vanish? 5

■ Empress Jito (645–702)

TRANSLATED BY KENNETH REXROTH AND IKUKO ATSUMI

This fine elegy was written by Empress Jito after the death of her husband Emperor Temmu in 686. She succeeded him to the throne, becoming Japan's forty-first sovereign. After ten years, she abdicated and was succeeded by her grandson, Emperor Mommu.

On the Death of the Emperor Temmu

Even flaming fire
can be snatched up, smothered
and carried in a bag.
Why then can't I
meet my dead lord again? 5

■ Kakinomoto Hitomaro (died c. 708–715)

Kakinomoto Hitomaro vies with Matsuo Basho for the title of Japan's finest poet. Two centuries after Hitomaro's death, Ki no Tsurayuki, a compiler of the famous Heian period *Kokinshu* anthology, gave him the appellation "the saint of poetry," and he is certainly the best poet of those represented in the *Manyoshu*. Yet he has left little historical trace. From his poems we may gather that he was a minor official who died before he was fifty. No direct evidence about his life exists in any text outside of the *Manyoshu*, but the Kakinomoto family had lived for generations in Ichinomoto, south of Nara. It appears that he was active in court life during the reigns of Emperor Temmu (r. 673–686), Empress Jito (r. 690–697), and Emperor Mommu (r. 697–707), that he held court offices, that he was an official in the provinces, and that he functioned at times as a court poet who wrote poems to celebrate outings or elegies for members of the royal family. He was married two or more times, and his first wife died before him.

Though his seventy *tanka* are excellent pieces, Hitomaro really excels in the longer form of *choka,* to which he brings an extraordinary narrative breadth and fluidity. He has both the directness of address and simple purity of the poets of the earlier period, as well as an acrobatic ability to leap from metaphor to metaphor. He is complex without being mannered. His poem about the temporary enshrinement of Prince Takechi (upon his death) is the longest poem in the *Manyoshu.* Takechi was the son of Emperor Temmu and Empress Jito, and he led their armies in the Jinshin War (672). The poem includes an explosive battle sequence that is unique in classical Japanese poetry in its detailed and extended presentation of the battle. His poems creatively refashion the worn rhetorical devices termed "pillow-words," which (like the Old English "kennings" in *Beowulf* or the formulaic expressions in Homer) are ornamental stock phrases that stand in for one or more words. These pillow-words run through Japanese poetry and have been used even in this century. The critics estimate that he either adapted or coined fifty percent of the pillow-words he used. Hitomaro brings the same genius to his personal poems that he does to his poems about public subjects, and his elegy on his first wife is among the most touching poems in any language.

FURTHER READING: Levy, Ian Hideo. *Hitomaro and the Birth of Japanese Lyricism,* 1984; tr. *The Ten Thousand Leaves: A Translation of the "Manyoshu," Japan's Premier Anthology of Classical Poetry,* 1981. Shinkokai, Nippon Gakujutsu, tr. *The Manyoshu,* 1965.

When She Walks

When she walks
by my door
she seems to say
"If love is killing you,
why aren't you dead yet?"   5

TRANSLATED BY TONY BARNSTONE AND WILLIS BARNSTONE

Just Let Me Take

Just let me take
her hand
and I won't care if words sprout
in gossiping mouths
like summer grass in the marsh.   5

TRANSLATED BY TONY BARNSTONE AND WILLIS BARNSTONE

Poem by Kakinomoto Hitomaro as He Shed Tears of Blood in His Grief following the Death of His Wife

On the Karu Road[1]
is the village of my wife,
and I desired to meet her intimately,
but if I went there too much
the eyes of others would cluster around us,   *5*
and if I went there too often
others would find us out.
And so I hoped
that later we would meet
like tangling vines,   *10*
trusted that we would
as I would trust a great ship,
and hid my love:
faint as jewel's light,
a pool walled in by cliffs.   *15*

Then came the messenger,
    his letter tied
    to a jewelled catalpa twig,
to tell me,
      in a voice   *20*
      like the sound
      of a catalpa bow,
that my girl,
who had swayed to me in sleep
like seaweed of the offing,   *25*
was gone
like the coursing sun
gliding into dusk,
like the radiant moon
secluding itself behind the clouds,   *30*
gone like the scarlet leaves of autumn.

I did not know what to say,
      what to do,
but simply could not listen
and so, perhaps to solace   *35*
a single thousandth
      of my thousand-folded longing,

---

1. "Karu" is preceded by the formal epithet *ama tobu ya*, "that soars through the sky," a pun on the word "*karu*" in its sense of "light" or "buoyant." It is essentially untranslatable.

I stood at the Karu market
where often she had gone,
and listened,   *40*
but could not even hear
the voices of the birds
that cry on Unebi Mountain,
    where the maidens
        wear strands of jewels,   *45*
and of the ones who passed me
on that road,
    straight as a jade spear,
not one resembled her.
I could do nothing   *50*
but call my wife's name
and wave my sleeves.

TRANSLATED BY IAN HIDEO LEVY

Poem by Kakinomoto Hitomaro at the Time of the Temporary Enshrinement of Prince Takechi at Kinoe

I hesitate to put it in words,
it is an awesome thing to speak.
Our Lord,
who, while we trembled,
fixed the far and heavenly   *5*
halls of his shrine
on the fields of Makami in Asuka
and, godlike, has secluded himself
    in the rocks there,
he,   *10*
who ruled the earth's eight corners,
crossed Fuwa Mountain,
lined with thick black pines,
in the northern land of his realm
and went down,   *15*
    as from heaven,
      to the provinces,
encamping on the plain of Wazami,
    Wazami
      of the Korean swords.   *20*
To hold sway over the realm under heaven

and bring his dominions to peace,
he gathered his soldiers
in the eastern country,
    where the cock cries,   25
and gave the task to his son,
he being an imperial prince:
to pacify the raging rebels
and subdue the defiant lands.
Then our Prince   30
girded his great body with his long sword
and took in his great hands his bow.
The sound of the drums,
calling the troops to ready,
boomed like the very voice of thunder,   35
and the echoing notes
of the signaller's flute
grew, to the terror of all,
like the roar of a tiger
with prey in its eyes.   40
The rippling of the high-held banners
was like the rippling of the fires
struck across every field
when spring comes, bursting winter's bonds,
and the roar of the bowstrings they plucked   45
was so fearful, we thought it a hurricane
whirling through a snowfallen winter forest.
When the arrows they let loose
swarmed like a blinding swirl of snow,
the resisters, standing defiant,   50
also resolved to perish,
    if they must,
like the dew and frost.
As they struggled
    like zooming birds,   55
the divine wind
from the Shrine of our offerings
at Ise in Watarai
blew confusion upon them,
hiding the very light of day   60
as clouds blanketed the heavens
in eternal darkness.
Thus pacifying this land,
abundant in ears of rice,
our Lord, sovereign   65
of the earth's eight corners,

a very god,
firmly drove his palace pillars
and proclaimed his rule
over the realm under heaven—   70
for ten thousand generations,
          we thought.
But just as his reign flourished
brilliant as the white bouquets
          of mulberry paper,   75
suddenly they deck his princely halls
to make a godly shrine,
and the courtiers who served him
now wear mourning clothes of white hemp.
On the fields   80
before the Haniyasu Palace gate
they crawl and stumble like deer
as long as the sun still streams its crimson,
and when pitch-black night descends
they crawl around like quail,   85
turning to look up at the great halls.
They wait upon him,
but they wait in vain,
and so they moan
like the plaintive birds of spring.   90
Before their cries can be stilled
or their mournful thoughts exhausted
the divine cortege
is borne from the Kudara Plain,
borne away.   95
Loftily he raises
the palace at Kinoe,
          good of hempen cloth,
as his eternal shrine.
A god, his soul is stilled there.   100
Yet could we even imagine
that his palace by Kagu Hill
          will pass away
in the ten thousand generations
he intended as he built?   105
I turn to gaze on it
as I would on the heavens,
bearing it in my heart
          like a strand of jewels,
preciously remembering,   110
awesome though it be.

Envoys

Although you rule
the far heavens now,
we go on longing for you,
unmindful of the passing
of sun and moon.   5

Not knowing where they will drift,
like the hidden puddles that run
on the banks of Haniyasu Pond,
the servingmen stand bewildered.

One Book Has for an Envoy,

Offering him sacred wine,
we pray at the shrine of Nakisawa,[1]
      the marsh of tears.
But our Lord is gone
to rule the high heavens.   5

TRANSLATED BY IAN HIDEO LEVY

■ The Priest Mansei (c. 720)

TRANSLATED BY AYAME FUKUDA

The Priest Mansei served Otomo Tabito, himself a noted poet and author of a famed series of drinking poems and father of Otomo Yakamochi, a compiler of the *Manyoshu*. Mansei was in charge of constructing the Kanzeonji Temple in Kyushu. Apart from this, little is known about him, but this poem is among the perfect gems of Japanese verse.

What Shall I Compare

What shall I compare
this world to?
At dawn

---

1. In the *Forest of Classified Verse,* the above poem is said to be "by Princess Hinokuma, in her anger at the Nakisawa Shrine (for the Prince's absence)." The *Nihonshoki* states that the later Crown Prince, Takechi, died in autumn, on the tenth day of the seventh month, in the tenth year of the reign (696).

a boat sails out.
The white wake fades. 5

Lady Ki (Eighth Century)

TRANSLATED BY AYAME FUKUDA

Lady Ki was the wife of Prince Aki, the great-grandson of Emperor Tenji, and a lover of Otomo Yakamochi. Her personal name was Ojika, and she was the daughter of Ki no Kahito, an official under Emperor Shomu (r. 724–748) and a minor *Manyoshu* poet. Twelve of her poems appear in the *Manyoshu,* five of them love poems sent to Otomo Yakamochi. Despite her slender representation in the collection, she is among the finest women poets in the *Manyoshu.*

Poem Sent to a Friend with a Gift

Across the beach
high winds whirl
but for you I cut
sleek seaweed,
drenching my sleeves. 5

Poem Sent by Lady Ki to Otomo Yakamochi in Response to His

Who flirted first?
Like water your passion
dams to a halt
halfway down the hill.
It reeks in ricebeds. 5

Otomo Yakamochi (716–785)

Otomo Yakamochi, from the illustrious Otomo clan, was the eldest son of Otomo Tabito, who was also a fine poet. Yakamochi held many posts in his life, in the war department, as governor of Inaba province, and as a military commander-in-chief. But he was as often demoted as promoted and, in fact, was posthumously stripped of rank because of the crime of a relative that effectively ended his family's political good fortune and caused his corpse to remain unburied for twenty days. In 806, twenty-one years after his death, he was granted a pardon. Even after his death, his fortunes were not stable. Four hundred and seventy-nine of his poems are collected in the *Manyoshu,* which he helped compile. He is one of the four principal

poets in the collection. He seems to have had many lovers, and he recorded these relationships in poem exchanges, many of which are included in
the *Manyoshu*. His poems are startlingly fresh today, though many of his
themes—the lover who appears in dreams, the desire to be "a jewel /
wrapped / around my lover's wrist"—are traditional themes that appear
repeatedly in this collection and in the works of later poets. Compare, for
example, this poem by an anonymous Lady, "Upon Emperor Tenji's Death"
(translated by Tony Barnstone and Ayame Fukuda):

> You are a god now
> and I am not fit to be with you.
> You are gone
> and I grieve for you this morning;
> you're gone and I miss you.   5
> If you were a jewel
> I'd wrap you around my wrist;
> if you were a robe
> I'd never take you off.
> My lord, whom I desire,   10
> I saw you last night
> in a dream.

FURTHER READING: Doe, Paula. *Warbler's Song in the Dusk: The Life and Work of Otomo
Yakamochi (716–785),* 1982.

In a Dream

In a dream
your smile
astounds me
and in my heart
burns   5

TRANSLATED BY AYAME FUKUDA

It Breaks Me

It breaks me
when I meet you in dream.
Startled awake
I grope for your body
through the empty air.   5

TRANSLATED BY TONY BARNSTONE

New Moon

I look up.
The new moon kindles
a memory.
A woman I met once.
Her painted eyebrows.   5

TRANSLATED BY TONY BARNSTONE

Wild Geese Cry

Wild geese cry
beyond clouds.
Like my love for you
a swarm descends
into ricefields.   5

TRANSLATED BY AYAME FUKUDA

A Long Life

I know my body
is like foam, vaporous,
yet I want it to live
a thousand years!

TRANSLATED BY TONY BARNSTONE

▪ Lady Kasa (Mid-Eighth Century)

Lady Kasa is a poet known for her twenty-nine *tanka* preserved in the *Manyoshu*, all of them love poems addressed to Otomo Yakamochi. She is an early figure of the passionate female poet who was to have so many incarnations in the history of Japanese poetry. Almost nothing is known about her life, but it has been surmised that her affair took place when Otomo Yakamochi was young, before he left the capital for the provinces. It is also thought, since the *Manyoshu* has only two love poems to her from him, that her love was to some extent unrequited.

Poems Sent to Otomo Yakamochi by Lady Kasa

In My Dream

In my dream
I held a sword
against my body.

What can it mean?
Are you coming soon?   5

To Love You

To love you
when you don't love me
is to worship
a hungry devil's ass
at the great temple.   5

Will I Never See You?

Will I never see you?
Only hear of you,
far,
a crane's cry
in the dark night?   5

My Keepsake

My keepsake—
look at it and think of me,
and I will love you
through the long years
strung like beads on a string   5

It's Not All Right

It's not all right, though
the years are gone
like a string of rough pearls.
Say nothing.
Bury even my name.   5

■ Lady Otomo Sakanoue (b. 695–701–died c. 750)

Lady Otomo Sakanoue was Yakamochi's aunt and the younger sister of Tabito. Eighty-four of her poems are in the *Manyoshu,* a number of which are love poems. Her passionate poetic persona influenced later women poets (such as Izumi Shikibu, Ono no Komachi, and Yosano Akiko), and some men (writing as women). This latter tradition—of men writing through female personae—was common to both China and Japan.

He Is So Handsome

He is so handsome
my heart
is a fast river breaking
through dams I put up
again and again   5

TRANSLATED BY TONY BARNSTONE

Unknown Love

Unknown love
is bitter
as a virgin lily
on the summer meadow,
blooming in bushes.   5

TRANSLATED BY WILLIS BARNSTONE

Heian Period

(794–1186)

■ Ki no Tsurayuki (c. 868–c. 946) (poems)

TRANSLATED BY BURTON WATSON

In his pristine observation of nature, of red leaves falling through moonlight and of human nature stained and intermingled with the tiniest motions in the landscape, Ki no Tsurayuki creates an elegantly crafted poetic that makes traditional themes new. He was a poet of the early Heian period and was one of the principal compilers of the *Kokinshu* (an abbreviation of the *Kokinwakashu,* or *Collection of Old and New Japanese Poems*), an extremely important early anthology, the first compilation ordered by Imperial decree. He came from a family steeped in the Chinese prose and poetry traditions, which he mastered himself. Though details about his life are scanty, we know that in 907 he held posts related to the preparation of the emperor's meals, that in the early 930s he was the governor of Tosa, and that he participated in a number of famous poetry matches. His preface to the *Kokinshu* was the first major essay in Japanese literary criticism. He was certainly the most famous poet in his time, and his work on the *Kokinshu* was a model for all subsequent compilations. His own poems appear in this and later collections and in a personal collection of his poetry, the *Tsurayuki Shu,* which appears in two versions, one of about seven hundred poems and one of about nine hundred. He is also well known for *The Tosa Diary* (c. 935), a diary of mixed prose and poetry that he writes from the point of view of a woman accompanying a governor on a trip from Tosa to the capital, a trip he took in 934. This essential work is the oldest piece of Japanese prose literature to come down to us in its original form. Both the preface to the *Kokinshu* and *The Tosa Diary* were written in the phonetic *kana* syllabary. The fact that two such central works were written not in Chinese characters but in a syllabary usually reserved for women's writings is extremely significant for the development of a purely Japanese literature. While his poetry still sings, Ki no Tsurayuki is a figure whose ultimate import lies in his pervasive influence on the evolution of Japanese letters.

FURTHER READING: McCullough, Helen Craig, tr. *Kokin Wakashu: The First Imperial Anthology of Japanese Poetry,* 1985. Miner, Earl, ed. and tr. *Japanese Poetic Diaries,* 1969, 1976.

from Preface to the Kokinshu[1]

Japanese poetry has its seeds in the human heart, and takes form in the countless leaves that are words. So much happens to us while we live in this world that we must voice the thoughts that are in our hearts, conveying them through the things we see and the things we hear. We hear the bush warbler singing in the flowers or the voice of the frogs that live in the water and know that among all living creatures there is not one that does not have its song. It is poetry that, without exerting force, can move heaven and earth, wake the feelings of the unseen gods and spirits, soften the relations between man and woman, and soothe the heart of the fierce warrior.

---

1. The opening paragraph is translated.

Five Tanka

Written When Visiting a Mountain Temple:

I found lodging
on the spring mountainside
and slept the night—
and in my dreams, too,
blossoms were falling   5

As autumn mists
rise up to veil them,
the red leaves
seem to drift down
in the dimness   5

Seeing someone off:
This thing called parting
has no color,
yet it seeps into our hearts
and stains them with loneliness   5

Along the Yodo
where they cut wild rice,
when it rains the marsh waters overflow,
like my love,
growing deeper than ever   5

Sixth month, cormorant fishing:
When torches cast their light,
in the depths of the night river
black as leopard-flower seeds,
the water bursts into flame   5

▪ Ono no Komachi (Ninth Century) (poems)

Although very little is known for certain about Ono no Komachi, she was the only woman included among the Six Poetic Geniuses (*rokkasen*), the six poets commented upon by Ki no Tsurayuki in his preface to the great early Heian poetry collection, the *Kokinshu,* the first of twenty-one anthologies compiled at the behest of various emperors. She and Ariwara Narihira are two of the six whose reputations have persisted, though Ki no Tsurayuki's praise of her poetry is rather backhanded: "Her poetry moves you in its enervation, like a gorgeous woman stricken with illness. This weakness probably comes from her sex." This assessment of her poems is echoed again and again by the stories and noh plays that have grown up about her life. It is difficult to extract her life from the legends that have surrounded her: various histories make her either the granddaughter of Ono no Takamura or the daughter of the district head of Dewa province, Ono no Yoshizane. Her most active periods could have been during the Jogan (859–877) or Showa (834–848) era. The name "Komachi" itself may not be a proper name but either a term applied to ladies-in-waiting or a diminutive, meaning "Little Machi," possibly referring to an older sister tentatively identified as Ono no Machi. The legends about her life depict her as a great beauty who rejected offers of marriage, hoping but failing to become an Imperial consort. Both her poems and the legends suggest that she was a great and passionate lover, and she exchanged poems with other great literary figures such as Ariwara Narihira, Sojo Henjo, and Funya Yasuhide, some of whom may have been her lovers. Later, when her beauty faded, she may have become a hunter's wife, and eventually a beggar, devoid of the graces she had hoped would gain her position. She was the subject of a number of noh plays, among them *Sotoba Komachi* and *Sekidera Komachi*. Arthur Waley's translation of *Sotoba Komachi* reads, in part: "Long ago I was full of pride / . . . I spoke with the voice of a nightingale that has sipped the dew. / I was lovelier than the petals of the wild-rose openstretched / In the hour before its fall. / But now I am grown loathsome even to sluts, / Poor girls of the people, and they and all men / Turn scornful from me." Her poetry is collected in a personal collection of one hundred and ten poems, the *Komachi Shu*, and they blaze off the page with such a mixture of intensity and delicate suggestion as to make her rank among the finest love poets in the world.

FURTHER READING: Hirshfield, Jane, with Mariko Aratani, trs. *The Ink Dark Moon: Love Poems by Ono no Komachi and Izumi Shikibu*, 1990. Rexroth, Kenneth, and Ikuko Atsumi, trs. *The Burning Heart: Women Poets of Japan*, 1977. Teele, Roy E., Nicholas J. Teele, and H. Rebecca Teele. *Ono no Komachi: Poems, Stories, No Plays*, 1993.

Doesn't He Realize

Doesn't he realize
that I am not
like the swaying kelp
in the surf,
where the seaweed gatherer   5
can come as often as he wants.

TRANSLATED BY KENNETH REXROTH AND IKUKO ATSUMI

I Fell Asleep Thinking of Him

I fell asleep thinking of him,
and he came to me.

If I had known it was only a dream
I would never have awakened.

He Does Not Come

He does not come.
Tonight in the dark of the moon
I wake wanting him.
My breasts heave and blaze.
My heart chars.   *5*

I Am So Lonely

I am so lonely
my body, a weed
severed at the root,
will drift on any current
that will have me.   *5*

The Autumn Night

The autumn night
is long only in name—
We've done no more
than gaze at each other
and it's already dawn.   *5*

How Invisibly

How invisibly
it changes color
in this world,
the flower
of the human heart.   *5*

■ Lady Ise (Ninth to Tenth Centuries) (poems)

Lady Ise came from the North branch of the Fujiwara family; her grandfather Fujiwara no Iemune is famous as the founder of the Hokai-ji in Hino, a very important temple in Japanese art history. Her father, Fujiwara no Tsugukage, was the governor of Ise and Yamato, and she came to be called Lady Ise because of her father's position. She acted as lady-in-waiting to Empress Onshi (872–907), was the consort of Emperor Uda, and was a literary figure for much of her adult life, spent at the Imperial court. She had a love affair with the empress's older brother, Fujiwara no Nakahira, and she later became a favorite of Emperor Uda and bore him a son who died at age seven. Eventually, she bore a daughter to Uda's fourth son, Prince Atsuyoshi, but after his death in 930, little is known of Lady Ise.

She was from a literary background. Both her uncle and her cousin were directors at the Imperial University, and her father graduated from the university's course in literature. Her delicate mastery and passion shine from her poems, and in her time she was an unusually distinguished female literary figure. One hundred and eighty of her poems are collected in the twenty-one Imperial anthologies, and there is a collection of poems bearing her name. She was selected to participate in a poetry match sponsored by Emperor Uda in 913, along with other eminent poets, including Ki no Tsurayuki. Like Ono no Komachi, she may have been a woman of considerable charm and beauty, and it can be seen that Lady Ise lived the life that Ono no Komachi dreamed of, as an Imperial consort.

Hanging from the Branches of a Green

Hanging from the branches of a green
willow tree,
the spring rain
is a
thread of pearls.   5

TRANSLATED BY WILLIS BARNSTONE

Like a Ravaged Sea

Like a ravaged sea
this bed.
Were I to smooth it,
the sleeve I press to it
would float back moist with foam.   5

TRANSLATED BY ETSUKO TERASAKI WITH IRMA BRANDEIS

Even in a Dream

Even in a dream
I don't want him to know
he's making love with me.
In the morning mirror
I see my face and blush.   5

TRANSLATED BY WILLIS BARNSTONE AND TONY BARNSTONE

■ *from* The Tales of Ise (Ninth to Tenth Centuries) (prose/poetry)

TRANSLATED BY HELEN CRAIG MCCULLOUGH

The Tales of Ise (Ise Monogatari) is a fascinating early Japanese work in which alternating poetry and prose set up a contrapuntal narrative of story and epiphany, consisting (in the most authoritative edition) of 209 poems in 125 sections. The central figure in these tales is the early Heian poet Ariwara Narihira (825–880), who becomes the model of the courtly lover in a number of the stories. In fact, during the Heian and medieval periods, the work was attributed to him, though later scholars discounted this possibility since the *Tales* contain the work of later poets and a poem on Narihira's death. Yet his famous poems, as well as poems written in response to them, are kernels around which some of the stories are written, and it is suggested that he may have been one of several authors who compiled the work between the late ninth and tenth centuries. As translator Helen Craig McCullough notes,

> *Tales of Ise* begins with an anecdote about a young nobleman recently come of age, continues with numerous episodes in which a male protagonist composes poems known to be by Narihira or is described as holding one of Narihira's known offices, and ends with Narihira's death poem. The picture that emerges from these sections, taken in conjunction with many others where the principal character is simply "a man," is that of a single recognizable individual who consistently demonstrates the sensitivity of the ideal aristocrat, especially in his relationships with women.[1]

Yet the tales are by no means a unified tribute to Narihira. Their unity comes, paradoxically, from their very variety and anonymity, which lend them a universal character. Though its author(s) remain unknown, the work has been enormously influential in the development of Japanese

---

1. Helen Craig McCullough, *Classical Japanese Prose: An Anthology* (Stanford, CA: Stanford University Press, 1990), 38–39.

literature, from Matsuo Basho's prose-poetry travelogue *Narrow Road to the Interior* to modern fiction stylists such as Kawabata Yasunari. Murasaki Shikibu is thought to have based Genji of her *The Tale of Genji* on Ariwara Narihira, a practice followed by many later authors of stories dealing with love. So popular was the work that many of its episodes appear on medieval scrolls, fans, and screens.

FURTHER READING: Harris, H. Jay, tr. *Tales of Ise,* 1972. McCullough, Helen Craig. *Classical Japanese Prose: An Anthology; Tales of Ise: Lyric Episodes from Tenth Century Japan,* 1968. Vos, Frits. *A Study of the Ise-monogatari,* 2 vols., 1957.

The Tales of Ise

12

Once there was a man who abducted someone's daughter. He was on his way to Musashi Plain with her when some provincial officials arrested him for theft. He had left the girl in a clump of bushes and run off, but the pursuers felt certain that he was on the plain, and they prepared to set fire to it. The girl recited this poem in great agitation:

> Light no fires today
> on the plain of Musashi,
>   for my young spouse,
> sweet as new grass, is hidden here,
> and I am hidden here too.

They heard her, seized her, and marched the two off together.

19

Once a man in the service of an imperial consort began to make love to one of the consort's attendants. Presently, the affair came to an end. When the two met in the course of their duties at the house, the man behaved as if the woman were invisible, even though she saw him plainly enough. She sent him this poem:

> Although you remain
> visible to the eye,
>   we are quite estranged:
> you have become as distant
> as a cloud in the heavens.

His reply:

> That I spend my days
> ever as distant from you
> as a cloud in the sky
> is the fault of the harsh wind
> on the hill where I would rest.

He meant that another man had been visiting her.

62

Once there was a woman whose husband had neglected her for years. Perhaps because she was not clever, she took the advice of an unreliable person and became a domestic in a provincial household. It happened one day that she served food to her former husband. That night, the husband told the master of the house to send her to him. "Don't you know me?" he asked. Then he recited:

> Where is the beauty
> you flaunted in days of old?
> Ah! You have become
> merely a cherry tree
> despoiled of its blossoms.

The woman was too embarrassed to reply. "Why don't you answer me?" he asked. "I am blind and speechless with tears," she said. He recited:

> Here is a person
> who has wished to be rid
> of her ties to me.
> Although much time has elapsed,
> her lot seems little improved.

He removed his cloak and gave it to her, but she left it and ran off—nobody knows where.

105

Once a man sent word to a woman, "I'll die if things go on like this." She answered:

> If the white dew
> must vanish, let it vanish.
> Even if it stayed,
> I doubt that anyone
> would string the drops like jewels.

The man considered the reply most discourteous, but his love for her increased.

125

Once a man was taken ill. Sensing the approach of death, he composed this poem:

> Upon this pathway,
> I have long heard it said,
>   man sets forth at last—
> yet I had not thought to go
> so very soon as today.

■ Sei Shonagon (c. 966–c. 1017) (memoir)

TRANSLATED BY IVAN MORRIS

The Pillow Book of Sei Shonagon is the earliest extant example of a particularly Japanese genre of writing called *zuihitsu* (random notes, occasional writings). *The Pillow Book* is Sei Shonagon's only known work, but it persists as one of the finest works in Japanese literature. We have almost no information about Sei Shonagon except what she herself writes in this compilation of idiosyncratic, witty, and daring observations. We do not even know her real name. Sei is the sinified reading of the character *kiyo*, the first character in her family name, and Shonagon is a court title. Recent research has suggested a possible first name for her: Nagiko. Her father was Kiyohara no Motosuke, who helped compile the *Gosenshu* (an Imperial anthology of poems), and it is possible that she married Tachibana no Norimitsu and bore him a son named Norinaga, but if so the marriage did not last long. She became a lady-in-waiting to Empress Sadako (also known as Teishi) in 990 and stayed in court service until 1000, when the empress died. Nothing is known for certain after her life in the court, but a legend has it that she became a Buddhist nun and died destitute and lonely. Translator Ivan Morris notes that such legends are probably the corrective invention of moralists who were shocked by her promiscuous life and worldly attitudes. Whoever she was, whatever her real name, Sei Shonagon lives through her book.

"Pillow book" seems to have been a term for informal collections of notes composed by men and women in their sleeping chambers in the evenings, journals that they may have kept in the drawers of their wooden pillows. Sei Shonagon's pillow book is distinguished for its clarity of observation and for the biting, charming intelligence of its author. She is considered a finer prose stylist than Murasaki Shikibu, particularly in her descriptions of nature. In addition to such descriptions, *The Pillow Book* contains anecdotes of court life, diary entries, observations on lovers, sketches of people high and low, and an incredible wealth of detail about aristocratic life in the Heian period. Perhaps her most famous and intriguing prose form is the "list." The book contains one hundred sixty-four lists of "hateful things," "people who look pleased with themselves," and even of "insects." Sei Shonagon was a sensitive woman but not without thorns. She is often cutting and dismissive, and her scorn for the lower classes is as excessive as her worship of the Imperial family; yet, as in the well-wrought snubs of Oscar Wilde or Gore Vidal, there are joys to be found in her negations.

Among the historical virtues of the Heian period is that major works by women were both written and preserved (in contrast to classical Latin literature from which, of many women authors, only seven poems by a poet who may have been called Sulpicia have been preserved). Sei Shonagon wrote at a time when the finest writers were aristocratic women of middle rank, and, with her contemporaries Izumi Shikibu and Murasaki Shikibu, she helped turn the middle Heian period into a moment of concentrated literary glory.

FURTHER READING: Morris, Ivan, tr. *The Pillow Book of Sei Shonagon,* 1967; *The World of the Shining Prince: Court Life in Ancient Japan,* 1969. Waley, Arthur. *The Pillow-Book of Sei Shonagon,* 1928.

from *The Pillow Book of Sei Shonagon*

That Parents Should Bring up Some Beloved Son

That parents should bring up some beloved son of theirs to be a priest is really distressing. No doubt it is an auspicious thing to do; but unfortunately most people are convinced that a priest is as unimportant as a piece of wood, and they treat him accordingly. A priest lives poorly on meagre food, and cannot even sleep without being criticized. While he is young, it is only natural that he should be curious about all sorts of things, and, if there are women about, he will probably peep in their direction (though, to be sure, with a look of aversion on his face). What is wrong about that? Yet people immediately find fault with him for even so small a lapse.

The lot of an exorcist is still more painful. On his pilgrimages to Mitake, Kumano, and all the other sacred mountains he often undergoes the greatest hardships. When people come to hear that his prayers are effective, they summon him here and there to perform services of exorcism: the more popular he becomes, the less peace he enjoys. Sometimes he will be called to see a patient who is seriously ill and he has to exert all his powers to cast out the spirit that is causing the affliction. But if he dozes off, exhausted by his efforts, people say reproachfully, 'Really, this priest does nothing but sleep.' Such comments are most embarrassing for the exorcist, and I can imagine how he must feel.

That is how things used to be; nowadays priests have a somewhat easier life.

The Cat Who Lived in the Palace

The cat who lived in the Palace had been awarded the headdress of nobility and was called Lady Myobu. She was a very pretty cat, and His Majesty saw to it that she was treated with the greatest care.[1]

One day she wandered on to the veranda, and Lady Uma, the nurse in charge of her, called out, 'Oh, you naughty thing! Please come inside at once.' But the cat paid no attention and went on basking sleepily in the sun. Intending to give her a scare, the nurse called for the dog, Okinamaro.

'Okinamaro, where are you?' she cried. 'Come here and bite Lady Myobu!' The foolish Okinamaro, believing that the nurse was in earnest, rushed at the cat, who, startled and terrified, ran behind the blind in the Imperial Dining Room, where the Emperor happened to be sitting. Greatly surprised, His Majesty picked up the cat and held her in his arms. He summoned his gentlemen-in-waiting. When Tadataka, the Chamberlain, appeared, His Majesty ordered that Okinamaro be chastised and banished to Dog Island. The attendants all started to chase the dog amid great confusion. His Majesty also reproached Lady Uma. 'We shall have to find a new nurse for our cat,' he told her. 'I no longer feel I can count on you to look after her.' Lady Uma bowed; thereafter she no longer appeared in the Emperor's presence.

The Imperial Guards quickly succeeded in catching Okinamaro and drove him out of the Palace grounds. Poor dog! He used to swagger about so happily. Recently, on the third day of the Third Month, when the Controller First Secretary paraded him through the Palace grounds, Okinamaro was adorned with garlands of willow leaves, peach blossoms on his head, and cherry blossoms round his body. How could the dog have imagined that this would be his fate? We all felt sorry for him. 'When Her Majesty was having her meals,' recalled one of the ladies-in-waiting, 'Okinamaro always used to be in attendance and sit opposite us. How I miss him!'

It was about noon, a few days after Okinamaro's banishment, that we heard a dog howling fearfully. How could any dog possibly cry so long? All the other dogs rushed out in excitement to see what was happening. Meanwhile a woman who served as a cleaner in the Palace latrines ran up to us. 'It's terrible,' she said. 'Two of the Chamberlains are flogging a dog. They'll surely kill him. He's being punished for having come back after he was banished. It's Tadataka and Sanefusa who are beating him.' Obviously the victim was Okinamaro. I was absolutely wretched and sent a servant to ask the

---

1. Cats had been imported from the Continent, and there are several references to them in Heian chronicles and literature. The diary of Fujiwara no Sanesuke, for instance, contains the momentous entry (on the nineteenth day of the Ninth Month in 999) that one of the Palace cats gave birth to a litter of kittens, that the birth-ceremony was attended by no lesser dignitaries than the Ministers of the Left and of the Right, and that Uma no Myobu was appointed nurse to the litter.

men to stop; but just then the howling finally ceased. 'He's dead,' one of the servants informed me. 'They've thrown his body outside the gate.'

That evening, while we were sitting in the Palace bemoaning Okinamaro's fate, a wretched-looking dog walked in; he was trembling all over, and his body was fearfully swollen.

'Oh dear,' said one of the ladies-in-waiting. 'Can this be Okinamaro? We haven't seen any other dog like him recently, have we?'

We called to him by name, but the dog did not respond. Some of us insisted that it was Okinamaro, others that it was not. 'Please send for Lady Ukon,' said the Empress, hearing our discussion. 'She will certainly be able to tell.' We immediately went to Ukon's room and told her she was wanted on an urgent matter.

'Is this Okinamaro?' the Empress asked her, pointing to the dog.

'Well,' said Ukon, 'it certainly looks like him, but I cannot believe that this loathsome creature is really our Okinamaro. When I called Okinamaro, he always used to come to me, wagging his tail. But this dog does not react at all. No, it cannot be the same one. And besides, wasn't Okinamaro beaten to death and his body thrown away? How could any dog be alive after being flogged by two strong men?' Hearing this, Her Majesty was very unhappy.

When it got dark, we gave the dog something to eat; but he refused it, and we finally decided that this could not be Okinamaro.

On the following morning I went to attend the Empress while her hair was being dressed and she was performing her ablutions. I was holding up the mirror for her when the dog we had seen on the previous evening slunk into the room and crouched next to one of the pillars. 'Poor Okinamaro!' I said. 'He had such a dreadful beating yesterday. How sad to think he is dead! I wonder what body he has been born into this time. Oh, how he must have suffered!'

At that moment the dog lying by the pillar started to shake and tremble, and shed a flood of tears. It was astounding. So this really was Okinamaro! On the previous night it was to avoid betraying himself that he had refused to answer to his name. We were immensely moved and pleased. 'Well, well, Okinamaro!' I said, putting down the mirror. The dog stretched himself flat on the floor and yelped loudly, so that the Empress beamed with delight. All the ladies gathered round, and Her Majesty summoned Lady Ukon. When the Empress explained what had happened, everyone talked and laughed with great excitement.

The news reached His Majesty, and he too came to the Empress's room. 'It's amazing,' he said with a smile. 'To think that even a dog has such deep feelings!' When the Emperor's ladies-in-waiting heard the story, they too came along in a great crowd. 'Okinamaro!' we called, and this time the dog rose and limped about the room with his swollen face. 'He must have a meal prepared for him,' I said. 'Yes,' said the Empress, laughing happily, 'now that Okinamaro has finally told us who he is.'

The Chamberlain, Tadataka, was informed, and he hurried along from the Table Room. 'Is it really true?' he asked. 'Please let me see for myself.' I sent a maid to him with the following reply: 'Alas, I am afraid that this is not the same dog after all.' 'Well,' answered Tadataka, 'whatever you say, I shall sooner or later have occasion to see the animal. You won't be able to hide him from me indefinitely.'

Before long, Okinamaro was granted an Imperial pardon and returned to his former happy state. Yet even now, when I remember how he whimpered and trembled in response to our sympathy, it strikes me as a strange and moving scene; when people talk to me about it, I start crying myself.

Hateful Things

One is in a hurry to leave, but one's visitor keeps chattering away. If it is someone of no importance, one can get rid of him by saying, 'You must tell me all about it next time'; but, should it be the sort of visitor whose presence commands one's best behaviour, the situation is hateful indeed.

One finds that a hair has got caught in the stone on which one is rubbing one's inkstick, or again that gravel is lodged in the inkstick, making a nasty, grating sound.

Someone has suddenly fallen ill and one summons the exorcist. Since he is not at home, one has to send messengers to look for him. After one has had a long fretful wait, the exorcist finally arrives, and with a sigh of relief one asks him to start his incantations. But perhaps he has been exorcizing too many evil spirits recently; for hardly has he installed himself and begun praying when his voice becomes drowsy. Oh, how hateful!

A man who has nothing in particular to recommend him discusses all sorts of subjects at random as though he knew everything.

An elderly person warms the palms of his hands over a brazier and stretches out the wrinkles. No young man would dream of behaving in such a fashion; old people can really be quite shameless. I have seen some dreary old creatures actually resting their feet on the brazier and rubbing them against the edge while they speak. These are the kind of people who in visiting someone's house first use their fans to wipe away the dust from the mat and, when they finally sit on it, cannot stay still but are forever spreading out the front of their hunting costume[2] or even tucking it up under their knees. One might suppose that such behaviour was restricted to people of humble station; but I have observed it in quite well-bred people, including a Senior Secretary of the Fifth Rank in the Ministry of Ceremonial and a former Governor of Suruga.

I hate the sight of men in their cups who shout, poke their fingers in their mouths, stroke their beards, and pass on the wine to their neighbours with great cries of 'Have some more! Drink up!' They tremble, shake their

---

2. Men's informal outdoor costume, originally worn for hunting.

heads, twist their faces, and gesticulate like children who are singing, 'We're off to see the Governor.' I have seen really well-bred people behave like this and I find it most distasteful.

To envy others and to complain about one's own lot; to speak badly about people; to be inquisitive about the most trivial matters and to resent and abuse people for not telling one, or, if one does manage to worm out some facts, to inform everyone in the most detailed fashion as if one had known all from the beginning—oh, how hateful!

One is just about to be told some interesting piece of news when a baby starts crying.

A flight of crows circle about with loud caws.

An admirer has come on a clandestine visit, but a dog catches sight of him and starts barking. One feels like killing the beast.

One has been foolish enough to invite a man to spend the night in an unsuitable place—and then he starts snoring.

A gentleman has visited one secretly. Though he is wearing a tall, lacquered hat,[3] he nevertheless wants no one to see him. He is so flurried, in fact, that upon leaving he bangs into something with his hat. Most hateful! It is annoying too when he lifts up the Iyo blind[4] that hangs at the entrance of the room, then lets it fall with a great rattle. If it is a head-blind, things are still worse, for being more solid it makes a terrible noise when it is dropped. There is no excuse for such carelessness. Even a head-blind does not make any noise if one lifts it up gently on entering and leaving the room; the same applies to sliding-doors. If one's movements are rough, even a paper door will bend and resonate when opened; but, if one lifts the door a little while pushing it, there need be no sound.

One has gone to bed and is about to doze off when a mosquito appears, announcing himself in a reedy voice. One can actually feel the wind made by his wings and, slight though it is, one finds it hateful in the extreme.

A carriage passes with a nasty, creaking noise. Annoying to think that the passengers may not even be aware of this! If I am travelling in someone's carriage and I hear it creaking, I dislike not only the noise but also the owner of the carriage.

One is in the middle of a story when someone butts in and tries to show that he is the only clever person in the room. Such a person is hateful, and so, indeed, is anyone, child or adult, who tries to push himself forward.

---

3. *Eboshi* (tall, lacquered hat): black, lacquered head-dress worn by men on the top of the head and secured by a mauve silk cord that was fastened under the chin; two long black pendants hung down from the back of the hat. The *eboshi* was a most conspicuous form of headgear and hardly suited for a clandestine visit.

4. Iyo blind: a rough type of reed blind manufactured in the province of Iyo on the Inland Sea. Head-blind: a more elegant type of blind whose top and edges were decorated with strips of silk. It also had thin strips of bamboo along the edges and was therefore heavier than ordinary blinds.

One is telling a story about old times when someone breaks in with a little detail that he happens to know, implying that one's own version is inaccurate—disgusting behaviour!

Very hateful is a mouse that scurries all over the place.

Some children have called at one's house. One makes a great fuss of them and gives them toys to play with. The children become accustomed to this treatment and start to come regularly, forcing their way into one's inner rooms and scattering one's furnishings and possessions. Hateful!

A certain gentleman whom one does not want to see visits one at home or in the Palace, and one pretends to be asleep. But a maid comes to tell one and shakes one awake, with a look on her face that says, 'What a sleepyhead!' Very hateful.

A newcomer pushes ahead of the other members in a group; with a knowing look, this person starts laying down the law and forcing advice upon everyone—most hateful.

A man with whom one is having an affair keeps singing the praises of some woman he used to know. Even if it is a thing of the past, this can be very annoying. How much more so if he is still seeing the woman! (Yet sometimes I find that it is not as unpleasant as all that.)

A person who recites a spell himself after sneezing.[5] In fact I detest anyone who sneezes, except the master of the house.

Fleas, too, are very hateful. When they dance about under someone's clothes, they really seem to be lifting them up.

The sound of dogs when they bark for a long time in chorus is ominous and hateful.

I cannot stand people who leave without closing the panel behind them.

How I detest the husbands of nurse-maids! It is not so bad if the child in the maid's charge is a girl, because then the man will keep his distance. But, if it is a boy, he will behave as though he were the father. Never letting the boy out of his sight, he insists on managing everything. He regards the other attendants in the house as less than human, and, if anyone tries to scold the child, he slanders him to the master. Despite this disgraceful behaviour, no one dare accuse the husband; so he strides about the house with a proud, self-important look, giving all the orders.

I hate people whose letters show that they lack respect for worldly civilities, whether by discourtesy in the phrasing or by extreme politeness to someone who does not deserve it. This sort of thing is, of course, most odious if the letter is for oneself, but it is bad enough even if it is addressed to someone else.

As a matter of fact, most people are too casual, not only in their letters but in their direct conversation. Sometimes I am quite disgusted at noting

---

5. Sneezing was a bad omen, and it was normal to counteract its effects by reciting some auspicious formula, such as wishing long life to the person who had sneezed (cf. 'Bless you!' in the West).

how little decorum people observe when talking to each other. It is particularly unpleasant to hear some foolish man or woman omit the proper marks of respect when addressing a person of quality; and, when servants fail to use honorific forms of speech in referring to their masters, it is very bad indeed. No less odious, however, are those masters who, in addressing their servants, use such phrases as 'When you were good enough to do such-and-such' or 'As you so kindly remarked.' No doubt there are some masters who, in describing their own actions to a servant, say, 'I presumed to do so-and-so'![6]

Sometimes a person who is utterly devoid of charm will try to create a good impression by using very elegant language; yet he only succeeds in being ridiculous. No doubt he believes this refined language to be just what the occasion demands, but, when it goes so far that everyone bursts out laughing, surely something must be wrong.

It is most improper to address high-ranking courtiers, Imperial Advisers, and the like simply by using their names without any titles or marks of respect; but such mistakes are fortunately rare.

If one refers to the maid who is in attendance on some lady-in-waiting as 'Madam' or 'that lady,' she will be surprised, delighted, and lavish in her praise.

When speaking to young noblemen and courtiers of high rank, one should always (unless Their Majesties are present) refer to them by their official posts. Incidentally, I have been very shocked to hear important people use the word 'I' while conversing in Their Majesties' presence.[7] Such a breach of etiquette is really distressing, and I fail to see why people cannot avoid it.

A man who has nothing in particular to recommend him but who speaks in an affected tone and poses as being elegant.

An inkstone with such a hard, smooth surface that the stick glides over it without leaving any deposit of ink.

Ladies-in-waiting who want to know everything that is going on.

Sometimes one greatly dislikes a person for no particular reason—and then that person goes and does something hateful.

A gentleman who travels alone in his carriage to see a procession or some other spectacle. What sort of a man is he? Even though he may not be a person of the greatest quality, surely he should have taken along a few of

---

6. *Owasu* ('good enough to do') and *notamau* ('kindly remarked') designate the actions of a superior; *haberu* (lit. 'to serve') is used to describe one's own or someone else's actions in relation to a superior. See *Dictionary of Selected Forms in Classical Japanese Literature until c. 1330*, App. IV. The correct use of honorific, polite, and humble locutions was of course enormously important in a strictly hierarchic society. In the present passage the sentence beginning 'No doubt . . .' is ironic.

7. Etiquette demanded that in the presence of the Emperor or Empress one referred to oneself by one's name rather than by the first person singular. One referred to other people by their real names; if Their Majesties were not present, however, one referred to these people by their offices (e.g., Major Counsellor). On the whole, personal pronouns were avoided and this added to the importance of correct honorific usage.

the many young men who are anxious to see the sights. But no, there he sits by himself (one can see his silhouette through the blinds), with a proud look on his face, keeping all his impressions to himself.

A lover who is leaving at dawn announces that he has to find his fan and his paper.[8] 'I know I put them somewhere last night,' he says. Since it is pitch dark, he gropes about the room, bumping into the furniture and muttering, 'Strange! Where on earth can they be?' Finally he discovers the objects. He thrusts the paper into the breast of his robe with a great rustling sound; then he snaps open his fan and busily fans away with it. Only now is he ready to take his leave. What charmless behaviour! 'Hateful' is an understatement.

Equally disagreeable is the man who, when leaving in the middle of the night, takes care to fasten the cord of his head-dress. This is quite unnecessary; he could perfectly well put it gently on his head without tying the cord. And why must he spend time adjusting his cloak or hunting costume? Does he really think someone may see him at this time of night and criticize him for not being impeccably dressed?

A good lover will behave as elegantly at dawn as at any other time. He drags himself out of bed with a look of dismay on his face. The lady urges him on: 'Come, my friend, it's getting light. You don't want anyone to find you here.' He gives a deep sigh, as if to say that the night has not been nearly long enough and that it is agony to leave. Once up, he does not instantly pull on his trousers. Instead he comes close to the lady and whispers whatever was left unsaid during the night. Even when he is dressed, he still lingers, vaguely pretending to be fastening his sash.

Presently he raises the lattice, and the two lovers stand together by the side door while he tells her how he dreads the coming day, which will keep them apart; then he slips away. The lady watches him go, and this moment of parting will remain among her most charming memories.

Indeed, one's attachment to a man depends largely on the elegance of his leave-taking. When he jumps out of bed, scurries about the room, tightly fastens his trouser-sash, rolls up the sleeves of his Court cloak, over-robe, or hunting costume, stuffs his belongings into the breast of his robe and then briskly secures the outer sash—one really begins to hate him.

It Is So Stiflingly Hot

It is so stiflingly hot in the Seventh Month that even at night one keeps all the doors and lattices open. At such times it is delightful to wake up when the moon is shining and to look outside. I enjoy it even when there is no

---

8. Elegant coloured paper that gentlemen carried in the folds of their clothes. It served for writing notes and was also used like an elegant sort of Kleenex.

moon. But to wake up at dawn and see a pale sliver of a moon in the sky—well, I need hardly say how perfect that is.

I like to see a bright new straw mat that has just been spread out on a well-polished floor.[9] The best place for one's three-foot curtain of state is in the front of the room near the veranda. It is pointless to put it in the rear of the room, as it is most unlikely that anyone will peer in from that direction.[10]

It is dawn and a woman is lying in bed after her lover has taken his leave. She is covered up to her head with a light mauve robe that has a lining of dark violet; the colour of both the outside and the lining is fresh and glossy.[11] The woman, who appears to be asleep, wears an unlined orange robe and a dark crimson skirt of stiff silk whose cords hang loosely by her side, as if they have been left untied. Her thick tresses tumble over each other in cascades, and one can imagine how long her hair must be when it falls freely down her back.[12]

Near by another woman's lover is making his way home in the misty dawn. He is wearing loose violet trousers, an orange hunting costume, so lightly coloured that one can hardly tell whether it has been dyed or not, a white robe of stiff silk, and a scarlet robe of glossy, beaten silk. His clothes, which are damp from the mist, hang loosely about him. From the dishevelment of his side locks one can tell how negligently he must have tucked his hair into his black lacquered head-dress when he got up. He wants to return and write his next-morning letter[13] before the dew on the morning

---

9. In the Heian period rooms were not covered with straw mats as became normal in later times; instead mats were spread out when and where they were needed for sleeping, sitting, etc.

10. *Kichō* (curtains of state) were usually classified in terms of the length of the horizontal wooden bar from which the curtains were suspended. A three-foot curtain of state normally had five widths of curtain.

On a hot summer night it was advisable to place one's *kichō* in as cool a part of the room as possible, i.e. near the veranda. Besides, since the main purpose of the *kichō* was to protect women from prying eyes, it would be illogical to place it in the rear of the room where people were unlikely to be looking at one from behind.

11. It was customary in Shōnagon's time to use clothes as bedcovers; also it was normal to sleep fully dressed. The two sets of clothing described in this paragraph are, respectively, the woman's bedclothes and her dress. The present scene evidently takes place in the Imperial Palace; the philandering gentleman is able to peep into the lady's quarters as he walks along the corridor on his way back from his own tryst.

12. Heian women usually let their long, thick hair hang loosely down their backs. The closer it reached the floor, the more beautiful they were considered.

13. It was an essential part of Heian etiquette for the man to write a love-letter to the lady with whom he had spent the night; it usually included a poem and was attached to a spray of some appropriate flower. The letter had to be sent as soon as the man returned home or, if he was on duty, as soon as he reached his office. The lady was of course expected to send a prompt reply. If the man failed to send a letter, it normally meant that he had no desire to continue the liaison.

glories has had time to vanish; but the path seems endless, and to divert himself he hums 'The sprouts in the flax fields.'[14]

As he walks along, he passes a house with an open lattice. He is on his way to report for official duty, but cannot help stopping to lift up the blind and peep into the room.[15] It amuses him to think that a man has probably been spending the night here and has only recently got up to leave, just as happened to himself. Perhaps that man too had felt the charm of the dew.[16]

Looking round the room, he notices near the woman's pillow an open fan with a magnolia frame and purple paper; and at the foot of her curtain of state he sees some narrow strips of Michinoku paper and also some other paper of a faded colour, either orange-red or maple.

The woman senses that someone is watching her and, looking up from under her bedclothes, sees a gentleman leaning against the wall by the threshold, a smile on his face. She can tell at once that he is the sort of man with whom she need feel no reserve. All the same, she does not want to enter into any familiar relations with him, and she is annoyed that he should have seen her asleep.[17]

'Well, well, Madam,' says the man, leaning forward so that the upper part of his body comes behind her curtains, 'what a long nap you're having after your morning adieu! You really are a lie-abed!'

'You call me that, Sir,' she replied, 'only because you're annoyed at having had to get up before the dew had time to settle.'

Their conversation may be commonplace, yet I find there is something delightful about the scene.

Now the gentleman leans further forward and, using his own fan, tries to get hold of the fan by the woman's pillow. Fearing his closeness, she

---

14. From the poem,

> The sprouts of the cherry flax
> In the flax fields
> Are heavy now with dew.
> I shall stay with you till dawn
> Though your parents be aware.

The expression 'cherry-flax' is found in a similar poem in the *Manyō Shū* and refers (i) to the fact that flax was sown at the same time that the cherries blossomed, (ii) to the similarity in appearance between cherry blossoms and the leaves of flax.

The gallant declares that he will stay with the girl until daylight, though this probably means that her parents will find out about his visit. His ostensible reason is that it is hard to make his way through the heavy morning dew (a standard euphemism); the real motive, of course, is his reluctance to leave the partner of his night's pleasures. 'Dew on the sprouts' may have a secondary erotic implication such as one frequently finds in early Japanese love poems.

15. I.e., the house of the woman with the long hair and the orange robe.

16. If the man was sensitive to the beauty of the dew, he would want to leave at early dawn before it had disappeared. The real reason for early departures, of course, was fear of discovery; but pretty conceits of this type were common.

17. As a rule a Heian woman of the upper class would not let herself be seen by a man unless she was actually having an affair with him—and not always then. They were usually protected by curtains of state, screens, fans, etc., and above all by the darkness of the rooms.

moves further back into her curtain enclosure, her heart pounding. The gentleman picks up the magnolia fan and, while examining it, says in a slightly bitter tone, 'How standoffish you are!'

But now it is growing light; there is a sound of people's voices, and it looks as if the sun will soon be up. Only a short while ago this same man was hurrying home to write his next-morning letter before the mists had time to clear. Alas, how easily his intentions have been forgotten!

While all this is afoot, the woman's original lover has been busy with his own next-morning letter, and now, quite unexpectedly, the messenger arrives at her house. The letter is attached to a spray of bush-clover, still damp with dew, and the paper gives off a delicious aroma of incense. Because of the new visitor, however, the woman's servants cannot deliver it to her.

Finally it becomes unseemly for the gentleman to stay any longer. As he goes, he is amused to think that a similar scene may be taking place in the house he left earlier that morning.

Elegant Things

A white coat worn over a violet waistcoat.
Duck eggs.
Shaved-ice mixed with liana syrup and put in a new silver bowl.
A rosary of rock crystal.
Wistaria blossoms. Plum blossoms covered with snow.
A pretty child eating strawberries.

Insects

The bell insect and the pine cricket; the grasshopper and the common cricket; the butterfly and the shrimp insect; the mayfly and the firefly.

I feel very sorry for the basket worm. He was begotten by a demon, and his mother, fearing that he would grow up with his father's frightening nature, abandoned the unsuspecting child, having first wrapped him in a dirty piece of clothing. 'Wait for me,' she said as she left. 'I shall return to you as soon as the autumn winds blow.' So, when autumn comes and the wind starts blowing, the wretched child hears it and desperately cries, 'Milk! Milk!'[18]

The clear-toned cicada.

The snap-beetle also impresses me. They say that the reason it bows while crawling along the ground is that the faith of Buddha has sprung up

---

18. *Chi-chi* is the characteristic sound of the basket worm as well as the word for 'milk.' The insect in question is a *psychidae;* it was called 'straw-coat insect' because of the nest in which it is wrapped. This nest is made chiefly of dirt.

in its insect heart. Sometimes one suddenly hears the snap-beetle tapping away in a dark place, and this is rather pleasant.

The fly should have been included in my list of hateful things; for such an odious creature does not belong with ordinary insects. It settles on everything, and even alights on one's face with its clammy feet. I am sorry that anyone should have been named after it.[19]

The tiger moth is very pretty and delightful. When one sits close to a lamp reading a story, a tiger moth will often flutter prettily in front of one's book.

The ant is an ugly insect; but it is light on its feet and I enjoy watching as it skims quickly over the surface of the water.

To Meet One's Lover

To meet one's lover summer is indeed the right season. True, the nights are very short, and dawn creeps up before one has had a wink of sleep. Since all the lattices have been left open, one can lie and look out at the garden in the cool morning air. There are still a few endearments to exchange before the man takes his leave, and the lovers are murmuring to each other when suddenly there is a loud noise. For a moment they are certain that they have been discovered; but it is only the caw of a crow flying past in the garden.

In the winter, when it is very cold and one lies buried under the bed-clothes listening to one's lover's endearments, it is delightful to hear the booming of a temple gong, which seems to come from the bottom of a deep well. The first cry of the birds, whose beaks are still tucked under their wings, is also strange and muffled. Then one bird after another takes up the call. How pleasant it is to lie there listening as the sound becomes clearer and clearer!

The Women's Apartments along the Gallery

The women's apartments along the gallery of the Imperial Palace are particularly pleasant. When one raises the upper part of the small half-shutters, the wind blows in extremely hard; it is cool even in summer, and in winter snow and hail come along with the wind, which I find agreeable. As the rooms are small, and as the page-boys (even though employed in such august precincts) often behave badly, we women generally stay hidden behind our screens or curtains. It is delightfully quiet there; for one cannot hear any of the loud talk and laughter that disturb one in other parts of the Palace.

---

19. In ancient Japan people were often named after animals. Haemaro (in which *hae* means 'fly') was probably given to members of the lower orders because of its unpleasant associations.

Of course we must always be on the alert when we are staying in these apartments. Even during the day we cannot be off our guard, and at night we have to be especially careful. But I rather enjoy all this. Throughout the night one hears the sound of footsteps in the corridor outside. Every now and then the sound will stop, and someone will tap on a door with just a single finger. It is pleasant to think that the woman inside can instantly recognize her visitor. Sometimes the tapping will continue for quite a while without the woman's responding in any way. The man finally gives up, thinking that she must be asleep; but this does not please the woman, who makes a few cautious movements, with a rustle of silk clothes, so that her visitor will know she is really there. Then she hears him fanning himself as he remains standing outside the door.

In the winter one sometimes catches the sound of a woman gently stirring the embers in her brazier. Though she does her best to be quiet, the man who is waiting outside hears her; he knocks louder and louder, asking her to let him in. Then the woman slips furtively towards the door where she can listen to him.

On other occasions one may hear several voices reciting Chinese or Japanese poems. One of the women opens her door, though in fact no one has knocked. Seeing this, several of the men, who had no particular intention of visiting this woman, stop on their way through the gallery. Since there is no room for them all to come in, many of them spend the rest of the night out in the garden—most charming.

I Remember a Clear Morning

I remember a clear morning in the Ninth Month when it had been raining all night. Despite the bright sun, dew was still dripping from the chrysanthemums in the garden. On the bamboo fences and criss-cross hedges I saw tatters of spider webs; and where the threads were broken the raindrops hung on them like strings of white pearls. I was greatly moved and delighted.

As it became sunnier, the dew gradually vanished from the clover and the other plants where it had lain so heavily; the branches began to stir, then suddenly sprang up of their own accord. Later I described to people how beautiful it all was. What most impressed me was that they were not at all impressed.

Things without Merit

An ugly person with a bad character.

Rice starch that has become mixed with water. . . . I know that this is a very vulgar item and everyone will dislike my mentioning it. But that should not stop me. In fact I must feel free to include anything, even tongs used for the parting-fires.[20] After all, these objects do exist in our world and people all know about them. I admit they do not belong to a list that others will see. But I never thought that these notes would be read by anyone else, and so I included everything that came into my head, however strange or unpleasant.[21]

The House Had a Spacious Courtyard

The house had a spacious courtyard and was shadowed by tall pine trees. To the south and east the lattice-windows were all wide open. It gave a cool feeling when one looked inside. In the main room was a four-foot curtain of state and in front of it a round hassock on which a priest was kneeling. He was in his early thirties and quite handsome. Over his grey habit he wore a fine silk stole — altogether the effect was magnificent. Cooling himself with a clove-scented fan, he recited the Magic Incantation of the Thousand Hands.[22]

I gathered that someone in the house was seriously ill, for now a heavily built girl with a splendid head of hair edged her way into the room. Clearly this was the medium to whom the evil spirit was going to be transferred. She was wearing an unlined robe of stiff silk and long, light-coloured trousers.

When the girl had sat down next to the priest in front of a small three-foot curtain of state, he turned round and handed her a thin, highly polished wand.[23] Then with his eyes tightly shut he began to read the mystic incantations, his voice coming out in staccato bursts as he uttered the sacred syllables. It was an impressive sight, and many of the ladies of the house came out from behind the screens and curtains and sat watching in a group.

---

20. Putting starch in laundered clothes was so plebeian an occupation that Shōnagon hesitates even to hint at its existence. She points out, however, that her notes were not intended for other people to see and that she would therefore be justified in including so inauspicious an item as parting-fire tongs (below), which were associated with death.

Tongs used for the parting fires: the Festival of the Dead (Urabon), which corresponded in some ways to All Souls' Day in the West, was celebrated from the thirteenth to the sixteenth of the Seventh Month. Sticks of peeled hemp were lit on the first day of the festival so that the souls of the dead might find their way to earth; on the last day, parting fires were again lit, this time to speed the ghostly visitors on their way back. On the fifteenth a special Buddhist service was held in intercession for the dead who were suffering in hell, especially for those who were undergoing the ordeal of Headlong Falling.

The wooden tongs used for the parting fires clearly deserved to be included among Things Without Merit. The tongs used for the welcoming fires could be used again at the end of the festival, but afterwards they had to be thrown away because of their inauspicious connotations.

21. Shōnagon is clearly defending herself from some criticism that she has received or expects to receive (e.g. 'Why do you write about such vulgar subjects as starching laundered clothes?').

22. Magic Incantation of the Thousand Hands: one section of the Thousand Hand Sutra, which was especially associated with Shingon. It was recited to ward off illnesses, discord, slander, and other evils.

23. A type of mace, particularly connected with Shingon and used by priests, exorcists, etc., who brandished it in all directions while reciting their prayers and magic formulae.

After a short time the medium began to tremble and fell into a trance. It was awesome indeed to see how the priest's incantations were steadily taking effect. The medium's brother, a slender young man in a long robe who had only recently celebrated his coming of age, stood behind the girl, fanning her.

Everyone who witnessed the scene was overcome with respect. It occurred to me how embarrassed the girl herself would feel to be exposed like this if she were in her normal state of mind. She lay there groaning and wailing in the most terrible way, and, though one realized that she was in no actual pain,[24] one could not help sympathizing with her. Indeed, one of the patients' friends, feeling sorry for the girl, went up to her curtain of state and helped to rearrange her disordered clothing.

Meanwhile it was announced that the patient was a little better. Some young attendants were sent to the kitchen to fetch hot water and other requisites. Even while they were carrying their trays they kept darting uneasy glances at the exorcist. They wore pretty unlined robes and formal skirts whose light mauve colour was as fresh as on the day they were dyed—it made a most charming effect.

By the Hour of the Monkey the priest had brought the spirit under control and, having forced it to beg for mercy, he now dismissed it. 'Oh!' exclaimed the medium. 'I thought I was behind the curtains and here I am in front. What on earth has happened?' Overcome with embarrassment, she hid her face in her long hair and was about to glide out of the room when the priest stopped her and, after murmuring a few incantations, said, 'Well, my dear, how do you feel? You should be quite yourself by now.' He smiled at the girl, but this only added to her confusion.

'I should have liked to stay a little longer,' said the priest, as he prepared to leave the house, 'but I am afraid it is almost time for my evening prayers.' The people of the house tried to stop him. 'Please wait a moment,' they said. 'We should like to make an offering.' But the priest was obviously in a great hurry and would not stay. At this point a lady of noble rank, evidently a member of the family, edged her way up to the priest's curtain of state and said, 'We are most grateful for your visit, Your Reverence. Our patient looked as if she might well succumb to the evil spirit, but now she is well on the way to recovery. I cannot tell you how delighted we are. If Your Reverence has any free time tomorrow, would you please call again?'

'I fear we are dealing with a very obstinate spirit,' the priest replied briefly, 'and we must not be off our guard. I am pleased that what I did

---

24. The groans and wails come from the evil spirit, which has temporarily been transferred to the medium and is now being painfully subdued by the priest's incantations.

today has helped the patient.' So saying, he took his leave with an air of such dignity that everyone felt the Buddha himself had appeared on earth.

When the Middle Captain

When the Middle Captain of the Left Guards Division was still Governor of Ise, he visited me one day at my home. There was a straw mat at the edge of the veranda, and I pulled it out for him. This notebook of mine happened to be lying on the mat, but I did not notice it in time. I snatched at the book and made a desperate effort to get it back; but the Captain instantly took it off with him and did not return it until much later. I suppose it was from this time that my book began to be passed about at Court.

It Is Getting So Dark

It is getting so dark that I can scarcely go on writing; and my brush is all worn out. Yet I should like to add a few things before I end.

I wrote these notes at home, when I had a good deal of time to myself and thought no one would notice what I was doing. Everything that I have seen and felt is included. Since much of it might appear malicious and even harmful to other people, I was careful to keep my book hidden. But now it has become public, which is the last thing I expected.

One day Lord Korechika, the Minister of the Centre, brought the Empress a bundle of notebooks. 'What shall we do with them?' Her Majesty asked me. 'The Emperor has already made arrangements for copying the "Records of the Historian".'[25]

'Let me make them into a pillow,' I said.[26]

'Very well,' said Her Majesty. 'You may have them.'

I now had a vast quantity of paper at my disposal, and I set about filling the notebooks with odd facts, stories from the past, and all sorts of other things, often including the most trivial material. On the whole I concentrated on things and people that I found charming and splendid; my notes are also full of poems and observations on trees and plants, birds and insects. I was sure that when people saw my book they would say, 'It's even worse than I expected. Now one can really tell what she is like.' After all, it is written entirely for my own amusement and I put things down exactly as they came to me. How could my casual jottings possibly bear comparison with the many impressive books that exist in our time? Readers have declared, however, that I can be proud of my work. This has surprised me greatly; yet I suppose it is not so strange that people should like it, for, as

---

25. It appears that Korechika also presented Emperor Ichijo with a quantity of paper (good paper being in short supply even at Court) and that the Emperor had decided to use his allotment for making a copy of the huge Chinese historical work, *Shih chi.*

26. A pillow book. Here we have one likely explanation of the title of Shōnagon's book.

will be gathered from these notes of mine, I am the sort of person who approves of what others abhor and detests the things they like.[27]

Whatever people may think of my book, I still regret that it ever came to light.

■ Izumi Shikibu (c. 974–c. 1034) (poems)

Izumi Shikibu was the major poet of her day. Her father, Oe no Masamune, was a provincial governor, and her mother may have been the daughter of Taira no Yasuhira, governor of Etchu. Around age twenty, she married Tachibana no Michisada, the governor of Izumi; her name comes from a combination of the place name *Izumi* and the appellation *Shikibu* (court lady). The marriage was not successful. She had many lovers, notably the two Imperial princes, Tamataka and his brother, Atsumichi. With Michisada she had a daughter, known as Naishi or Ko-shikibu (meaning "Shikibu's child"), herself a fine poet who died young, before her mother. Both of Izumi Shikibu's Imperial lovers died young, and she writes passionately about Atsumichi in particular in her diary (*Izumi Shikibu Nikki*), a literary classic of the Heian period. A personal collection of her poetry exists in five recensions, containing between 647 and 902 poems. Her scandalous and overt affairs soon caused her to be permanently separated from her husband. Prince Atsumichi, who died when he was twenty-seven, was her great love, and she mourns him in more than one hundred poems, some of the most striking in her collection: "It would console me / if you returned / even for the length of the flash — / seen and then gone — / of lightning at dusk" (translated by Jane Hirshfield and Mariko Aratani). At some time after his death, she became a lady-in-waiting to the Empress Shoshi, whose retinue included many brilliant writers, such as Murasaki Shikibu. While in the empress's service, she married Fujiwara no Yasumasa (958–1036), a man of great military fame. According to some sources, late in life she became a nun, and in her poems she questions whether she should "leave this burning house / of ceaseless thought" and enter Buddhist service.

Since the romantic custom at court was to initiate an affair by sending a poem — and acceptance was signaled through a poem sent in return — it helped for great lovers to be great poets. Izumi Shikibu was certainly both and was, in fact, Japan's finest female poet. Her poems of love are fresh and saucy, flames that burn fiercely in the mind — five lines of absolute heat. Her poems of loss are as absolute. Mourning or in love, a Buddhist sense of the world as illusion permeates the poetry, a counterpoint to the pattern of joy and loss that was her life: "The fleeting world / of white dew, / fox fires,

---

27. Since Shōnagon's judgment tended to be the exact opposite of other people's, it was only natural that they should praise a book (her own) which she considered to be deficient in so many respects.

dreams—/ all last long, / compared with love" (translated by Jane Hirshfield and Mariko Aratani).

FURTHER READING: Cranston, Edwin A., tr. *The Izumi Shikibu Diary: A Romance of the Heian Court*, 1969. Hirshfield, Jane, and Mariko Aratani, trs. *The Ink Dark Moon: Love Poems by Ono no Komachi and Izumi Shikibu, Women of the Ancient Court of Japan*, 1986. Miner, Earl, tr. *Japanese Poetic Diaries*, 1969.

I'm in Such Bad Shape

I'm in such bad shape
that when a firefly rises
out of the marsh grass
I feel my soul leaping out
of my body in desire.   5

TRANSLATED BY TONY BARNSTONE

I Don't Care about These

I don't care about these
wild tangles in my black hair.
I just lie back down
in bed and ache for your hands
which no longer brush them smooth.   5

TRANSLATED BY TONY BARNSTONE

I Throw Myself Away

I throw myself away
and don't care.
A heart in love
is a ravine
that has no end.   5

TRANSLATED BY TONY BARNSTONE AND WILLIS BARNSTONE

In This World

In this world
love has no color—
yet how deeply
my body
is stained by yours.   5

TRANSLATED BY JANE HIRSHFIELD AND MARIKO ARATANI

I Cannot Say

I cannot say
which is which:
the glowing
plum blossom is
the spring night's moon.   *5*

TRANSLATED BY JANE HIRSHFIELD AND MARIKO ARATANI

This Heart

This heart,
longing for you,
breaks
to a thousand pieces—
I wouldn't lose one.   *5*

TRANSLATED BY JANE HIRSHFIELD AND MARIKO ARATANI

Mourning Naishi

*Around the time Naishi [Shikibu's daughter] died, snow fell, then
melted away*

Why did you vanish
into empty sky?
Even the fragile snow,
when it falls,
falls in this world.   *5*

TRANSLATED BY JANE HIRSHFIELD AND MARIKO ARATANI

On Nights When Hail

On nights when hail
falls noisily
on bamboo leaves,
I completely hate
to sleep alone.   *5*

TRANSLATED BY WILLIS BARNSTONE

Since That Night

Since that night
I cannot know myself.
I go to unheard of places
and sleep recklessly
on a strange bed.   5

TRANSLATED BY WILLIS BARNSTONE

You Wear the Face

You wear the face
of someone awake
in the icy air,
seeing the moon we saw
in our night of no sleep.   5

TRANSLATED BY WILLIS BARNSTONE

When You Broke from Me

When you broke from me
I thought I let the thread
of my life break,
yet now, for you,
I don't want to die.   5

TRANSLATED BY WILLIS BARNSTONE

If You Have No Time

If you have no time
to come, I'll go.
I want to learn the way
of writing poems
as a way to you.   5

TRANSLATED BY WILLIS BARNSTONE

If You Love Me

If you love me,
come. The road
I live on

is not forbidden
by impetuous gods.   5

TRANSLATED BY WILLIS BARNSTONE

On This Winter Night

On this winter night
my eyes were closed
with ice.
I wore out the darkness
until lazy dawn.   5

TRANSLATED BY WILLIS BARNSTONE

Here in This World

Here in this world
I won't live
one minute more,
where pain is rank
like black bamboo.   5

TRANSLATED BY WILLIS BARNSTONE

■ Murasaki Shikibu (978–c. 1015) (novel)

Murasaki Shikibu came from a distinguished literary line, a minor branch of the influential Fujiwara clan, which produced many of the empresses, high government officials, and court ladies through most of the Heian period. Her great-grandfather Kanesuke (877–933) and her grandfather Masatada (c. 910–962) were associated with Ki no Tsurayuki, and a number of their poems appear in Imperial anthologies. Her father began his career as a student of literature and went on to serve in the upper strata of government, becoming the governor of Echizen and later of Echigo. He retired in 1016 and turned to the priesthood. In her diary, Murasaki Shikibu records how she came to gain a classical Chinese education, which was very unusual for women at that time. Her brother Nobunori was being tutored and "on these occasions I was always present, and so quick was I at picking up the language that I was soon able to prompt my brother whenever he got stuck. At this my father used to sigh and say to me: 'If only you were a boy, how proud and happy I should be.'" She was also well read in Japanese works and in Buddhist literature and was a talented calligrapher, painter, and musician. She seems to have accompanied her father to the provinces when he became governor of Echizen in 996 and returned to the capital in her early twenties to marry her kinsman Fujiwara no Nobutaka. He was a lieutenant in the Imperial guard and at least twenty years older than she. They had one daughter, Nobutaka, who died in 1001. Around that time Murasaki Shikibu began writing what was to be her masterpiece, *The Tale of Genji*. She served as a lady-in-waiting to the Empress Akiko (or Shoshi) at the Kyoto court from around 1005, and much of the novel seems to have been written by this time. Shoshi's court, along with that of Teishi, was the center of literary culture. Izumi Shikibu, the finest poet of that time, was also at Shoshi's court, and Sei Shonagon was at Teishi's court. Murasaki Shikibu may have been the consort of Empress Akiko's father, Michinaga, and in any case, he certainly courted her; he, along with Ariwara Narihira (hero of the *Tales of Ise*) and Shotoku Taishi, has been put forward as a historical model for Prince Genji. In addition to *The Tale of Genji*, Murasaki Shikibu kept a diary describing events at the court from 1008–1010 and wrote a number of poems. These works are of lesser importance than her great novel. Her name may be explained in several ways. *Shikibu* designates an appointment in the court hierarchy that her father probably held. As for *Murasaki* ("purple"), it may be a nickname alluding to the color of wisteria (*fuji*, the first character of the surname *Fujiwara*), or it may be taken from Murasaki, the character who is Prince Genji's great love in *The Tale of Genji*. Details of her later life are sketchy, and the last known mention of her is in 1013, when she was in her mid-thirties.

The Tale of Genji is the world's first great novel and one of the world's longest. It is distinguished for the complex characterization that Murasaki brings to her huge cast of characters, at a time when characterization was a poorly developed art in China, as in Japan. *The Tale of Genji* belongs to a form of Japanese narrative termed "monogatari," which was normally written by men to be read by women. This novel breaks that pattern, not only through its female author but by the fact that it was read by Murasaki's male contemporaries and, of course, by succeeding generations. The first forty-one chapters tell the story of Prince Genji, son of the emperor and an obscure court lady who has gained the emperor's favor. Genji is so handsome and talented that he is given the appellation "The Shining Prince." The last ten chapters are concerned with Kaoru, whom Genji thought was his son, though his father was actually the emperor. Although it seems the entire novel was written by Murasaki Shikibu, between these sections are three intermediary chapters that may be spurious (written by a later author). The action of the novel takes place within a period of about seventy-five years. Much of the first part of the novel treats Genji's love affairs and wives and his attempt to raise a girl who will be the perfect woman. The chapter presented here takes place early in the novel; Genji and his friends debate what characteristics make up the perfect woman Genji later tries to create, illustrating their points with anecdotes. The end of the chapter deals with Genji's attempts at courting a reluctant woman. Though the novel might be described generally as a romantic depiction of courtly love, it can also be seen as a Buddhist allegory about the decline of dharma, or Buddhist law, in which the relatively anemic and ambivalent relations of Kaoru make him seem a pale reflection of Genji, the great man of the past. Or the novel could be a Buddhist parable of karmic retribution in which, years after cuckolding his own father, Genji finds himself cuckolded by his best friend's son. In spite of its romantic character, the novel seems to present a pessimistic view of the world as shot through with tragedy, a view that a number of the characters share. Commentators have also pointed out the running theme of a quest for origins—as Genji pursues the image of his dead mother in the women he loves, so Kaoru is consumed with the search for a father. *The Tale of Genji* is of interest as an anthropological window on the attitudes, surroundings, and behavior of men and women inhabiting a lost world; more important, it still reads as a great novel today.

FURTHER READING: Bowring, Richard, tr. *Murasaki Shikibu: Her Diary and Poetic Memoirs*, 1982. Morris, Ivan. *The World of the Shining Prince: Court Life in Ancient Japan*, 1964. Puette, William J. *A Guide to the Tale of Genji by Murasaki Shikibu*, 1983. Seidensticker, Edward, tr. *The Tale of Genji*, 1981. Waley, Arthur, tr. *The Tale of Genji*, 1935.

from *The Tale of Genji*

TRANSLATED BY ARTHUR WALEY

The Broom-Tree

Genji the Shining One . . . He knew that the bearer of such a name could not escape much scrutiny and jealous censure and that his lightest dallyings would be proclaimed to posterity. Fearing then lest he should appear to after ages as a mere good-for-nothing and trifler, and knowing that (so accursed is the blabbing of gossips' tongues) his most secret acts might come to light, he was obliged always to act with great prudence and to preserve at least the outward appearance of respectability. Thus nothing really romantic ever happened to him and Katano no Shosho[1] would have scoffed at his story.

While he was still a Captain of the Guard and was spending most of his time at the Palace, his infrequent visits to the Great Hall[2] were taken as a

---

1. The hero of a lost popular romance. It is also referred to by Murasaki's contemporary Sei Shonagon in Chapter 145 of her *Makura na Soshi.*

2. His father-in-law's house, where his wife Princess Aoi still continued to live.

sign that some secret passion had made its imprint on his heart. But in reality the frivolous, commonplace, straight-ahead amours of his companions
did not in the least interest him, and it was a curious trait in his character
that when on rare occasions, despite all resistance, love did gain a hold
upon him, it was always in the most improbable and hopeless entangle-
ment that he became involved.

It was the season of the long rains. For many days there had not been a
fine moment and the Court was keeping a strict fast. The people at the
Great Hall were becoming very impatient of Genji's long residence at the
Palace, but the young lords, who were Court pages, liked waiting upon
Genji better than upon anyone else, always managing to put out his clothes
and decorations in some marvellous new way. Among these brothers his
greatest friend was the Equerry, To no Chujo, with whom above all other
companions of his playtime he found himself familiar and at ease. This
lord too found the house which his father-in-law, the Minister of the Right,
had been at pains to build for him, somewhat oppressive, while at his father's house he, like Genji, found the splendours somewhat dazzling, so
that he ended by becoming Genji's constant companion at Court. They
shared both studies and play and were inseparable companions on every
sort of occasion, so that soon all formalities were dispensed with between
them and the inmost secrets of their hearts freely exchanged.

It was on a night when the rain never ceased its dismal downpour.
There were not many people about in the palace and Genji's rooms
seemed even quieter than usual. He was sitting by the lamp, looking at various books and papers. Suddenly he began pulling some letters out of the
drawers of a desk which stood near by. This aroused To no Chujo's curiosity. 'Some of them I can show to you' said Genji 'but there are others which
I had rather . . .' 'It is just those which I want to see. Ordinary, commonplace letters are very much alike and I do not suppose that yours differ
much from mine. What I want to see are passionate letters written
in moments of resentment, letters hinting consent, letters written at
dusk . . .'

He begged so eagerly that Genji let him examine the drawers. It was
not indeed likely that he had put any very important or secret documents
in the ordinary desk; he would have hidden them away much further from
sight. So he felt sure that the letters in these drawers would be nothing to
worry about. After turning over a few of them, 'What an astonishing variety!' To no Chujo exclaimed and began guessing at the writers' names, and
made one or two good hits. More often he was wrong and Genji, amused by
his puzzled air, said very little but generally managed to lead him astray. At
last he took the letters back, saying 'But you too must have a large collection. Show me some of yours, and my desk will open to you with better will.'
'I have none that you would care to see,' said To no Chujo, and he continued:'I have at last discovered that there exists no woman of whom one can
say "Here is perfection. This is indeed she." There are many who have the
superficial art of writing a good running hand, or if occasion requires of

making a quick repartee. But there are few who will stand the ordeal of any further test. Usually their minds are entirely occupied by admiration for their own accomplishments, and their abuse of all rivals creates a most unpleasant impression. Some again are adored by over-fond parents. These have been since childhood guarded behind lattice windows[3] and no knowledge of them is allowed to reach the outer-world, save that of their excellence in some accomplishment or art; and this may indeed sometimes arouse our interest. She is pretty and graceful and has not yet mixed at all with the world. Such a girl by closely copying some model and applying herself with great industry will often succeed in really mastering one of the minor and ephemeral arts. Her friends are careful to say nothing of her defects and to exaggerate her accomplishments, and while we cannot altogether trust their praise we cannot believe that their judgment is entirely astray. But when we take steps to test their statements we are invariably disappointed.'

He paused, seeming to be slightly ashamed of the cynical tone which he had adopted, and added 'I know my experience is not large, but that is the conclusion I have come to so far.' Then Genji, smiling: 'And are there any who lack even one accomplishment?' 'No doubt, but in such a case it is unlikely that anyone would be successfully decoyed. The number of those who have nothing to recommend them and of those in whom nothing but good can be found is probably equal. I divide women into three classes. Those of high rank and birth are made such a fuss of and their weak points are so completely concealed that we are certain to be told that they are paragons. About those of the middle class everyone is allowed to express his own opinion, and we shall have much conflicting evidence to sift. As for the lower classes, they do not concern us.'

The completeness with which To no Chujo disposed of the question amused Genji, who said 'It will not always be so easy to know into which of the three classes a woman ought to be put. For sometimes people of high rank sink to the most abject positions; while others of common birth rise to be high officers, wear self-important faces, redecorate the inside of their houses and think themselves as good as anyone. How are we to deal with such cases?'

At this moment they were joined by Hidari no Uma no Kami and To Shikibu no Jo, who said they had also come to the Palace to keep the fast. As both of them were great lovers and good talkers, To no Chujo handed over to them the decision of Genji's question, and in the discussion which followed many unflattering things were said. Uma no Kami spoke first. 'However high a lady may rise, if she does not come of an adequate stock, the world will think very differently of her from what it would of one born

---

3. Japanese houses were arranged somewhat differently from ours and for many of the terms which constantly recur in this book (*kicho, sudare, sunoko*, etc.) no exact English equivalents can be found. In such cases I have tried to use expressions which without being too awkward or unfamiliar will give an adequate general idea of what is meant.

to such honours; but if through adverse fortune a lady of highest rank finds herself in friendless misery, the noble breeding of her mind is soon forgotten and she becomes an object of contempt. I think then that taking all things into account, we must put such ladies too into the "middle class." But when we come to classify the daughters of Zuryo,[4] who are sent to labour at the affairs of distant provinces—they have such ups and downs that we may reasonably put them too into the middle class.

'Then there are Ministers of the third and fourth classes without Cabinet rank. These are generally thought less of even than the humdrum, ordinary officials. They are usually of quite good birth, but have much less responsibility than Ministers of State and consequently much greater peace of mind. Girls born into such households are brought up in complete security from want or deprivation of any kind, and indeed often amid surroundings of the utmost luxury and splendour. Many of them grow up into women whom it would be folly to despise; some have been admitted at Court, where they have enjoyed a quite unexpected success. And of this I could cite many, many instances.'

'Their success has generally been due to their having a lot of money,' said Genji smiling. 'You should have known better than to say that,' said To no Chujo, reproving him, and Uma no Kami went on: 'There are some whose lineage and reputation are so high that it never occurs to one that their education could possibly be at fault; yet when we meet them, we find ourselves exclaiming in despair "How can they have contrived to grow up like this?"

'No doubt the perfect woman in whom none of those essentials is lacking must somewhere exist and it would not startle me to find her. But she would certainly be beyond the reach of a humble person like myself, and for that reason I should like to put her in a category of her own and not to count her in our present classification.

'But suppose that behind some gateway overgrown with vine-weed, in a place where no one knows there is a house at all, there should be locked away some creature of unimagined beauty—with what excitement should we discover her! The complete surprise of it, the upsetting of all our wise theories and classifications, would be likely, I think, to lay a strange and sudden enchantment upon us. I imagine her father rather large and gruff; her brother, a surly, ill-looking fellow. Locked away in an utterly blank and uninteresting bedroom, she will be subject to odd flights of fancy, so that in her hands the arts that others learn as trivial accomplishments will seem strangely full of meaning and importance; or perhaps in some particular art she will thrill us by her delightful and unexpected mastery. Such a one may perhaps be beneath the attention of those of you who are of flawless lineage. But for my part I find it hard to banish her . . .' and here he looked

---

4. Provincial officials. Murasaki herself came of this class.

at Shikibu no Jo, who wondered whether the description had been meant to apply to his own sisters, but said nothing. 'If it is difficult to choose even out of the top class . . .' thought Genji, and began to doze.

He was dressed in a suit of soft white silk, with a rough cloak carelessly slung over his shoulders, with belt and fastenings untied. In the light of the lamp against which he was leaning he looked so lovely that one might have wished he were a girl; and they thought that even Uma no Kami's 'perfect woman,' whom he had placed in a category of her own, would not be worthy of such a prince as Genji.

The conversation went on. Many persons and things were discussed. Uma no Kami contended that perfection is equally difficult to find in other spheres. The sovereign is hard put to it to choose his ministers. But he at least has an easier task than the husband, for he does not entrust the affairs of his kingdom to one, two or three persons alone, but sets up a whole system of superiors and subordinates.

But when the mistress of a house is to be selected, a single individual must be found who will combine in her person many diverse qualities. It will not do to be too exacting. Let us be sure that the lady of our choice possesses certain tangible qualities which we admire; and if in other ways she falls short of our ideal, we must be patient and call to mind those qualities which first induced us to begin our courting.

But even here we must beware; for there are some who in the selfishness of youth and flawless beauty are determined that not a dust-flick shall fall upon them. In their letters they choose the most harmless topics, but yet contrive to colour the very texture of the written signs with a tenderness that vaguely disquiets us. But such a one, when we have at last secured a meeting, will speak so low that she can scarcely be heard, and the few faint sentences that she murmurs beneath her breath serve only to make her more mysterious than before. All this may seem to be the pretty shrinking of girlish modesty; but we may later find that what held her back was the very violence of her passions.

Or again, where all seems plain sailing, the perfect companion will turn out to be too impressionable and will upon the most inappropriate occasions display her affections in so ludicrous a way that we begin to wish ourselves rid of her.

Then there is the zealous housewife, who regardless of her appearance twists her hair behind her ears and devotes herself entirely to the details of our domestic welfare. The husband, in his comings and goings about the world, is certain to see and hear many things which he cannot discuss with strangers, but would gladly talk over with an intimate who could listen with sympathy and understanding, someone who could laugh with him or weep if need be. It often happens too that some political event will greatly perturb or amuse him, and he sits apart longing to tell someone about it. He suddenly laughs at some secret recollection or sighs audibly. But the wife only says lightly 'What is the matter?' and shows no interest.

This is apt to be very trying.

Uma no Kami considered several other cases. But he reached no definite conclusion and sighing deeply he continued: 'We will then, as I have suggested, let birth and beauty go by the board. Let her be the simplest and most guileless of creatures so long as she is honest and of a peaceable disposition, that in the end we may not lack a place of trust. And if some other virtue chances to be hers we shall treasure it as a godsend. But if we discover in her some small defect, it shall not be too closely scrutinized. And we may be sure that if she is strong in the virtues of tolerance and amiability her outward appearance will not be beyond measure harsh.

'There are those who carry forbearance too far, and affecting not to notice wrongs which cry out for redress seem to be paragons of misused fidelity. But suddenly a time comes when such a one can restrain herself no longer, and leaving behind her a poem couched in pitiful language and calculated to rouse the most painful sentiments of remorse, she flies to some remote village in the mountains or some desolate seashore, and for a long while all trace of her is lost.

'When I was a boy the ladies-in-waiting used to tell me sad tales of this kind. I never doubted that the sentiments expressed in them were real, and I wept profusely. But now I am beginning to suspect that such sorrows are for the most part affectation. She has left behind her (this lady whom we are imagining) a husband who is probably still fond of her; she is making herself very unhappy, and by disappearing in this way is causing him unspeakable anxiety, perhaps only for the ridiculous purpose of putting his affection to the test. Then comes along some admiring friend crying "What a heart! What depth of feeling!" She becomes more lugubrious than ever, and finally enters a nunnery. When she decided on this step she was perfectly sincere and had not the slightest intention of ever returning to the world. Then some female friend hears of it and "Poor thing" she cries; "in what an agony of mind must she have been to do this!" and visits her in her cell. When the husband, who has never ceased to mourn for her, hears what she has become, he bursts into tears, and some servant or old nurse, seeing this, bustles off to the nunnery with tales of the husband's despair, and "Oh Madam, what a shame, what a shame!" Then the nun, forgetting where and what she is, raises her hand to her head to straighten her hair, and finds that it has been shorn away. In helpless misery she sinks to the floor, and do what she will, the tears begin to flow. Now all is lost; for since she cannot at every moment be praying for strength, there creeps into her mind the sinful thought that she did ill to become a nun and so often does she commit this sin that even Buddha must think her wickeder now than she was before she took her vows; and she feels certain that these terrible thoughts are leading her soul to the blackest Hell. But if the karma of their past lives should chance to be strongly weighted against a parting, she will be found and captured before she has taken her final vows. In such a case their life will be beyond endurance unless she be fully determined, come good or ill, this time to close her eyes to all that goes amiss.

'Again there are others who must needs be forever mounting guard over their own and their husband's affections. Such a one, if she sees in him not a fault indeed but even the slightest inclination to stray, makes a foolish scene, declaring with indignation that she will have no more to do with him.

'But even if a man's fancy should chance indeed to have gone somewhat astray, yet his earlier affection may still be strong and in the end will return to its old haunts. Now by her tantrums she has made a rift that cannot be joined. Whereas she who when some small wrong calls for silent rebuke, shows by a glance that she is not unaware; but when some large offence demands admonishment knows how to hint without severity, will end by standing in her master's affections better than ever she stood before. For often the sight of our own forbearance will give our neighbour strength to rule his mutinous affections.

'But she whose tolerance and forgiveness know no bounds, though this may seem to proceed from the beauty and amiability of her disposition, is in fact displaying the shallowness of her feeling: "The unmoored boat must needs drift with the stream." Are you not of this mind?'

To no Chujo nodded. 'Some' he said 'have imagined that by arousing a baseless suspicion in the mind of the beloved we can revive a waning devotion. But this experiment is very dangerous. Those who recommend it are confident that so long as resentment is groundless one need only suffer it in silence and all will soon be well. I have observed however that this is by no means the case.

'But when all is said and done, there can be no greater virtue in woman than this: that she should with gentleness and forbearance meet every wrong whatsoever that falls to her share.' He thought as he said this of his own sister, Princess Aoi; but was disappointed and piqued to discover that Genji, whose comments he awaited, was fast asleep.

Uma no Kami was an expert in such discussions and now stood preening his feathers. To no Chujo was disposed to hear what more he had to say and was now at pains to humour and encourage him.

'It is with women' said Uma no Kami 'as it is with the works of craftsmen. The wood-carver can fashion whatever he will. Yet his products are but toys of the moment, to be glanced at in jest, not fashioned according to any precept or law. When times change, the carver too will change his style and make new trifles to hit the fancy of the passing day. But there is another kind of artist, who sets more soberly about his work, striving to give real beauty to the things which men actually use and to give to them the shapes which tradition has ordained. This maker of real things must not for a moment be confused with the carver of idle toys.

'In the Painters' Workshop too there are many excellent artists chosen for their proficiency in ink-drawing; and indeed they are all so clever it is hard to set one above the other. But all of them are at work on subjects intended to impress and surprise. One paints the Mountain of Horai; another a raging sea-monster riding a storm; another, ferocious animals from the

Land beyond the sea, or faces of imaginary demons. Letting their fancy run wildly riot they have no thought of beauty, but only of how best they may astonish the beholder's eye. And though nothing in their pictures is real, all is probable. But ordinary hills and rivers, just as they are, houses such as you may see anywhere, with all their real beauty and harmony of form—quietly to draw such scenes as this, or to show what lies behind some intimate hedge that is folded away far from the world, and thick trees upon some unheroic hill, and all this with befitting care for composition, proportion, and the like—such works demand the highest master's utmost skill and must needs draw the common craftsman into a thousand blunders. So too in handwriting, we see some who aimlessly prolong their cursive strokes this way or that, and hope their flourishes will be mistaken for genius. But true penmanship preserves in every letter its balance and form, and though at first some letters may seem but half-formed, yet when we compare them with the copy-books we find that there is nothing at all amiss.

'So it is in these trifling matters. And how much the more in judging of the human heart should we distrust all fashionable airs and graces, all tricks and smartness, learnt only to please the outward gaze! This I first understood some while ago, and if you will have patience with me I will tell you the story.'

So saying, he came and sat a little closer to them, and Genji woke up. To no Chujo, in wrapt attention, was sitting with his cheek propped upon his hand. Uma no Kami's whole speech that night was indeed very much like a chaplain's sermon about the ways of the world, and was rather absurd. But upon such occasions as this we are easily led on into discussing our own ideas and most private secrets without the least reserve.

'It happened when I was young, and in an even more humble position than I am today' Uma no Kami continued. 'I was in love with a girl who (like the drudging, faithful wife of whom I spoke a little while ago) was not a full-sail beauty; and I in my youthful vanity thought she was all very well for the moment, but would never do for the wife of so fine a fellow as I. She made an excellent companion in times when I was at a loose end; but she was of a disposition so violently jealous, that I could have put up with a little less devotion if only she had been somewhat less fiercely ardent and exacting.

'Thus I kept thinking, vexed by her unrelenting suspicions. But then I would remember her ceaseless devotion to the interests of one who was after all a person of no account, and full of remorse I made sure that with a little patience on my part she would one day learn to school her jealousy.

'It was her habit to minister to my smallest wants even before I was myself aware of them; whatever she felt was lacking in her she strove to acquire, and where she knew that in some quality of mind she still fell behind my desires, she was at pains never to show her deficiency in such a way as might vex me. Thus in one way or another she was always busy in forwarding my affairs, and she hoped that if all down to the last dew-drop (as they say) were conducted as I should wish, this would be set down to her credit and help to balance the defects in her person which meek and obliging as she might be could not (she fondly imagined) fail to offend me; and at this time she even hid herself from strangers lest their poor opinion of her looks should put me out of countenance.

'I meanwhile, becoming used to her homely looks, was well content with her character, save for this one article of jealousy; and here she showed no amendment. Then I began to think to myself "Surely, since she seems so anxious to please, so timid, there must be some way of giving her a fright which will teach her a lesson, so that for a while at least we may have a respite from this accursed business." And though I knew it would cost me dear, I determined to make a pretence of giving her up, thinking that since she was so fond of me this would be the best way to teach her a lesson. Accordingly I behaved with the greatest coldness to her, and she as usual began her jealous fit and behaved with such folly that in the end I said to her, "If you want to be rid for ever of one who loves you dearly, you are going the right way about it by all these endless poutings over nothing at all. But if you want to go on with me, you must give up suspecting some deep intrigue each time you fancy that I am treating you unkindly. Do this, and you may be sure I shall continue to love you dearly. It may well be that as time goes on, I shall rise a little higher in the world and then . . ."

'I thought I had managed matters very cleverly, though perhaps in the heat of the moment I might have spoken somewhat too roughly. She smiled faintly and answered that if it were only a matter of bearing for a while with my failures and disappointments, that did not trouble her at all, and she would gladly wait till I became a person of consequence. "But it is a hard task" she said "to go on year after year enduring your coldness and waiting the time when you will at last learn to behave to me with some decency; and therefore I agree with you that the time has come when we had better go each his own way." Then in a fit of wild and uncontrollable jealousy she began to pour upon me a torrent of bitter reproaches, and with a woman's savagery she suddenly seized my little finger and bit deep into it. The unexpected pain was difficult to bear, but composing myself I said tragically, "Now you have put this mark upon me I shall get on worse than ever in polite society; as for promotion, I shall be considered a disgrace to the meanest public office and unable to cut a genteel figure in any capacity, I shall be obliged to withdraw myself completely from the world. You and I at any rate shall certainly not meet again," and bending my injured finger as I turned to go, I recited the verse "As on bent hand I count the times that we have met, it is not one finger only that bears witness to my pain." And she, all of a sudden bursting into tears . . . "If still in your heart only you look for pains to count, then were our hands best employed in parting." After a few more words I left her, not for a moment thinking that all was over.

'Days went by, and no news. I began to be restless. One night when I had been at the Palace for the rehearsal of the Festival music, heavy sleet was falling; and I stood at the spot where those of us who came from the

Palace had dispersed, unable to make up my mind which way to go. For in no direction had I anything which could properly be called a home. I might of course take a room in the Palace precincts; but I shivered to think of the cheerless grandeur that would surround me. Suddenly I began to wonder what she was thinking, how she was looking; and brushing the snow off my shoulders, I set out for her house. I own I felt uneasy; but I thought that after so long a time her anger must surely have somewhat abated. Inside the room a lamp showed dimly, turned to the wall. Some undergarments were hung out upon a large, warmly-quilted couch, the bed-hangings were drawn up, and I made sure that she was for some reason actually expecting me. I was priding myself on having made so lucky a hit, when suddenly, "Not at home!"; and on questioning the maid I learnt that she had but that very night gone to her parents' home, leaving only a few necessary servants behind. The fact that she had till now sent no poem or conciliatory message seemed to show some hardening of heart, and had already disquieted me. Now I began to fear that her accursed suspiciousness and jealousy had but been a stratagem to make me grow weary of her, and though I could recall no further proof of this I fell into great despair. And to show her that, though we no longer met, I still thought of her and planned for her, I got her some stuff for a dress, choosing a most delightful and unusual shade of colour, and a material that I knew she would be glad to have. "For after all" I thought "she cannot want to put me altogether out of her head." When I informed her of this purchase she did not rebuff me nor make any attempt to hide from me, but to all my questions she answered quietly and composedly, without any sign that she was ashamed of herself.

'At last she told me that if I went on as before, she could never forgive me; but if I would promise to live more quietly she would take me back again. Seeing that she still hankered after me I determined to school her a little further yet, and said that I could make no conditions and must be free to live as I chose. So the tug of war went on; but it seems that it hurt her far more than I knew, for in a little while she fell into a decline and died, leaving me aghast at the upshot of my wanton game. And now I felt that, whatever faults she might have had, her devotion alone would have made her a fit wife for me. I remembered how both in trivial talk and in consideration of important matters she had never once shown herself at a loss, how in the dyeing of brocades she rivalled the Goddess of Tatsuta who tints the autumn leaves, and how in needlework and the like she was not less skillful than Tanabata, the Weaving-lady of the sky.'

Here he stopped, greatly distressed at the recollection of the lady's many talents and virtues.

'The Weaving-lady and the Herd boy' said To no Chujo 'enjoy a love that is eternal. Had she but resembled the Divine Sempstress in this, you would not, I think, have minded her being a little less skilful with her needle. I wonder that with this rare creature in mind you pronounce the world to be so blank a place.'

'Listen' replied Uma no Kami. 'About the same time there was another lady whom I used to visit. She was of higher birth than the first; her skill in poetry, cursive writing, and lute-playing, her readiness of hand and tongue were all marked enough to show that she was not a woman of trivial nature; and this indeed was allowed by those who knew her. To add to this she was not ill-looking and sometimes, when I needed a rest from my unhappy persecutress, I used to visit her secretly. In the end I found that I had fallen completely in love with her. After the death of the other I was in great distress. But it was no use brooding over the past and I began to visit my new lady more and more often. I soon came to the conclusion that she was frivolous and I had no confidence that I should have liked what went on when I was not there to see. I now visited her only at long intervals and at last decided that she had another lover.

'It was during the Godless Month,[5] on a beautiful moonlight night. As I was leaving the Palace I met a certain young courtier, who, when I told him that I was driving out to spend the night at the Dainagon's, said that my way was his and joined me. The road passed my lady's house and here it was that he alighted, saying that he had an engagement which he should have been very sorry not to fulfil. The wall was half in ruins and through its gaps I saw the shadowy waters of the lake. It would not have been easy (for even the moonbeams seemed to loiter here!) to hasten past so lovely a place, and when he left his coach I too left mine.

'At once this man (whom I now knew to be that other lover whose existence I had guessed) went and sat unconcernedly on the bamboo skirting of the portico and began to gaze at the moon. The chrysanthemums were just in full bloom, the bright fallen leaves were tumbling and tussling in the wind. It was indeed a scene of wonderful beauty that met our eyes. Presently he took a flute out of the folds of his dress and began to play upon it. Then putting the flute aside, he began to murmur. "Sweet is the shade"[6] and other catches. Soon a pleasant-sounding native zithern[7] began to tune up somewhere within the house and an ingenious accompaniment was fitted to his careless warblings. Her zithern was tuned to the autumn-mode, and she played with so much tenderness and feeling that though the music came from behind closed shutters it sounded quite modern and passionate,[8] and well accorded with the soft beauty of the moonlight. The courtier was ravished, and as he stepped forward to place himself right under her window he turned to me and remarked in a self-satisfied way that among the fallen leaves no other footstep had left its mark. Then plucking a chrysanthemum, he sang:

---

5. The tenth month.

6. From the *saibara* ballad, *The Well of Asuka:* 'Sweet is the shade, the lapping waters cool, and good the pasture for our weary steeds. By the Well of Asuka, here let us stay.'

7. The 'Japanese zithern'; also called *wagon*. A species of *koto*.

8. As opposed to the formal and traditional music imported from China.

> Strange that the music of your lute,
> These matchless flowers and all the beauty of the night,
> Have lured no other feet to linger at your door!

and then, beseeching her pardon for his halting verses, he begged her to play again while one was still near who longed so passionately to hear her. When he had paid her many other compliments, the lady answered in an affected voice with the verse:

> Would that I had some song that might detain
> The flute that blends its note
> With the low rustling of the autumn leaves.

and after these blandishments, still unsuspecting, she took up the thirteen-stringed lute, and tuning it to the *Banjiki* mode[9] she clattered at the strings with all the frenzy that fashion now demands. It was a fine performance no doubt, but I cannot say that it made a very agreeable impression upon me.

'A man may amuse himself well enough by trifling from time to time with some lady at the Court; will get what pleasure he can out of it while he is with her and not trouble his head about what goes on when he is not there. This lady too I only saw from time to time, but such was her situation that I had once fondly imagined myself the only occupant of her thoughts. However that night's work dissolved the last shred of my confidence, and I never saw her again.

'These two experiences, falling to my lot while I was still so young, early deprived me of any hope from women. And since that time my view of them has but grown the blacker. No doubt to you at your age they seem very entrancing, these "dewdrops on the grass that fall if they are touched," these "glittering hailstones that melt if gathered in the hand." But when you are a little older you will think as I do. Take my advice in this at least; beware of caressing manners and soft, entangling ways. For if you are so rash as to let them lead you astray, you will soon find yourselves cutting a very silly figure in the world.'

To no Chujo as usual nodded his assent, and Genji's smile seemed such as to show that he too accepted Uma no Kami's advice. 'Your two stories were certainly very dismal' he said, laughing. And here To no Chujo interposed: 'I will tell you a story about myself. There was a lady whose acquaintance I was obliged to make with great secrecy. But her beauty well rewarded my pains, and though I had no thought of making her my wife, I grew so fond of her that I soon found I could not put her out of my head and she seemed to have complete confidence in me. Such confidence indeed that when from time to time I was obliged to behave in such a way as might well have aroused her resentment, she seemed not to notice that anything was amiss, and even when I neglected her for many weeks, she treated me as though I were still coming every day. In the end indeed I

---

9. See *Encyclopédie de la Musique*, p. 247. Under the name Nan-lu this mode was frequently used in the Chinese love-dramas of the fourteenth century. It was considered very wild and moving.

found this readiness to receive me whenever and however I came very painful, and determined for the future to merit her strange confidence.

'Her parents were dead and this was perhaps why, since I was all she had in the world, she treated me with such loving meekness, despite the many wrongs I did her. I must own that my resolution did not last long, and I was soon neglecting her worse than before. During this time (I did not hear of it till afterwards) someone who had discovered our friendship began to send her veiled messages which cruelly frightened and distressed her. Knowing nothing of the trouble she was in, although I often thought of her I neither came nor wrote to her for a long while. Just when she was in her worst despair a child was born, and at last in her distress she plucked a blossom of the flower that is called "Child of my Heart" and sent it to me.'

And here To no Chujo's eyes filled with tears.

'Well' said Genji 'and did she write a message to go with it?' 'Oh nothing very out-of-the-ordinary' said To no Chujo. 'She wrote: "Though tattered be the hillman's hedge, deign sometimes to look with kindness upon the Child-flower that grows so sweetly there." This brought me to her side. As usual she did not reproach me, but she looked sad enough, and when I considered the dreary desolation of this home where every object wore an aspect no less depressing than the wailing voices of the crickets in the grass, she seemed to me like some unhappy princess in an ancient story, and wishing her to feel that it was for the mother's sake and not the child's that I had come, I answered with a poem in which I called the Child-flower by its other name "Bed-flower," and she replied with a poem that darkly hinted at the cruel tempest which had attended this Bed-flower's birth. She spoke lightly and did not seem to be downright angry with me; and when a few tears fell she was at great pains to hide them, and seemed more distressed at the thought that I might imagine her to be unhappy than actually resentful of my conduct towards her. So I went away with an easy mind and it was some while before I came again. When at last I returned she had utterly disappeared, and if she is alive she must be living a wretched vagrant life. If while I still loved her she had but shown some outward sign of her resentment, she would not have ended thus as an outcast and wanderer; for I should never have dared to leave her so long neglected, and might in the end have acknowledged her and made her mine for ever. The child too was a sweet creature, and I have spent much time in searching for them, but still without success.

'It is, I fear, as sorrowful a tale as that which Uma no Kami has told you. I, unfaithful, thought that I was not missed; and she, still loved, was in no better case than one whose love is not returned. I indeed am fast forgetting her; but she, it may be, cannot put me out of her mind and I fear there may be nights when thoughts that she would gladly banish burn fiercely in her breast; for now I fancy she must be living a comfortless and unprotected life.'

'When all is said and done' said Uma no Kami, 'my friend, though I pine for her now that she is gone, was a sad plague to me while I had her, and we must own that such a one will in the end be sure to make us wish ourselves well rid of her. The zithern-player had much talent to her credit, but was a great deal too light-headed. And your diffident lady, To no Chujo, seems to me to be a very suspicious case. The world appears to be so constructed that we shall in the end be always at a loss to make a reasoned choice; despite all our picking, sifting and comparing we shall never succeed in finding this in all ways and to all lengths adorable and impeccable female.'

'I can only suggest the Goddess Kichijo'[10] said To no Chujo 'and I fear that intimacy with so holy and majestic a being might prove to be impracticable.'

At this they all laughed and To no Chujo continued: 'But now it is Shikibu's turn and he is sure to give us something entertaining. Come Shikibu, keep the ball rolling!' 'Nothing of interest ever happens to humble folk like myself' said Shikibu; but To no Chujo scolded him for keeping them waiting and after reflecting for a while which anecdote would best suit the company, he began: 'While I was still a student at the University, I came across a woman who was truly a prodigy of intelligence. One of Uma no Kami's demands she certainly fulfilled, for it was possible to discuss with her to advantage both public matters and the proper handling of one's private affairs. But not only was her mind capable of grappling with any problems of this kind; she was also so learned that ordinary scholars found themselves, to their humiliation, quite unable to hold their own against her.

'I was taking lessons from her father, who was a Professor. I had heard that he had several daughters, and some accidental circumstance made it necessary for me to exchange a word or two with one of them who turned out to be the learned prodigy of whom I have spoken. The father, hearing that we had been seen together, came up to me with a wine-cup in his hand and made an allusion to the poem of The Two Wives.[11] Unfortunately I did not feel the least inclination towards the lady. However I was very civil to her; upon which she began to take an affectionate interest in me and lost no opportunity of displaying her talents by giving me the most elaborate advice how best I might advance my position in the world. She sent me marvelous letters written in a very far-fetched epistolary style and entirely in Chinese characters; in return for which I felt bound to visit her, and by making her my teacher I managed to learn how to write Chinese poems. They were wretched, knock-kneed affairs, but I am still grateful to her for it. She was not however at all the sort of woman whom I should have cared to have as a wife, for though there may be certain disadvantages in marrying a complete dolt, it is even worse to marry a bluestocking. Still less do princes like you and Genji require so huge a stock of intellect and erudition for your support! Let her but be one to whom the karma of our past

---

10. Goddess of Beauty.

11. A poem by Po Chu-i pointing out the advantages of marrying a poor wife.

lives draws us in natural sympathy, what matter if now and again her ignorance distresses us? Come to that, even men seem to me to get along very well without much learning.'

Here he stopped, but Genji and the rest, wishing to hear the end of the story, cried out that for their part they found her a most interesting woman. Shikibu protested that he did not wish to go on with the story, but at last after much coaxing, pulling a comical wry face he continued: 'I had not seen her for a long time. When at last some accident took me to the house, she did not receive me with her usual informality but spoke to me from behind a tiresome screen. Ha, Ha, thought I foolishly, she is sulking; now is the time to have a scene and break with her. I might have known that she was not so little of a philosopher as to sulk about trifles; she prided herself on knowing the ways of the world and my inconstancy did not in the least disturb her.

'She told me (speaking without the slightest tremor) that having had a bad cold for some weeks she had taken a strong garlic-cordial, which had made her breath smell rather unpleasant and that for this reason she could not come very close to me. But if I had any matter of special importance to discuss with her she was quite prepared to give me her attention. All this she had expressed with solemn literary perfection. I could think of no suitable reply, and with an "at your service" I rose to go. Then, feeling that the interview had not been quite a success, she added, raising her voice, "Please come again when my breath has lost its smell." I could not pretend I had not heard. I had however no intention of prolonging my visit, particularly as the odour was now becoming definitely unpleasant, and looking cross I recited the acrostic "On this night marked by the strange behaviour of the spider, how foolish to bid me come back tomorrow"[12] and calling over my shoulder "There is no excuse for you!" I ran out of the room. But she, following me, "If night by night and every night we met, in daytime too I should grow bold to meet you face to face." Here in the second sentence she had cleverly concealed the meaning, "If I had had any reason to expect you, I should not have eaten garlic."'

'What a revolting story!' cried the young princes, and then, laughing, 'He must have invented it.' 'Such a woman is quite incredible; it must have been some sort of ogress. You have shocked us, Shikibu!' and they looked at him with disapproval. 'You must try to tell us a better story than that.' 'I do not see how any story could be better' said Shikibu, and left the room.

'There is a tendency among men as well as women' said Uma no Kami 'so soon as they have acquired a little knowledge of some kind, to want to display it to the best advantage. To have mastered all the difficulties in the Three Histories and Five Classics is no road to amiability. But even a woman

---

12. There is a reference to an old poem which says: 'I know that tonight my lover will come to me. The spider's antics prove it clearly.' Omens were drawn from the behaviour of spiders. There is also a pun on *hiru* 'day' and *hiru* 'garlic,' so that an ordinary person would require a few moments' reflection before understanding the poem.

cannot afford to lack all knowledge of public and private affairs. Her best way will be without regular study to pick up a little here and a little there, merely by keeping her eyes and ears open. Then, if she has her wits at all about her, she will soon find that she has amassed a surprising store of information. Let her be content with this and not insist upon cramming her letters with Chinese characters which do not at all accord with her feminine style of composition, and will make the recipient exclaim in despair "If only she could contrive to be a little less mannish!" And many of these characters, to which she intended the colloquial pronunciation to be given, are certain to be read as Chinese, and this will give the whole composition an even more pedantic sound than it deserves. Even among our ladies of rank and fashion there are many of this sort, and there are others who, wishing to master the art of verse-making, in the end allow it to master them, and, slaves to poetry, cannot resist the temptation, however urgent the business they are about or however inappropriate the time, to make use of some happy allusion which has occurred to them, but must needs fly to their desks and work it up into a poem. On festival days such a woman is very troublesome. For example on the morning of the Iris Festival, when everyone is busy making ready to go to the temple, she will worry them by stringing together all the old tags about the "matchless root";[13] or on the 9th day of the 9th month, when everyone is busy thinking out some difficult Chinese poem to fit the rhymes which have been prescribed, she begins making metaphors about the "dew on the chrysanthemums," thus diverting our attention from the far more important business which is in hand. At another time we might have found these compositions quite delightful; but by thrusting them upon our notice at inconvenient moments, when we cannot give them proper attention, she makes them seem worse than they really are. For in all matters we shall best commend ourselves if we study men's faces to read in them the "Why so?" or the "As you will" and do not, regardless of times and circumstances, demand an interest and sympathy that they have not leisure to give.

'Sometimes indeed a woman should even pretend to know less than she knows, or say only a part of what she would like to say . . .'

All this while Genji, though he had sometimes joined in the conversation, had in his heart of hearts been thinking of one person only, and the more he thought the less could he find a single trace of those shortcomings and excesses which, so his friends had declared, were common to all women. 'There is no one like her' he thought, and his heart was very full. The conversation indeed had not brought them to a definite conclusion, but it had led to many curious anecdotes and reflections. So they passed the night, and at last, for a wonder, the weather had improved. After this long residence at the Palace Genji knew he would be expected at the Great

---

13. The irises used for the Tango festival (5th day of 5th month) had to have nine flowers growing on a root.

Hall and set out at once. There was in Princess Aoi's air and dress a dignified precision which had something in it even of stiffness; and in the very
act of reflecting that she, above all women, was the type of that single-hearted
and devoted wife whom (as his friends had said last night) no sensible man
would lightly offend, he found himself oppressed by the very perfection of
her beauty, which seemed only to make all intimacy with her the more
impossible.

He turned to Lady Chunagon, to Nakatsukasa and other attendants of
the common sort who were standing near and began to jest with them. The
day was now very hot, but they thought that flushed cheeks became Prince
Genji very well. Aoi's father came, and standing behind the curtain, began
to converse very amiably. Genji, who considered the weather too hot for visits, frowned, at which the ladies-in-waiting tittered. Genji, making furious
signs at them to be quiet, flung himself on to a divan. In fact, he behaved
far from well.

It was now growing dark. Someone said that the position of the Earth
Star[14] would make it unlucky for the Prince to go back to the Palace that
night; and another: 'You are right. It is now set dead against him.' 'But my
own palace is in the same direction!' cried Genji. 'How vexing! where then
shall I go?' and promptly fell asleep. The ladies-in-waiting, however, agreed
that it was a very serious matter and began discussing what could be done.
'There is Ki no Kami's house' said one. This Ki no Kami was one of Genji's
gentlemen-in-waiting. 'It is in the Middle River' she went on; 'and delightfully cool and shady, for they have lately dammed the river and made it flow
right through the garden.' 'That sounds very pleasant' said Genji, waking
up, 'besides they are the sort of people who would not mind one's driving
right in at the front gate, if one had a mind to.'[15]

He had many friends whose houses lay out of the unlucky direction.
But he feared that if he went to one of them, Aoi would think that, after ab-
senting himself so long, he was now merely using the Earth Star as an excuse for returning to more congenial company. He therefore broached the
matter to Ki no Kami, who accepted the proposal, but stepping aside whispered to his companions that his father Iyo no Kami, who was absent on
service, had asked him to look after his young wife.[16] 'I am afraid we have
not sufficient room in the house to entertain him as I could wish.' Genji,
overhearing this, strove to reassure him, saying 'It will be a pleasure to me
to be near the lady. A visit is much more agreeable when there is a hostess
to welcome us. Find me some corner behind her partition . . . !' 'Even then,
I fear you may not find . . .' but breaking off Ki no Kami sent a runner to his
house, with orders to make ready an apartment for the Prince. Treating a
visit to so humble a house as a matter of no importance, he started at once,

14. The 'Lord of the Centre,' i.e. the planet Saturn.

15. I.e., people with whom one can be quite at ease. It was usual to unharness one's bulls at the
gate.

16. Ki no Kami's stepmother.

without even informing the Minister, and taking with him only a few trusted body-servants. Ki no Kami protested against the precipitation, but in vain.

The servants dusted and aired the eastern side-chamber of the Central Hall and here made temporary quarters for the Prince. They were at pains to improve the view from his windows, for example by altering the course of certain rivulets. They set up a rustic wattled hedge and filled the borders with the choicest plants. The low humming of insects floated on the cool breeze; numberless fireflies wove inextricable mazes in the air. The whole party settled down near where the moat flowed under the covered bridge and began to drink wine.

Ki no Kami went off in a great bustle, saying that he must find them something to eat. Genji, quietly surveying the scene, decided this was one of those middle-class families which in last night's conversation had been so highly commended. He remembered that he had heard the lady who was staying in the house well spoken of and was curious to see her. He listened and thought that there seemed to be people in the western wing. There was a soft rustling of skirts, and from time to time the sound of young and by no means disagreeable voices. They did not seem to be much in earnest in their efforts to make their whispering and laughter unheard, for soon one of them opened the sliding window. But Ki no Kami crying 'What are you thinking of?' crossly closed it again. The light of a candle in the room filtered through a crack in the paper-window. Genji edged slightly closer to the window in the hope of being able to see through the crack, but found that he could see nothing. He listened for a while, and came to the conclusion that they were sitting in the main women's apartments, out of which the little front room opened. They were speaking very low, but he could catch enough of it to make out that they were talking about him.

'What a shame that a fine young Prince should be taken so young and settled down for ever with a lady that was none of his choosing!'

'I understand that marriage does not weigh very heavily upon him' said another. This probably meant nothing in particular, but Genji, who imagined they were talking about what was uppermost in his own mind, was appalled at the idea that his relations with Lady Fujitsubo were about to be discussed. How could they have found out? But the subsequent conversation of the ladies soon showed that they knew nothing of the matter at all, and Genji stopped listening. Presently he heard them trying to repeat the poem which he had sent with a nosegay of morning-glory to Princess Asagao, daughter of Prince Momozono.[17] But they got the lines rather mixed up, and Genji began to wonder whether the lady's appearance would turn out to be on a level with her knowledge of prosody.

---

17. We learn later that Genji courted this lady in vain from his seventeenth year onward. Though she has never been mentioned before, Murasaki speaks of her as though the reader already knew all about her. This device is also employed by Marcel Proust.

At this moment Ki no Kami came in with a lamp which he hung on the wall. Having carefully trimmed it, he offered Genji a tray of fruit. This was all rather dull and Genji by a quotation from an old folk-song hinted that he would like to meet Ki no Kami's other guests. The hint was not taken. Genji began to doze, and his attendants sat silent and motionless.

There were in the room several charming boys, sons of Ki no Kami, some of whom Genji already knew as pages at the Palace. There were also numerous sons of Iyo no Kami; with them was a boy of twelve or thirteen who particularly caught Genji's fancy. He began asking whose sons the boys were, and when he came to this one Ki no Kami replied 'He is the youngest son of the late Chunagon, who loved him dearly, but died while this boy was still a child. His sister married my father and that is why he is living here. He is quick at his books, and we hope one day to send him to Court, but I fear that his lack of influence . . .'

'Poor child!' said Genji. 'His sister, then, is your stepmother, is that not so? How strange that you should stand in this relationship with so young a girl! And now I come to think of it there was some talk once of her being presented at Court, and I once heard the Emperor asking what had become of her. How changeable are the fortunes of the world.' He was trying to talk in a very grown-up way.

'Indeed, Sir' answered Ki no Kami; 'her subsequent state was humbler than she had reason to expect. But such is our mortal life. Yes, yes, and such has it always been. We have our ups and downs—and the women even more than the men.'

Genji: 'But your father no doubt makes much of her?'

Ki no Kami: 'Makes much of her indeed! You may well say so. She rules his house, and he dotes on her in so wholesale and extravagant a fashion that all of us (and I among the foremost) have had occasion before now to call him to order, but he does not listen.'

Genji: 'How comes it then that he has left her behind in the house of a fashionable young Courtier? For he looks like a man of prudence and good sense. But pray, where is she now?'

Ki no Kami: 'The ladies have been ordered to retire to the common room, but they have not yet finished all their preparations.'

Genji's followers, who had drunk heavily, were now all lying fast asleep on the verandah. He was alone in his room, but could not get to sleep. Having at last dozed for a moment, he woke suddenly and noticed that someone was moving behind the paper-window of the back wall. This, he thought, must be where she is hiding, and faintly curious he sauntered in that direction and stood listening. 'Where are you?' I say 'Where are you?' whispered someone in a quaint, hoarse voice, which seemed to be that of the boy whom Genji had noticed earlier in the evening. 'I am lying over here' another voice answered. 'Has the stranger gone to sleep yet? His room must be quite close to this; but all the same how far off he seems!' Her sleepy voice was so like the boy's that Genji concluded this must be his sister.

'He is sleeping in the wing, I saw him tonight. All that we have heard of him is true enough. He is as handsome as can be' whispered the boy. 'I wish it were tomorrow; I want to see him properly' she answered drowsily, her voice seeming to come from under the bed clothes. Genji was rather disappointed that she did not ask more questions about him. Presently he heard the boy saying 'I am going to sleep over in the corner-room. How bad the light is' and he seemed to be trimming the lamp. His sister's bed appeared to be in the corner opposite the paper-window. 'Where is Chujo?' she called. 'I am frightened, I like to have someone close to me.' 'Madam' answered several voices from the servants' room, 'she is taking her bath in the lower house. She will be back presently.' When all was quiet again, Genji slipped back the bolt and tried the door. It was not fastened on the other side. He found himself in an ante-room with a screen at the end, beyond which a light glimmered. In the half-darkness he could see clothes boxes and trunks strewn about in great disorder. Quietly threading his way among them, he entered the inner room from which the voices had proceeded. One very minute figure was couched there who, to Genji's slight embarrassment, on hearing his approach pushed aside the cloak which covered her, thinking that he was the maid for whom she had sent. 'Madam, hearing you call for Chujo[18] I thought that I might now put at your service the esteem in which I have long secretly held you.' The lady could make nothing of all this, and terrified out of her wits tried hard to scream. But no sound came, for she had buried her face in the bed clothes.

'Please listen' said Genji. 'This sudden intrusion must of course seem to you very impertinent. You do not know that for years I have waited for an occasion to tell you how much I like and admire you, and if tonight I could not resist the temptation of paying this secret visit, pray take the strangeness of my behaviour as proof of my impatience to pay a homage that has long been due.' He spoke so courteously and gently and looked so kind that not the devil himself would have taken umbrage at his presence. But feeling that the situation was not at all a proper one for a married lady she said (without much conviction) 'I think you have made a mistake.' She spoke very low. Her bewildered air made her all the more attractive, and Genji, enchanted by her appearance, hastened to answer: 'Indeed I have made no mistake; rather, with no guide but a long-felt deference and esteem, I have found my way unerringly to your side. But I see that the suddenness of my visit has made you distrust my purpose. Let me tell you then that I have no evil intentions and seek only for someone to talk with me for a while about a matter which perplexes me.' So saying he took her up in his arms (for she was very small) and was carrying her through the ante-room when suddenly Chujo, the servant for whom she had sent before, entered the bedroom. Genji gave an astonished cry and the maid, wondering who could have entered the ante-room, began groping her way towards them.

---

18. Chujo means 'Captain,' which was Genji's rank at the time.

But coming closer she recognized by the rich perfume of his dress that this could be none other than the Prince. And though she was sorely puzzled to know what was afoot, she dared not say a word. Had he been an ordinary person, she would soon have had him by the ears. 'Nay' she thought 'even if he were not a Prince I should do best to keep my hands off him; for the more stir one makes, the more tongues wag. But if I should touch this fine gentleman . . . ,' and all in a flutter she found herself obediently following Genji to his room. Here he calmly closed the door upon her, saying as he did so 'You will come back to fetch your mistress in the morning.' Utsusemi herself was vexed beyond measure at being thus disposed of in the presence of her own waiting-maid, who could indeed draw but one conclusion from what she had seen. But to all her misgivings and anxieties Genji, who had the art of improvising a convincing reply to almost any question, answered with such a wealth of ingenuity and tender concern, that for a while she was content. But soon becoming again uneasy, 'This must all be a dream—that you, so great a Prince, should stoop to consider so humble a creature as I, and I am overwhelmed by so much kindness. But I think you have forgotten what I am. A Zuryo's wife! there is no altering that, and you . . . !' Genji now began to realize how deeply he had distressed and disquieted her by his wild behaviour, and feeling thoroughly ashamed of himself he answered: 'I am afraid I know very little about these questions of rank and precedence. Such things are too confusing to carry in one's head. And whatever you may have heard of me I want to tell you for some reason or other I have till this day cared nothing for gallantry nor ever practised it, and that even you cannot be more astonished at what I have done tonight than I myself am.' With this and a score of other speeches he sought to win her confidence. But she, knowing that if once their talk became a jot less formal, she would be hard put to it to withstand his singular charm, was determined, even at the risk of seeming stiff and awkward, to show him that in trying so hard to put her at her ease he was only wasting his time, with the result that she behaved very boorishly indeed. She was by nature singularly gentle and yielding, so that the effort of steeling her heart and despite her feelings, playing all the while the part of the young bamboo-shoot which though so green and tender cannot be broken, was very painful to her; and finding that she could no longer think of arguments with which to withstand his importunity, she burst into tears; and though he was very sorry for her, it occurred to him that he would not gladly have missed that sight. He longed however to console her, but could not think of a way to do so, and said at last, 'Why do you treat me so unkindly? It is true that the manner of our meeting was strange, yet I think that Fate meant us to meet. It is harsh that you should shrink from me as though the World and you had never met.' So he chided her, and she: 'If this had happened long ago before my troubles, before my lot was cast, perhaps I should have been glad to take your kindness while it lasted, knowing that you would soon think better of your strange condescension. But now that my course is fixed, what can such meetings bring me save misery and regret? *Tell none that you have seen my home*' she ended, quoting the old song.[19] 'Small wonder that she is sad' thought Genji, and he found many a tender way to comfort her. And now the cock began to crow. Out in the courtyard Genji's men were staggering to their feet, one crying drowsily 'How I should like to go to sleep again,' and another 'Make haste there, bring out his Honour's coach.' Ki no Kami came out into the yard, 'What's all this hurry? It is only when there are women in his party that a man need hasten from a refuge to which the Earth Star has sent him. Why is his Highness setting off in the middle of the night?'

Genji was wondering whether such an opportunity would ever occur again. How would he be able even to send her letters? And thinking of all the difficulties that awaited him, he became very despondent. Chujo arrived to fetch her mistress. For a long while he would not let her go, and when at last he handed her over, he drew her back to him saying 'How can I send news to you? For, Madam' he said, raising his voice that the maid Chujo might hear, 'such love as mine, and such pitiless cruelty as yours have never been seen in the world before.' Already the birds were singing in good earnest. She could not forget that she was no one and he a Prince. And even now, while he was tenderly entreating her, there came unbidden to her mind the image of her husband Iyo no Suke, about whom she generally thought either not at all or with disdain. To think that even in a dream he might see her now, filled her with shame and terror.

It was daylight. Genji went with her to the partition door. Indoors and out there was a bustle of feet. As he closed the door upon her, it seemed to him a barrier that shut him out from all happiness. He dressed, and went out on to the balcony. A blind in the western wing was hastily raised. There seemed to be people behind who were looking at him. They could only see him indistinctly across the top of a partition in the verandah. Among them was one, perhaps, whose heart beat wildly as she looked . . . ?

The moon had not set, and though with dwindled light still shone crisp and clear in the dawn. It was a daybreak of marvellous beauty. But in the passionless visage of the sky men read only their own comfort or despair; and Genji, as with many backward glances he went upon his way, paid little heed to the beauty of the dawn. He would send her a message? No, even that was utterly impossible. And so, in great unhappiness he returned to his wife's house.

He would gladly have slept a little, but could not stop trying to invent some way of seeing her again; or when that seemed hopeless, imagining to himself all that must now be going on in her mind. She was no great beauty, Genji reflected, and yet one could not say that she was ugly. Yes, she was in every sense a member of that Middle Class upon which Uma no Kami had given them so complete a dissertation.

---

19. *Kokinshu* 811, an anonymous love-poem.

He stayed for some while at the Great Hall, and finding that, try as he might, he could not stop thinking about her and longing for her, at last in despair he sent for Ki no Kami and said to him 'Why do you not let me have that boy in my service—the Chunagon's son, whom I saw at your house? He is a likely looking boy, and I might make him my body-servant, or even recommend him to the Emperor.' 'I am sensible of your kindness' said Ki no Kami. 'I will mention what you have said to the boy's sister.' This answer irritated Genji, but he continued: 'And has this lady given you stepbrothers my lord?' 'Sir, she has been married these two years, but has had no child. It seems that in making this marriage she disobeyed her father's last injunctions, and this has set her against her husband.'

Genji: 'That is sad indeed. I am told that she is not ill-looking. Is that so?'

Ki no Kami: 'I believe she is considered quite passable. But I have had very little to do with her. Intimacy between stepchildren and stepparents is indeed proverbially difficult.'

Five or six days afterwards Ki no Kami brought the boy. He was not exactly handsome, but he had great charm and (thought Genji) an air of distinction. The Prince spoke very kindly to him and soon completely won his heart. To Genji's many questions about his sister he made such answers as he could, and when he seemed embarrassed or tongue-tied Genji found some less direct way of finding out what he wanted to know, and soon put the boy at his ease. For though he vaguely realized what was going on and thought it rather odd, he was so young that he made no effort to understand it, and without further question carried back a letter from Genji to his sister.

She was so much agitated by the sight of it that she burst into tears and, lest her brother should perceive them, held the letter in front of her face while she read it. It was very long. Among much else it contained the verse 'Would that I might dream that dream again! Alas, since first this wish was mine, not once have my eyelids closed in sleep.'

She had never seen such beautiful writing, and as she read, a haze clouded her eyes. What incomprehensible fate had first dragged her down to be the wife of a Zuryo, and then for a moment raised her so high? Still pondering, she went to her room.

Next day, Genji again sent for the boy, who went to his sister saying 'I am going to Prince Genji. Where is your answer to his letter?' 'Tell him' she answered 'that there is no one here who reads such letters.' The boy burst out laughing. 'Why, you silly, how could I say such a thing to him. He told me himself to be sure to bring an answer.' It infuriated her to think that Genji should have thus taken the boy into his confidence and she answered angrily, 'He has no business to talk to you about such things at your age. If that is what you talk about you had better not go to him any more.' 'But he sent for me' said the boy, and started off.

'I was waiting for you all yesterday' said Genji when the boy returned. 'Did you forget to bring the answer? Did you forget to come?' The child blushed and made no reply. 'And now?' 'She said there is no one at home who reads such letters.' 'How silly, what can be the use of saying such things?' and he wrote another letter and gave it to the boy, saying: 'I expect you do not know that I used to meet your sister before her marriage. She treats me in this scornful fashion because she looks upon me as a poor-spirited, defenceless creature. Whereas she has now a mighty Deputy Governor to look after her. But I hope that you will promise to be my child, not his. For he is very old, and will not be able to take care of you for long.'

The boy was quite content with this explanation, and admired Genji more than ever. The Prince kept him always at his side, even taking him to the Palace. And he ordered his Chamberlain to see to it that he was provided with a little Court suit. Indeed he treated him just as though he were his own child.

Genji continued to send letters; but she, thinking that the boy, young as he was, might easily allow a message to fall into the wrong hands and that then she would lose her fair name to no purpose, feeling too (that however much he desired it) between persons so far removed in rank there could be no lasting union, she answered his letters only in the most formal terms.

Dark though it had been during most of the time they were together, she yet had a clear recollection of his appearance, and could not deny to herself that she thought him uncommonly handsome. But she very much doubted if he on his side really knew what she was like; indeed she felt sure that the next time they met he would think her very plain and all would be over.

Genji meanwhile thought about her continually. He was for ever calling back to memory each incident of that one meeting, and every recollection filled him with longing and despair. He remembered how sad she had looked when she spoke to him of herself, and he longed to make her happier. He thought of visiting her in secret. But the risk of discovery was too great, and the consequences likely to be more fatal to her even than to himself.

He had been many days at the Palace, when at last the Earth Star again barred the road to his home. He set out at once, but on the way pretended that he had just remembered the unfavourable posture of the stars. There was nothing to do but seek shelter again in the house on the Middle River. Ki no Kami was surprised but by no means ill pleased, for he attributed Genji's visit to the amenity of the little pools and fountains which he had constructed in his garden.

Genji had told the boy in the morning that he intended to visit the Middle River, and since he had now become the Prince's constant companion, he was sent for at once to wait upon him in his room. He had already given a message to his sister, in which Genji told her of his plan. She could not but feel flattered at the knowledge that it was on her account he had contrived this ingenious excuse for coming to the house. Yet she had, as we have seen, for some reason got it into her head that at a leisurely meeting she would not please him as she had done at that first fleeting and dream-like encounter, and she dreaded adding a new sorrow to the burden of her thwarted and unhappy existence. Too proud to let him think that she had posted herself in waiting for him, she said to her servants (while the boy was busy in Genji's room) 'I do not care to be at such close quarters with our guest, besides I am stiff, and would like to be massaged; I must go where there is more room,' and so saying she made them carry her things to the maid Chujo's bedroom in the cross-wing.

Genji had purposely sent his attendants early to bed, and now that all was quiet, he hastened to send her a message. But the boy could not find her. At last when he had looked in every corner of the house, he tried the cross-wing, and succeeded in tracking her down to Chujo's room. It was too bad of her to hide like this, and half in tears he gasped out, 'Oh how can you be so horrid? What will he think of you?' 'You have no business to run after me like this,' she answered angrily. 'It is very wicked for children to carry such messages. But,' she added, 'you may tell him I am not well, that my ladies are with me, and I am going to be massaged . . .' So she dismissed him; but in her heart of hearts she was thinking that if such an adventure had happened to her while she was still a person of consequence, before her father died and left her to shift for herself in the world, she would have known how to enjoy it. But now she must force herself to look askance at all his kindness. How tiresome he must think her! And she fretted so much at not being free to fall in love with him, that in the end she was more in love than ever. But then she remembered suddenly that her lot had long ago been cast. She was a wife. There was no sense in thinking of such things, and she made up her mind once and for all never again to let foolish ideas enter her head.

Genji lay on his bed, anxiously waiting to see with what success so young a messenger would execute his delicate mission. When at last the answer came, astonished at this sudden exhibition of coldness, he exclaimed in deep mortification, 'This is a disgrace, a hideous disgrace,' and he looked very rueful indeed. For a while he said no more, but lay sighing deeply, in great distress. At last he recited the poem — 'I knew not the nature of the strange tree[20] that stands on Sono plain, and when I sought the comfort of its shade, I did but lose my road,' and sent it to her. She was still awake, and answered with the poem 'Too like am I in these my outcast years to the dim tree that dwindles from the traveller's approaching gaze.' The boy was terribly sorry for Genji and did not feel sleepy at all, but he was afraid people would think his continual excursions very strange. By this time, however, everyone else in the house was sound asleep. Genji alone lay plunged in the blackest melancholy. But even while he was raging at the inhuman stubbornness of her new-found and incomprehensible resolve, he found that he could not but admire her the more for this invincible tenacity. At last he grew tired of lying awake; there was no more to be done. A

20. The *hahakigi* or 'broom-tree' when seen in the distance appears to offer ample shade; but when approached turns out to be a skimpy bush.

moment later he had changed his mind again, and suddenly whispered to the boy, 'Take me to where she is hiding!' 'It is too difficult,' he said, 'she is locked in and there are so many people there. I am afraid to go with you.' 'So be it,' said Genji, 'but you at least must not abandon me,' and he laid the boy beside him on his bed. He was well content to find himself lying by this handsome young Prince's side, and Genji, we must record, found the boy no bad substitute for his ungracious sister.

■ Saigyo (1118–1190) (poems)

TRANSLATED BY BURTON WATSON

Saigyo (born Sato Norikiyo) was a member of the illustrious Fujiwara clan, which had dominated the government but was beginning to decline. His branch of the clan was a prosperous warrior family, and as a young man, he became an expert in the martial arts. However, he entered the priesthood at age twenty-two for reasons that can only be surmised: perhaps a devastating love affair (his work does include passionate love poems), a death in the family, or disillusionment with court life. Or perhaps he was simply uneasy about the wide-reaching changes that were beginning to transform Japanese society in the decades before the decline of the Imperial system and the rise of the Taira and Minamoto military conflict recorded in *Tales of the Heike.* After joining the priesthood, Saigyo took the name Eni, and later, Saigyo. He traveled across Japan in his role as priest, which gave him access to all social classes. He appears to have spent part of his life near Mount Koya, the center of the Shingon sect of Buddhism, to which he belonged. He also was a member of several poetry circles, including one centered on Fujiwara Shunzei. He was highly regarded in his time both as a poet and as a priest, and his reputation has never declined.

More than two thousand of his *tanka* are extant, and ninety-four of his poems are included in the important Imperial collection, the *Shinkokinshu* (*New Collection of Old and New Japanese Poems*), making him by far the best-represented poet in the anthology. His poetry precisely observes the smallest motions in nature, sudden epiphanies in natural beauty, sorrow at the passing of the seasons, and the poet's loneliness in his ascetic seclusion. Yet, he wrote beautiful poems of longing for an absent lover, whose face he sees "printed on the moon." He is a poet of the world and out of the world, of love and of asceticism, a poet who chooses seclusion and is lonely in it. Warrior, poet, priest, he is fully involved in the complexity and quandary of being human: "The priest chastens / his heart but can't deny / this deep, melancholy beauty: / a longbill lifts from the marsh / and fades in autumn dusk" (translated by Tony Barnstone). Perhaps this is the source of his lasting appeal.

FURTHER READING: Watson, Burton, tr. *Saigyo: Poems of a Mountain Home,* 1991.

The Plum Tree at My Mountain Hut

Take note:
the plum by my rustic hedge
halted in his tracks
a total stranger
who happened by   5

Living Alone

Living alone
in the shade of a remote mountain,
I have you for my companion
now the storm has passed,
moon of the winter night!   5

Her Face When We Parted

Her face when we parted,
a parting
I can never forget—
And for keepsake she left it
printed on the moon   5

When the Moon Shines

When the moon shines
without the smallest blemish,
I think of her—
and then my heart disfigures it,
blurs it with tears.   5

As Rays of Moonlight Stream

As rays of moonlight stream
through a sudden gap
in the rain clouds—
if we could meet even
for so brief a moment!   5

I Know

"I know
how you must feel!"
And with those words
she grows more hateful
than if she'd never spoken at all   5

On the Phrase "All Phenomena Are Fleeting"[1]

I think of past times,
so swift
in their vanishing,
the present soon to follow—
dew on the morning-glory   5

Fishermen

Fishermen
by a rocky shore,
winds blowing wildly,
in a boat unmoored—
such is our condition!   5

In This Mountain Village

In this mountain village
where I've given up
all hope of visitors,
how drab life would be
without my loneliness   5

The Loneliness

The loneliness
of my ramshackle
grass hut,
where no one but the wind
comes to call   5

Since I No Longer Think

Since I no longer think
of reality
as reality,
what reason would I have
to think of dreams as dreams?   5

---

1. From the famous verse in the seventh chapter of the *Nirvana Sutra:* "All phenomena are fleeting, / this is the law of birth and death. / When you have wiped out birth and death, / nirvana is your joy."

In a Mountain Village

In a mountain village
when I'm lost in the dark
of the mind's dreaming,
the sound of the wind
blows me to brightness   5

Kamakura/Nambokucho Periods

(1186–1392)

■ The Middle Counselor of the Riverbank's Stories (Eleventh to Twelfth Centuries)

TRANSLATED BY ROBERT L. BACKUS

This late Heian collection of ten stories and a fragment was originally attributed to Fujiwara Kanesuke (877–933), who held the title of Middle Counselor (a high office in the government of the central court). In 1939, however, one of the stories was positively dated as having been written in 1055 by a court woman in a story-writing contest at Princess Baishi's court. Authorities differ on whether the entire collection derived from the aristocratic women who participated in this contest or whether some of the stories may have been composed by men. Perhaps the title derives from the fact that middle counselors are often the heroes of tales in this genre, and the fact that no such hero appears in these stories may be an early example of false attribution for ironic purposes (as in the fiction of Jorge Luis Borges). The story presented here, "The Lady Who Admired Vermin," is a broad parody of a self-important intellectual woman who cares more for essences than for the elaborate rituals and appearances that an aristocratic woman was supposed to embody. For the courtly audience, nothing could be more grotesque than a woman who refused to blacken her teeth and pluck her eyebrows in order to present a beautiful front. She is a woman who prefers caterpillars to butterflies, function to aesthetics, essence to surface. This woman who rejects cosmetics, leaves her hair uncombed, speaks loudly and pontificates, and allows herself to be revealed to the eyes of men would in her time be a laughable creature. Clearly, at this end of history and through the lens of another culture, the parodied woman becomes the hero to the modern reader. Yet, as several commentators have noted, this peculiar individualist gets the better of her parents and the men she debates, suggesting at least a hidden sympathy on the part of the anonymous author.

FURTHER READING: Backus, Robert L. *The Riverside Counselor's Stories: Vernacular Fiction of Late Heian Japan,* 1985. McCullough, Helen Craig, ed. *Classical Japanese Prose: An Anthology,* 1990.

The Lady Who Admired Vermin

Next to the place where lived the lady who admired butterflies was the daughter of the Inspector-Major Counselor, whose parents tended her with such infinite care that she grew up to be a creature of intriguing and exceptional beauty.

This lady collected great numbers of frightful-looking vermin. "The way people lose themselves in admiration of blossoms and butterflies is positively silly and incomprehensible," she would say. "It is the person who wants the truth and inquires into the essence of things who has an interesting mind."

And she put them into different kinds of screened boxes to see how they would develop. "What intrigues me the most is the caterpillars, which have a certain appeal," she would say, and she would lay them out on the palm of her hand and watch them from morning till evening with her hair drawn back behind her ears.

Since her young ladies were dismayed at this behavior, she gathered around her a band of fearless and disreputable boys, and amused herself by giving them the vermin in the boxes to hold, asking their names and assigning names to the unfamiliar ones.

"As a rule it is wrong for people to make themselves up," she would say, and never plucked her eyebrows, and never applied tooth blackening because she thought it was bothersome and dirty. And she doted on the vermin from morning till night, all the while showing the gleaming white of her teeth in a smile.

Whenever people fled from her in consternation, this "lady" would shout at them in a very peculiar manner. The people thus frightened she would transfix with a stare from under heavy black eyebrows, calling them "Disgraceful!" "Vulgar!" so that they were bewildered all the more.

"That she should be so peculiar and behave so differently!" her parents thought. But at the same time they wondered, "Can there be some meaning in this that she has comprehended? Whenever we think that something she does is odd and tell her about it, she contradicts us no end. It makes one feel so intimidated!" And they were very embarrassed by this behavior too. "That may be," they told her. "But you are getting a strange reputation. What people like is good looks. If society were to hear that you enjoy playing with weird-looking caterpillars, it would put you in a very peculiar light."

"I don't care. Only when one examines all things and looks at their outcome do things have significance. That's being very childish, because caterpillars turn into butterflies." She took out some in which that phase was emerging, and as she showed them, said, "The clothes that people wear by the name of 'silk' are produced by worms before they grow wings, and when they become butterflies, why then they are completely ignored and are worthless!" Against this they could find no argument and were confounded.

Nevertheless, she was lady enough not to display herself even to her parents, and she held the opinion that "Devils and women are better invisible to the eyes of mankind." Thus would she deliver herself so cleverly from behind a curtain stand set out by a slightly raised blind in the main chamber of the house.

Her young ladies would listen to all of this. "She puts on quite a show, but leaves you positively bewildered. These playthings of hers! I wonder what kind of people serve the lady who admires butterflies," said one of them who was called Hyoe, and recited:

> What means have I
> to make her understand?
>   Oh, to go away!
> I would never look upon those things
> in their caterpillar stage again.

Another, who was called Little Tayu, recited laughing:

>   I do envy them.
> "Ah, the blossoms! Ah, the butterflies!"
>   they will be exclaiming;
> while what have we to look upon
> but a world that reeks of caterpillars!

"Too harsh, really," said one who was called Sakon. "Her eyebrows look like furry caterpillars all right, but her bare teeth you would think have been skinned.

>   In wintertime
> we can depénd on having coats
>   however cold it is,
> in a place like this where one can see
> so many worms with furry skins.

We could easily get along without clothes, you know."

They were overheard telling each other such things by a faultfinding woman, who said, "Whatever are you young people saying! I find nothing at all admirable about a person who is supposed to admire butterflies. You are quite inexcusable! And besides, would anyone line up caterpillars and call them butterflies? It's just that they molt; you know. She examines that stage. That is good sense. When you catch a butterfly, its dust sticks to your hand and makes it very unpleasant, you know. Also, they say that if you catch a butterfly, it gives you the ague. Horrid things!"

But this only made them even more malicious in their remarks to one another.

To the boys who caught the vermin the lady gave interesting things, things they desired; and so they collected various kinds of frightful-looking creatures and presented them to her. Although the caterpillars had fine-looking fur and all, they did not suggest anything to her imagination, and for that reason she found them lacking. So they would collect such things as mantises and snails, and she had them sing loud songs about them for her to hear, and raised her voice herself to chant the ditty:

> Why do the horns of the snail
> battle each other to no avail?

She was disappointed to find that the boys' names were so ordinary, and so she named them after insects and other low creatures. She employed them under such names as Mole Cricket, Toady, Dragonfly, Grasshopper, and Millipede.

Such things became known in public, and there were people who said very disagreeable things, among them a certain young man well connected by marriage, who was high-spirited, fearless, and personable. Hearing about the lady, he said, "Well, I bet she will be afraid of this." And he fashioned the end of a sash—very beautiful to look at—into the close likeness of a snake, fixed it so that it could move and all, put it into a bag that had a scaly pattern and a string to draw it closed, and tied a note to it which read:

> Ever so slowly
> creeping, creeping would I follow
> by my lady's side,
> I who am long in faithfulness
> that stretches on without an end.

When they saw what was written, they brought it into her presence in all innocence. "These bags are always so strangely heavy just to lift!" they remarked as they drew it open. And there was the snake with its head raised up. Her people cried out in bewilderment, but the lady was very calm. "Praised be Amida Buddha! Praised be Amida Buddha!" she intoned.

"It must be an ancestor reborn in this present form. Don't carry on so!" she quavered; and averting her face, she muttered as she drew it close to her, "Right now, while it is still so young and lovely, I want to have a feeling of kinship for it. How low-minded all of you are!"

But even a woman of her temperament felt so afraid that she fidgeted up and down like a butterfly, and the strained voice in which she spoke made a terribly funny sound, so that her people broke into laughter as they fled noisily away. Whereupon the news spread.

"What an appalling, unearthly thing is this I am hearing!" exclaimed His Lordship. "How unnatural that all of them should have left her with such a creature right there in front of their eyes!" And he rushed to her, sword in hand. When he looked at the thing closely, he saw that the gentleman had fashioned it into a very good likeness; and so, taking it into his hands, he said, "How very good this person is at making things! Apparently he has done this because he heard about the wise airs you put on and the kind of things you appreciate. Write an answer and send it to him at once." And with that he took his leave.

When her people heard that it was artificial they said angrily, "What an outrageous thing to do!"

"He will be left in suspense if you don't answer him," everyone told her, and so she wrote an answer on a very stiff and coarse piece of paper. Since she had never written in a cursive hand, it was done in the angular script.

In the Garden of Bliss

If we are bound by fate,
one day I shall encounter you
in that good paradise.
No easy thing to get involved with
is the shape of a lowly creature.

When the young man, who was the Assistant Director of the Stables of the Right, saw it, he thought, "What a curious and different sort of letter this is!" And hoping to find some way to have a look at her, he made an arrangement with a certain Middle Captain whereby they disguised themselves as common women, proceeded to the home of the Inspector-Major Counselor at a time when he was out, and watched from a position by a latticework on the north side of the quarters where the lady resided. They noticed some boys who were doing nothing unusual, loitering about and walking among the grasses and trees, when one of them said, "Look! Here's a whole bunch of them crawling all over this tree! These are very fine ones!"

"Would you look at these?" they said, raising one of the blinds. "We've got some wonderful caterpillars for you!"

"Oh what fun!" said the lady in a brisk voice. "Bring them here!"

"I don't think we can sort them out. Would you just come and look at them here?"

At that she trod brusquely into the open.

As the men watched her push the blind outward and stare wide-eyed at the branches, they saw that she wore a mantelet over her head; and her hair, though the sidelocks made a pretty curve downward, had a prickly look about it, perhaps because she did not groom it, while her eyebrows stood out very dark in gaudy relief and looked crisp. Her mouth was attractively formed and pretty, but since she did not apply tooth blackening, it was most unconventional. One felt that had she used cosmetics she would certainly be good-looking. How depressing! What a pity it was to see that she had let herself go so badly, yet was not unattractive, but looked quite different from the ordinary, was remarkably genteel, and had an air of brightness about her. She wore robes of figured silk in pale yellow under the outer robe with a katydid design, and preferred her trousers white.[1]

She went out because she wanted to examine the worms as closely as possible. "What a splendid sight!" she said. "They are coming this way because it hurts them to be burned in the sun. Round them up, boys, and don't miss a single one!"

As the boys knocked them off they fluttered to the ground. She held out a white fan with calligraphy on it that she had practiced in black strokes of India ink. "Pick them up and put them on this," she commanded, and the boys got them out.

The two gentlemen were appalled. "How extraordinary in a place that has misfortune enough!" they thought; and in their opinion of her, as far as the gentlemen were concerned, she was incredible.

One of the boys, who was standing there, looked at them suspiciously and said, "Over there alongside that latticework some good-looking but strangely dressed men are standing and peeking at us!"

"How awful! I fear Milady is exposed to view because of her interest in playing with vermin the way she does. I shall go and inform her," said Lady Tayu; and when she came into her mistress's presence she found her outside the blind as usual, shouting and having the caterpillars brushed off so that they fell to the ground. Since they frightened her very much, she announced without coming too close, "Come inside, Madam! The veranda is exposed to view."

Believing that she spoke only to restrain her from what she was doing, the lady replied, "Well, what of it! I am not ashamed."

"Oh, what a sorry business! Do you think I am lying? Why do you act this way when they say that some very magnificent-looking persons are over by the latticework! Come inside and look!"

"Mole Cricket, go over there and take a look!" said the lady.

He ran over and then reported, "They are really there!"

At this the lady jumped to her feet, and the caterpillars she gathered up and put into her sleeve before she ran inside. Her figure was nicely proportioned, and her hair fell very abundantly the full length of her robes. Since it was untrimmed at the edges, it did not form a cluster, yet it flowed evenly and looked only the more beautiful.

"Most people are not this well favored. Is it so regrettable that they try to improve their personal appearance and manner? One ought really to be repelled by her appearance, yet she is very nice looking and genteel, and it is surely only her troublesome qualities that make her different. Oh, how regrettable! Why does she have such a weird mind, and when she looks so nice too!"

So the gentlemen thought. The Assistant Director was highly dissatisfied with the prospect of just going away. He would at least let her know

---

1. The pale colors were appropriate for a middle-aged or older woman.

that he had seen her. Therefore he used the juice of a plant to write on a sheet of folded paper:

> Now that I have seen
> significant depths in caterpillar fur,
>   I have every hope
> that I may keep yours in hand for good
> to watch and guard with tender care!

He tapped with his fan, whereupon a boy appeared. "Present this to the lady," he said, giving it to him.

The lady called Tayu accepted it from the boy as he told her, "The person standing over there says to present this to Her Ladyship."

"Oh, how awful!" she said. "This does indeed seem to be the work of the Assistant Director of the Stables of the Right. He must have seen your face, Madam, while you were amusing yourself with those wretched bugs!" And she told her mistress a thing or two.

To which the lady replied, "When one thinks things through, one realizes that nothing is shameful. Who among men can stay long enough in this dreamlike and illusory world to look at bad things or look at the good and wonder about them?"

There was no point in saying anything to that, and her young people turned to each other in despair. The men stood by for a while on the off chance that there might be a reply, but the ladies called all the boys inside. "A sorry business!" they said to one another.

There must have been some among those present who understood what was required, for one of them did rise to the occasion and out of sympathy wrote:

> The depths of a heart
> so unlike the hearts of other human
> beings
>   I certainly wish to reveal;
> but only when I have asked the person's
> name
> as I do with caterpillars whom I do not
> know.

The Assistant Director recited:

> No one at all
> could equal the tip of a single hair
>   growing on those eyebrows,
> which are all but indistinguishable
> from furry caterpillar forms!

Then, laughing, he apparently went home.

What happened next you shall read in Scroll Two.

■ Tales of Times Now Past (Late Eleventh to Early Twelfth Centuries) (stories)

TRANSLATED BY MARIAN URY

Tales of Times Now Past is a late Heian collection of more than twelve hundred brief tales (or *setsuwa*) that is considered a Japanese literary classic. Though the tales are traditionally attributed to Minamoto Takakuni (1004–1077), it is by no means certain that he was either the compiler or the sole author. Each story begins "At a time now past . . ." and ends ". . . so it's been handed down." The collection contains stories set in India and China as well as secular and supernatural tales set in Japan, including Buddhist Jataka tales (tales of the Buddha's previous lives), Buddhist parables, miracle tales, tales of visits to hell, secular histories, warrior stories, tales of supernatural creatures, tales of robbery, and many other sorts of stories. The didactic nature of a number of these stories suggests that the collection may have been put together as a sourcebook for priests to help them with their sermons, though the substantial number of secular stories puts this in question as well. The collection is meticulously arranged into chapters consisting of a number of stories that develop a particular theme or set of themes arranged in thematic pairs that also have a rapport with adjacent stories. As a compilation of folktales, legends, real history, and miracle stories, this collection is a great example of the value of popular traditions, as opposed to the refined works of the courtly tradition. It has been very influential in the development of later Japanese literature, often serving as a sourcebook for playwrights in the noh, kabuki, and bunraku theaters.

FURTHER READING: Jones, S. W. *Ages Ago: Thirty-seven Tales from the Konjaku Monogatari Collection*, 1959. Kelsey, W. Michael. "*Konjaku Monogatari-shu:* Toward an Understanding of Its Literary Qualities," *Monumenta Nipponica*, 30, 1975. Nakamura, Kyoko Motomichi. *Miraculous Stories from the Japanese Buddhist Tradition: The Nihon ryo of the Monk Kyōkai*, 1973. Ury, Marian, tr. *Tales of Times Now Past: Sixty-two Stories from a Medieval Japanese Collection*, 1979.

How an Invisible Man Regained Corporeal Form through Kannon's Aid[1]

At a time now past—when it was I do not know—there lived in the capital a young, low-ranking samurai. He went regularly to the Rokkakudō[2] and worshipped there earnestly.

---

1. "Kannon" is the Japanese name for the female bodhisattva Avalokiteshvara, who is spoken of in the Lotus Sutra and is known in China as Quan Yin, the goddess of mercy [Editor].

2. A hall in the Chōhōji, in Kyoto, in which a celebrated image of Kannon was enshrined.

On the last day of the twelfth month[3] it happened that at nightfall he went to the house of a friend. He set out for home after it was quite dark and went west down First Avenue. As he was crossing the bridge over Horikawa[4] he saw ahead of him a great many men carrying lighted torches. "It must be some high nobleman," he thought and hurried under the bridge. He waited in its shadow as the torch-bearers came toward him and passed over it eastward. He raised his eyes for a quiet look—and what should he see but that it was not men at all but a procession of dreadful oni![5] Some had one eye; some had horns; some had extra hands; and some had only one foot and hopped. At the sight, the man felt as though he were no longer alive; his mind went numb and he just stood there as the oni went by. They had all gone past except for one last, and he said, "There are signs of a man here." "We can't see any," some said. "Catch him and bring him here," said yet others.

"It's all over with me," the man thought. One of the oni ran and grabbed him and pulled him up. The others said, "This man's offense is not serious. Let him go." Four or five of them spat on him, and then they all went past.

The man was glad that he hadn't been killed. He felt funny and his head hurt, but he pulled himself together. "I'll go straight home and tell my wife about it," he thought. He hurried home, but once he was indoors his wife and children said not a word to him although they were looking right at him; nor did they answer when he addressed them. The man thought this strange and went up close to them, but even though he was standing beside them they had no idea he was there. Now he understood. "So that's it! When the oni spat on me my body disappeared!" His distress was boundless. He saw other people just as before and heard them talk as clearly as ever, but other people did not see him or hear his voice. He took food to eat which his family had set out, and none of them knew it. Thus he passed the night; at dawn his wife and children were saying that they were sure he had been murdered the night before.

Days passed—and what was he to do? With no other remedy, he went to the Rokkakudō and went into retreat there. "Kannon, save me!" he prayed. "For many years now I have worshipped you and put my trust in you; as proof of it let me regain my original corporeal form." He ate the food of others who were in retreat there and took rice from their offerings, but none of the people beside him were aware of it.

Thus he spent twice seven days. One night shortly before dawn he had a dream. A venerable monk appeared near the curtains of the sacred image and came to his side. The monk said, "Leave this place as soon as it is morning and do as the first person you meet tells you to." At this, the man awoke.

---

3. In ancient times the spirits of the dead were thought to return on this night.

4. First Avenue was the northern boundary of Kyoto; Horikawa was to the west.

5. Demons [Editor].

At dawn he left the temple. At the foot of the gate he met a herdboy whose appearance was fearsome in the extreme, leading a great ox. The boy looked at him and said, "Well, sir, you're to come along with me." The man was overjoyed at being spoken to, for he thought, "I have become visible again," and, trusting in his dream, followed the boy happily. They walked westward for about two-thirds of a mile and came to a large gabled gate, which was shut fast. The boy tied his ox to it and started to slip through a space between the doors too narrow for a human being to enter. He tugged at the man. "Come in with me," he said. "How on earth can I get through that?" said the man. "Never mind," said the boy, "just go in"— and taking the man's hand, he pulled him in along with him. The man saw that they were within the walls of a great, thronging mansion.

The boy took him up onto the veranda floor and straight inside. Not a person spoke up to challenge them. They went into the inner-most recesses of the house, and there the man saw a fine young lady lying sick and in pain. Her maids sat side by side behind her pillow and at her feet, nursing her. The oxboy led the man to the sick lady, made him hold a small mallet, sat him down beside her, and made him strike her head and hips, so that she shook her head in agony. "This illness will be the end of her," her parents said, and they wept. As the man looked on, they read sutras, and also they sent for [a certain][6] worthy exorcist. Soon the priest arrived. Sitting close to the sick girl, he intoned the Heart Sutra. The man felt boundless veneration. His hair stood on end, and a chill went through his body. But no sooner did the oxboy catch sight of the priest than he, for his part, ran out of the house at full speed.

The priest read a dharani of Fudō's realm of fire.[7] When he pronounced the formula and made mystic signs over the patient, the man's clothing caught fire. It burned and burned, and as it burned he screamed. At that moment he became fully visible. Everyone in the household, from the parents down to the maids, saw to their amazement a man obviously of very lowly station sitting next to the sufferer. Before anything else, they took hold of him and dragged him away. "What is this?" they demanded, and he told them what had happened, from the very beginning. "What a queer business!" they thought. But then it turned out that when the man had become visible the lady had recovered: it was as though her illness had been simply wiped away. The joy of the household was unbounded. The exorcist then said: "Do not blame this man, for he has benefited from the favor of the Kannon of Rokkakudō. Release him at once." And so they let him go free.

---

6. Bracketed words bridge a lacuna; literally, "a worthy exorcist called———."

7. Through chanting, mystic gestures, and meditation on Fudō, the adept produced a magic fire to drive out demons. The passage that follows may be unique in literature in describing an exorcism essentially from the point of view of the supernatural being who is exorcised.

The man went home and told his story, and his wife was glad and thought how uncanny it all was. The oxboy was in fact the attendant of a deity. He had afflicted the lady because someone had persuaded him to.

Neither the lady nor the man was ever ill afterward; this resulted from the miraculous power of the realm of fire dharani.

Among the benefits with which Kannon favors his worshippers are marvels of this sort. So the tale's been told, and so it's been handed down.

■ Tale of the Heike (Twelfth to Fourteenth Centuries) (prose)

TRANSLATED BY HELEN CRAIG MCCULLOUGH

The *Tale of the Heike* is the finest Japanese military epic. Its original author seems to have been a minor noble named Nakayama Yukinari (c. 1164–?), but there are more than a hundred recensions, and the standard twelve-book text (plus sequel) is the product of centuries of modification by professional chanters who took the story across Japan and chanted it to audiences with musical accompaniment. The work can be described as at least in part verse-prose, since it often has the seven-five syllable pattern that is basic to Japanese verse. The subject of this tale, which is as familiar to the Japanese as the *Iliad* is to the West, is the rise and eventual fall of the Taira clan (the Heike) in the second part of the twelfth century. The Taira fall to their rivals, the Minamoto clan (Genji), in the Gempei War of 1180–1185, leading to the establishment of the Minamoto shogunate. The Taira bring on themselves karmic punishment for the arrogance and pride of their leader Kiyomori and for their attempts to supplant the powerful Fujiwara clan and change their station in life. The story must be read not as fiction but as a dramatization of history, based on actual events, characters, and historical accounts. There is a balance between Buddhist morality and swashbuckling celebration of feats of courage, treacheries, and honor. This epic tale has been a fertile source for cultural production in many other fields from noh, kabuki, and bunraku plays to modern movies and novels. It is second only to *The Tale of Genji* as a masterpiece of Japanese storytelling. In the selections presented here we see the famous Buddhist opening chapter; a self-contained tale about Tadamori, clan head of the Taira, and father of Kiyomori; and in "The Death of Etchū no Zenji" we see a fascinating account of battlefield etiquette and betrayal.

FURTHER READING: Kitagawa, Hiroshi, and Paul Tsuchida, trs. *The Tale of the Heike: "Heike Monogatari,"* 1977. McCullough, Helen Craig, tr. *The Tale of the Heike,* 1988. Sadler, A. L. *The Ten Foot Square Hut and Tales of the Heike,* 1971.

Gion Shōja

The sound of the Gion Shōja bells echoes the impermanence of all things; the color of the *śāla* flowers reveals the truth that the prosperous must decline. The proud do not endure, they are like a dream on a spring night; the mighty fall at last, they are as dust before the wind.

In a distant land, there are the examples set by Zhao Gao of Qin, Wang Mang of Han, Zhu Yi of Liang, and Lushan of Tang, all of them men who prospered after refusing to be governed by their former lords and sovereigns, but who met swift destruction because they disregarded admonitions, failed to recognize approaching turmoil, and ignored the nation's distress. Closer to home, there have been Masakado of Shōhei, Sumitomo of Tengyō, Yoshichika of Kōwa, and Nobuyori of Heiji, every one of them proud and mighty. But closest of all, and utterly beyond the power of mind to comprehend or tongue to relate, is the tale of Taira no Ason Kiyomori, the Rokuhara Buddhist Novice and Former Chancellor.

Kiyomori was the oldest son and heir of Punishments Minister Tadamori. He was a grandson of the Sanuki Governor Masamori, who was a descendant in the ninth generation from Prince Kazurahara of First Rank, the Minister of Ceremonial and fifth son of Emperor Kanmu. Prince Kazurahara's son, Prince Takami, died without office or rank. The clan received the Taira surname in the time of Prince Takami's son, Prince Takamochi, who left the imperial clan to become a subject soon after he was named Vice-Governor of Kazusa Province. Prince Takamochi's son was the Defense Garrison Commander Yoshimochi, who changed his name to Kunika in later life. During the six generations from Kunika to Masamori, members of the clan held provincial governorships but were not permitted to have their names on the duty-board in the Courtiers' Hall.

The Night Attack at the Courtiers' Hall

But Tadamori, during his term as Bizen Governor, built a Buddhist hall thirty-three bays long, enshrined therein a thousand and one holy images, and offered it in fulfillment of Retired Emperor Toba's vow to found a temple, the Tokujōjuin. The dedication took place on the Thirteenth of the Third Month in the first year of Tenshō. Orders were issued to reward Tadamori with a province, and Tajima, which happened to be available, was given to him. The delighted Retired Emperor also granted him courtier privileges at the imperial palace. Tadamori set foot in the Courtiers' Hall for the first time at the age of thirty-six.

Angered by those marks of favor, the courtiers and senior nobles conspired to attack Tadamori under cover of darkness on the night of the Gosechi Flushed Faces Banquet, which was to be held on the Twenty-Third of the Twelfth Month in that same year. But Tadamori made preparations of his own on hearing of the plot. "I am not a civil functionary," he thought. "I belong to a warrior house. It would be a grief to my family and to me if I let myself be humiliated through lack of foresight. Besides, the book says, 'Take care of yourself so you can serve your master.'"

When Tadamori entered the palace, he brought along a large dagger, thrust loosely under his court robes. Turning toward a spot where the lamplight was dim, he drew the weapon with deliberation and held it alongside his head, its blade gleaming like ice. None of those present failed to mark the act. Furthermore, his retainer Sahyōe-no-jō Iesada came and sat at attention in the small side garden, dressed in a green-laced corselet under a pale green hunting robe, with a sword and an attached bowstring bag under his arm. Iesada was a son of Shinnosaburō Dayū Suefusa and a grandson of Assistant Director of the Carpentry Bureau Sadamitsu, who had been a member of the Taira clan.

In great perturbation, the Head Chamberlain and his staff sent a Chamberlain of Sixth Rank to rebuke Iesada. "Who is this person in an unfigured hunting robe waiting beyond the rainspout near the bell pull? You are misbehaving. Get out of there!"

Iesada kept his seat. "I have been told that my hereditary lord, the honorable Governor of Bizen, is to be cut down in the dark tonight. I am here to witness his fate; I cannot leave." Perhaps the conspirators lost heart, for there was no attack that night.

Later during the same occasion, when it was Tadamori's turn to dance as part of the informal entertainment, the gentlemen put new words to a song, chanting, "The Ise wine bottles are vinegar jars." Although the Taira were descended from the great Emperor Kanmu, they had not frequented the capital in the recent past, but had become *jige* with roots in Ise Province. Thus the singers chanted of Ise bottles, punning on a kind of vessel produced in that province. And because Tadamori suffered from a squint, they introduced the second pun.[1] Since Tadamori had no means of retaliation, he decided to slip away before the affair ended. He went to the north corner of the Shishinden, and there, within sight of the other courtiers, he called over a woman from the Bureau of Grounds and put the dagger in her charge. Then he left.

"How did things go?" Iesada asked. Tadamori wanted to tell him the truth, but Iesada was the kind of man who would leap into the Courtiers' Hall itself, slashing and cutting, if he were to hear such a story, so he replied, "Nothing much happened."

People are expected to confine themselves to amusing trifles like "White tissue paper, deep-dyed paper, corded brushes, and lacquered brushes" during the singing and dancing at Gosechi entertainments. In the relatively recent past, to be sure, there had been an incident involving the Dazaifu Provisional Governor-General Suenaka, whose swarthy complexion

---

1. *Heiji* can mean both "wine bottle" and "Taira clan"; *sugame*, "vinegar jar" and "squint eye."

had caused him to be nicknamed the "Black Governor." Suenaka had danced at a Gosechi party during his tenure as Head Chamberlain, and the singers had improvised, "Ah, black, black, black is the head! Who applied the lacquer?"[2] There had also been the case of the Kazan'in Former Chancellor Tadamasa. Orphaned at ten by the death of his father, Middle Counselor Tadamune, Tadamasa had been taken as a son-in-law and maintained in luxury by the late Naka-no-mikado Middle Counselor, Fujiwara no Ienari, who was then Governor of Harima Province. When Tadamasa danced during the Gosechi festivities, the singers chanted, "Can the Harima rice be a scouring rush or a *muku* leaf? Ah, how it polishes up the wardrobe!"[3] Nothing had come of such affairs, people remarked now—but who could tell what might happen in these latter days of the Law?[4] It was a worrisome business.

As was to have been anticipated, all the courtiers presented complaints after the Gosechi ceremonies ended. "Rules and regulations are supposed to determine who may wear a weapon to an official banquet, and who may go in and out of the palace accompanied by Escorts," they said. "It has always been accepted that neither may be done without explicit imperial authorization. But Tadamori stationed a warrior wearing a hunting robe at the small garden outside the Courtiers' Hall, on the pretext that the man was a hereditary retainer, and he also attended a formal banquet with a weapon at his waist. Both actions were unprecedented breaches of conduct. A person who commits a double offense must not escape punishment. Tadamori must have his name removed from the duty-board and lose his official position at once."

In great surprise, the Retired Emperor summoned Tadamori for questioning. "To begin with," Tadamori explained, "I had no idea that my retainer had posted himself in the small garden. But it has seemed recently that there has been some kind of plot against me. Iesada has been in my service for many years; he must have heard about it and gone there without my knowledge, in the hope of sparing me embarrassment. That is not something I could have done anything about. If Iesada deserves censure, shall I call him in and turn him over to you? Next, as regards the dagger, I gave it to one of the servants from the Bureau of Grounds to keep for me. Before judgment is rendered, would it not be well to summon the woman and see whether it is a real weapon?"

The Retired Emperor found the suggestion reasonable; he called for the dagger and inspected it. The scabbard was of black lacquer, but the blade proved to be silver foil over wood.

---

2. The song puns on *tō* ("face," "head") and Suenaka's official title, *kurōdo no tō* (Head Chamberlain).

3. "Harima rice" is a metaphor for the Governor. Scouring rushes (*tokusa*) and the bristly leaves of the muku tree (*Aphananthe aspera*) were used as polishing agents.

4. *Matsudai.* In Buddhist thought, a 10,000-year age of moral degeneration, culminating in the disappearance of the Law (doctrine) itself. In the 12th century, it was generally believed that the age had begun around 1050.

"He wanted to avoid humiliation, so he made a show of carrying a dagger," the Retired Emperor said. "But he wore a wooden blade because he knew there would be complaints later. That is a sign of admirable resourcefulness—precisely what one would desire in a warrior. His retainer's foray into the garden was the kind of thing warriors' retainers do. Tadamori is not to blame for it." In view of his evident approval, there was no more talk of punishment.

The Death of Etchū no Zenji

In reckless disregard of their lives, the warriors from Musashi and Sagami took the offensive on both the main front and the seaward side. The Kodama League sent a messenger from the mountain flank to the New Middle Counselor Tomomori, who was fighting with his face toward the east. "The men of the Kodama League tell you this because you were once Governor of Musashi: look behind you!" On doing so, Tomomori and the others saw a cloud of black smoke advancing toward them. "Ah! The western front has fallen!" They all fled in desperate haste.

Etchū no Zenji Moritoshi, the Samurai Commander on the cliffward side, halted his mount and sat motionless, perhaps because he believed it was too late to try to escape. Inomata no Koheiroku Noritsuna marked him as a worthy adversary, galloped forward with flailing whip and flapping stirrups, rode up alongside him, gripped him with all his strength, and crashed with him to the ground. Noritsuna was a man renowned in the Eight Provinces for his great strength, a warrior who was said to have once torn apart a deer's double-branched antlers with ease. Moritoshi allowed others to consider him merely as strong as twenty or thirty ordinary men, but in actuality he could haul up or send down a vessel that required sixty or seventy men for the working. Thus, Moritoshi succeeded in gripping Noritsuna and holding him still. Noritsuna, lying underneath, tried to draw his dagger but could not grasp the hilt with his splayed fingers, tried to speak but was pinned too tight to utter a word. But although his head was about to be cut off, and despite his physical inferiority, his valor did not flag. He collected his breath calmly for a few instants and then spoke in an offhand manner.

"Did you hear me announce my name? A man who kills an enemy does not perform a great exploit unless he takes the head after identifying himself and requiring the other to do the same. What will you gain by taking an anonymous head?"

Moritoshi may have thought that he was right. "I am Etchū no Zenji Moritoshi, born a Taira but now become a samurai because of my inadequacies. Who are you? Announce your name: I would like to hear it."

"I am Inomata no Koheiroku Noritsuna, a resident of Musashi Province." Noritsuna continued, "If we look at the present state of affairs, it seems that the Genji are the stronger, and that you on the Heike side face defeat. Unless your masters prosper, you will reap no rewards by taking heads to show them. Stretch a point and spare me. I will use my exploits to save the lives of any number of Heike men—dozens, if you like."

Moritoshi was outraged. "In spite of all my shortcomings, I belong to the house of Taira. I have no intention of turning to the Genji for help, and no intention whatsoever of helping one of them. Your proposal is ignoble." He prepared to cut off Noritsuna's head.

"You are disgracing yourself! How can you decapitate a man who has already surrendered?" Noritsuna said.

"Very well, I will spare you." Moritoshi raised Noritsuna to his feet, and the two sat down to rest on a footpath, with a hard, sun-baked field in front and a deep, muddy rice paddy to their rear.

Presently, a warrior attired in a suit of armor with black leather lacing came galloping toward them on a whitish horse. Moritoshi eyed him suspiciously. "Don't worry," Noritsuna said. "That is Hitomi no Shirō, a friend of mine. He must have seen me." But to himself Noritsuna thought, "If I begin wrestling with Etchū no Zenji after Shirō gets close, Shirō will be sure to attack him, too." He bided his time.

The rider meanwhile advanced until he was a mere thirty-five feet away. At first, Moritoshi tried to keep one eye on each of the two men, but the galloping foe engaged his full attention as he gradually approached, and he lost track of Noritsuna. Noritsuna seized the opportunity. He sprang to his feet with a yell, dealt a powerful blow to Moritoshi's breastplate with the combined force of his two hands, and toppled him backwards into the rice paddy behind. As Moritoshi struggled to rise, Noritsuna clamped him between his legs, snatched the dagger from Moritoshi's waist, lifted his adversary's armor skirt, plunged the weapon into his flesh three times, hilt, fist, and all, and took his head.

Hitomi no Shirō had come up in the meantime. "It is cases like this that give rise to disputes," Noritsuna thought. He impaled the head on the tip of his sword, held it high, and announced his name in a mighty voice. "Inomata no Koheiroku Noritsuna has slain Etchū no Zenji Moritoshi, the Heike samurai known in these days as a demon god!" His name led that day's list of exploits.

■ Kamo no Chomei (c. 1155–1216) (memoir)

TRANSLATED BY HELEN CRAIG MCCULLOUGH

An Account of My Hermitage by Kamo no Chomei is a masterly Buddhist essay and a classic of Japanese literature. Like Henry David Thoreau retreating to his cabin by Walden Pond, Chomei records his attempt to simplify his life and become self-reliant. He was born to a family that traced its ancestry to a god who lived at Kamo in legendary times, and traditionally family members were lesser courtiers and priests in the shrines of the Kamo area. His father was the head priest of the Lower Kamo Shrine, but he died when Chomei was eighteen. Chomei was appointed by the Retired Emperor Gotoba to the Poetry Office, which was responsible for organizing the compilation of the *Shinkokinshu,* an important Imperial poetry anthology. In his early twenties, he gave up his active court life and devoted himself to the arts of poetry and the lute. Later he took Buddhist vows, severed his connection with the Poetry Office, and went to live as a recluse near Mount Hiei. Around 1208, he built his famous ten-foot-square hut in the solitary mountains at Himo in the Uji region (made famous in the last chapters of *The Tale of Genji*), where he lived till his death. In addition to *An Account of My Hermitage,* his most famous piece, Chomei wrote poems, *The Nameless Treatise* (a work on poetics), and *A Collection of Religious Awakenings* (a collection of didactic stories).

Chomei lived through the turbulent years of warfare between the Taira and Minamoto clans and through a series of natural disasters. In *An Account of My Hermitage,* which he wrote in 1212, he recounts the violence of nature and of human nature in a series of striking depictions of prevailing misery in a changing world. Since life is evanescent as "bubbles on the water" and since all his early pampered existence cannot protect him from natural and human disasters, Chomei moves to ever smaller and simpler residences and finds protection from loss in owning very little. Like the Chinese poets Han Shan and Tao Yuanming, Chomei is a model for later Buddhist recluses.

FURTHER READING: McCullough, Helen Craig, ed. *Classical Japanese Prose: An Anthology,* 1990. Ury, Marian. "Recluses and Eccentric Monks: Tales from the *Hosshinshu* by Kamo no Chomei," *Monumenta Nipponica,* 27, 1972.

An Account of My Hermitage

1

The waters of a flowing stream are ever present but never the same; the bubbles in a quiet pool disappear and form but never endure for long. So it is with men and their dwellings in the world.

The houses of the high and the low seem to last for generation after generation, standing with ridgepoles aligned and roof-tiles jostling in the magnificent imperial capital, but investigation reveals that few of them existed in the past. In some cases, a building that burned last year has been replaced this year; in others, a great house has given way to a small one. And it is the same with the occupants. The places are unchanged, the population remains large, but barely one or two survive among every twenty or thirty of the people I used to know. Just as with the bubbles on the water, someone dies at night and someone else is born in the morning. Where do they come from and where do they go, all those who are born and die? And for whose benefit, for what reason, does a man take enormous pains to build a temporary shelter pleasing to the eye? The master in his dwelling is like the dewdrop vying in ephemerality with the morning glory where it forms. The flower may remain after the dew evaporates, but it withers in the morning sun; the flower may droop before the moisture vanishes, but the dew does not survive until nightfall.

2

I have witnessed a number of remarkable occurrences in the more than forty years since I began to understand the nature of things. Around the Hour of the Dog [7:00 P.M.–9:00 P.M.] on a very windy night—I believe it was the Twenty-eighth of the Fourth Month in the third year of Angen [1177]—a fire broke out in the southeastern part of the capital and burned toward the northwest. In the end, it spread to Suzaku Gate, the Great Hall of State, the Academy, and the Ministry of Popular Affairs, reducing them all to ashes overnight. Its source is said to have been a temporary structure housing some dancers, located near the Higuchi–Tomi-no-kōji intersection. Spread here and there by an erratic wind, it burned in a pattern resembling an open fan, narrow at the base and wide at the outer edge. Suffocating smoke engulfed distant houses; wind-whipped flames descended to earth everywhere near at hand. The sky was red to the horizon with ashes lit by the fiery glare, and winged flames leaped a block or two at a time in the lurid atmosphere, torn free by the irresistible force of the gale. Everything must have seemed as unreal as a dream to the people in the fire's path. Some of them fell victim to the smoke. Others died instantly in the embrace of the flames. Still others managed to escape with their lives but failed to rescue their belongings, and all their cherished treasures turned to ashes. The value of so much property may be imagined! The fire claimed the houses of sixteen senior nobles, to say nothing of countless others of less importance. It was reported that fully one-third of the capital had been destroyed. Dozens of men and women were killed; innumerable horses and oxen perished.

All human enterprises are pointless, but it must be counted an act of supreme folly for a man to consume his treasure and put himself to endless trouble merely to build a house in a place as dangerous as the capital.

Again, around the Fourth Month in the fourth year of Jishō [1180], a great whirlwind sprang up near the Nakamikado–[Higashi] Kyōgoku intersection and swept all the way to Rokujō Avenue. Not a house, large or small, escaped destruction within the area of three or four blocks where the blast wreaked its full fury. In some cases, entire buildings were flattened; in others, only crossbeams and pillars were spared. Gates were caught up and deposited four or five blocks distant; fences were blown away and neighboring properties merged. And I need hardly mention what happened to smaller objects. Everything inside a house mounted to the skies; cypress-bark thatch and shingles whirled like winter leaves in the wind. Dust ascended like smoke to blind the eye; the terrible howl of the storm swallowed the sound of voices. It seemed that even the dread karma-wind of hell could be no worse. Not only were houses damaged or destroyed, but countless men suffered injury or mutilation while the buildings were being reconstructed. The wind moved toward the south-southeast, visiting affliction on innumerable people.

Whirlwinds are common, but not ones such as that. Those who experienced it worried that it might be an extraordinary phenomenon, a warning from a supernatural being.

Again, around the Sixth Month in the fourth year of Jishō, the court moved suddenly to a new capital.[1] Nobody had dreamed of such a thing. When we consider that more than 400 years had elapsed since the establishment of the present imperial seat during Emperor Saga's reign, surely a new one ought not to have been chosen without exceptional justification. It was more than reasonable that people should have felt disquiet and apprehension.

But complaints were useless. The Emperor, the Ministers of State, the senior nobles, and all the others moved. Nobody remained in the old capital who held even a minor court position. Those who aspired to office and rank, or who relied on the favor of patrons, strove to move with all possible dispatch; those who had lost the opportunity to succeed in life, or who had been rejected by society, stayed behind, sunk in gloom. The dwellings that had once stood eave to eave grew more dilapidated with every passing day. Houses were dismantled and sent floating down the Yodo River, and their former locations turned into fields before the onlookers' eyes.

In a complete reversal of values, everyone prized horses and saddles and stopped using oxen and carriages. Properties in the Western and Southern Sea circuits were sought; those in the Eastern Sea and Northern Land circuits were considered undesirable.

It happened that something took me to the new capital in Settsu Province. The cramped site, too small for proper subdivision, rose high on the north where it bordered the hills and sank low on the south beside the sea. The breaking waves never ceased to clamor; the wind from the sea blew with peculiar fury. The imperial palace struck me as unexpectedly novel

---

1. The move took place soon after the suppression of a preliminary attempt to overthrow the Taira. The new capital was at Fukuhara (now a part of Kōbe), where Taira no Kiyomori had established his principal residence some years earlier.

and interesting, situated in the hills as it was, and I asked myself whether Empress Saimei's log house might not have been rather similar.[2]

I wondered where people were erecting the whole houses that were being sent downstream daily, their numbers great enough to clog the river. There were still many empty parcels of land and few houses. The old capital was already in ruins; the new one had yet to take form. Not a soul but felt as rootless as a drifting cloud. The original inhabitants grieved over the loss of their land; the new arrivals worried about plaster and lumber. On the streets, those who ought to have used carriages rode horseback; those who ought to have worn court dress or hunting robes appeared in *hitatare*. The customs of the capital had been revolutionized overnight, and people behaved like rustic warriors.

I have heard that such changes portend civil disturbance—and that was precisely what happened. With every passing day, the world grew more unsettled, people lost more of their composure, and the common folk felt more apprehension. In the end, a crisis brought about a return to the old capital during the winter of the same year.[3] But who knows what became of the houses that had been torn down everywhere? They were not rebuilt in their former style.

We are told that the sage Emperors of old ruled with compassion. They roofed their palaces with thatch, neglecting even to trim the eaves; they remitted the already modest taxes when they saw the commoners' cooking-fires emit less smoke than before. The reason was simply that they cherished their subjects and wished to help them. To compare the present to the past is to see what kind of government we have today.

Again, there was a dreadful two-year famine. (I think it was around the Yōwa era [1181–82], but it was too long ago to be sure.) The grain crops were ruined as one calamity followed another: drought in the spring and summer, typhoons and floods in the autumn. It was vain for the farmers to till the fields in the spring or set out plants in the summer; there was no reaping in the fall, no bustle of storage in the winter. Some rural folk abandoned their land and wandered off; others deserted their homes to live in the hills. Prayers were begun and extraordinary rituals were performed, but they accomplished nothing.

The capital had always depended on the countryside for every need. Now, with nothing coming in, people were beside themselves with anxiety. In desperation, they offered all their treasures at bargain rates, but nobody took any notice. The rare person who was willing to trade thought little of gold and much of grain. The streets were overrun with mendicants; lamentations filled the air.

---

2. The log house was a temporary residence in Kyūshū used by Empress Saimei (594–661) when the Japanese were preparing to attack the Korean state of Silla in 661.

3. The rebellions of provincial Minamoto leaders had produced serious military disturbances.

The first of the two years dragged to a close. But just as everyone was anticipating a return to normal in the new year, a pestilence came along to make matters even worse. Like fish gasping in a puddle, the starving populace drew closer to the final extremity with every passing day, until at last people of quite respectable appearance, clad in hats and leggings, begged frantically from house to house. These wretched, dazed beings fell prostrate even as one marveled at their ability to walk.

Countless people perished of starvation by the wayside or died next to tile-capped walls. Since there was no way to dispose of the bodies, noisome stenches filled the air, and innumerable decomposing corpses shocked the eye. Needless to say, the dead lay so thick in the Kamo riverbed that there was not even room for horses and ox-carriages to pass.

With the woodsmen and other commoners too debilitated to perform their usual functions, a shortage of firewood developed, and people who possessed no other means of support broke up their own houses to sell in the market. The amount a man could carry brought less than enough to sustain him for a day. It was shocking to see pieces of wood covered with red lacquer or gold and silver leaf jumbled together with the rest. On inquiry, one learned that desperate people were going to old temples, stealing the sacred images, tearing away the fixtures from the halls, and breaking up everything for firewood. It is because I was born in a degenerate age that I have been forced to witness such disgraceful sights.

Some deeply moving things also happened. Whenever a couple were too devoted to part, the one whose love was greater was the first to die. This was because he or she put the spouse's welfare first and gave up whatever food came to hand. Similarly, a parent always predeceased a child. One sometimes saw a recumbent child sucking at his mother's breast, unaware that her life had ended. Grieved that countless people should be perishing in that manner, Dharma Seal Ryūgyō of Ninnaji Temple sought to help the dead toward enlightenment by writing the Sanskrit letter "A" on the forehead of every corpse he saw.[4]

The authorities kept track of the deaths in the Fourth and Fifth Months. During that period, there were more than 42,300 bodies on the streets in the area south of Ichijō, north of Kujō, west of Kyōgoku, and east of Suzaku. Of course, many others died before and afterward. And there would be no limit to the numbers if we were to count the Kamo riverbed, Shirakawa, the western sector, and the outlying districts, to say nothing of the provinces in the seven circuits.

People say there was something similar during the reign of Emperor Sutoku, around the Choshō era [1132–35], but I know nothing about that. I witnessed this phenomenal famine with my own eyes.

---

4. In esoteric Buddhism, of which Ninnaji was a center, "A," the first syllable in the Sanskrit syllabary, was regarded as symbolic of the unity of all things.

If I remember correctly, it was at more or less the same time that a terrible seismic convulsion occurred. It was no ordinary earthquake. Mountains crumbled and buried streams; the sea tilted and immersed the land. Water gushed from fissures in the earth; huge rocks cracked and rolled into valleys. Boats being rowed near the shoreline tossed on the waves; horses journeying on the roads lost their footing. Not a Buddhist hall or stupa remained intact anywhere in the vicinity of the capital. Some crumbled, others fell flat. Dust billowed like smoke; the shaking earth and collapsing houses rumbled like thunder. If people stayed indoors, they were crushed at once; if they ran outside, the ground split apart. If men had been dragons, they might have ridden the clouds, but they lacked the wings to soar into the heavens. It was then that I came to recognize an earthquake as the most terrible of all terrible things.

The violent shaking subsided fairly soon, but aftershocks followed for some time. No day passed without twenty or thirty earthquakes of an intensity that would ordinarily have caused consternation. The intervals lengthened after ten or twenty days, and then there were tremors four or five times a day, or two or three times a day, or once every other day, or once every two or three days. It must have been about three months before they ceased.

Of the four constituents of the universe, water, fire, and wind create constant havoc, but the earth does not usually give rise to any particular calamities. To be sure, there were some dreadful earthquakes in the past (for instance, the great shock that toppled the head of the Tōdaiji Buddha during the Saikō era [854–57]), but none of them could compare with this. Immediately after the event, people all talked about the meaninglessness of life and seemed somewhat more free from spiritual impurity than usual. But nobody even mentioned the subject after the days and months had accumulated and the years had slipped by.

Such, then, is the difficulty of life in this world, such the ephemerality of man and his dwellings. Needless to say, it would be utterly impossible to list every affliction that stems from individual circumstance or social position. If a man of negligible status lives beside a powerful family, he cannot make a great display of happiness when he has cause for heartfelt rejoicing, nor can he lift his voice in lamentation when he experiences devastating grief. In all that he does, he is ill at ease; like a sparrow near a hawk's nest, he pursues his daily activities in fear and trembling. If a poor man lives next door to a wealthy house, he abases himself before the neighbors and agonizes over his wretched appearance whenever he goes out in the morning or returns in the evening. Forced to witness the envy of his wife, children, and servants, and to hear the rich household dismiss him with contempt, he is forever agitated, constantly distraught.

He who lives in a crowded area cannot escape calamity when a fire breaks out nearby; he who settles in a remote spot suffers many hardships in his travels to and fro and puts himself at grave risk from robbers. The powerful man is consumed by greed; the man who refuses to seek a patron becomes an object of derision. The man who owns many possessions knows many worries; the impoverished man seethes with envy.

He who depends on another belongs to another; he who takes care of another is chained by human affection. When a man observes the conventions, he falls into economic difficulties; when he flouts them, people wonder if he is mad. Where can we live, what can we do, to find even the briefest of shelters, the most fleeting peace of mind?

3

For a long time, I lived in a house inherited from my paternal grandmother. Later, my fortunes declined through lack of connections, and I found myself unable to remain in society, despite many nostalgic associations. Shortly after I entered my thirties, I moved voluntarily into a simple new dwelling one-tenth the size of the old place. I built only a personal residence, with no fashionable auxiliary structures, and although I managed an encircling earthen wall, my means did not extend to a gate. The carriage-shelter was supported by bamboo pillars, and the house was unsafe in a snowfall or windstorm. The site was near the riverbed, which left it vulnerable to floods, and there was also danger from robbers.

For more than thirty miserable years, I endured an existence in which I could not maintain my position. Every setback during that time drove home the realization that I was not blessed by fortune. And thus, at fifty, I became a monk and turned my back on the world. Having never had a wife or children, I was not bound to others by ties difficult to break; lacking office and stipend, I possessed no attachments to which to cling.

During the next five springs and autumns, I sojourned among the clouds of the Ōhara hills, leading a life devoid of spiritual progress.

Now at sixty, with the dew nearing its vanishing point, I have built a new shelter for the tree's last leaves, just as a traveler might fashion a single night's resting place or an old silkworm spin a cocoon. It is not a hundredth the size of my second house. Indeed, while I have sat around uttering idle complaints, my age has increased with every year, and my house has shrunk with every move.

This house is unusual in appearance. It is barely ten feet square, and its height is less than seven feet. The location was a matter of indifference to me; I did not divine to select a site. I built a foundation and a simple roof, and attached hinges to all the joints so that I could move easily if cause for dissatisfaction arose. There would be no trouble about rebuilding. The house would barely fill two carts, and the carters' fees would be the only expense.

After settling on my present place of retirement in the Hino hills, I extended the eastern eaves about three feet to provide myself with a convenient spot in which to break up and burn firewood. On the south side of the building, I have an open bamboo veranda with a holy water shelf at the west end. Toward the north end of the west wall, beyond a freestanding screen, there is a picture of Amida Buddha, with an image of Fugen alongside and a copy of the *Lotus Sutra* in front. At the east end of the room, some dried bracken serves as a bed. South of the screen on the west side, a bamboo shelf suspended from the ceiling holds three leather-covered bamboo baskets, in which I keep excerpts from poetry collections and critical treatises, works on music, and religious tracts like *Collection of Essentials on Rebirth in the Pure Land.* A zither and a lute stand next to the shelf. The zither is of the folding variety; the handle of the lute is detachable. Such is the appearance of my rude temporary shelter.

To turn to the surroundings: I have made a rock basin in which to collect water from an elevated conduit south of the hermitage, and I gather ample supplies of firewood in a neighboring stand of trees. The locality is called Toyama, "the foothills." Vines cover the paths. The valley is thickly forested, but there is open land to the west.

Aids to contemplation abound. In the spring, lustrous cascades of wisteria burgeon in the west like purple clouds. In the summer, every song of the cuckoo conveys a promise of companionship in the Shide Mountains. In the autumn, the incessant cries of the cicadas seem to lament the transitoriness of worldly things. And in the winter, the accumulating and melting snows suggest poignant comparisons with sins and hindrances.[5]

When I tire of reciting the sacred name or find myself intoning a sutra in a perfunctory manner, I rest as I please, I fall idle as I see fit. There is nobody to interfere, nobody to shame me. Although I do not make a point of performing silent austerities, I can control speech-induced karma because I live alone; although I do not make a fuss about obeying the commandments, I have no occasion to break them because mine is not an environment conducive to transgression.

On mornings when I compare my existence to a white wake in the water, I borrow Mansei's style while watching boats come and go at Okanoya; on evenings when the wind rustles the maple leaves, I imitate Tsunenobu's practice while recalling the Xinyang River.[6] If my interest does

---

5. Amida and his attendants were thought to descend, riding on a purple cloud, to escort the believer to the Western Paradise at the moment of death. Possibly because the cuckoo's cry included notes that sounded like *shide,* the bird was considered a messenger from the land of the dead, which lay beyond the Shide Mountains. Sins and hindrances to enlightenment piled up in the course of daily life and were discharged periodically by repentance rites and confessions before a Buddha.

6. Mansei (8th c.) was the author of a frequently quoted poem on ephemerality: yo no naka o / nani ni tatoen / asaborake / kogiyuku fune no / ato no shiranami ("To what shall I compare life in this world—the white wake of a boat rowing off at break of day"). Tsunenobu (1016–97) was a major poet known also as an expert lute player. Chōmei alludes to the first two lines of Bo Juyi's "Lute Song": "As I see off a guest at night near the Xinyang River, / The autumn wind rustles through maple leaves and reed plumes."

not flag, I often perform "Song of the Autumn Wind" as an accompaniment to the murmur of the pines, or play "Melody of the Flowing Spring" to harmonize with the sound of the water. I am not an accomplished musician, but my playing is not designed for the pleasure of others. I merely pluck the strings alone and chant alone to comfort my own spirit.

At the foot of the hill, there is a brush-thatched cottage, the abode of the mountain warden. The small boy who lives there pays me an occasional visit, and if I chance to feel at loose ends, I set out for a ramble with him as my companion. He is ten, I am sixty. Our ages differ greatly, but we take pleasure in the same things. Sometimes we pull out reed-flower sprouts, pick *iwanashi* berries, heap up yam sprouts, or pluck herbs. Or we may go to the rice fields at the foot of the mountains, glean ears left by the reapers, and fashion sheafs. When the weather is balmy, we scramble up to a peak from which I can look toward the distant skies over my old home and see Kohatayama, Fushimi-no-sato, Toba, and Hatsukashi. Nobody owns the view; there is nothing to keep me from enjoying it.

When the going is easy and I feel like taking a long walk, I follow the peaks past Sumiyama and Kasatori to worship at Iwama or Ishiyama. Or I may traverse Awazu Plain, visit the site of Semimaru's dwelling, cross the Tanakami River, and seek out Sarumaru's grave.[7] On the way home, I search for cherry blossoms, pick autumn leaves, gather bracken, or collect fruit and nuts, depending on the season. Some of my trophies I present to the Buddha; others I treat as useful souvenirs.

On peaceful nights, I long for old friends while gazing at the moon through the window, or weep into my sleeve at the cry of a monkey. Sometimes I mistake fireflies in the bushes for fish lures burning far away at Maki-no-shima Island, or think that a gale must be scattering the leaves when I hear rain just before dawn. The *horohoro* call of a pheasant makes me wonder if the bird might be a parent; the frequent visits of deer from the peaks attest to the remoteness of my abode.[8] Sometimes I stir up the banked fire and make it a companion for the wakefulness of old age. The mountains are so little intimidating that even the owl's hoot sounds moving rather than eerie. Indeed, there is no end to the delights of the changing seasons in these surroundings. A truly reflective man, blessed with superior powers of judgment, would undoubtedly find many more pleasures than the ones I have described.

---

7. Semimaru and Sarumaru were semilegendary poets.

8. Gyōki (Gyōgi): yamadori no / horohoro to naku / koe kikeba / chichi ka to zo omou / haha ka to zo omou ("When I hear the voice of the pheasant, mountain bird, crying *horohoro,* I think, 'Might it be a father? Or might it be a mother?'"). Saigyō: yama fukami / naruru kasegi no / kejikasa ni / yo ni tōzakaru / hodo zo shiraruru ("To see at close hand deer grown accustomed to me deep in the mountains is to know my remoteness from the affairs of the world").

4

When I first began to live here, I thought it would not be for long, but five years have already elapsed. My temporary hermitage has gradually become a home, its eaves covered with rotted leaves and its foundation mossy. Whenever I happen to hear news of the capital, I learn that many illustrious personages have breathed their last since my retreat to these mountains. And it would be quite impossible to keep track of all the unimportant people who have died. A great many houses have also suffered destruction in recurrent conflagrations. Only in my temporary hermitage is life peaceful and safe. The quarters are cramped, but I have a place where I can lie at night and another where I can sit in the daytime. There is ample room for one person. The hermit crab likes a small shell because it knows its own size; the osprey lives on the rocky coast because it fears man. It is the same with me. Knowing myself and knowing the world, I harbor no ambitions and pursue no material objectives. Quietude is what I desire; the absence of worries is what makes me happy.

Men do not usually build houses for their own benefit. Some build for wives, children, relatives, and servants, some for friends and acquaintances, some for masters, for teachers, or even for household goods, treasures, oxen, and horses. But I have built for myself this time, not for anybody else. Because of present conditions and my own situation, I possess neither a family to share my dwelling nor servants to work for me. If I had built a great house, whom would I have lodged in it, whom would I have established there?

Friends esteem wealth and look for favors; they do not necessarily value sincere friendship or probity. I prefer to make friends of music and nature. Servants prize lavish rewards and unstinting generosity; they do not care about protection, affection, or a safe, tranquil existence. I prefer to make my own body my servant. How do I do it? If there is work to perform, I use my body. True, I may grow weary, but it is easier than employing and looking after someone else. If there is walking to do, I walk. It is burdensome, but less so than worrying over horses, saddles, oxen, and carriages. I divide my body and put it to two uses: it suits me very well to employ hands as servants and feet as conveyances. My mind understands my body's distress: I allow the body to rest when it is distressed and use it when it feels energetic. I use it but do not make a habit of pushing it to extremes. If it finds a task irksome, I am not perturbed. It is surely a healthful practice to walk constantly and work constantly. What would be the point of idling away the time? To make others work creates bad karma. Why should I borrow their strength?

It is the same with food and clothing. I hide my nakedness under a rough fiber robe, a hemp quilt, or whatever comes to hand; I survive by eating starwort from the fields and nuts from the peaks. Because I do not mingle with others, I need not chide myself for having felt ashamed of my appearance. Because I possess little food, I find coarse fare tasty.

I do not describe such pleasures as a means of criticizing the wealthy; I merely compare my own former life with my present existence. "The triple world is but one mind."[9] If the mind is not at peace, elephants, horses, and the seven treasures are trash; palatial residences and stately mansions are worthless. I feel warm affection for my present lonely dwelling, my tiny cottage. My beggarly appearance is a source of embarrassment on the infrequent occasions when something takes me to the capital, but after my return I feel pity for those who pursue worldly things. If anyone doubts my sincerity, let him consider the fish and the birds. A fish never tires of water, but only another fish can understand why. A bird seeks trees, but only another bird can understand why. It is the same with the pleasures of retirement. Only a recluse can understand them.

5

The moon of my life is setting; my remaining years approach the rim of the hills. Very soon, I shall face the darkness of the Three Evil Paths. Which of my old disappointments is worth fretting over now? The Buddha teaches us to reject worldly things. Even my affection for this thatched hut is a sin; even my love of tranquility must be accounted an impediment to rebirth. Why do I waste time in descriptions of inconsequential pleasures?

As I reflect on these things in the quiet moments before dawn, I put a question to myself:

You retired to the seclusion of remote hills so that you might discipline your mind and practice the Way, but your impure spirit belies your monkish garb. Your dwelling presumes to imitate the abode of the honorable Yuima, but you are worse than Suddhipanthaka when it comes to obeying the commandments. Is this because you let yourself be troubled by karma-ordained poverty, or has your deluded mind finally lost its sanity?

The question remains unanswered. I can do no other than use my impure tongue for three or four repetitions of Amida's sacred name. Then I fall silent.

Late in the Third Month of the second year of Kenryaku [1212]
Set down by the monk Ren'in in the hermitage at Toyama[10]

---

9. *Kegon Sutra:* "The triple world is but one mind. Outside mind there is nothing; mind, Buddha, and all the living, these three are no different."

10. Ren'in was Chōmei's Buddhist name.

■ Fujiwara no Teika (Sadaie) (1162–1241) (poems)

TRANSLATED BY TONY BARNSTONE AND WILLIS BARNSTONE

The son of poet Fujiwara no Shunzei, Fujiwara no Teika was among the finest *tanka* poets, a teacher of *tanka,* and an influential essayist on poetry who, more than anyone else, set the standards of taste for his time and times to come. He is considered to rank with Basho, Saigyo, and Kakinomoto Hitomaro as among Japan's finest poets. Associating himself with retired Emperor Gotoba, in 1201 he was appointed to the Bureau of Poetry and later was the compiler of two of the Imperial anthologies, the *Shinkokinshu* and the *Shinchokusenshu.* He edited *The Tale of Genji* among other famous works, and it is thought that he also compiled the famous collection of *One Hundred Poems by One Hundred Poets,* which is Japan's most popular anthology of poetry.

FURTHER READING: "Eighty-four Tanka" and "An Outline for Composing Tanka, with a compendium of good tanka (complete translation)," in Hiroaki Sato and Burton Watson, eds. *From the Country of Eight Islands: An Anthology of Japanese Poetry,* 1981.

Like Seaweed Burnt for Salt

Like seaweed burnt for salt
I blaze for him.
He doesn't come.
In night calm at the inlet
my body smoulders.

In the Infinite Night

In the infinite night
your restless hair
spills blackly
across our sleeves
like random dew.

Wind Pierces

Wind pierces
transparently.
Frost forms

on the evening moon's
light.

Stars Must Be Clear

Stars must be clear
beyond this wind.
I listen
to random hailstones
clatter.

◼ Dogen (1200–1253) (poems)

TRANSLATED BY BRIAN UNGER AND KAZUAKI TANAHASHI

Dogen is the founder of the Soto School of Japanese Zen Buddhism, which is one of the two largest Zen Buddhist orders in Japan (along with Rinzai Zen). He was born in Kyoto in 1200, apparently the son of an influential court minister. His father died when he was three, his mother when he was eight. Faced with these deaths, he abandoned the prospect of a career in court for a life of Buddhism. At a time when militarism and commercialism had permeated the monastic culture, many Buddhists considered it "the age of the decline of dharma." It was a time ripe for the introduction of new practices, and Dogen, who went to China in 1223 to study with Soto master Ju-ching (1163–1228), brought back Soto practice with him in 1227. He was responsible for disseminating this Zen teaching through his writings and by founding a practice center in Fukakusa in 1233 and Daibutsu Monastery in Echizen province a decade later. Though he is mainly known for his treatises on Zen, he also left behind a number of poems in Chinese and Japanese forms. Soto Zen emphasizes meditative practice and a view of time in which eternity rests on the knife blade of the instant. It states that all things contain a hidden "Buddha-nature," to which Zen practice awakens one. Thus, his poetry, like that of Ryokan (1758–1831), is infused with Zen insight into the natural world. For Dogen, a dewdrop reflecting moonlight is an image of Zen meditation (as the moon can be reflected in this tiny ball of water, so the whole universe resides in each human being). As Emily Dickinson says:

> The Brain—is wider than the Sky—
> For—put them side by side—
> The one the other will contain
> With ease—and You—beside—

FURTHER READING: Tanahashi, Kazuaki, ed. *Moon in a Dewdrop: Writings of Zen Master Dogen,* 1985.

Mountain Seclusion

I won't even stop
at the valley's brook
for fear that
my shadow
may flow into the world.

Bowing Formally

A snowy heron
on the snowfield
where winter grass is unseen
hides itself
in its own figure.

On Nondependence of Mind

Water birds
going and coming
their traces disappear
but they never
forget their path.

■ Zen Stories *from* Sand and Pebbles (and other collections) (Thirteenth Century and Later) (wisdom stories)

TRANSLATED BY NYOGEN SENZAKI AND PAUL REPS

These stories derive from the wealth of wacky, humorous, profound, and startling Zen literature collected into various story (*setsuwa*) compilations. Translators Nyogen Senzaki and Paul Reps are drawing in the main on *Sand and Pebbles* (*Shasekishu*), a thirteenth-century compilation of anecdotes written and compiled by Muju, a Rinzai Zen priest who lived at the Chojobi temple near the Atsuta Shrine in Nagoya.

FURTHER READING: Reps, Paul, ed. *Zen Flesh, Zen Bones*, 1989.

The Moon Cannot Be Stolen

Ryokan, a Zen master, lived the simplest kind of life in a little hut at the foot of a mountain. One evening a thief visited the hut only to discover there was nothing in it to steal.

Ryokan returned and caught him. "You may have come a long way to visit me," he told the prowler, "and you should not return empty-handed. Please take my clothes as a gift."

The thief was bewildered. He took the clothes and slunk away.

Ryokan sat naked, watching the moon. "Poor fellow," he mused, "I wish I could give him this beautiful moon."

Muddy Road

Tanzan and Ekido were once traveling together down a muddy road. A heavy rain was still falling.

Coming around a bend, they met a lovely girl in a silk kimono and sash, unable to cross the intersection.

"Come on, girl," said Tanzan at once. Lifting her in his arms, he carried her over the mud.

Ekido did not speak again until that night when they reached a lodging temple. Then he no longer could restrain himself. "We monks don't go near females," he told Tanzan, "especially not young and lovely ones. It is dangerous. Why did you do that?"

"I left the girl there," said Tanzan. "Are you still carrying her?"

A Parable

Buddha told a parable in a sutra:

A man traveling across a field encountered a tiger. He fled, the tiger after him. Coming to a precipice, he caught hold of the root of a wild vine and swung himself down over the edge. The tiger sniffed at him from above. Trembling, the man looked down to where, far below, another tiger was waiting to eat him. Only the vine sustained him.

Two mice, one white and one black, little by little started to gnaw away the vine. The man saw a luscious strawberry near him. Grasping the vine with one hand, he plucked the strawberry with the other. How sweet it tasted!

Joshu's Zen

Joshu began the study of Zen when he was sixty years old and continued until he was eighty, when he realized Zen.

He taught from the age of eighty until he was one hundred and twenty.

A student once asked him: "If I haven't anything in my mind, what shall I do?"

Joshu replied: "Throw it out."

"But if I haven't anything, how can I throw it out?" continued the questioner.

"Well," said Joshu, "then carry it out."

The Stone Mind

Hogen, a Chinese Zen teacher, lived alone in a small temple in the country. One day four traveling monks appeared and asked if they might make a fire in his yard to warm themselves.

While they were building the fire, Hogen heard them arguing about subjectivity and objectivity. He joined them and said: "There is a big stone. Do you consider it to be inside or outside your mind?"

One of the monks replied: "From the Buddhist viewpoint everything is an objectification of mind, so I would say that the stone is inside my mind."

"Your head must feel very heavy," observed Hogen, "if you are carrying around a stone like that in your mind."

Nothing Exists

Yamaoka Tesshu, as a young student of Zen, visited one master after another. He called upon Dokuon of Shokoku.

Desiring to show his attainment, he said: "The mind, Buddha, and sentient beings, after all, do not exist. The true nature of phenomena is emptiness. There is no realization, no delusion, no sage, no mediocrity. There is no giving and nothing to be received."

Dokuon, who was smoking quietly, said nothing. Suddenly he whacked Yamaoka with his bamboo pipe. This made the youth quite angry.

"If nothing exists," inquired Dokuon, "where did this anger come from?"

■ Muso Soseki (1275–1351) (poems)

TRANSLATED BY W. S. MERWIN AND SOIKU SHIGEMATSU

Thirteenth-century Zen roshi Muso Soseki was born in the province of Ise in 1275 to a Buddhist family. Like Zeus coming to Danae in a shower of gold coins, or like Jehovah coming to Mary, legend has it that the Bodhisattva Avalokiteshvara came to Muso's barren mother in a dream as a golden light and thirteen months later he was born. His mother died when he was three, and when he was nine his father took him to the Shingon temple in Kai to lead the religious life of a Mantrayana Buddhist. At eighteen, he took vows as a monk in Nara, but before he was twenty he left the sect and became a student of Zen. In the summer of 1305, he is said to have received enlightenment in a garden, after which he wrote his satori poem and was certified by his master Koho as enlightened. In his life, he founded fourteen temples and had more than thirteen thousand students. He is considered the father of Zen rock gardening, an aesthetic practice equally linked to architecture and spirituality. After his death, his writings were collected by his followers into three volumes of conversations, sermons, and poems. His poems were written both in Japanese and in Chinese. Though he is not well known in the West, his poetry, with a minimum of dogma, is a marvelous evocation of the world seen through Zen eyeglasses, and it reads well next to the work of other great mystical poets: Rumi, Kabir, and Wang Wei.

FURTHER READING: Merwin, W. S., and Shigematsu Soiku, trs. *Sun at Midnight: Poems and Sermons by Muso Soseki,* 1989.

Three-Step Waterfall

At dangerous places
    awesome ledges
      three barriers
The loud water rushes
    The spray of the fall hovers
      It's hard to find the way
So many fish
    have fallen back
      with the stamp of failure on their foreheads
Who knows that this
    wind of blood
      is lashing the whole universe

Toki-no-Ge (Satori Poem)

Year after year
    I dug in the earth
      looking for the blue of heaven
only to feel
    the pile of dirt
      choking me
until once in the dead of night
    I tripped on a broken brick
      and kicked it into the air
and saw that without a thought
    I had smashed the bones
      of the empty sky

Beyond Light

The clear mirror
    and its stand
      have been broken
There is no dust
    in the eyes
      of the blind donkey

Dark
> dark everywhere
>> the appearance of subtle Zen
Let it be
> The garden lantern
>> opens its mouth laughing

▪ Kenko (c. 1283–1350) (prose)

TRANSLATED BY DONALD KEENE

The author we know by the name Kenko (which is his name as a Buddhist priest) was also called Urabe no Kaneyoshi or Yoshida no Kaneyoshi (because he lived for a long time at Yoshida in Kyoto). He is among Japan's finest writers of *zuihitsu* prose, or prose consisting of a miscellany of meditations, anecdotes, and observations, as in Sei Shonagon's *Pillow Book*. He was born into a family of Shinto priests of medium rank and became a priest in his own right, but his work reveals an ability to temper Buddhist doctrine that probably makes the work more attractive to a lay audience. He had a reputation as a poet of medium worth in his own time, whereas *Essays in Idleness* was unknown to his public; today, however, his essays seem to shine much brighter than the poems and, in fact, remain popular reading for schoolchildren and literati alike. A tale told about its composition, probably apocryphal, says that Kenko was in the habit of writing down his meditations on paper scraps and pasting them on his cottage walls. General Imagawa Ryoshun is credited with removing the scraps and arranging them into the work we know today, consisting of 243 sections of varying length.

FURTHER READING: Keene, Donald, tr. *Essays in Idleness: The Tsurezuregusa of Kenko,* 1967. Sansom, George, tr. "The Tzuredzure of Yoshida no Kaneyoshi," *Transactions, Asiatic Society of Japan,* 39, 1911.

from *Essays in Idleness*

3

A man may excel at everything else, but if he has no taste for lovemaking, one feels something terribly inadequate about him, as if he were a valuable winecup without a bottom. What a charming figure is the lover, his clothes drenched with dew or frost, wandering about aimlessly, so fearful of his parents' reproaches or people's gossip that he has not a moment's peace of mind, frantically resorting to one unsuccessful stratagem after another; and for all that, most often sleeping alone, though never soundly. But it is best that a man not be given over completely to fleshly pleasures, and that women not consider him an easy conquest.

41

On the fifth day of the fifth month I went to see the horse race at the Kamo Shrine.[1] There was such a mob before our carriage, between us and the view, that we could see nothing. We all got out of the carriage and pushed towards the railing, but the crowd was particularly dense in that area, and there seemed no chance of making our way to the fore. Just then we noticed a priest perched in the crotch of an ōchi[2] tree across the way, watching the race. Even as he clung to the tree he was nodding drowsily, again and again waking himself just as he seemed about to fall.

People, observing the priest, laughed at his folly. "What an idiot! Imagine anyone being able to sleep so peacefully when he's sitting on such a dangerous branch!" It suddenly occurred to me, however, "The hour of death may be upon us at any moment. To spend our days in pleasure-seeking, forgetful of this truth, is even more foolish." I blurted out the words, and some people standing before me said, "That's certainly true. It is a most stupid way to behave." Turning round towards us, they said, "Please come through here," and made room, urging us to take their places.

Anybody at all might have made the same observation, but probably it came as a surprise at that particular moment and struck home. Man, not being made of wood or stone, is at times not without emotional reactions.

45

Kin'yo,[3] an officer of the second rank, had a brother called the High Priest Ryogaku,[4] an extremely bad-tempered man. Next to his monastery grew a large nettle-tree which occasioned the nickname people gave him, the Nettle-tree High Priest. "That name is outrageous," said the high priest, and cut down the tree. The stump still being left, people referred to him now as the Stump High Priest. More furious than ever, Ryogaku had the stump dug up and thrown away, but this left a big ditch. People now called him the Ditch High Priest.

---

1. A feature of the Kamo Festival is the horse race from the first to the second *torii* of the Upper Kamo Shrine.

2. The azedarach, also called bead tree, etc.

3. Fujiwara no Kin'yo (died 1301) was a poet.

4. Ryogaku Sōjō (died about 1305) was a distinguished poet. He is here called *sōjō* but elsewhere is referred to as *daisōjō*, a position at the top of the Buddhist hierarchy.

51

The cloistered emperor, having decided to introduce water from the Ōi River into the pond of his Kameyama palace,[5] commanded the inhabitants of Ōi to build a waterwheel. He paid them generously, and the men worked hard for several days to construct it. But when the wheel was put in place it failed to turn at all. The men tried in various ways to repair it, but it stood there useless, stubbornly refusing to turn. The emperor thereupon summoned some villagers from Uji and ordered them to build a waterwheel. They put one together without difficulty and presented it. The wheel turned perfectly and was splendidly efficient at drawing up water.

Expert knowledge in any art is a noble thing.

71

As soon as I hear a name I feel convinced I can guess what the owner looks like, but it never happens, when I actually meet the man, that his face is as I had supposed. I wonder if everybody shares my experience of feeling, when I hear some story about the past, that the house mentioned in the story must have been rather like this or that house belonging to people of today, or that the persons of the story resemble people I see now. It has happened on various occasions too that I have felt, just after someone has said something or I have seen something or thought of something, that it has occurred before. I cannot remember *when* it was, but I feel absolutely certain that the thing has happened. Am I the only one who has such impressions?

97

There are innumerable instances of things which attach themselves to something else, then waste and destroy it. The body has lice; a house has mice; a country has robbers; inferior men have riches; superior men have benevolence and righteousness; priests have the Buddhist law.[6]

---

5. This detached palace, used by the Cloistered Emperors Go-Saga (1220–1272) and Kameyama (1249–1305), stood near the present Tenryuji, west of Kyoto. The Ōi River flows nearby at Arashiyama. The cloistered emperor of this episode could be either Go-Saga or Kameyama.

6. The thought is Taoist, inspired by the passage in *Tao Te Ching:* "It was when the Great Way declined / That human kindness and morality arose" (Arthur Waley's translation). Kenko seems to mean that superior men (*kunshi*) are so puffed up with their virtues that they become incapable of practical action, and that priests are so bound by the letter of the Buddhist law that they become inhuman.

142

Even a man who seems devoid of intelligence occasionally says an apt word. A fierce-looking brute of a soldier once asked a companion, "Have you got any kids?" "Not one," replied the other. "Then," said the soldier, "I don't suppose you know what deep feelings are. You probably haven't a drop of human warmth in you. That's a frightening thought! It's having children that makes people understand the beauty of life." He was right. Would any tenderness of feeling exist in such a man's heart if not for the natural affection between parent and child? Even the man with no sense of duty towards his parents learns what parental solicitude means when he has a child of his own.

It is wrong for anyone who has abandoned the world and is without attachments to despise other men burdened with many encumbrances for their deep-seated greed and constant fawning on others. If he could put himself in the place of the men he despises, he would see that, for the sake of their parents, wives, and children, whom they truly love, they forget all sense of shame and will even steal. I believe therefore that it would be better, instead of imprisoning thieves and concerning ourselves only with punishing crimes, to run the country in such a way that no man would ever be hungry or cold. When a man lacks steady employment, his heart is not steady, and in extremity he will steal. As long as the country is not properly governed and people suffer from cold and hunger, there will never be an end to crime. It is pitiful to make people suffer, to force them to break the law, and then to punish them.

How then may we help the people? If those at the top would give up their luxury and wastefulness, protect the people, and encourage agriculture, those below would unquestionably benefit greatly. The real criminal is the man who commits a crime even though he has a normal share of food and clothing.

149

You should never put the new antlers of a deer to your nose and smell them. They have little insects that crawl into the nose and devour the brain.

235

A man with no business will never intrude into an occupied house simply because he so pleases. If the house is vacant, on the other hand, travelers journeying along the road will enter with impunity, and even creatures like foxes and owls, undisturbed by any human presence, will take up their abodes, acting as if the place belonged to them. Tree spirits and other apparitions will also manifest themselves.

It is the same with mirrors: being without color or shape of their own, they reflect all manner of forms. If mirrors had color and shape of their own, they would probably not reflect other things.

Emptiness accommodates everything. I wonder if thoughts of all kinds intrude themselves at will on our minds because what we call our minds are vacant? If our minds were occupied, surely so many things would not enter them.

243

When I turned eight years old I asked my father, "What sort of thing is a Buddha?" My father said, "A Buddha is what a man becomes." I asked then, "How does a man become a Buddha?" My father replied, "By following the teachings of Buddha." "Then, who taught the Buddha to teach?" He again replied, "He followed the teachings of the Buddha before him." I asked again, "What kind of Buddha was the first Buddha who began to teach?" At this my father laughed and answered, "I suppose he fell from the sky or else he sprang up out of the earth."

My father told other people, "He drove me into a corner, and I was stuck for an answer." But he was amused.

Muromachi/Momoyama Periods

(1392–1603)

■ Zeami Motokiyo (1363–1443) (noh play, prose)

Noh theater is a total theatrical experience, incorporating music, chanting, dance, poetry, prose, mime, and masks to create an ethereal atmosphere and to suggest the sublime experience of other worlds. This sublime beauty is called *yugen*, a term derived from Zen. *Yugen* is what lies underneath surfaces, hints of the supernatural, glimmers of a lost past, a ghostly world, or a hidden truth. Zeami writes that "the actor must consider *yugen* as the most important aspect of his art, and study to perfect his understanding of it." Dance, music, gesture, even an actor's display of anger, must be balanced, aestheticized, and made into an elegant show of virtuosity. The word *noh* means "accomplishment" and refers to a virtuoso performance. Noh was developed in the fourteenth century, primarily as a result of the efforts of Kan'ami Kiyotsugu (1333–1384), the father of Zeami Motokiyo. He was instrumental in blending ritual ceremonies and popular forms of entertainment into one art—the sources of noh include folk dance, Buddhist chanting, popular songs, ritual Shinto dance, and the variety show. In 1374, Kan'ami showed his newly synthesized art form to the shogun, Ashikaga Yoshimitsu, who became his patron, converting noh into an entertainment for the aristocracy. Kan'ami's son Zeami was an extraordinary actor from the age of seven and the noh theater's finest playwright; he took noh to its highest form, and his treatises on the art of noh theater are masterpieces of Japanese aesthetics. Zeami was so important a figure that a huge number of plays were attributed to him, though now only fifty (some scholars say a dozen) seem likely to have been written by him. Distinguished scholar Donald Keene suggests that twenty-five is a plausible number, and since certainty is impossible, it seems wise to go with this compromise figure.

Noh plays often read well on the page, but the reader should be aware that (even more than in the Western theater) the shift from performance to literature has its costs. Many plays derive from classical tales, and the very fact that the audience is familiar with the story helps to take the emphasis off plot and put it onto psychology and mood instead. Some time after Zeami's death, noh performances were categorized into types and presented in a slate of five plays of five specific categories: god plays, warrior plays, woman plays, realistic (or mad) plays, and demon plays. The contemporary noh theater, however, performs its plays at a slower pace, so that the full slate of five plays has been shortened. *Semimaru* is a play of the fourth kind. The different character of the plays creates a varied theatrical experience, and short farcical skits take place between plays. The actor's lines are spoken in a stylized manner that makes no attempt at realistic voice inflections. As Donald Keene notes, "Every inflection of the actor's voice and every move of his body is prescribed by long traditions that have as their object the revelation of the ultimate meanings of the text, but these meanings transcend the meaning of any one line, and it is therefore possible for an actor to deliver a line perfectly without understanding it."[1] The actors are all men, and the principal actor often wears a beautifully crafted mask; the costumes are also works of art. Authors' lines are accompanied by three drummers and a flute player, who utter percussive, rhythmic noises, and the chorus sings for the main actor at moments of deep emotion and at the climax of the play when his movements turn into dance. Noh theater has excited considerable interest in the West—both William Butler Yeats and Bertolt Brecht wrote experimental noh plays, while Ezra Pound adapted a number of the major noh plays (with changes so radical that "translation" would not be the appropriate word). Twentieth-century Japanese fiction writer Mishima Yukio also wrote a number of modern noh plays.

FURTHER READING: Fenollosa, Ernest, and Ezra Pound. *The Classical Noh Theatre of Japan*, 1959. Keene, Donald. *Twenty Plays of the No Theatre*, 1970. Ueda, Makoto, tr. *The Old Pine Tree and Other Noh Plays*, 1962. Waley, Arthur, tr. *The No Plays of Japan*, 1921.

---

1. Donald Keene, *Twenty Plays of the No Theatre* (New York: Columbia University Press, 1970), 2.

Semimaru

TRANSLATED BY SUSAN MATISOFF

PERSONS
Prince Semimaru (tsure)
Kiyotsura, An Imperial Envoy (waki)
Two Palanquin Bearers (wakizure)
Hakuga No Sammi (kyōgen)
Princess Sakagami, Semimaru's Sister (shite)

PLACE
Mt. Ōsaka in Ōmi Province

TIME
The Reign of Emperor Daigo; The Eighth Month

(The stage assistant places a representation of a hut at the waki-position. Semimaru enters, wearing the semimaru mask. He is flanked by two Palanquin Bearers who hold a canopy over him. Kiyotsura follows them.)

KIYOTSURA: The world is so unsure, unknowable;
    Who knows—our griefs may hold our greatest hopes.
    This nobleman is the Prince Semimaru
    Fourth child of the Emperor Daigo.

KIYOTSURA AND ATTENDANTS: Truly in this uncertain world
    All that befalls us comes our way
    As recompense for what we've done before.
    In his previous existence
    He observed intently the laws of Buddha
    And in this life was born a prince,
    Yet why was it—ever since he lay,
    An infant wrapped in swaddling clothes
    His eyes have both been blind: For him
    The sun and moon in heaven have no light;
    In the black of night his lamp is dark;
    The rain before the dawn never ends.

KIYOTSURA: His nights and days have been spent this way,
    But now what plan has the Emperor conceived?
    He ordered us to escort the Prince in secret,
    To abandon him on Mount Ōsaka
    And to shave his head in priestly tonsure.
    The Emperor's words, once spoken
    Are final—what immense pity I feel!
    Yet, such being the command, I am powerless;

KIYOTSURA AND ATTENDANTS: Like lame-wheeled carriages
    We creep forth reluctantly

On the journey from the Capital;
How hard it is to say farewell
As dawn clouds streak the east!
Today he first departs the Capital
When again to return? His chances are as fragile
As unraveled threads too thin to intertwine.
Friendless, his destination is unknown.
Even without an affliction
Good fortune is elusive in this world,
Like the floating log the turtle gropes for
Once a century: The path is in darkness
And he, a blind turtle, must follow it.[1]
Now as the clouds of delusion rise
We have reached Mount Ōsaka
We have reached Mount Ōsaka.

(Semimaru sits on a stool before the Chorus. Kiyotsura kneels at the shite-pillar. The Bearers exit through the slit door.)

SEMIMARU: Kiyotsura!

KIYOTSURA: I am before you.

(From his kneeling position, he bows deeply.)

SEMIMARU: Are you to leave me on this mountain?

KIYOTSURA: Yes, your highness. So the Emperor has commanded, and I have
　　brought you this far.
But I wonder just where
I should leave you.
Since the days of the ancient sage kings
Our Emperors have ruled the country wisely,
Looking after its people with compassion—
But what can his Majesty have had in mind?
Nothing could have caught me so unprepared.

SEMIMARU: What a foolish thing to say, Kiyotsura. I was born blind because I
　　was lax in my religious duties in a former life.
That is why the Emperor, my father,
Ordered you to leave me in the wilderness,
Heartless this would seem, but it's his plan
To purge in this world my burden from the past,

---

1. In certain Buddhist texts the rarity of meeting a Buddha is compared to the difficulty of a blind seaturtle's chances of bumping into a log to float on. The turtle emerges to the surface only once a century and tries to clutch the log, but it has a hole and eludes his grasp; this was a simile for the difficulty of obtaining good fortune.

And spare me suffering in the world to come.
This is a father's true kindness.
You should not bewail his decree.

KIYOTSURA: Now I shall shave your head.
His Majesty has so commanded.

SEMIMARU: What does this act signify?

KIYOTSURA: It means you have become a priest,
A most joyous event.

(Seminaru rises. The stage assistant removes his nobleman's outer robe and places a priest's hat on his head.)

SEMIMARU: Surely Seishi's poem described such a scene:
"I have cut my fragrant scented hair
My head is pillowed half on sandalwood."[2]

KIYOTSURA: Such splendid clothes will summon thieves, I fear.
Allow me to take your robe and give you instead
This cloak of straw they call a *mino*.

(Semimaru mines receiving the mino.)

SEMIMARU: Is this the mino mentioned in the lines.
"I went to Tamino Island when it rained"?[3]

KIYOTSURA: And I give you this *kasa* rainhat
To protect you also from the rain and dew.

(He takes a kasa *from the stage assistant and hands it to Semimaru.)*

SEMIMARU: Then this must be the *kasa* of the poem
"Samurai—take a *kasa* for your lord."[4]

(Semimaru puts down the kasa.*)*

KIYOTSURA: And this staff will guide you on your way.
Please take it in your hands.

---

2. The poem referred to is by Li Ho and is actually a description of Hsi-shih (Seishi) rather than a poem by her. The meaning of the original verses was that Seishi's fragrant locks rivaled the perfume of cloves or sandalwood; however, the dramatist here misunderstood the Chinese and interpreted it as meaning she had cut her locks and now would have to rest her head on a hard pillow of sandalwood. (See commentary by Tanaka Makoto in Yōkyoku Shu, III, 205 [Nihon Koten Zensho series].)

3. From the poem by Ki no Tsurayuki, no. 918 in the *Kokinshū*.

4. From the anonymous poem, no. 1091 in the *Kokinshū*.

(He takes a staff from the stage assistant and hands it to Semimaru.)

SEMIMARU: Is this the staff about which Henjō wrote:
"Since my staff was fashioned by the gods
I can cross the mountain of a thousand years"?[5]

(Kiyotsura kneels at the shite-pillar.)

KIYOTSURA: His staff brought a thousand prosperous years,[6]

SEMIMARU: But here the place is Mount Ōsaka,

KIYOTSURA: A straw-thatched hut by the barrier;

SEMIMARU: Bamboo pillars and staff, my sole support.

KIYOTSURA: By your father, the Emperor,

SEMIMARU: Abandoned,

CHORUS: I meet my unsure fate at Mount Ōsaka.
You who know me, you who know me not[7]
Behold—this is how a prince, Daigo's son,
Has reached the last extremity of grief.

(He lowers his head to give a sad expression to his mask.)

Travelers and men on horses
Riding to and from the Capital,
Many people, dressed for their journeys,
Will drench their sleeves in sudden showers;
How hard it is to abandon him,
To leave him all alone;
How hard it is to abandon him,
To tear ourselves away.

(Kiyotsura bows to Semimaru.)

But even farewells must have an end;
By the light of the daybreak moon
Stifling tears that have no end, they depart.

(Weeping, Kiyotsura goes to the bridgeway.)

---

5. From the poem by the priest Henjō, no. 348 in the *Kokinshū.*

6. There is a pivot-word embedded here: *chitose no saka,* the slope of a thousand years; and *saka yuku tsue,* the staff that brings steady prosperity.

7. An allusion to the poem, attributed to Semimaru himself, no. 1091 in the *Gosenshū.* The poem, about the Barrier of Ōsaka, originally had a meaning something like: "This is the Barrier where people come and go exchanging farewells; for friends and strangers alike this is Meeting Barrier."

Semimaru, the Prince, left behind alone,
Takes in his arms his lute, his one possession,
Clutches his staff and falls down weeping.

(Semimaru picks up the staff and kasa, *comes forward, and turns toward the departing Kiyotsura. Kiyotsura stops at the second pine and looks back at him, then exits. Semimaru retreats, kneels, drops his kasa and staff, and weeps. Hakuga no Sammi enters and stands at the naming-place.)*

HAKUGA: I am Hakuga no Sammi.[8] I have learned that Prince Semimaru has been abandoned on Mount Ōsaka, and it pains me so much to think of him at the mercy of the rain and dew that I have decided to build a straw hut where he may live. (He opens the door of the hut, then goes to Semimaru at the shite-pillar.) The hut is ready at last, I shall inform him of this. (He bows to Semimaru.) Pardon me, sir; Hakuga is before you. If you stay here in this way, you will be soaked by the rain. I have built you a straw hut and I hope you will live in it. Please, come with me. (He takes Semimaru's hand and leads him inside the hut, then steps back and bows.) If ever you need anything, you have only to summon me, Hakuga no Sammi. I shall always be ready to serve you. I take my leave of you for now.

(He closes the door of the hut, then exits. Sakagami enters wearing the zō mask. Her robe is folded back from her right shoulder indicating that she is deranged. She stops at the first pine.)

SAKAGAMI: I am the third child of the Emperor Daigo,
The one called Sakagami, Unruly Hair.
Though born a princess, some deed of evil
From my unknown past in former lives
Causes my mind at times to act deranged.
And in my madness I wander distant ways.
My blueblack hair grows skywards;
Though I stroke it, it will not lie flat.

(She smooths down her hair.)

Those children over there—what are they laughing at?

(She looks to the right as if watching passersby.)

What? You find it funny that my hair stands on end? Yes,
I suppose hair that grows upside down is funny.
My hair is disordered, but much less than you—
Imagine, commoners laughing at me!

How extraordinary it is that so much before our eyes is upside down.
Flower seeds buried in the ground rise up to grace the branches of a

---

8. Hakuga no Sammi was in fact the grandson of the Emperor Daigo; and lived from 919 to 980; but here he is demoted to the position of a rustic, in inverse proportion to Semimaru's rise in position from being a menial to being Daigo's son.

thousand trees. The moon hangs high in the heavens, but its light sinks to the bottom of countless waters.

(She looks up and down.)

I wonder which of all these should be said to go in the proper direction and which is upside down?

> I am a princess, yet I have fallen,
> And mingle with the ruck of common men;

(She proceeds to the stage while chanting.)

> My hair, rising upward from my body,
> Turns white with the touch of stars and frost:
> The natural order or upside down?
> How amazing that both should be within me!

(She enters the stage.)

> The wind combs even the willows' hair
> But neither can the wind untangle,
> Nor my hand separate this hair.

(She takes hold of her hair and looks at it.)

> Shall I rip it from my head? Throw it away?
> I lift my sleeved hands—what is this?
> The hair-tearing dance?[9] How demeaning!

(She begins to dance, in a deranged manner.)

CHORUS: As I set forth from the flowery Capital
> From the flowery Capital,
> At Kamo River what were those mournful cries?[10]
> The river ducks? Not knowing where I went
> I crossed the river Shirakawa
> And when I reached Awataguchi, I wondered,
> "Whom shall I meet now at Matsuzaka?"[11]
> I thought I had yet to pass the barrier
> But soon Mount Otowa fell behind me
> How sad it was to leave the Capital!
> Pine crickets, bell crickets, grasshoppers,
> How they cried in the dusk at Yamashina!
> I begged the villagers, "Don't scold me, too!"
> I may be mad, but you should know

---

9. The *batō* dance is described thus in *The Pillow Book of Sei Shōnagon* (translation by Ivan Morris): "In the Dance of the Pulled Head the dancer's hair is in disorder and he has a fierce look in his eyes; but the music is delightful."

10. The name of the river, *kamo*, meant a species of duck.

11. The name Matsuzaka contains the familiar pivot-word *matsu*, to wait.

My heart is a pure rushing stream:
"When in the clear water
At Ōsaka Barrier
It sees its reflection
The tribute horse from Mochizuki
Will surely shy away."[12]
Have my wanderings brought me to the same place?
In the running stream I see my reflection.
Though my own face, it horrifies me:
Hair like tangled briers crowns my head
Eyebrows blackly twist—yes, that is really
Sakagami's reflection in the water.
Water, they say, is a mirror,
But twilight ripples distort my face.

(Sakagami sits at the stage assistant's position, indicating she has arrived at Mount Ōsaka. Semimaru, inside the hut, opens his fan and holds it in his left hand as if playing his lute.)

SEMIMARU: The first string and the second wildly sound[13]—
The autumn wind brushes the pines and falls
With broken notes; the third string and the fourth—
The fourth is myself, Semimaru,
And four are the strings of the lute I play
As sudden strings of rain drive down on me—
How dreadful is this night!
"All things in life
In the end are alike;
Whether in a palace or a hovel
We cannot live forever."[14]

(While Semimaru is speaking Sakagami comes before the shite-pillar. Semimaru inclines his head toward her as she speaks.)

SAKAGAMI: How strange—I hear music from this straw-thatched hut,
The sounds of a *biwa*, elegantly plucked—
To think a hovel holds such melodies!
But why should the notes evoke this sharp nostalgia?
With steps silent as the rain beating on the thatch
She stealthily approaches, stops and listens.

(She silently comes to stage center. Semimaru folds his fan.)

---

12. A poem by Ki no Tsurayuki, no. 118 in the Shūishū. The horse referred to was presented as tribute to the moon in a special ceremony held at the height of autumn on the night of the full moon. The headnote in Shūishū attributes this practice to the reign of the Emperor Daigo.

13. An allusion to the poem by Po Chū-i, no. 463 in the Wakan Rōei Shū.

14. From the poem attributed to Semimaru, no. 1851 in the Shinkokinshū.

SEMIMARU: Who is there? Who's making that noise outside my hut?
Hakuga no Sammi, lately you've been coming
From time to time to visit me — is that you?

SAKAGAMI: As I approach and listen carefully—that's the voice of my
brother, the Prince!
It's Sakagami! I'm here!
Semimaru, is that you inside?

SEMIMARU: Can it be my sister, the Princess?
Amazed, he opens the door of his hut.

(Taking his staff he rises and opens the door.)

SAKAGAMI: Oh—how wretched you look!

(She comes up to Semimaru as he emerges from the hut.)

SEMIMARU: They take each other hand in hand

(They place their hands on each other's shoulders and kneel.)

SAKAGAMI: My royal brother,
is that indeed you?

SEMIMARU: My royal sister,
is that indeed you?

CHORUS: They speak each other's names as in one voice.
Birds are also crying, here at Ōsaka,
Barrier of meeting — but no barrier
Holds back the tears that soak each other's sleeves.

(Both weep. During the following passage Sakagami returns to the middle of the stage and kneels.)

CHORUS: They say that sandalwood reveals its fragrance
From the first two leaves[15] — but how much closer still
Are we who sheltered beneath a single tree![16]
The wind rising in the orange blossoms[17]
Awakens memories we shall preserve

---

15. An expression used proverbially to indicate that genius can be recognized even in early youth. Here used to mean that a noble person reveals his character spontaneously.

16. Taking shelter beneath the same tree was an illustration of the concept that even casual contact in a previous existence might bring a karmic connection between people in their next incarnation. Because of some connection in a previous life Semimaru and Sakagami were born in this life as brother and sister.

17. The fragrance of orange *(tachibana)* blossoms was believed to summon up remembrance of people one once knew; here the memories are those shared by brother and sister.

We who flowered once on linking branches!
The love between brothers is told abroad:
Jōzō and Jōgen, Sōri and Sokuri;[18]
And nearer at hand, in Japan
The children of Emperor Ōjin,
The princes Naniwa and Uji,[19]
Who yielded the throne, each to the other:
All these were brothers and sisters
Bound in love, like us, like linking branches.

SAKAGAMI: But did I imagine my brother
    Would ever live in such a hovel?

CHORUS: Had no music come from that straw-thatched hut
    How should I have known? But I was drawn
    By the music of those four strings,

SAKAGAMI: Drawn like the water offered to the gods

CHORUS: From deep wells of love and far-reaching ties.
    The world may have reached its final phase[20]
    But the sun and moon have not dropped to the ground.
    Things are still in their accustomed place, I thought,
    But how can it be, then, that you and I
    Should cast away our royalty and live like this,
    Unable even to mingle with common men?
    A mad woman, I have come wandering now
    Far from the Capital girdled by clouds,
    To these rustic scenes, a wretched beggar,
    By the roads and forests, my only hope
    The charity of rustics and travelers.
    To think it was only yesterday you lived
    In jeweled pavilions and golden halls;
    You walked on polished floors and wore bright robes.
    In less time than it takes to wave your sleeve,
    Today a hovel is your sleeping-place.

---

18. Jōzō and Jōgen were siblings mentioned in the *Lotus Sutra*. Sōri and Sokuri were the son and daughter of a Brahman king of southern India. They were abandoned by their stepmother. After their death, their father found and recognized their skeletons on the island where they had been abandoned. The story is mentioned in the *Taiheiki* and the *Gempei Seisuiki*.

19. Sons of the Emperor Ōjin. The younger, Prince Uji, had been designated by Ōjin as his heir, but declined, saying the office belonged by rights to his elder brother. Prince Uji died first, and the empire went to Prince Naniwa, known posthumously as Emperor Nintoku.

20. A familiar concept. Believers in the medieval Pure Land Buddhism were convinced that the world had reached the period of the end of the Buddhist Law (*mappō*). According to one method of calculation, this period began about 1000 A.D., and was to continue for another thousand years.

Bamboo posts and bamboo fence, crudely fashioned
Eaves and door: straw your window, straw the roof,
And over your bed, the quilts are mats of straw:
Pretend they are your silken sheets of old.

SEMIMARU: My only visitors—how rarely they come—
Are monkeys on the peak, swinging in the trees;
Their doleful cries soak my sleeve with tears.
I tune my lute to the sound of the showers,
I play for solace, but tears obscure the sounds.
Even rain on the straw roof makes no noise.
Through breaks in the eaves moonlight seeps in.
But in my blindness, the moon and I are strangers.
In this hut I cannot even hear the rain—
How painful to contemplate life in this hut!

(Both weep.)

SAKAGAMI: Now I must go; however long I stayed
The pain of parting never would diminish.
Farewell, Semimaru.

(Both rise.)

SEMIMARU: If sheltering under a single tree
Were our only tie, parting would still be sad;
How much sadder to let my sister go!
Imagine what it means to be alone!

(Sakagami moves toward the shite-pillar.)

SAKAGAMI: Truly I pity you; even the pain
Of wandering may provide distraction,
But remaining here—how lonely it will be!
Even as I speak the evening clouds have risen,
I rise and hesitate; I stand in tears.

(She weeps.)

SEMIMARU: The evening crows call on the barrier road,
Their hearts unsettled

SAKAGAMI: As my raven hair,
My longing unabated, I must go.

SEMIMARU: Barrier of Meeting, don't let her leave!

SAKAGAMI: As I pass by the grove of cedars . . .

(She goes to the first pine.)

SEMIMARU: Her voice grows distant . . .

SAKAGAMI: By the eaves of the straw hut . . .

SEMIMARU: I stand hesitant.

CHORUS: "Farewell," she calls to him, and he responds,
  "Please visit me as often as you can."
(Sakagami goes to the third pine and turns back to look at Semimaru.)

  Her voice grows faint but still he listens,

(Sakagami starts to exit. Semimaru takes a few steps forward, stops and listens. His blind eyes gaze in her direction.)

  She turns a final time to look at him.
  Weeping, weeping they have parted,
  Weeping, weeping they have parted.

(Sakagami exits, weeping. Semimaru also weeps.)

The One Mind Linking All Powers

TRANSLATED BY DONALD KEENE

Sometimes spectators of the *Nō* say that the moments of "no action" are the most enjoyable. This is one of the actor's secret arts. Dancing and singing, movements on the stage, and the different types of miming are all acts performed by the body. Moments of "no action" occur in between. When we examine why such moments without action are enjoyable, we find that it is due to the underlying spiritual strength of the actor which unremittingly holds the attention. He does not relax the tension when the dancing or singing comes to an end or at intervals between the dialogue and the different types of miming, but maintains an unwavering inner strength. This feeling of inner strength will faintly reveal itself and bring enjoyment. However, it is undesirable for the actor to permit this inner strength to become obvious to the audience. If it is obvious, it becomes an act, and is no longer "no action." The actions before and after an interval of "no action" must be linked by entering the state of mindlessness in which the actor conceals even from himself his own intent. The ability to move audiences depends, thus, on linking all the artistic powers with one mind.

  "Life and death, past and present—
  Marionettes on a toy stage.

When the strings are broken,
Behold the broken pieces!"[1]

This is a metaphor describing human life as it transmigrates between life and death. Marionettes on a stage appear to move in various ways, but in fact it is not they who really move—they are manipulated by strings. When these strings are broken, the marionettes fall and are dashed to pieces. In the art of the *Nō* too, the different types of miming are artificial things. What holds the parts together is the mind. This mind must not be disclosed to the audience. If it is seen, it is just as if a marionette's strings were visible. The mind must be made the strings which hold together all the powers of the art. If this is done the actor's talent will endure. This effort must not be confined to the times when the actor is appearing on the stage: day or night, wherever he may be, whatever he may be doing, he should not forget it, but should make it his constant guide, uniting all his powers. If he persistently strives to perfect this, his talent will steadily grow. This article is the most secret of the secret teachings.

Tokugawa/Edo Periods

(1603–1868)

■ Ihara Saikaku (1642–1693) (novel)

TRANSLATED BY IVAN MORRIS

Ihara Saikaku was born into a wealthy merchant family in Osaka and appears to have lived a well-heeled life, though the death of his wife and later of his blind daughter brought him personal tragedy. He started off as a haiku poet and was such a prolific writer that he is said to have composed 23,500 verses in a single twenty-four-hour period. None of his poems is considered of particularly good quality. In 1682, he began writing prose in the phonetic syllabary *kana* and became the dominant writer of *ukiyo-zoshi*, or "tales of the floating world." Many of these tales were erotic in nature, and they described contemporary events and society, some of them fictional, some based on real occurrences. He was contemporaneous with the master haiku poet Basho and enjoyed the long, peaceful Tokugawa period, during which the spread of literacy and printing methods and the growth of urban

---

1. Poem by an unknown Zen master. The last two lines may mean, "When life comes to an end the illusions of this world also break into pieces."

centers and the merchant class allowed writers to break away from the patronage system and write for direct remuneration. He was an immensely popular writer, the author of such tales as *The Man Who Loved Love, Five Women Who Loved Love,* and *The Life of an Amorous Woman,* whose concubine heroine, struggling for money and survival, is Japanese literature's equivalent to Daniel Defoe's Moll Flanders. Like Moll Flanders, the protagonist of *The Life of an Amorous Woman* tells a series of ribald anecdotes about her life, strung together in picaresque fashion. In the chapter given, the protagonist narrates her life as a young courtesan; as the novel progresses and her beauty diminishes, her life takes a downward turn as she becomes a prostitute of the street.

FURTHER READING: Ihara, Saikaku. *Five Women Who Loved Love.* Translated by Wm. Theodore de Bary, 1995; *The Scheming World.* Translated by Masanori Takatsuka and David C. Stubbs, 1965. Morris, Ivan, tr. *The Life of an Amorous Woman and Other Writings by Ihara Saikaku,* 1963.

from *The Life of an Amorous Woman**

A Beauty of Easy Virtue

By the West Gate of the Kiyomizu Temple a woman sat strumming on her *samisen.* And as she played, I heard her sing these words:

> "Bitter is the Floating World[1]
> And pitiful this frame of mine!
> Would that I could alter into dew
> My life that I prize so little."

Her voice was gentle. She was a beggar woman.

Wretched indeed was her appearance! One could imagine that in the summer she must wear heavy padded clothes, and that in the winter, when the mountain winds blow fiercely from all directions, she would have nothing to protect her but an unlined summer dress. Seeing her in this present condition, I inquired what manner of person she had been in the past, and

---

*The translator's notes have been shortened in places.

1. *The Floating World* (ukiyo-gura). *Ukiyo* (floating world) was the conventional image used by writers, both lay and clerical, to convey the transitoriness of present life; in Saikaku's time it also suggested the fugitive pleasures of the demimonde; hence *ukiyo-e,* the genre paintings. By further extension, *ukiyo* meant "fashionable," "up-to-date," as in *ukiyo-motoyui* (fashionable type of paper cord for tying the hair). It also had the sense of "depraved" as in *ukiyo-dera* (the temple of a depraved priest).

was told that, in the days when the gay quarters had been at the Sixth Avenue,[2] this woman had flourished as one of the great courtesans,[3] being known as Katsuragi the Second. Since then she had fallen on bad days, as indeed is the way of this world, and finally reached her present state. In the autumn, when I went to view the cherry trees in their russet tints, I and the others of my party pointed at this woman and laughed. Little do we know what fate has prepared for us!

At about this time my parents fell into sorrowful adversity; they had unthinkingly become surety at the request of a certain man, who had then disappeared without a trace, leaving my parents much embarrassed over how they might obtain the money for which they were now held answerable. Finding no other means to extricate themselves, they sold me to the Kambayashi in Shimabara[4] for fifty gold koban,[5] and thus it was that I unexpectedly found myself in this profession. I was now just fifteen years old and, being in the fullness of my beauty, was—or so my new employer[6] said as she looked with rejoicing to the future—unequalled in the Moon Capital.[7]

As a rule, the floating trade[8] is one that a girl learns, by means of observation and without any special lessons, from the time that she is first employed as apprentice[9] in a house of pleasure. But I, being a "midway

---

2. *at the Sixth Avenue* (Rokujō ni). In 1602 the licensed quarter was moved from Yanagi-machi to Muromachi at the Sixth Avenue; in 1641 it was established at Shimabara, northwest of the Nishi Honganji (Temple).

3. *the great courtesans* (tayū). *Jorō* is the term for "a girl of pleasure," a generic term including the entire gamut of professional women, from the most exalted courtesan (tayū) whose nightly hire was the equivalent of about $58 (£21), to the meanest strumpet (hashi-jorō), who might cost a mere 40 cents (3 s). "High (-ranking)," "top (-ranking)" or "great" courtesan in the text will invariably refer to *tayū*.

4. *Kambayashi.* Famous house of assignation (*ageya*) in the Shimabara district.

5. *fifty gold koban* (gojū-ryō). The equivalent of about $2,300 (£820).

6. *employer* (oyakata). Being an *age-jorō* (high-class courtesan), she did not, like the lowly *mise-jorō*, live in the house where she practised her trade, but was called to the various *ageya* as her services were required. The *age-jorō*, a number of whom normally lived together in the house of their employer, were called out to entertain guests in various *ageya* (houses of assignation), as opposed to the far less dignified *mise-jorō*, who plied their trade in the houses (*mise*) where they lived. In this sense the *age-jorō* belonged more to the category of professional entertainer than to that of mere prostitute, the latter class being represented by *mise-jorō*, *yaha-tsu* (streetwalkers), etc. In Saikaku's time, the term *geisha* was not used in its modern sense (it referred to any person, male or female, whose profession was based on artistic accomplishment), nor was there any real equivalent to the present-day *geisha* institution. Even the most exalted and artistically accomplished *tayū* could be hired by the night for sexual purposes, although it is true that she might on occasion turn down a client if he was too displeasing, a luxury which her less elevated colleagues could ill afford.

7. *Moon Capital* (Tsuki no Miyako). "Moon" is used here (i) as a conventional epithet (*engo*) in relation with Kyōto, (ii) to imply that the heroine's beauty, now that she has reached the age of 16 (Japanese count), is fully developed like that of the 16-day-old moon.

8. *the floating trade* (nagare no kotowaza). Euphemism for prostitution; the image is the same as in *ukiyo*. See note 1 above.

9. *apprentice* (kaburo). The young apprentices in question (called *kaburo*) were employed in the brothels and other houses of pleasure to entertain visitors, pour their *sake*, etc.; they themselves normally became courtesans when they reached the proper age.

starter,"[10] had to learn the new fashions all at once. These, I may say, differ in every respect from the ways of ordinary townsfolk. A courtesan shaves her eyebrows, paints heavily above her forehead and eyes with an ink stick, wears her hair in a great Shimada without inserting any wooden support;[11] she secures her coiffure with a single hidden paper cord, decorating it outside with a wide band that she has folded into a narrow strip, and, forbidding even one stray wisp, she plucks her hair carefully from the back of her neck. Her long hanging sleeves are cut in the modern fashion, measuring two and a half feet at the bottom; no padding is used at the hips, and the bottom of her skirt is wide. The courtesan's buttocks should look flat as an open fan. A wide, unpadded sash is tied loosely about her and artlessly secures her three layers of clothing. Underneath she wears a petticoat of triple width, tying it rather higher than do women who are not of the profession.

A courtesan, also, has many special ways of walking. When she sallies forth, she usually wears no socks and adopts a floating walk;[12] on reaching the house of assignation,[13] she trips in nimbly; in the parlour she uses the soft-footed gait; this is followed by a hasty gait as she goes up the stairs. When it comes to leaving, she lets the servant arrange her sandals for her and slips them on without even looking; in the street she walks with her head held high and does not step aside for anyone.

There are many ways of winning a man's favour. The "amorous gaze," as they call it, consists of looking at some man, even though he be a complete stranger, in such a fashion as to make him believe that one finds him most attractive. Again, when evening comes at the house of assignation, one may go out on the front veranda and, if one sees some man of one's acquaintance on the street, one can throw him a distant glance; thereafter one sits down casually and, being sure that the man does not notice, gives one's hand to the town drum-holder[14] who has accompanied him on his jaunt; one praises the crest on the drum-holder's coat, or again his hair style, his modish fan or any other mark of elegance that may catch one's attention.

---

10. *"midway starter"* (*tsukidashi*). Tsukidashi, as used in the present context, were girls who became courtesans without having gone through the apprenticeship of being *kaburo*.

11. *wooden support* (komakura). Lit., "little pillow," a thin strip of wood normally used to prepare and raise the Shimada coiffure. Courtesans, with their very luxuriant hair, did not need to raise their Shimada artificially by inserting a support.

12. *a floating walk* (uke-ayumi). Coquettish style of walking affected by courtesans. The woman would walk slowly along the street, her body turned slightly aside, and her feet moving as though she were kicking up something with the tips of her toes.

13. *the house of assignation* (yadoya). Same as *ageya* (note 6 above).

14. *town drum-holder* (machi no taiko). This refers to an amateur *taiko-mochi* from outside the gay quarters, as opposed to those professional *taiko-mochi* who lived within the Shimabara area. Both kinds accompanied customers on their visits to houses of assignation and played a central role in the world of courtesans by recommending them to potential clients or, alternatively, by pointing out their defects. It was important, therefore, for these women to be on the best of terms with the *taiko-mochi*, and we are here given an example of an effort to cultivate good relations.

"You're a fellow to capture any woman's heart! From whom, pray tell me, did you learn that style of hair?" So saying, one strikes him smartly[15] on the back and returns into the house. However much experienced this drum-holder may be in the ways of the world, he is bound to succumb to such flattery from a woman; he now feels sure that, if he woos her at the proper opportunity, he will have her for himself. In anticipation he casts aside all desire for selfish gain: he sings her praises in the company of great men, and, should some bad rumour be noised abroad about her, he will put his own name in pawn to see her cleared.

One way to cause pleasure to a man is to tear up some letter that one does not need, crumple it into a ball and throw it at him.[16] The method is simple and requires no special material; yet there is many a dull-witted courtesan who cannot even manage this.

There were girls, I remember, who, though they were every jot as comely as the others, had no customer on the appointed day of payment[17] and were bidden to make their personal offerings[18] to the house. Such a courtesan will try to have the others think that she does in fact have an appointed lover, for whom she is now waiting; but her pretence is to no effect and everyone in the house treats the unwanted girl with disdain. She sits alone in a corner of the room, without even a proper table, munching her cold rice and her eggplant pickles flavoured with raw soy sauce. So long as no one sees her, she can bear the humiliation; yet it is all most painful. When she returns to her abode and sees her employer's expression,[19] she assumes a timid air and softly asks the maid to heat the water.[20] There are indeed many painful sides to a courtesan's life; but we can have no sympathy with

---

15. *strikes him smartly on the back* (pisshari pon to tataki). Standard coquettish gesture favoured by Japanese women.

16. *throw it at him* (kore wo uchitsukete). For a Japanese woman to throw some light object (a ball of paper, a match, etc.) playfully at a man is another coquettish gesture (cf. note 15 above) and is supposed to indicate that she is interested in him.

17. *day of payment* (mombi). The established days on which the courtesan was expected to receive a customer; if no man came for her, she was obliged to pay the fee (which he would normally have given to the proprietor of the establishment) out of her own pocket. This, of course, was considered a great humiliation for the girl in question, apart from the financial loss involved.

18. *personal offerings* (miagari). Payment by a courtesan to the proprietor of the fee that would normally be paid for her services. This was done on occasions when the girl preferred to rest and to reimburse the proprietor for the money which she would otherwise have earned; or again, when she was receiving a man to whom she was emotionally attached and preferred to pay the proprietor herself, rather than to have her lover do so; or, as in the present case, when no customer came on the appointed day of payment.

19. *employer's* (naigi no). This refers to the madam to whom the girl has been sold, and who is now highly disgruntled as a result of the latter's failure to obtain a customer on the day of payment.

20. *to heat the water* (gyozui tore). Courtesans always washed themselves thoroughly with hot water on returning from their visits to houses of assignation (ageya). Thus this girl prepares to wash herself even though she has had no customer. Perhaps she hopes to delude the other inmates of the house into thinking that she has really had an encounter. She is not too sure of herself, however, and addresses the maid softly (kogoe natte), instead of in the imperious manner customary for high-ranking courtesans.

those foolish women who slight a money-spending customer because he is not exactly to their taste, and who pass their time in idleness. Such women bring trouble on their masters and disregard their own standing in the world. Nor should a courtesan, when she is entertaining a customer at sakè, lard her conversation with over-clever repartee and display her parts with much ingenious talk. Such tactics may avail if her companion is a real gallant and well versed in the ways of the world; but, if he is an inexperienced man who has only dabbled in these paths, he will be abashed by such a show and will acquit himself ill with the woman. When they retire to bed, he may be gasping with excitement; yet he will be too overawed to perform the proper motions; his occasional remarks will be uttered in a quivering voice; and, though he should by rights be enjoying what he has bought with his own money, yet he finds it all most trying. He is just like a man who knows nothing about the art of the tea ceremony, yet finds himself thrust into the seat of honour.[21]

All this is not to say that a courtesan should turn down such a man because he is not to her liking; there are other ways to handle him. Since he has chosen from the beginning[22] to give himself the airs of a man of the world, the woman should use him with the greatest decorum. When they reach the bedchamber, she is most polite in her bearing to the customer; but she does not undo her sash,[23] and soon she pretends to fall asleep. Seeing this, the man will as a rule move closer to her and lay his leg on hers. The courtesan still lies there quietly, waiting to see what may happen next. Her customer starts to tremble with nervousness and breaks into a sweat.

Then he pricks up his ears to listen to the happenings in the next-door room. Here things are advancing far more smoothly, perhaps because the customer next door is already intimate with his courtesan, or perhaps again, because he is an experienced man, who even at their first meeting has caused her to throw off all restraint. Listening in the dark, he hears the woman say, "Your naked body feels plumper than I had expected from seeing you in your clothes." Next comes the sound of amorous embraces. The man's actions become more vehement, and in his onset he pays little heed

---

21. *seat of honour* (joza). I.e., the chief guest at the tea ceremony (*cha no yu*), who first receives the tea bowl from the host and who leads the other guests in the various traditional formalities. For a sophisticated courtesan to dazzle a tyro with her verbal coruscations is as foolish as to choose someone who knows nothing about the tea ceremony for the role of chief guest.

22. *Since he has chosen from the beginning* . . . (kashira ni). What follows is clearly a description of the heroine's own behaviour on such an occasion. As becomes clear later in the narrative, she was in the habit of treating tyros and other uncongenial customers with the greatest disdain; this, in fact, was the origin of her downfall.

23. *does not undo her sash* (obi wo mo tokazu). The *obi* (sash) is the most crucial part of a woman's attire and came to have a highly suggestive meaning in Japanese literature, especially drama. The voluntary untying of the sash suggested that the woman was ready to accept a man's advances; it was customary for lovers to undo each other's sashes. In the present context the undone sash is positive proof to Osan that her honour has been compromised.

to the pillow or to the surrounding screen. The woman lets out a cry of heart-felt delight. In her spontaneous joy she throws aside the pillow and there is the sound of the ornamental comb in her hair as it snaps in two.

Meantime, from the floor above comes the voice, "Ah, ah, what bliss that was!" followed by the rustling of paper handkerchiefs.[24] And in yet another room a man who has been pleasantly asleep is tickled awake by his partner, who says to him, "Already it is growing light outside. Will you not leave me one more remembrance of this night?" Hearing this, the man, still half asleep, says, "Pray forgive me, but I cannot do another thing!" One wonders whether it can be that he has drunk too much sakè the night before; but then one hears the sound of his loincloth being undone. This hussy is clearly of a more sensual nature than most. Is it not truly a blessing for a courtesan to be endowed with a hearty appetite for love?

With all these pleasant diversions afoot in the nearby rooms the unsuccessful customer cannot catch a wink of sleep. In the end he awakens his companion and says, "The Festival of the Ninth Moon[25] will soon be with us. May I inquire whether you have any special friend who will visit you on that day?"

Such words are a cheering tonic for a courtesan. But his purpose is too transparent for her and brusquely she replies, "I shall be taken care of in the Ninth Moon—and in the First Moon, too."

Now the man is at a loss for anything to say that might bring him closer to her; and, alas, the time has come when she must get up and leave, like all the other courtesans. Then she is greeted with a comical sight as her customer unties his hair and secures it loosely into a whisk,[26] and also redoes his sash—all this to make others believe that his night has been crowned with the joys of intimacy.

As a rule a customer who has been used in such a heartless fashion will regard this courtesan with bitterness. On his next visit to the house he may call for another girl and spend five or even seven days there, indulging in lavish entertainment, thus causing the most lively regret to the courtesan who treated him so coldly. Or again, he may for once and all renounce these quarters and determine henceforth to consort for his pleasure with

---

24. *paper handkerchiefs* (hanagami). Paper handkerchiefs were used for blowing the nose, wiping the face and other purposes. They almost invariably figure in descriptions of erotic scenes and are a standard adjunct of the so-called Spring Pictures, the success of the amorous encounter being in proportion to the number of such handkerchiefs depicted.

25. *Festival of the Ninth Moon* (Kugatsu no sekku). I.e., the Chrysanthemum Festival; this was one of the fixed days of payment (*mombi*) in the Shimabara, the pleasure quarters of Kyoto, when courtesans were obliged to receive customers. The unsuccessful customer is, as a last resource, trying to win her favours by suggesting that he will visit her on this day. She, however, rebuffs his heavy-handed overtures.

26. *a whisk* (chasen). Informal style of tying the queue into a bunch. Standing straight out at the back with a tuft at the end, and resembling the split-bamboo whisk used in preparing ground tea (*matcha*), a loose informal hair style, such as would be adopted by a man who has become thoroughly dishevelled after a successful night in the gay quarters.

young actors.[27] As he leaves the house, he will call flurriedly for the friend who accompanied him here, and, paying no heed to the latter's reluctance at being dragged at dawn from the arms of his fair companion, he will say, "Come, let us quit this place and hasten our return!" With no further ado he takes leave of his disobliging courtesan.

But there are also ways to prevent this. One may, for instance, tweak the man's ear in the presence of his friends and, while smoothing his ruffled side-locks, whisper to him: "What a heartless rogue you are to leave like this with no regard for a woman's true feelings — ay, without even having bidden her undo her sash!" So saying, one strikes him on the back before hurrying back into the house. His companions, having taken note, will say to him, "You lucky dog! How do you manage to enravish a woman at the very first meeting?"

Delighted, the man replies, "Ah yes, I'm her lover and I'll warrant she'd give her life for me now! The attentions she showered on me last night were amazing. She even insisted on rubbing my shoulder that has been so stiff these past few days. Frankly, I can't understand why she was so taken with me. Surely you spoke to her in my favour and told her I was a man of property?"

"No indeed," his friends answer him. "No courtesan will use a man with so much warmth out of mere avarice. You'll have a hard time ridding yourself of her now!"

Thus they flatter him, and in due course the woman's stratagem has effect. If things can turn out well even after such an inauspicious start, how much better if she uses her client with true regard from the outset! Aye, he will be ready to give his very life for her!

If some undistinguished customer asks a courtesan to spend the night with him, she should not turn him down just because this is their first meeting. However, a man may be overawed in the presence of a high-ranking courtesan like herself and at the crucial moment he may let slip his opportunity. Should this happen, he will get up and leave, the amorous spell having been broken.

A woman of the floating trade[28] should not let herself be drawn to a man because of his handsome looks. So long as he is of high standing in

---

27. *with young actors* (yaro-gurui). I.e., consort with professional catamites from the theatre. The term *yarō* originally referred to the type of close-cropped hairstyle that the government obliged young actors to adopt in order to reduce their homosexual attractions. Kabuki actors of the time (c. 1670–1690), were well known for taking the parts of women (*onnagata*). The theatre in Saikaku's time was a centre of paederasty.

Until 1652 young Kabuki actors (*wakashu*) continued to wear the forelock, or frontlet worn by boys until celebrating the ceremony of assuming manhood (*gembuku*) at the age of about 15, and this was one of the main aspects of their charms so far as male admirers were concerned; in that year the government, alarmed at the incidence of male immorality in the theatre, ordered actors to shave their heads like other men. A forelock continued to be the distinguishing mark of homosexuals.

28. *A woman of the floating trade* (nagare no mi). I.e., courtesan (note 8 above).

the capital, she should willingly accept him, even if he be a greybeard or a priest. A young man who is liberal with his gifts and to boot boasts of a handsome appearance is a courtesan's natural ideal. But where is one to find a customer equipped only with such excellent attributes?

The appearance that an up-to-date courtesan favours in a man is as follows: his kimono, of which both the outside and the lining are of the same yellow silk, is dyed with fine stripes; over this he wears a short black crested jacket of Habutaé silk. His sash is wrought of light yellowish-brown Ryumon, and his short coat is of reddish-brown Hachijo pongee, lined at the bottom with the same material. His bare feet are shod in a pair of straw sandals, and he dons a new pair each time that he goes out. In the parlour he bears himself with dignity. The short sword by his side protrudes slightly from its scabbard; he wields his fan so that the air is blown inside his hanging sleeves.

Though the stone basin may already be full of water, he has it filled afresh; then he washes his hands in a leisurely fashion, gargles softly and performs his other ablutions with like elegance. Having completed his toilet, he bids one of the girl assistants fetch his tobacco, which his attendant has brought along wrapped in white Hosho paper.[29] After a few puffs he lays a handkerchief of Nobé paper by his knees, uses it with artless elegance and throws it away.

Next he summons an assistant courtesan,[30] and, telling her that he would fain borrow her hand for a moment, he has her slip it up his sleeve to scratch the moxa that has been applied for the cramp in his shoulder muscles. Now he calls upon a drum courtesan[31] to perform the Kaga Air,[32] though paying but little attention to her as she strums on her samisen and sings; instead, in the middle of the tune, he turns to the jester[33] who is in

---

29. *Hosho paper* . . . Nobé paper (Hōsho . . . Nobe). Nobe was one type of Hōsho, the latter being thick Japanese hand-made paper, originally used for important government documents. The dandy in question here uses it to wipe his face after a few puffs of tobacco. He is, of course, kneeling on the floor in the Japanese fashion; hence, "by his knees" (hiza chikaku).

30. *assistant courtesan* (hikifune-jorō). Lit., "tow-boat courtesan." The *hikifune-jorō* were of the same rank as the *kakoi* and their fee was the same; they accompanied the *tayū* to the house of assignation (*ageya*) and helped to entertain the guests. The *kakoi* ranked third (after *tayū* and *tenjin*) in the hierarchy of *age-jorō* (high-class courtesans) in Kyōto and Ōsaka. In a town like Murotsu where there were no *tayū* or *tenjin*, the *kakoi* occupied the highest rank. In Shimabara (Kyōto) the *kakoi's* fee was 18 *momme* of silver (equivalent to about $14; £5).

31. *drum courtesan* (taiko-joro). Courtesan who helped to entertain a tayu's guests by playing the samisen, singing, etc. Her rank and fee were the same as that of a *kakoi*.

32. *Kaga Air* (Kaga-bushi). Ballad especially popular during the 1660s.

33. *jester* (massha). Lit., "subordinate shrine," another word for "drum-holder" (*taikomochi*). In the Edo Period drum-holders were professional male entertainers, corresponding (very roughly) to European jesters, buffoons or "allowed fools"; they would accompany customers on drinking expeditions to the gay quarters, where they often had the role of elegant panders. They would frequently supervise the entertainment at parties and had considerable influence over the courtesans.

attendance and says, "In yesterday's performance of *The Seaweed Gatherer*,[34] the supporting actor truly put Takayasu to shame with his skill." Or again, he may remark, "When I inquired of the Chief Councillor[35] about that old verse I was mentioning the other day, he confirmed that it was indeed the work of Ariwara no Motokata."[36]

In the presence of a customer who—without giving himself airs—starts out with some elegant conversation of this kind, and who in all things shows an attitude of perfect dignity and composure, even a top-ranking courtesan is overawed and inspired with a new spirit of modesty. Everything that the man does seems to her admirable and she looks on him with awe; the result is that she quite throws off her usual haughty air and comes to humour his every whim.

The pride displayed by courtesans of high rank is always due to their having been pampered by customers. In the palmy days of the gay quarters at Edo there was a connoisseur of fashion named Sakakura who grew intimate with the great courtesan Chitosé. This woman was much given to drinking saké; as a side dish she relished the so-called flower crabs, to be found in the Mogami River in the East, and these she had pickled in salt for her enjoyment. Knowing this, Sakakura commissioned a painter of the Kano School[37] to execute her bamboo crest[38] in powdered gold on the tiny shells of these crabs; he fixed the price of each painted shell at one rectangular piece of gold[39] and presented them to Chitosé throughout the year, so that she never lacked for them.

Again, in Kyoto there was a connoisseur called Ishiko. This man was much smitten with the high-ranking courtesan Nokazé, for whom he would purchase the most rare and fashionable wares, hastening to do so before

---

34. *The Seaweed Gatherer* (Mekari). *Nō* play by Zenchiku (1405–1468). The supporting actor or deutaroginist in a *Nō* play is known as the *waki;* he is second in importance and usually acts as a foil to the main character, the *shite.* Takayasu belonged to a famous family of *waki* actors that lasted until the Meiji Period. The dandy is making a show of his artistic discrimination by preferring a lesser-known actor to the established master.

35. *Chief Councillor* (Dainagon). One of the high court officials in Kyōto. Since real power had long since passed out of the hands of the court, these aristocratic officials concentrated on ceremonial functions and also on the preservation of classical learning and artistic forms. A Chief Councillor would therefore be an appropriate person to consult about the authorship of an old verse. By mentioning that he has done so, the dandy not only makes further show of his artistic interests, but suggests that he is familiar with court circles, and is also something of a scholar.

36. *Ariwara no Motokata.* Heian poet and grandson of Narihira. He is the author of the first poem in the *Kokinshū* anthology.

37. *Kano School* (Kanō no fude). Famous academic school of painting that flourished in the Momoyama and Edo Periods.

38. *her bamboo crest* (sasa no maru no jōmon). High-ranking courtesans all had their own crests and these were familiar to the habitués of the gay quarters.

39. *one rectangular piece of gold* (kinsu ichibu). I.e., I *ichibu-koban.* In other words, each little crab that Chitosé ate cost the equivalent of about $11 (£4). There were numerous stories in Saikaku's time of this type of extravagance.

anyone else could acquire them. On one occasion, Nokazé received a wadded autumn kimono dyed with pale scarlet; the silk was of fully dappled design and in the centre of each dapple a hole had been burned with a taper, so that one could see through the surface of the dress into the scarlet-tinted wadding. This material was of matchless elegance, and the single kimono was said to have cost close upon twenty-five pounds of silver.

In Osaka, too, there was a man, since deceased, who called himself Nisan, and who had made Dewa of the Nagasaki House into his private courtesan.[40] During one gloomy autumn he made show of his great compassion by paying for numerous courtesans in the Kuken-cho[41] who were not in demand by other customers; this merciful usage of her colleagues afforded much comfort to Dewa. On another occasion, when the clover bloomed profusely outside the house, Dewa noticed that some of the water which had been sprinkled in the garden had come to rest on the leaf tips; it sparkled just like early morning dew, and Dewa was deeply moved by its beauty.

"I have heard," she said to Nisan, "that loving couples of deer are wont to lie behind clover bushes. How I should like to see this in real life! Surely these animals cannot be dangerous, for all they are equipped with horns."

Hearing this, her lover is said to have replied that nothing could be simpler than to grant her wish; he then — so the story has it — ordered the back part of her parlour to be demolished and had numerous clover bushes planted there, thus making the room into a veritable field; next he sent word during the night to people in the mountains of Tamba and had them round up wild deer of both sexes, who were dispatched to the house. On the following day he was able to show them to Dewa; after which he had the parlour restored to its former state. Surely Heaven will someday punish men like these, who, though endowed with little virtue, permit themselves luxury that even noblemen can ill afford![42]

Now, concerning my own career as a top courtesan, though I sold my body to men who were not to my taste, yet I never yielded myself to them. Indeed, I used these men harshly, so that they came to regard me as a cold-hearted woman and to turn their backs on me. Day after day the number of my customers diminished; I was thus inevitably eclipsed by the other courtesans of my rank, and I began fondly to remember my past glory.

---

40. *private courtesan* (agezume ni seshi). Nisan paid a sufficient sum to Dewa's employer so that he might visit her daily if so desired, and so that no one else might be allowed to enjoy her favours. This was a normal procedure for wealthy men if they had some favourite courtesan, and the system carries over into the present-day *geisha* institution.

41. *Kuken-cho.* A centre of houses of assignation in Shinmachi.

42. *Surely Heaven will someday punish . . .* (Ten mo itsu zo wa togame-tamawan). A conventional condemnation of bourgeois extravagance of the type that the Tokugawa authorities used to issue (with little effect) in the form of sumptuary edicts.

Truly, a courtesan can only afford to dislike a man while she herself is in great favour; for once she is no longer in demand, any customer will be welcome, not excepting servants, mendicant priests, cripples and men with harelips. When one comes to think of it, there is no calling in the world so sad as this one.

■ Matsuo Basho (1644–1694) (poems, travel diary)

Matsuo Basho is Japan's best-loved poet and is considered the world's unparalleled haiku poet. In Basho's time, haiku was not considered a form in itself, as in the modern era; rather, it was the initial stanza of a longer linked-verse poem (*haikai*) composed by several poets in collaboration and was termed *hokku* (see discussion under Matsuo Basho and His School). Until the mid-seventeenth century, hokku was most often a comic verse, composed by the senior poet; it is required to include a *kigo,* or "season word," which explicitly or indirectly suggests a season. Basho was responsible for elevating this form from a trivial diversion to a serious art form. He also wrote some of the finest *haibun* (prose combined with hokku) in Japanese literature; his *Essay on the Unreal Dwelling* is particularly fine.

Matsuo Munefusa, who later took the literary name Basho, was born in Ueno, Iga province, in 1644. When he was between nine and twelve, he became a personal companion to Yoshitada, the third son of the local samurai lord, and with him studied linked verse of the Teimon school. Yoshitada died when Basho was twenty-two, and the young poet left feudal service, drifting for a period of five or six years. He settled in Edo around 1672. There he was influenced by Nishiyama Soin, founder of the Danrin school of haikai, a style generally comic and allusive, emphasizing conceptual linkages between haikai stanzas rather than the verbal connection that the Teimon school championed. In Edo, he gained recognition as a poet, gathering students around him with whom he composed haikai. Around 1680, he settled in the countryside near Edo in a hut built for him by a disciple, which was named Basho-an (meaning "Banana Tree Retreat") after a banana tree he planted beside his door. From this retreat he took the literary name by which he is best known. For the remainder of his life, he lived in this retreat (and in two others of the same name) and took frequent journeys across Japan, which he recorded in a series of magnificent travel diaries. The best of these, and the finest product in its genre, is his *Narrow Road to the Interior.* He died on such a journey in 1694, when he was fifty years old, composing his death poem at that time: "I fall sick traveling. / But through withered fields / my dream still wanders."

Basho's work shows the influence of the Daoist thought of Zhuangzi and Laozi and of Zen Buddhism, which he studied under a master called Butcho. Though he was influenced by Danrin and Teimon haikai, he developed his own style, and a Basho school of poetry survived him; without the supporting genius of the master, however, this style became moribund and lost dominance to the former two schools. In his own work, he moved from a more decorative poetics to an ideal of *sabi*, or a mood of desolate and lonely beauty, the Japanese sublime. In his last years Basho shifted toward an ideal he termed *karumi*, or lightness. This was an even simpler style, and it often celebrated the utterly humble and ordinary. Basho's poetry blazes with sudden and total presence, each word hinting at chasms of meaning that flicker at the edges of consciousness. "Words," says American poet William Carlos Williams, "are keys that unlock the mind." Each little hokku by Basho opens a hidden door and gives us entryway to what was always inside: the smallest processes of nature and the largest movements of the universe, which are often one and the same.

Oku no Hosomichi, the *Narrow Road to the Interior*, is Basho's famed travel diary. He had already composed a number of these, such as his *Journey to Sarashina* of 1688 and his *Essay from a Wanderer's Book-Satchel*, in which he linked the form of his diaries, prose interspersed with *hokku*, to the tradition of Ki no Tsurayuki's famous *Tosa Diary* of around 935. In the spring of 1699, he set out with his friend Iwanami Sora on a journey north from Edo along the Pacific coastline, across the island, down the Japan Sea coastline, and then across the island again. On this journey they suffered illness and dangers and dressed as Buddhist monks to assure their safety. The journal reflects these hardships as well as a spartan style of travel that may not reflect the realities of the journey, since Basho and Sora were entertained and put up by wealthy patrons along the way. Sora kept a more factual account that reveals that key events in Basho's version were fictional and that others were altered. This exaggeration (like the Sunday dinners at his mother's house that Henry David Thoreau artfully left out of his account of his spartan life in Walden) must be seen as part of the conversion of experience into art. After all, he revised the journal for years after the actual journey, and it is clear, as translator Sam Hamill notes, that he wanted the physical journey to the "interior country" to open doors to the "spiritual interior" and to put more structure into the journey of the reader through his text than he may have encountered on the road. In spite of (or because of) this, *Narrow Road to the Interior* remains a remarkable blending of poetry and prose, the premier example of the travel diary in Japanese literature.

FURTHER READING: Keene, Donald. *World within Walls: Japanese Literature of the Pre-Modern Era, 1600–1867*, 1976. Matsuo Basho. *Back Roads to Far Towns: Basho's Oku-no-hosomichi*. With a translation and notes by Cid Corman and Kamaike Susumu, 1968, 1986; *A Haiku Journey, Basho's Narrow Road to a Far Province*. Translated and introduced by Dorothy Britton, 1980; *The Narrow Road to the Deep North, and Other Travel Sketches*. Translated from the Japanese with an introduction by Nobuyuki Yuasa, 1966; *Narrow Road to the Interior*. Translated by Sam Hamill; illustrated by Stephen Addiss, 1991. Miner, Earl. *Japanese Poetic Diaries*, 1969. Stryf, Lucian, tr. *On Love and Barley: Haiku of Basho*, 1985. Veda, Makoto. *Basho and His Interpreters: Selected Hokku, with Commentary*, 1991.

Twenty-one Haiku

TRANSLATED BY TONY BARNSTONE

In the cicada cry
nothing
of how soon it will die.

A high mountain path
where plum scent hangs in air.
Suddenly the sun!

A sound so crystal
it pierces constellations.
Someone beating clothes.

Above the garden
winter moon thins to a thread
as insects wail.

Dragonfly
trying to land
on a blade of grass.

No moon,
not even flowers, so I drink sake
alone.

A cuckoo sings
in wild bamboo.
Moonlight trickles through.

The bell hushes
and flower aromas swell
the evening.

Lightning.
Through dark air
a night heron screams.

How admirable
as lightning cracks
not to think life is brief.

Cicada shell;
it sang itself
away.

A night so icy
I burst from sleep
as the water jar cracks.

Rough sea,
and the river of heaven pours forever
over Sado Island.

As the sea darkens
wild duck cries
seem faint and white.

A frog leaps
into the ancient pond
—plop![1]

The bee emerges
from deep within the peony
—reluctantly!

On the dead limb
a crow alights
in autumn evening.

First cold rain.
Even the monkey seems to want
a straw raincoat.

---

1. Basho's most famous poem, often imitated.

Not even a hat
as the cold rain falls.
Who cares?

Even in Kyoto
I long for Kyoto
when the cuckoo sings.

Basho's Death Poem
I fall sick traveling,
but through withered fields
my dream still wanders.

---

from **Narrow Road to the Interior**

TRANSLATED BY SAM HAMILL

The moon and sun are eternal travelers.[1] Even the years wander on. A lifetime adrift in a boat, or in old age leading a tired horse into the years, every day is a journey, and the journey itself is home. From the earliest times there have always been some who perished along the road.[2] Still I have always been drawn by windblown clouds into dreams of a lifetime of wandering. Coming home from a year's walking tour of the coast last autumn, I swept the cobwebs from my hut on the banks of the Sumida just in time for New Year, but by the time spring mists began to rise from the fields, I longed to cross the Shirakawa Barrier into the Northern Interior. Drawn by the wanderer-spirit Dosojin, I couldn't concentrate on things. Mending my cotton pants, sewing a new strap on my bamboo hat, I daydreamed. Rubbing moxa into my legs to strengthen them, I dreamed a bright moon rising over Matsushima. So I placed my house in another's hands and moved to my patron Mr. Sampu's summer house in preparation for my journey. And I left a verse by my door:

---

1. "The moon and sun are eternal travelers." This line echoes the famous preface to a poem ("Peach Garden Banquet on a Spring Night") by the T'ang-dynasty poet Li Po.

2. "some who perished along the road." Bashō is thinking of T'ang poet Tu Fu (712–770) and the wandering monk Saigyō (1118–1190).

Even this grass hut
may be transformed
into a doll's house[3]

Very early on the twenty-seventh morning of the third moon, under a
predawn haze, transparent moon still visible,[4] Mount Fuji just a shadow, I
set out under the cherry blossoms of Ueno and Yanaka. When would I see
them again? A few old friends had gathered in the night and followed
along far enough to see me off from the boat. Getting off at Senju, I felt
three thousand miles rushing through my heart, the whole world only a
dream. I saw it through farewell tears.

Spring passes
and the birds cry out—
tears in the eyes of fishes

With these first words from my brush, I started. Those who remain behind watch the shadow of a traveler's back disappear.

* * *

The second year of Genroku [1689], I think of the long way leading into
the Northern Interior under Go stone skies.[5] My hair may turn white as
frost before I return from those fabled places—or maybe I won't return at
all. By nightfall, we come to Sōka, bony shoulders sore from heavy pack,
grateful for warm night robe, cotton bathing gown, writing brush, ink
stone, necessities. The pack made heavier by farewell gifts from friends. I
couldn't leave them behind.

* * *

The last night of the third moon, an inn at the foot of Mount Nikkō. The
innkeeper is called Hoteke Gozaemon—Joe Buddha. He says his honesty
earned him the name and invites me to make myself at home. A merciful
buddha like an ordinary man, he suddenly appeared to help a pilgrim
along his way. His simplicity's a great gift, his sincerity unaffected. A model
of Confucian rectitude, my host is a saint.

* * *

On the first day of the fourth moon, climbed to visit the shrines on a mountain once called Two Wildernesses, renamed by Kūkai[6] when he dedicated
the shrine. Perhaps he saw a thousand years into the future, this shrine

---

3. "Even this grass hut / may be transformed / into a doll's house." This image—of Bashō's
tiny thatched hut dwarfed by his patron's mansion—refers to Hina Matsuri, the Girls' Festival
4. "transparent moon still visible." This is an allusion to a line from *The Tale of Genji*.
5. "Go stone skies." Go is an ancient Chinese board game played with black and white pieces
called "stones," which create patterns as the game progresses.
6. Kūkai, also called Kōbō Daishi (774–835), founded the Shingon Buddhist sect. The temple
at Nikkō was actually founded by Shōdō (737–817).

under sacred skies, his compassion endlessly scattered through the eight directions, falling equally, peaceably, on all four classes of people. The greater the glory, the less these words can say.

> Speechless before
> these budding green spring leaves
> in blazing sunlight

✳   ✳   ✳

Mount Kurokami still clothed in snow, faint in the mist, Sora wrote:

> Head shaven
> at Black Hair Mountain
> we change into summer clothes

Sora was named Kawai Sōgorō; Sora's his nom de plume. At my old home—called Basho (plantain tree)—he carried water and wood. Anticipating the pleasures of seeing Matsushima and Kisagata, we agreed to share the journey, pleasure and hardship alike. The morning we started, he put on Buddhist robes, shaved his head, and changed his name to Sogo, the Enlightened. So the "changing clothes" in his poem is pregnant with meaning.[7]

A hundred yards uphill, the waterfall plunged a hundred feet from its cavern in the ridge, falling into a basin made by a thousand stones. Crouched in the cavern behind the falls, looking out, I understood why it's called Urami-no-Taki, "View-from-behind-Falls."

> Stopped awhile
> inside a waterfall:
> the summer begins[8]

✳   ✳   ✳

A friend lives in kurobane on the far side of the broad Nasu Moor. Tried a shortcut running straight through, but it began to rain in the early evening, so we stopped for the night at a village farmhouse and continued again at dawn. Out in the field, a horse, and nearby a man cutting grass. I stopped to ask directions. Courteous, he thought awhile, then said, "Too many intersecting roads. It's easy to get lost. Best to take that old horse as far as he'll go. He knows the road. When he stops, get off, and he'll come back alone."

Two small children danced along behind, one with the curious name of Kasane, same as the pink flower. Sora wrote:

> With this *kasane*
> she's doubly pink
> a fitting name

---

7. "his poem is pregnant with meaning." Japanese poets often changed their names, as had Bashō himself. Traveling in Buddhist robes was both safer and in keeping with Bashō's spiritual pilgrimage.

8. "Stopped awhile / inside a waterfall: / the summer begins." This verse refers to Shinto-Buddhist spring ritual bathing.

Arriving at a village, I tied a small gift to the saddle and the horse turned back.

* * *

Set out to see the Murder Stone, Sesshō-seki, on a borrowed horse, and the man leading it asked for a poem, "Something beautiful, please."

> The horse lifts his head:
> from across deep fields
> the cuckoo's cry

Sesshō-seki lies in dark mountain shadow near a hot springs emitting bad gases. Dead bees and butterflies cover the sand.

* * *

Over the pass, we crossed the Abukuma River, Mount Aizu to the left, the villages of Iwaki, Sōma, and Miharu on the right, divided from the villages of Hitachi and Shimotsuke by two small mountain ranges. At Kagenuma, the Mirror Pond, a dark sky blurred every reflection.

We spent several days in Sukagawa with the poet Tōkyū, who asked about the Shirakawa Barrier. "With mind and body sorely tested," I answered, "busy with other poets' lines, engaged in splendid scenery, it's hardly surprising I didn't write much":

> Culture's beginnings:
> from the heart of the country
> rice-planting songs

"From this opening verse," I told him, "we wrote three linked-verse poems."

* * *

Staying the night in Iizuka, we bathed in a mineral hot springs before returning to thin straw sleeping mats on bare ground—a true country inn. Without a lamp, we made our beds by firelight, in flickering shadows, and closed our tired eyes. Suddenly a thunderous downpour and leaky roof aroused us, fleas and mosquitoes everywhere. Old infirmities tortured me throughout the long, sleepless night.

At first light, long before dawn, we packed our things and left, distracted, tired, but moving on. Sick and worried, we hired horses to ride to the town of Kori. I worried about my plans. With every pilgrimage one encounters the temporality of life. To die along the road is destiny. Or so I told myself. I stiffened my will and, once resolute, crossed Ōkido Barrier in Date Province.

* * *

We stopped along the Tama River at Noda, and at the huge stone in the lake, Oki-no-ishi, both made famous in poems. On Mount Sue-no-matsu, we found a temple called Masshozan. There were graves everywhere among the pines, underscoring Po Chu-i's famous lines quoted in *The Tale of Genji*, "wing and wing, branch and branch," and I thought, "Yes, what we all must come to," my sadness heavy.

At Shiogama Beach, a bell sounded evening. The summer rain-sky cleared to reveal a pale moon high over Magaki Island. I remembered the "fishing boats pulling together" in a *Kokinshū* poem, and understood it clearly for the first time.

Along the Michinoku
every place is wonderful,
but in Shiogama
fishing-boats pulling together
are most amazing of all

That night we were entertained by a blind singer playing a lute to boisterous back-country ballads one hears only deep inside the country, not like the songs in *The Tale of the Heike* or the dance songs. A real earful, but pleased to hear the tradition continued.

* * *

Rose at dawn to pay respects at Myōjin Shrine in Shiogama. The former governor rebuilt it with huge, stately pillars, bright-painted rafters, and a long stone walkway rising steeply under a morning sun that danced and flashed along the red lacquered fence. I thought, "As long as the road is, even if it ends in dust, the gods come with us, keeping a watchful eye. This is our culture's greatest gift." Kneeling at the shrine, I noticed a fine old lantern with this inscribed on its iron grate:

In the Third Year of the Bunji Era [1187]
Dedicated by Izumi Saburō

Suddenly, five long centuries passed before my eyes. A trusted, loyal man martyred by his brother; today there's not a man alive who doesn't revere his name. As he himself would say, a man must follow the Confucian model—renown will inevitably result.

* * *

Sun high overhead before we left the shrine, we hired a boat to cross to Matsushima, a mile or more away. We disembarked on Ojima Beach.

As many others often observed, the views of Matsushima take one's breath away. It may be—along with Lake Tung-t'ing and West Lake in China—the most beautiful place in the world. Islands in a three-mile bay, the sea to the southeast entering like floodtide on the Ch'ien-t'ang River in Chekiang. Small islands, tall islands pointing at the sky, islands on top of islands, islands like mothers with baby islands on their backs, islands cradling islands in the bay. All covered with deep green pines shaped by salty winds, trained into sea-wind bonsai. Here one is almost overcome by the sense of intense feminine beauty in a shining world. It must have been the mountain god Ōyamazumi who made this place. And whose words or brush could adequately describe a world so divinely inspired?

* * *

Here three generations of the Fujiwara clan passed as though in a dream. The great outer gates lay in ruins. Where Hidehira's manor stood, rice fields grew. Only Mount Kinkei remained. I climbed the hill where Yoshitsune died; I saw the Kitakami, a broad stream flowing down through the Nambu Plain, the Koromo River circling Izumi Castle below the hill before joining the Kitakami. The ancient ruins of Yasuhira—from the end of the Golden Era—lie out beyond the Koromo Barrier where they stood guard against the Ainu people. The faithful elite remained bound to the castle, for all their valor, reduced to ordinary grass. Tu Fu wrote:

> The whole country devastated,
> only mountains and rivers remain.
> In springtime, at the ruined castle,
> the grass is always green.

We sat awhile, our hats for a seat, seeing it all through tears.

> Summer grasses:
> all that remains of great soldiers'
> imperial dreams

Sora wrote:

> Kanefusa's
> own white hair
> seen in blossoming briar[9]

* * *

The road through the Nambu Plain visible in the distance, we stayed the night in Iwate, then trudged on past Cape Oguro and Mizu Island, both along the river. Beyond Narugo Hot Springs, we crossed Shitomae Barrier and entered Dewa Province. Almost no one comes this way, and the barrier guards were suspicious, slow, and thorough. Delayed, we climbed a steep mountain in falling dark and took refuge in a guard shack. A heavy storm pounded the shack with wind and rain for three miserable days.

> Eaten alive by lice and fleas
> now the horse
> beside my pillow pees

* * *

The guard told us, "To get to Dewa, you'd better take a guide. There's a high mountain and a hard-to-find trail." He found us a powerful young

---

9. "Kanefusa's / own white hair / seen in blossoming briar." Kanefusa (1127–1189), although old, fought beside Yoshitsune.

man, short sword on his hip and oak walking stick in hand, and off we went, not without a little trepidation. As forewarned, the mountain was steep, the trail narrow, not even a birdcall to be heard. We made our way through deep forest dark as night, reminding me of Tu Fu's poem about "clouds bringing darkness." We groped through thick bamboo, waded streams, climbed through rocks, sweaty, fearful, and tired, until we finally came to the village of Mogami. Our guide, turning back, said again how the trail was tough. "Happy you didn't meet many surprises!" And departed. Hearing this, our hearts skipped another beat.

✳   ✳   ✳

In Yamagata province, the ancient temple founded by Jikaku Daishi in 860, Ryūshaku Temple, is stone quiet, perfectly tidy. Everyone told us to see it. It meant a few miles extra, doubling back toward Obanazawa to find shelter. Monks at the foot of the mountain offered rooms, then we climbed the ridge to the temple, scrambling up through ancient gnarled pine and oak, smooth gray stones and moss. The temple doors, built on rocks, were bolted. I crawled among boulders to make my bows at shrines. The silence was profound. I sat, feeling my heart begin to open.

> Lonely silence
> a single cicada's cry
> sinking into stone

✳   ✳   ✳

Today we came through places with names like Children-Desert-Parents, Lost Children, Send-Back-the-Dog, and Turn-Back-the-Horse — some of the most fearsomely dangerous places in all the North Country. And well named. Weakened and exhausted, I went to bed early but was roused by the voices of two young women in the room next door. Then an old man's voice joined theirs. They were prostitutes from Niigata in Echigo Province and were on their way to Ise Shrine in the south, the old man seeing them off at this barrier, Ichiburi. He would turn back to Niigata in the morning, carrying their letters home. One girl quoted the *Shinkokinshū* poem,[10] "On the beach where white waves fall, / we all wander like children into every circumstance, / carried forward every day...." And as they bemoaned their fate in life, I fell asleep.

In the morning, preparing to leave, they came to ask directions. "May we follow along behind?" they asked. "We're lost and not a little fearful. Your robes bring the spirit of the Buddha to our journey." They had mistaken us for priests. "Our way includes detours and retreats," I told them. "But follow anyone on this road, and the gods will see you through." I hated to leave them in tears and thought about them hard for a long time after we left. I told Sora, and he wrote down:

---

10. The *Shinkokinshū* is the eighth imperial anthology of "new and old poems," and the primary source for Bashō's study of Saigyō's poetry.

Under one roof, prostitute and priest,
we all sleep together:
moon in a field of clover

* * *

Here we visited Tada Shrine to see Sanemori's helmet[11] and a piece of his
brocade armor-cloth presented to him by Lord Yoshitomo when he served
the Genji clan. His helmet was no common soldier's gear: engraved with
chrysanthemums and ivy from eyehole to earflap, crowned with a dragon's
head between two horns. After Sanemori died on the battlefield, Kiso
Yoshinaka sent it with a prayer, hand-carried to the shrine by Higuchi Jiro,
Sanemori's friend. The story's inscribed on the shrine.

Ungraciously, under
a great soldier's empty helmet,
a cricket sings

* * *

Sora, suffering from persistent stomach ailments, was forced to return to
his relatives in Nagashima in Ise Province. His parting words:

Sick to the bone
if I should fall
I'll lie in fields of clover

He carries his pain as he goes, leaving me empty. Like paired geese parting
in the clouds.[12]

Now falling autumn dew
obliterates my hatband's
"We are two"[13]

* * *

I stayed at zenshō-ji, a temple near the castle town of Daishōji in Kaga
Province. It was from this temple that Sora departed here the night before,
leaving behind:

All night long
listening to autumn winds
wandering in the mountains

One night like a thousand miles, as the proverb says, and I too listened to fall
winds howl around the same temple. But at dawn, the chanting of sutras, gongs
ringing, awakened me. An urgent need to leave for distant Echizen Province. As

---

11. Sanemori's story is told in *The Tale of the Heike* and in a Noh play by Zeami.

12. "Like paired geese parting in the clouds" recalls a poem of Basho's written while still in his
teens following the death of his lord, Yoshitada; it also carries echoes of Tu Fu.

13. "Now falling autumn dew / obliterates my hatband's / 'We are two'" It was a custom for
travelers to wear inscribed hatbands saying that they traveled "with the Buddha," thereby reducing risks.

I prepared to leave the temple, two young monks arrived with ink stone and paper in hand. Outside, willow leaves fell in the wind.

> Sweep the garden
> all kindnesses
> falling willow leaves repay

My sandals already on, I wrote it quickly and departed.

*   *   *

At the Echizen province border, at an inlet town called Yoshizaki, I hired a boat and sailed for the famous pines of Shiogoshi. Saigyō wrote:

> All the long night
> salt-winds drive
> storm-tossed waves
> and moonlight drips
> through Shiogoshi pines

This one poem says enough. To add another would be like adding a sixth finger to a hand.[14]

*   *   *

Mount Shirane faded behind us and Mount Hina began to appear. We crossed Asamuzu Bridge and saw the legendary "reeds of Tamae" in bloom. We crossed Uguisu Barrier at Yuno-o Pass and passed by the ruins of Hiuchi Castle. On Returning Hill we heard the first wild geese of autumn. We arrived at Tsuruga Harbor on the evening of the fourteenth day of the eighth moon. The harbor moonlight was marvelously bright.

I asked at the inn, "Will we have this view tomorrow night?" The innkeeper said, "Can't guarantee weather in Koshiji. It may be clear, but then again it may turn overcast. It may rain." We drank sake with the innkeeper, then paid a late visit to the Kehi Myōjin Shrine honoring the second-century Emperor Chūai. A great spirituality—moonlight in pines, white sands like a touch of frost. In ancient times Yugyō, the second high priest, himself cleared away the grounds, carried stones, and built drains. To this day, people carry sands to the shrine. "*Yugyō-no-sunamochi,*" the innkeeper explained, "Yugyō's sand-bringing."

> Transparent moonlight
> shines over Yugyō's sand
> perfectly white

*   *   *

On the fifteenth, just as the innkeeper warned, it rained:

---

14. "To add another would be like adding a sixth finger to a hand." This image is derived from *Chuang Tzu*, chapter 8.

Harvest moon —
true North Country weather —
nothing to view

*　　*　　*

A disciple, Rotsū, had come to Tsuruga to travel with me to Mino Province. We rode horses into the castle town of Ōgaki. Sora returned from Ise, joined by Etsujin, also riding a horse. We gathered at the home of Jokō, a retired samurai. Lord Zensen, the Keiko family men, and other friends arrived by day and night, all to welcome me as though I'd come back from the dead. A wealth of affection!

Still exhausted and weakened from my long journey, on the sixth day of the darkest month, I felt moved to visit Ise Shrine, where a twenty-one-year Rededication Ceremony was about to get under way. At the beach, in the boat, I wrote:

Clam ripped from its shell
I move on to Futami Bay:
passing autumn

■ Matsuo Basho and His School (linked verse)

TRANSLATED BY EARL MINER AND HIROKO ODAGIRI

During the seventeenth and eighteenth centuries, the art of haikai, or sequential composition of individual poems, evolved from an amusement to a serious pastime in which a number of poets would collaborate to create an individual sequence. Of the haikai poets, Matsuo Basho is considered Japan's finest. *Throughout the Town,* composed in 1690, is a kazen, or sequence of thirty six stanzas. A haiku is a three-line poem of 5–7–5 syllables, and a tanka adds two lines of 7 syllables each to that; in a sense, then, these are the building blocks from which Basho's school made its haikai. An initial stanza of 5–7–5 is joined to a lower stanza of 7–7, then that stanza of 7–7 syllables is joined to another stanza of 5–7–5, then another of 7–7 is joined in turn to that, and so the sequence is extended. The initial stanza, or hokku, is considered so important that it was sometimes thought of as an independent poem, like modern haiku, which share the hokku's syllabic form.

FURTHER READING: Keene, Donald. *World within Walls: Japanese Literature of the Pre-Modern Era, 1600–1867,* 1976. Mayhew, Lenore, tr. *Monkey's Raincoat = Sarumino: Linked Poetry of the Basho School with Haiku Selections,* 1985. Miner, Earl, and Hiroko Odagiri, trs., *The Monkey's Straw Raincoat and Other Poetry of the Basho School.* Introduced and translated by Earl Miner and Hiroko Odagiri, 1981.

from **Throughout the Town**

1

Throughout the town
above the welter of smelly things
the summer moon

BONCHŌ

2

Throughout the town
above the welter of smelly things
the summer moon
how hot it is, how hot it is
says a voice at every house gate

BASHŌ

3

How hot it is, how hot it is
says a voice at every farm gate
although the weeds
have not been worked a second time
the rice comes into ear

KYORAI

4

Although the weeds
have not been worked a second time
the rice has come to ear
the charcoal ash is shaken off
the dried sardine broiled at noon

BONCHŌ

5

The charcoal ash is shaken off
the dried sardine broiled at noon

but in this back country
the use of coins is not yet heard of
what a bother it is

BASHŌ

6

In this back country
the use of coins is not yet heard of
what a bother it is
but he is an odd one to be talking
and swagger with an enormous sword

KYORAI

7

He is an odd one to carry on
swaggering with an enormous sword
he quakes in fright
from a frog croaking in the weeds
as twilight thickens

BONCHŌ

8

She jumps with fright
at the frog's croaking in the weeds
as twilight thickens
so in search of butterburr shoots
her shaking hand puts out the lamp

BASHŌ

9

While hunting butterburr shoots
I shook the lamp and put it out
my waking to the Way
came long ago at that season
of budding flowers

KYORAI

10

His waking to the Way
came long ago at that season
   of budding flowers
now at Nanao Bay in Noto
the winter cold is hard to bear

BONCHŌ

11

At Nanao Bay in Noto
the winter cold is hard to bear
   all that I can do
is suck upon the bones of fish
   and think of old age

BASHŌ

12

All that he can do
is suck upon the bones of fish
   thinking of his age
as he lets the mistress' lover
through the side gate with his key

KYORAI

13

The mistress' lover was let in
through the side gate with a key
   stretching for a peek
the young maidservants overturn
   the folding screen

BONCHŌ

14

As they stretch forward
the young maidservants overturn
   the folding screen

the split bamboo drainboard gives
a forlorn appearance to the bath

BASHŌ

15

The split bamboo drainboard gave
a forlorn appearance to the bath
        and to the seeds of fennel
that are all blown off their plants
        by the evening storm

KYORAI

16

    The seeds of fennel
are all blown off their plants
        by the evening storm
will the priest return to the temple
as he feels the cold increasing

BONCHŌ

17

Will the priest return to the temple
as he feels the cold increasing
        the monkey master
ages with his monkey and the world
        beneath the autumn moon

BASHŌ

■ Chikamatsu Monzaemon (1653–1725) (play, prose)

TRANSLATED BY DONALD KEENE

Chikamatsu Monzaemon has often been called the Japanese Shakespeare, and his play *The Love Suicides at Amijima* is considered to be his masterpiece. But the theater of Chikamatsu was considerably different from that of Shakespeare. He wrote most of his hundred-odd plays for the puppet theater (*joruri*, now called *bunraku*), in which a chanter performs all roles and all voices, accompanied by the music of a *samisen* (something like a small guitar), while black-clothed handlers move the jointed wooden puppets across the stage.

Chikamatsu was born in Echizen province to a lesser samurai family, which moved to Kyoto when he was in his teens. He writes of his life, "I was born into a hereditary family of samurai but left the martial profession. I served in personal attendance on the nobility but never obtained the least court rank. I drifted in the market place but learned nothing of trade."[1] He was born Sugimori Nobumori but apparently took the stage name Chikamatsu after staying at Chikamatsu Temple in Omi province when young. His play *Kagekiyo Victorious* transformed the puppet theater from rudimentary skits to what it is now. For a period of his life, he wrote for the live actor theater (kabuki), tailoring his plays to fit Sakata Tojuro, the premier actor of his day. He wrote *The Love Suicides at Amijima* in 1703, which was a great success; after Sakata Tojuro retired in 1705, Chikamatsu devoted himself to the puppet theater for the remainder of his life.

Like the other dramatists of his day, Chikamatsu would often dramatize recent sensational events in his play. In the case of *The Love Suicides at Amijima,* he actually interviewed people associated with the case. The tragic crux of his plays often lies in the conflict between the culturally powerful concept of *giri,* or duty, and natural human emotions. Since what constitutes such obligation and its hold over people is necessarily culture bound, there are times when modern Western readers (or viewers) of his plays will find themselves frustrated, but no more frustrated, ultimately, than they are by examples of duty that seem exaggerated and outmoded in the Western tradition, such as the Puritan *giri* of Nathaniel Hawthorne's Hester Prynne, which keeps her suffering in a repressive and narrow-minded society long after any external constraints on her have faded. Chikamatsu's plays are remarkably modern to Western tastes in part because they represent ordinary people, prostitutes and oil shop attendants, as seriously as Shakespeare would have written of royalty, and with the zest of Shakespeare's Falstaff.

FURTHER READING: Dunn, C. J. *The Early Japanese Puppet Drama,* 1966. Keene, Donald. *The Battles of Coxinga: Chikamatsu's Puppet Play, Its Background and Importance,* 1951; *Bunraku: The Art of the Japanese Puppet Theatre,* 1965; tr. *Four Major Plays of Chikamatsu,* 1961; tr. *Major Plays of Chikamatsu,* 1961. Shively, Donald H., tr. *The Love Suicides at Amijima,* 1953.

---

1. Donald Keene, tr. *Four Major Plays of Chikamatsu* (New York: Columbia University Press, 1961), 3.

The Love Suicides at Amijima

First performed on January 3, 1721. No source for this play, often acclaimed as Chikamatsu's masterpiece, has been determined, but traditional (though unreliable) accounts state that the suicides at Amijima occurred on November 13, 1720, one day earlier than in the drama. Takano Masami, a recent Japanese critic, has suggested that *The Love Suicides at Amijima* was a reworking of *The Love Suicides at Umeda* (1706) by Chikamatsu's rival, Ki no Kaion. There are striking points of resemblance between the two plays, and it may be that Chikamatsu, when shaping into dramatic form the events that took place at Amijima, borrowed from the earlier work. Chikamatsu's play has in turn been many times revised. The version most commonly performed today dates from the early nineteenth century.

CAST OF CHARACTERS
Kamiya Jihei, aged 28, a paper merchant
Konaya Magoemon, his brother, a flour merchant
Gozaemon, Jihei's father-in-law
Tahei, a rival for Koharu
Dembei, proprietor of the Yamato House
Sangoro, Jihei's servant
Kantarō, aged 6, Jihei's son
A Minstrel Priest
Porters, Fishermen, Persons of the Quarter
Koharu, aged 19, a courtesan at the Kinokuni House in Sonezaki
Osan, Jihei's wife
Osan's Mother (who is also Jihei's aunt), aged 56
Osue, aged 4, Jihei's daughter
Proprietress at Kawachi House
Kiyo, a receptionist
Tama, Osan's servant
Sugi, Koharu's maid
Maids, Prostitutes, Servants

ACT ONE

Scene One:

A street in Sonezaki New Quarter, Osaka.

TIME:
November 4, 1720.

NARRATOR:
Sanjo bakkara fungoro nokkoro
Chokkoro fungoro de
Mate tokkoro wakkara yukkuru

Wakkara yukkuru ta ga
Kasa wo wanga ranga ra su
Sora ga kunguru kunguru mo
Renge rengere bakkara fungoro.[1]

The love of a prostitute is deep beyond measure; it's a bottomless sea of affection that cannot be emptied or dried. By Shell River,[2] love songs in every mood fill the air, and hearts stop short at the barrier[3] of doorway lanterns. Men roam the streets in high spirits, humming snatches of puppet plays, mimicking the actors, or singing bawdy ballads as they pass; others are drawn into the houses by samisens played in upstairs rooms. But here is a visitor who hides his face, avoiding the gift day.[4] See how he creeps along, afraid to be forced into spending too much!

Kiyo, the receptionist, notices him.[5]

KIYO: Who's this trying to avoid me?

NARRATOR: She snatches again and again at his hood-flap; he dodges her twice or thrice, but this is a valuable customer, and she refuses to let him escape. At last she pounces on him with the cry:

KIYO: No more of your nonsense! Come along!

NARRATOR: And the customer, caught flap and cap, is trapped into folly by this female Kagekiyo.

Among the flowers on display—even the bridges are called Plum and Cherry Blossom—[6] here is Koharu of the Kinokuni House, now graduated from the smock of a bath attendant in the South[7] to the garments of love in the New Quarter. Is her name "Second Spring"[8] a sign that she is fated to leave behind a fleeting name in November?

---

1. Japanese scholars have puzzled over these curious syllables for years, and many explanations of them have been offered. Their meaning, if any, is less important than the lively rhythm, which evokes the atmosphere of the Sonezaki Quarter.

2. Shijimi River, frequently mentioned in the course of the play, flowed along the border of the Sonezaki Quarter. Its name *shijimi* means the *corbicula*, a small mollusc related to the clam. There is a play on words here: the sea cannot be emptied by ladling it with tiny clam shells.

3. A play on words: *moji ga seki* (the barrier of Chinese characters) suggests that customers stop short when they read on doorway lanterns the names in characters of their favorite teahouses; *Moji ga seki* (the Barrier of Moji) refers to the Straits of Shimonoseki.

4. Festive days in the gay quarter on which customers were required to make presents to the teahouses. For a detailed description, see Donald H. Shively, *The Love Suicides at Amijima*, p. 100.

5. The following few lines are based on a passage in the Nō play *Kagekiyo*. See Arthur Waley, *The No Plays of Japan*, p. 98. The maid's name Kiyo suggests that of Kagekiyo, and the effect is one of burlesque.

6. References to Umeda Bridge and Sakura Bridge over the Shijimi River.

7. The "south" refers to Shimanouchi Quarter, a section of low-class brothels which originally had been bathhouses. Sonezaki Quarter was north of this section.

8. The name Koharu, literally "little spring," means Indian summer.

"Who has sent for me tonight?" she wonders, uncertain as a dove in the uncertain light of a standing lantern. A prostitute passes her, then turns back.

PROSTITUTE: Is that you, Koharu? Where have you been keeping yourself? We don't get invited to the same parties any more, and I never see you or hear a word from you. Have you been sick? Your face looks thinner. Somebody was telling me that the master at your place now gives all your customers a thorough examination and hardly lets you out of the house, all on account of your Kamiji.[9] But I've also heard that you're to be ransomed by Tahei and go live with him in the country—in Itami, was it? Is it true?

KOHARU: I'd be much obliged if you'd please stop talking about Itami! The relations between Jihei and myself, I'm sorry to say, are not as close as people suppose. It's that loud-mouthed Tahei who's started the rumors and spread them everywhere, until every last customer has deserted me. The master blames Kamiya Jihei, and he's done everything to keep us from meeting. Why, I'm not even allowed to receive letters from Jihei. Tonight, strangely enough, I've been sent to Kawasho.[10] My customer's a samurai, I'm told. But I keep worrying that I might meet that dreadful Tahei on the way. I feel exactly as if I had some mortal enemy. Do you suppose he might be over there?

PROSTITUTE: If you feel that way about Tahei, you'd better hide quickly. Look—coming out of the first block—there's one of those street minstrels, singing his nonsense hymns.[11] I can see in the crowd round him a dissolute-looking fellow with his hair tricked up in some funny style— the stuck-up swell! I'm sure it's Tahei. Oh—they're heading this way!

NARRATOR: A moment later the defrocked priest, in a flat cap and ink-black robes with the sleeves tucked back, comes bumbling along, surrounded by a crowd of idlers. He bangs at random on his bell, mixing his nonsense with the burden of a hymn.

MINSTREL:
"Fan Kuai's style was no great shakes—
See how Asahina of Japan used to break down gates!"
He rips through the gate bars and tangle of felled trees,
Slays Uryōko and Saryōko and passes the barrier,
As time passes by.[12]
Namamida Namaida Namamida Namaida.
Ei Ei Ei Ei Ei.

---

9. A familiar contraction for Kamiya Jihei.

10. A contraction of Kawachi House and the owner's name, which began with the syllable "Shō."

11. Sections from popular puppet dramas with a quasi-religious refrain.

12. Adapted from *The Battles of Coxinga*. Keene, *Four Major Plays of Chikamatsu*, p. 118.

"Though I wander all over,
The sad world holds no one
Who looks like my dear Matsuyama!"[13]
—He weeps, he howls, only to burst into laughs.
"How wretched that I must end my life in madness!"
He falls prostrate, the grass for his pallet,
A sight too sad for the eyes to behold.
Namamida Namaida Namamida Namaida.
Ei Ei Ei Ei Ei.
Tokubei of the dyer's shop,
Since he first fell in love with Fusa,
Has yielded to passion that absorbs his fortune,
A love stained so deep lye itself cannot cleanse it.[14]
Namamida Namaida Namamida Namaida
Namamida Namaida.

SUGI: Excuse me, priest.

MINSTREL: What is it?

SUGI: It's bad luck to sing those songs, just when stories about love suicides in the Quarter have at last quieted down. Why don't you give us instead a *nembutsu* song on the journey from *The Battles of Coxinga?*

NARRATOR: Sugi offers him some coins from her sleeve.

MINSTREL:
For a mere one or two coppers
You can't expect to travel all the way,
Three thousand leagues to the Land of Great Ming!
It doesn't pay, it doesn't pray Amida Buddha.

NARRATOR: Grumbling in this strain, he moves on.

Scene Two:

The Kawachi House, a Sonezaki teahouse.

NARRATOR: Koharu slips away, under cover of the crowd, and hurries into the Kawachi House.

---

13. From the play *Wankyū Sue no Matsuyama* (1707). See Shively, p. 104.

14. From the festive epilogue to "Yosaku from Tamba," in Keene, *Major Plays of Chikamatsu*, and see also Shively, pp. 104–105.

PROPRIETRESS: Well, well, I hadn't expected you so soon.—It's been ages even since I've heard your name mentioned. What a rare visitor you are, Koharu! And what a long time it's been!

NARRATOR: The proprietress greets Koharu cheerfully.

KOHARU: Oh—you can be heard as far as the gate. Please don't call me Koharu in such a loud voice. That horrible Ri Tōten[15] is out there. I beg you, keep your voice down.

NARRATOR: Were her words overheard? In bursts a party of three men.

TAHEI: I must thank you first of all, dear Koharu, for bestowing a new name on me, Ri Tōten. I never was called *that* before. Well, friends, this is the Koharu I've confided to you about—the goodhearted, good-natured, good-in-bed Koharu. Step up and meet the whore who's started all the rivalry! Will I soon be the lucky man and get Koharu for my wife? Or will Kamiya Jihei ransom her?

NARRATOR: He swaggers up.

KOHARU: I don't want to hear another word. If you think it's such an achievement to start unfounded rumors about someone you don't even know, throw yourself into it, say what you please. But I don't want to hear.

NARRATOR: She steps away suddenly, but he sidles up again.

TAHEI: You may not want to hear me, but the clink of my gold coins will make you listen! What a lucky girl you are! Just think—of all the many men in Temma and the rest of Osaka, you chose Jihei the paper dealer, the father of two children, with his cousin for his wife and his uncle for his father-in-law! A man whose business is so tight he's at his wits' ends every sixty days merely to pay the wholesalers' bills! Do you think he'll be able to fork over nearly ten *kamme*[16] to ransom you? That reminds me of the mantis who picked a fight with an oncoming vehicle![17] But look at me—I haven't a wife, a father-in-law, a father, or even an uncle, for that matter. Tahei the Lone Wolf—that's the name I'm known by. I admit that I'm no match for Jihei when it comes to bragging about myself in the Quarter, but when it comes to money, I'm an easy winner. If I pushed with all the strength of my money, who knows what I might conquer?—How about it, men?—Your customer tonight, I'm sure, is

---

15. The villain of the play *The Battles of Coxinga*. See Keene, pp. 60 ff.

16. This would amount to over $5,000 in current purchasing power. The price is unusually high; no doubt Tahei is exaggerating.

17. A simile, derived ultimately from ancient Chinese texts, for someone who does not know his own limitations. See Shively, p. 107.

none other than Jihei, but I'm taking over. The Lone Wolf's taking over. Hostess! Bring on the saké! On with the saké!

PROPRIETRESS: What are you saying? Her customer tonight is a samurai, and he'll be here any moment. Please amuse yourself elsewhere.

NARRATOR: But Tahei's look is playful.

TAHEI: A customer's a customer, whether he's a samurai or a townsman. The only difference is that one wears swords and the other doesn't. But even if this samurai wears his swords he won't have five or six — there'll only be two, the broadsword and dirk. I'll take care of the samurai and borrow Koharu afterwards. (*To Koharu.*) You may try to avoid me all you please, but some special connection from a former life must have brought us together. I owe everything to that ballad-singing priest — what a wonderful thing the power of prayer is! I think I'll recite a prayer of my own. Here, this ashtray will be my bell, and my pipe the hammer. This is fun.

> *Chan Chan Cha Chan Chan.*
> *Ei Ei Ei Ei Ei.*
> Jihei the paper dealer —
> Too much love for Koharu
> Has made him a foolscap,
> He wastepapers sheets of gold
> Till his fortune's shredded to confetti
> And Jihei himself is like scrap paper
> You can't even blow your nose on!
> Hail, Hail Amida Buddha!
> Namaida Namaida Namaida.

NARRATOR: As he prances wildly, roaring his song, a man appears at the gate, so anxious not to be recognized that he wears, even at night, a wicker hat.[18]

TAHEI: Well, Toilet paper's showed up! That's quite a disguise! Why don't you come in, Toilet paper? If my prayer's frightened you, say a Hail Amida![19] Here, I'll take off your hat!

NARRATOR: He drags the man in and examines him: it is the genuine article, a two-sworded samurai, somber in dress and expression, who glares at Tahei through his woven hat, his eyeballs round as gongs. Tahei, unable to utter either a Hail or an Amida, gasps "Haaa!" in dismay, but his face is unflinching.

---

18. Customers visiting the Quarter by day wear these deep wicker hats (which virtually conceal the face) in order to preserve the secrecy of their visits; but this customer wears a hat even at night, when the darkness normally is sufficient protection.

19. A play on words devolving on the syllables *ami*, part of the name Amida and on *amigasa*, meaning "woven hat."

TAHEI: Koharu, I'm a townsman. I've never worn a sword, but I've lots of New Silver[20] at my place, and I think that the glint could twist a mere couple of swords out of joint. Imagine that wretch from the toilet paper shop, with a capital as thin as tissue, trying to compete with the Lone Wolf! That's the height of impertinence! I'll wander down now from Sakura Bridge to Middle Street, and if I meet that Wastepaper along the way, I'll trample him under foot. Come on, men.

NARRATOR: Their gestures, at least, have a cavalier assurance as they swagger off, taking up the whole street.

    The samurai customer patiently endures the fool, indifferent to his remarks because of the surroundings, but every word of gossip about Jihei, whether for good or ill, affects Koharu. She is so depressed that she stands there blankly, unable even to greet her guest. Sugi, the maid from the Kinokuni House, runs up from home, looking annoyed.

SUGI: When I left you here a while ago, Miss Koharu, your guest hadn't appeared yet, and they gave me a terrible scolding when I got back for not having checked on him. I'm very sorry, sir, but please excuse me a minute.

NARRATOR: She lifts the woven hat and examines the face.

SUGI: Oh—it's not him! There's nothing to worry about, Koharu. Ask your guest to keep you for the whole night, and show him how sweet you can be. Give him a barrelful of nectar![21] Good-by, madam, I'll see you later, honey.

NARRATOR: She takes her leave with a cloying stream of puns. The extremely hard-baked[22] samurai is furious.

SAMURAI: What's the meaning of this? You'd think from the way she appraised my face that I was a tea canister or a porcelain cup! I didn't come here to be trifled with. It's difficult enough for me to leave the Residence even by day, and in order to spend the night away I had to ask the senior officer's permission and sign the register. You can see how complicated the regulations make things. But I'm in love, miss, just from hearing about you, and I wanted very badly to spend a night with you. I came here a while ago without an escort and made the arrangements with the teahouse. I had been looking forward to your kind reception, a memory to last me a lifetime, but you haven't so much as smiled at me or said a word of greeting. You keep your head

---

20. Good-quality coinage of about 1720. It was necessary to specify the kind of silver one meant because devaluations and revaluations altered the value of coins of nominally the same denomination.

21. I have altered the imagery used by the maid from puns on saltiness (soy sauce, green vegetables, etc.) to puns on sweetness, somewhat easier to manage in English.

22. A technical term of pottery making, meaning "hard-fired." Here used to introduce the mention of "tea canister" and "porcelain cup."

down, as if you were counting money in your lap. Aren't you afraid of getting a stiff neck? Madam—I've never heard the like. Here I come to a teahouse, and I must play the part of night nurse in a maternity room!

PROPRIETRESS: You're quite right, sir. Your surprise is entirely justified, considering that you don't know the reasons. This girl is deeply in love with a customer named Kamiji. It's been Kamiji today and Kamiji tomorrow, with nobody else allowed a chance at her. Her other customers have scattered in every direction, like leaves in a storm. When two people get so carried away with each other, it often leads to trouble, for both the customer and the girl. In the first place, it intefers with business, and the owner, whoever he may be, is bound to prevent it. That's why all her guests are examined. Koharu is naturally depressed—it's only to be expected. You are annoyed, which is equally to be expected. But, speaking as the proprietress here, it seems to me that the essential thing is for you to meet each other halfway and cheer up. Come, have a drink.—Act a little more lively, Koharu.

NARRATOR: Koharu, without answering, lifts her tear-stained face.

KOHARU: Tell me, samurai, they say that, if you're going to kill yourself anyway, people who die during the Ten Nights[23] are sure to become Buddhas. Is that really true?

SAMURAI: How should I know? Ask the priest at your family temple.

KOHARU: Yes, that's right. But there's something I'd like to ask a samurai. If you're committing suicide, it'd be a lot more painful, wouldn't it, to cut your throat rather than hang yourself?

SAMURAI: I've never tried cutting my throat to see whether or not it hurt. Please ask more sensible questions.—What an unpleasant girl!

NARRATOR: Samurai though he is, he looks nonplussed.

PROPRIETRESS: Koharu, that's a shocking way to treat a guest the first time you meet him. I'll go and get my husband. We'll have some saké together. That ought to liven things a bit.

NARRATOR: The gate she leaves is illumined by the evening moon low in the sky; the clouds and the passers in the street have thinned.

For long years there has lived in Temma, the seat of the mighty god,[24] though not a god himself, Kamiji,[25] a name often bruited by the

---

23. A period from the sixth to the sixteenth nights of the tenth moon when special Buddhist services were conducted in temples of the Pure Land (Jōdo) Sect. It was believed that persons who died during this period immediately became Buddhas.

24. Temma, one of the principal districts of Osaka, was the site of the Tenjin Shrine, to the memory of the deified Sugawara no Michizane (845–993).

25. The word *kami* for "paper" is the homophone of *kami*, "god." We have thus "Kami who is not a *kami*"—the paper dealer who is not a god.

gongs of worldly gossip, so deeply, hopelessly, is he tied to Koharu by the ropes[26] of an ill-starred love. Now is the tenth moon, the month when no gods will unite them;[27] they are thwarted in their love, unable to meet. They swore in the last letters they exchanged that if only they could meet, that day would be their last. Night after night Jihei, ready for death, trudges to the Quarter, distractedly, as though his soul had left a body consumed by the fires of love.

At a roadside eating stand he hears people gossiping about Koharu. "She's at Kawasho with a samurai customer," someone says, and immediately Jihei decides, "It will be tonight!"

He peers through the latticework window and sees a guest in the inside room, his face obscured by a hood. Only the moving chin is visible, and Jihei cannot hear what is said.

JIHEI: Poor Koharu! How thin her face is! She keeps it averted from the lamp. In her heart she's thinking only of me. I'll signal her that I'm here, and we'll run off together. Then which will it be—Umeda or Kitano?[28] Oh—I want to tell her I'm here. I want to call her.

NARRATOR: He beckons with his heart, his spirit flies to her, but his body, like a cicada's cast-off shell, clings to the latticework. He weeps with impatience.

The guest in the inside room gives a great yawn.

SAMURAI: What a bore, playing nursemaid to a prostitute with worries on her mind!—The street seems quiet now. Let's go to the end room. We can at least distract ourselves by looking at the lanterns. Come with me.

NARRATOR: They go together to the outer room. Jihei, alarmed, squeezes into the patch of shadow under the lattice window. Inside they do not realize that anyone eavesdrops.

SAMURAI: I've been noticing your behavior and the little things you've said this evening. It's plain to me that you intend a love suicide with Kamiji, or whatever his name is—the man the hostess mentioned. I'm sure I'm right. I realize that no amount of advice or reasoning is likely to penetrate the ears of somebody bewitched by the god of death, but I must say that you're exceedingly foolish. The boy's family won't blame him for his recklessness, but they will blame and hate you. You'll be shamed by the public exposure of your body. Your parents may be dead, for all I know, but if they're alive, you'll be punished in hell as a wicked daughter. Do you suppose that you'll become a Buddha? You and your

---

26. The sacred ropes (*mishimenawa*) at a Shinto shrine. Here mentioned (like the gongs) as a word related to the imagery of Shinto.

27. The tenth month, called *kannazuki* (literally "month of no gods") was a time when the gods were believed to gather at Izumo; they were thus absent from the rest of Japan.

28. Both places had well-known cemeteries.

lover won't even be able to fall smoothly into hell together! What a pity—and what a tragedy! This is only our first meeting but, as a samurai, I can't let you die without trying to save you. No doubt money's the problem. I'd like to help, if five or ten *ryō* would be of service. I swear by the god Hachiman and by my good fortune as a samurai that I will never reveal to anyone what you tell me. Open your heart without fear.

NARRATOR: He whispers these words. She joins her hands and bows.

KOHARU: I'm extremely grateful. Thank you for your kind words and for swearing an oath to me, someone you've never had for a lover or even a friend. I'm so grateful that I'm crying.—Yes, it's as they say, when you've something on your mind it shows on your face. You were right. I have promised Kamiji to die with him. But we've been completely prevented from meeting by my master, and Jihei, for various reasons, can't ransom me at once. My contracts with my former master[29] and my present one still have five years to run. If somebody else claimed me during that time, it would be a blow to me, of course, but a worse disgrace to Jihei's honor. He suggested that it would be better if we killed ourselves, and I agreed. I was caught by obligations from which I could not withdraw, and I promised him before I knew what I was doing. I said, "We'll watch for a chance, and I'll slip out when you give the signal." "Yes," he said, "slip out somehow." Ever since then I've been leading a life of uncertainty, never knowing from one day to the next when my last hour will come.

I have a mother living in a back alley south of here. She has no one but me to depend on, and she does piecework to eke out a living. I keep thinking that after I'm dead she'll become a beggar or an outcast, and maybe she'll die of starvation. That's the only sad part about dying. I have just this one life. I'm ashamed that you may think me a coldhearted woman, but I must endure the shame. The most important thing is that I don't want to die. I beg you, please help me to stay alive.

NARRATOR: As she speaks the samurai nods thoughtfully. Jihei, crouching outside, hears her words with astonishment; they are so unexpected to his manly heart that he feels like a monkey who has tumbled from a tree. He is frantic with agitation.

JIHEI (*to himself*): Then was everything a lie? Ahhh—I'm furious! For two whole years I've been bewitched by that rotten she-fox! Shall I break in and kill her with one blow of my sword? Or shall I satisfy my anger by shaming her to her face?

NARRATOR: He gnashes his teeth and weeps in chagrin. Inside the house Koharu speaks through her tears.

---

29. The master at the bathhouse where Koharu formerly worked.

KOHARU: It's a curious thing to ask, but would you please show the kindness of a samurai and become my customer for the rest of this year and into next spring? Whenever Jihei comes, intent on death, please interfere and force him to postpone and postpone his plan. In this way our relations can be broken quite naturally. He won't have to kill himself, and my life will also be saved.—What evil connection from a former existence made us promise to die? How I regret it now!

NARRATOR: She weeps, leaning on the samurai's knee.

SAMURAI: Very well, I'll do as you ask. I think I can help you.—But there's a draft blowing. Somebody may be watching.

NARRATOR: He slams shut the latticework *shōji*. Jihei, listening outside, is in a frenzy.

JIHEI: Exactly what you'd expect from a whore, a cheap whore! I misjudged her foul nature. She robbed the soul from my body, the thieving harlot! Shall I slash her down or run her through? What am I to do?

NARRATOR: The shadows of two profiles fall on the *shōji*.

JIHEI: I'd like to give her a taste of my fist and trample her.—What are they chattering about? See how they nod to each other! Now she's bowing to him, whispering and sniveling. I've tried to control myself—I've pressed my chest, I've stroked it—but I can't stand any more. This is too much to endure!

NARRATOR: His heart pounds wildly as he unsheathes his dirk, a Magoroku of Seki. "Koharu's side must be here," he judges, and stabs through an opening in the latticework. But Koharu is too far away for his thrust, and though she cries out in terror, she remains unharmed. Her guest instantly leaps at Jihei, grabs his hands, and jerks them through the latticework. With his sword knot he quickly and securely fastens Jihei's hands to the window upright.

SAMURAI: Don't make any outcry, Koharu. You are not to look at him.

NARRATOR: At this moment the proprietor and his wife return. They exclaim in alarm.

SAMURAI: This needn't concern you. Some ruffian ran his sword through the *shōji*, and I've tied his arms to the latticework. I have my own way of dealing with him. Don't untie the cord. If you attract a crowd, the place is sure to be thrown in an uproar. Let's all go inside. Come with me, Koharu. We'll go to bed.

NARRATOR: Koharu answers, "Yes," but she recognizes the handle of the dirk, and the memory—if not the blade—transfixes her breast.

KOHARU: There's always people doing crazy things in the Quarter when they've had too much to drink. Why don't you let him go without making any trouble? I think that's best, don't you, Kawasho?

SAMURAI: Out of the question. Do as I say—inside, all of you. Koharu, come along.

NARRATOR: Jihei can still see their shadows even after they enter the inner room, but he is bound to the spot, his hands held in fetters which grip him the tighter as he struggles, his body beset by suffering as he tastes a living shame worse than a dog's.[30] More determined than ever to die, he sheds tears of blood, a pitiful sight.

Tahei the Lone Wolf returns from his carousing.

TAHEI: That's Jihei standing by Kawasho's window. I'll give him a tossing.

NARRATOR: He catches Jihei by the collar and starts to lift him over his back.

JIHEI: Owww!

TAHEI: Owww? What kind of weakling are you? Oh, I see—you're tied here. You must've been pulling off a robbery. You dirty pickpocket! You rotten pickpocket!

NARRATOR: He drubs Jihei mercilessly.

TAHEI: You burglar! You convict!

NARRATOR: He kicks him wildly.

TAHEI: Kamiya Jihei's been caught burgling, and they've tied him up!

NARRATOR: Passersby and people of the neighborhood, attracted by his shouts, quickly gather. The samurai rushes from the house.

SAMURAI: Who's calling him a burglar? You? Tell what Jihei's stolen! Out with it!

NARRATOR: He seizes Tahei and forces him into the dirt. Tahei rises to his feet only for the samurai to kick him down again and again. He grips Tahei.

SAMURAI: Jihei! Trample him to your heart's content!

NARRATOR: He pushes Tahei under Jihei's feet. Bound though he is, Jihei stamps furiously over Tahei's face. Tahei, thoroughly trampled and covered with mire, gets to his feet and glares around him.

TAHEI (*to bystander*): How could you fools stand there calmly and let him step on me? I've memorized every one of your faces, and I intend to pay you back. Remember that!

NARRATOR: He makes his escape, still determined to have the last word. The spectators burst out laughing.

---

30. A proverb of Buddhist origin, "Suffering follows one like a dog," is imbedded in the text.

VOICES: Listen to him brag, even after he's been trampled on! Let's throw him from the bridge and give him a drink of water! Don't let him get away!

NARRATOR: They chase after him. When the crowd has dispersed, the samurai approaches Jihei and unfastens the knots. He shows his face with his hood removed.

JIHEI: Magoemon! My brother! How shaming!

NARRATOR: He sinks to the ground and weeps, prostrating himself in the dirt.

KOHARU: Are you his brother, sir?

NARRATOR: Koharu runs to them. Jihei, catching her by the front of the kimono, forces her to the ground.

JIHEI: Beast! She-fox! I'd sooner trample on you than on Tahei!

NARRATOR: He raises his foot, but Magoemon calls out.

MAGOEMON: That's the kind of foolishness responsible for all your trouble. A prostitute's business is to deceive men. Have you just now waked up to that? I've seen to the bottom of her heart the very first time I met her, but you're so scatter-brained that in over two years of intimacy with the woman you never discovered what she was thinking. Instead of stamping on Koharu, why don't you use your feet on your own misguided disposition? — It's deplorable. You're my younger brother, but you're almost thirty, and you've got a six-year-old boy and a four-year-old girl, Kantarō and Osue. You run a shop with a thirty-six foot frontage[31] but you don't seem to realize that your whole fortune's collapsing. You shouldn't have to be lectured to by your brother. Your father-in-law is your aunt's husband, and your mother-in-law is your aunt. They've always been like real parents to you. Your wife Osan is my cousin too. The ties of marriage are multiplied by those of blood. But when the family has a reunion the only subject of discussion is our mortification over your incessant visits to Sonezaki. I feel sorry for our poor aunt. You know what a stiff-necked gentleman of the old school her husband Gozaemon is. He's forever flying into a rage and saying, "We've been tricked by your nephew. He's deserted our daughter. I'll take Osan back and ruin Jihei's reputation throughout Temma." Our aunt, with all the heartache to bear herself, sometimes sides with him and sometimes with you. She's worried herself sick. What an ingrate, not to appreciate how she's defended you in your shame! This one offense is enough to make you the target for Heaven's future punishment!

---

31. It was customary to refer to the size of shops by giving their frontage on the street.

I realized that your marriage couldn't last much longer at this rate. I decided, in the hopes of relieving our aunt's worries, that I'd see with my own eyes what kind of woman Koharu was, and work out some sort of solution afterwards. I consulted the proprietor here, then came myself to investigate the cause of your sickness. I see now how natural it was that you should desert your wife and children. What a faithful prostitute you discovered! I congratulate you!

And here I am, Magoemon the Miller,[32] known far and wide for my paragon of a brother, dressed up like a masquerader at a festival or maybe a lunatic! I put on swords for the first time in my life, and announced myself, like a bit player in a costume piece, as an officer at a residence. I feel like an absolute idiot with these swords, but there's nowhere I can dispose of them now.—It's so infuriating—and ridiculous—that it's given me a pain in the chest.

NARRATOR: He gnashes his teeth and grimaces, attempting to hide his tears. Koharu, choking the while with emotion, can only say:

KOHARU: Yes, you're entirely right.

NARRATOR: The rest is lost in tears. Jihei pounds the earth with his fist.

JIHEI: I was wrong. Forgive me, Magoemon. For three years I've been possessed by that witch. I've neglected my parents, relatives—even my wife and children—and wrecked my fortune, all because I was deceived by Koharu, that sneak thief! I'm utterly mortified. But I'm through with her now, and I'll never set foot here again. Weasel! Vixen! Sneak thief! Here's proof that I've broken with her!

NARRATOR: He pulls out the amulet bag which has rested next to his skin.

JIHEI: Here are the written oaths we've exchanged, one at the beginning of each month, twenty-nine in all. I return them. This means our love and affection are over. Take them.

NARRATOR: He flings the notes at her.

JIHEI: Magoemon, collect from her my pledges. Please make sure you get them all. Then burn them with your own hands. (*To Koharu.*) Hand them to my brother.

KOHARU: As you wish.

NARRATOR: In tears, she surrenders the amulet bag. Magoemon opens it.

MAGOEMON: One, two, three, four . . . ten . . . twenty-nine. They're all here. There's also a letter from a woman. What's this?

NARRATOR: He starts to unfold it.

---

32. Magoemon is a dealer in flour (for noodles). His shop name Konaya—"the flour merchant"—is used almost as a surname, in the manner that Jihei is known as Kamiya Jihei.

KOHARU: That's an important letter. I can't let you see it.

NARRATOR: She clings to Magoemon's arm, but he pushes her away. He holds the letter to the lamplight and examines the address, "To Miss Koharu from Kamiya Osan." As soon as he reads the words, he casually thrusts the letter into his kimono.

MAGOEMON: Koharu. A while ago I swore by my good fortune as a samurai, but now Magoemon the Miller swears by his good fortune as a businessman that he will show this letter to no one, not even his wife. I alone will read it, then burn it with the oaths. You can trust me. I will not break this oath.

KOHARU: Thank you. You save my honor.

NARRATOR: She bursts into tears again.

JIHEI (*laughs contemptuously*): Save your honor! You talk like a human being! (*To Magoemon.*) I don't want to see her cursed face another minute. Let's go. No—I can't hold so much resentment and bitterness! I'll kick her one in the face, a memory to treasure for the rest of my life. Excuse me, please.

NARRATOR: He strides up to Koharu and stamps on the ground.

JIHEI: For three years I've loved you, delighted in you, longed for you, adored you, but today my foot will say my only farewells.

NARRATOR: He kicks her sharply on the forehead and bursts into tears. The brothers leave, forlorn figures. Koharu, unhappy woman, raises her voice in lament as she watches them go. Is she faithful or unfaithful? Her true feelings are hidden in the words penned by Jihei's wife, a letter no one has seen. Jihei goes his separate way without learning the truth.[33]

ACT TWO

SCENE:
The house and shop of Kamiya Jihei.

TIME:
Ten days later.

NARRATOR: The busy street that runs straight to Tenjin Bridge[34] named for the god of Temma, bringer of good fortune, is known as the Street Before the Kami,[35] and here a paper shop does business under the name

---

33. An extremely complicated set of word plays runs through the last two sentences. See Shively, p. 113.

34. The reference is to Temma Tenjin, the name as a deity of Sugawara no Michizane.

35. Again a play on the words *kami* (god) and *kami* (paper).

Kamiya Jihei. The paper is honestly sold, the shop well situated; it is a long-established firm, and customers come thick as raindrops.

Outside crowds pass in the street, on their way to the Ten Nights service, while inside the husband dozes in the kotatsu,[36] shielded from draughts by a screen at his pillow. His wife Osan keeps solitary, anxious watch over shop and house.

OSAN: The days are so short—it's dinnertime already, but Tama still hasn't returned from her errand to Ichinokawa.[37] I wonder what can be keeping her. That scamp Sangorō isn't back either. The wind is freezing. I'm sure the children will both be cold. He doesn't even realize that it's time for Osue to be nursed. Heaven preserve me from ever becoming such a fool! What an infuriating creature!

NARRATOR: She speaks to herself.

KANTARŌ: Mama, I've come back all by myself.

NARRATOR: Her son, the older child, runs up to the house.

OSAN: Kantarō—is that you? What's happened to Osue and Sangorō?

KANTARŌ: They're playing by the shrine. Osue wanted her milk and she was bawling her head off.

OSAN: I was sure she would. Oh—your hands and feet are frozen stiff as nails! Go and warm yourself at the kotatsu. Your father's sleeping there.—What am I to do with that idiot?

NARRATOR: She runs out impatiently to the shop just as Sangorō shuffles back, alone.

OSAN: Come here, you fool! Where have you left Osue?

SANGORŌ: You know, I must've lost her somewhere. Maybe somebody's picked her up. Should I go back for her?

OSAN: How could you? If any harm has come to my precious child, I'll beat you to death!

NARRATOR: But even as she screams at him, the maid Tama returns with Osue on her back.

TAMA: The poor child—I found her in tears at the corner. Sangorō, when you're supposed to look after the child, do it properly.

OSAN: You poor dear. You must want your milk.

NARRATOR: She joins the others by the kotatsu and suckles the child.

---

36. A source of heat in which a charcoal burner is placed under a low, quilt-covered table.

37. Ichinokawa was the site of a large vegetable market near the north end of Tenjin Bridge.

OSAN: Tama—give that fool a taste of something that he'll remember![38]

NARRATOR: Sangorō shakes his head.

SANGORŌ: No, thanks. I gave each of the children two tangerines just a while ago at the shrine, and I tasted five myself.

NARRATOR: Fool though he is, bad puns come from him nimbly enough, and the others can only smile despite themselves.

TAMA: Oh—I've become so involved with this half-wit that I almost forgot to tell you, ma'am, that Mr. Magoemon and his aunt[39] are on their way here from the west.

OSAN: Oh dear! I'll have to wake Jihei in that case. (*To Jihei.*) Please get up. Mother and Magoemon are coming. They'll be upset again if you let them see you, a businessman, sleeping in the afternoon, with the day so short as it is.

JIHEI: All right.

NARRATOR: He struggles to a sitting position and, with his abacus in one hand, pulls his account book to him with the other.

JIHEI: Two into ten goes five, three into nine goes three, three into six goes two, seven times eight is fifty-six.

NARRATOR: His fifty-six-year old aunt enters with Magoemon.

JIHEI: Magoemon, aunt. How good of you. Please come in. I was in the midst of some urgent calculations. Four nines makes thirty-six *momme*. Three sixes make eighteen *fun*. That's two *momme* less two *fun*.[40] Kantarō! Osue! Granny and Uncle have come! Bring the tobacco tray! One times three makes three. Osan, serve the tea![41]

NARRATOR: He jabbers away.

AUNT: We haven't come for tea or tobacco. Osan, you're young I know, but you're the mother of two children, and your excessive forbearance does you no credit. A man's dissipation can always be traced to his wife's carelessness. Remember, it's not only the man who's disgraced when he goes bankrupt and his marriage breaks up. You'd do well to take notice of what's going on and assert yourself a bit more.

MAGOEMON: It's foolish to hope for any results, aunt. The scoundrel even deceives me, his elder brother. Why should he take to heart criticism

---

38. A pun on the two meanings of *kurawasu:* "to cause to eat" and "to beat".

39. Magoemon's (and Jihei's) aunt, but Osan's mother.

40. Meaningless calculations. Twenty *fun* made two *momme*.

41. The name Osan echoes the word *san* (three).

from his wife? Jihei—you played me for a fool. After showing me how you returned Koharu's pledges, here you are, not ten days later, redeeming her! What does this mean? I suppose your urgent calculations are of Koharu's debts! I've had enough!

NARRATOR: He snatches away the abacus and flings it clattering into the hallway.

JIHEI: You're making an enormous fuss without any cause. I haven't crossed the threshold since the last time I saw you except to go twice to the wholesalers in Imabashi and once to the Tenjin Shrine. I haven't even thought of Koharu, much less redeemed her.

AUNT: None of your evasions! Last evening at the Ten Nights service I heard the people in the congregation gossiping. Everybody was talking about the great patron from Temma who'd fallen in love with a prostitute named Koharu from the Kinokuni House in Sonezaki. They said he'd driven away her other guests and was going to ransom her in the next couple of days. There was all kinds of gossip about the abundance of money and fools even in these days of high prices.

My husband Gozaemon has been hearing about Koharu constantly, and he's sure that her great patron from Temma must be you, Jihei. He told me, "He's your nephew, but for me he's a stranger, and my daughter's happiness is my chief concern. Once he ransoms the prostitute he'll no doubt sell his wife to a brothel. I intend to take her back before he starts selling her clothes."

He was halfway out of the house before I could restrain him. "Don't get so excited. We can settle this calmly. First we must make sure whether or not the rumors are true."

That's why Magoemon and I are here now. He was telling me a while ago that the Jihei of today was not the Jihei of yesterday—that you'd broken all connections with Sonezaki and completely reformed. But now I hear that you've had a relapse. What disease can this be?

Your father was my brother. When the poor man was on his deathbed, he lifted his head from the pillow and begged me to look after you, as my son-in-law and nephew. I've never forgotten those last words, but your perversity has made a mockery of his request!

NARRATOR: She collapses in tears of resentment. Jihei claps his hands in sudden recognition.

JIHEI: I have it! The Koharu everybody's gossiping about is the same Koharu, but the great patron who's to redeem her is a different man. The other day, as my brother can tell you, Tahei—they call him the Lone Wolf because he hasn't any family or relations—started a fight and was trampled on. He gets all the money he needs from his home town, and he's been trying for a long time to redeem Koharu. I've always prevented him, but I'm sure he's decided that now is his chance. I have nothing to do with it.

NARRATOR: Osan brightens at his words.

OSAN: No matter how forbearing I might be—even if I were an angel—you don't suppose I'd encourage my husband to redeem a prostitute! In this instance at any rate there's not a word of untruth in what my husband has said. I'll be a witness to that, Mother.

NARRATOR: Husband's and wife's words tally perfectly.

AUNT: Then it's true?

NARRATOR: The aunt and nephew clap their hands with relief.

MAGOEMON: Well, I'm happy it's over, anyway. To make us feel doubly reassured, will you write an affidavit which will dispel any doubts your stubborn uncle may have?

JIHEI: Certainly. I'll write a thousand if you like.

MAGOEMON: Splendid! I happen to have bought this on the way here.

NARRATOR: Magoemon takes from the fold of his kimono a sheet of oath-paper from Kumano, the sacred characters formed by flocks of crows.[42] Instead of vows of eternal love, Jihei now signs under penalty of Heaven's wrath an oath that he will sever all ties and affections with Koharu. "If I should lie, may Bonten and Taishaku above, and the Four Great Kings below afflict me!"[43] So the text runs, and to it is appended the names of many Buddhas and gods. He signs his name, Kamiya Jihei, in bold characters, imprints the oath with a seal of blood, and proffers it.

OSAN: It's a great relief to me too. Mother, I have you and Magoemon to thank. Jihei and I have had two children, but this is his firmest pledge of affection. I hope you share my joy.

AUNT: Indeed we do. I'm sure that Jihei will settle down and his business will improve, now that he's in this frame of mind. It's been entirely for his sake and for love of the grandchildren that we've intervened. Come, Magoemon, let's be on our way. I'm anxious to set my husband's mind at ease.—It's become chilly here. See that the children don't catch cold.—This too we owe to the Buddha of the Ten Nights. I'll say a prayer of thanks before I go. Hail, Amida Buddha!

NARRATOR: She leaves, her heart innocent as Buddha's. Jihei is perfunctory even about seeing them to the door. Hardly have they crossed the

---

42. The charms issued by the Shinto shrine at Kumano were printed on the face with six Chinese characters, the strokes of which were in the shape of crows. The reverse side of these charms was used for writing oaths. See Shively, p. 116, for a fuller description.

43. A formal oath. Bonten (Brahma) and Taishaku (Sakra), though Hindu gods, were considered to be protective deities of the Buddhist law. The four Deva kings served under Sakra and were also protectors of Buddhism.

threshold than he slumps down again at the *kotatsu*. He pulls the checked quilting over his head.

OSAN: You still haven't forgotten Sonezaki, have you?

NARRATOR: She goes up to him in disgust and tears away the quilting. He is weeping; a waterfall of tears streams along the pillow, deep enough to bear him afloat. She tugs him upright and props his body against the *kotatsu* frame. She stares into his face.

OSAN: You're acting outrageously, Jihei. You shouldn't have signed that oath if you felt so reluctant to leave her. The year before last, on the middle day of the Boar of the tenth moon,[44] we lit the first fire in the *kotatsu* and celebrated by sleeping here together, pillow to pillow. Ever since then—did some demon or snake creep into my bosom that night?—for two whole years I've been condemned to keep watch over an empty nest. I thought that tonight at least, thanks to Mother and Magoemon, we'd share sweet words in bed as husbands and wives do, but my pleasure didn't last long. How cruel of you, how utterly heartless! Go ahead, cry your eyes out, if you're so attached to her. Your tears will flow into Shijimi River and Koharu, no doubt, will ladle them out and drink them! You're ignoble, inhuman.

NARRATOR: She embraces his knees and throws herself over him, moaning in supplication. Jihei wipes his eyes.

JIHEI: If tears of grief flowed from the eyes and tears of anger from the ears, I could show my heart without saying a word. But my tears all pour in the same way from my eyes, and there's no difference in their color. It's not surprising that you can't tell what's in my heart. I have not a shred of attachment left for that vampire in human skin, but I bear a grudge against Tahei. He has all the money he wants, no wife or children. He's schemed again and again to redeem her, but Koharu refused to give in, at least until I broke with her. She told me time and again, "You have nothing to worry about. I'll never let myself be redeemed by Tahei, not even if my ties with you are ended and I can no longer stay by your side. If my master is induced by Tahei's money to deliver me to him, I'll kill myself in a way that'll do you credit!" But think—not ten days have passed since I broke with her, and she's to be redeemed by Tahei! That rotten whore! That animal! No, I haven't a trace of affection left for her, but I can just hear how Tahei will be boasting. He'll spread the word around Osaka that my business has come to a standstill and I'm hard pressed for money. I'll meet with contemptuous stares from the wholesalers. I'll be dishonored. My heart is broken and my body burns with shame. What a disgrace! How maddening! I've passed the stage of

---

44. It was customary to light the first fire of the winter on this day, which would generally be towards the end of November in the Western calendar.

shedding hot tears, tears of blood, sticky tears—my tears now are of molten iron!

NARRATOR: He collapses with weeping. Osan pales with alarm.

OSAN: If that's the situation, poor Koharu will surely kill herself.

JIHEI: You're too well bred, despite your intelligence, to understand her likes! What makes you suppose that faithless creature would kill herself? Far from it—she's probably taking moxa treatments and medicine to prolong her life!

OSAN: No, that's not true. I was determined never to tell you so long as I lived, but I'm afraid of the crime I'd be committing if I concealed the facts and let her die with my knowledge. I will reveal my great secret. There is not a grain of deceit in Koharu. It was I who schemed to end the relations between you. I could see signs that you were drifting towards suicide. I felt so unhappy that I wrote a letter, begging her as one woman to another to break with you, though I knew how painful it would be. I asked her to save your life. The letter must have moved her. She answered that she would give you up, though you were more precious than life itself, because she could not shirk her duty to me. I've kept her letter with me ever since—it's been like a protective charm. Could such a noble-hearted woman violate her promise and brazenly marry Tahei? When a woman—I no less than another—has given herself completely to a man, she does not change. I'm sure she'll kill herself. I'm sure of it. Ahhh—what a dreadful thing to have happened! Save her, please.

NARRATOR: Her voice rises in agitation. Her husband is thrown into a turmoil.

JIHEI: There was a letter in an unknown woman's hand among the written oaths she surrendered to my brother. It must have been from you. If that's the case, Koharu will surely commit suicide.

OSAN: Alas! I'd be failing in the obligations I owe her as another woman if I allowed her to die. Please go to her at once. Don't let her kill herself.

NARRATOR: Clinging to her husband, she melts in tears.

JIHEI: But what can I possibly do? It'd take half the amount of her ransom in earnest money merely to keep her out of Tahei's clutches. I can't save Koharu's life without administering a dose of 750 *momme* in New Silver.[45] How could I raise that much money in my present financial straits? Even if I crush my body to powder, where will the money come from?

---

45. The medical images are occasioned by considering Koharu's plight as a sickness. If 750 *me* is half the sum needed to redeem Koharu, the total of 1,500 *me* (or 6,000 *me* in Old Silver) is considerably less than the 10 *kamme*, or 10,000 *me* in Old Silver, mentioned by Tahei. See footnote 16.

OSAN: Don't exaggerate the difficulties. If that's all you need, it's simple enough.

NARRATOR: She goes to the wardrobe, and opening a small drawer takes out a bag fastened with cords of twisted silk. She unhesitantly tears it open and throws down a packet which Jihei retrieves.

JIHEI: What's this? Money? Four hundred *momme* in New Silver? How in the world—

NARRATOR: He stares astonished at this money he never put there.

OSAN: I'll tell you later where this money came from. I've scraped it together to pay the bill for Iwakuni paper that falls due the day after tomorrow. We'll have to ask Magoemon to help us keep the business from betraying its insolvency. But Koharu comes first. The packet contains 400 *momme*. That leaves 350 *momme* to raise.

NARRATOR: She unlocks a large drawer. From the wardrobe lightly fly kite-colored Hachijō silks;[46] a Kyoto crepe kimono lined in pale brown, insubstantial as her husband's life which flickers today and may vanish tomorrow; a padded kimono of Osue's, a flaming scarlet inside and out—Osan flushes with pain to part with it; Kantarō's sleeveless, unlined jacket—if she pawns this, he'll be cold this winter. Next comes a garment of striped Gunnai silk lined in pale blue and never worn, and then her best formal costume—heavy black silk dyed with her family crest, an ivy leaf in a ring. They say that those joined by marriage ties can even go naked at home, though outside the house clothes make the man: she snatches up even her husband's finery, a silken cloak, making fifteen articles in all.

OSAN: The very least the pawnshop can offer is 350 *momme* in New Silver.

NARRATOR: Her face glows as though she already held the money she needs; she hides in the one bundle her husband's shame and her own obligation, and puts her love in besides.

OSAN: It doesn't matter if the children and I have nothing to wear. My husband's reputation concerns me more. Ransom Koharu. Save her. Assert your honor before Tahei.

NARRATOR: But Jihei's eyes remain downcast all the while, and he is silently weeping.

JIHEI: Yes, I can pay the earnest money and keep her out of Tahei's hands. But once I've redeemed her, I'll either have to maintain her in a separate establishment or bring her here. Then what will become of you?

---

46. Hachijō silks were woven with a warp of brown and a woof of yellow thread to give a color like that of the bird called the kite. "Kite" also suggests that the material flies out of the cupboard.

NARRATOR: Osan is at a loss to answer.

OSAN: Yes, what shall I do? Shall I become your children's nurse or the cook? Or perhaps the retired mistress of the house?

NARRATOR: She falls to the floor with a cry of woe.

JIHEI: That would be too selfish. I'd be afraid to accept such generosity. Even if the punishment for my crimes against my parents, against Heaven, against the gods and the Buddhas fails to strike me, the punishment for my crimes against my wife alone will be sufficient to destroy all hope for the future life. Forgive me, I beg you.

NARRATOR: He joins his hands in tearful entreaty.

OSAN: Why should you bow before me? I don't deserve it. I'd be glad to rip the nails from my fingers and toes, to do anything which might serve my husband. I've been pawning my clothes for some time in order to scrape together the money for the paper wholesalers' bills. My wardrobe is empty, but I don't regret it in the least. But it's too late now to talk of such things. Hurry, change your cloak and go to her with a smile.

NARRATOR: He puts on an under kimono of Gunnai silk, a robe of heavy black silk, and a striped cloak. His sash of figured damask holds a dirk of middle length worked in gold: Buddha surely knows that tonight it will be stained with Koharu's blood.

JIHEI: Sangorō! Come here!

NARRATOR: Jihei loads the bundle on the servant's back, intending to take him along. Then he firmly thrusts the wallet next to his skin and starts towards the gate.

VOICE: Is Jihei at home?

NARRATOR: A man enters, removing his fur cap. They see—good heavens!—that it is Gozaemon.

OSAN and JIHEI: Ahhh—how fortunate that you should come at this moment!

NARRATOR: Husband and wife are upset and confused. Gozaemon snatches away Sangorō's bundle and sits heavily. His voice is sharp.

GOZAEMON: Stay where you are, harlot!—My esteemed son-in-law, what a rare pleasure to see you dressed in your finest attire, with a dirk and a silken cloak! Ahhh—that's how a gentleman of means spends his money! No one would take you for a paper dealer. Are you perchance on your way to the New Quarter? What commendable perseverance! You have no need for your wife, I take it.—Give her a divorce. I've come to take her home with me.

NARRATOR: He speaks needles and his voice is bitter. Jihei has not a word to reply.

OSAN: How kind of you, Father, to walk here on such a cold day. Do have a cup of tea.

NARRATOR: Offering the teacup serves as an excuse for edging closer.

OSAN: Mother and Magoemon came here a while ago, and they told my husband how much they disapproved of his visits to the New Quarter. Jihei was in tears and he wrote out an oath swearing he had reformed. He gave it to Mother. Haven't you seen it yet?

GOZAEMON: His written oath? Do you mean this?

NARRATOR: He takes the paper from his kimono.

GOZAEMON: Libertines scatter vows and oaths wherever they go, as if they were monthly statements of accounts. I thought there was something peculiar about this oath, and now that I am here I can see I was right. Do you still swear to Bonten and Taishaku? Instead of such nonsense, write out a bill of divorcement!

NARRATOR: He rips the oath to shreds and throws down the pieces. Husband and wife exchange looks of alarm, stunned into silence. Jihei touches his hands to the floor and bows his head.

JIHEI: Your anger is justified. If I were still my former self, I would try to offer explanations, but today I appeal entirely to your generosity. Please let me stay with Osan. I promise that even if I become a beggar or an outcast and must sustain life with the scraps that fall from other people's chopsticks, I will hold Osan in high honor and protect her from every harsh and bitter experience. I feel so deeply indebted to Osan that I cannot divorce her. You will understand that this is true as time passes and I show you how I apply myself to my work and restore my fortune. Until then please shut your eyes and allow us to remain together.

NARRATOR: Tears of blood stream from his eyes and his face is pressed to the matting in contrition.

GOZAEMON: The wife of an outcast! That's all the worse. Write the bill of divorcement at once! I will verify and seal the furniture and clothes Osan brought in her dowry.

NARRATOR: He goes to the wardrobe. Osan is alarmed.

OSAN: My clothes are all here. There's no need to examine them.

NARRATOR: She runs up to forestall him, but Gozaemon pushes her aside and jerks open a drawer.

GOZAEMON: What does this mean?

NARRATOR: He opens another drawer: it too is empty. He pulls out every last drawer, but not so much as a foot of patchwork cloth is to be seen. He tears open the wicker hampers, long boxes, and clothes chests.

GOZAEMON: Stripped bare, are they?

NARRATOR: His eyes set in fury. Jihei and Osan huddle under the striped kotatsu quilts, ready to sink into the fire with humiliation.[47]

GOZAEMON: This bundle looks suspicious.

NARRATOR: He unties the knots and dumps out the contents.

GOZAEMON: As I thought! You were sending these to the pawnshop, I take it. Jihei—you'd strip the skin from your wife's and your children's bodies to squander the money on your whore! Dirty thief! You're my wife's nephew, but an utter stranger to me, and I'm under no obligation to suffer for your sake. I'll explain to Magoemon what has happened and ask him to make good whatever inroads you've already made on Osan's belongings. But first, the bill of divorcement!

NARRATOR: Even if Jihei could escape through seven padlocked doors, eight thicknesses of chains, and a hundred girdling walls, he could not evade so stringent a demand.

JIHEI: I won't use a brush to write the bill of divorcement. Here's what I'll do instead! Good-by, Osan.

NARRATOR: He lays his hand on his dirk, but Osan clings to him.

OSAN: Father—Jihei admits that he's done wrong and he's apologized in every way. You press your advantage too hard. Jihei may be a stranger, but his children are your grandchildren. Have you no affection for them? I will not accept a bill of divorcement.

NARRATOR: She embraces her husband and raises her voice in tears.

GOZAEMON: Very well. I won't insist on it. Come with me, woman.

NARRATOR: He pulls her to her feet.

OSAN: No, I won't go. What bitterness makes you expose to such shame a man and wife who still love each other? I will not suffer it.

NARRATOR: She pleads with him, weeping, but he pays her no heed.

GOZAEMON: Is there some greater shame? I'll shout it through the town!

NARRATOR: He pulls her up, but she shakes free. Caught by the wrist she totters forward when—alas!—her toes brush against her sleeping children. They open their eyes.

CHILDREN: Mother dear, why is Grandfather, the bad man, taking you away? Whom will we sleep beside now?

NARRATOR: They call out after her.

---

47. I have omitted here an irrelevant allusion to Urashima Tarō. See Shively, p. 85.

OSAN: My poor dears! You've never spent a night away from Mother's side since you were born. Sleep tonight beside your father. (*To Jihei.*) Please don't forget to give the children their tonic before breakfast.—Oh, my heart is broken!

NARRATOR: These are her parting words. She leaves her children behind, abandoned as in the woods; the twin-trunked bamboo of conjugal love is sundered forever.

ACT THREE

Scene One:

Sonezaki New Quarter, in front of the Yamato House.

TIME:
That night.

NARRATOR: This is Shijimi River, the haunt of love and affection. Its flowing water and the feet of passersby are stilled now at two in the morning, and the full moon shines clear in the sky. Here in the street a dim doorway lantern is marked "Yamatoya Dembei" in a single scrawl. The night watchman's clappers take on a sleepy cadence as he totters by on uncertain legs. The very thickness of his voice crying, "Beware of fire! Beware of fire!" tells how far advanced the night is. A serving woman from the upper town comes along, followed by a palanquin. "It's terribly late," she remarks to the bearers as she clatters open the side door of the Yamato House and steps inside.

SERVANT: I've come to take back Koharu of the Kinokuni House.

NARRATOR: Her voice is faintly heard outside. A few moments later, after hardly time enough to exchange three or four words of greeting, she emerges.

SERVANT: Koharu is spending the night. Bearers, you may leave now and get some rest. (*To proprietress, inside the doorway.*) Oh, I forgot to tell you, madam. Please keep an eye on Koharu. Now that the ransom to Tahei has been arranged and the money's been accepted, we're merely her custodians. Please don't let her drink too much saké.

NARRATOR: She leaves, having scattered at the doorway the seeds that before morning will turn Jihei and Koharu to dust.

At night between two and four even the teahouse kettle rests; the flame flickering in the low candle stand narrows; and the frost spreads in the cold river-wind of the deepening night. The master's voice breaks the stillness.

DEMBEI (*to Jihei*): It's still the middle of the night. I'll send somebody with you. (*To servants.*) Mr. Jihei is leaving. Wake Koharu. Call her here.

NARRATOR: Jihei slides open the side door.

JIHEI: No, Dembei, not a word to Koharu. I'll be trapped here till dawn if she hears I'm leaving. That's why I'm letting her sleep and slipping off this way. Wake her up after sunrise and send her back then. I'm returning home now and will leave for Kyoto immediately on business. I have so many engagements that I may not be able to return in time for the interim payment.[48] Please use the money I gave you earlier this evening to clear my account. I'd like you also to send 150 *me* of Old Silver to Kawashō for the moon-viewing party last month. Please get a receipt. Give Saietsubo[49] from Fukushima one piece of silver as a contribution to the Buddhist altar he's bought, and tell him to use it for a memorial service. Wasn't there something else? Oh yes — give Isoichi a tip of four silver coins. That's the lot. Now you can close up and get to bed. Good-by. I'll see you when I return from Kyoto.

NARRATOR: Hardly has he taken two or three steps than he turns back.

JIHEI: I forgot my dirk. Fetch it for me, won't you? — Yes, Dembei, this is one respect in which it's easier being a townsman. If I were a samurai and forgot my sword, I'd probably commit suicide on the spot!

DEMBEI: I completely forgot that I was keeping it for you. Yes, here's the knife with it.

NARRATOR: He gives the dirk to Jihei, who fastens it firmly into his sash.

JIHEI: I feel secure as long as I have this. Good night!

NARRATOR: He goes off.

DEMBEI: Please come back to Osaka soon! Thank you for your patronage!

NARRATOR: With this hasty farewell Dembei rattles the door bolt shut; then not another sound is heard as the silence deepens. Jihei pretends to leave, only to creep back again with stealthy steps. He clings to the door of the Yamato House. As he peeps within he is startled by shadows moving towards him. He takes cover at the house across the way until the figures pass.

    Magoemon the Miller, his heart pulverized with anxiety over his younger brother, comes first, followed by the apprentice Sangorō with Jihei's son Kantarō on his back. They hurry along until they spy the lantern of the Yamato House. Magoemon pounds on the door.

MAGOEMON: Excuse me. Kamiya Jihei's here, isn't he? I'd like to see him a moment.

---

48. On the last day of the tenth moon (November 29, 1720). This day was one of the times established during the course of the year for making payments.

49. The name of a male entertainer in the Quarter. Fukushima was west of Sonezaki.

NARRATOR: Jihei thinks, "It's my brother!" but dares not stir from his place of concealment. From inside a man's sleep-laden voice is heard.

DEMBEI: Jihei left a while ago saying he was going up to Kyoto. He's not here.

NARRATOR: Not another sound is heard. Magoemon's tears fall unchecked.

MAGOEMON (*to himself*): I ought to have met him on the way if he'd been going home. I can't understand what takes him to Kyoto. Ahhh—I'm trembling all over with worry. I wonder if he didn't take Koharu with him.

NARRATOR: The thought pierces his heart; unable to bear the pain, he pounds again on the door.

DEMBEI: Who is it, so late at night? We've gone to bed.

MAGOEMON: I'm sorry to disturb you, but I'd like to ask one more thing. Has Koharu of the Kinokuni House left? I was wondering if she mightn't have gone with Jihei.

DEMBEI: What's that? Koharu's upstairs, fast asleep.

MAGOEMON: That's a relief, anyway. There's no fear of a lovers' suicide. But where is he hiding himself causing me all this anxiety? He can't imagine the agony of suspense that the whole family is going through on his account. I'm afraid that bitterness towards his father-in-law may make him forget himself and do something rash. I brought Kantarō along, hoping he would help to dissuade Jihei, but the gesture was in vain. I wonder why I failed to meet him?

NARRATOR: He murmurs to himself, his eyes moist with tears. Jihei's hiding place is close enough for him to hear every word. He chokes with emotion, but can only swallow his tears.

MAGOEMON: Songorō! Where does the fool go night after night? Don't you know anywhere else?

NARRATOR: Sangorō imagines that he himself is the fool referred to.

SANGORŌ: I know a couple of places, but I'm too embarrassed to mention them.

MAGOEMON: You know them? Where are they? Tell me.

SANGORŌ: Please don't scold me when you've heard. Every night I wander down below the warehouses by the market.

MAGOEMON: Imbecile! Who's asking about that? Come on, let's search the back streets. Don't let Kantarō catch a chill. The poor kid's having a cold time of it, thanks to that useless father of his. Still, if the worst the boy experiences is the cold I won't complain. I'm afraid that Jihei may cause him much greater pain. The scoundrel!

NARRATOR: But beneath the rancor in his heart of hearts is profound pity.

MAGOEMON: Let's look at the back street!

NARRATOR: They pass on. As soon as their figures have gone off a distance Jihei runs from his hiding place. Standing on tiptoes he gazes with yearning after them and cries out in his heart.

JIHEI: He cannot leave me to my death, though I am the worst of sinners! I remain to the last a burden to him! I'm unworthy of such kindness!

NARRATOR: He joins his hands and kneels in prayer.

JIHEI: If I may make one further request of your mercy, look after my children!

NARRATOR: These are his only words; for a while he chokes with tears.

JIHEI: At any rate, our decision's been made. Koharu must be waiting.

NARRATOR: He peers through a crack in the side door of the Yamato House and glimpses a figure.

JIHEI: That's Koharu, isn't it? I'll let her know I'm here.

NARRATOR: He clears his throat, their signal. "Ahem, ahem"—the sound blends with the clack of wooden clappers as the watchman comes from the upper street, coughing in the night wind. He hurries on his round of fire warning, "Take care! Beware!" Even this cry has a dismal sound to one in hiding. Jihei, concealing himself like the god of Katsuragi,[50] lets the watchman pass. He sees his chance and rushes to the side door, which softly opens from within.

JIHEI: Koharu?

KOHARU: Were you waiting? Jihei—I want to leave quickly.

NARRATOR: She is all impatience, but the more hastily they open the door, the more likely people will be to hear the casters turning. They lift the door; it gives a moaning that thunders in their ears and in their hearts. Jihei lends a hand from the outside, but his fingertips tremble with the trembling of his heart. The door opens a quarter of an inch, a half, an inch—an inch ahead are the tortures of hell, but more than hell itself they fear the guardian-demon's eyes. At last the door opens, and with the joy of New Year's morn[51] Koharu slips out. They catch each other's hands. Shall they go north or south, west or east? Their pounding hearts urge them on, though they know not to what destination: turning their backs on the moon reflected in Shijimi River, they hurry eastward as fast as their legs will carry them.

---

50. The god was so ashamed of his ugliness that he ventured forth only at night.

51. Mention of New Year is connected with Koharu's name, in which *haru* means "spring."

Scene Two:

The farewell journey of many bridges.

NARRATOR:

The running hand in texts of Nō is always Konoe style;
An actor in a woman's part is sure to wear a purple hat.[52]
Does some teaching of the Buddha as rigidly decree
That men who spend their days in evil haunts must end like this?

Poor creatures, though they would discover today their destiny in the Sutra of Cause and Effect,[53] tomorrow the gossip of the world will scatter like blossoms the scandal of Kamiya Jihei's love suicide, and, carved in cherry wood,[54] his story to the last detail will be printed in illustrated sheets.

Jihei, led on by the spirit of death—if such there be among the gods—is resigned to this punishment for neglect of his trade. But at times—who could blame him?—his heart is drawn to those he has left behind, and it is hard to keep walking on. Even in the full moon's light, this fifteenth night of the tenth moon,[55] he cannot see his way ahead—a sign perhaps of the darkness in his heart? The frost now falling will melt by dawn but, even more quickly than this symbol of human frailty, the lovers themselves will melt away. What will become of the fragrance that lingered when he held her tenderly at night in their bedchamber?

This bridge, Tenjin Bridge, he has crossed every day, morning and night, gazing at Shijimi River to the west. Long ago, when Tenjin, then called Michizane,[56] was exiled to Tsukushi, his plum tree, following its master, flew in one bound to Dazaifu, and here is Plum-field Bridge.[57] Green Bridge recalls the aged pine that followed later, and Cherry

---

52. The Konoe style of calligraphy, originated by Konoe Nobutada (1565–1614), was invariably used in books of Nō texts. Custom also decreed that young actors playing the parts of women cover their foreheads with a square of purple cloth to disguise the fact that they were shaven.

53. A sacred text of Buddhism (Karma Sūtra); Chikamatsu here alludes to the line from that text: "If you wish to know the past cause, look at the present effect; if you wish to know the future effect, look at the present cause." See Shively, p. 125.

54. The blocks from which illustrated books were printed were frequently of cherry wood. The illustrated sheets mentioned here featured current scandals, such as lovers' suicides.

55. November 14, 1720. In the lunar calendar the full moon occurs on the fifteenth of the month.

56. Sugawara no Michizane, unfairly abused at court, was exiled to Dazaifu in Kyushu. When he was about to depart he composed a poem of farewell to his favorite plum tree. The tree, moved by this honor, flew after him to Kyushu. The cherry tree in his garden withered away in grief. Only the pine seemed indifferent, as Michizane complained in another poem. The pine thereupon also flew to Kyushu. See also n. 24, above.

57. Umeda Bridge. "Green Bridge" is Midori-bashi.

Bridge the tree that withered away in grief over parting. Such are the tales still told, bespeaking the power of a single poem.[58]

JIHEI: Though born the parishioner of so holy and mighty a god, I shall kill you and then myself. If you ask the cause, it was that I lacked even the wisdom that might fill a tiny Shell Bridge.[59] Our stay in this world has been short as an autumn day. This evening will be the last of your nineteen, of my twenty-eight years. The time has come to cast away our lives. We promised we'd remain together faithfully, till you were an old woman and I an old man, but before we knew each other three full years, we have met this disaster. Look, there is Ōe Bridge. We follow the river from Little Naniwa Bridge to Funairi Bridge. The farther we journey, the closer we approach the road to death.

NARRATOR: He laments. She clings to him.

KOHARU: Is this already the road to death?

NARRATOR: Falling tears obscure from each the other's face and threaten to immerse even the Horikawa bridges.

JIHEI: A few steps north and I could glimpse my house, but I will not turn back. I will bury in my breast all thoughts of my children's future, all pity for my wife. We cross southward over the river. Why did they call a place with as many buildings as a bridge has piers "Eight Houses"? Hurry, we want to arrive before the down-river boat from Fushimi comes—with what happy couples sleeping aboard!

Next is Temma Bridge, a frightening name[60] for us about to depart this world. Here the two streams Yodo and Yamato join in one great river, as fish with water, and as Koharu and I, dying on one blade will cross together the River of Three Fords.[61] I would like this water for our tomb offering!

KOHARU: What have we to grieve about? Though in this world we could not stay together, in the next and through each successive world to come until the end of time we shall be husband and wife. Every summer for my devotions[62] I have copied the All Compassionate and All Merciful

---

58. The poem by Michizane bewailing the inconstancy of his pine tree.

59. Shijimi Bridge. Twelve bridges are mentioned in the *michiyuki*. The lovers' journey takes them along the north bank of Shijimi River to Shijimi Bridge, where they cross to Dōjima. At Little Naniwa Bridge they cross back again to Sonezaki. Continuing eastward, they cross Horikawa, then cross the Temma Bridge over the Ōkawa. At "Eight Houses" (Hakkenya) they journey eastward along the south bank of the river as far as Kyō Bridge. They cross this bridge to the tip of land at Katamachi, and then take the Onari Bridge to Amijima.

60. The characters used for Temma mean literally "demon."

61. A river in the Buddhist underworld which had to be crossed to reach the world of the dead. Mention here is induced arithmetically: one blade plus two people equal three fords.

62. It was customary for Buddhist monks and some of the laity in Japan to observe a summer retreat from the sixteenth day of the fourth moon to the fifteenth day of the seventh moon, a period of ninety days. During this time they practiced various austerities and copied out the holy books or wrote the Buddha's name over and over.

Chapter of the Lotus Sutra, in the hope that we may be reborn on one lotus.

NARRATOR: They cross over Kyō Bridge and reach the opposite shore.[63]

KOHARU: If I can save living creatures at will when once I mount a lotus calyx in Paradise and become a Buddha, I want to protect women of my profession, so that never again will there be love suicides.

NARRATOR: This unattainable prayer stems from worldly attachment, but it touchingly reveals her heart.

They cross Onari Bridge.[64] The waters of Noda Creek are shrouded with morning haze; the mountain tips show faintly white.

JIHEI: Listen—the voices of the temple bells begin to boom. How much farther can we go on this way? We are not fated to live any longer—let us make an end quickly. Come this way.

NARRATOR: Tears are strung with the 108 beads of the rosaries in their hands. They have come now to Amijima, to the Daichō Temple; the overflowing sluice gate of a little stream beside a bamboo thicket will be their place of death.

Scene Three:

Amijima.

JIHEI: No matter how far we walk, there'll never be a spot marked "For Suicides." Let us kill ourselves here.

NARRATOR: He takes her hand and sits on the ground.

KOHARU: Yes, that's true. One place is as good as another to die. But I've been thinking on the way that if they find our dead bodies together people will say that Koharu and Jihei committed a lovers' suicide. Osan will think then that I treated as mere scrap paper the letter I sent promising her, when she asked me not to kill you, that I would not, and vowing to break all relations. She will be sure that I lured her precious husband into a lovers' suicide. She will despise me as a one-night prostitute, a false woman with no sense of decency. I fear her contempt more than the slander of a thousand or ten thousand strangers. I can imagine how she will resent and envy me. That is the greatest obstacle to my salvation. Kill me here, then choose another spot, far away, for yourself.

NARRATOR: She leans against him. Jihei joins in her tears of pleading.

---

63. "Opposite shore" suggests the Buddhist term *higan* (nirvana).

64. The name Onari is used here for the bridge more properly called Bizenjima because of a play on words meaning "to become a Buddha."

JIHEI: What foolish worries! Osan has been taken back by my father-in-law. I've divorced her. She and I are strangers now. Why should you feel obliged to a divorced woman? You were saying on the way that you and I will be husband and wife through each successive world until the end of time. Who can criticize us, who can be jealous if we die side by side?

KOHARU: But who is responsible for your divorce? You're even less reasonable than I. Do you suppose that our bodies will accompany us to the afterworld? We may die in different places, our bodies may be pecked by kites and crows, but what does it matter as long as our souls are twined together? Take me with you to heaven or to hell!

NARRATOR: She sinks again in tears.

JIHEI: You're right. Our bodies are made of earth, water, fire, and wind, and when we die they revert to emptiness. But our souls will not decay, no matter how often reborn. And here's a guarantee that our souls will be married and never part!

NARRATOR: He whips out his dirk and slashes off his black locks at the base of the top knot.

JIHEI: Look, Koharu. As long as I had this hair I was Kamiya Jihei, Osan's husband, but cutting it has made me a monk. I have fled the burning house of the three worlds of delusion; I am a priest, unencumbered by wife, children, or worldly possessions. Now that I no longer have a wife named Osan, you owe her no obligations either.

NARRATOR: In tears he flings away the hair.

KOHARU: I am happy.

NARRATOR: Koharu takes up the dirk and ruthlessly, unhesitantly, slices through her flowing Shimada coiffure. She casts aside the tresses she has so often washed and combed and stroked. How heartbreaking to see their locks tangled with the weeds and midnight frost of this desolate field!

JIHEI: We have escaped the inconstant world, a nun and a priest. Our duties as husband and wife belong to our profane past. It would be best to choose quite separate places for our deaths, a mountain for one, the river for the other. We will pretend that the ground above this sluice gate is a mountain. You will die there. I shall hang myself by this stream. The time of our deaths will be the same, but the method and place will differ. In this way we can honor to the end our duty to Osan. Give me your under sash.

NARRATOR: Its fresh violet color and fragrance will be lost in the winds of impermanence; the crinkled silk long enough to wind twice round her body will bind two worlds, this and the next. He firmly fastens one end to the crosspiece of the sluice, then twists the other into a noose for his neck. He will hang for love of his wife like the "pheasant in the hunting grounds."[65]

Koharu watches Jihei prepare for his death. Her eyes swim with tears, her mind is distraught.

KOHARU: Is that how you're going to kill yourself?—If we are to die apart, I have only a little while longer by your side. Come near me.

NARRATOR: They take each other's hands.

KOHARU: It's over in a moment with a sword, but I'm sure you'll suffer. My poor darling!

NARRATOR: She cannot stop the silent tears.

JIHEI: Can suicide ever be pleasant, whether by hanging or cutting the throat? You mustn't let worries over trifles disturb the prayers of your last moments. Keep your eyes on the westward-moving moon, and worship it as Amida himself.[66] Concentrate your thoughts on the Western Paradise. If you have any regrets about leaving the world, tell me now, then die.

KOHARU: I have none at all, none at all. But I'm sure you must be worried about your children.

JIHEI: You make me cry all over again by mentioning them. I can almost see their faces, sleeping peacefully, unaware, poor dears, that their father is about to kill himself. They're the one thing I can't forget.

NARRATOR: He droops to the ground with weeping. The voices of the crows leaving their nests at dawn rival his sobs. Are the crows mourning his fate? The thought brings more tears.

JIHEI: Listen to them. The crows have come to guide us to the world of the dead. There's an old saying that every time somebody writes an oath on the back of a Kumano charm, three crows of Kumano die on the holy mountain. The first words we've written each New Year have been vows of love, and how often we've inscribed oaths at the beginning of the month! If each oath has killed three crows, what a multitude must have perished! Their cries have always sounded like "beloved, beloved," but hatred for our crime of taking life makes their voices ring tonight "revenge, revenge!"[67] Whose fault is it they demand revenge? Because of me you will die a painful death. Forgive me!

---

65. A reference to a poem by Ōtomo no Yakamochi (718–785): "The pheasant foraging in the fields of spring reveals his whereabouts to man as he cries for his mate" (Shuishu, no. 21).

66. Amida's paradise lies in the west. The moon is also frequently used as a symbol of Buddhist enlightenment.

67. The cries have always sounded like *kawai, kawai*, but now they sound like *mukui, mukui*. These Japanese sounds seem more within the range of a crow's articulatory powers than "beloved" and "revenge."

NARRATOR: He takes her in his arms.

KOHARU: No, it's my fault!

NARRATOR: They cling to each other, face pressed to face; their sidelocks, drenched with tears, freeze in the winds blowing over the fields. Behind them echoes the voice of the Daichō Temple.

JIHEI: Even the long winter night seems short as our lives.

NARRATOR: Dawn is already breaking, and matins can be heard. He draws her to him.

JIHEI: The moment has come for our glorious end. Let there be no tears on your face when they find you later.

KOHARU: There won't be any.

NARRATOR: She smiles. His hands, numbed by the frost, tremble before the pale vision of her face, and his eyes are first to cloud. He is weeping so profusely that he cannot control the blade.

KOHARU: Compose yourself—but be quick!

NARRATOR: Her encouragement lends him strength; the invocations to Amida carried by the wind urge a final prayer. *Namu Amida Butsu.* He thrusts in the saving sword.[68] Stabbed, she falls backwards, despite his staying hand, and struggles in terrible pain. The point of the blade has missed her windpipe, and these are the final tortures before she can die. He writhes with her in agony, then painfully summons his strength again. He draws her to him, and plunges his dirk to the hilt. He twists the blade in the wound, and her life fades away like an unfinished dream at dawning.

He arranges her corpse head to the north, face to the west, lying on her right side,[69] and throws his cloak over her. He turns away at last, unable to exhaust with tears his grief over parting. He pulls the sash to him and fastens the noose around his neck. The service in the temple has reached the closing section, the prayers for the dead. "Believers and unbelievers will equally share in the divine grace," the voices proclaim, and at the final words Jihei jumps from the sluice gate.

JIHEI: May we be reborn on one lotus! Hail Amida Buddha!

NARRATOR: For a few moments he writhes like a gourd swinging in the wind, but gradually the passage of his breath is blocked as the stream is dammed by the sluice gate, where his ties with this life are snapped.

---

68. The invocation of Amida's name freed one from spiritual obstacles, just as a sword freed one from physical obstacles. Here the two images are blended.

69. The dead were arranged in this manner because Shakyamuni Buddha chose this position when he died.

Fishermen out for the morning catch find the body in their net.[70]

FISHERMEN: A dead man! Look, a dead man! Come here, everybody!

NARRATOR: The tale is spread from mouth to mouth. People say that they who were caught in the net of Buddha's vow immediately gained salvation and deliverance, and all who hear the tale of the Love Suicides at Amijima are moved to tears.

Chikamatsu on the Art of the Puppet Stage

[from *Naniwa Miyage*] *by Hozumi Ikan*[1]

This is what Chikamatsu told me when I visited him many years ago:

Jōruri differs from other forms of fiction in that, since it is primarily concerned with puppets, the words must all be living and full of action. Because *jōruri* is performed in theatres that operate in close competition with those of the *kabuki*, which is the art of living actors, the author must impart to lifeless wooden puppets a variety of emotions, and attempt in this way to capture the interest of the audience. It is thus generally very difficult to write a work of great distinction.

Once when I was young and reading a story about the court,[2] I came across a passage which told how, on the occasion of a festival, the snow had fallen heavily and piled up. An order was given to a guard to clear away the snow from an orange tree. When this happened, the pine next to it, apparently resentful that its boughs were still bent with snow, recoiled its branches. This was a stroke of the pen which gave life to the inanimate tree. It did so because the spectacle of the pine, resentful that the snow had been cleared from the orange tree, recoiling its branches and shaking off the snow that bends it down, is one which creates the feeling of a living, moving thing. Is that not so?

From this model I learned how to put life into my *jōruri*. Thus, even descriptive passages like the *michiyuki*,[3] to say nothing of the narrative phrases and dialogue, must be charged with feeling or they will be greeted with scant applause. This is the same thing as what is called evocative power in poetry. For example, if a poet should fail to bring emotion to his praise of

---

70. "Net" (*ami*) is mentioned because of the connection with fishermen. It is echoed a few lines later in the mention of the name *Amijima*. The vow of the Buddha to save all living creatures is likened to a net which catches people in its meshes. For a further explanation of this image (and of the title of the play), see Shively, p. 41.

---

1. The following account of Chickamatsu's views on the *jōruri*, or puppet stage, was written after his death, in 1738, by a friend. It is one of the most important examples of dramatic criticism in the literature.

2. "The Tale of Genji." The particular reference is to a passage in the chapter translated by Waley as "The Village of Falling Flowers."

3. The journey, such as that of the lovers in "The Love Suicides at Sonezaki."

even the superb scenery of Matsushima or Miyajima in his poem, it would be like looking at the carelessly drawn portrait of a beautiful woman. For this reason, it should be borne in mind that feeling is the basis of writing.

When a composition is filled with particles, its literary quality is somehow lowered. Authors of no merit inevitably try to cast their writings exactly in the form of *waka* or linked-verse, stringing together alternating lines of five and seven syllables. This naturally results in the use of many unnecessary particles. For example, when one should say "*Toshi mo yukanu musume wo*," they say such things as "*Toshiha mo yukanu, musume wo ba*." This comes from concerning one's self with the syllable count, and naturally causes the language to sound vulgar. Thus, while verse is generally written by arranging long and short lines in order, the *jōruri* is basically a musical form, and the length of the lines recited is therefore determined by the melody. If an author adheres implicitly to the rules of metrics, his lines may prove awkward to recite. For this reason I am not concerned with metrics in my writings and I use few particles.

The old *jōruri* was just like our modern street storytelling,[4] and was without either flower or fruit. From the time I first began to write *jōruri*, I have used care in my works, which was not true of the old *jōruri*. As a result, the medium was raised considerably. For example, inasmuch as the nobility, the samurai, and the lower classes all have different social stations, it is essential that they be distinguished in their representation from their appearance down to their speech. Similarly, even within the same samurai class, there are both daimyō [feudal lords] and retainers, as well as others of lower rank, each rank possessed of its distinct qualities; such differences must be established. This is because it is essential that they be well pictured in the emotions of the reader.

In writing *jōruri*, one attempts first to describe facts as they really are, but in so doing one writes things which are not true, in the interest of art. In recent plays many things have been said by female characters which real women could not utter. Such things fall under the heading of art; it is because they say what could not come from a real woman's lips that their true emotions are disclosed. If in such cases the author were to model his character on the ways of a real woman and conceal her feelings, such realism, far from being admired, would permit no pleasure in the work. Thus, if one examines a play without paying attention to the question of art, one will certainly criticize it for containing many unpleasant words which are not suitable for women. But such things should be considered art. In addition, there are numerous instances in the portrayal of a villain as excessively cowardly, or of a clown as funny, which are outside the truth and which must be regarded as art. The spectator must bear this consideration in mind.

---

4. These were popular recitations of ballads, gossip, etc., which flourished particularly about this time.

There are some who, thinking that pathos is essential to a *jōruri*, make frequent use of such expressions as "It was touching" in their writing, or who when chanting do so in voices thick with tears. This is foreign to my style. I take pathos to be entirely a matter of restraint. It is moving when the whole of a play is controlled by the dramatic situation, and the stronger and firmer the melody and words, the sadder will be the impression created. For this reason, when one says of something which is sad that it is sad, one loses the implications, and in the end, even the impression of sadness is slight. It is essential that one not say of a thing that "it is sad," but that it be sad of itself. For example, when one praises a place renowned for its scenery such as Matsushima by saying, "Ah, what a fine view!" one has said in one phrase all that one can about the sight, but without effect. If one wishes to praise the view, and one says numerous things indirectly about its appearance, the quality of the view may be known of itself, without one's having to say, "It is a fine view." This is true of everything of its kind.

Someone said, "People nowadays will not accept plays unless they are realistic and well reasoned out. There are many things in the old stories which people will not now tolerate. It is thus that such people as *kabuki* actors are considered skilful to the degree that their acting resembles reality. The first consideration is to have the retainer in the play resemble a real retainer, and to have the daimyō look like a real daimyō. People will not stand for childish nonsense as they did in the past." I answered, "Your view seems plausible, but it is a theory which does not take into account the real methods of art. Art is something which lies in the slender margin between the real and the unreal. Of course it seems desirable, in view of the current taste for realism, to have the retainer in the play copy the gestures and speech of a real retainer, but in that case should a real retainer put rouge and powder on his face like an actor? Or, would it prove entertaining if an actor, on the grounds that real retainers do not make up their faces, were to appear on the stage and perform with his beard growing wild and his head shaven? This is what I mean by the slender margin between the real and the unreal. It is unreal, and yet it is not unreal; it is real, and yet it is not real. Entertainment lies between the two."

In this connection, there is the story of a certain court lady who had a lover. The two loved each other very passionately, but the lady lived far deep in the women's palace, and the man could not visit her quarters. She could see him therefore only very rarely, from between the cracks of her screen of state at the court. She longed for him so desperately that she had a wooden image carved of the man. Its appearance was not like that of an ordinary doll, but did not differ in any particle from the man. It goes without saying that the color of his complexion was perfectly rendered; even the pores of his skin were delineated. The openings in his ears and nostrils were fashioned, and there was no discrepancy even in the number of teeth in the mouth. Since it was made with the man posing beside it, the only difference between the man and this doll was the presence in one, and the absence in the other, of a soul. However, when the lady drew the doll close to her and looked at it, the exactness of the reproduction of the living man chilled her, and she felt unpleasant and rather frightened. Court lady that she was, her love was also chilled, and as she found it distressing to have the doll by her side, she soon threw it away.

In view of this we can see that if one makes an exact copy of a living being, even if it happened to be Yang Kuei-fei, one will become disgusted with it. If when one paints an image or carves it of wood there are, in the name of artistic license, some stylized parts in a work otherwise resembling the real form; this is, after all, what people love in art. The same is true of literary composition. While bearing resemblance to the original, it should have stylization; this makes it art, and is what delights men's minds. Theatrical dialogue written with this in mind is apt to be worth while.

■ Yosa Buson (Taniguchi Buson) (1716–1783) (poems)

Yosa Buson was born in the village of Kema (Settsu province, in present-day Osaka prefecture) as Taniguchi Buson, taking the name Yosa in midlife after spending three years in Yosa, a village in Tango province, his mother's hometown. At age twenty, he moved to Edo (modern Tokyo) and studied painting and poetry; his teacher was Hayano Hajin, a disciple of Kikaku and Ransetsu, who themselves had been disciples of Basho. After stays in Uki and Utsunomiya, Buson moved to Kyoto for several years; he then spent three years in Yosa, eventually moving back to Kyoto. In Kyoto, he became the center of a group of disciples and formed a haiku association called the Sankasha. He died at age sixty-six.

Yosa Buson was equally famous as a painter and as a poet. He ranks second only to Basho in the pantheon of great Japanese haiku poets and was the essential figure in the revival of the form, which had become moribund after the death of Basho in 1694. In fact, his dedication to this form caused the period from 1743 until his death to be named the "Haikai Revival." Throughout his life, though, he was known primarily as the most famous painter of the classical Chinese literati style (*bunjinga*). However, he remained devoted to both these arts, and in addition was a master calligrapher, fluent in Chinese, and dedicated to the Chinese ideal of being a gentleman scholar, adept at many arts. There is a particularly "cool" feeling to Buson's poetry; unlike Issa, he did not see it as a forum for airing his personal griefs. In addition to writing haiku, he wrote a few poems in the Chinese style and throughout his work showed a deep indebtedness to the classical Chinese poets (and to Du Fu in particular), whose lines he would often echo. Buson advocated Basho as the ideal haiku writer, and his motto was "Return to Basho!" Yet, this allusive quality in his work, his devotion to the work and ideals of great poets of the past, is an essential difference between his work and that of Basho. Buson was an aesthete, separating art from life, whereas Basho seems to immerse himself wholly in the smallest events of the actual world in his art. Finally, the exact meaning of "Return to Basho!" is unclear, but in general it referred to the need to hold the art of haiku to the highest possible standard, to emulate Basho's serious devotion to the art. Buson shines particularly in the individual *hokku,* and has been criticized for so perfecting the stanzas he contributed to linked-verse poems (*haikai*) as to threaten the integrity of the whole.

FURTHER READING: French, Calvin L. *The Poet-Painters: Buson and His Followers,* 1974. Sawa, Yuki, and Edith Marcombe Shiffert, trs. *Haiku Master Buson: Translations from the Writings of Yosa Buson—Poet and Artist—with Related Materials,* 1978. Suzuki, S. *Poet-Painter Buson,* 1958. Watson, Wm. *Yosa-no-Buson,* 1960. Yasuhara, Eri Fujita. *Buson and Haishi: A Study of Free-Form Haikai Poetry in Eighteenth Century Japan,* 1982. Yonezawa Yoshiho and Yoshizawa Chu. *Japanese Painting in the Literati Style,* 1974.

Twenty-one Haiku

Spring sea,
day and night, undulating
undulating.

Bright moon to the west.
Shadows of cherryblossoms
stroll east.

No underwear,
a gust of spring wind shows
my bare ass.

Blossoming pear tree.
a woman reading a letter
by moonlight.

On the temple bell
sleeps
a butterfly.

Brief night:
on the hairy caterpillar
beads of dew.

On each thorn
a drop
of white dew.

Lightning flash.
Drip, drip
of dew through bamboo.

Whale diving,
its tail
rising and rising!

Morning breeze
stirs
the caterpillar's hair.

So cool
to nap at noon,
feet against the wall.

In the old well
a fish leaps for a gnat.
The water sound is dark.

It hurts to step
in the bedroom
on my dead wife's comb.

Cool morning.
The voice of the bell
is leaving the bell.

Avoiding fishnet
and fishing lines,
moon on the water.

At the old pond
the frog is aging
among fallen leaves.[1]

---

1. A play on Basho's most famous poem.

Scent of plum-blossoms
rising.
Halo round the moon.

Cold night:
sliver of
thinning moon.

I pull the ice
off my writing brush
with my teeth.

Crow after crow
settling
in autumn dusk.

Red plum flowers
burn
on horse plop.

TRANSLATED BY TONY BARNSTONE

Three Haiku

The Grand Abbot
is shitting
in the barren field.

I seize
in the mind's darkness
a firefly.

Leak
in the footwashing tub.
Spring drains away.

TRANSLATED BY AYAME FUKUDA

■ Ryokan (1758–1831) (poems)

Ryokan (*ryo,* "good"; *kan,* "generosity"), also known by the literary name Daigu ("Big Fool"), is, in his elegant simplicity, one of the world's great mystical poets. He was born in the village of Izumozaki in Echigo province (today's Niigata prefecture) in 1758 and passed up the opportunity to follow his father in the role of village headman, instead shaving his head and entering the life of a Zen Buddhist monk in 1777. His father, who in addition to his political role was a haiku poet and a Shinto priest, was very unhappy with the military government in Edo, supporting the emperor instead and, perhaps in protest, drowned himself in 1795 in the Katsura River in Kyoto. From 1790 to 1795, Ryokan traveled on a number of pilgrimages, until, on hearing of his father's death, he set up a hermitage on Mount Kugami, near Izumozaki, where he lived until his own death thirty-four years later. Soon he became a familiar figure in town plying his begging bowl or playing with the children who appear in so many of his poems.

He practiced Soto Zen, which was brought to Japan from China by Dogen in the thirteenth century. As translator John Stevens notes: "Dogen's teaching emphasized two main points: (1) *shikantaza,* themeless sitting in zazen, that is, abandoning all thoughts of good or bad, enlightenment or illusion, and just sitting; and (2) *shusho ichigyo,* 'practice and enlightenment are one.' There is no sudden enlightenment, and enlightenment cannot be separated from one's practice. For these reasons Soto Zen is usually contrasted with Rinzai Zen, with its use of koans during zazen and its striving for *kensho,* an instantaneous, profound insight into reality."[1] Late in life he had an affair, or a close friendship, it is hard to tell which, with a young nun named Teishin, with whom he wrote poetry and who is responsible for collecting the poems of his that have come down to us today. He wrote haiku, waka, Manyo poems, and folk songs as well as poems in classical Chinese forms. The Chinese poet Han Shan, whose work and character resonates with his so strongly, was one of his favorite poets.

FURTHER READING: Ryokan. *Between the Floating Mist: Poems of Ryokan.* Translated by Dennis Maloney and Hide Oshiro, 1992; *One Robe, One Bowl: The Zen Poetry of Ryokan.* Translated by John Stevens, 1981; *Ryokan: Zen Monk-Poet of Japan.* Translated by Burton Watson, 1977.

Who Says My Poem Is a Poem?

Who says my poem is a poem?
My poem, in fact, is not poem.

---

1. John Stevens, tr., *One Robe, One Bowl: The Zen Poetry of Ryokan* (New York and Tokyo: Weatherhill, 1981), 15.

When you realize that my poem is not poem,
then we can discuss poetry.

TRANSLATED BY DENNIS MALONEY AND HIDE OSHIRO

For an Old Man, a Dream Is Easily Broken

For an old man, a dream is easily broken.
Waking, I enter the empty room
lit by an oil lamp, but soon
the lamp is exhausted leaving the long winter night.

TRANSLATED BY DENNIS MALONEY AND HIDE OSHIRO

Shaggy Hair Past the Ears

Shaggy hair past the ears,
A worn-out robe resembling white clouds and dark smoke.
Half drunk, half sober, I return home,
Children all around, guiding me along the Way.

TRANSLATED BY JOHN STEVENS

The Thief Left It Behind

The thief left it behind—
The moon
At the window.

TRANSLATED BY JOHN STEVENS

Last Night's Dream Was a Lie

Last night's dream was a lie.
I can't explain what I saw.
It lied like truth.
I wake up inside the dream.

TRANSLATED BY TONY BARNSTONE

The New Pond

The new pond,
a frog jumps in,
—no sound![1]

TRANSLATED BY DENNIS MALONEY AND HIDE OSHIRO

■ Issa (Kobayashi Issa) (1763–1827) (poems)

Kobayashi Issa was born Yataro Kobayashi in Kashiwabara, a small mountain village in central Japan. He was the first son of a moderately well off farmer. In 1765 his mother died, and in 1770 his father remarried. After the birth of his half-brother in 1773, a fierce, lifelong battle with his stepmother began. He studied at the village school under a haiku (*hokku*) poet whose pen name was Shimpo; when his family situation became unbearable, his father sent him to Edo to be an apprentice. After ten years, he enrolled at the school of Nirokuan Chikua, where he studied haiku under Nirokuan (a poet strongly influenced by Basho), and in 1790, after his teacher's death, Issa became the new master. Issa (meaning "cup of tea") is one of many pen names he took and the one by which he is best known. He spent the decade of his thirties wandering across Japan, like Basho, devoting himself to composing haiku and putting out occasional collections. When Issa's father fell ill with typhoid in 1801, Issa returned home and nursed him, but he died. After his father's death, there was a bitter struggle over the will, which left Issa the majority of the property; as a result, Issa was denied his birthright by his stepmother and half-brother until he was fifty years old. At that time, he finally settled into his ancestral home and married a village girl named Kiku. They had four sons and a daughter, but none of them lived through infancy. The *haibun* (haiku mixed with prose) journal he wrote about the death of his daughter Sato is his best-known work—*A Year of My Life* (1819). In 1823, the year his fourth son died, Kiku died as well, and Issa's poems about her are among his most touching: "Night moon, / if only she were here / to grumble." He briefly remarried in 1824, but it did not work out, and a year later he married for the last time to a woman named Yao. In 1827, Issa died, sixty-five years old, with his daughter, Yata, the only one fated to survive, still in her mother's womb.

Issa was a Pure Land Buddhist, a form of Buddhism that emphasizes living like common folk while worshiping Amida Buddha. His work reflects an earthy, humorous, Buddhist consciousness, never preachy: "I pray to Buddha/while smashing/flies." The tragedies he lived through are recorded in his haiku, yet they are balanced by his ability to record lightning-flash glimpses of children, animals, insects, and the Japanese landscapes he traveled through. Hokku had become by this time essentially the same

---

1. A commentary on Basho's most famous poem.

as the modern haiku, though it could still be used as the initial stanza in a series or integrated into prose as haibun. Issa's hokku is his best work, and he ranks with Basho, Buson, and Shiki as one of its four supreme masters.

FURTHER READING: Lewis, Richard. *Of This World: A Poet's Life in Poetry*, 1968. MacKenzie, Lewis, tr. *The Autumn Wind: A Selection from the Poems of Issa*, 1957, 1984. Maloney, Dennis, tr. *Dusk Lingers: Haiku of Issa*, 1986. Merrill, Jean and Ronni Solbert, eds. *A Few Flies and I: Haiku by Issa*, 1969. Stryk, Lucien, and Noboru Fujiwara, trs. *The Dumpling Field: Haiku of Issa*, 1981. Williams, C. K., tr. *The Lark, the Thrush, the Starling: Poems from Issa*, 1983. Yuasa, Nobuyuki, tr. *The Year of My Life*, 1972.

Twenty-one Haiku

Don't smash the fly!
He's wringing his hands,
and even his feet!

Red moon,
something a child
would own.

Three day moon
warped
by the cold.

Snow melting.
The village floods
with children.

Spring rain.
Through the trees blows
a discarded letter.

Out the nose
of the Great Buddha
flies a sparrow.

Through a sudden shower
I ride naked
on a naked horse!

Even one-foot waterfall
makes the evening
sound cool.

Big firefly:
flicker, flicker,
gone.

Snail climbing
up Mount Fuji
slowly! slowly!

Distant mountains
reflected in the eye
of a dragonfly.

Wonderful to see
through a torn paper window
the star river.

I piss through the door
making a neat hole
in the snow.

She counts flea bites
while her baby
sucks.

So young,
even her flea bites
are beautiful!

The cat stretches
yawns wide,
goes out to make love.

In the garden the baby
crawls toward a butterfly. It flutters off.
Crawls again. Flutter.

Mosquito in the bedroom
humming,
burnt!

The toad
seems about to belch
out a cloud!

"The peony was this big"
says the small girl
opening her arms wide.

Hell

A bright autumn moon.
Pond snails wailing
in the saucepan.

TRANSLATED BY TONY BARNSTONE

Three Haiku

Bright full moon.
A child weeps
"Get it for me!"

Mountain village:
bright moon
in my soup.

Song of bell,
waterbird wail,
darkening night.

TRANSLATED BY AYAME FUKUDA

Modern Period

(1868–present)

■ Natsume Soseki (1867–1916) (story)

TRANSLATED BY AIKO ITO AND GRAEME WILSON

Natsume Soseki is a supremely important figure in the development of the modern Japanese novel. Most of his novels are revered as classics, and he anticipated the psychological and realistic novel in Japan. He was born Natsume Kinnosuke in 1867 in Edo (modern-day Tokyo), the fifth son of a merchant family. He was an unwanted child, and his father put him out for adoption when he was two; when his new parents separated after seven years, his birth father took him back, albeit reluctantly. His early education was in Chinese, but he studied English literature at Tokyo University. In 1889, he became close friends with a fellow student, the famous haiku poet Masaoka Shiki. After teaching for several years, he spent the years 1900–1903 in England on a government scholarship, studying literature with tutors. He lived in bitter poverty, terribly alienated from the society of English gentlemen (he was, he wrote "lonely as a stray dog in a pack of wolves"), and so he made a life of the intense study of a huge range of books in English. While in England, he had a kind of nervous breakdown, and he suffered from a nervous disorder for the remainder of his life. Returning to Japan, he became Lecturer in English Literature at Tokyo University, taking over that position from Lafcadio Hearn. In 1907, he resigned from his prestigious scholarly position and became the literary editor of the *Asahi Shimbun,* a newspaper that agreed to serialize his novels. Late in life he was a mentor to Akutagawa Ryunosuke and other younger writers.

Two of his famous novels that show the range and development of his career are the immensely popular *Botchan,* a parodic account of a Tokyo youth's picaresque adventures teaching in a provincial boys' school, and the serious later novel *Kokoro,* meaning "heart" or "spirit." It is a story about the quest for meaning and connection in the bleak and materialist modern world. His fiction has stylistic and imagistic debts to the classical poetry of China and Japan, while the deeper structures of his novels derive significantly from Western fiction. The brief and beautiful piece presented here comes from the early period of his fiction, from a collection of linked allegorical dreams titled *Ten Nights of Dream.* Though it does not represent the psychological depth and deep social concern of his later work, it shows his extraordinary talent for description, his need to make sense of a life's journey, and something of his pessimism.

FURTHER READING: Aiko, Ito, and Graeme Wilson, trs. *Ten Nights of Dream, Hearing Things, The Heredity of Taste,* 1974. Field, Norma Moore, tr. *And Then: Natsume Soseki's Novel Sorekara,* 1978. Katsue, Shibata, and Motonari Kai, tr. *I Am a Cat,* 1961. Kingo, Ochiai, and Sanford Goldstein, trs. *To the Spring Equinox and Beyond,* 1985. Mathy, Francis, tr. *Mon: The Gate,* 1972. McClellan, Edwin, tr. *Kokoro,* 1957. Rubin, Jay, tr. *Sanshiro: A Novel,* 1977. Turney, Alan, tr. *Botchan,* 1972; tr. *The Three Cornered World,* 1965. Viglielmo, V. H., tr. *Light and Darkness: An Unfinished Novel,* 1971.

The Seventh Night

It seems that I'm aboard some massive ship. The ship plows forward, shearing the waves away, day after day, night after night, continuously emitting, without one second's break, a stream of inky smoke. The noise is tremendous: but the destination utterly unknown. All I know is that the sun, burning red like red-hot tongs, bulges up from the bottom of the sea. It rises, seems to hover briefly dead above the tall ship's mast, and then, before we realize what's happening, overtakes the shuddering ship and, plunging dead ahead, sinks back with a sizzling sound, the sound of red-hot tongs, down to the bottom of the sea. Each time it sinks, the blue waves far ahead seethe to a blackish red. The ship, making its tremendous noise, pursues the sinking sun. But it never catches up.

One day I buttonholed a sailor, and I asked him "Is this ship steering west?"

The sailor, a curiously uncertain expression on his face, studied me briefly and then answered "Why?"

"Because it seems concerned to chase the setting sun."

The sailor burst into a roar of laughter; and then left me.

I heard the sound of jolly voices chanting:

"Does the sun that travels west
End up in the east?
Is that really true?
Has the sun that leaves the east
Its real home in the west?
Is that also true?
We that on the ocean live,
Rudders for a pillow,
Sail and sail, on and on."

I went up into the bows where I found a watch of sailors hauling at the halyards.

I began to feel most terribly forlorn. There was no way of knowing when one might get ashore. And, worse, no way of knowing whither we were bound. The only certainties were the streaming of black smoke and the shearing of the sea. The waves stretched wide as wide, blue in their boundlessness. Sometimes they grew purple though, close to the sliding ship, they slavered and were white. I felt most terribly forlorn. I even thought it would be better to throw myself into the sea than to stick with such a ship.

There were many fellow-passengers, most, or so it seemed, foreigners though each had a different cast of feature. One day when the sky was clouded and the ship rolling, I saw a woman leaning on the rail, and crying bitterly. The handkerchief with which she wiped her eyes looked white, and her dress, a sort of calico, carried a printed pattern. Seeing her weep, I realized that I was not the only person sad.

One evening when I was alone on deck, watching the stars, a foreigner came up and asked if I knew anything about astronomy. Since I was already contemplating suicide as a means of escape from boredom, it scarcely seemed necessary for me to be acquainted with matters such as astronomy. So I made no answer. The foreigner then told me the story of the seven stars in the neck of the constellation of the Bull; and went on to inform me that the stars and the sea were all of God's creation. He finally asked me if I believed in God. I looked at the sky and said nothing.

Once as I was entering the saloon, I saw a gaily dressed young woman playing the piano, with her back toward me. At her side a tall most splendid-looking man stood singing. His mouth appeared inordinately large. They seemed completely indifferent to all things other than themselves. They seemed even to have forgotten their being on this ship.

I grew more bored than ever. Finally, I determined to put an end to myself and, one convenient evening when no one was about, I jumped with resolution over the side. However, in that moment when my feet left the deck and my link with the ship was severed, suddenly then life became peculiarly precious. From the bottom of my heart I regretted my rash action. But by then it was too late. Will-nilly I was committed to the deep. But, possibly because of the ship's high freeboard, my feet for some long time failed to touch water although my body had abandoned ship. Nonetheless, since nothing could check my fall, I dropped closer and closer to the sea. However much I drew in my legs, nearer and still nearer came the sea. The color of the sea was black.

Meanwhile the ship, still as usual streaming its black smoke, steamed steadily away. I would have been far better off aboard, even though that ship had no known destination. When I came to that realization, it was no longer possible to make use of my belated wisdom. And so I went down quietly, infinitely regretful, infinitely afraid, down to the black of waves.

■ Shiki (Masaoka Shiki) (1867–1902) (poems)

TRANSLATED BY BURTON WATSON

Masaoka Shiki was extremely influential in resuscitating the moribund haiku form of poetry, and his ideas were instrumental in reforming both the tanka and prose writing. He advocated a theory of narrative based on description, on "direct copying from life," which should be understood both as a form of empirical observation and as an attempt to get at the essence of things through observation. He was born in Matsuyama in 1867, and he wrote prose and poetry from his childhood on. In 1883, he moved to Tokyo and in the following year entered the University Preparatory College. In 1889, he suffered the first attack of the tuberculosis that was to plague him throughout his life and eventually confine him to his bed. During this year, he took on the literary pen name Shiki. During the Sino-Japanese War of 1894–1895 he was a war correspondent in China, but this experience only accelerated his illness. His studies, *The Essence of Haikai* (1895) and *Buson, Haiku Poet* (1897), were essential in spreading his ideas about the need for including contemporary life and colloquial speech in the haiku. He helped found the important magazine *Hototogisu* (*The Cuckoo*) in 1897, which served as a forum for his work. He was critical of Basho's poetry, preferring that of Buson, and perceived his own work as hearkening back to what he saw as the less-contrived spirit of the *Manyoshu* poets.

FURTHER READING: Behn, Harry, tr. *Cricket Songs,* 1960. Blyth, R. H. *A History of Haiku.* Vol. 2, 1964. Brower, Robert H. "Masaoka Shiki and Tanka Reform" in Donald Shively, ed., *Tradition and Modernization in Japanese Culture,* 1971. Corman, Cid. *Born of a Dream: 50 Haiku by Basho, Buson, Taigi, Issa, Shiki,* 1988. Miner, Earl. *Japanese Poetic Diaries,* 1969.

Thirteen Haiku

From the firefly
in my hands,
cold light

A cricket singing
somewhat back of
the shoe closet

Lonely sound—
simmering in the firepit,
wood chips with snow on them

Getting lazy—
taking my socks off
after I get in bed

Fluttering, fluttering,
butterflies yellow
over the water

Summer storm—
all the sheets of blank paper
blown off my desk

Country road—
boys whacking at a snake,
wheat in autumn

Morning fog—
one man's got a fire going—
construction workers' shed

Peeling pears—
sweet juice drips
from the knife blade

Summer grass—
way in the distance
people playing baseball

A stray cat
shits in my
winter garden

Crickets—
in the corner of the garden
where we buried the dog

Clog with a broken thong
discarded in the
winter paddy

■ **Yosano Akiko (1878–1942) (poems)**

TRANSLATED BY SANFORD GOLDSTEIN AND SEISHI SHINODA

Yosano Akiko was the finest practitioner of the "new tanka." The five
lines of the tanka (based on syllable counts of $5-7-5-7-7$) constitute the
form that has dominated Japanese poetry from the time of the *Manyoshu*
until Western forms were introduced in the modern era. Late-nineteenth-
and early-twentieth-century tanka was dominated by the practitioners of
the Poetry Bureau School, a traditionalist school based at the Imperial Poetry Bureau. In the Meiji era, however, contact with the West and increasing

industrial progress were changing the nature of life in Japan, and the Bureau School's nature-centered aesthetic was inadequate to the need of poetry to express life as lived.

Yosano Akiko was born to the family of a famous confectioner in Sakai City, Osaka prefecture. Her father, expecting a male child and mourning the death of a son, so hated his daughter that for the first three years of her life she was sent to be raised by an aunt. Later, however, he repented (after the birth of a new brother) and came to admire his bright daughter, providing the best possible education for her. In other aspects, however, he raised her extremely traditionally—locking her in her bedroom at night and making sure she never went out without a chaperone. But Akiko was a firm believer in social and sexual emancipation for women, which is apparent later in her life in the frankly erotic nature of her tanka. She married Yosano Hiroshi, son of a Buddhist priest, who rejected the priesthood to become first a teacher and then a writer under the pen name Tekkan. One of the most important theorists and popularizers of the new tanka, he had a strong early reputation as a "manly" practitioner of tanka, who wrote about his experiences in the Sino-Japanese War (1894–1895), but his reputation steadily declined as it became apparent that the real talent in the family belonged to Akiko. They were both in love with one of Tekkan's students, a young woman named Yamakawa Tomiko, who died young of tuberculosis in 1909.

In addition to poetry, Akiko wrote novels, essays, and children's stories and translated *The Tale of Genji* into modern Japanese. Akiko's most famous book of poems is *Midaregami* (*Tangled Hair*), a term that, as in Robert Herrick's "Delight in Disorder" or the tangled tresses of women in Pre-Raphaelite paintings, has erotic undertones—not dishevelment but release from constraints. Such release characterizes her poetry, which celebrates love and the flesh and chastizes the priests whom, in another context, William Blake criticizes for "binding with briars, my joys & desires."

FURTHER READING: Goldstein, Sanford, and Seishi Shinoda, trs. *Tangled Hair: Selected Tanka from Midaregami by Akiko Yosana*, 1987.

You Have Yet to Touch

You have yet to touch
This soft flesh,
This throbbing blood—
Are you not lonely,
Expounder of the Way?

5

Without Returning

Without returning . . .
O my feelings
In this gathering darkness of spring,
And against my koto
My tangled, tangled hair.   *5*

In My Bath

In my bath—
Submerged like some graceful lily
At the bottom of a spring,
How beautiful
This body of twenty summers.   *5*

Now

Now
Thinking back
On the course of my passion,
I was like one blind,
Unafraid of the dark.   *5*

Whispering Goodnight

Whispering goodnight
This spring evening
And leaving the room,
I take from the rack
His kimono and try it on.   *5*

Softly I Pushed Open

Softly I pushed open
That door
We call a mystery,
These full breasts
Held in both my hands.   *5*

Was It So Long Ago

Was it so long ago
All innocent I smiled
In the full-length mirror
As I dressed
After my bath?   *5*

Inside the Coffin

Inside the coffin
Of my beautiful
Friend,
The flowers
A riot of color.   5

Sleeve Raised

Sleeve raised
As if to strike her love,
She tries to turn the gesture
Into
A dance!   5

Spring Is Short!

Spring is short!
Nothing endures!
I cried,
Letting him touch
These supple breasts!   5

To Punish

To punish
Men for their endless sins,
God gave me
This fair skin,
This long black hair!   5

■ Tanizaki Junichiro (1886–1965) (story)

TRANSLATED BY HOWARD HIBBET

Tanizaki Junichiro was born in 1886 in the heart of downtown Tokyo's old merchant quarter to a father who owned a printing establishment but failed in a series of business enterprises. Tanizaki attended Tokyo Imperial University, where he studied Japanese literature, but never completed his degree, leaving school to become a successful writer and to live a vigorous bohemian life. In this period, he was powerfully influenced by fin de siècle decadent aestheticism and by the work of Charles-Pierre Baudelaire, Edgar Allan Poe, and Oscar Wilde. "The Tattooer" (*Shisei*), the story presented here, launched his literary career in 1910 and is still a favorite. Today, he is considered by many the greatest modern Japanese novelist, and Mishima Yukio was a fierce admirer of his work. The two authors shared a personal flamboyance that shocked their contemporaries, a fascination with sado-masochistic themes in their work, and an aesthetic pursuit of ultimate beauty, a beauty often gendered female. These themes can be seen in "The Tattooer," a kind of perverse meditation on the costs and rewards of art, the tale of a twisted Pygmalion. In the context of this story of a beauty printed over with a tattoer's art, it is interesting to note that Tanizaki's mother was herself a beauty, portrayed in Japanese woodcut prints.

Tanizaki left Tokyo after the 1923 earthquake for the Kansai region, a move from the new capital to the region of Kyoto, the old capital, where he was surrounded by the culture, the architecture, the temples, and the gardens of old Japan. At this time, he moved away from his earlier Westernized work and became fascinated with the Japanese past. Much of his fiction transports the reader into Japanese historical settings, and he devoted years to translating the great work of classical Japanese fiction, *The Tale of Genji*, into modern Japanese.

Tanizaki was, like other intellectual fiction writers, criticized by leftist writers known as the Proletarian Writers for being "bourgeois, decadent, reactionary." Though he was able to pass through the difficult war years without much hardship, his novel *The Makioka Sisters* was censored by the military during this period. He was awarded the Imperial Culture Prize in 1949, the highest official honor for Japanese writers. In 1964, he was the first Japanese writer to be elected to honorary membership in the American Academy and Institute of Arts and Letters. Among his other well-known works are *A Fool's Love* (1924), *Some Prefer Nettles* (1929), *Captain Shigemoto's Mother* (1949), *The Key* (1956), and *Diary of a Mad Old Man* (1962).

FURTHER READING: Harper, Thomas J., and Edward G. Seidensticker, trs. *In Praise of Shadows*, 1977. Hibbett, Howard, tr. *Seven Japanese Tales*, 1963. McCarthy, Paul, tr. *A Cat, a Man, and Two Women: Stories*, 1990. Petersen, Gwenn Boardman. *The Moon in Water: Understanding Tanizaki, Kawabata, and Mishima*, 1979.

The Tattooer

It was an age when men honored the noble virtue of frivolity, when life was not such a harsh struggle as it is today. It was a leisurely age, an age when professional wits could make an excellent livelihood by keeping rich or wellborn young gentlemen in a cloudless good humor and seeing to it that the laughter of Court ladies and geisha was never stilled. In the illustrated romantic novels of the day, in the Kabuki theater, where rough masculine heroes like Sadakuro and Jiraiya were transformed into women—everywhere beauty and strength were one. People did all they could to beautify themselves, some even having pigments injected into their precious skins. Gaudy patterns of line and color danced over men's bodies.

Visitors to the pleasure quarters of Edo preferred to hire palanquin bearers who were splendidly tattooed; courtesans of the Yoshiwara and the Tatsumi quarter fell in love with tattooed men. Among those so adorned were not only gamblers, firemen, and the like, but members of the merchant class and even samurai. Exhibitions were held from time to time; and the participants, stripped to show off their filigreed bodies, would pat themselves proudly, boast of their own novel designs, and criticize each other's merits.

There was an exceptionally skillful young tattooer named Seikichi. He was praised on all sides as a master the equal of Charibun or Yatsuhei, and the skins of dozens of men had been offered as the silk for his brush. Much of the work admired at the tattoo exhibitions was his. Others might be more noted for their shading, or their use of cinnabar, but Seikichi was famous for the unrivaled boldness and sensual charm of his art.

Seikichi had formerly earned his living as an ukiyoye painter of the school of Toyokuni and Kunisada, a background which, in spite of his decline to the status of a tattooer, was evident from his artistic conscience and sensitivity. No one whose skin or whose physique failed to interest him could buy his services. The clients he did accept had to leave the design and cost entirely to his discretion—and to endure for one or even two months the excruciating pain of his needles.

Deep in his heart the young tattooer concealed a secret pleasure, and a secret desire. His pleasure lay in the agony men felt as he drove his needles into them, torturing their swollen, blood-red flesh; and the louder they groaned, the keener was Seikichi's strange delight. Shading and vermilioning—these are said to be especially painful—were the techniques he most enjoyed.

When a man had been pricked five or six hundred times in the course of an average day's treatment and had then soaked himself in a hot bath to bring out the colors, he would collapse at Seikichi's feet half dead. But Seikichi would look down at him coolly. "I dare say that hurts," he would remark with an air of satisfaction.

Whenever a spineless man howled in torment or clenched his teeth and twisted his mouth as if he were dying, Seikichi told him: "Don't act like a child. Pull yourself together—you have hardly begun to feel my needles!" And he would go on tattooing, as unperturbed as ever, with an occasional sidelong glance at the man's tearful face.

But sometimes a man of immense fortitude set his jaw and bore up stoically, not even allowing himself to frown. Then Seikichi would smile and say: "Ah, you are a stubborn one! But wait. Soon your body will begin to throb with pain. I doubt if you will be able to stand it. . . ."

For a long time Seikichi had cherished the desire to create a master-piece on the skin of a beautiful woman. Such a woman had to meet various qualifications of character as well as appearance. A lovely face and a fine body were not enough to satisfy him. Though he inspected all the reigning beauties of the Edo gay quarters he found none who met his exacting demands. Several years had passed without success, and yet the face and figure of the perfect woman continued to obsess his thoughts. He refused to abandon hope.

One summer evening during the fourth year of his search Seikichi happened to be passing the Hirasei Restaurant in the Fukagawa district of Edo, not far from his own house, when he noticed a woman's bare milk-white foot peeping out beneath the curtains of a departing palanquin. To his sharp eye, a human foot was as expressive as a face. This one was sheer perfection. Exquisitely chiseled toes, nails like the iridescent shells along the shore at Enoshima, a pearl-like rounded heel, skin so lustrous that it seemed bathed in the limpid waters of a mountain spring—this, indeed, was a foot to be nourished by men's blood, a foot to trample on their bodies. Surely this was the foot of the unique woman who had so long eluded him. Eager to catch a glimpse of her face, Seikichi began to follow the palanquin. But after pursuing it down several lanes and alleys he lost sight of it altogether.

Seikichi's long-held desire turned into passionate love. One morning late the next spring he was standing on the bamboo-floored veranda of his home in Fukagawa, gazing at a pot of *omoto* lilies, when he heard someone at the garden gate. Around the corner of the inner fence appeared a young girl. She had come on an errand for a friend of his, a geisha of the nearby Tatsumi quarter.

"My mistress asked me to deliver this cloak, and she wondered if you would be so good as to decorate its lining," the girl said. She untied a saffron-colored cloth parcel and took out a woman's silk cloak (wrapped in a sheet of thick paper bearing a portrait of the actor Tojaku) and a letter.

The letter repeated his friend's request and went on to say that its bearer would soon begin a career as a geisha under her protection. She hoped that, while not forgetting old ties, he would also extend his patronage to this girl.

"I thought I had never seen you before," said Seikichi, scrutinizing her intently. She seemed only fifteen or sixteen, but her face had a strangely ripe beauty, a look of experience, as if she had already spent years in the gay quarter and had fascinated innumerable men. Her beauty mirrored the dreams of the generations of glamorous men and women who had lived and died in this vast capital, where the nation's sins and wealth were concentrated.

Seikichi had her sit on the veranda, and he studied her delicate feet, which were bare except for elegant straw sandals. "You left the Hirasei by palanquin one night last July, did you not?" he inquired.

"I suppose so," she replied, smiling at the odd question. "My father was still alive then, and he often took me there."

"I have waited five years for you. This is the first time I have seen your face, but I remember your foot. . . . Come in for a moment, I have something to show you."

She had risen to leave, but he took her by the hand and led her upstairs to his studio overlooking the broad river. Then he brought out two picture scrolls and unrolled one of them before her.

It was a painting of a Chinese princess, the favorite of the cruel Emperor Chou of the Shang Dynasty. She was leaning on a balustrade in a languorous pose, the long skirt of her figured brocade robe trailing halfway down a flight of stairs, her slender body barely able to support the weight of her gold crown studded with coral and lapis lazuli. In her right hand she held a large wine cup, tilting it to her lips as she gazed down at a man who was about to be tortured in the garden below. He was chained hand and foot to a hollow copper pillar in which a fire would be lighted. Both the princess and her victim—his head bowed before her, his eyes closed, ready to meet his fate—were portrayed with terrifying vividness.

As the girl stared at this bizarre picture her lips trembled and her eyes began to sparkle. Gradually her face took on a curious resemblance to that of the princess. In the picture she discovered her secret self.

"Your own feelings are revealed here," Seikichi told her with pleasure as he watched her face.

"Why are you showing me this horrible thing?" the girl asked, looking up at him. She had turned pale.

"The woman is yourself. Her blood flows in your veins." Then he spread out the other scroll.

This was a painting called "The Victims." In the middle of it a young woman stood leaning against the trunk of a cherry tree: she was gloating over a heap of men's corpses lying at her feet. Little birds fluttered about her, singing in triumph; her eyes radiated pride and joy. Was it a battlefield or a garden in spring? In this picture the girl felt that she had found something long hidden in the darkness of her own heart.

"This painting shows your future," Seikichi said, pointing to the woman under the cherry tree—the very image of the young girl. "All these men will ruin their lives for you."

"Please, I beg of you to put it away!" She turned her back as if to escape its tantalizing lure and prostrated herself before him, trembling. At last she spoke again. "Yes, I admit that you are right about me—I am like that woman. . . . So please, please take it away."

"Don't talk like a coward," Seikichi told her, with his malicious smile. "Look at it more closely. You won't be squeamish long."

But the girl refused to lift her head. Still prostrate, her face buried in her sleeves, she repeated over and over that she was afraid and wanted to leave.

"No, you must stay—I will make you a real beauty," he said, moving closer to her. Under his kimono was a vial of anesthetic which he had obtained some time ago from a Dutch physician.

The morning sun glittered on the river, setting the eight-mat studio ablaze with light. Rays reflected from the water sketched rippling golden waves on the paper sliding screens and on the face of the girl, who was fast asleep. Seikichi had closed the doors and taken up his tattooing instruments, but for a while he only sat there entranced, savoring to the full her uncanny beauty. He thought that he would never tire of contemplating her serene masklike face. Just as the ancient Egyptians had embellished their magnificent land with pyramids and sphinxes, he was about to embellish the pure skin of this girl.

Presently he raised the brush which was gripped between the thumb and last two fingers of his left hand, applied its tip to the girl's back, and, with the needle which he held in his right hand, began pricking out a design. He felt his spirit dissolve into the charcoal-black ink that stained her skin. Each drop of Ryukyu cinnabar that he mixed with alcohol and thrust in was a drop of his lifeblood. He saw in his pigments the hues of his own passions.

Soon it was afternoon, and then the tranquil spring day drew toward its close. But Seikichi never paused in his work, nor was the girl's sleep broken. When a servant came from the geisha house to inquire about her, Seikichi turned him away, saying that she had left long ago. And hours later, when the moon hung over the mansion across the river, bathing the houses along the bank in a dreamlike radiance, the tattoo was not yet half done. Seikichi worked on by candlelight.

Even to insert a single drop of color was no easy task. At every thrust of his needle Seikichi gave a heavy sigh and felt as if he had stabbed his own heart. Little by little the tattoo marks began to take on the form of a huge black-widow spider; and by the time the night sky was paling into dawn this weird, malevolent creature had stretched its eight legs to embrace the whole of the girl's back.

In the full light of the spring dawn boats were being rowed up and down the river, their oars creaking in the morning quiet; roof tiles glistened in the sun, and the haze began to thin out over white sails swelling in the early breeze. Finally Seikichi put down his brush and looked at the tattooed spider. This work of art had been the supreme effort of his life. Now that he had finished it his heart was drained of emotion.

The two figures remained still for some time. Then Seikichi's low, hoarse voice echoed quaveringly from the walls of the room:

"To make you truly beautiful I have poured my soul into this tattoo. Today there is no woman in Japan to compare with you. Your old fears are gone. All men will be your victims."

As if in response to these words a faint moan came from the girl's lips. Slowly she began to recover her senses. With each shuddering breath, the spider's legs stirred as if they were alive.

"You must be suffering. The spider has you in its clutches."

At this she opened her eyes slightly, in a dull stare. Her gaze steadily brightened, as the moon brightens in the evening, until it shone dazzlingly into his face.

"Let me see the tattoo," she said, speaking as if in a dream but with an edge of authority to her voice. "Giving me your soul must have made me very beautiful."

"First you must bathe to bring out the colors," whispered Seikichi compassionately. "I am afraid it will hurt, but be brave a little longer."

"I can bear anything for the sake of beauty." Despite the pain that was coursing through her body, she smiled.

"How the water stings! . . . Leave me alone—wait in the other room! I hate to have a man see me suffer like this!"

As she left the tub, too weak to dry herself, the girl pushed aside the sympathetic hand Seikichi offered her, and sank to the floor in agony, moaning as if in a nightmare. Her disheveled hair hung over her face in a wild tangle. The white soles of her feet were reflected in the mirror behind her.

Seikichi was amazed at the change that had come over the timid, yielding girl of yesterday, but he did as he was told and went to wait in his studio. About an hour later she came back, carefully dressed, her damp, sleekly combed hair hanging down over her shoulders. Leaning on the veranda rail, she looked up into the faintly hazy sky. Her eyes were brilliant; there was not a trace of pain in them.

"I wish to give you these pictures too," said Seikichi, placing the scrolls before her. "Take them and go."

"All my old fears have been swept away—and you are my first victim!" She darted a glance at him as bright as a sword. A song of triumph was ringing in her ears.

"Let me see your tattoo once more," Seikichi begged.

Silently the girl nodded and slipped the kimono off her shoulders. Just then her resplendently tattooed back caught a ray of sunlight and the spider was wreathed in flames.

■ Akutagawa Ryunosuke (1892–1927) (story)

TRANSLATED BY TAKASHI KOJIMA

Fiction writer Akutagawa Ryunosuke was born in Tokyo in 1892, the son of a milkman. Seven months later his mother went mad and, not long after, died. Her brother and his wife, the Akutagawas, adopted him into their cultivated and priestly family, but he feared throughout his life that his mother's madness might be in him as well. He studied English literature at Tokyo University from 1913 to 1916, graduating with high honors. At college and throughout his short life, he read widely in both Eastern and Western literatures. He was a disciple of novelist Natsume Soseki, whose attention was captured by Akutagawa's early stories "Rashomon" (1915) and "The Nose" (1916), and he attended Natsume's weekly literary salon.

After a brief period teaching English, he devoted himself entirely to literature, and his reputation as a master of the short story was soon established. When he was thirty-five years old, he shocked his contemporaries by drinking poison. He was found with a Bible next to his pillow and with letters in which he gave no better reason for killing himself than (as in some existential short story) "a vague uneasiness."

His fiction is known for its grotesque yet psychologically well observed depictions, for its dark sensitivity and mordant outlook, as well as for his adaptations of classical Chinese fiction and of traditional *setsuwa*, or "brief narratives," from classical Japanese collections. "Rashomon," for example, was adapted from *Tales of Times Now Past* and later became (with his short story "In a Grove") the basis for the 1950 movie of that name by Akira Kurosawa. He was of a school of intellectual writers who were in conflict with the political fiction of the Proletarian Writers and the confessional, first-person stories of the contemporary world promoted by the Naturalistic School. As is commonly noted, Akutagawa's style eschews the subjectivity of confession and the crude moralizing of political prose, preferring to hide behind a mask of objectivity, embedding his views subtly in tone and perspective—the deft evasions of a masterful style. Thus, in spite of its "cool" surface, his work was not removed from the concerns of his day: the relativistic perspective in a story such as "In a Grove" and the distancing of placing many of his stories at a historical remove are a screen behind which the author's often biting satire of contemporary Japan resides. This satire of Japanese culture is much more explicit in his short novel *Kappa,* which is a sort of mixture of "Rip Van Winkle" and *Gulliver's Travels.* "Hell Screen," another of his finest works, is a story about the artist as misfit, sacrificer of his own family, and suicide.

FURTHER READING: Bownas, Geoffrey, tr. *Kappa: A Satire,* 1971. Kojima, Takashi, tr. *Rashomon and Other Stories,* 1952. Norman, W. H. H., tr. *Hell Screen and Other Stories,* 1948. Peterson, Will, tr. *A Fool's Life,* 1970.

Rashōmon[1]

It was a chilly evening. A servant of a samurai stood under the Rashōmon, waiting for a break in the rain.

No one else was under the wide gate. On the thick column, its crimson lacquer rubbed off here and there, perched a cricket. Since the Rashōmon

---

1. The "Rashōmon" was the largest gate in Kyoto, the ancient capital of Japan. It was 106 feet wide and 26 feet deep, and was topped with a ridge-pole; its stone-wall rose 75 feet high. This gate was constructed in 789 when the then capital of Japan was transferred to Kyoto. With the decline of West Kyoto, the gate fell into bad repair, cracking and crumbling in many places, and became a hide-out for thieves and robbers and a place for abandoning unclaimed corpses.

stands on Sujaku Avenue, a few other people at least, in sedge hat or no-bleman's headgear, might have been expected to be waiting there for a break in the rain storm. But no one was near except this man.

For the past few years the city of Kyōto had been visited by a series of calamities, earthquakes, whirlwinds, and fires, and Kyōto had been greatly devastated. Old chronicles say that broken pieces of Buddhist images and other Buddhist objects, with their lacquer, gold, or silver leaf worn off, were heaped up on roadsides to be sold as firewood. Such being the state of af-fairs in Kyōto, the repair of the Rashōmon was out of the question. Taking advantage of the devastation, foxes and other wild animals made their dens in the ruins of the gate, and thieves and robbers found a home there too. Eventually it became customary to bring unclaimed corpses to this gate and abandon them. After dark it was so ghostly that no one dared approach.

Flocks of crows flew in from somewhere. During the daytime these caw-ing birds circled round the ridgepole of the gate. When the sky overhead turned red in the afterlight of the departed sun, they looked like so many grains of sesame flung across the gate. But on that day not a crow was to be seen, perhaps because of the lateness of the hour. Here and there the stone steps, beginning to crumble, and with rank grass growing in their crevices, were dotted with the white droppings of crows. The servant, in a worn blue kimono, sat on the seventh and highest step, vacantly watching the rain. His attention was drawn to a large pimple irritating his right cheek.

As has been said, the servant was waiting for a break in the rain. But he had no particular idea of what to do after the rain stopped. Ordinarily, of course, he would have returned to his master's house, but he had been dis-charged just before. The prosperity of the city of Kyōto had been rapidly declining, and he had been dismissed by his master, whom he had served many years, because of the effects of this decline. Thus, confined by the rain, he was at a loss to know where to go. And the weather had not a little to do with his depressed mood. The rain seemed unlikely to stop. He was lost in thoughts of how to make his living tomorrow, helpless incoherent thoughts protesting an inexorable fate. Aimlessly he had been listening to the pattering of the rain on the Sujaku Avenue.

The rain, enveloping the Rashōmon, gathered strength and came down with a pelting sound that could be heard far away. Looking up, he saw a fat black cloud impale itself on the tips of the tiles jutting out from the roof of the gate.

He had little choice of means, whether fair or foul, because of his help-less circumstances. If he chose honest means, he would undoubtedly starve to death beside the wall or in the Sujaku gutter. He would be brought to this gate and thrown away like a stray dog. If he decided to steal . . . His mind, after making the same detour time and again, came finally to the conclusion that he would be a thief.

But doubts returned many times. Though determined that he had no choice, he was still unable to muster enough courage to justify the conclu-sion that he must become a thief.

After a loud fit of sneezing he got up slowly. The evening chill of Kyōto made him long for the warmth of a brazier. The wind in the evening dusk howled through the columns of the gate. The cricket which had been perched on the crimson-lacquered column was already gone.

Ducking his neck, he looked around the gate, and drew up the shoulders of the blue kimono which he wore over his thin underwear. He decided to spend the night there, if he could find a secluded corner sheltered from wind and rain. He found a broad lacquered stairway leading to the tower over the gate. No one would be there, except the dead, if there were any. So, taking care that the sword at his side did not slip out of the scabbard, he set foot on the lowest step of the stairs.

A few seconds later, halfway up the stairs, he saw a movement above. Holding his breath and huddling cat-like in the middle of the broad stairs leading to the tower, he watched and waited. A light coming from the upper part of the tower shone faintly upon his right cheek. It was the cheek with the red, festering pimple visible under his stubbly whiskers. He expected only dead people inside the tower, but he had only gone up a few steps before he noticed a fire above, about which someone was moving. He saw a dull, yellow, flickering light which made the cobwebs hanging from the ceiling glow in a ghostly way. What sort of person would be making a light in the Rashōmon . . . and in a storm? The unknown, the evil terrified him.

As quietly as a lizard, the servant crept up to the top of the steep stairs. Crouching on all fours, and stretching his neck as far as possible, he timidly peeped into the tower.

As rumor had said, he found several corpses strewn carelessly about the floor. Since the glow of the light was feeble, he could not count the number. He could only see that some were naked and others clothed. Some of them were women, and all were lolling on the floor with their mouths open or their arms outstretched showing no more signs of life than so many clay dolls. One would doubt that they had ever been alive, so eternally silent they were. Their shoulders, breasts, and torsos stood out in the dim light; other parts vanished in shadow. The offensive smell of these decomposed corpses brought his hand to his nose.

The next moment his hand dropped and he stared. He caught sight of a ghoulish form bent over a corpse. It seemed to be an old woman, gaunt, gray-haired, and nunnish in appearance. With a pine torch in her right hand, she was peeping into the face of a corpse which had long black hair.

Seized more with horror than curiosity, he even forgot to breathe for a time. He felt the hair of his head and body stand on end. As he watched, terrified, she wedged the torch between two floor boards and, laying hands on the head of the corpse, began to pull out the long hairs one by one, as a monkey kills the lice of her young. The hair came out smoothly with the movement of her hands.

As the hair came out, fear faded from his heart, and his hatred toward the old woman mounted. It grew beyond hatred, becoming a consuming antipathy against all evil. At this instant if anyone had brought up the question of whether he would starve to death or become a thief—the question which had occurred to him a little while ago—he would not have hesitated to choose death. His hatred toward evil flared up like the piece of pine wood which the old woman had stuck in the floor.

He did not know why she pulled out the hair of the dead. Accordingly, he did not know whether her case was to be put down as good or bad. But in his eyes, pulling out the hair of the dead in the Rashōmon on this stormy night was an unpardonable crime. Of course it never entered his mind that a little while ago he had thought of becoming a thief.

Then, summoning strength into his legs, he rose from the stairs and strode, hand on sword, right in front of the old creature. The hag turned, terror in her eyes, and sprang up from the floor, trembling. For a small moment she paused, poised there, then lunged for the stairs with a shriek.

"Wretch! Where are you going?" he shouted, barring the way of the trembling hag who tried to scurry past him. Still she attempted to claw her way by. He pushed her back to prevent her . . . they struggled, fell among the corpses, and grappled there. The issue was never in doubt. In a moment he had her by the arm, twisted it, and forced her down to the floor. Her arms were all skin and bones, and there was no more flesh on them than on the shanks of a chicken. No sooner was she on the floor than he drew his sword and thrust the silver-white blade before her very nose. She was silent. She trembled as if in a fit, and her eyes were open so wide that they were almost out of their sockets, and her breath came in hoarse gasps. The life of this wretch was his now. This thought cooled his boiling anger and brought a calm pride and satisfaction. He looked down at her, and said in a somewhat calmer voice:

"Look here, I'm not an officer of the High Police Commissioner. I'm a stranger who happened to pass by this gate. I won't bind you or do anything against you, but you must tell me what you're doing up here."

Then the old woman opened her eyes still wider, and gazed at his face intently with the sharp red eyes of a bird of prey. She moved her lips, which were wrinkled into her nose, as though she were chewing something. Her pointed Adam's apple moved in her thin throat. Then a panting sound like the cawing of a crow came from her throat:

"I pull the hair . . . I pull out the hair . . . to make a wig."

Her answer banished all unknown from their encounter and brought disappointment. Suddenly she was only a trembling old woman there at his feet. A ghoul no longer: only a hag who makes wigs from the hair of the dead—to sell, for scraps of food. A cold contempt seized him. Fear left his heart, and his former hatred entered. These feelings must have been sensed by the other. The old creature, still clutching the hair she had pulled off the corpse, mumbled out these words in her harsh broken voice:

"Indeed, making wigs out of the hair of the dead may seem a great evil to you, but these that are here deserve no better. This woman, whose beautiful black hair I was pulling, used to sell cut and dried snake flesh at the guard barracks, saying that it was dried fish. If she hadn't died of the plague, she'd be selling it now. The guards liked to buy from her, and used to say her fish was tasty. What she did couldn't be wrong, because if she hadn't, she would have starved to death. There was no other choice. If she knew I had to do this in order to live, she probably wouldn't care."

He sheathed his sword, and, with his left hand on its hilt, he listened to her meditatively. His right hand touched the big pimple on his cheek. As he listened, a certain courage was born in his heart—the courage which he had not had when he sat under the gate a little while ago. A strange power was driving him in the opposite direction of the courage which he had had when he seized the old woman. No longer did he wonder whether he should starve to death or become a thief. Starvation was so far from his mind that it was the last thing that would have entered it.

"Are you sure?" he asked in a mocking tone, when she finished talking. He took his right hand from his pimple, and, bending forward, seized her by the neck and said sharply:

"Then it's right if I rob you. I'd starve if I didn't."

He tore her clothes from her body and kicked her roughly down on the corpses as she struggled and tried to clutch his leg. Five steps, and he was at the top of the stairs. The yellow clothes he had wrested off were under his arm, and in a twinkling he had rushed down the steep stairs into the abyss of night. The thunder of his descending steps pounded in the hollow tower, and then it was quiet.

Shortly after that the hag raised up her body from the corpses. Grumbling and groaning, she crawled to the top stair by the still flickering torchlight, and through the gray hair which hung over her face, she peered down to the last stair in the torch light.

Beyond this was only darkness . . . unknowing and unknown.

■ Kawabata Yasunari (1899–1972) (stories)

In 1968, Kawabata Yasunari became the first Japanese writer to win the Nobel Prize in literature. Four years later, he committed suicide in his studio, leaving no note. He was born in Osaka in 1899, and a tragic childhood in which he lost his sister, parents, grandmother, and in his teens, his grandfather, informs his work with a pervasive sadness. He studied English and Japanese literature at Tokyo University and graduated in 1924. Throughout his life, he wrote the extremely short stories to which he gave the name "palm-of-the-hand stories," and these brief tales quickly established his reputation after his graduation. In addition to the masterful short story "The Mole," one of these palm-of-the-hand stories, "Eggs," is included here.

He was early on associated with a group of writers known as the Neosensualists, who launched a journal called *Age of the Arts,* and who strove for startling, sometimes surreal, images, and a compact, suggestive fiction, a reaction to the dominant mode of naturalism in the early part of the century. Many of his short stories grew into novels, and he even created one palm-of-the-hand story from an already extant novel (*Gleanings from Snow Country*). Translator J. Martin Holman considers the palm-of-the-hand story to be Kawabata's "basic unit of composition from which his longer works were built, after the manner of linked-verse poetry, in which discreet verses are joined to form a longer poem, the linkage between each dependent on subtle shifts as the poem continues."[1] Kawabata had a fantastic instinct for capturing psychologically revelatory dialogue and events, and in his stories life often tilts suddenly into the strange so that ordinary objects, such as a mole or an egg, can become fetishes, or icons of terror. He is best known in the West for his novels *Snow Country* (1947) and *A Thousand Cranes* (1949–1951).

FURTHER READING: Kawabata, Yasunari. *The Izu Dancer and Other Stories*, 1974; *Palm-of-the-Hand Stories*. Translated by Lane Dunlop and J. Martin Holman, 1988; *Snow Country*. Translated by Edward Seidensticker, 1981; *Snow Country, and Thousand Cranes; the Nobel Prize Edition of Two Novels*. Translated by Edward G. Seidensticker, 1969; *The Sound of the Mountain*. Translated by Edward G. Seidensticker, 1981. Petersen, Gwenn Boardman. *The Moon in the Water: Understanding Tanizaki, Kawabata, and Mishima*, 1979.

The Mole

TRANSLATED BY EDWARD SEIDENSTICKER

Last night I dreamed about that mole.

I need only write the word for you to know what I mean. That mole—how many times have I been scolded by you because of it.

It is on my right shoulder, or perhaps I should say high on my back.

"It's already bigger than a bean. Go on playing with it and it will be sending out shoots one of these days."

You used to tease me about it. But as you said, it was large for a mole, large and wonderfully round and swollen.

As a child I used to lie in bed and play with that mole. How ashamed I was when you first noticed it.

I even wept, and I remember your surprise.

"Stop it, Sayoko. The more you touch it the bigger it will get." My mother scolded me too. I was still a child, probably not yet thirteen, and afterwards I kept the habit to myself. It persisted after I had all but forgotten about it.

---

1. Kawabata Yasunari. *Palm-of-the-Hand Stories*. Translated by Lane Dunlop and J. Martin Holman (San Francisco: North Point Press, 1988), xiii.

When you first noticed it, I was still more child than wife. I wonder if you, a man, can imagine how ashamed I was. But it was more than shame. This is dreadful, I thought to myself. Marriage seemed at that moment a fearful thing indeed.

I felt as though all my secrets had been discovered—as though you had bared secret after secret of which I was not even conscious myself—as though I had no refuge left.

You went off happily to sleep, and sometimes I felt relieved, and a little lonely, and sometimes I pulled myself up with a start as my hand traveled to the mole again.

"I can't even touch my mole any more," I thought of writing to my mother, but even as I thought of it I felt my face go fiery red.

"But what nonsense to worry about a mole," you once said. I was happy, and I nodded, but looking back now, I wonder if it would not have been better if you had been able to love that wretched habit of mine a little more.

I did not worry so very much about the mole. Surely people do not go about looking down women's necks for moles. Sometimes the expression "unspoiled as a locked room" is used to describe a deformed girl. But a mole, no matter how large it is, can hardly be called a deformity.

Why do you suppose I fell into the habit of playing with that mole?

And why did the habit annoy you so?

"Stop it," you would say. "Stop it." I do not know how many hundred times you scolded me.

"Do you have to use your left hand?" you asked once in a fit of irritation.

"My left hand?" I was startled by the question.

It was true. I had not noticed before, but I always used my left hand.

"It's on your right shoulder. Your right hand should be better."

"Oh?" I raised my right hand. "But it's strange."

"It's not a bit strange."

"But it's more natural with my left hand."

"The right hand is nearer."

"It's backwards with my right hand."

"Backwards?"

"Yes, it's a choice between bringing my arm in front of my neck or reaching around in back like this." I was no longer agreeing meekly with everything you said. Even as I answered you, though, it came to me that when I brought my left arm around in front of me it was as though I were warding you off, as though I were embracing myself. I have been cruel to him, I thought.

I asked quietly, "But what is wrong with using my left hand?"

"Left hand or right hand, it's a bad habit."

"I know."

"Haven't I told you time and time again to go to a doctor and have the thing removed?"

"But I couldn't. I'd be ashamed to."

"It would be a very simple matter."

"Who would go to a doctor to have a mole removed?"

"A great many people seem to."

"For moles in the middle of the face, maybe. I doubt if anyone goes to have a mole removed from the neck. The doctor would laugh. He would know I was there because my husband had complained."

"You could tell him it was because you had a habit of playing with it."

"Really. . . . Something as insignificant as a mole, in a place where you can't even see it. I should think you could stand at least that much."

"I wouldn't mind the mole if you wouldn't play with it."

"I don't mean to."

"You are stubborn, though. No matter what I say, you make no attempt to change yourself."

"I do try. I even tried wearing a high-necked nightgown so that I wouldn't touch it."

"Not for long."

"But is it so wrong for me to touch it?" I suppose I must have seemed to be fighting back.

"It's not wrong, especially. I only ask you to stop because I don't like it."

"But why do you dislike it so?"

"There's no need to go into the reasons. You don't need to play with that mole, and it's a bad habit, and I wish you would stop."

"I've never said I won't stop."

"And when you touch it you always get that strange, absent-minded expression on your face. That's what I really hate."

You're probably right—something made the remark go straight to my heart, and I wanted to nod my agreement.

"Next time you see me doing it, slap my hand. Slap my face even."

"But doesn't it bother you that even though you've been trying for two or three years you haven't been able to cure a trivial little habit like that by yourself?"

I did not answer. I was thinking of your words, "That's what I really hate."

That pose, with my left arm drawn up around my neck—it must look somehow dreary, forlorn. I would hesitate to use a grand word like "solitary." Shabby, rather, and mean, the pose of a woman concerned only with protecting her own small self. And the expression on my face must be just as you described it, "strange, absent-minded."

Did it seem a sign that I had not really given myself to you, as though a space lay between us? And did my true feelings come out on my face when I touched the mole and lost myself in reverie, as I had done since I was a child?

But it must have been because you were already dissatisfied with me that you made so much of that one small habit. If you had been pleased with me you would have smiled and thought no more about it.

That was the frightening thought. I trembled when it came to me of a sudden that there might be men who would find the habit charming.

It was your love for me that first made you notice. I do not doubt that even now. But it is just this sort of small annoyance, as it grows and becomes distorted, that drives its roots down into a marriage. To a real husband and wife personal eccentricities have stopped mattering, and I suppose that on the other hand there are husbands and wives who find themselves at odds on everything. I do not say that those who accommodate themselves to each other necessarily love each other, and that those who constantly disagree hate each other. I do think, though, and I cannot get over thinking, that it would have been better if you could have brought yourself to overlook my habit of playing with the mole.

You actually came to beat me and to kick me. I wept and asked why you could not be a little less violent, why I had to suffer so because I touched my mole. That was only surface. "How can we cure it?" you said, your voice trembling, and I quite understood how you felt and did not resent what you did. If I had told anyone of this, no doubt you would have seemed a violent husband. But since we had reached a point where the most trivial matter added to the tension between us, your hitting me actually brought a sudden feeling of release.

"I will never get over it, never. Tie up my hands." I brought my hands together and thrust them at your chest, as though I were giving myself, all of myself, to you.

You looked confused, your anger seemed to have left you limp and drained of emotion. You took the cord from my sash and tied my hands with it.

I was happy when I saw the look in your eyes, watching me try to smooth my hair with my bound hands. This time the long habit might be cured, I thought.

Even then, however, it was dangerous for anyone to brush against the mole.

And was it because afterwards the habit came back that the last of your affection for me finally died? Did you mean to tell me that you had given up and that I could very well do as I pleased? When I played with the mole, you pretended you did not see, and you said nothing.

Then a strange thing happened. Presently the habit which scolding and beating had done nothing to cure—was it not gone? None of the extreme remedies worked. It simply left of its own accord.

"What do you know—I'm not playing with the mole any more." I said it as though I had only that moment noticed. You grunted, and looked as if you did not care.

If it mattered so little to you, why did you have to scold me so, I wanted to ask; and I suppose you for your part wanted to ask why, if the habit was to be cured so easily, I had not been able to cure it earlier. But you would not even talk to me.

A habit that makes no difference, that is neither medicine nor poison—go ahead and indulge yourself all day long if it pleases you. That is what the expression on your face seemed to say. I felt dejected. Just to annoy you, I thought of touching the mole again there in front of you, but, strangely, my hand refused to move.

I felt lonely. And I felt angry.

I thought too of touching it when you were not around. But somehow that seemed shameful, repulsive, and again my hand refused to move.

I looked at the floor, and I bit my lip.

"What's happened to your mole?" I was waiting for you to say, but after that the word "mole" disappeared from our conversation.

And perhaps many other things disappeared with it.

Why could I do nothing in the days when I was being scolded by you? What a worthless woman I am.

Back at home again, I took a bath with my mother.

"You're not as good-looking as you once were, Sayoko," she said. "You can't fight age, I suppose."

I looked at her, startled. She was as she had always been, plump and fresh-skinned.

"And that mole used to be rather attractive."

I have really suffered because of that mole—but I could not say that to my mother. What I did say was: "They say it's no trouble for a doctor to remove a mole."

"Oh? For a doctor . . . but there would be a scar." How calm and easy-going my mother is! "We used to laugh about it. We said that Sayoko was probably still playing with that mole even now that she was married."

"I was playing with it."

"We thought you would be."

"It was a bad habit. When did I start?"

"When do children begin to have moles, I wonder. You don't seem to see them on babies."

"My children have none."

"Oh? But they begin to come out as you grow up, and they never disappear. It's not often you see one this size, though. You must have had it when you were very small." My mother looked at my shoulder and laughed.

I remembered how, when I was very young, my mother and my sisters sometimes poked at the mole, a charming little spot then. And was that not why I had fallen into the habit of playing with it myself?

I lay in bed fingering the mole and trying to remember how it was when I was a child and a young woman.

It was a very long time since I had last played with it. How many years, I wonder.

Back in the house where I was born, away from you, I could play with it as I liked. No one would stop me.

But it was no good.

As my finger touched the mole, cold tears came to my eyes.

I meant to think of long ago, when I was young, but when I touched the mole all I thought of was you.

I have been damned as a bad wife, and perhaps I shall be divorced; but it would not have occurred to me that here in bed at home again I should have only these thoughts of you.

I turned over my damp pillow—and I even dreamed of the mole.

I could not tell after I awoke where the room might have been, but you were there, and some other woman seemed to be with us. I had been drinking. Indeed I was drunk. I kept pleading with you about something.

My bad habit came out again. I reached around with my left hand, my arm across my breast as always. But the mole—did it not come right off between my fingers? It came off painlessly, quite as though that were the most natural thing in the world. Between my fingers it felt exactly like the skin of a roast bean.

Like a spoiled child I asked you to put my mole in the pit of that mole beside your nose.

I pushed my mole at you. I cried and clamored, I clutched at your sleeve and hung on your chest.

When I awoke the pillow was still wet. I was still weeping.

I felt tired through and through. And at the same time I felt light, as though I had laid down a burden.

I lay smiling for a time, wondering if the mole had really disappeared. I had trouble bringing myself to touch it.

That is all there is to the story of my mole.

I can still feel it like a black bean between my fingers.

I have never thought much about that little mole beside your nose, and I have never spoken of it, and yet I suppose I have had it always on my mind.

What a fine fairy story it would make if your mole really were to swell up because you put mine in it.

And how happy I would be if I thought you in your turn had dreamed of my mole.

I have forgotten one thing.

"That's what I hate," you said, and so well did I understand that I even thought the remark a sign of your affection for me. I thought that all the meanest things in me came out when I fingered the mole.

I wonder, however, if a fact of which I have already spoken does not redeem me: it was perhaps because of the way my mother and sisters petted me that I first fell into the habit of fingering the mole.

"I suppose you used to scold me when I played with the mole," I said to my mother, "a long time ago."

"I did—it was not so long ago, though."

"Why did you scold me?"

"Why? It's a bad habit, that's all."

"But how did you feel when you saw me playing with the mole?"

"Well . . ." My mother cocked her head to one side. "It wasn't becoming."

"That's true. But how did it look? Were you sorry for me? Or did you think I was nasty and hateful?"

"I didn't really think about it much. It just seemed as though you could as well leave it alone, with that sleepy expression on your face."

"You found me annoying?"

"It did bother me a little."

"And you and the others used to poke at the mole to tease me?"

"I suppose we did."

If that is true, then wasn't I fingering the mole in that absent way to remember the love my mother and sisters had for me when I was young?

Wasn't I doing it to think of the people I loved?

This is what I must say to you.

Weren't you mistaken from beginning to end about my mole?

Could I have been thinking of anyone else when I was with you?

Over and over I wonder whether the gesture you so disliked might not have been a confession of a love that I could not put into words.

My habit of playing with the mole is a small thing, and I do not mean to make excuses for it; but might not all of the other things that turned me into a bad wife have begun in the same way? Might they not have been in the beginning expressions of my love for you, turned to unwifeliness only by your refusal to see what they were?

Even as I write I wonder if I do not sound like a bad wife trying to seem wronged. Still there are these things that I must say to you.

Eggs

TRANSLATED BY J. MARTIN HOLMAN

The husband and wife had both caught colds and were sleeping side by side.

The wife always took the older grandchild to bed with her, but her husband hated to be awakened early, so it was rare that they slept side by side.

The husband had caught his cold in a funny way. He had a favorite old hot-spring resort at Tōnosawa in Hakone where he went even in the winter. This year he had gone at the beginning of February. On the third day of his stay, he had hurriedly gotten up and gone to the bath, thinking it was already one-thirty in the afternoon. When he had returned, the maid was putting charcoal in the brazier, looking as though she were half-asleep.

"What's going on this morning? I'm surprised to see you awake so early."

"What? You're being facetious."

"It's still only just past seven. You got up at five after seven."

"What?" He was bewildered. "Oh, I see. I confused the big hand and the little hand on my watch. That's quite a mistake. My eyes are getting old."

"Down at the desk I was worried that a thief or something had gotten into your room."

When he looked up, he saw the maid was wearing a lined *meisen* kimono over her nightgown. Awakened where she slept, she must have had no time to change. He had called the desk to notify them that he was up, but the reason he had gotten no response was that she had been asleep.

"I'm sorry I got you up so early."

"That's all right. It was time to get up anyway. But will you be going back to bed? Shall I get your bedding out again?"

"Well, let me see . . ." He held his hands over the brazier. Now that she mentioned it, he did feel sleepy, but he thought the cold would awaken him.

He had left the inn while the morning was still chilly. And he had caught a cold.

The cause of his wife's cold was not so clear, but colds had been going around, so she had probably caught it from someone else.

By the time the husband had come home, his wife was already in bed.

When the husband had told the story about getting up too early after mistaking the hands of his watch, the whole family had had a good laugh. They had all passed around the pocket watch to have a look at it.

It was a rather large pocket watch; however, they had come to the conclusion that one could confuse the big hand and the little hand in the dim bedside light with sleepy eyes, since the two hands were shaped the same with circles at the tips. They had turned the hands to test whether five after seven could be confused with one-thirty.

"Father needs a watch that glows in the dark," the youngest daughter had said.

Feeling languid and feverish, the husband had decided to sleep beside his wife. "To keep you company," he had said.

"You could probably take the medicine I got for myself from the doctor. After all, we have the same thing."

When they awoke the next morning, the wife asked, "How was Hakone?"

"Well, it was cold," the husband said, summing it all up. "Last night you coughed terribly and it woke me up, but all I had to do was clear my throat and you started up in a fright. I was quite surprised."

"Really? I didn't know."

"You were sleeping well."

"But I wake up right away if I'm sleeping with our grandson."

"Jumping up startled like that at your age."

"Was I that startled?"

"Yes."

"Maybe it's instinctive, even in a woman my age. If there's a foreign body at your side, you go to sleep and forget, and then—"

"Foreign body? Have I become a 'foreign body'?" Her husband smiled bitterly, but then he added, "That's right. One night in Hakone—I think it was Saturday—a lot of people came to the inn together. After a banquet, one group of guests came to the next room to sleep, but a geisha who had come with them was so dead drunk that her speech was slurred. She was grumbling on the telephone with a geisha in another room. She was screeching and her speech was slurred, so I couldn't understand what she was saying, but it sounded like 'I'm going to lay an egg, I'm going to lay an egg.' It was funny how she said that."

"That's pathetic."

"Pathetic? Her voice was booming."

"Then you looked at your watch, half-asleep, and got up, right?"

"No, stupid." The husband smiled bitterly.

They heard footsteps.

"Mother," the youngest daughter, Akiko, called from beyond the sliding partition, "are you awake?"

"Yes."

"Father, too?"

"Yes, he is."

"May I come in?"

"Yes."

Their fifteen-year-old daughter came in and sat down at her mother's side.

"I had a bad dream."

"What about?"

"I had died. I was a dead person. I knew it was me."

"What a horrible dream!"

"Yes, it was. I was wearing a light kimono, all white. I was going down a straight road. Both sides of the road were foggy. The road seemed to be floating, and I floated when I walked. A strange old woman was following me. She followed me all the way. There was no sound of footsteps. I was so scared I couldn't look back, but I knew she was there. I couldn't get away. Mother, was it the god of death?"

"Of course not," she said as she looked at her husband. "Then what happened?"

"Then, as I walked along, houses began to appear here and there at the roadside. They were low houses like barracks—all the same gray color and all in gentle, rounded shapes. I ducked inside one of the houses. The old woman mistakenly went inside a different house. Good, I thought to myself. But there wasn't anyplace to sleep in the house—just eggs piled everywhere."

"Eggs?" the wife said, exhaling.

"Eggs. I think they were eggs."

"Really? Then what happened?"

"I'm not certain, but I think I was taken up to heaven, away from that house and its eggs. Just as I thought, 'I'm going to heaven,' I woke up."

The girl then looked at her father.

"Father, am I going to die?"

"Of course not." Surprised by her question, he answered the same way his wife had. He had been pondering whether fifteen-year-olds usually have such dreams of death when she had mentioned the eggs. He had almost cried out—it was so bizarre.

"Oh, it was so scary. . . . It still is," the girl said.

"Akiko, yesterday when my throat hurt, I thought it would be good to swallow some raw egg. You went to buy some, and that's why you had the dream about eggs."

"Could that be? Shall I bring you some now? Would you eat some?" The girl went out.

"You were thinking about your good-for-nothing egg geisha, so those eggs appeared in her dream. How pathetic," his wife said.

"Hmm," her husband was looking at the ceiling. "Does Akiko often dream about death?"

"I don't know. It's the first time, I think."

"Did something happen?"

"I don't know."

"But it was the eggs that made her ascend to heaven, wasn't it?"

Their daughter brought the eggs. She broke one and handed it to her mother. "Here you are," she said, then left the room.

The wife glanced sideways at the egg. "It seems somehow repulsive. I can't swallow it. Here—you take it."

The husband also looked at the egg out of the corner of his eye.

■ Nakamoto Takako (1903–1991) (story)

TRANSLATED BY YUKIKO TANAKA

Nakamoto Takako is a writer only now beginning to be reassessed after years in which her work was ignored, in contrast with the work of male Japanese fiction writers. Her father was a retired army officer and a high school gym teacher. She came from an extremely poor background; when she was young her family moved from a small village to the city of Yamaguchi, where she completed her schooling through high school. After teaching at primary school for a while, she moved to Tokyo to pursue her goal of becoming a writer. There, she worked for one of the leading publishing houses and began to publish her stories. She was associated with the journal *Women and the Arts,* which was a magazine started in 1928 as a forum for women writers. In 1929, she published "The Female Bell-Cricket" in

Women in the Arts, which caused a sensation and gave Nakamoto instant visibility. The story, as translator Tanaka Yukiko notes, "was the first story written by a Japanese woman that openly depicted a woman's sexual desire."[1] Yet the message about the powerful woman in this story, who becomes a kind of man-devouring insect (like Tanizaki's geisha in "The Tattooer"), is far from clear. Is this a feminist story, as Tanaka suggests—a "militant expression of a woman's need to control her life"—or does the terror of the devouring, selfish, femme fatale depicted here effectively counteract this message?

Women in the Arts soon shifted heavily to the left, this being the heyday of the Proletarian School of writers, and Nakamoto herself did union organizing of textile workers, mostly young women from the country working in Tokyo mills. She was arrested in 1930, among hundreds of other women, for fighting police and company thugs with makeshift weapons after a dispute over large layoffs. After her thirty-one days in prison, she became a Communist Party sympathizer and was soon arrested by the secret police, interrogated, tortured, and upon her mental collapse sent to a mental hospital. Her trouble with the police was not over, however; she went to work in a ceramic tile factory in Kawasaki, a violation of her probation conditions, and was sentenced to three years in prison. During this time, she wrote a novel about her experiences with the mill workers and published it in *Women in the Arts* as *Factory Number Four, the Toyo Muslin.* She had become a committed Communist by this time but was forced to recant her beliefs as Japan slipped further into military rule. In the 1930s, she published two more novels, *Nanbu Iron Kettle Makers* (1938) and *Dark and Bright Sides of Construction* (1939). In the 1940s, she married and had two children (her husband lost his civil service job under United States military occupation for being a Communist). Though she did not write through most of the war and postwar period, she began publishing again in the 1950s, and her novel *Runways* was serialized in the Japanese Communist Party's daily, *Red Flag.* She continued publishing novels through the 1960s.

The Female Bell-Cricket

In a corner of the last streetcar of the day, Tomoko sat, her chin buried deep in the collar of her overcoat. She felt as if her voice were caught in her throat, like a broken musical instrument. The streetcar was nearly empty but the air was filled with the smell of sour alcohol. Each time the train jerked, Tomoko's lackluster hair swayed, disturbing her shadow on the wall. She felt as if the train were hurling her into the depths of the ocean; it was

---

1. Tanaka Yukiko, ed. *To Live and to Write* (Seattle: Seal Press, 1987), 710.

difficult to breathe. Inhaling greedily, her nostrils flaring, Tomoko gazed inquisitively at the passengers.

Men! They are all hefty men! she thought. Moved by this sudden realization of their male sex, she was breathless. For a moment she forgot that her stomach was empty, shrunken like a paper balloon—she had been wandering around all day. The next moment she heard her own voice scolding her for being helplessly attracted to men, even after Akita, her common-law husband, had betrayed and left her.

Tomoko got off the train and started walking briskly, her thin shoulders braced as if the air were assaulting her. Stone buildings stood indifferent and cold, making the street look as narrow as a fjord. The bare branches lining the street sliced the cold air. As she walked along, following her black shadow, Tomoko felt like spitting on herself out of hostility and self-disgust.

The roof on the other side of the bridge was lower, making the town look much less intimidating. But the pressure of the wind grew stronger, and Tomoko felt her body being pushed along. She was already at the outskirts of the city. After the cold concrete pavement, the resilience and the rich smell of soil overwhelmed her. At the left side of the road was a huge pile of dirt, fenced off with a rope. Inside the enclosure, a lantern illuminated a close-cropped head and a shovel going up and down in a regular rhythm. Occasionally the tip of the shovel flashed an icy glitter. Walking on, she felt something cold on the end of her nose; she stuck out her hand and some chilly drops of water fell onto her palm. No sooner did she realize what this was than she was enveloped in rain, which beat down on the rooftops with increasing force. Blown by the wind, the rain pelted against the ground with the strength of horses' hooves. The driving rain spashed in Tomoko's face as she stood in the middle of the road. She pulled up the collar of her coat and hurried on, her body bent so low that she was almost crawling under the eaves of the houses. The rain trickled through her collar and down her back. The sole reason for her being out late on a night like this was the same as for all the other nights: to indulge in sex with Akita before he took his new bride, to feel superior to the bride-to-be. Akita's parents had refused to recognize Tomoko as their son's common-law wife.

The house she was returning to stood in front of her, shabby as a small paper box, desolate and trembling in the gusty wind. The first thing that Tomoko sensed as her shivering hand pulled the door open was the smell of a male body. She was once again overcome by self-disgust as she remembered how she had reacted earlier to the odor of men in the streetcar. She went in, noisily. Under the dim light of the lamp, Miki sat hunched over his desk. This man, poor and gentle as a doe, had rescued Tomoko and was providing her with shelter and food. She stood in front of him and stared coldly at his pale forehead, half-covered by hair. She directed her pent-up anger at him, ready to explode.

"Look, I'm drenched," she said, shaking herself hard and pulling at the sleeve of her coat. She looked around the room. Finding no charcoal left in the brazier and therefore no fire with which to dry herself, she went to the closet and yanked a dress out of her wicker trunk. Seeing Tomoko's anger, Miki looked at her apologetically.

"You must be cold. I'm sorry I don't have a fire," he said.

Without responding, Tomoko took off her wet clothes in front of him and dried herself with a towel. When her body had regained its warmth and color, she put on dry clothes. The wind outside had begun to blow harder against the houses and the ground.

Sullenly she went to the kitchen to find something to eat. In a pot was a bit of cold rice, gleaming faintly in the light. There was also some salted seaweed in a sake cup.

"Have you eaten?" she asked Miki, glancing at the food.

"Yes, I have," he said firmly. But she knew that he hadn't. The rice in the pan was the same as it had been when she left the house. Realizing that Miki had saved the food for her even though he was hungry himself, she was filled with an even stronger contempt for him. She felt no gratitude for his kindness and gentleness. She knew where his ambition lay, she could see it more clearly everyday. Men are all kind and gentle until they get what they want from a woman, she thought. She went ahead and ate the food as if she were entitled to it.

Tomoko's body, which had been chilled to the bone, now felt warmer. After she had eaten what little food there was, she began spreading the quilts out next to Miki, who was still sitting at the desk. On the desert of the sheet Tomoko found a pubic hair. I shall let this lie modestly in a piece of tissue paper, she thought, and held it in her palm to inspect it under the light. She sighed deep and long, a sigh long as a comet's tail.

Tomoko grew plump as the days went by and her skin became silky. Miki, on the other hand, became pale and skinny. He had only a few books left; his violin had been exchanged long ago for rice and charcoal. His cloak had flown away like a butterfly, transformed into a piece of steak, into hot chicken with rice, into colorful salads. The only regular income Miki had was from writing a few pages of poetry, which he sold for ten yen to a stationery outfit in Kanda. The poems adorned the covers of stationery, intended to inspire the hearts of naive teenage girls. The money earned was quickly changed into meat and vegetables; the only trace of his labors was the faint smell of fat at the bottom of a cooking pan. Miki also worked long hours as a copyist, but even so he could not keep up with Tomoko's appetite. Still, he was pleased that Tomoko had stopped chasing after Akita and was no longer going out so often, instead spending most of her time lying beside him.

Tomoko felt dried up, like a scab on an old wound. She had no desire to work; respectable jobs all seemed absurd, and any effort of a philosophical nature she considered useless. Look at the way people live in this large city, she thought: they flourish like cryptogamous plants; they conceal strange bacteria as they live day to day. She spent her days observing the man gasping beside her, indifferent to what she saw; she could have been watching a plastic doll. Sometimes she stared at his fine Roman nose, thinking that she would some day kill this man and eat him, just as the female bell-cricket devours her mate.

Tomoko sat on the sunny windowsill, her clothes slipped down to her waist. She was hunting for fleas in her underwear. The fleas, which had been hiding inside the seams, jumped in small, perfect arcs on the faded pink fabric. She pursued them with concentration. Miki watched, enjoying the curves of Tomoko's body—from her forehead to her nose, then to her chin, from her neck down to her breasts. When his eyes reached her two shiny cones, he quickly averted them, blinking; he felt his cigarette burning his fingertips and threw it away. He returned his gaze to Tomoko, but by this time the cones were hidden behind her arms, the wonderful opportunity to enjoy her was lost. His face revealed his desire to lie in her arms and suck at her breast, as he had at his mother's. But this was a fantasy, he knew, and he forced himself to go back to his book.

After she had killed all the fleas she could find, Tomoko slipped her soft body back into her clothes and spanned her waist with her hands to measure it. Then she went over to Miki and, squatting down by his desk, moved her knees back and forth like a pet dog wagging its tail.

"I feel like eating a steak tonight," she said.

"Tonight?" Miki said nervously. "But we had chicken cutlets last night, so . . . "

"That was yesterday."

"But . . . " The man still hesitated. Tomoko kept staring at him as he turned his face away.

"But there's no money. Is that what you're saying? There are many ways to get money."

Miki bit his lip and lowered his head, supporting it in his hands and staring at the vacant space in front of him. He saw before him the shadow of this woman whose body had filled out and whose skin was now lustrous. Tomoko was aware of her power over Miki, who sat silently. She watched him indifferently, smoking her cigarette.

"You haven't got your pay from that place in Kanda, have you?"

"I got it for the work I did this month. And the day before yesterday I took in the work I was supposed to do for next month," he said, slowly opening his eyes. His voice was low and sad, like the sound a cat makes when it's been smacked on the forehead.

"How about asking to get paid for that work? You have to be a bit aggressive about these things."

"I see."

"This is what I don't like," she said, shaking her head. Her face was tense, her muscles tight. "Men are attractive when they're pushy and tough. Being timid and reserved like you doesn't impress anyone."

She exhaled as she lifted her chin. The smoke came out of her tilted nose and floated upward. She felt pleased with herself.

"And your poems—they are no good. So old-fashioned. They're sentimental, too. You ought to change your approach altogether."

"I'll go to Kanda, then, even though I don't think I can get any more money," said Miki, who had been listening to Tomoko with his chin resting on his hand. He shook his thin shoulders. Tomoko sat puffing smoke rings while he went out the door.

When Miki came back that evening, he handed her, with a deep sigh, a mere one yen bill. He must have begged it from the stationery store. Saying he had a stomach ache, he let Tomoko eat the whole steak, shining with fat. The thick, warm steak titillated Miki's nose with its wonderful smell, while satisfying juices fell on Tomoko's tongue. She enjoyed every bite while she watched Miki clutching his stomach, which she knew was growling from hunger. Does he feel heroic and self-satisfied? she wondered. If so I'll kick him in the back.

The next day Tomoko found the announcement of Akita's wedding in the newspaper, accompanied by a photograph. He had transformed himself back into the son of a comfortable middle-class family. How painlessly he had taken a lovely maiden for his wife. In the photograph the bride and groom looked like a pair of butterflies, like insect specimens. Tomoko wanted to spit on the picture and throw it at Miki. Instead, she cut it out and pinned it on the wall. She decided to congratulate the pair of butterflies with rowdy laughter, but soon her laughter turned to crying, the tears dripping down and making dark spots on her knees.

Miki watched without a word from where he sat on the windowsill, cleaning his ears. It was a nice day and Tomoko invited him to take a walk to an open field nearby. They sat with their legs stretched out on the withered grass. The late November sun cast soft, transparent rays on their backs. Tomoko's lavishly padded hips overshadowed Miki's pencil-thin body. He sat quietly with his eyes half closed, basking in the sun and the pressure of her body and female odor, and tried to conjure up some poetic sentiment to suit his mood.

As the days passed, Tomoko grew fatter; she sprawled immodestly in front of the man. She had a double chin now, and her hips were as full and solid as the body of a female moth. Miki grew thinner, his bones showed beneath his skin. Exhaling black breath from his rancid lungs and suffering from anemic dizziness, he would not give up his woman, whose splendid energy and strength was a pleasure to his eyes.

And indeed Tomoko's body was deserving of admiration. Her supple skin was as smooth and shiny as rare Occidental parchment, and in the darkness he was sure he could see a halo around her body. When the small crimson lips above her chin—as full as those of an image of Buddha—were open, her small, well-shaped white teeth gleamed. Her inner thighs were as taut as newly strung rackets, revealing their marvelous flexibility, and when she leaned back in a certain way, her private parts glistened. Living with this glorious female finally led Miki to idolize and worship her.

Tomoko only despised him even more, laughing at his hopeless romanticism. She coldly watched as this male bell-cricket became emaciated with the approach of autumn, ready to be eaten by his female.

It became impossible to get money in any way. The copy work done by this man with rancid lungs no longer provided food to satisfy the woman's glorious body. Tossing his pen away, Miki rolled on the floor with his legs and arms pulled up to his chest. Tomoko simply watched him, puffing on her cigarette as she sat on the windowsill.

"What's the matter? You're lazy," she said.

"I can't do it. I'll never catch up," he moaned, gasping his bad breath.

"You're a coward," said Tomoko, and left the window. She went to the mirror to make up her face. Then she changed her clothes and left the house. The man lay on the floor, holding his arms and legs against his abdomen, until she returned late that night.

Tomoko glanced at Miki and sat down next to him on the floor, exposing her nicely shaped legs. Then she took a five-yen bill from her pocket and threw it at him. He got up, about to take the money, and stopped himself. He frowned and stared at the bill for a moment, his eyes filled with doubt. Having reached a conclusion, he stood up, went to the window and took a deep breath. The clear air outside stung him with the sharpness of a needle. Looking from the man to the money a few times, Tomoko began to laugh loudly so that her shoulders shook. Her laughter sounded empty, like bones being shaken in a canister.

"You are a fool," she said.

Miki turned around. His unshaven face grew paler. He tried to say something, but no sound came from his distorted mouth. The fact that some physical exercises she had performed earlier that evening had been transformed into a five-yen bill was of no significance to Tomoko. She despised all things that belonged to the abstract arena anyway; she hunted them down like fleas. She had simply thrown her glorious body at a man, a pug-nosed bourgeois, who'd had his eyes on her for some time. That's how she had gotten the money. Ever since losing Akita to another woman, Tomoko felt like a movie screen: after the film of her metaphysical life was finished, the screen reflected only an empty reality. No matter who tried to project an image on the screen, no matter who tried to stir up a physical sensation, the screen remained blank, empty. She picked up the money, looked at it, and started laughing again, loudly.

"What are you thinking, you fool?" She snapped the paper money with her fingers, enjoying its sound, and put it back in her pocket. Then she turned her smile to Miki, who was rubbing his face in confusion. He closed the window and lay down on the floor again. Tomoko lay down next to him.

Tomoko reflected over her current state, comparing it to a few hours earlier, when she had still had a foot in the metaphysical arena. Tomoko discovered that she had neither sadness nor regret. She was now living in a place free of complex thoughts and emotion—and it was far easier. She could blot out her obsessive attachment to Akita and her bitterness toward the city that had engulfed and altered him. But she also felt an even stronger revulsion toward Miki's romanticism, his amiable and timid personality. If he blamed her for what she had done and loved her less because of it, she would grab him like a wild bear, tear his throat with her sharp claws and spill his warm blood.

Moving closer to Miki, Tomoko cornered him; slowly he was backed against the wall. Then she reached out to grab his face and pull it toward her. He looked up with tearful eyes, then suddenly pushed her away, shaking his head fiercely. As she fell backward, he saw her uncovered breast, her arched neck, and the shining hair under her armpits. But even the sight of this did not make Miki want to touch her. Tomoko, who liked being handled roughly, waited in vain for him to grab her. She looked at this man who had turned his back on her, then got up and left the room.

There was a thick fog outside, falling like heavy, milk-colored breath, settling on the ground as it fell. The bare branches of the trees, stretching out like a nervous system, were quickly being covered. Tomoko walked, feeling drops of water form on her eyelids. Night was for those who want to believe in mystery and superstition, she thought. She walked for some time with her hands in her pockets, taking a deep breath once in a while, and then she went back to the house. She went to bed without a word.

With the one yen Tomoko had given him, Miki left the house early in the morning. A day without him seemed emptier than mere physical hunger. She was in anguish all day long; she leaned against the desk and felt like a morning glory in evening. That night she left the door unlocked and waited for him. The clock struck three, then came the first crowing of a cock, but Miki did not return. Toward dawn she fell asleep, still leaning against the desk. When she awakened, Miki was there, the bright morning sunlight on his back.

He stood with the veins showing through the pale skin of his face, his hair mussed. His eyes were wide open. He must have been watching me while I slept, Tomoko thought. His clenched hands shook. Tomoko felt revulsion and anger, but this soon turned to pity and contempt. She couldn't tell whether he had been walking the streets all night or if he'd gone somewhere to buy a prostitute. Either way, she felt he deserved her scorn. He looked at her in confusion, and this made her feel tense; she stared back at him. Unable to bear her gaze, he threw himself to the floor, folded his arms over his chest, and sighed like a person in great distress. His sigh then turned into painful sobbing. Pretending that she didn't understand, Tomoko continued to stare at him reproachfully. She lit a cigarette and smoked it slowly, her chin cupped on her hand, all the while staring at him. When he moved, his kimono fell open, and she spotted what looked like dried semen on his thigh. From his body came the rank odor of rotten flesh.

"Why don't you go to the bathhouse today. You haven't washed in weeks. You ought to clean yourself up," she said, exhaling smoke toward him.

His eyes closed, Miki lay still for a while, and then, suddenly, he moved, gripping his throat. Gasping hard, as if something were forcing its way from his chest, he covered his mouth with a handkerchief. When he took it away from his mouth, he saw a clot of blood, dark red, staring up at his darkened eyes. He folded the handkerchief and feebly threw his head down against his outstretched arms. Tomoko sat by this man, still smoking, watching him coolly.

■ Sakaki Nanao (1922–) (poems)

TRANSLATED BY AUTHOR

Sakaki Nanao is a fascinating paradox, a Japanese writer whose life and work has become inextricably linked with that of the great American Beat poets, Gary Snyder and Allen Ginsberg. It is well known in the West that Gary Snyder went to Japan to study in a Zen monastery for years, but much less known that Sakaki and a few other like-minded artists, photographers, and writers of the Japanese counterculture came to America and became associated with the flower children and the Beat scene. Sakaki is also the founder of an agricultural community called the Banyan Ashram. The seventh son in a large family, he was born in a village near Kagoshima and was drafted into the Japanese army in World War II, serving as a radar analyst. As Gary Snyder recounts,

> He sat in on the farewell parties for young kamikaze pilots leaving dawn the next day for their death, and identified the B-29 that was on its way to bomb Nagasaki on his radar screen. Upon the announcement of the surrender of Japan his outfit's senior officer ordered the men to prepare to commit mass suicide. Someone luckily turned on the radio, to hear the Emperor himself command, in almost incomprehensibly archaic Japanese, that there was no need for soldiers to kill themselves.[1]

He first came to the United States in 1969 and traveled extensively in the West and Southwest, where a number of his poems are set. He is at once a cosmopolitan poet and a throwback to the poet mystics of the Chinese and Japanese past—Wang Wei, Ryokan, and Saigyo. Like Snyder, he is a lone voice for spiritual values and environmental politics, a cantankerous,

---

1. Sakaki Nanao, *Break the Mirror: The Poems of Nanao Sakaki.* Foreword by Gary Snyder (San Francisco: North Point Press, 1987), ix.

hilarious, excremental, dedicated poet-activist, running counter to the prevailing wind of avarice and consumption.

His excellent poem "Future Knows" shows Sakaki at his best—anecdotal, with an understated but savage irony. His more polemical poems succeed less, for example, "Ancestor of the Japanese," in which he compares the Japanese consumer to a cockroach: "The Japanese cockroach is also gulping down / the Amazonian rain forest for toilet paper. / For future generations, / they work vigorously and joyously / leaving the soil full of agrichemicals, / leaving rivers and lakes terribly polluted / leaving graveyards of coral reefs." But through all his poems, koans, and polemical tracts can be seen Sakaki's big heart and his big spirit, the voice of a modern wild man shouting uncomfortable truths from the margins of society. His book *Break the Mirror* (1987) is available from North Point Press. *Real Play* was published by Tooth of Time Books, and *Bellyfulls* was published in 1966 by Toad Press.

Future Knows

Thus I heard:

Oakland, California—
To teacher's question
An eleven-year-old girl answered,
"The ocean is
A huge swimming pool with cement walls." 5

On a starry summer night
At a camping ground in Japan
A nine-year-old boy from Tokyo complained,
"Ugly, too many stars." 10

At a department store in Kyoto
One of my friends bought a beetle
For his son, seven years old.

A few hours later
The boy brought his dead bug
To a hardware store, asking 15
"Change battery please."

Small People

"inch by inch
little snail,
creep up and up Mt. Fuji."
—Issa, 19th century Haiku poet.

. . . "a Navaho woman identifies 5
801 specimens of desert insects."
an American scientist recorded — 1948.

3,000,000 abandoned children
in big Brazilian cities, I heard.

300,000,000 soldiers 10
in Red China, I heard.

a Pennsylvanian sea lily fossil
300,000,000 years old
from the Santa Fe basin,
now paperweight on my desk. 15

I want to be a lightning bug
for the next 300,000,000
light years' dark age.

■ Tamura Ryuichi (1923–) (poems)

TRANSLATED BY CHRISTOPHER DRAKE

Tamura Ryuichi is one of modern Japan's most interesting poets, a peculiar writer of great intelligence and deep humanity. He is one of the
poets originally associated with the modernist magazine *Wasteland,* and his
work shows influence from both Western modernism and Japanese humorous traditions. As he noted in a conversation with translator Christopher
Drake,

> We wanted to question the basic principles behind an industrial society
> based on the illusion of the isolated individual and the deification of
> economic growth based on war and imperialism. I tried to make my
> poems holes or windows that would let me see through the indefinable
> spiritual waste as well as the obvious spiritual destruction.[1]

He writes an extremely self-conscious, wacky, humorous, conceptual
poetry, but if the "house" of "Human House" is "built of . . . words," and if
the "body" of "Green Conceptual Body" explores the dream within dream
within dream of human conceptual systems, such poems always come back
to human truths and human nightmares. He attempts to deal, as Western

---

1. Ooka Makoto and Thomas Fitzsimmons, eds., *A Play of Mirrors: Eight Major Poets of Modern Japan* (Rochester, MI: Katydid Books, Oakland University, 1987), 63.

authors did, with a peculiarly Japanese version of the modernist wasteland. Tamura sees "angelic missiles and beautiful hydrogen bombs" as symptoms of a diseased mode of thinking. For Tamura, such human nightmares derive from flawed, hubris-filled humanity, "Feverish decaying matter / standing on two legs / giddy with sky in its pores,"[2] and even the actual nuclear nightmares that led to Hiroshima and Nagasaki are human brainchilds, so that "I myself am the nightmare." Yet, in his poetry there is the possibility of peace if we can see past the hall of mirrors of conceptual systems and are able "Just once / with eyes not human / to see, experience," and affirm "the taste of ice cream."

FURTHER READING: Fitzsimmons, Thomas. *Japanese Poetry Now,* 1972. Keene, Donald, tr. *The Modern Japanese Prose Poem: An Anthology of Six Poets,* 1980. Kijima, Hajime. *The Poetry of Postwar Japan,* 1975. Makoto, Ooka, and Thomas Fitzsimmons, eds. *A Play of Mirrors: Eight Major Poets of Modern Japan,* 1987.

Green Conceptual Body

Dogs run inside dogs
cats sleep inside cats
birds fly inside birds nailed to the sky
fish swim inside fish across deserts and pant in water

But people can't run inside inner people   5
so they run inside conceptual bodies
they can't dream free-form cat dreams
so they watch insomniac dreams
they can't swim like fish
so they labor to float concepts   10
and they can't fly like birds
so they put wings on concepts
to feel the pleasure of crashing

Sometimes people
are inside rooms   15
but they never live
inside people (inside bodies)
people sleep inside different concepts,
choose vegetables over meat,
boil, fry, make eating a chore;   20
concepts peer into the blood,
make people need forks and chopsticks

---

2. From his poem "Green Thought," translated by Christopher Drake.

people even need shovels to bury corpses
stopping to lick ice cream as they work

People go out walking   25
on nice days in early summer
leaving the people inside themselves in their rooms;
these shut-in bodies measure their blood pressure and spoon out
    honey
and lead thoughts across their voices;
what does the spirit, shut in, do?   30
what went out walking
weren't bodies, weren't spirit
were conceptual bodies with legs
they built the vertical nightmare of medieval Gothic
the ascending nightmare knotting heaven and earth   35
invisible ropes
hierarchical classes
wings for angels
ivory horns for devils
the materials had to be combustible   40
the dream irreversible

I walk a small path through the field
and come out by the Tama River
on the other side two men tend fishing lines
no conceptual bodies: people   45
drowsy, I lie down in the grass — that instant
the vertical axis swings, the horizontal
pushes through my conceptual body
the Gothic collapses
voluptuous curves and colors spurt out   50
the smell of water comes this far

Sun directly overhead
objects but no shadows
my conceptual body turns cat — indeterminate
its footsteps   55
utterly soundless

Leaving one dream to enter another,
you can hardly call that waking;
I have no Globe to world
my thoughts to actors on a stage —   60
I'd rather look, for a split-second,
at the most modern nightmare, nuclear war
but the moment I saw it
because I had come to the edge of the field
they would be watching me: eyes in   65

angelic missiles and beautiful hydrogen bombs;
I'm not a passerby, not a spectator
I myself am the nightmare

All I still want
is, on the tongues of gravediggers,   70
the taste of ice cream

Human House

I guess I'll be back late
I said and left the house
my house is made of words
an iceberg floats in my old wardrobe
unseen horizons wait in my bathroom   5
from my telephone: time, a whole desert
on the table: bread, salt, water
a woman lives in the water
hyacinths bloom from her eyeballs
of course she is metaphor herself   10
she changes the way words do
she's as free-form as a cat
I can't come near her name

I guess I'll be back late
no, no business meeting   15
not even a reunion
I ride ice trains
walk fluorescent underground arcades
cut across a shadowed square
ride in a mollusk elevator   20
violet tongues and gray lips in the trains
rainbow throats and green lungs underground
in the square, bubble language
foaming bubble information, informational information
adjectives, all the hollow adjectives   25
adverbs, paltry begging adverbs
and nouns, crushing, suffocating nouns
all I want is a verb
but I can't find one anywhere
I'm through with a society   30
built only of the past and future
I want the present tense

Because you open a door
doesn't mean there has to be a room

because there are windows 35
doesn't mean there's an interior
doesn't mean there's a space
where humans can live and die—
so far I've opened and shut
countless doors, going out each one 40
so I could come in through another
telling myself each time
what a wonderful new world lies just beyond
what do I hear? from the paradise on the other side
dripping water 45
wingbeats
waves thudding on rocks
sounds of humans and beasts breathing
the smell of blood

Blood 50
it's been a while
I'd almost forgotten what it smells like
silence gathers around a scream
on the tip of a needle
as he walks slowly toward me 55
the surgeon puts on his rubber gloves
I close my eyes, open them again
things falling through my eyes
both arms spread like wings
hair streaming out full length 60
things descending momentary gaps of light
connecting darkness and darkness
I rise slowly from a table in a bar
not pulled by a political slogan or religious belief
it's hard enough trying to find my eyes 65
to see the demolition of the human house
the dismemberment of my language

My house, of course, isn't made of your words
my house is built of my words

■ Abe Kobo (1924–) (story)

TRANSLATED BY ALISON KIBRICK

Abe Kobo was born in 1924 in Tokyo, the son of a doctor, but he grew up in the city of Mukden in Manchuria, where his father practiced. He felt alienated from the aggressive, imperialistic Japan of the war years and even changed his name (to Kobo from Kimfusa) to make it sound more Chinese. He received an M.D. from Tokyo University in 1948 and published his first novel the same year, but he never practiced medicine. In an early phase, Abe was a Marxist playwright. In 1951, he received the prestigious Akutagawa prize, and in 1963 the film version of his novel *The Woman in the Dunes* received the Jury Prize at the Cannes Film Festival. He has also received the Kishida and the Kanizaki prizes for drama. He is best known in the West for *The Woman in the Dunes* (Random House, 1972), but many of his other novels have been translated and well received, such as *The Ruined Map* (Putnam, 1969, 1981) and his extraordinary experimental novel *The Box Man* (Putnam, 1974, 1981). Most recently, editions of his short stories have appeared in English translation, notably *Beyond the Curve* (Kodansha International, 1991). His fiction is relentlessly strange and takes great chances, as obsessed with nightmare as Franz Kafka, as darkly sexual as Mishima Yukio, and as magically cerebral as Jorge Luis Borges. His relationship to the new generation of postmodern Japanese fiction writers (such as Murakami Haruki) is like that of J. G. Ballard to Cyberpunk—precursor, first explorer, metaphysician of the fantastic—and Abe ranks with Eugene Ionesco and Samuel Beckett as one of the great masters of the absurd and the grotesque.

The Magic Chalk

Next door to the toilet of an apartment building on the edge of the city, in a room soggy with roof leaks and cooking vapors, lived a poor artist named Argon.

The small room, nine feet square, appeared to be larger than it was because it contained nothing but a single chair set against the wall. His desk, shelves, paint box, even his easel had been sold for bread. Now only the chair and Argon were left. But how long would these two remain?

Dinnertime drew near. "How sensitive my nose has become!" Argon thought. He was able to distinguish the colors and proximity of the complex aromas entering his room. Frying pork at the butcher's along the streetcar line: yellow ocher. A southerly wind drifting by the front of the fruit stand: emerald green. Wafting from the bakery: stimulating chrome yellow. And the fish the housewife below was broiling, probably mackerel: sad cerulean blue.

The fact is, Argon hadn't eaten anything all day. With a pale face, a wrinkled brow, an Adam's apple that rose and fell, a hunched back, a sunken abdomen, and trembling knees, Argon thrust both hands into his pockets and yawned three times in succession.

His fingers found a stick in his pocket.

"Hey, what's this? Red chalk. Don't remember it being there."

Playing with the chalk between his fingers, he produced another large yawn.

"Aah, I need something to eat."

Without realizing it, Argon began scribbling on the wall with the chalk. First, an apple. One that looked big enough to be a meal in itself. He drew a paring knife beside it so that he could eat it right away. Next, swallowing hard as baking smells curled through the hallway and window to permeate his room, he drew bread. Jam-filled bread the size of a baseball glove. Butter-filled rolls. A loaf as large as a person's head. He envisioned glossy browned spots on the bread. Delicious-looking cracks, dough bursting through the surface, the intoxicating aroma of yeast. Beside the bread, then, a stick of butter as large as a brick. He thought of drawing some coffee. Freshly brewed, steaming coffee. In a large, jug-like cup. On a saucer, three matchbox-size sugar cubes.

"Damn it!" He ground his teeth and buried his face in his hands. "I've got to eat!"

Gradually his consciousness sank into darkness. Beyond the window-pane was a bread and pastry jungle, a mountain of canned goods, a sea of milk, a beach of sugar, a beef and cheese orchard—he scampered about until, fatigued, he fell asleep.

A heavy thud on the floor and the sound of smashing crockery woke him up. The sun had already set. Pitch black. Bewildered, he glanced toward the noise and gasped. A broken cup. The spilled liquid, still steaming, was definitely coffee, and near it were the apple, bread, butter, sugar, spoon, knife, and (luckily unbroken) the saucer. The pictures he had chalked on the wall had vanished.

"How could it . . .?"

Suddenly every vein in his body was wide awake and pounding. Argon stealthily crept closer.

"No, no, it can't be. But look, it's real. Nothing fake about the smoth-ering aroma of this coffee. And here, the bread is smooth to the touch. Be bold, taste it. Argon, don't you believe it's real even now? Yes, it's real. I believe it. But frightening. To believe it is frightening. And yet, it's real. It's ed-ible!"

The apple tasted like an apple (a "snow" apple). The bread tasted like bread (American flour). The butter tasted like butter (same contents as the label on the wrapper—not margarine). The sugar tasted like sugar (sweet). Ah, they all tasted like the real thing. The knife gleamed, reflecting his face.

By the time he came to his senses, Argon had somehow finished eating and heaved a sigh of relief. But when he recalled why he had sighed like this, he immediately became confused again. He took the chalk in his fingers and stared at it intently. No matter how much he scrutinized it, he couldn't understand what he didn't understand. He decided to make sure by trying it once more. If he succeeded a second time, then he would have to concede that it had actually happened. He thought he would try to draw something different, but in his haste just drew another familiar-looking apple. As soon as he finished drawing, it fell easily from the wall. So this is real after all. A repeatable fact.

Joy suddenly turned his body rigid. The tips of his nerves broke through his skin and stretched out toward the universe, rustling like fallen leaves. Then, abruptly, the tension eased, and, sitting down on the floor, he burst out laughing like a panting goldfish.

"The laws of the universe have changed. My fate has changed, misfortune has taken its leave. Ah, the age of fulfillment, a world of desires realized . . . God, I'm sleepy. Well, then, I'll draw a bed. This chalk has become as precious as life itself, but a bed is something you always need after eating your fill, and it never really wears out, so no need to be miserly about it. Ah, for the first time in my life I'll sleep like a lamb."

One eye soon fell asleep, but the other lay awake. After today's contentment he was uneasy about what tomorrow might bring. However, the other eye, too, finally closed in sleep. With eyes working out of sync he dreamed mottled dreams throughout the night.

Well, this worrisome tomorrow dawned in the following manner.

He dreamed that he was being chased by a ferocious beast and fell off a bridge. He had fallen off the bed . . . No. When he awoke, there was no bed anywhere. As usual, there was nothing but that one chair. Then what had happened last night? Argon timidly looked around the wall, tilting his head.

There, in red chalk, were drawings of a cup (it was broken!), a spoon, a knife, apple peel, and a butter wrapper. Below these was a bed — a picture of the bed off which he was supposed to have fallen.

Among all of last night's drawings, only those he could not eat had once again become pictures and returned to the wall. Suddenly he felt pain in his hip and shoulder. Pain in precisely the place he should feel it if he had indeed fallen out of bed. He gingerly touched the sketch of the bed where the sheets had been rumpled by sleep and felt a slight warmth, clearly distinguishable from the coldness of the rest of the drawing.

He brushed his finger along the blade of the knife picture. It was certainly nothing more than chalk; there was no resistance, and it disappeared leaving only a smear. As a test he decided to draw a new apple. It neither turned into a real apple and fell nor even peeled off like a piece of unglued paper, but rather vanished beneath his chafed palm into the surface of the wall.

His happiness had been merely a single night's dream. It was all over, back to what it was before anything had happened. Or was it really? No, his misery had returned fivefold. His hunger pangs attacked him fivefold. It seemed that all he had eaten had been restored in his stomach to the original substances of wall and chalk powder.

When he had gulped from his cupped hands a pint or so of water from the communal sink, he set out toward the lonely city, still enveloped in the mist of early dawn. Leaning over an open drain that ran from the kitchen of a restaurant about a hundred yards ahead, he thrust his hands into the viscous, tarlike sewage and pulled something out. It was a basket made of wire netting. He washed it in a small brook nearby. What was left in it seemed edible, and he was particularly heartened that half of it looked like rice. An old man in his apartment building had told him recently that by placing the basket in the drain one could obtain enough food for a meal a day. Just about a month ago the man had found the means to afford bean curd lees, so he had ceded the restaurant drain to the artist.

Recalling last night's feast, this was indeed muddy, unsavory fare. But it wasn't magic. What actually helped fill his stomach was precious and so could not be rejected. Even if its nastiness made him aware of every swallow, he must eat it. Shit. This was the real thing.

Just before noon he entered the city and dropped in on a friend who was employed at a bank. The friend smiled wryly and asked, "My turn today?"

Stiff and expressionless, Argon nodded. As always, he received half of his friend's lunch, bowed deeply and left.

For the rest of the day, Argon thought.

He held the chalk lightly in his hand, leaned back in the chair, and as he sat absorbed in his daydreams about magic, anticipation began to crystallize around that urgent longing. Finally, evening once again drew near. His hope that at sunset the magic might take effect had changed into near confidence.

Somewhere a noisy radio announced that it was five o'clock. He stood up and on the wall drew bread and butter, a can of sardines, and coffee, not forgetting to add a table underneath so as to prevent anything from falling and breaking as had occurred the previous night. Then he waited.

Before long darkness began to crawl quietly up the wall from the corners of the room. In order to verify the course of the magic, he turned on the light. He had already confirmed last night that electric light did it no harm.

The sun had set. The drawings on the wall began to fade, as if his vision had blurred. It seemed as if a mist was caught between the wall and his eyes. The pictures grew increasingly faint, and the mist grew dense. And soon, just as he had anticipated, the mist had settled into solid shapes—success! The contents of the pictures suddenly appeared as real objects.

The steamy coffee was tempting, the bread freshly baked and still warm.

"Oh! Forgot a can opener."

He held his left hand underneath to catch it before it fell, and, as he drew, the outlines took on material form. His drawing had literally come to life.

All of a sudden, he stumbled over something. Last night's bed "existed" again. Moreover, the knife handle (he had erased the blade with his finger), the butter wrapper, and the broken cup lay fallen on the floor.

After filling his empty stomach, Argon lay down on the bed.

"Well, what shall it be next? It's clear now that the magic doesn't work in daylight. Tomorrow I'll have to suffer all over again. There must be a simple way out of this. Ah, yes! a brilliant plan—I'll cover up the window and shut myself in darkness."

He would need some money to carry out the project. To keep out the sun required some objects that would not lose their substance when exposed to sunlight. But drawing money is a bit difficult. He racked his brains, then drew a purse full of money . . . The idea was a success, for when he opened up the purse he found more than enough bills stuffed inside.

This money, like the counterfeit coins that badgers made from tree leaves in the fairy tale, would disappear in the light of day, but it would leave no trace behind, and that was a great relief. He was cautious nonetheless and deliberately proceeded toward a distant town. Two heavy blankets, five sheets of black woolen cloth, a piece of felt, a box of nails, and four pieces of squared lumber. In addition, one volume of a cookbook collection that caught his eye in a secondhand bookstore along the way. With the remaining money he bought a cup of coffee, not in the least superior to the coffee he had drawn on the wall. He was (why?) proud of himself. Lastly, he bought a newspaper.

He nailed the door shut, then attached two layers of cloth and a blanket. With the rest of the material, he covered the window, and he blocked the edges with the wood. A feeling of security, and at the same time a sense of being attacked by eternity, weighed upon him. Argon's mind grew distant, and, lying down on the bed, he soon fell asleep.

Sleep neither diminished nor neutralized his happiness in the slightest. When he awoke, the steel springs throughout his body were coiled and ready to leap, full of life. A new day, a new time . . . tomorrow wrapped in a mist of glittering gold dust, and the day after tomorrow, and more and more overflowing armfuls of tomorrows were waiting expectantly. Argon smiled, overcome with joy. Now, at this very moment, everything, without any hindrance whatsoever, was waiting eagerly among myriad possibilities to be created by his own hand. It was a brilliant moment. But what, in the depths of his heart, was this faintly aching sorrow? It might have been the sorrow that God had felt just before Creation. Beside the muscles of his smile, smaller muscles twitched slightly.

Argon drew a large wall clock. With a trembling hand he set the clock precisely at twelve, determining at that moment the start of a new destiny.

He thought the room was a bit stuffy, so he drew a window on the wall facing the hallway. Hm, what's wrong? The window didn't materialize. Perplexed for a moment, he then realized that the window could not acquire any substance because it did not have an outside; it was not equipped with all the conditions necessary to make it a window.

"Well, then, shall I draw an outside? What kind of view would be nice? Shall it be the Alps or the Bay of Naples? A quiet pastoral scene wouldn't be bad. Then again, a primeval Siberian forest might be interesting." All the beautiful landscapes he had seen on postcards and in travel guides flickered before him. But he had to choose one from among them all, and he couldn't make up his mind. "Well, let's attend to pleasure first," he decided. He drew some whiskey and cheese and, as he nibbled, slowly thought about it.

The more he thought, the less he understood.

"This isn't going to be easy. It could involve work on a larger scale than anything I—or anyone—has ever tried to design. In fact, now that I think about it, it wouldn't do simply to draw a few streams and orchards, mountains and seas, and other things pleasing to the eye. Suppose I drew a mountain; it would no longer be just a mountain. What would be beyond it? A city? A sea? A desert? What kind of people would be living there? What kind of animals? Unconsciously I would be deciding those things. No, making this window a window is serious business. It involves the creation of a world. Defining a world with just a few lines. Would it be right to leave that to chance? No, the scene outside can't be casually drawn. I must produce the kind of picture that no human hand has yet achieved."

Argon sank into deep contemplation.

The first week passed in discontent as he pondered a design for a world of infinitude. Canvases once again lined his room, and the smell of turpentine hung in the air. Dozens of rough sketches accumulated in a pile. The more he thought, however, the more extensive the problem became, until finally he felt it was all too much for him. He thought he might boldly leave it up to chance, but in that case his efforts to create a new world would come to nothing. And if he merely captured accurately the inevitability of partial reality, the contradictions inherent in that reality would pull him back into the past, perhaps trapping him again in starvation. Besides, the chalk had a limited life-span. He had to capture the world.

The second week flew by in inebriation and gluttony.

The third week passed in a despair resembling insanity. Once again his canvases lay covered with dust, and the smell of oils had faded.

In the fourth week Argon finally made up his mind, a result of nearly total desperation. He just couldn't wait any longer. In order to evade the responsibility of creating with his own hand an outside for the window, he decided to take a great risk that would leave everything to chance.

"I'll draw a door on the wall. The outside will be decided by whatever is beyond the door. Even if it ends in failure, even if it turns out to be the same apartment scene as before, it'll be far better than being tormented by this responsibility. I don't care what happens, better to escape."

Argon put on a jacket for the first time in a long while. It was a ceremony in honor of the establishment of the world, so one couldn't say he was being extravagant. With a stiff hand he lowered the chalk of destiny. A picture of the door. He was breathing hard. No wonder. Wasn't the sight beyond the door the greatest mystery a man could contemplate? Perhaps death was awaiting him as his reward.

He grasped the knob. He took a step back and opened the door.

Dynamite pierced his eyes, exploding. After a while he opened them fearfully to an awesome wasteland glaring in the noonday sun. As far as he could see, with the exception of the horizon, there was not a single shadow. To the extent that he could peer into the dark sky, not a single cloud. A hot dry wind blew past, stirring up a dust storm.

"Aah . . . It's just as though the horizon line in one of my designs had become the landscape itself. Aah . . ."

The chalk hadn't resolved anything after all. He still had to create it all from the beginning. He had to fill this desolate land with mountains, water, clouds, trees, plants, birds, beasts, fish. He had to draw the world all over again. Discouraged, Argon collapsed onto the bed. One after another, tears fell unceasingly.

Something rustled in his pocket. It was the newspaper he had bought on that first day and forgotten about. The headline on the first page read, "Invasion Across 38th Parallel!" On the second page, an even larger space devoted to a photograph of Miss Nippon. Underneath, in small print, "Riot at N Ward Employment Security Office," and "Large-scale Dismissals at U Factory."

Argon stared at the half-naked Miss Nippon. What intense longing. What a body. Flesh of glass.

"This is what I forgot. Nothing else matters. It's time to begin everything from Adam and Eve. That's it—Eve! I'll draw Eve!"

Half an hour later Eve was standing before him, stark naked. Startled, she looked around her.

"Oh! Who are you? What's happened? Golly, I'm naked!"

"I am Adam. You are Eve." Argon blushed bashfully.

"I'm Eve, you say? Ah, no wonder I'm naked. But why are you wearing clothes? Adam, in Western dress—now that's weird."

Suddenly her tone changed.

"You're lying! I'm not Eve. I'm Miss Nippon."

"You're Eve. You really are Eve."

"You expect me to believe this is Adam—in those clothes—in a dump like this? Come on, give me back my clothes. What am I doing here anyway? I'm due to make a special modeling appearance at a photo contest."

"Oh, no. You don't understand. You're Eve, I mean it."

"Give me a break, will you? Okay, where's the apple? And I suppose this is the Garden of Eden? Ha, don't make me laugh. Now give me my clothes."

"Well, at least listen to what I have to say. Sit down over there. Then I'll explain everything. By the way, can I offer you something to eat?"

"Yes, go ahead. But hurry up and give me my clothes, okay? My body's valuable."

"What would you like? Choose anything you want from this cookbook."

"Oh, great! Really? The place is filthy, but you must be pretty well fixed. I've changed my mind. Maybe you really are Adam after all. What do you do for a living? Burglar?"

"No, I'm Adam. Also an artist, and a world planner."

"I don't understand."

"Neither do I. That's why I'm depressed."

Watching Argon draw the food with swift strokes as he spoke, Eve shouted, "Hey, great, that's great. This is Eden, isn't it? Wow. Yeah, okay, I'll be Eve. I don't mind being Eve. We're going to get rich — right?"

"Eve, please listen to me."

In a sad voice, Argon told her his whole story, adding finally, "So you see, with your cooperation we must design this world. Money's irrelevant. We have to start everything from scratch."

Miss Nippon was dumbfounded.

"Money's irrelevant, you say? I don't understand. I don't get it. I absolutely do not understand."

"If you're going to talk like that, well, why don't you open this door and take a look outside."

She glanced through the door Argon had left half open.

"My God! How awful!"

She slammed the door shut and glared at him.

"But how about this door," she said, pointing to his real, blanketed door. "Different, I'll bet."

"No, don't. That one's no good. It will just wipe out this world, the food, desk, bed, and even you. You are the new Eve. And we must become the father and mother of our world."

"Oh no. No babies. I'm all for birth control. I mean, they're such a bother. And besides, I won't disappear."

"You will disappear."

"I won't. I know myself best. I'm me. All this talk about disappearing — you're really weird."

"My dear Eve, you don't know. If we don't re-create the world, then sooner or later we're faced with starvation."

"What? Calling me 'dear' now, are you? You've got a nerve. And you say I'm going to starve. Don't be ridiculous. My body's valuable."

"No, your body's the same as my chalk. If we don't acquire a world of our own, your existence will just be a fiction. The same as nothing at all."

"Okay, that's enough of this junk. Come on, give me back my clothes. I'm leaving. No two ways about it, my being here is weird. I shouldn't be here. You're a magician or something. Well, hurry up. My manager's probably fed up with waiting. If you want me to drop in and be your Eve every now and then, I don't mind. As long as you use your chalk to give me what I want."

"Don't be a fool! You can't do that."

The abrupt, violent tone of Argon's voice startled her, and she looked into his face. They both stared at each other for a moment in silence. Whatever was in her thoughts, she then said calmly, "All right, I'll stay. But, in exchange, will you grant me one wish?"

"What is it? If you stay with me, I'll listen to anything you have to say."

"I want half of your chalk."

"That's unreasonable. After all, dear, you don't know how to draw. What good would it do you?"

"I do know how to draw. I may not look like it, but I used to be a designer. I insist on equal rights."

He tilted his head for an instant, then straightening up again, said decisively, "All right, I believe you."

He carefully broke the chalk in half and gave one piece to Eve. As soon as she received it, she turned to the wall and began drawing.

It was a pistol.

"Stop it! What are you going to do with that thing?"

"Death, I'm going to make death. We need some divisions. They're very important in making a world."

"No, that'll be the end. Stop it. It's the most unnecessary thing of all."

But it was too late. Eve was clutching a small pistol in her hand. She raised it and aimed directly at his chest.

"Move and I'll shoot. Hands up. You're stupid, Adam. Don't you know that a promise is the beginning of a lie? It's you who made me lie."

"What? Now what are you drawing?"

"A hammer. To smash the door down."

"You can't!"

"Move and I'll shoot!"

The moment he leaped the pistol rang out. Argon held his chest as his knees buckled and he collapsed to the floor. Oddly, there was no blood.

"Stupid Adam."

Eve laughed. Then, raising the hammer, she struck the door. The light streamed in. It wasn't very bright, but it was real. Light from the sun. Eve was suddenly absorbed, like mist. The desk, the bed, the French meal, all disappeared. All but Argon, the cookbook which had landed on the floor, and the chair were transformed back into pictures on the wall.

Argon stood up unsteadily. His chest wound had healed. But something stronger than death was summoning him, compelling him—the wall. The wall was calling him. His body, which had eaten drawings from the wall continuously for four weeks, had been almost entirely transformed by them. Resistance was impossible now. Argon staggered toward the wall and was drawn in on top of Eve.

The sound of the gunshot and the door being smashed were heard by others in the building. By the time they ran in, Argon had been completely absorbed into the wall and had become a picture. The people saw nothing but the chair, the cookbook, and the scribblings on the wall. Staring at Argon lying on top of Eve, someone remarked, "Starved for a woman, wasn't he."

"Doesn't it look just like him, though?" said another.

"What was he doing, destroying the door like that? And look at this, the wall's covered with scribbles. Huh. He won't get away with it. Where in the world did he disappear to? Calls himself a painter!"

The man grumbling to himself was the apartment manager.

After everyone left, there came a murmuring from the wall.

"It isn't chalk that will remake the world . . ."

A single drop welled out of the wall. It fell from just below the eye of the pictorial Argon.

■ Mishima Yukio (1925–1970) (story)

TRANSLATED BY JOHN BESTER

Mishima Yukio is the pen name of Hiraoka Kimitake, who was born in Tokyo in 1925, the son of a high government official. A teenage prodigy, he had written a novel by the time he was thirteen and published his first short story collection, a decorative and romantic book, titled *The Forest in Full Bloom* in 1944 while still a student at the prestigious Peers' School. He studied law at Tokyo University and took a position at the Ministry of Finance but resigned after only eight months to devote himself to writing. For the remainder of his life, he was a prolific writer in many literary forms, writing twenty novels, thirty-three plays, and countless stories, articles, essays, film scripts, and travel books. He was also a film director, designer, stage producer, and actor; he won a number of prestigious prizes for his fiction and drama and was a leading candidate for the Nobel Prize in literature. His autobiographical novel *Confessions of a Mask* (1949) traces his life through the time he gave up his government job and recounts both his dawning realization of his homosexuality and his masochistic self-identification with Saint Sebastian, pierced by arrows and fetishizing his martyrdom, and it shows early on Mishima's equation of beauty and death.

Mishima was steeped in the literature and culture of old Japan and felt betrayed after World War II by what he saw as his country's shift toward materialism and moral corruption. In *The Temple of the Golden Pavilion* (1956), the protagonist, a young Buddhist acolyte, sets fire to the fourteenth-century Kyoto landmark, the Kinkakuji. Obsessed by its sacred beauty, he destroys this quintessential example of the aesthetic perfection of premodern Japan. Mishima himself moved from nihilism to a fanatic love of an idealized samurai culture of the premodern era. In later years, he organized a private army of young men into a paramilitary "Shield Society," planned a military *coup d'état,* and in November 1970, dressed in a self-designed uniform, broke into a Tokyo barracks of the Self-Defense Force. There, after failing to incite the soldiers to revolt, haranguing them from a balcony about their need to regain their lost cultural heritage, he committed ritual suicide *(seppuku),* and then was clumsily beheaded by his right-hand man, who then killed himself as well.

In 1985, his life became the subject of a well-known film by Paul Schrader, titled *Mishima.* Among his best-known works are the love story

Thirst for Love (1950); *Forbidden Colors* (1951), a novel about Tokyo's homosexual subculture; *The Sound of Waves* (1954), an idyllic love story on a Japanese island; *The Sailor Who Fell from Grace with the Sea* (1963), which was made into a popular movie in America; and *Runaway Horses* (1968), one of a quartet of novels called *The Sea of Fertility*. His 1960 novella *Patriotism*, which foretold his own fate, describes a historical incident culminating in the suicides of an army officer and his wife who attempted a coup to restore power to the emperor in 1936. "Martyrdom" is a story that brings together many of Mishima's themes—homosexuality, sadomasochism, and a hint of necrophilia—and like all of his prose, it is beautifully written.

FURTHER READING: Bester, John, tr. *Acts of Worship: Seven Stories,* 1989. Mishima, Yukio. *Death in Midsummer and Other Stories,* 1966. Miyoshi, Masao. *Accomplices of Silence: The Modern Japanese Novel,* 1974. Nathan, John. *Mishima: A Biography,* 1974. Petersen, Gwenn Boardman. *The Moon in Water: Understanding Tanizaki, Kawabata, and Mishima,* 1979. Scott-Stokes, Henry. *The Life and Death of Mishima,* 1974.

Martyrdom

A diminutive Demon King ruled over the dormitory. The school in question was a place where large numbers of sons of the aristocracy were put through their paces. Equipped by the age of thirteen or fourteen with a coldness of heart and an arrogance of spirit worthy of many a grown-up, they were placed in this dormitory in their first year at middle school in order to experience communal life; this was one of the traditions of the spartan education devised several decades earlier by the principal of the school, General Ogi. The members of any one year had all been to the same primary school, so that their training in mischief had taken thorough effect in the six years before entering the dormitory, and facilitated an astonishing degree of collaboration among them. A "graveyard" would be arranged in a corner of the classroom with a row of markers bearing the teachers' names; a trap would be set so that when an elderly, bald teacher came into the room a blackboard duster fell precisely onto his bald patch, coating it with white; on a winter morning, a lump of snow would be flung to stick on the ceiling, bright in the morning sun, so that it dripped steadily onto the teacher's platform; the matches in the teachers' room would be mysteriously transformed into things that spouted sparks like fireworks when struck; a dozen drawing pins would be introduced into the chair where the teacher sat, with their points just showing above the surface—these and a host of other schemes that seemed the work of unseen elves were all in fact carried out by two or three masterminds and a band of well-trained terrorists.

"Come on—let's see it! What's wrong with showing me anyway?"

The older boy who had turned up in the lunch break lounged astride the broken dormitory chair. He could sense the itching curiosity in himself that crawled vaguely, like soft incipient beard, right up to his ears, but in trying to conceal it from the other, his junior by a year, he was only making his face turn all the pinker. At the same time, it was necessary to sit in as slovenly a way as possible in order to show his independence of the rules.

"I'll show you, don't worry. But you'll have to wait another five minutes. What's up, K?—it's not like you to be so impatient."

The Demon King spoke boldly, gazing steadily at the older boy with mild, beautiful eyes. He was well developed for a mere fourteen, and looked in fact at least sixteen or seventeen. He owed his physique to something called the "Danish method" of child rearing—which involved among other things dangling the baby by one leg and kneading its soft, plump body like so much dough—and to the fact that he'd been brought up in a Western house with huge plate-glass windows standing on high ground in the Takanawa district of Tokyo, where breezes borne on bright wings from the distant sea would occasionally visit the lawn. Naked, he had the figure of a young man. During physical check-ups, when the other boys were pale with dire embarrassment, he was a Daphnis surveying his nanny goats with cool, scornful eyes.

The dormitory was the farthest from the main school buildings, and the Demon King's room on the second floor looked out over the shimmering May woods covering the gentle slope of the school grounds. The long grass and undergrowth seemed almost tipsy as it swayed in the wind. It was morning, and the chirping of the birds in the woods was particularly noisy. Now and again, a pair of them would take off from the sea of young foliage and fly up like fish leaping from its surface, only to produce a sudden, furious twittering, turn a somersault, and sink down again between the waves of greenery.

When K, his senior, came to see him in his room bearing sandwiches and the like, it had been instantly apparent to the Demon King—young Hatakeyama—that the motive was a desire to see the book that everyone found so fascinating. To tease a senior pupil over something of this sort gave him a sweet sense of complicity, as though he too were being teased.

"Five minutes is up."

"No it isn't—it's only three minutes yet."

"It's five minutes!"

Quite suddenly, Hatakeyama gave him an almost girlish smile, the vulnerable smile of someone who had never yet had anyone be rude to him.

"Oh well, I suppose it can't be helped," he said. "I'll let you see it."

With his left hand thrust in his trouser pocket, as was his usual habit (in imitation of a cousin, a college student, whom he'd much admired for the way he let his shiny metal watchstrap show between the pocket and his sweater), he went lazily to open the bookcase. There, among the textbooks that he'd never once laid hands on after returning to the dorm, and the books his parents had bought for him—a grubby *Collected Boys' Tales,* the

Jungle Book, and *Peter Pan* in paperback editions—there ought to have stood a volume with *"Plutarch's Lives"* inscribed in immature lettering on its spine. This book, whose red cover he had wrapped in uninviting brown paper and labeled with a title that he had memorized from a work of about the same thickness seen in the library, was constantly being passed from hand to hand, during classes and in recess alike. People would have been startled to find, on the page that should have portrayed a statue of Alexander the Great, an odd, complex sectional diagram in color.

"It's no use suddenly pretending you can't find it!" Gazing at the Demon King's rear view as he ferreted through the contents of the bookshelves, K was less concerned with the desire to see the book as such than with making sure, first, that he wasn't cheated by this formidable younger schoolmate, and then that he didn't put himself at a disadvantage by clumsy bullying.

"Somebody's stolen it!" shouted Hatakeyama, standing up. He'd been looking down as he searched, and his face was flushed, his eyes gleaming. Rushing to his desk, he frantically opened and closed each drawer in turn, talking to himself all the while:

"I made a point of getting everyone who came to borrow that book to sign for it. I mean, I couldn't have people taking my stuff out without my permission, could I? That book was the class's special secret. It meant a lot to everybody. I was particularly careful with it—I'd never have let anyone I didn't like read it. . . ."

"It's a bit late to get so angry about it, surely," said K with an assumed maturity, then, noticing the brutal glint in Hatakeyama's eye, suddenly shut up. More than anything, the look reminded him of a child about to kill a snake.

"I'm *sure* it's Watari," said his crony Komiyama, writing the name "Watari" twice in small letters on the blackboard and pointing to the bright-lit doorway through which the boy in question, by himself as usual, had just gone out into the school yard. Beyond the doorway a cloud was visible, smooth and glossy, floating in the sky beyond the spacious playground. Its shadow passed ponderously across the ground.

"Watari? Come off it! What does a kid like him understand about a book like that?"

"A lot—you wait and see! Haven't you ever heard of the quiet lecher? It's types with saintly expressions like him who're most interested in that kind of thing. Try barging in on him in his room tonight before supper, when all the rest have gone for exercise and there's nobody in the dorm. You'll see!"

Alone of their group, Watari had come to them from another primary school, and was thus a comparative outsider. There was something about him that kept others at a distance. Although he was particular about his clothes—he changed his shirt every day—he would go for weeks without cutting his nails, which were always an unhealthy black. His skin was a yellowish, lusterless white like a gardenia. His lips, in contrast, were so red that you wanted to rub them with your finger to see if he was wearing lipstick. Seen close to, it was an astonishingly beautiful face, though from a distance quite unprepossessing. He reminded you of an art object in which excessive care over detail has spoiled the effect of the whole; the details were correspondingly seductive in a perverse way.

He had begun to be bullied almost as soon as he appeared at the school. He gave the impression of looking disapprovingly on the tendency, common to all boys, to worship toughness as a way of making up for their awareness of the vulnerability peculiar to their age. If anything, Watari sought to preserve the vulnerability. The young man who seeks to be himself is respected by his fellows; the boy who tries to do the same is persecuted by other boys, it being a boy's business to become something else just as soon as he can.

Watari had the habit, whenever he was subjected to particularly vile treatment by his companions, of casting his eyes up at the clear blue sky. The habit was itself another source of mockery.

"Whenever he's picked on, he stares up at the sky as if he was Christ," said M, the most persistent of his tormentors. "And you know, when he does it, his nose tips back so you can see right up his nostrils. He keeps his nose so well blown, it's a pretty pink color round the edges inside. . . ."

Watari was, of course, banned from seeing *"Plutarch's Lives."*

The sun had set on all but the trees in the woods. The dark mass of foliage, minutely catching the lingering rays of the setting sun, trembled like the flame of a guttering candle. As he stealthily opened the door and went in, the first thing Hatakeyama saw was the wavering trees through the window directly ahead. The sight of Watari registered next; he was seated at his desk, gazing down with his head in his delicate white hands, intent on something. The open pages of the book and the hands stood out in white relief.

He turned around at the sound of footsteps. The next instant, his hands covered the book with an obstinate strength.

Moving swiftly and easily across the short space that separated them, Hatakeyama had seized him by the scruff of the neck almost before he realized it himself. Watari's large, expressionless eyes, wide open like a rabbit's, were suddenly close to his own face. He felt his knees pressing into the boy's belly, eliciting a strange sound from it as he sat on the chair; then he knocked aside the hands that tried to cling to him, and dealt a smart slap to his cheek. The flesh looked soft, as though it might stay permanently dented. For one moment, indeed, Watari's face seemed to tilt in the direction in which it had been struck, assuming an oddly placid, helpless expression. But then the cheek rapidly flooded with red and a thin, stealthy trickle of blood ran from the finely shaped nostrils. Seeing it, Hatakeyama felt a kind of pleasant nausea. Taking hold of the collar of Watari's blue shirt, he dragged him toward the bed, moving with unnecessarily large strides as though dancing. Watari let himself be dragged, limp as a puppet;

curiously, he didn't seem to grasp the situation he was in, but gazed steadily at the evening sky over the woods with their lingering light. Or perhaps those big, helpless eyes simply let in the evening light quite passively, taking in the sky without seeing anything. The blood from his nose, though, cheerfully seemed to flaunt its glossy brightness as it dribbled down his mouth and over his chin.

"You thief!"

Dumping Watari on the bed, Hatakeyama climbed onto it himself and started trampling and kicking him. The bed creaked, sounding like ribs breaking. Watari had his eyes shut in terror. At times, he bared his over-regular teeth and gave a thin wail like a small sick bird. Hatakeyama thumped him in the side for a while, then, seeing that he had turned toward the wall and gone still, like a corpse, jumped down from the bed in one great leap. As a finishing touch, he remembered to thrust one guilty hand elegantly into the pocket of his narrow slacks and tilt himself slightly to one side. Then, whisking up *"Plutarch's Lives"* from the desk with his right hand, he tucked it stylishly under his arm and ran up the stairs to his second-floor room.

He had read the dubious book in question quite a few times. Each time, the first frenzied excitement seemed to fade a little. Recently in fact he had begun to get more pleasure, if anything, out of observing the powerful spell the book exerted over his friends as they read it for the first time. But now, reading it again himself after getting it back and roughing up Watari in the process, the original, wild excitement emerged as a still fiercer pleasure. He couldn't get through a single page at a time. Each appearance of one of those words of almost mystic power brought a myriad associations crowding, plunged him into an ever deeper intoxication. His breath grew shallower, his hand trembled, the bell for supper that happened just then to resound through the dormitory almost made him panic: how could he appear before the others in this state? He had entirely forgotten Watari.

That night, a dream woke Hatakeyama from a troubled sleep. The dream had led him to the lairs of various illnesses that he had suffered from in childhood. In actual fact, few children could have been healthier than he: the only illnesses he'd succumbed to were of the order of whooping cough, measles, and intestinal catarrh. Nevertheless, the diseases in his dream were all acquainted with him, and greeted him accordingly. Whenever one of them approached him, there was a disagreeable smell; if he tried to shove it away, "disease" transferred itself stickily to his hand like oil paint. One disease was even tickling his throat with its finger. . . .

When he awoke, he found himself staring, wide-eyed like a rabbit, in just the way that Watari had done earlier that day. And there, floating above the covers, was Watari's startled face, a mirror of his own. As their eyes met, the face rose slowly into the air.

Hatakeyama let out a high-pitched yell. At least, he thought he did: in fact his voice rose only as far as his throat.

Something was pressing down steadily, with cold hands, on his throat; yet the pressure was slight enough to be half pleasant. Deciding that it was a continuation of his dream after all, he extracted a hand unhurriedly from the bedclothes and stroked himself experimentally around the neck. It appeared that something like a cloth sash, about two inches wide, had been wrapped snugly around it.

He had the courage and good sense to fling it off without further ado. He sat up in bed, looking much older than he was, more like a young man of twenty. A chain of ivory clouds, lit up by the moon, was passing across the window outside, so that he was silhouetted against it like the statue of some god of old.

The thing that crouched like a dog at the foot of the bed had a white, human face turned resolutely toward him. It seemed to be breathing heavily, for the face as a whole appeared to swell and shrink; the eyes alone were still, overflowing with a shining light as they gazed, full of hostility (or was it longing?), at Hatakeyama's shadowed features.

"Watari. You came to get even, didn't you?"

Watari said nothing, the lips that were like a rose in the dark night quivering painfully. Finally, he said as though in a dream:

"I'm sorry."

"You wanted to kill me, I suppose."

"I'm sorry." He made no attempt to run away, simply repeating the same phrase.

Without warning, Hatakeyama flew at him and, propelled by the bedsprings, carried him face down onto the floor. There, kneeling astride him, he subjected him to a full twenty minutes' violence. "I'm going to make sure you feel ashamed in front of everyone in the bath!" he promised, then splashed his bare buttocks with blue-black ink; prodded them with the points of a pair of compasses to see their reaction; reared up, hauling the boy up by the ears as he did so. . . . He was brilliantly methodical, as though everything had been thought out in advance. There was no chance, even, for Watari to look up at the sky this time. He lay still, his cheek pressed against a join in the linoleum.

Two boys were allotted to each room in the dormitory, but Hatakeyama's roommate was home on sick leave. So long as he was careful not to be overheard downstairs, Hatakeyama could do as he wished.

Eventually, both of them began to tire. Before they realized it they were dozing, sprawled on the floor; Watari had even forgotten to cover his pale behind.

Their nap lasted no more than a moment. Hatakeyama awoke first. Pillowing his chin on clasped hands, he gazed at the moonlit window. All that was visible from the floor where he lay was the sky. The moon was below the frame of the window, but two or three clouds could be seen in the sky's fullness of limpid light. The scene had the impersonal clarity, precision, and fineness of detail of a scene reflected in the polished surface of a piece of machinery. The clouds seemed stationed as immovably as some majestic man-made edifice.

An odd desire awoke in Hatakeyama, taking him by surprise. It wasn't so much a break with the mood of tranquility as a natural transition from it, and in a strange way it was linked with the terrifying sensation of the cord around his neck that he'd experienced a while before. This, he thought, is the fellow who tried to kill me. And suddenly a peculiar sense of both superiority and inferiority, a nagging humiliation at not in fact having been killed, made it impossible for him to stay still.

"You asleep?" he said.

"No," said Watari. As he replied, his eyes turned to look straight at Hatakeyama. He began to stretch out his thin right arm, then drew it in again and pressed it to his side, saying,

"It hurts here."

"Really? Does it *really* hurt?"

Hatakeyama rolled over twice. It brought him a little too close, so that he was lying half on top of Watari. Just as this happened, the latter gave a faint little chuckle, a sound—like the cry of a shellfish—he had never heard before. The Demon King sought out the sound, then pressed his whole face against Watari's lips and the soft down around them.

There was something going on between Hatakeyama and Watari: their classmates passed on the rumor in hushed voices. The scandal possessed a mysterious power; thanks to it, Hatakeyama became increasingly influential, and even Watari was taken into their circle. The process was similar to that whereby a woman so far generally ignored suddenly acquires value in everyone's eyes if the dandy of the group takes a fancy to her. And it was totally unclear how Hatakeyama himself responded to this general reaction.

Before long, it was felt that his authority as Demon King required some kind of strict legal system. They would draft the necessary laws during their English and spelling lessons. The criminal code, for example, must be an arbitrary one, based on the principle of intimidation. A strong urge to self-regulation had awoken in the boys. One morning in the dormitory, the gang insisted that their leader pick out someone for them to punish. They were sitting in their chairs in a variety of bizarre postures; some were not so much seated in them as clinging to them. One first-grader had turned his chair upside down and was sitting holding on to two projecting legs.

"Hatakeyama—you've got to name somebody. You name him, and the rest of us'll deal with him. Isn't there anyone who's been getting above himself lately?"

"No, no one." He spoke in a surly voice, his mature-looking back turned to them.

"You sure? Then we'll choose the person ourselves."

"Wait a minute! What I said wasn't true. Listen: I'll name someone. But I won't say why."

They waited breathlessly; there wasn't one of them who didn't want to hear his own name mentioned.

"Where's Watari?"

"Watari? — he went off somewhere just now."

"OK, it's him. He's been getting uppish. If we don't put a stop to it, he'll get completely out of hand."

This was pure imitation of fifth-grader talk. Even so, having got it out, Hatakeyama looked cheerfully relieved, like someone remembering something till then forgotten. It provoked a happy clamor among the others:

"Let's fix the time — the lunch break!"

"And the place — by Chiarai Pond."

"I'll take my jackknife."

"And I'll bring a rope. If he struggles we can tie him up."

On a pond already green with slime the surrounding trees spread an even reflection of lush young foliage, so that anyone who walked beside it was steeped in its green light. They were all privately enjoying the important sound of their own feet tramping through the bamboo grass, and the party with Hatakeyama and Watari at its center exchanged no words. Watari showed no sign of fear as he walked, a fact that had a disturbing effect on his classmates, as though they were watching a very sick man, supposedly on his last legs, suddenly striding along. From time to time, he glanced up at the sky visible through the new leaves of the treetops. But the others were all too sunk in their own thoughts for anyone to remark on his behavior. Hatakeyama walked with long strides, head bent, left hand in pocket. He avoided looking at Watari.

Halting, Hatakeyama raised both arms in their rolled-up sleeves above his head:

"Stop! Quiet!"

An elderly gardener was pushing a wheelbarrow along the path above them toward the flower beds.

"Well, well — up to some mischief, I suppose," he said, seeing them.

"Dirty old scrounger!" someone replied. It was rumored that the old man lived off free dormitory leftovers.

"He's gone." M gave a signal with his eyes.

"Right. Here, Watari — "

For the first time, Hatakeyama looked straight into his eyes. Both Watari and his companions had unusually grave expressions.

"You've been getting too big for your boots."

No more was said: the sentence was passed; but nothing was done to carry it out. The judge stood with bare arms folded, slowly stroking them with his fingertips. . . . At that moment, Watari seemed to see his chance. Quite suddenly, he lunged toward Hatakeyama as though about to cling to him. Behind the latter lay the pond. As he braced his legs, stones and soil rolled down into it with a faint splashing. That was the only sound; to those around them, the two seemed locked in an embrace, silently consoling each other. But in steadying himself to avoid falling backward, Hatakeyama had exposed his arms to an attack already planned. Watari's teeth —

regular and sharp as a girl's, or perhaps a cat's—sank into his young flesh. Blood oozed out along the line between teeth and skin, yet biter and bitten remained still. Hatakeyama didn't even groan.

A slight movement separated them. Wiping his lips, more crimson than ever with the blood, Watari stood still, his eyes fixed on Hatakeyama's wound. A second or two before the members of the group had grasped what had happened, Watari had started running. But his pursuers were six tough boys. He lost his footing on the clay by the pond. He resisted, so that his blue shirt tore to give a glimpse of one shoulder, almost pathologically white. The boy with the rope tied his hands behind his back. His trousers, soiled by the red clay, were an oddly bright, shiny color.

Hatakeyama had made no move to chase him. His left hand was thrust casually into his pocket, with no care for his wound. The blood dripped down steadily, making a red rim around the glass of his wristwatch, then seeping from his fingertips into the bottom of his pocket. He felt no pain, aware only of something that hardly seemed like blood, something warm and familiar and intensely personal, caressing the surface of his skin as it went. But he had made up his mind on one thing: in his friends' faces when they brought Watari back, he would see nothing but an embodiment of his own decision, inviting him to proceed.

After that, he didn't look at Watari but gazed steadily at the long rope to which he was tied, with the slack wound round and round him and its end held in the hand of one of his classmates.

"Let's go somewhere quiet," he said. "The little wood behind the pigeon lofts."

Prodded, Watari began walking. As they filed along the red clay path, he staggered again and fell to his knees. With a coarse "heave-ho," they yanked him to his feet. His shoulder stood out so white in the light reflected from the foliage that it was as though the bone was sticking out of the rent in his blue shirt.

All the time as Watari walked, the incorrigible M hung about him, tickling him under the arms, pinching his backside, roaring with laughter because the boy, he said, had looked up at the sky. What if he had known that only two things in the whole world were visible to Watari's eyes: the blue sky—the eye of God, forever striking down into men's eyes through the green leaves of the treetops—and the precious blood spilled on his own account down here on earth, the lifeblood staining Hatakeyama's arm? His gaze went continually from one to the other of these two things. Hatakeyama was looking straight ahead, walking with a confident step more adult than any adult's. On his left arm, just in front of Watari, the blood was slowly drying, showing up a bright purple whenever it passed through the sun's rays.

The grove behind the pigeon lofts was a sunny patch of widely spaced trees, little frequented, where the pigeons often came to pass the time. An undistinguished collection of smallish deciduous trees, it had, at its very center, one great pine with gently outstretched branches on which the birds were fond of lining up to coo at one another. The rays of the after-noon sun picked out the trunk of the pine in a bright, pure light so that the resin flowing from it looked like veins of agate.

Hatakeyama came to a halt and said to the boy holding the rope:

"All right—this'll do. Take the rope off Watari. But don't let him get away. Throw the thing up like a lasso and put it over that big branch on the pine tree."

The rich jest of this sent the others into ecstasies. Watari was being held down by two of them. The remaining four danced like little demons on the grass as they helped hitch up the rope. One end of it was tied in a loop. Then one of the boys mounted a handy tree stump, poked his head through the noose, and stuck out his tongue.

"That's no good—it'll have to be higher."

The boy who'd stuck his tongue out was the shortest of them all. Watari would need at least another two or three inches.

They were all scared, scared by the occasional, shadowy suggestion that their prank might possibly be in earnest. As they led Watari, pale and trem-bling slightly, to the waiting noose, one waggish youth delivered a funeral address. All the while, Watari continued to gaze up at the sky with his idiot-ically wide-open eyes.

Abruptly, Hatakeyama raised a hand by way of a signal. His eyes were shut tight.

The rope went up.

Startled by the sudden beating of many pigeons' wings and by the glow on Watari's beautiful face, astonishingly high above them, they fled the grove, each in a different direction, unable to bear the thought of staying at the scene of such dire murder.

They ran at a lively pace, each boyish breast still swelling with the pride of having killed someone.

A full thirty minutes later, they reentered the wood as though by agree-ment and, huddling together, gazed up fearfully at the branch of the great pine.

The rope was dangling free, the hanged corpse nowhere to be seen.

■ Shiraishi Kazuko (1931–) (poem)

TRANSLATED BY KENNETH REXROTH AND IKUKO ATSUMI

Shiraishi Kazuko was born in Vancouver, Canada, and her family moved to Japan just before World War II. Her wild, sexy, sometimes surreal poetry, originally associated with the avant-garde magazine *Vou*, comes out of the new Japan of the postwar period. She is a Japanese Beat, a perform-ance poet who sometimes reads her poetry to jazz, who writes, as translator

Kenneth Rexroth notes, not "of the *ukiyo*, The Floating World, now utterly gone, but of a maelstrom, a typhoon, in which lost men and women whirl through toppling towers of neon."[1]

FURTHER READING: Rexroth, Kenneth, ed. *Seasons of Sacred Lust: The Selected Poems of Kazuko Shiraishi.* Translated by Ikuko Atsumi, John Solt, Carol Tinker, Yasuyo Morita, and Kenneth Rexroth. Wilson, Graeme, and Ikuko Atsumi, trs. *Three Contemporary Japanese Poets: Anzai Hitoshi, Shiraishi Kazuko, Tanikawa Shuntaro,* 1972.

The Man Root

For Sumiko's Birthday

God if he exists
Or if he doesn't
Still has a sense of humor
Like a certain type of man

So this time   5
He brings a gigantic man root
To join the picnic
Above the end of the sky of my dreams
Meanwhile
I'm sorry   10
I didn't give Sumiko anything for her birthday
But now I wish I could at least
Set the seeds of that God given penis
In the thin, small, and very charming voice of Sumiko
On the end of the line   15

Sumiko, I'm so sorry
But the penis shooting up day by day
Flourishes in the heart of the galaxy
As rigid as a wrecked bus
So that if   20
You'd like to see
The beautiful sky with all its stars
Or just another man instead of this God given cock
A man speeding along a highway
With a hot girl   25
You'll have to hang
All the way out of the bus window

---

1. Kenneth Rexroth, ed., *Seasons of Sacred Lust: The Selected Poems of Kazuko Shiraishi.* Translated by Ikuko Atsumi, John Solt, Carol Tinker, Yasuyo Morita, and Kenneth Rexroth (New York: New Directions, 1978), vi.

With your eyes peeled
It's spectacular when the cock
Starts nuzzling the edge of the cosmos   30
At this time
Dear Sumiko
The lonely way the stars of night shine
And the curious coldness of noon
Penetrates my gut   35
Seen whole
Or even if you refused to look
You'd go crazy
Because you can trace
The nameless, impersonal and timeless penis   40
In the raucous atmosphere
Of the passers-by
That parade it in a portable shrine
In that stir of voices
You can hear an immensity of savage   45
Rebellion, the curses of
Heathen gism
Sometimes
God is in conference or out to lunch
It seems he's away   50
Absconding from debts but leaving his penis.

So now
The cock abandoned by God
Trots along
Young and gay   55
And full of callow confidence
Amazingly like the shadow
Of a sophisticated smile

The penis bursting out of bounds
And beyond measure   60
Arrives here
Truly unique and entirely alone
Seen from whatever perspective
It's faceless and speechless
I would like to give you, Sumiko   65
Something like this for your birthday

When it envelops your entire life
And you've become invisible even to yourself
Occasionally you'll turn into the will
Of exactly this penis   · 70
And wander
Ceaselessly

I want to catch in my arms
Forever
Someone like you   75

◼ Tanikawa Shuntaro (1931–) (poems)

TRANSLATED BY HAROLD WRIGHT

Tanikawa Shuntaro is probably the best-known poet in Japan today, respected by the general public and by literary cognoscenti alike. He was born in Tokyo in 1931, the only son of philosopher Tanikawa Tetsuzo. He started writing poetry when he was eighteen, but he so loathed schooling that he went from the top of his class to being such a poor student that the family decided not to send him on to the university. With college out of the picture, Tanikawa needed a new direction; his father sent his poetry notebooks to Miyoshi Tatsuji, at that time Japan's leading poet, and the next day Miyoshi came to their house. Through his influence, several of Tanikawa's poems were published in *Bungakkai* (*Literary World*). Tanikawa was profoundly disturbed by the cultural turmoil in Japan during World War II and by the destruction wrought upon Tokyo by Allied air raids in 1945, which he witnessed as he bicycled through the ruined city and encountered the charred corpses of neighbors. In the postwar period, Tanikawa was deeply influenced by Western writers and has said that it was while listening to Beethoven that he realized that "life is possible," and he came back to art with faith in humanistic possibilities.

Tanikawa is a relentlessly innovative poet who writes in many, many forms—from the prose poem to the lyric to the experimental sonnet. In the 1960s, he broadened his creative output to drama, film, children's songs, and works combining poetry with paintings and photographs. He has translated a five-volume *Mother Goose* and has been the translator of the comic strip "Peanuts" since 1969. His poems have a similar childlike whimsy and irony and a determined faith in human possibility. A prolific writer, he has published, in his words, "a disgusting number" of books and has, throughout his life, tried to bring poetry back to the people through the mass media, giving poetry readings, and even shouting his poems through a bullhorn from the windows of office buildings. His cosmic view of the relationship of the universe and humanity has caused him to be embraced by a new generation and to take on a new label as a "New Age" poet. *His Selected Poems,* translated by Harold Wright, has appeared from North Point Press.

FURTHER READING: Elliot, William I., and Kazuo Kawamura, trs. *Coca-Cola Lessons,* 1986. Elliot, William I., and Kazuo Kawamura, trs. *Floating the River in Melancholy,*

1988. Keene, Donald, tr. *The Modern Japanese Prose Poem: An Anthology of Six Poets,* 1980. Wilson, Graeme, and Ikuko Atsumi, trs. *Three Contemporary Japanese Poets,* 1972.

Museum

stone axes and the like
lie quietly beyond the glass

constellations rotate endlessly
many of us become extinct
many of us appear   5

then
comets endlessly miss collision
lots of dishes and the like are broken
Eskimo dogs walk over the South Pole
great tombs are built both east and west   10
books of poems are often dedicated
recently
the atom's being smashed to bits
the daughter of a president is singing
such things as these   15
have been happening

stone axes and the like
lie absurdly quiet beyond the glass

Growth

Drawing a meaningless line,
a child says it's an apple.

Painting an apple just like an apple,
a painter says it's an apple.

Painting an apple unlike an apple,   5
an artist says it's truly an apple.

Not painting an apple or anything else
members of the Academy of Art
slurp up apple sauce.

Apples, apples, red apples,   10
are apples bitter? Are they sour?

Ten Yen Coin

With his last ten yen coin
the boy wanted to make a phone call.
He wanted to talk to someone close
    in a rowdy language,
but none of his friends had telephones.   5
The ten yen coin was wet in his palm
and smelled of metal.
(Why should I buy gum?
    This ten yen coin will be used
        for something more important.)   10
Then the boy saw the car,
a haughty car like a beautiful woman,
a fierce car like an unreachable happiness . . .
and before he knew it himself,
the boy, taking the ten yen coin in his hand,   15
    cut into that beautiful finish,
a long deep gash —
Then the boy threw the ten yen coin,
with all his might,
    into the city's congestion.   20

■ Oe Kenzaburo (1935–) (story)

TRANSLATED BY JOHN NATHAN

In 1994, Oe Kenzaburo, a masterful writer considered the voice of his generation in Japan (though little known in the West and translated into only four languages), won the Nobel Prize for literature. Oe's work has been decisively formed by two cataclysmic events, the Japanese surrender at the close of World War II when he was ten years old and the birth of his son, Hikari, a boy with serious brain damage. The first event transformed the sense of the values that regulated his childhood in a mountain village in Shikoku Island and led directly to the sense of betrayal, cynicism, and social commentary that pervades his novels and political essays. Translator John Nathan describes this event:

> On August 15, 1945, Emperor Hirohito went on to the radio to announce the surrender and deprived Oe of his innocence. Until that day, like all Japanese schoolchildren, he had been taught to fear the Emperor as a living god. Once a day his turn had come to be called to the front of the classroom and asked, "What would you do if the Emperor commanded you to die?" And Oe had replied, knees shaking, "I would die, Sir, I would cut open my belly and die."

When he heard the emperor's human voice on the radio, he found himself angry, humiliated, and deceived. The second event, the birth of his retarded son, is, at least nominally, the subject of the story appearing here and of his novel *A Personal Matter*. In *A Personal Matter*, the protagonist Bird conspires with a doctor to kill his two-headed son. In actuality Oe and his wife Yukari turned down the doctors who counseled them to let their son die. The name Hikari means "light," and Hikari's nickname is Pooh (after Winnie the Pooh); recently he has partially overcome his handicap and become a composer.

Oe is the quintessential postwar Japanese writer, obsessed with the nuclear destruction visited upon Hiroshima and Nagasaki by American bombers at the close of World War II, critical of Japanese militarism, and presenting in his novels a world radically off-kilter. He has edited an anthology entitled *The Crazy Iris and Other Stories of the Atomic Aftermath* (1985) and published two dozen novels, only a few of which are available in English translation. At the end of his introduction to *The Crazy Iris*, Oe states, "The fundamental condition of life, then, is that we are assailed by overwhelming fear yet, at the same time, beckoned by the necessity to rebuild hope, however difficult, in defiance of that fear."

FURTHER READING: Oe, Kenzaburo. *A Personal Matter*, 1958; *Hiroshima Notes*, 1963; *The Silent Cry*, 1974; *Teach Us to Outgrow Our Madness*, 1977; ed., *The Crazy Iris and Other Stories of the Atomic Aftermath*, 1984; *Japan's Dual Identity: A Writer's Dilemma*, 1988.

Aghwee the Sky Monster

Alone in my room, I wear a piratical black patch over my right eye. The eye may look all right, but the truth is I have scarcely any sight in it. Scarcely, I say; it isn't totally blind. The consequence is that when I look at this world with both eyes I see two worlds perfectly superimposed, a vague and shadowy world on top of one that's bright and vivid. I can be walking down a paved street when a sense of peril and unbalance will stop me, like a rat just scurried out of a sewer, dead in my tracks. Or I'll discover a film of unhappiness and fatigue on the face of a cheerful friend and clog the flow of an easy chat with my sluggish stutter. I suppose I'll get used to this eventually. If I don't I intend to wear my patch not only in my room when I'm alone but on the street and with my friends. Strangers may pass with condescending smiles—what an old-fashioned joke!—but I'm old enough not to be annoyed by every little thing.

The story I intend to tell is about my first experience earning money; I began with my right eye because the memory of that experience ten years ago revived in me abruptly and quite out of context when violence was done to my eye last spring. Remembering, I should add, I was freed from the hatred uncoiling in my heart and beginning to fetter me. At the very end I'll talk about the accident itself.

Ten years ago I had twenty-twenty vision. Now one of my eyes is ruined. *Time* shifted, launched itself from the springboard of an eyeball squashed by a stone. When I first met that sentimental madman I had only a child's understanding of *time*. I was yet to have the cruel awareness of *time* drilling its eyes into my back and *time* lying in wait ahead.

Ten years ago I was eighteen years old and weighed one hundred and ten pounds, had just entered college and was looking for a part-time job. Although I still had trouble reading French, I wanted to buy a clothbound edition in two volumes of *L'Âme Enchanté*. It was a Moscow edition I wanted, with not only a foreword but footnotes and even the colophon in Russian, and wispy lines like bits of thread connecting the letters of the French text. It was a curious edition all right, but far sturdier and more elegant than the French, and much cheaper. At the time I discovered it in a bookstore specializing in East European publications I had no interest in Romain Rolland, yet I went immediately into action to make the volumes mine. In those days I often succumbed to some curious passion and it never bothered me, I had the feeling there was nothing to worry about so long as I was sufficiently obsessed.

As I had just entered college and wasn't registered at the employment center, I looked for work by making the rounds of people I knew. Finally my uncle introduced me to a banker who came up with an offer. "Did you happen to see a movie called *Harvey?*" he asked. I said yes, and tried for a smile of moderate but unmistakable dedication, appropriate for someone about to be employed for the first time. *Harvey* was that Jimmy Stewart film about a man living with an imaginary rabbit as big as a bear; it had made me laugh so hard I thought I would die. The banker didn't return my smile. "Recently, my son has been having the same sort of delusions about living with a monster. He's stopped working and stays in his room. I'd like him to get out from time to time, but of course he'd need a—chaperon. Would you be interested?"

I knew quite a bit about the banker's son. He was a young composer whose avant-garde music had won prizes in France and Italy and who was generally included in the photo roundups in the weekly magazines, the kind of article they always called "Japan's Artists of Tomorrow." I had never heard his major works, but I had seen several films for which he had done the music. There was one about the adventures of a juvenile delinquent that had a short, lyrical theme played on the harmonica. It was beautiful. Watching the picture, I remember feeling vaguely troubled by the idea of an adult nearly thirty years old (in fact, the composer was twenty-eight when he hired me, my present age) working out a theme for the harmonica. Because my own harmonica had become my little brother's property when I had entered elementary school. And possibly because I knew more about the composer, whose name was D, than just public facts; I knew he had created a scandal. Generally, I have nothing but contempt for scandals, but I knew that the composer's infant child had died, that he had gotten divorced as a result, and that he was rumored to be involved with a certain movie actress. I hadn't known that he was in the grips of something like the rabbit in Jimmy Stewart's movie, or that he had stopped working and secluded himself in his room. How serious was his condition, I wondered, was it a case of nervous breakdown, or was he clearly schizophrenic?

"I'm not certain I know just what you mean by chaperon," I said, reeling in my smile. "Naturally, I'd like to be of service if I can." This time, concealing my curiosity and apprehension, I tried to lend my voice and expression as much sympathy as possible without seeming forward. It was only a part-time job, but it was the first chance of employment I had had and I was determined to do my accommodating best.

"When my son decides he wants to go somewhere in Tokyo, you go along—just that. There's a nurse at the house and she has no trouble handling him, so you don't have to worry about violence." The banker made me feel like a soldier whose cowardice has been discovered. I blushed and said, trying to recover lost ground: "I'm fond of music, and I respect composers more than anyone, so I look forward to accompanying D and talking with him."

"All he thinks about these days is this thing in his head, and apparently that's all he talks about!" The banker's brusqueness made my face even redder. "You can go out to see him tomorrow," he said.

"At—your house?"

"That's right, did you think he was in an asylum?" From the banker's tone of voice I could only suppose that he was at bottom a nasty man.

"If I should get the job," I said with my eyes on the floor, "I'll drop by again to thank you." I could easily have cried.

"No, he'll be hiring you" (All right then, I resolved defiantly, I'll call D my employer!), "so that won't be necessary. All I care about is that he doesn't get into any trouble outside that might develop into a scandal. There's his career to think about. Naturally, what he does reflects on me—"

So that was it! I thought, so I was to be a moral sentinel guarding the banker's family against a second contamination by the poisons of scandal. Of course I didn't say a thing, I only nodded dependably, anxious to warm the banker's chilly heart with the heat of reliance on me. I didn't even ask the most pressing question, something truly difficult to ask, namely: This monster haunting your son, sir, is it a rabbit like Harvey, nearly six feet tall? A creature covered in bristly hair like an Abominable Snowman? What kind of a monster is it? In the end I remained silent and consoled myself with the thought that I might be able to pry the secret out of the nurse if I made friends with her.

Then I left the executive's office, and as I walked along the corridor grinding my teeth in humiliation as if I were Julien Sorel after a meeting with someone important, I became self-conscious to the tips of my fingers and tried assessing my attitude and its effectiveness. When I got out of college I chose not to seek nine-to-five employment, and I do believe the memory of my dialogue with that disagreeable banker played a large part in my decision.

Even so, when classes were over the next day, I took a train out to the residential suburb where the composer lived. As I passed through the gate of that castle of a house, I remember a roaring of terrific beasts, as at a zoo in the middle of the night. I was dismayed, I cowered, what if those were the screams of my employer? A good thing it didn't occur to me then that those savage screams might have been coming from the monster haunting D like Jimmy Stewart's rabbit. Whatever they were, it was so clear that the screaming had rattled me that the maid showing me the way was indiscreet enough to break into a laugh. Then I discovered someone else laughing, voicelessly, in the dimness beyond a window in an annex in the garden. It was the man who was supposed to employ me; he was laughing like a face in a movie without a sound track. And boiling all around him was that howling of wild beasts. I listened closely and realized that several of the same animals were shrieking in concert. And in voices too shrill to be of this world. Abandoned by the maid at the entrance to the annex, I decided the screaming must be part of the composer's tape collection, regained my courage, straightened up, and opened the door.

Inside, the annex reminded me of a kindergarten. There were no partitions in the large room, but two pianos, an electric organ, several tape recorders, a record-player, something we had called a "mixer" when I was in the high-school radio club—there was hardly room to thread your way through. What looked like a dog asleep on the floor, for example, turned out to be a tuba of reddish brass. It was just as I had imagined a composer's studio; I even had the illusion I had seen the place before. D had stopped working and secluded himself in his room—could his father have been mistaken about all that?

The composer was just bending to switch off the tape recorder. Enveloped in a chaos that was not without its own order, he moved his hands swiftly and in an instant those beastly screams were sucked into a dark hole of silence. Then he straightened and turned to me with a truly tranquil smile.

Having glanced around the room and seen that the nurse was not present, I was a little wary, but the composer gave me no reason in the world to expect that he was about to get violent.

"My father told me about you. Come in, there's room over there," he said in a low resonant voice.

I took off my shoes and stepped up onto the rug without putting on slippers. Then I looked around for a place to sit, but except for round stools in front of the pianos and the organ, there wasn't a bit of furniture in the room, not even a cushion. So I brought my feet together between a pair of bongo drums and some empty tape boxes and stood there uncomfortably. The composer was standing too, arms hanging at his sides. I wondered if he ever sat down. He didn't ask me to be seated either, just stood there silent and smiling.

"Could those have been monkey voices?" I said, trying to crack a silence that threatened to set more quickly than any cement.

"Rhinoceros—they sounded that way because I speeded the machine up. And I had the volume way up, too. At least I think they're rhinoceros—rhino is what I asked for when I had this tape made—of course I can't really be sure. But now that you're here, I'll be able to go to the zoo myself."

"I may take that to mean that I'm employed?"

"Of course! I didn't have you come out here to test you. How can a madman test a normal person?" The man who was to be my employer said this objectively and almost as if he were embarrassed. Which made me feel disgusted with the obsequiousness of what I had said—I may take that to mean that I'm employed?—I had sounded like a shopkeeper! The composer was different from his businessman father and I should have been more direct with him.

"I wish you wouldn't call yourself a madman. It's awkward for me." Trying to be frank was one thing, but what a brainless remark! But the composer met me halfway. "All right, if that's how you feel. I suppose that would make work easier."

Work is a vague word, but, at least during those few months when I was visiting him once a week, the composer didn't get even as close to work as going to the zoo to record a genuine rhino for himself. He merely wandered around Tokyo in various conveyances or on foot and visited a variety of places. When he mentioned work, he must therefore have had me in mind. And I worked quite a lot; I even went on a mission for him, all the way to Kyoto.

"Then when should I begin?" I said.

"Right away if it suits you. Now."

"That suits me fine."

"I'll have to get ready—would you wait outside?"

Head lowered cautiously, as though he were walking in a swamp, my employer picked his way to the back of the room past musical instruments and sound equipment and piles of manuscripts to a black wooden door which he opened and then closed behind him. I got a quick look at a woman in a nurse's uniform, a woman in her early forties with a longish face and heavy shadows on her cheeks that might have been wrinkles or maybe scars. She seemed to encircle the composer with her right arm as she ushered him inside, while with her left hand she closed the door. If this was part of the routine, I would never have a chance to talk with the nurse before I went out with my employer. Standing in front of the closed door, in the darkest part of that dim room, I shuffled into my shoes and felt my anxiety about this job of mine increase. The composer had smiled the whole time and when I had prompted him he had replied. But he hadn't volunteered much. Should I have been more reserved? I wondered. Since "outside" might have meant two things, and since I was determined that everything should be perfect on my first job, I decided to wait just inside the main gate, from where I could see the annex in the garden.

D was a small, thin man, but with a head that seemed larger than most. To make the bony cliff of his forehead seem a little less forbidding, he combed his pale, well-washed, and fluffy hair down over his brow. His mouth and jaw were small, and his teeth were horribly irregular. And yet, probably due to the color of his deeply recessed eyes, there was a static correctness about his face that went well with a tranquil smile. As for the overall impression, there was something canine about the man. He wore flannel trousers and a sweater with stripes like rows of fleas. His shoulders were a little stooped, his arms outlandishly long.

When he came out of the back door of the annex, my employer was wearing a blue wool cardigan over his other sweater and a pair of white tennis shoes. He reminded me of a grade-school music teacher. In one hand he held a black scarf, and as if he were puzzling whether to wrap it around his neck, there was perplexity in his grin to me as I waited at the gate. For as long as I knew D, except at the very end when he was lying in a hospital bed, that was how he dressed. I remember his outfit so well because I was always struck by something comical about an adult man wearing a cardigan around his shoulders, as if he were a woman in disguise. Its shapelessness and nondescript color made that sweater perfect for him. As the composer pigeon-toed toward me past the shrubbery, he absently lifted the hand that held the scarf and signaled me with it. Then he wrapped the scarf resolutely around his neck. It was already four in the afternoon and fairly cold out of doors.

D went through the gate, and as I was following him (our relationship was already that of employer and employee), I had the feeling I was being watched and turned around: behind the same window through which I had discovered my employer, that forty-year-old nurse with the scarred—or were they wrinkled?—cheeks was watching us the way a soldier remaining behind might see a deserter off, her lips clamped shut like a turtle. I resolved to get her alone as soon as I could to question her about D's condition. What was wrong with the woman, anyway? Here she was taking care of a young man with a nervous condition, maybe a madman, yet when her charge went out she had nothing to say to the chaperon accompanying him. Wasn't that professional negligence? Wasn't she at least obliged to fill in the new man on the job? Or was my employer a patient so gentle and harmless that nothing had to be said?

When he got to the sidewalk D shuttered open his tired-looking eyes in their deep sockets and glanced swiftly up and down the deserted residential street. I didn't know whether it was an indication of madness or what—sudden action without any continuity seemed to be a habit of his. The composer looked up at the clear, end-of-autumn sky, blinking rapidly. Though they were sunken, there was something remarkably expressive about his deep brown eyes. Then he stopped blinking and his eyes seemed to focus, as though he were searching the sky. I stood obliquely behind him, watching, and what impressed me most vividly was the movement of his Adam's apple, which was large as any fist. I wondered if he had been destined to become a large man; perhaps something had impeded his growth in infancy and now only his head from the neck up bespoke the giant he was meant to be.

Lowering his gaze from the sky, my employer found and held my puzzled eyes with his own and said casually, but with a gravity that made objection impossible: "On a clear day you can see things floating up there very well. I see him up there with them, and frequently he comes down to me when I go outdoors."

Instantly I felt threatened. Looking away from my employer, I wondered how to survive this first ordeal that had confronted me so quickly. Should I pretend to believe in what this man called "him," or would that be a mistake? Was I dealing with a raving madman, or was the composer just a poker-faced humorist trying to have some fun with me? As I stood there in distress, he extended me a helping hand: "I know you can't see the figures floating in the sky, and I know you wouldn't be aware of him even if he were right here at my side. All I ask is that you don't act amazed when he comes down to earth, even if I talk to him. Because you'd upset him if you were to break out laughing all of a sudden or were to try to shut me up. And if you happen to notice when we're talking that I want some support from you, I'd appreciate it if you'd chime right in and say something, you know, affirmative. You see, I'm explaining Tokyo to him as if it were a paradise. It might seem a lunatic paradise to you, but maybe you could think of it as satire and be affirmative anyway, at least when he's down here with me."

I listened carefully and thought I could make out at least the contours of what my employer expected of me. Then was "he" a rabbit as big as a man after all, nesting in the sky? But that wasn't what I asked; I restrained myself to asking only: "How will I know when he's down here with you?"

"Just by watching me; he only comes down when I'm outside."

"What about when you're in a car?"

"In a car or train, as long as I'm next to an open window he's likely to show up. There have been times when he's appeared when I was in the house, just standing next to an open window."

"And . . . right now?" I asked uncomfortably. I must have sounded like the class dunce who simply cannot grasp the multiplication principle.

"Right now it's just you and me," my employer said graciously. "Why don't we ride in to Shinjuku today? I haven't been on a train in a long time."

We walked to the station, and all the way I kept an eye peeled for a sign that something had appeared at my employer's side. But before I knew it we were on the train and, so far as I could tell, nothing had materialized. One thing I did notice: the composer ignored the people who passed us on the street even when they greeted him. As if he himself did not exist, as if the people who approached with hellos and how-are-yous were registering an illusion which they mistook for him, my employer utterly ignored all overtures to contact.

The same thing happened at the ticket window; D unilaterally declined to relate to other people. Handing me one thousand yen, he told me to buy tickets and then refused to take his own even when I held it out to him. I had to stop at the gate and have both our tickets punched while D swept through the turnstile onto the platform with the freedom of the invisible man. Even on the train, he behaved as if the other passengers were no more aware of him than of the atmosphere; huddling in a seat in the farthest corner of the car, he rode in silence with his eyes closed. I stood in front of him and watched in growing apprehension for whatever it was to float in through the open window and settle at his side. Naturally, I didn't believe in the monster's existence. It was just that I was determined not to miss the instant when D's delusions took hold of him; I felt I owed him that much in return for the money he was paying me. But, as it happened, he sat like some small animal playing dead all the way to Shinjuku Station, so I could only surmise that he hadn't had a visit from the sky. Of course, supposition was all it was: as long as other people were around us, my employer remained a sullen oyster of silence. But I learned quickly enough that my guess had been correct. Because when the moment came, it was more than apparent (from D's reaction, I mean) that something was visiting him.

We had left the station and were walking down the street. It was that time of day a little before evening when not many people are out; we ran across a small crowd gathered on a corner. We stopped to look; surrounded by the crowd, an old man was turning around and around in the street without so much as a glance at anyone. A dignified-looking old man, he was spinning in a frenzy, clutching a briefcase and an umbrella to his breast, mussing his gray, pomaded hair a little as he stamped his feet and shouted like a seal. The faces in the watching crowd were lusterless and dry in the evening chill that was stealing into the air; the old man's face alone was flushed, and sweating, and seemed about to steam.

Suddenly I noticed that D, who should have been standing at my side, had taken a few steps back and thrown one arm around the shoulders of an invisible something roughly his own height. Now he was peering affectionately into the space slightly above the empty circle of his arm. The crowd was too intent on the old man to be concerned with D's performance, but I was terrified. Slowly the composer turned to me, as if he wanted to introduce me to a friend. I didn't know how to respond; all I could do was panic and blush. It was like forgetting your silly lines in the junior-high-school play. The composer continued to stare at me, and now there was annoyance in his eyes. He was seeking an explanation for that intent old man turning singlemindedly in the street, for the benefit of his visitor from the sky. A paradisiacal explanation! But all I could do was wonder stupidly whether the old man might have been afflicted with Saint Vitus's dance.

When I sadly shook my head in silence, the light of inquiry went out of my employer's eyes. As if he were taking leave of a friend, he dropped his arm. Then he slowly shifted his gaze skyward until his head was all the way back and his large Adam's apple stood out in bold relief. The phantom had soared back into the sky and I was ashamed; I hadn't been equal to my job.

As I stood there with my head hanging, the composer stepped up to me and indicated that my first day of work was at an end: "We can go home now. He's come down once today already, and you must be pretty tired." I did feel exhausted after all that tension.

We rode back in a taxi with the windows rolled up, and as soon as I'd been paid for the day, I left. But I didn't go straight to the station; I waited behind a telephone pole diagonally across from the house. Dusk deepened, the sky turned the color of a rose, and just as the promise of night was becoming fact, the nurse, in a short-skirted, one-piece dress of a color indistinct in the dimness, appeared through the main gate pushing a brand-new bicycle in front of her. Before she could get on the bicycle, I ran over to her. Without her nurse's uniform she was just an ordinary little woman in her early forties; vanished from her face was the mystery I had discovered through the annex window. And my appearance had unsettled her. She couldn't climb on the bike and pedal away, but neither would she stand still; she had begun to walk the bike along when I demanded that she explain our mutual employer's condition. She resisted, peevishly, but I had a good grip on the bicycle seat and so in the end she gave in. When she began to talk, her formidable lower jaw snapped shut at each break in the sentence; she was absolutely a talking turtle.

"He says it's a fat baby in a white cotton nightgown. Big as a kangaroo, he says. It's supposed to be afraid of dogs and policemen and it comes down out of the sky. He says its name is Aghwee! Let me tell you something, if you happen to be around when that spook gets hold of him, you'd better just play dumb, you can't afford to get involved—don't forget you're dealing with a loony! And another thing, don't you take him anyplace funny, even if he wants to go. On top of everything else, a little gonorrhea is all we need around here!"

I blushed and let go of the bicycle seat. The nurse, jangling her bell, pedaled away into the darkness as fast as she could go with legs as tubular as handlebars. Ah, a fat baby in a white cotton nightgown, big as a kangaroo!

When I showed up at the house the following week, the composer fixed me with those clear brown eyes of his and rattled me by saying, though not especially in reproof: "I hear you waited for the nurse and asked her about my visitor from the sky. You really take your work seriously."

That afternoon we took the same train in the opposite direction, into the country for half an hour to an amusement park on the banks of the Tama River. We tried all kinds of rides and, luckily for me, the baby as big as a kangaroo dropped out of the sky to visit D when he was up by himself in the Sky Sloop, wooden boxes shaped like boats that were hoisted slowly into the air on the blades of a kind of windmill. From a bench on the ground, I watched the composer talking with an imaginary passenger at his side. And until his visitor had climbed back into the sky, D refused to come down; again and again a signal from him sent me running to buy him another ticket.

Another incident that made an impression on me that day occurred as we were crossing the amusement park toward the exit, when D accidentally stepped in some wet cement. When he saw that his foot had left an imprint he became abnormally irritated, and until I had negotiated with the workmen, paid them something for their pains and had the footprint troweled away, he stubbornly refused to move from the spot. This was the only time the composer ever revealed to me the least violence in his nature. On the way home on the train, I suppose because he regretted having barked at me, he excused himself in this way: "I'm not living in present time anymore, at least not consciously. Do you know the rule that governs trips into the past in a time machine? For example, a man who travels back ten thousand years in time doesn't dare do anything in that world that might remain behind him. Because he doesn't exist in time ten thousand years ago, and if he left anything behind him there the result would be a warp, infinitely slight maybe but still a warp, in all of history from then until now, ten thousand years of it. That's the way the rule goes, and since I'm not living in present time, I mustn't do anything here in this world that might remain or leave an imprint."

"But why have you stopped living in present time?" I asked, and my employer sealed himself up like a golf ball and ignored me. I regretted my loose tongue; I had finally exceeded the limits permitted me, because I was too concerned with D's problem. Maybe the nurse was right; playing dumb was the only way, and I couldn't afford to get involved. I resolved not to.

We walked around Tokyo occasionally after that, and my new policy was a success. But the day came when the composer's problems began to involve me whether I liked it or not. One afternoon we got into a cab together and, for the first time since I had taken the job, D mentioned a specific destination, a swank apartment house in Daikan Yama laid out like a hotel. When we arrived, D waited in the coffee shop in the basement while I went up in the elevator alone to pick up something that was waiting for me. I was to receive it from D's former wife, who was now living alone in the apartment.

I knocked on a door that made me think of the cell blocks at Sing Sing (I was always going to the movies in those days; I have the feeling that about 95 percent of what I knew came directly from the movies) and it was opened by a short woman with a pudgy, red face on top of a neck that was just as pudgy, as round as a cylinder. She ordered me to take my shoes off and step inside, and pointed to a sofa near the window where I was to sit. This must be the way high society receives a stranger, I remember thinking at the time. For me, the son of a poor farmer, refusing her invitation and asking for delivery at the door would have taken the courage to defy Japanese high society, the courage of that butcher who threatened Louis XIV. I did as I was told, and stepped for the first time in my life into an American-style studio apartment.

The composer's former wife poured me some beer. She seemed somewhat older than D, and although she gestured grandly and intoned when she spoke, she was too round and overweight to achieve dignity. She was wearing a dress of some heavy cloth with the hem of the skirt unraveled in the manner of a squaw costume, and her necklace of diamonds set in gold looked like the work of an Inca craftsman (now that I think about them, these observations, too, smell distinctly of the movies). Her window overlooked the streets of Shibuya, but the light pouring through it into the room seemed to bother her terrifically; she was continually shifting in her chair, showing me legs as round and bloodshot as her neck, while she questioned me in the voice of a cross-examiner. I suppose I was her only source of information about her former husband. Sipping my black, bitter beer as if it were hot coffee, I answered her as best I could, but my knowledge of D was scant and inaccurate and I couldn't satisfy her. Then she started asking about D's actress girlfriend, whether she came to see him and things like that, and there was nothing I could say. Annoyed, I thought to myself, what business was it of hers, didn't she have any feminine pride?

"Does D still see that phantom?" she said at last.

"Yes, it's a baby the size of a kangaroo in a white cotton nightgown and he says its name is Aghwee; the nurse was telling me about it," I said enthusiastically, glad to encounter a question I could do justice to. "It's usually floating in the sky, but sometimes it flies down to D's side."

"Aghwee, you say? Then it must be the ghost of our dead baby. You know why he calls it Aghwee? Because our baby spoke only once while it was alive and that was what it said—Aghwee. That's a pretty mushy way to name the ghost that's haunting you, don't you think?" The woman spoke derisively; an ugly, corrosive odor reached me from her mouth. "Our baby was born with a lump on the back of its head that made it look as if it had two heads. The doctor diagnosed it as a brain hernia. When D heard the news he decided to protect himself and me from a catastrophe, so he got together with the doctor, and they killed the baby—I think they only gave it sugar water instead of milk no matter how loud it screamed. My husband killed the baby because he didn't want us to be saddled with a child who could only function as a vegetable, which is what the doctor had predicted! So he was acting out of fantastic egotism more than anything else. But then there was an autopsy and the lump turned out to be a benign tumor. That's when D began seeing ghosts; you see, he'd lost the courage he needed to sustain his egotism, so he declined to live his own life, just as he had declined to let the baby go on living. Not that he committed suicide, he just fled from reality into a world of phantoms. But once your hands are all bloody with a baby's murder, you can't get them clean again just by running from reality, anybody knows that. So here he is, hands as filthy as ever and carrying on about Aghwee."

The cruelty of her criticism was hard to bear, for my employer's sake. So I turned to her, redder in the face than ever with the excitement of her loquacity, and struck a blow for D. "Where were you while all this was going on? You were the mother, weren't you?"

"I had a Caesarean, and for a week afterwards I was in a coma with a high fever. It was all over when I woke up," said D's former wife, leaving my gauntlet on the floor. Then she stood up and moved toward the kitchen. "I guess you'll have some more beer?"

"No, thank you, I've had enough. Would you please give me whatever I'm supposed to take to D?"

"Of course, just let me gargle. I have to gargle every ten minutes, for pyorrhea—you must have noticed the smell?"

D's former wife put a brass key into a business envelope and handed it to me. Standing behind me while I tied my shoes, she asked what school I went to and then, mentioning a certain newspaper, added proudly: "I hear there's not even one subscriber in the dormitories there. You may be interested to know that my father will own that paper soon."

I let silence speak for my contempt.

I was about to get into the elevator when doubt knifed through me as though my chest were made of butter. I had to think. I let the elevator go and decided to use the stairs. If his former wife had described D's state of mind correctly, how could I be sure he wouldn't commit suicide with a pinch of cyanide or something taken from a box this key unlocked? All the way down the stairs I wondered what to do, and then I was standing in front of D's table and still hadn't arrived at a conclusion. The composer sat there with his eyes tightly shut, his tea untouched on the table. I suppose it wouldn't do for him to be seen drinking substances of this time, now that he had stopped living in it and had become a traveler from another.

"I saw her," I began, resolved all of a sudden to lie, "and we were talking all this time but she wouldn't give me anything."

My employer looked up at me placidly and said nothing, though doubt clouded his puppy eyes in their deep sockets. All the way back in the cab I sat in silence at his side, secretly perturbed. I wasn't sure whether he had seen through my lie. In my shirt pocket the key was heavy.

But I only kept it a week. For one thing, the idea of D's suicide began to seem silly; for another, I was worried he might ask his wife about the key. So I put it in a different envelope and mailed it to him special delivery. The next day I went out to the house a little worried and found my employer in the open space in front of the annex, burning a pile of music manuscripts. They must have been his own compositions: that key had unlocked the composer's music.

We didn't go out that day. Instead I helped D incinerate his whole opus. We had burned everything and had dug a hole and I was burying the ashes when suddenly D began to whisper. The phantom had dropped out of the sky. And until it left I continued working, slowly burying those ashes. That afternoon the sky monster called Aghwee (and there was no denying it was a mushy name) remained at my employer's side for fully twenty minutes.

From that day on, since I either stepped to one side or dropped behind whenever the phantom baby appeared, the composer must have realized that I was complying with only the first of his original instructions, not to act amazed, while his request that I back him up with something affirmative was consistently ignored. Yet he seemed satisfied, and so my job was made easier. I couldn't believe D was the kind of person to create a disturbance in the street; in fact his father's word of warning began to seem ridiculous, our tours of Tokyo together continued so uneventfully. I had already purchased the Moscow edition of *L'Âme Enchanté* I wanted, but I no longer had any intention of giving up such a marvelous job. My employer and I went everywhere together. D wanted to visit all the concert halls where works of his had been performed and all the schools he had ever been to. We would make special trips to places where he used to amuse himself — bars, movie theaters, indoor swimming pools — and then we would turn back without going inside. And the composer had a passion for all of Tokyo's many forms of public transportation; I'm sure we rode the entire metropolitan subway system. Since the monster baby couldn't descend from the sky while we were underground, I could enjoy the subway in peace of mind. Naturally, I tensed whenever we encountered dogs or officers of the law, remembering what the nurse had told me, but those encounters never coincided with an appearance by Aghwee. I discovered that I was loving my job. Not loving my employer or his phantom baby the size of a kangaroo. Simply loving my job.

One day the composer approached me about making a trip for him. He would pay traveling expenses, and my daily wage would be doubled; since I would have to stay overnight in a hotel and wouldn't be back until the second day, I would actually be earning four times what I usually made. Not only that, the purpose of the trip was to meet D's former girlfriend the movie actress, in D's place. I accepted eagerly, I was delighted. And so began that comic and pathetic journey.

D gave me the name of the hotel the actress had mentioned in a recent letter and the date she was expecting him to arrive. Then he had me learn a message to the girl: my employer was no longer living in present time; he was like a traveler who had arrived here in a time machine from a world ten thousand years in the future. Accordingly, he couldn't permit himself to create a new existence with his own signature on it through such acts as writing letters.

I memorized the message, and then it was late at night and I was sitting opposite a movie actress in the basement bar of a hotel in Kyoto, with a chance first to explain why D hadn't come himself, next to persuade his mistress of his conception of time, and finally to deliver his message. I concluded: "D would like you to be careful not to confuse his recent divorce with another divorce he once promised you he would get and since he isn't living in present time anymore, he says it's only natural that he won't be seeing you again." I felt my face color; for the first time I had the sensation that I had a truly difficult job.

"Is that what D-boy says? And what do you say? How do you feel about all this, that you'd run an errand all the way to Kyoto?"

"Frankly, I think D is being mushy."

"That's the way he is—I'd say he's being pretty mushy with you, too, asking this kind of favor!"

"I'm employed; I get paid by the day for what I do."

"What are you drinking there? Have some brandy."

I had some. Until then I'd been drinking the same dark beer D's former wife had given me, with an egg in it to thin it down. By some queer carom of a psychological billiard ball, I'd been influenced by a memory from D's former wife's apartment while waiting to meet his mistress. The actress had been drinking brandy from the start. It was the first imported brandy I'd ever had.

"And what's all this about D-boy seeing a ghost, a baby as big as a kangaroo? What did you call it, Raghbee?"

"Aghwee! The baby only spoke once before it died and that was what it said."

"And D thought it was telling him its name? Isn't that darling! If that baby had been normal, it was all decided that D was going to get a divorce and marry me. The day the baby was born we were in bed together in a hotel room and there was a phone call and then we knew something awful had happened. D jumped out of bed and went straight to the hospital. Not a word from him since—" The actress gulped her brandy down, filled her glass to the brim from the bottle of Hennessy on the table as if she were pouring fruit juice, and drained her glass again.

Our table was hidden from the bar by a display case full of cigarettes. Hanging on the wall above my shoulder was a large color poster with the actress's picture on it, a beer advertisement. The face in the poster glittered like gold, no less than the beer. The girl sitting opposite me was not quite so dazzling, there was even a depression in her forehead, just below the hairline, that looked deep enough to contain an adult thumb. But it was precisely the fault that made her more appealing than her picture.

She couldn't get the baby off her mind.

"Look, wouldn't it be terrifying to die without memories or experiences because you'd never done anything human while you were alive? That's how it would be if you died as an infant—wouldn't that be terrifying?"

"Not to the baby, I don't imagine," I said deferentially.

"But think about the world after death!" The actress's logic was full of leaps.

"The world after death?"

"If there is such a thing, the souls of the dead must live there with their memories for all eternity. But what about the soul of a baby who never knew anything and never had any experiences? I mean, what memories can it have?"

At a loss, I drank my brandy in silence.

"I'm terribly afraid of death, so I'm always thinking about it—you don't have to be disgusted with yourself because you don't have a quick answer for me. But you know what I think? The minute that baby died, I think D-boy decided not to create any new memories for himself, as if he had died, too, and that's why he stopped living, you know, positively, in present time. And I bet he calls that ghost baby down to earth all over Tokyo so he can create new memories for it!"

At the time I thought she must be right. This tipsy movie actress with a dent in her forehead big enough for a thumb is quite an original psychologist, I thought to myself. And much more D's type, I thought, than the pudgy, tomato-faced daughter of a newspaper baron. All of a sudden I realized that, even here in Kyoto with hundreds of miles between us, I, the model of a faithful employee, was thinking exclusively about D. No, there was something else, too, there was D's phantom. I realized that the baby whose appearance I waited for nervously every time my employer and I went out together hadn't been off my mind for a minute.

It was time for the bar to close and I didn't have a room. I'd managed to get as old as I was without ever staying in a hotel and I knew nothing about reservations. Luckily, the actress was known at the hotel, and a word from her got me a room. We went up in the elevator together, and I started to get off at my floor when she suggested we have one last drink and invited me to her room. From that point on I have only muddled comic and pathetic memories. When she had seated me in a chair, the actress returned to the door and looked up and down the hall, then went through a whole series of nervous motions, flounced on the bed as if to test the springs, turned lights on and switched them off, ran a little water in the tub. Then she poured me the brandy she had promised and, sipping a Coca Cola, she told me about another man chasing her during her affair with D, and finally going to bed with him, and D slapping her so hard the teeth rattled in her mouth. Then she asked if I thought today's college students went in for "heavy petting"? It depended on the student, I said—suddenly the actress had become a mother scolding a child for staying up too late and was telling me to find my own room and go to sleep. I said good night, went downstairs, and fell asleep immediately. I woke up at dawn with a fire in my throat.

The most comic and pathetic part was still to come. I understood the minute I opened my eyes that the actress had invited me to her room intending to seduce a college student who was wild for heavy petting. And with that understanding came rage and abject desire. I hadn't slept with a woman yet, but this humiliation demanded that I retaliate. I was drunk on what must have been my first Hennessy VSOP, and I was out of my head with the kind of poisonous desire that goes with being eighteen. It was only five o'clock in the morning and there was no sign of life in the halls. Like a panther wild with rage I sped to her door on padded feet. It was ajar. I stepped inside and found her seated at the dresser mirror with her back to me. Creeping up directly behind her (to this day I wonder what I was trying to do), I lunged at her neck with both hands. The actress whirled around with a broad smile on her face, rising as she turned, and then she had my hands in her own and was pumping them happily up and down as if she were welcoming a guest and singsonging: "Good morning! Good morning! Good morning!" Before I knew it I had been seated in a chair and we were sharing her toast and morning coffee and reading the newspaper together. After a while the movie actress said in a tone of voice she might have used to discuss the weather: "You were trying to rape me just now, weren't you." She went back to her makeup and I got out of there, fled downstairs to my own room and burrowed back into bed, trembling as though I had malaria. I was afraid that a report of this incident might reach D, but the subject of the movie actress never came up again. I continued to enjoy my job.

Winter had come. Our plan that afternoon was to bicycle through D's residential neighborhood and the surrounding fields. I was on a rusty old bike and my employer had borrowed the nurse's shiny new one. Gradually we expanded the radius of a circle around D's house, riding into a new housing development and coasting down hills in the direction of the fields. We were sweating, relishing the sensation of liberation, more and more exhilarated. I say "we" and include D because that afternoon it was evident that he was in high spirits, too. He was even whistling a theme from a Bach sonata for flute and harpsichord called *Siciliana.* I happened to know that because when I was in high school, I had played flute. I never learned to play well, but I did develop a habit of thrusting out my upper lip the way a tapir does. Naturally, I had friends who insisted my buck teeth were to blame. But the fact is, flutists frequently look like tapirs.

As we pedaled down the street, I picked up the tune and began to whistle along with D. Siciliana is a sustained and elegant theme, but I was out of breath from pedaling and my whistle kept lapsing into airy sibilance. Yet D's phrasing was perfect, absolutely legato. I stopped whistling then, ashamed to go on, and the composer glanced over at me with his lips still pursed in a whistle like a carp puckering up to breathe and smiled his tranquil smile. Granted there was a difference in the bikes, it was still unnatural and pathetic that an eighteen-year-old student, skinny maybe, but tall, should begin to tire and run short of breath before a twenty-eight-year-old composer who was a little man and sick besides. Unjust is what it was, and infuriating. My mood clouded instantly and I felt disgusted with the whole job. So I stood up on the pedals all of a sudden and sped away as furiously as a bicycle racer. I even turned, purposely, down a narrow gravel path between two vegetable fields. When I looked back a minute later, my employer was hunched over the handle bars, his large, round head nodding above his narrow shoulders, churning the gravel beneath his wheels in hot pursuit of me. I coasted to a stop, propped a foot on the barbed wire fence that bordered the field, and waited for D to catch up. I was already ashamed of my childishness.

His head still bobbing, my employer was approaching fast, and then I knew the phantom was with him. D was racing his bike down the extreme left of the gravel path, his face twisted to the right so that he was almost looking over his right shoulder, and the reason his head appeared to bob was that he was whispering encouragement to something running, or maybe flying, alongside the bicycle. Like a marathon coach pacing one of his runners. Ah, I thought, he's doing that on the premise that Aghwee is neck and neck with his speeding bike. The monster as large as a kangaroo, the fat, funny baby in a white cotton nightgown was bounding—like a kangaroo!—down that gravel path. I shuddered, then I kicked the barbed wire fence and slowly pedaled away, waiting for my employer and the monster in his imagination to catch up.

Don't think I'd let myself begin to believe in Aghwee's existence. I had taken the nurse's advice, sworn not to lose the anchor on my common sense, not to give way to lunacy as in those slightly solemn slapstick comedies where, say, the keeper of the madhouse goes mad; and, consciously derisive, I was thinking to myself that the neurotic composer was putting on a show with his bicycle just to follow up a lie he had told me once, and what a lot of trouble to go to! In other words, I was keeping a clinical distance between myself and D's phantom monster. Even so, there occurred a strange alteration in my state of mind.

It began this way: D had finally caught up and was biking along a few feet behind me when, as unexpectedly as a cloudburst and quite inescapably, we were enveloped by the belling of a pack of hounds. I looked up and saw them racing toward me down the gravel path, young adult Dobermans that stood two feet high, more than ten of them. Running breathlessly behind the pack, the thin black leather leashes grasped in one hand, was a man in overalls, chasing the dogs perhaps, or maybe they were dragging him along. Jet-black Dobermans, sleek as wet seals, with just a dusting of dry chocolate on their chests and jowls and pumping haunches. And down on us they howled, filling the gravel path, keening for the attack at such a forward tilt they looked about to topple on their foaming snouts. There was a meadow on the other side of the field; the man in overalls must have been training the beasts there and now he was on his way home with them.

Trembling with fear, I got off my bike and helplessly surveyed the field on the other side of the fence. The barbed wire came up to my chest. I might have had a chance myself but I would never have been able to boost the little composer to safety on the other side. The poisons of terror were beginning to numb my head, but for one lucid instant I could see the catastrophe that was bound to occur in a few seconds. As the Dobermans neared, D would sense that Aghwee was being attacked by a pack of the animals it most feared. He would probably hear the baby's frightened crying. And certainly he would meet the dogs head on, in defense of his baby. Then the Dobermans would rip him to pieces. Or he would try to escape with the baby and make a reckless leap to clear the fence and be just as cruelly torn. I was rocked by the pity of what I knew must happen. And while I stood there dumbly without a plan, those giant black-and-chocolate devils were closing in on us, snapping the air with awful jaws, so close by now that I could hear their alabaster claws clicking on the gravel. Suddenly I knew I could do nothing for D and his baby, and with that knowledge I went limp, unresisting as a pervert when he is seized in the subway, and was swallowed whole in the darkness of my fear. I backed off the gravel path until the barbed wire was a fire in my back, pulled my bike in front of me as if it were a wall, and shut my eyes tight. Then an animal stench battered me, together with the howling of the dogs and the pounding of their feet, and I could feel tears seeping past my eyelids. I abandoned myself to a wave of fear and it swept me away . . .

On my shoulder was a hand gentle as the essence of all gentleness; it felt like Aghwee touching me. But I knew it was my employer; he had let those fiendish dogs pass and no catastrophe of fear had befallen him. I continued crying anyway, with my eyes closed and my shoulders heaving. I was too old to cry in front of other people. I suppose the shock of fright had induced some kind of infantile regression in me. When I stopped crying, we walked our bikes past that barbed wire fence like prisoners in a concentration camp, in silence, our heads hanging, to the meadow beyond the field where strangers were playing ball and exercising dogs (D wasn't occupied with Aghwee anymore; the baby must have left while I was crying). We laid our bikes down and then sprawled on the grass ourselves. My tears had flooded away my pretensions and my rebelliousness and the perverse suspicion in my heart. And D was no longer wary of me. I lay back on the grass and clasped my hands beneath my head, curiously light and dry after all that crying. Then I closed my eyes and listened quietly while D peered down at me with his chin in his hand and spoke to me of Aghwee's world.

"Do you know a poem called 'Shame' by Nakahara Chuya? Listen to the second verse:

> The mournful sky
> high where branches tangle
> teems with dead baby souls;
> I blinked and saw
> above the distant fields
> fleece knit into a dream
> of mastodons.

"That's one aspect of the world of the dead baby I see. There are some Blake engravings, too, especially one called 'Christ Refusing the Banquet Offered by Satan'—have you ever seen it? And there's another, 'The Morning Stars Singing Together.' In both there are figures in the sky who have the same reality about them as the people on the ground, and whenever I look at them I'm sure Blake was hinting at an aspect of this other world. I once saw a Dali painting that was close, too, full of opaque beings floating in the sky about a hundred yards above the ground and glowing with an ivory-white light. Now that's exactly the world I see. And you know what those glowing things are that fill the sky? Beings we've lost from our lives down here on earth, and now they float up there in the sky about a hundred yards above the ground, quietly glowing like amoebas under a microscope. And sometimes they descend the way our Aghwee does." (My employer said it and I didn't protest, which doesn't mean I acquiesced.) "But it takes a sacrifice worthy of them to acquire the eyes to see them floating there and the ears to detect them when they descend to earth, and yet there are moments when suddenly we're endowed with that ability without any sacrifice or even effort on our part. I think that's what happened to you a few minutes ago."

Without any sacrifice or even effort on my part, just a few tears of expiation, my employer seemed to have wanted to say. The truth was I had shed tears out of fear and helplessness and a kind of vague terror about my future (my first job, an experiment in a kind of microcosm of life, was guarding this mad composer, and since I had failed to do that adequately, it was predictable that situations which left me stupefied because I couldn't cope with them would recur as one of the patterns of my life), but instead of interrupting with a protest, I continued to listen docilely.

"You're still young; probably you haven't lost anything in this world that you can never forget, that's so dear to you that you're aware of its absence all the time. Probably the sky a hundred yards or so above your head is still nothing more than sky to you. But all that means is that the storehouse happens to be empty at the moment. Or have you lost something that was really important to you?"

The composer paused for my answer, and I found myself remembering his former mistress, that movie actress with a dent in her forehead as big as an adult thumb. Naturally, no crucial loss of mine could have had anything to do with her; all that crying had eroded my head and a sentimental honey was seeping into the crevices.

"Well, have you?" For the first time since we had met, my employer was insistent. "Have you lost anything that was important to you?"

Suddenly I had to say something silly to cover my embarrassment.

"I lost a cat," I tried.

"A Siamese or what?"

"Just an ordinary cat with orange stripes; he disappeared about a week ago."

"If it's only been a week he might come back. Isn't it the season for them to wander?"

"That's what I thought, too, but now I know he won't be back."

"Why?"

"He was a tough tom with his own territory staked out. This morning I saw a weak-looking cat walking up and down his block and it wasn't even on its guard—my cat won't be coming back." When I'd stopped talking I realized I'd told a story intended for laughs in a voice that was hoarse with sadness.

"Then there's a cat floating in your sky," my employer said solemnly.

Through closed eyes I pictured an opaque cat as large as an ad balloon, glowing with an ivory-white light as it floated through the sky. It was a comical flight all right, but it also made me wistful.

"The figures floating in your sky begin to increase at an accelerating rate. That's why I haven't been living in present time ever since that incident with the baby, so I could stop that spreading. Since I'm not living in our time, I can't discover anything new, but I don't lose anything, either — the state of my sky never changes." There was profound relief in the composer's voice.

But was my own sky really empty except for one bloated cat with orange stripes? I opened my eyes and started to look up at the clear, now almost evening sky, when dread made me close my eyes again. Dread of myself, for what if I had seen a glowing herd of numberless beings we had lost from time down here on earth?

We lay on the grass in that meadow for quite a while, ringed by the passive affinity two people have for one another when the same gloom is gripping them. And gradually I began to get my perspective back. I reproached myself: how unlike the eighteen-year-old pragmatist I really was to have let myself be influenced by a mad composer! I'm not suggesting my equilibrium was perfectly restored. The day I succumbed to that strange panic, I drew closer than ever to the sentiments of my employer and to that glowing herd in the sky one hundred yards above the ground. To an extent, what you might call the aftereffects remained with me.

And then the final day came. It was Christmas Eve. I'm certain about the date because D gave me a wristwatch with a little apology about being a day early. And I remember that a powdery snow fell for about an hour just after lunch. We went down to the Ginza together but it was already getting crowded, so we decided to walk out to Tokyo harbor. D wanted to see a Chilean freighter that was supposed to have docked that day. I was eager to go, too; I pictured a ship with snow blanketing her decks. We had left the Ginza crowds and were just passing the Kabuki Theater when D looked up at the dark and still snowy sky. Then Aghwee descended to his side. As usual, I walked a few steps behind the composer and his phantom. We came to a wide intersection. D and the baby had just stepped off the curb when the light changed. D stopped, and a fleet of trucks as bulky as elephants heaved into motion with their Christmas freight. That was when it happened. Suddenly D cried out and thrust both arms in front of him as if he were trying to rescue something; then he leaped in among those trucks and was struck to the ground. I watched stupidly from the curb.

"That was suicide; he just killed himself!" said a shaky voice at my side.

But I had no time to wonder whether it might have been suicide. In a minute that intersection had become backstage at a circus, jammed with milling trucks like elephants, and I was kneeling at D's side, holding his bloody body in my arms and trembling like a dog. I didn't know what to do; a policeman had dashed up and then disappeared on the run again.

D wasn't dead, it was more awful than that. He was dying, lying there in the filthy wet that had been a light snow, oozing blood and something like tree sap. The dark and snowy pattern of the sky ripped open and the stately light of a Spanish pietà made my employer's blood glisten like stupid grease. By that time a crowd had gathered, snatches of "Jingle Bells" wheeled above our heads like panic-stricken pigeons, and I knelt at D's side listening hard for nothing in particular and hearing screaming in the distance. But the crowd just stood there silently in the cold, as if indifferent to the screams. I have never listened so hard on a street corner again, nor again heard screams like that.

An ambulance finally arrived and my employer was lifted inside unconscious. He was caked with blood and mud, and shock seemed to have withered his body. In his white tennis shoes, he looked like an injured blind man. I climbed into the ambulance with a doctor and an orderly and a young man about my age who seemed haughty and aloof. He turned out to be the driver of the long-distance truck that had hit D. The congestion was getting worse all the time as the ambulance cut across the Ginza (according to some statistics I saw recently, there were record crowds that Christmas Eve). Those who heard the siren and stopped to watch us pass, nearly all of them, shared a look of circumspectly solemn concern. In one corner of my dazed head I reflected that the so-called inscrutable Japanese smile, while it seemed likely to exist, did not. Meanwhile D lay unconscious on that wobbly stretcher, bleeding his life away.

When we arrived at the hospital, orderlies rushed D away to some recess of the building. The same policeman as before appeared again out of nowhere and calmly asked me a lot of questions. Then I was permitted to go to D. The young truckdriver had already found the room and was sitting on a bench in the corridor next to the door. I sat down beside him and we waited for a long time. At first he only muttered about all the deliveries he still had to make, but after two hours or so he began to complain of being hungry in a surprisingly childish voice, and my hostility toward him dwindled. We waited some more, then the banker arrived with his wife and three daughters, who were all dressed up to go to a party. Ignoring us, they went inside. All four of the women had fat, squat bodies and red faces; they reminded me of D's former wife. I continued to wait. It had been hours by then, and the whole time I had been tormented by suspicion: hadn't my employer intended to kill himself from the beginning? Before taking his life he had settled things with his ex-wife and former mistress, burned his manuscripts, toured the city saying good-by to places he would miss—hadn't he hired me because he needed some good-natured help with those chores? Kept me from seeing through his plan by inventing a monster baby floating in the sky? In other words, wasn't it the case that my only real function had been to help D commit suicide? The young truckdriver had fallen asleep with his head on my shoulder and every minute or two he would be convulsed as though in pain. He must have been having a nightmare about running over a man with his truck.

It was pitch black outside when the banker appeared in the door and called me. I eased my shoulder from under the driver's head and stood up. The banker paid me my salary for the day and then let me into the room. D lay on his back with rubber tubes in his nostrils, as if for a joke. His face gave me pause; it was black as smoked meat. But I couldn't help voicing the doubt that had me so afraid. I called out to my dying employer: "Did you hire me just so you could commit suicide? Was all that about Aghwee just a cover-up?" Then my throat was clogged with tears and I was surprised to hear myself shouting: "I was about to believe in Aghwee!"

At that moment, as my tear-filled eyes began to dim, I saw a smile appear on D's darkened, shriveled face. It might have been a mocking smile or it might have been a smile of friendly mischief. The banker led me out of the room. The young man from the truck was stretched out on the bench asleep. On my way out, I slipped the thousand yen I had earned into his jacket pocket. I read in the evening paper the next day that the composer was dead.

And then it was this spring and I was walking down the street when a group of frightened children suddenly started throwing stones. It was so sudden and unprovoked, I don't know what I had done to threaten them. Whatever it was, fear had turned those children into killers, and one of them hit me in the right eye with a rock as big as a fist. I went down on one knee, pressed my hand to my eye and felt a lump of broken flesh. With my good eye I watched my dripping blood suck in the dirt in the street as though magnetically. It was then that I sensed a being I knew and missed leave the ground behind me—a being the size of a kangaroo—and soar into the teary blue of a sky that retained its winter brittleness. Good-by, Aghwee, I heard myself whispering in my heart. And then I knew that my hatred of those frightened children had melted away and that time had filled my sky during those ten years with figures that glowed with an ivory-white light, I suppose not all of them purely innocent. When I was wounded by those children and sacrificed my sight in one eye, so clearly a gratuitous sacrifice, I had been endowed, if for only an instant, with the power to perceive a creature that had descended from the heights of my sky.

■ Murakami Haruki (1949–) (novel)

TRANSLATED BY ALFRED BIRNBAUM

Murakami Haruki was born in Kyoto in 1949 and grew up in Kobe. He studied classical Greek drama at Waseda University and from 1974 to 1981 managed a Tokyo jazz bar and published his first three novels. He lives now in Cambridge, Massachusetts, and is well known in the West as Haruki Murakami, the English name order that his books in translation carry, in contrast to normal Japanese name order (family name first, personal name last). For his third novel, *A Wild Sheep Chase* (1982; English translation, 1989), he won the Noma Literary Award for New Writers; he was also awarded the prestigious Tanizaki Prize for his fourth novel, *Hard-Boiled Wonderland and the End of the World* (1985; English translation, 1991). His next novel, *Norwegian Wood* (1987), sold more than four million copies, making him Japan's highest-selling novelist. His recent work includes *Dance, Dance, Dance*, which is a sequel to *A Wild Sheep Chase*, and *The Elephant Vanishes* (English translation, 1993), a book of short stories. Murakami is also the prolific translator of such authors as F. Scott Fitzgerald, Paul Theroux, Raymond Carver, John Irving, and Truman Capote, among others.

Like Abe Kobo, Murakami is a wildly innovative author, wacky, surreal, postmodern, and experimental. He has a hip and warped style and a talent for the strangely apt comparison ("Atop the telephone poles, crows gave a flap or two of their wings, their beaks shiny as credit cards"). "Elevator, Silence, Overweight" is the opening chapter of *Hard-Boiled Wonderland and the End of the World*, a novel that, like its split-brained protagonist, carries on a dual storyline in alternating chapters. In Murakami's world, the resolutely strange is perfectly normal, and the pleasure of reading him lies in witnessing his attitude, verbal ingenuity, and each bizarre tangent opening like an unexpected room off the strange corridor of his narration.

FURTHER READING: Murakami, Haruki. *A Wild Sheep Chase*, 1989; *Hard-Boiled Wonderland and the End of the World*, 1991; *Norwegian Wood* (in Japanese), 1987; *Dance, Dance, Dance; The Elephant Vanishes*, 1993.

from *Hard-Boiled Wonderland and the End of the World*

Elevator, Silence, Overweight

The elevator continued its impossibly slow ascent. Or at least I imagined it was ascent. There was no telling for sure: it was so slow that all sense of direction simply vanished. It could have been going down for all I knew, or maybe it wasn't moving at all. But let's just assume it was going up. Merely a guess. Maybe I'd gone up twelve stories, then down three. Maybe I'd circled the globe. How would I know?

Every last thing about this elevator was worlds apart from the cheap die-cut job in my apartment building, scarcely one notch up the evolutionary scale from a well bucket. You'd never believe the two pieces of machinery had the same name and the same purpose. The two were pushing the outer limits conceivable as elevators.

First of all, consider the space. This elevator was so spacious it could have served as an office. Put in a desk, add a cabinet and a locker, throw in a kitchenette, and you'd still have room to spare. You might even squeeze in three camels and a mid-range palm tree while you were at it. Second, there was the cleanliness. Antiseptic as a brand-new coffin. The walls and ceiling were absolutely spotless polished stainless steel, the floor immaculately carpeted in a handsome moss-green. Third, it was dead silent. There wasn't a sound—literally not one sound—from the moment I stepped inside and the doors slid shut. Deep rivers run quiet.

Another thing, most of the gadgets an elevator is supposed to have were missing. Where, for example, was the panel with all the buttons and switches? No floor numbers to press, no DOOR OPEN and DOOR CLOSE, no EMERGENCY STOP. Nothing whatsoever. All of which made me feel utterly defenseless. And it wasn't just no buttons; it was no indication of advancing floor, no posted capacity or warning, not even a manufacturer's nameplate. Forget about trying to locate an emergency exit. Here I was, sealed in. No way this elevator could have gotten fire department approval. There are norms for elevators after all.

Staring at these four blank stainless-steel walls, I recalled one of Houdini's great escapes I'd seen in a movie. He's tied up in how many ropes and chains, stuffed into a big trunk, which is wound fast with another thick chain and sent hurtling, the whole lot, over Niagara Falls. Or maybe it was an icy dip in the Arctic Ocean. Given that I wasn't all tied up, I was doing okay; insofar as I wasn't clued in on the trick, Houdini was one up on me.

Talk about not clued in, I didn't even know if I was moving or standing still.

I ventured a cough, but it didn't echo anything like a cough. It seemed flat, like clay thrown against a slick concrete wall. I could hardly believe that dull thud issued from my own body. I tried coughing one more time. The result was the same. So much for coughing.

I stood in that hermetically sealed vault for what seemed an eternity. The doors showed no sign of ever opening. Stationary in unending silence, a still life: *Man in Elevator*.

I started to get nervous. What if the machinery had malfunctioned? Or suppose the elevator operator—assuming there was one in the building—forgot I was here in this box? People have lost track of me before.

I strained to hear something, anything, but no sound reached my ears. I pressed my ear against the stainless-steel wall. Sure enough, not a sound. All I managed was to leave an outline of my ear on the cold metal. The elevator was made, apparently, of a miracle alloy that absorbed all noise. I tried whistling *Danny Boy*, but it came out like a dog wheezing with asthma.

There was little left to do but lean up against a wall and count the change in my pockets. For someone in my profession, knowing how to kill time is as important a method of training as gripping rubber balls is for a boxer. Although, in any strict sense, it's not killing time at all. For only through assiduous repetition is it possible to redistribute skewed tendencies.

I always come prepared with pockets full of loose change. In my right pocket I keep one-hundred- and five-hundred-yen coins, in my left fifties and tens. One-yen and five-yen coins I carry in a back pocket, but as a rule these don't enter into the count. What I do is thrust my hands simultaneously into both pockets, the right hand tallying the hundreds and five-hundreds in tandem with the left hand adding up the fifties and tens.

It's hard for those who've never attempted the procedure to grasp what it is to calculate this way, and admittedly it is tricky at first. The right brain and the left brain each keep separate tabs, which are then brought together like two halves of a split watermelon. No easy task until you get the hang of it.

Whether or not I really do put the right and left sides of my brain to separate accounts, I honestly can't say. A specialist in neurophysiology might have insights to offer on the matter. I'm no neurophysiologist, however. All I know is that when I'm actually in the midst of counting, I feel like I'm using the right side and left side of my brain differently. And when I'm through counting, it seems the fatigue that sets in is qualitatively quite distinct from what comes with normal counting. For convenience sake, I think of it as right-brain-totals-right-pocket, left-brain-totals-left-pocket.

On the whole, I think of myself as one of those people who take a convenience-sake view of prevailing world conditions, events, existence in general. Not that I'm such a blasé, convenience-sake sort of guy—although I do have tendencies in that direction—but because more often than not I've observed that convenient approximations bring you closest to comprehending the true nature of things.

For instance, supposing that the planet earth were not a sphere but a gigantic coffee table, how much difference in everyday life would that make? Granted, this is a pretty far-fetched example; you can't rearrange facts of life so freely. Still, picturing the planet earth, for convenience sake, as a gigantic coffee table does in fact help clear away the clutter—those practically pointless contingencies such as gravity and the international dateline and the equator, those nagging details that arise from the spherical view. I mean, for a guy leading a perfectly ordinary existence, how many times in the course of a lifetime would the equator be a significant factor?

But to return to the matter at hand—or rather, hands, the right and the left each going about its own separate business—it is by no means easy to keep running parallel counts. Even for me, to get it down took the longest time. But once you do, once you've gotten the knack, it's not something you lose. Like riding a bike or swimming. Which isn't to say you can't always use a little more practice. Repetition can improve your technique and refine your style. If for no other reason than this, I always keep my hands busy.

This time I had three five-hundred-yen coins and eighteen hundreds in the one pocket, and seven fifties and sixteen tens in the other. Making a grand total of three-thousand eight-hundred-ten yen. Calculations like this are no trouble at all. Simpler than counting the fingers on my hands. Satisfied, I leaned back against the stainless-steel wall and looked straight ahead at the doors. Which were still not opening.

What could be taking so long? I tentatively wrote off both the equipment-malfunction theory and the forgotten-by-operator theory. Neither very realistic. This was not to say that equipment malfunction or operator negligence couldn't realistically occur. On the contrary, I know for a fact that such accidents are all too common in the real world. What I mean to say is that in a highly exceptional reality—this ridiculously slick elevator a case in point—the non-exceptional can, for convenience sake, be written off as paradoxically exceptional. Could any human being capable of designing this Tom Swift elevator fail to keep the machinery in working order or forget the proper procedures once a visitor stepped inside?

The answer was obvious. No.

Never happen.

Not after *they* had been so meticulous up to that point. They'd seen to minute details, measuring each step I'd taken virtually to the millimeter. I'd been stopped by two guards at the entrance to the building, asked whom I was there to see, matched against a visitors' list, made to produce my driver's license, logged into a central computer for verification, after which I was summarily pushed into this elevator. You don't get this much going over when you visit the Bank of Japan. It was unthinkable that they, having done all that, should slip up now.

The only possibility was that they had intentionally placed me in this particular situation. They *wanted* the elevator's motions to be opaque to me. They *wanted* the elevator to move so slowly I wouldn't be able to tell if it were going up or down. They were probably watching me with a hidden TV camera now.

To ward off the boredom, I thought about searching for the camera lens. But on second thought, what would I have to gain if I found it? That would alert them, they'd halt the elevator, and I'd be even later for my appointed hour.

So I decided to do nothing. I was here in proper accordance with my duties. No need to worry, no cause for alarm.

I leaned against the elevator wall, thrust my hands in my pockets, and once more counted my change. Three-thousand seven-hundred-fifty yen. Nothing to it. Done in a flash.

Three-thousand seven-hundred-fifty yen?

Something was wrong.

I'd made a mistake somewhere.

My palms began to sweat. In three years of counting, never once had I screwed up. This was a bad sign.

I shut my eyes and made my right brain and left brain a blank, in a way you might clean your glasses. Then withdrawing both hands from my pockets, I spread my fingers to dry the sweat. Like Henry Fonda in *Warlock,* where he steels himself before a gunfight.

With palms and fingers completely dry, both hands dived into my pockets to do a third count. If the third sum corresponded to either of the other sums I'd feel better. Everybody makes mistakes. Under the peculiar conditions I found myself, I may have been anxious, not to mention a little overconfident. That was my first mistake. Anyway, an accurate recount was all I needed to remedy the situation, to put things right.

But before I could take the matter in hand, the elevator doors opened. No warning, no sound, they just slid open to either side. I was concentrating so hard on the critical recount that I didn't even notice. Or more precisely, my eyes had seen the opening doors, but I didn't fully grasp the significance of the event. Of course, the doors' opening meant the linking of two spaces previously denied accessible continuity by means of those very doors. And at the same time, it meant the elevator had reached its destination.

I turned my attention to what lay beyond the doors. There was a corridor and in the corridor stood a woman. A young woman, turned out in a pink suit, wearing pink high heels. The suit was coutured of a polished material, her face equally polished. The woman considered my presence, then nodded succinctly. "Come this way," she seemed to indicate. I gave up all hope of that recount, and removing my hands from my pockets, I exited the elevator. Whereupon the elevator doors closed behind me as if they'd been waiting for me to leave.

Standing there in the corridor, I took a good look around, but I encountered no hint of the nature of my current circumstances. I did seem to be in an interior passage of a building, but any school kid could have told you as much.

The interior was gloomy, featureless. Like the elevator. Quality materials throughout; no sign of wear. Marble floors buffed to a high luster; the walls a toasted off-white, like the muffins I eat for breakfast. Along either side of the corridor were tall wooden doors, each affixed with metal room numbers, but out of order. 936 was next to 213 next to 26. Something was screwy. Nobody numbers rooms like that.

The young woman hardly spoke. "This way, please," was all she told me, but it was more her lips forming the words than speaking, because no sound came out. Having taken two months of lipreading since starting this line of work, I had no problem understanding what she said. Still, I thought there was something wrong with my ears. After the dead silence of the elevator, the flattened coughs and dessicated whistling, I had to be losing my hearing.

So I coughed. It sounded normal. I regained some confidence in my hearing. Nothing's happened to my ears. The problem must be with the woman's mouth.

I walked behind her. The clicks of her pointy high heels echoed down the empty corridor like an afternoon at the quarry. Her full, stockinged legs reflected clearly in the marble.

The woman was on the chubby side. Young and beautiful and all that went with it, but chubby. Now a young, beautiful woman who is, shall we say, plump, seems a bit off. Walking behind her, I fixated on her body.

Around young, beautiful, fat women, I am generally thrown into confusion. I don't know why. Maybe it's because an image of their dietary habits naturally congeals in my mind. When I see a goodly sized woman, I have visions of her mopping up that last drop of cream sauce with bread, wolfing down that final sprig of watercress garnish from her plate. And once that happens, it's like acid corroding metal: scenes of her eating spread through my head and I lose control.

Your plain fat woman is fine. Fat women are like clouds in the sky. They're just floating there, nothing to do with me. But your young, beautiful, fat woman is another story. I am demanded to assume a posture toward her. I could end up sleeping with her. That is probably where all the confusion comes in.

Which is not to say that I have anything against fat women. Confusion and repulsion are two different things. I've slept with fat women before and on the whole the experience wasn't bad. If your confusion leads you in the right direction, the results can be uncommonly rewarding. But of course, things don't always take the right course. Sex is an extremely subtle undertaking, unlike going to the department store on Sunday to buy a thermos. Even among young, beautiful, fat women, there are distinctions to be made. Fleshed out one way, they'll lead you in the right direction; fleshed out another way, they'll leave you lost, trivial, confused.

In this sense, sleeping with fat women can be a challenge. There must be as many paths of human fat as there are ways of human death.

This was pretty much what I was thinking as I walked down the corridor behind this young, beautiful, fat woman.

A white scarf swirled around the collar of her chic pink suit. From the fullness of her earlobes dangled square gold earrings, glinting with every step she took. Actually, she moved quite lightly for her weight. She may have strapped herself into a girdle or other paraphernalia for maximum visual effect, but that didn't alter the fact that her wiggle was tight and cute. In fact, it turned me on. She was my kind of chubby.

Now I'm not trying to make excuses, but I don't get turned on by that many women. If anything, I think of myself as more the non-turn-on type. So when I do get turned on, I don't trust it; I have to investigate the source.

I scooted up next to her and apologized for being eight or nine minutes late for the appointment. "I had no idea the entrance procedures would take so long," I said. "And then the elevator was so slow. I was ten minutes early when I got to the building."

She gave me a brisk I-know sort of nod. A hint of *eau de cologne* drifted from her neckline. A scent reminiscent of standing in a melon patch on a summer's morn. It put me in a funny frame of mind. A nostalgic yet impossible pastiche of sentiments, as if two wholly unrelated memories had threaded together in an unknown recess. Feelings like this sometimes come over me. And most often due to specific scents.

"Long corridor, eh?" I tried to break the ice. She glanced at me, but kept walking. I guessed she was twenty or twenty-one. Well-defined features, broad forehead, clear complexion.

It was then that she said, "Proust."

Or more precisely, she didn't pronounce the word "Proust," but simply moved her lips to form what ought to have been "Proust." I had yet to hear a genuine peep out of her. It was as if she were talking to me from the far side of a thick sheet of glass.

Proust?

"*Marcel* Proust?" I asked her.

She gave a look. Then she repeated, "Proust." I gave up on the effort and fell back in line behind her, trying for the life of me to come up with other lip movements that corresponded to "Proust." *Truest? . . . Brew whist? . . . Blue is it? . . .* One after the other, quietly to myself, I pronounced strings of meaningless syllables, but none seemed to match. I could only conclude that she had indeed said, "Proust." But what I couldn't figure was, what was the connection between this long corridor and Marcel Proust?

Perhaps she'd cited Marcel Proust as a metaphor for the length of the corridor. Yet, supposing that were the case, wasn't it a trifle flighty—not to say inconsiderate—as a choice of expression? Now if she'd cited this long corridor as a metaphor for the works of Marcel Proust, that much I could accept. But the reverse was bizarre.

A corridor as long as Marcel Proust?

Whatever, I kept following her down that long corridor. Truly, a long corridor. Turning corners, going up and down short flights of stairs, we must have walked five or six ordinary buildings' worth. We were walking around and around, like in an Escher print. But walk as we might, the surroundings never seemed to change. Marble floors, muffin-white walls, wooden doors with random room numbers. Stainless-steel door knobs. Not a window in sight. And through it all, the same staccato rhythm of her heels, followed by the melted rubber gumminess of my jogging shoes.

Suddenly she pulled to a halt. I was now so tuned in to the sound of my jogging shoes that I walked right into her backside. It was wonderfully cushioning, like a firm rain cloud. Her neck effused that melon *eau de cologne.* She was tipping forward from the force of my impact, so I grabbed her shoulders to pull her back upright.

"Excuse me," I said. "I was somewhere else in my thoughts."

The chubby young woman blushed. I couldn't say for sure, but she didn't seem at all bothered. "*Tozum'sta,*" she said with a trace of a smile. Then she shrugged her shoulders and added, "*Sela.*" She didn't actually say that, but need I repeat, her lips formed the words.

"*Tozum'sta?*" I pronounced to myself. "*Sela?*"

"*Sela,*" she said with conviction.

Turkish perhaps? Problem was, I'd never heard a word of Turkish. I was so flustered, I decided to forget about holding a conversation with her. Lip reading is very delicate business and not something you can hope to master in two months of adult education classes.

She produced a lozenge-shaped electronic key from her suit pocket and inserted it horizontally, just so, into the slot of the door bearing the number 728. It unlocked with a click. Smooth.

She opened the door, then turned and bid me, "*Saum'te, sela.*"

Which, of course, is exactly what I did.

Acknowledgments

■

Section 1: India, Pakistan, and Bangladesh

Excerpts from *The Upanishads*, tr. Juan Mascaró (Penguin Classics, 1965). Copyright © Juan Mascaró, 1965. Reproduced by permission of Penguin Books Ltd.

Excerpts from Theravada Buddhist Texts: *Visuddhi-Magga, Sainyutta-Nikaya, Milindapañha,* and *Maha-Vagga*, tr. Henry Clarke Warren from *Buddhism in Translation.* Copyright © 1896 by Harvard University. Reprinted by permission of Harvard University Press.

From *The Dhammapada: The Path of Perfection*, tr. Juan Mascaró (Penguin Classics, 1973). Copyright © Juan Mascaró, 1973. Reproduced by permission of Penguin Books Ltd.

"The Parable of the Burning House," tr. Burton Watson from *The Lotus Sutra*, edited by Burton Watson. Copyright © 1993. Reprinted by permission of Columbia University Press.

Excerpts from Volume II, Aranya Kanda, Chapters 17–18, 32–35, 46–48; and Volume III, Yuddha Kanda, Chapters 100–102, 110. Translated by Hari Prasad Shastri, 1957, from *The Ramayana of Valmiki*, in three volumes. Available from the publishers, Shanti Sadan, 29 Chepstow Villas, London W11 3DR, U.K.

Poems of Love and War, *Akam Poems*, "What She Said," by Kaccipettu Nannakaiyer, "What Her Friend Said to Him," by Kannan, "What She Said" by Kalporu Cirunuraiyar, tr. A.K. Ramanujan; *Puram Poems*, "Harvest of War," by Kappiyarrukkappiyanar; "A King's Last Words, in Jail, before He Takes His Life," by Ceraman Kanaikkal Irumporai; "A Woman and Her Dying Warrior," by Vanparanar, tr. A.K. Ramanujan, from *Poems of Love and War*, edited by A.K. Ramanujan. Copyright © 1985. Reprinted by permission of Columbia University Press.

The Gatha Saptashati, "Nineteen quatrains," tr. David Ray from *Not Far from the River: Poems from the Gatha-Saptasati*. Translation copyright © 1993 by David Ray. Reprinted by permission of Copper Canyon Press, P.O. Box 271, Port Townsend, WA 98368.

Vijjika, "Friends," tr. Willis Barnstone from *A Book of Women Poets from Antiquity to Now*, edited by Willis and Aliki Barnstone. Copyright © 1980 by Schocken Books Inc. Reprinted by permission of Schocken Books, published by Pantheon Books, a division of Random House, Inc.

Vijjika, "Ominous Clouds" and "To Her Daughter," tr. Andrew Schelling. Reprinted by permission of the translator.

Amaru, "Ingenue" and "Finesse," tr. V.N. Misra, L. Nathan, and S.H. Vatsyayan from *The Indian Poetic Tradition: An Anthology of Poetry from the Vedic Period to the Seventeenth Century*, edited by S.H. Vatsyayan, V.N. Misra, and L. Nathan. Reprinted by permission of Y.K. Publishers, Agra, India.

Amaru, "Somehow She Got," tr. Andrew Schelling. Reprinted by permission of the translator.

Basavanna, "The Pot is a God," tr. A.K. Ramanujan from *Speaking of Siva* (Penguin Classics, 1973). Copyright © A.K. Ramanujam, 1973. Reproduced by permission of Penguin Books Ltd.

Excerpts from *Speaking of Siva*, tr. A.K. Ramanujan (Penguin Classics, 1973). Copyright © A.K. Ramanujan, 1973. Reproduced by permission of Penguin Books Ltd.

Jayadeva, excerpts from *The Gitagovinda*, tr. Barbara Stoler Miller from *Love Song of the Dark Lord*, edited by Barbara Stoller Miller. Copyright © 1977. Reprinted by permission of Columbia University Press.

Lalla, "Dance, Lalla, with Nothing On," "Whatever Your Name, Shiva, Vishnu," and "The Soul, Like the Moon," tr. Coleman Barks. Reprinted by permission of the translator.

Kabir, "Between the Conscious and the Unconscious," "I Have Been Thinking of the Difference," and "Are You Looking for Me?" tr. Robert Bly from *The Kabir Book* by Robert Bly. Copyright © 1971, 1977 by Robert Bly. Reprinted by permission of Beacon Press and Robert Bly.

Excerpts from Mirabai, tr. Willis Barnstone and Usha Nilsson from *A Book of Women Poets from Antiquity to Now*, edited by Willis and Aliki Barnstone. Copyright © 1980 by Schocken Books Inc. Reprinted by permission of Schocken Books, published by Pantheon Books, a division of Random House, Inc.

Rabindranath Tagore, "The Sick-Bed," "Recovery," and "On My Birthday," tr. William Radice from *Selected Poems* by Rabindranath Tagore (Penguin Books, 1985). Copyright © William Radice, 1985. Reproduced by permission of Penguin Books Ltd.

Mahatma Gandhi, "Passive Resistance" (*Indian Home Rule*) from *The Gandhi Reader: A Sourcebook of His Life and Writings*, edited by Homer Jack. Reprinted courtesy of Alex Jack.

Sarat Chandra Chatterjee, "Drought," tr. S. Sinha from *Profiles in Faith* (Indus/HarperCollins India, 1997). Reprinted by permission of the publisher.

Premchand, "The Shroud," from *Deliverance and Other Stories*, translated from the Hindi by David Rubin. Reprinted by permission of Penguin Books India Pvt. Ltd. and the translator.

Jibanananda Das, "Grass," tr. Chidananda Das Gupta. Reprinted by permission of Donald Junkins.

R.K. Narayan, "Forty-five a Month," from *Malgudi Days*. Copyright © 1972, 1975, 1978, 1980, 1981, 1982 by R.K. Narayan. Used by permission of Viking Penguin, a division of Penguin Books USA Inc.

Faiz Ahmed Faiz, "Before You Came" and "Prison Meeting," tr. Naomi Lazard from *The True Subject: Selected Poems of Faiz Ahmed Faiz*. Copyright © 1988 by Princeton University Press. Reprinted by permission of Princeton University Press.

Ruth Prawer Jhabvala, "Picnic with Moonlight and Mangoes" from *How I Became a Holy Mother and Other Stories*. © Ruth Prawer Jhabvala 1976, 1984. Used by permission of Harriet Wasserman Literary Agency, Inc., as agent for author.

Bharati Mukherjee, "Buried Lives" from *The Middleman and Other Stories*. Copyright © 1988 by Bharati Mukherjee. Reprinted by permission of Grove/Atlantic, Inc. and the author.

Salman Rushdie, "The Perforated Sheet" from *Midnight's Children* by Salman Rushdie. Copyright © 1981 by Salman Rushdie. Reprinted by permission of Alfred A. Knopf, Inc. and The Wylie Agency, Inc.

Section 2: China

Excerpts from *The Book of Songs*, tr. Tony Barnstone and Chou Ping. Reprinted by permission of the translators.

Confucius, "The Analects," tr. Raymond Dawson from *Confucius: The Analects* (World's Classic, 1993). © Raymond Dawson 1993. Reprinted by permission of Oxford University Press.

Laozi, "The Dao De Jing," tr. Gia-fu Feng and Jane English from *Tao Te Ching: A New Translation* by Lao Tsu. Copyright © 1972 by Gia-fu Feng and Jane English. Reprinted by permission of Alfred A. Knopf, Inc.

Zhuangzi, "The Zhuangzi," tr. Burton Watson from *Chuang Tzu*. Copyright © 1964. Reprinted by permission of Columbia University Press.

Qu Yuan, "The Fisherman," tr. David Hawkes from *The Songs of the South: An Anthology of Ancient Chinese Poems by Qu Yuan and Other Poets* (Penguin Classics, 1985). Copyright © David Hawkes, 1985. Reproduced by permission of Penguin Books Ltd.

Liu Xijun, "Lament," tr. Tony Barnstone and Chou Ping. Reprinted by permission of the translators.

Anonymous Folk Songs from the Music Bureau, "The East Gate" and "A Sad Tune," tr. Tony Barnstone and Chou Ping. Reprinted by permission of the translators.

Lu Ji, "The Art of Writing," tr. Tony Barnstone and Chou Ping. Reprinted by permission of the translators.

Tao Qian, "Return to My Country Home" and poem from the Series "Drinking Wine," tr. Tony Barnstone and Chou Ping. Reprinted by permission of the translators.

Tao Qian, "Preface to the Poem on the Peach Blossom Spring," tr. Burton Watson from *The Columbia Book of Chinese Poetry*. Copyright © 1984. Reprinted by permission of Columbia University Press.

Excerpts from Wang Wei, tr. Tony Barnstone, Willis Barnstone, and Xu Haixin from *Laughing Lost in the Mountains: Poems of Wang Wei.* © 1992 University Press of New England. Reprinted by permission of the publisher.

Excerpts from Li Bai, tr. Willis Barnstone, Tony Barnstone, and Chou Ping. Reprinted by permission of the translators.

Excerpts from Du Fu, tr. Tony Barnstone and Chou Ping. Reprinted by permission of the translators.

Du Fu, "P'eng-ya Road," tr. Sam Hamill from *Facing the Snow: Visions of Tu Fu* (White Pine Press, 1988). Reprinted by permission of Sam Hamill.

Du Fu, "Broken Boat," tr. Stephen Owen from *Traditional Chinese Poetry and Poetics: Omen of the World.* © 1985. Reprinted by permission of The University of Wisconsin Press.

Meng Jiao, "Autumn Meditations," tr. James A. Wilson. Cf. *Shanti: Chinese and Chinese-American Poetry*, Vol. 10, No. 1 (Winter-Spring 1995), edited by Tony Barnstone and Ayame Fukuda. Reprinted by permission of James A. Wilson.

Han Yu, "Mountain Rocks," tr. Tony Barnstone and Chou Ping. Reprinted by permission of the translators.

Xue Tao, "Spring-Gazing Song," tr. Carolyn Kizer from *A Book of Women Poets from Antiquity to Now,* edited by Willis and Aliki Barnstone. Copyright © 1980 by Schocken Books Inc. Reprinted by permission of Schocken Books, published by Pantheon Books, a division of Random House, Inc.

Xue Tao, "Seeing a Friend Off," tr. Tony Barnstone and Chou Ping. Reprinted by permission of the translators.

Li Gongzuo, "The Governor of Southern-Bough," tr. Chou Ping. Reprinted by permission of the translator.

Excerpts from Bo Juyi, tr. Tony Barnstone and Chou Ping. Reprinted by permission of the translators.

Bo Juyi, "At the End of Spring" and "On His Baldness," tr. Arthur Waley from Po Chu-i, *Translations from the Chinese* (1919, 1941). Copyright secured by Alfred A. Knopf. Reprinted by permission of John Robinson for the Arthur Waley Estate.

Bo Juyi, "Light Furs, Fat Horses," tr. Burton Watson from *The Columbia Book of Chinese Poetry*. Copyright © 1984. Reprinted with permission of Columbia University Press.

Excerpts from Liu Zongyuan, tr. Tony Barnstone and Chou Ping. Reprinted by permission of the translators.

Liu Zongyuan, "The Donkey of Guizhou" and "The Snake-Catcher," tr. Chou Ping. Reprinted by permission of the translator.

Yuan Zhen, "When Told Bai Juyi Was Demoted and Sent to Jiangzhou," tr. Tony Barnstone and Chou Ping. Reprinted by permission of the translators.

Sikong Tu, excerpts from *The Twenty-four Modes of Poetry*, tr. Tony Barnstone and Chou Ping. Reprinted by permission of the translators.

Yu Xuanji, "To Tzu-an" and "Letting My Feelings Out," tr. Geoffrey Waters from *A Book of Women Poets from Antiquity to Now*, edited by Willis and Aliki Barnstone. Copyright © 1980 by Schocken Books Inc. Reprinted by permission of Schocken Books, published by Pantheon Books, a division of Random House, Inc.

Excerpts from Li Yu, tr. Tony Barnstone and Chou Ping. Reprinted by permission of the translators.

Li Yu, "To the Tune of 'Crows Cawing at Night'" and "To the Tune of 'Encountering Joy,'" tr. Brendan Connell and Marty Jiang. Reprinted by permission of the translators.

Mei Yaochen, "Sorrow," tr. Kenneth Rexroth from *One Hundred Poems from the Chinese*. Copyright © 1971 by Kenneth Rexroth. Reprinted by permission of New Directions Publishing Corp.

Ouyang Xiu, "You Cannot Hold It," tr. J.P Seaton from *Love and Time: The Poems of Ou-Yang Hsiu*. Translation © 1989 by J.P. Seaton. Reprinted by permission of Copper Canyon Press, P.O. Box 271, Port Townsend, WA 98368.

Ouyang Xiu, "The Autumn Sound," tr. Ch'u Chai and Winberg Chai from *A Treasury of Chinese Literature: A New Prose Anthology Including Fiction and Drama* (New York: Appleton-Century, 1965). Reprinted by permission of Winberg Chai.

Excerpts from Su Dongpo, tr. Tony Barnstone and Chou Ping. Reprinted by permission of the translators.

Excerpts from Li Qingzhao, tr. Tony Barnstone and Chou Ping. Reprinted by permission of the translators.

Excerpts from *Poets' Jade Dust*, tr. Tony Barnstone and Chou Ping. Reprinted by permission of the translators.

Excerpts from Ma Zhiyuan, tr. Tony Barnstone and Chou Ping. Reprinted by permission of the translators.

Ma Zhiyuan "Autumn Moon on the Tung T'ing Lake," tr. Gary Gachard and C.H. Kwock from *Renditions* Nos. 21 & 22 (Spring & Autumn 1984). Hong Kong: Research Centre for Translation of the Chinese University of Hong Kong, p. 222. Reprinted by permission.

Shi Naian and Luo Guanzhong, excerpt from *Outlaws of the Marsh*, tr. Sidney Shapiro from *Outlaws of the Marsh*. Reprinted by permission of Indiana University Press.

Wu Chengen, excerpt tr. Arthur Waley from *Monkey: A Folk Novel of China* by Wu Ch'eng-en. Copyright © 1943 by John Day Company. Used by permission of Grove/Atlantic, Inc.

Pu Songling, "The Cricket," tr. Yang Xianyi and Gladys Yang from *Selected Tales of Liao Zhai* by Pu Songling. Reprinted by permission of China Books and Periodicals, Inc., 2929 24th Street, San Francisco, CA 94110, Phone: 415/282-2994, Fax: 415/282-0994. Catalog available.

Yuan Mei, Four Zen Poems, tr. J.P. Seaton from *I Don't Bow to Buddhas*, © 1997 by J.P. Seaton, reprinted by permission of Copper Canyon Press, P.O. Box 271, Port Townsend, WA 98368.

Li Ruzhen, excerpt tr. Lin Tai-yi from *Flowers in the Mirror* by Li Ju-chen. Reprinted by permission of Peter Owen Ltd., Publishers.

Cao Xueqin, excerpt from Chapter 82, tr. John Minford from *Dream of the Red Chamber:* Vol. 4: "The Debt of Tears" (Penguin Classics, 1982). Copyright © John Minford, 1982. Reprinted by permission of Penguin Books Ltd.

Excerpts from Mao Zedong, tr. Willis Barnstone and Ko Ching-Po. Copyright Willis Barnstone. Reprinted by permission.

Wen Yiduo, "Miracle," tr. Arthur Sze; first appeared in *Two Ravens* (Tooth of Time Books, 1984). Copyright © Arthur Sze, 1984. Reprinted by permission of the translator.

Lao She, "Filling a Prescription," tr. Don J. Cohn from *Selected Tales of Liao Zhai* by Pu Songling, translated by Yang Xianyi and Gladys Yang. Reprinted by permission of China Books and Periodicals, Inc., 2929 24th Street, San Francisco, CA 94110, Phone: 415/282-2994, Fax: 415/282-0994. Catalog available.

Wang Meng, "Anecdotes of Minister Maimaiti: A Uygur Man's Black Humor," tr. Qinyun Wu from *Return Trip Tango* by Frank MacShane and Lori M. Carlson. Copyright © 1992. Reprinted by permission of Columbia University Press.

Chen Rong, "Regarding the Problem of Newborn Piglets in Winter," tr. Chun-Ye Shih from *The Rose Colored Dinner* (Hong Kong: Joint Publishing [H.K.] Co. Ltd., 1988). Copyright © by the publisher, transferred to Shen Rong. Reprinted by permission of Shen Rong.

Bei Dao, "Sweet Tangerines," tr. James A. Wilson from *August Sleepwalker.* Copyright © 1988 by Bei Dao. Reprinted by permission of New Directions Publishing Corp.

Bei Dao, "Coming Home at Night," tr. Bonnie McDougall and Chen Maiping from *Old Snow.* Copyright © 1991 by Bei Dao. Reprinted by permission of New Directions Publishing Corp.

Bei Dao, "Night: Theme and Variations," tr. Tony Barnstone and Newton Liu from *Old Snow.* Copyright © 1991 by Bei Dao. Reprinted by permission of New Directions Publishing Corp.

Bei Dao, "Beyond," tr. Donald Finkel and Xueliang Chen from *Old Snow.* Copyright © 1991 by Bei Dao. Reprinted by permission of New Directions Publishing Corp.

Shu Ting, "Two or Three Incidents Recollected," tr. Chou Ping from *Out of the Howling Storm: The New Chinese Poetry,* edited by Tony Barnstone. © 1993 by Wesleyan University, used by permission of University Press of New England.

Liang Heng and Judith Shapiro, excerpts from *Son of the Revolution.* Copyright © 1983 by Liang Heng and Judith Shapiro. Reprinted by permission of Alfred A. Knopf, Inc.

Yang Lian, "An Ancient Children's Tale," tr. Tony Barnstone and Newton Liu from *Out of the Howling Storm: The New Chinese Poetry,* edited by Tony Barnstone. © 1993 by Wesleyan University, used by permission of University Press of New England.

Ha Jin, "My Best Soldier," published in *Ocean of Words: Army Stories* by Ha Jin (Zoland Books, 1996). Reprinted by permission of Ha Jin.

Chou Ping, "Ways of Looking at a Poet," from *Out of the Howling Storm: The New Chinese Poetry,* edited by Tony Barnstone. © 1993 by Wesleyan University, used by permission of University Press of New England.

Tang Yaping, excerpt from *Black Desert Suite,* tr. Tony Barnstone and Newton Liu from *Out of the Howling Storm: The New Chinese Poetry,* edited by Tony Barnstone. © 1993 by Wesleyan University, used by permission of University Press of New England.

Section 3: Japan

Empress Iwanohime, excerpts from *Missing Emperor Nintoku,* tr. Ayame Fukuda. Reprinted by permission of the translator.

Empress Jito, "On the Death of the Emperor Temmu," tr. Kenneth Rexroth and Ikuko Atsumi, from *Women Poets of Japan.* Copyright © 1977 by Kenneth Rexroth and Ikuko Atsumi. Reprinted by permission of New Directions Publishing Corp.

Kakinomoto Hitomaro, "Poem by Kakinomoto Hitomaro as He Shed Tears of Blood in His Grief following the Death of His Wife" and "Poem by Kakinomoto Hitomaro at the Time of the Temporary Enshrinement of Prince Takechi at Kinoe," tr. Ian Hideo Levy from *Ten Thousand Leaves.* Copyright © 1981 by Princeton University Press. Reprinted by permission of Princeton University Press.

The Priest Mansei, "What Shall I Compare," tr. Ayame Fukuda. Reprinted by permission of the translator.

Lady Ki, "Poem Sent to a Friend with a Gift" and "Poem Sent by Lady Ki to Otomo Yakamochi in Response to His," tr. Ayame Fukuda. Reprinted by permission of the translator.

Otomo Yakamochi, "In a Dream" and "Wild Geese Cry," tr. Ayame Fukuda. Reprinted by permission of the translator.

Lady Kasa, *Poems Sent to Otomo Yakamochi by Lady Kasa,* "My Keepsake," tr. Burton Watson from *The Country of Eight Islands* by Hiroaki Sato and Burton Watson. Copyright © 1981 by Hiroaki Sato and Burton Watson. Used by permission of Doubleday, a division of Bantam Doubleday Dell Publishing Group, Inc.

Ki no Tsurayuki, from *Preface to the Kokinshu,* "Five Tanka," tr. Burton Watson from *The Country of Eight Islands* by Hiroaki Sato and Burton Watson. Copyright © 1981 by Hiroaki Sato and Burton Watson. Used by permission of Doubleday, a division of Bantam Doubleday Dell Publishing Group, Inc.

Ono no Komachi, "Doesn't He Realize," "I Fell Asleep Thinking of Him," and "He Does Not Come," tr. Kenneth Rexroth and Ikuko Atsumi, from *Women Poets of Japan.* Copyright © 1977 by Kenneth Rexroth and Ikuko Atsumi. Reprinted by permission of New Directions Publishing Corp.

Ono no Komachi, "I Am So Lonely," tr. Ayame Fukuda and Tony Barnstone. Reprinted by permission of the translators.

Ono no Komachi, "The Autumn Night" and "How Invisibly," tr. Jane Hirshfield and Mariko Aratani from *The Ink Dark Moon* by Jane Hirshfield and Mariko Aratani. Copyright © 1990 by Jane Hirshfield and Mariko Aratani. Reprinted by permission of Vintage Books, a division of Random House, Inc.

Lady Ise, "Like a Ravaged Sea," tr. Etsuko Terasaki and Irma Brandies from *A Book of Women Poets from Antiquity to Now,* edited by Willis and Aliki Barnstone. Copyright © 1980 by Schocken Books Inc. Reprinted by permission of Schocken Books, published by Pantheon Books, a division of Random House, Inc.

The Tales of Ise, tr. Helen Craig McCullough from *The Tales of Ise,* translated, with an Introduction and Notes, by Helen Craig McCullough. © 1986 by the Board of Trustees of the Leland Stanford Junior University. Reprinted by permission of Stanford University Press.

Sei Shonagon, excerpts from *The Pillow Book of Sei Shonagon,* tr. Ivan Morris. Copyright © 1991 by Columbia University Press. Reprinted by permission of the publisher.

Izumi Shikibu, "In This World," "I Cannot Say," "This Heart," and "Mourning Naishi," tr. Jane Hirshfield and Mariko Aratani from *The Ink Dark Moon* by Jane Hirshfield and Mariko Aratani. Copyright © 1990 by Jane Hirshfield and Mariko Aratani. Reprinted by permission of Vintage, Books, a division of Random House, Inc.

Izumi Shikibu, "On Nights When Hail," "Since That Night," "You Wear the Face," "When You Broke from Me," "If You Have No Time," "If You Love Me," "On This Winter Night," and "Here in This World," tr. Willis Barnstone from *A Book of Women Poets from Antiquity to Now,* edited by Willis and Aliki Barnstone. Copyright © 1980 by Schocken Books Inc. Reprinted by permission of Schocken Books, published by Pantheon Books, a division of Random House, Inc.

Murasaki Shikibu, "The Broom-Tree" from *The Tale of Genji* by Lady Murasaki, tr. Arthur Waley (Tokyo: Charles C. Tuttle, 1971). Copyright Alison Waley. Reprinted by permission of John Robinson for the Estate of Arthur Waley.

Saigyo, excerpts from *Poems of a Mountain Home* by Saigyo, tr. Burton Watson. Copyright © 1991. Reprinted by permission of Columbia University Press.

The Middle Councilor of the Riverbank, "The Lady Who Admired Vermin" from *The Riverside Counselor's Stories: Vernacular Fiction of Late Heian Japan,* translated, with an Introduction and Notes, by Robert L. Backus. © 1985 by the Board of Trustees of the Leland Stanford Junior University. Reprinted by permission of Stanford University Press.

"How an Invisible Man Regained Corporeal Form through Kannon's Aid," tr. Marian Ury from *Tales of Time Now Past: Sixty-two Stories from a Medieval Japanese Collection* (Berkeley: University of California Press, 1979). Reprinted by permission of Marian Ury.

Excerpts from *The Tale of the Heike,* translated, with an Introduction, by Helen Craig McCullough. © 1988 by the Board of Trustees of the Leland Stanford Junior University. Reprinted by permission of Stanford University Press.

Kamo no Chomei, "An Account of My Hermitage" tr. Helen Craig McCullough from *Classical Japanese Prose: An Anthology,* compiled and edited by Helen Craig McCullough. © 1990 by the Board of Trustees of the Leland Stanford Junior University. Reprinted by permission of Stanford University Press.

Dogen, tr. Brian Unger and Kazuaki Tanahashi, excerpts from *Moon in a Dewdrop: Writings of Zen Master Dogen,* edited by Kazuaki Tanahashi. Translation copyright © 1985 by the San Francisco Zen Center. Reprinted by permission of North Point Press, a division of Farrar, Straus & Giroux, Inc.

Zen stories from *Sand and Pebbles,* from *Zen Flesh, Zen Bones* by Nyogen Senzaki and Paul Reps, translated by Paul Reps. © 1989. Reprinted by permission of Charles E. Tuttle Co., Inc., Rutland, Vermont and Tokyo, Japan.

Muso Soseki, tr. W.S. Merwin and Soiku Shigematsu from *Muso Soseki (1275–1351).* Reprinted by permission of the translators.

Kenko, excerpt from *Essays in Idleness; the Tsurezuregusa of Kenko,* tr. Donald Keene. Copyright © 1967. Reprinted by permission of Columbia University Press.

Zeami Motokiyo, "Semimaru," tr. Susan Matisoff from *Twenty Plays of the No Theatre,* translated by Donald Keene. Copyright © 1970. Reprinted by permission of Columbia University Press.

Zeami Motokiyo, "The One Mind Linking All Powers," tr. Donald Keene from *Anthology of Japanese Literature,* edited by Donald Keene. Copyright © 1955 by Grove Press, Inc. Reprinted by permission of Grove/Atlantic, Inc.

Ihara Saikaku, "A Beauty of Easy Virtue," tr. Ivan Morris from *The Life of an Amorous Woman* in *The Life of an Amorous Woman and Other Writings.* Copyright © 1963 by New Directions Publishing Corp. Reprinted by permission of New Directions Publishing Corp.

Matsuo Basho, excerpt from *Narrow Road to the Interior,* tr. Sam Hamill. © 1991. Reprinted by arrangement with Shambhala Publications, Inc., 300 Massachusetts Ave., Boston, MA 02115.

Matsuo Basho and His School, from "Throughout the Town," tr. Earl Miner and Hiroko Odagiri from *The Monkey's Straw Raincoat* by Earl Miner and Hiroko Odagiri. Reprinted by permission of Earl Miner.

Chikamatsu Monzaemon, "The Love Suicides at Amijima" and "Chikamatsu on the Art of the Puppet Stage," tr. Donald Keene from *Four Major Plays of Chikamatsu.* Copyright © 1961. Reprinted by permission of Columbia University Press.

Yosa Buson, "Three Haiku," tr. Ayame Fukuda. Reprinted by permission of the translator.

Ryokan, "Who Says My Poem Is a Poem?" "The New Pond," and "For an Old Man, a Dream Is Easily Broken," tr. Dennis Maloney and Hide Oshiro from *Between the Floating Mist: Poems of Ryokan* (Buffalo, NY: Springhouse Editions, an imprint of White Pine Press, Fredonia, NY, 1992). Reprinted by permission of White Pine Press.

Ryokan, "Shaggy Hair Past the Ears" and "The Thief Left It Behind," tr. John Stevens from *One Robe One Bowl: The Zen Poetry of Ryokan,* translated by John Stevens. Reprinted by permission of Weatherill, Publishers.

Issa, "Three Haiku," tr. Ayame Fukuda. Reprinted by permission of the translator.

Natsume Soseki, "The Seventh Night," tr. Aiko Ito and Graeme Wilson from *Ten Nights of Dream, Hearing Things, the Heredity of Taste* by Natsume Soseki. © 1974. Published by Charles E. Tuttle Co., Inc., Rutland, Vermont and Tokyo, Japan.

Shiki, "Thirteen Haiku," tr. Burton Watson from *The Country of Eight Islands* by Hiroaki Sato and Burton Watson. Copyright © 1981 by Hiroaki Sato and Burton Watson. Used by permission of Doubleday, a division of Bantam Doubleday Dell Publishing Group, Inc.

Yosano Akiko, excerpts from *Tangled Hair,* tr. Sanford Goldstein and Seishi Shinoda. Reprinted by permission of Charles E. Tuttle Co., Inc., Tokyo.

Tanizaki Junichiro, "The Tattooer," tr. Howard Hibbet from *Seven Japanese Tales.* Copyright © 1963 and renewed 1991 by Alfred A. Knopf, Inc. Reprinted by permission of Alfred A. Knopf, Inc.

Akutagawa Ryunosuke, "Rashomon," tr. Takashi Kojima from *Rashomon and Other Stories.* Copyright 1952 by Charles E. Tuttle Co. English translation copyright 1952 by Liveright Publishing Corporation. Reprinted by permission of Liveright Publishing Corporation.

Kawabata Yasunari, "The Mole," tr. Edward Seidensticker from *Modern Japanese Literature,* edited by Donald Keene. Copyirght © 1956 by Grove Press, Inc. Used by permission of Grove/Atlantic, Inc.

Kawabata Yasunari, "Eggs," tr. J. Martin Holman from *Palm-of-the-Hand Stories.* Translation copyright © 1988 by Lane Dunlop and J. Martin Holman. Reprinted by permission of North Point Press, a division of Farrar, Straus & Giroux, Inc.

Nakamoto Takako, "The Female Bell-Cricket," tr. Yukiko Tanaka from *To Live and to Write: Selections by Japanese Women Writers, 1913–1938,* edited by Yukiko Tanaka. Reprinted by permission of Seal Press.

Sakaki Nanao, "Future Knows" and "Small People," tr. Sakaki Nanao. © Nanao Sakaki, 1989. Reprinted by permission.

Tamura Ryuichi, "Green Conceptual Body" and "Human House," tr. Christopher Drake from *A Play of Mirrors: Eight Major Poets of Modern Japan* (Rochester, MI: Katydid Books, 1987). Reprinted by permission of Thomas Fitzsimmons.

Abe Kobo, "The Magic Chalk," tr. Alison Kibrick from *Other Voices, Other Vistas: Short Stories from Africa, China, India, Japan and Latin America,* edited by Barbara Solomon. Copyright © 1950 by Kobo Abe in Japan. Copyright © 1982 in English translation by Alison Kibrick. Reprinted by permission of International Creative Management, Inc.

Mishima Yukio, "Martydom (*Junkyo*)," tr. John Bester. © 1948 Iichiro Hiraoka, from *Acts of Worship: Seven Stories* by Yukio Mishima. Published by Kodansha International Ltd. The anthology copyright © 1989 by Kodansha International Ltd. Reprinted by permission. All rights reserved.

Shiraishi Kazuko, "The Man Root," from *Women Poets of Japan.* Copyright © 1977 by Kenneth Rexroth and Ikuko Atsumi. Reprinted by permission of New Directions Publishing Corp.

Tanikawa Shuntaro, "Museum," "Growth," and "Ten Yen Coin," tr. Harold Wright. Reprinted by permission of Bonnie R. Crown.

Oe Kenzaburo, "Aghwee the Sky Monster," tr. John Nathan from *Teach Us to Outgrow Our Madness.* Copyright © 1977 by John Nathan. Used by permission of Grove/Atlantic, Inc.

Murakami Haruki, from *Hard-Boiled Wonderland and the End of the World,* "Elevator, Silence, Overweight," tr. Alfred Birnbaum. Published by Kodansha International Ltd. Copyright © 1991 by Kodansha International Ltd. Reprinted by permission. All rights reserved.

I N D E X